European Business

Although not without significant problems, European integration is the deepest and most advanced case of regional integration in the contemporary world. But Europe cannot be fully understood without considering how the component parts of Europe – the member states – affect policy and strategy, and how Europe itself interacts with the rest of the world.

European Business highlights what is unique about the European business environment – integration – especially market integration and explores how it has affected the strategy and behaviour of businesses with a European presence. The second edition of this established text has been fully updated to cover topics such as the Single European Market, the single currency and related policy issues. However, it also covers issues that have not been well covered elsewhere such as:

- the European consumer
- entrepreneurship
- sustainability
- Europe's relationship with emerging economies such as China.

Attractively designed and engagingly written, the book contains numerous topical case studies that demonstrate the objectives, discussion questions, boxed supporting information, and extensive up-to-date further reading and resources. A supporting website provides further material for both lecturers and students. Visit www.routledge.com/textbooks/9780415351355 .

Debra Johnson is a Senior Lecturer at Hull University Business School. She has written a number of books and articles on a range of European and international business issues. Her current research interests include energy, challenges arising from EU enlargement and trans-European networks.

Colin Turner is a lecturer at International Business and Strategy at University Business School. He has written a number of books and articles on European and international business issues. Current research interests include telecommunications strategy and trans-European networks.

European Business

SECOND EDITION

Debra Johnson and Colin Turner

Routledge
Taylor & Francis Group

LONDON AND NEW YORK

First edition published 2000 by Routledge

Second edition published 2006
by Routledge
2 Park Square, Milton Park, Abingdon, Oxon OX14 4RN

Simultaneously published in the USA and Canada
by Routledge
270 Madison Ave, New York, NY 10016

Routledge is an imprint of the Taylor & Francis Group, an informa business

© 2000, 2006 Debra Johnson and Colin Turner

Typeset in Perpetua and Bell Gothic by
Florence Production Ltd, Stoodleigh, Devon
Printed and bound in Great Britain by
Antony Rowe Ltd, Chippenham, Wiltshire

British Library Cataloguing in Publication Data
A catalogue record for this book is available from the British Library

Library of Congress Cataloging in Publication Data
Johnson, Debra, 1957–
    European business/Debra Johnson and Colin Turner.
       p. cm.
     Includes bibliographical references and index.
    1. European Union countries – Commercial policy. 2. Industrial policy –
European Union countries. 3. European Union countries – Economic
policy. 4. Business enterprises – European Union countries. 5. European
Union countries – Economic integration. 6. Competition, International.
I. Turner, Colin, 1967–   II. Title.
    HF1531.J64 2006
337.1'42 – dc22   2006014633

ISBN10: 0–415–35134–0 (hbk)
ISBN13: 978–0–415–35134–8 (hbk)

ISBN10: 0–415–35135–9 (pbk)
ISBN13: 978–0–415–35135–3 (pbk)

ISBN10: 0–203–69692–1 (ebk)
ISBN13: 978–0–203–69692–7 (ebk)

Contents

CONTENTS

Illustrations

CASE STUDIES

BOXES

TABLES

FIGURES

Preface

The first edition of this book was written because, despite the existence of many excellent books on Europe and European integration, the majority of these books were written for political scientists or economists. There was an extremely limited choice of texts that analysed European business per se and, in particular, those aspects that distinguish business in Europe from business in other regions – namely, long-lived and ambitious regional integration. This has had a profound effect both on businesses based in Europe and on those businesses based outside Europe but which seek to enter the European market, through either trade or investment. Furthermore, the European business environment demonstrates how political, economic and social factors can have a profound effect on business strategy and on the environment: the transformation of Central and Eastern Europe (CEE) and the subsequent enlargement of the European Union from 15 to 25 states is a prime example of this. It is the absence of the link with the business world in many books about Europe that led us to write the first edition of this book. Several years later, the situation remains the same and the need for a second edition is overdue.

The book is published at a time when Europe appears to be at a crossroads: in particular, the draft constitutional treaty, in its original form at least, is dead following its rejection in the French and Dutch referendums in 2005 but the way forward remains unclear at the present time. This situation is complicated by the apparent divergence of opinion regarding Europe's future among member states: some of which wish to continue with the liberalisation agenda whereas others appear to want to pull back from it. There has also been the re-emergence of the debate about multi-speed Europe and the possibility of an inner core of countries pushing ahead with deeper integration. At the global level, Europe is wrestling with how to engage with the emerging commercial powerhouses of China and India.

The book is, therefore, published at a time of great change in Europe. This change of pace has necessitated major re-writes, rather than minor alterations, in the second edition. In addition to content changes, the second edition is also different from, and we hope an improvement on, the first edition in two ways. First, although European policy and integration remains a key theme of the book, we have tried to place an even greater emphasis on the business implications of the integration process. We have tried to achieve this both within the main body of the text and by the use of sectoral and corporate case studies. Second, we have, through the more extensive use of case studies, complete with case questions, and general questions and recommended activities, tried to upgrade the pedagogical features of the text.

Our primary aims remain to explore the European business environment; to identify and analyse its major characteristics; and to set the development and establishment of policy within the context of the business environment and to foster greater awareness of the interaction of European public policy with business. Accordingly, common themes permeate the chapters. Market access, deregulation and liberalisation, therefore, appear in various guises as a theme in most chapters. Moreover, EU policy is not formed in a vacuum and reflects pressures from three inter-related levels – the national, the European and the global. Therefore, in several instances, the chapters reflect the pressures on the EU from member states and how different national approaches influence European policy. Increasingly, however, it is global factors that are having a major impact on the business environment. As liberalisation advances into new areas of the international arena and technological changes facilitate more effective and efficient communication and transactions, so the global economy is becoming more and more interdependent and wielding a greater influence on European business and the determination of EU policy – a theme that runs through many chapters.

The book is essentially divided into four parts:

Part I: perspectives on Europe – national, regional and global;

Part II: market integration;
Part III: inputs and factors of production;
Part IV: Europe and the rest of the world.

Part I establishes key contextual material for the rest of the book by analysing the various levels that influence European business. The first chapter establishes the scope and characteristics of the European economy and its constituent national markets. In particular, it explores the themes of diversity that exists in Europe at a national level – a diversity that expresses itself through differing cultures, business systems and practices – and highlights similarities and differences that affect business in European nations. The second chapter explores the European-level influences on business – the unifying influence on the text, and provides a context for later policy-driven chapters. It achieves this by discussing the theoretical drivers of integration and how integration has evolved from the post-war settlements through to the draft constitutional treaty in recognition of the fact that the integration process and its associated policies did not emerge out of thin air but arose from a specific set of economic and political circumstances. The chapter concludes with a survey of how the European institutions work (important for business lobbyists) and preliminary ideas about the implications of integration for business. The remainder of the book raises these ideas in more depth. Chapter 3 discusses globalisation – a process that is increasingly affecting European business and shaping the process of integration itself. Indeed, differences about the appropriate response to globalisation are contributing to the debate about the future evolution of Europe.

An abiding theme of European integration is market integration and unification. Part II deals with the broad framework of integration process and the horizontal policies, such as the single currency and competition policy, that cut across sectors and which define the overall nature of market integration within Europe. Chapter 4 deals with the ongoing construction of the single market, the effects of which continue to unfold. Chapter 5 is concerned with competition policy, an important factor in the integrity of the single market. Chapter 6 discusses Europe's elusive industrial policy with an emphasis on attempts to achieve a European competitiveness policy. Chapter 7 discusses similar themes to the previous chapter but with a particular emphasis on small and medium-sized enterprises. Chapter 8 is concerned with economic and monetary union – a policy that has moved on significantly since the first edition. The final chapter in Part II is on trans-European networks – that is, the attempts by the EU to confer upon Europe's physical infrastructures, which have traditionally grown up within the constraints of national boundaries, a trans-European dimension to support and facilitate the integration of European markets.

The chapters in Part III act as sectoral case studies of the single market and of broader integration initiatives in practice. They also deal with key inputs and factors of production that are important to all business such as transport, energy and information – the subject matter of Chapters 10, 11 and 12 respectively. Chapter 13 discusses Europe's labour markets from the perspective of social dumping and labour rights, key themes of the 1990s, but with a much greater emphasis on European demographic and labour mobility trends than in the first edition. The issue of labour market flexibility is also discussed; an issue that has even greater salience since the launch of the single currency and the need for reforms in some of the larger European countries. Chapter 14 is concerned with the environment. Part III finishes with a completely new chapter on the European citizen/consumer – a theme which, in our view, is becoming more important as a result of the greater attention being paid to consumer issues at the European level and the need to engage the European populace more with European issues.

Part IV reflects Europe's commercial and economic interaction with the rest of the world. Chapter 16 is about enlargement and CEE. Although it could be argued that the biggest enlargement to date is complete and the need for a separate chapter has disappeared, we decided to keep a specific chapter on this part of Europe to focus on the transformation that has taken place in that part of the world and on the response of business in the old and the new EU to the much expanded market. Chapter 17 is on European business in a global context and looks at the more generic issues raised in Chapter 3 from an applied perspective. In particular, it establishes Europe's place in the world as part of the triad and as an important actor in multilateral organisations such as the World Trade Organisation (WTO). It also investigates Europe's key economic and commercial relationships with other parts of the developed world, particularly the US and Japan. Chapter 18 explores how Europe is responding to the challenge of developing trade and investment links with transitional and developing countries. Indeed, how the EU chooses to engage with countries such as Russia, India and China is becoming increasingly important to Europe's long-term well-being.

The intention in writing individual chapters was not to present an exhaustive description of individual policies (as well as being a lengthy process, it would also be extremely tedious for the reader). Rather, we have aimed to highlight key themes in contemporary debates. In other words, we have endeavoured to ensure that the text of chapters reflects the broad sweep of policies and the ideas and themes surrounding them: more detailed analysis of individual policies is confined to boxes, a device that is also used to present case studies relating to the impact of policy changes on individual sectors or companies.

A degree of cross-referencing across chapters is included: this highlights common themes across chapters and encourages the reader to consider and appreciate linkages between policies. Each chapter finishes with a summary of key points, questions and suggestions for further reading. We also encourage students to consult key policy documents directly, many of which are now available in full text form on the Internet, and have included references to them in the suggested reading.

The reader is the best judge of the extent to which we have achieved our original aims and attained an appropriate balance within and between chapters.

Debra Johnson and Colin Turner
Hull, March 2006

Abbreviations

3G	third generation	ECB	European Central Bank
ACEA	European Automobile Manufacturers Association	ECJ	European Court of Justice
		ECN	European Competition Network
ACP	African Caribbean Pacific	ECSC	European Coal and Steel Community
BSE	bovine spongiform encephalopathy		
CAP	Common Agricultural Policy	ecu	European currency unit
CCP	Common Commercial Policy	EEA	European Economic Area
CEE	Central and Eastern Europe	EEC	European Economic Community
CEES	Common European Economic Space	EFSA	European Food Safety Authority
		EFTA	European Free Trade Area
Cefic	European Chemical Industry Council	EIB	European Investment Bank
		EIF	European Investment Fund
CFI	Court of First Instance	EIT	European Institute of Technology
CFSP	Common Foreign and Security Policy	ELV	end-of-life vehicle
		EMAS	Eco-Management and Audit Scheme
CIS	Commonwealth of Independent States		
		EMCF	European Monetary Cooperation Fund
CMEA	Council for Mutual Economic Assistance		
		EMI	European Monetary Institute
CO_2	carbon dioxide	EMS	environmental management scheme
CoR	Committee of the Regions		
Coreper	Committee of Permanent Representatives	EMS	European monetary system
		EMU	economic and monetary union
CSR	corporate social responsibility	EP	European Parliament
CTP	Common Transport Policy	EPC	European political cooperation
EAP	Environmental Action Programme	EPO	European Patent Office
EBRD	European Bank for Reconstruction and Development	ERM	Exchange Rate Mechanism
		ESC	Economic and Social Committee
EC	European Community	ESCB	European System of Central Banks

ESF	European Social Fund	ISO	International Standardisation Organisation
ESI	electricity supply industry	IT	information technology
ETS	emissions trading scheme	LNG	liquefied natural gas
EU	European Union	LSE	large-scale enterprise
Euratom	European Atomic Energy Community	M&A	mergers and acquisitions
FDI	foreign direct investment	MCR	Merger Control Regulation
FECC	European Chemical Distributors Association	MEP	Member of the European Parliament
FEMIP	Facility for Euro-Mediterranean Investment and Partnership	MFN	Most Favoured Nation
		MNC	multinational corporation
FSA	Food Standards Agency	MNE	multinational enterprise
FSAP	Financial Services Action Plan	NAFTA	North American Free Trade Area
FSC	Foreign States Corporation	NATO	North Atlantic Treaty Organisation
FT	France Telecom	NGO	non-governmental organisation
FYRM	Former Yugoslav Republic of Macedonia	NRA	national regulatory authority
		NSI	Network Spread Index
GATT	General Agreement on Tariffs and Trade	NTA	New Transatlantic Agenda
		NTB	non-tariff barrier
GDP	gross domestic product	OCA	optimal currency area
GHG	greenhouse gas	OECD	Organisation for Economic Cooperation and Development
GM	genetically modified (as in food)		
GM	General Motors	OSCE	Organisation for Security and Cooperation in Europe
GMO	genetically modified organisms		
GPSD	General Product Safety Directive	PCA	Partnership and Cooperation Agreement
GSM	Global System for Mobile Communications		
		PPP	polluter pays principle
GSP	Generalised System of Preferences	PPP	public private partnership
		PPS	purchasing power standard
HLG	High-Level Group	PSO	public service obligation
IATA	International Air Transport Agreement	QMV	qualified majority voting
		QSP	Quick Start Programme
ICC	International Chamber of Commerce	R&D	research and development
		REACH	Registration, Evaluation and Authorisation of Chemicals
ICN	International Competition Network		
		RTD	research and technological development
ICT	information and communication technology		
		SAP	Social Action Programme
IEM	internal energy market	SARS	severe acute respiratory syndrome
IGC	Intergovernmental Conference		
IIT	intra-industry trade	SBM	single buyer model
IMF	International Monetary Fund	SCP	structure–conduct–performance
IPP	integrated product policy	SEA	Single European Act
IPR	intellectual property rights	SEM	Single European Market

SGP	Stability and Growth Pact	TPA	third-party access
SLIM	Simpler Legislation for the Internal Market	UMTS	Universal Mobile Telecommunications System
SME	small and medium-sized enterprise	UN	United Nations
		UNCTAD	United Nations Conference for Trade and Development
SOE	state-owned enterprise		
SPORT	Strategic Partnership on REACH Testing	USSR	Union of Soviet Socialist Republics
STP	strategic trade policy	VAT	value-added tax
TBR	Trade Barriers Regulation	vCJD	variant Creutzfeld-Jakob disease
TENs	trans-European networks		
TEU	Treaty on European Union	VDA	Association of the German Automotive Industry
TNC	transnational corporation		
TNI	Transnationality Index	WTO	World Trade Organisation

Part I

Europe
The national, regional and global dimensions

Why European business? What is different about European business or business in Europe from American business or Asian business or business in any other part of the world? Clearly, businesses have much in common whatever their origin. They are all trying to find the best way to compete in a world that is becoming increasingly open and competitive. However, although their overall objective may be similar, business strategies are shaped and influenced by the culture, traditions, economies, political and institutional frameworks, etc. of their home base and these vary tremendously from country to country and from region to region. European business is no different and the first part of this volume establishes the context in which European business operates and which provides it with the platform from which it engages with the rest of the world.

Part I of this text explores the three different levels – the national, regional and global levels – which are both separate and which also interact with each other to form a unique set of influences to shape the European business environment. The first chapter opens with a broad brush portrait of Europe that sketches the scope and main characteristics of the European economy and markets. In the process, some of the main similarities and differences among European countries are highlighted, particularly, but not only, in terms of the major social and economic models that co-exist in Europe. The chapter concludes with a discussion of the competitive challenges facing Europe and some of the responses to these challenges that have been developed. Although the main focus of the text is on the regional level, the national dimension is important: there is frequent tension between the national and the regional. In short, Europe is the sum of its many and varied constituent parts. It is not a homogeneous territory and it is important to remember that when considering the regional and international perspectives of European business.

What really makes European business unique, however, is the depth, level and ambitiousness of the regional integration that shapes its operating environment. Indeed, in international business literature, regional integration is an important factor in business location and the example and experiences (both good and bad) of European integration can help other regions that are not so far down the integration road, or even individual countries that are struggling to overcome market fragmentation. The second chapter discusses four general themes in the regional dimension of European business – theoretical aspects, the historical aspects (that is, how and why the European Union has arrived at its present degree of integration), institutional aspects (that is, the role of the main institutions of the European Union) and the general business response to these stimuli. The intention is not to explore these facets in exhaustive detail but to provide students with sufficient background that they can place later, more specific chapters into their broader context – that is, how they fit into the overall integration process and what are the implications for business.

The third and final chapter of this part is concerned with the global dimension of European business – a theme that is returned to in Part IV. Just as European integration and policy is the outcome of a wide array of national inputs, so one of the main purposes of European integration, and market integration in particular, is to help European business engage fully and effectively in the international market place. The third chapter discusses Europe's role in the global economy and how regional integration helps European business contend with the international integration (often referred to as 'globalisation') that is taking place.

Chapter 1

A portrait of Europe
Challenge and change

The real problem, which our contemporaries by and large do not see, is that Europe has been in historical decline since the First World War.

Jacques Delors, President of the European Commission (1985–95)

This chapter will help you to understand:

- key features of the modern EU economy;
- characteristics of the different European social models;
- the key competitiveness issues facing the EU;
- the rationale and key elements behind the Lisbon Strategy;
- the process of national reform.

Much of the excitement and interest in the sub-field of regional studies within the broad domain of international business is currently focused on China and, to a lesser extent, India. To business practitioners, academics and students, the emergence of these states has aroused considerable interest primarily because of their tremendous potential in terms of trade and investment and because they represent two-fifths of humanity and are benefiting from shifting power within the global economy. To many, the emergence of these states and the anticipated shift in power

represent a serious strategic challenge for those 25 small states occupying a relatively small area of land at the far end of the Eurasian plate.

A cursory examination of the business press highlights the essence of the challenges facing Europe. The fashion among the press is to portray Europe as the 'old continent' that is unwilling to face up to the process of relative decline and, when it does, is bereft of any commitment to undertake necessary reforms. No matter what contemporary trends suggest, Europe will remain a pivotal

3

player in the global economic system – a position cemented by the ongoing process of European integration.

In historical terms, one cannot underplay the significance of the 'old continent'. For centuries, Europe has been the source of ideas that have shaped business practice. The spread of Europeans throughout the globe has been crucial in shaping the contemporary environment to which Europe must now respond. The challenge for Europe is that it must be a good place to do business. To this end, Europe has to undergo a process of adjustment. This means a transformation of how it creates and sustains employment, the types of jobs it creates and how it enables its businesses to expand and develop.

Within the context of the rest of this text, this chapter addresses a number of objectives. The first is to offer a portrait of contemporary Europe and an examination of the economic structures prevalent within the continent. The second is to elaborate upon the various social models within Europe – the focus of much commercial debate across the continent. These models are important in terms of setting the context within which businesses operate. The chapter then moves on to examine the core competitive challenges for Europe before moving on to how the EU sought to address these challenges within the Lisbon Strategy. The chapter concludes with a brief and tentative examination of the process of reform at the member state level.

PORTRAIT OF EUROPE

The bulk of contemporary Europe's business environment is organised within the framework of European integration in the form of the European Union (EU). In 2006, in Western Europe, only Switzerland and Norway plus a few smaller independent nations such as Andorra and Liechtenstein stand outside this framework. The 2004 EU enlargement absorbed eight Central and Eastern countries and two more – Bulgaria and Romania – look set to join the EU in 2007. The situation is more complex in south-east Europe with several Balkan states aspiring to join but needing to vanquish the negative legacies from the conflicts of the 1990s. Further eastwards, Turkey is engaged in negotiations with the EU over membership.

The EU in 2006 is comprised of 25 nation states with a combined population of over 450 million people (see Table 1.1). Europe's main traditional economic rivals – the United States and Japan – have populations of almost 300 million and 130 million respectively. A major thrust of Europe's integration process has been to create a Single European Market (SEM) (see Chapters 2 and 4) within which European businesses can compete with each other on equal terms and which creates a strong domestic market that European business can use as a platform to compete with businesses in the rest of the world.

Figures 1.1 and 1.2 go some way to explain why a key thrust of European integration is to end the fragmentation of the European market place. Europe's economies range widely in terms of their size. The big three are Germany, France and the UK. Their economic power helps explain their centrality in many EU policy debates and also the concerns of the smaller states to get their own concerns heard. However, in an international context, the US is 4.5 times bigger than Germany, Europe's biggest economy. It is only through acting as an integrated unit that Europe can match the US in terms of market size and influence (see Figure 1.2). However, in terms of

Table 1.1 Portrait of the EU

	Population in millions − 2005	Population density − inhabitants per km² − 2003	GDP per head − PPS[a] (EU-25 = 100) − 2005	Social protection expenditure as a % of GDP − 2003*	Social protection expenditure in PPS[a] per capita − 2003*	Labour productivity per person employed (EU-25 = 100)
Austria	8.2	96.8	122.2	29.5	7,700	109.8
Belgium	10.4	340.0	118.1	29.7	7,476	128.8
Cyprus	0.7	126.9	83.8	16.4[b]	2,904[b]	76.8
Czech Rep.	10.2	132.1	73.3	20.1	2,964	72.5
Denmark	5.4	125.1	123.9	30.9	8,115	107.0
Estonia	1.4	31.2	54.9	13.4	1,411	60.1
Finland	5.2	17.1	112.7	26.9	6,560	110.2
France	59.9	110.4	109.0	30.9	7,434	119.6
Germany	82.5	231.2	108.2	30.2	7,086	99.8
Greece	11.1	83.7	83.7	26.3	4,567	99.1
Hungary	10.1	108.9	61.9	21.4	2,783	73.4
Ireland	4.0	58.4	138.1	16.5	4,814	132.6
Italy	57.9	191.2	103.7	26.4	6,024	108.0
Latvia	2.3	37.3	46.8	13.4	1,341	51.0
Lithuania	3.5	52.9	51.0	13.6	1,341	56.2
Luxembourg	0.5	174.0	230.8	23.8	10,905	148.2
Malta	0.4	1,263.0	69.5	18.5	2,879	80.0
Netherlands	16.3	480.3	123.6	28.1	7,604	108.4
Poland	38.2	122.2	49.8	21.6	2,121	65.3
Portugal	10.5	113.6	71.2	24.3	4,076	64.7
Slovakia	5.4	109.7	54.2	18.4	2,063	65.5
Slovenia	2.0	99.1	80.9	24.6	4,076	80.8
Spain	42.4	83.0	98.0	19.7	4,186	92.4
Sweden	9.0	21.8	118.5	33.5	8,258	109.3
UK	59.8	244.3	116.0	26.7	6,812	108.1
EU-15	382.7	−	108.2	28.3	6,926	105.3
Eurozone	308.7	−	106.1	28.1	6,564	104.5
EU-25	456.9	117.5	100.0	28.0	6,012	100.0
Japan	127.3	−	111.0	−	−	95.8
US	291.7	−	152.3	−	−	139.0

Notes
a   PPS = Purchasing Power Standards – a form of measurement that is expressed in a common currency
    and corrects for differences in price levels.
b   Refers to 2002 figures.

Source: Eurostat on-line; * Eurostat (2006) *European Social Statistics: Social Protection – Expenditure and Receipts (Data 1995–2003).*

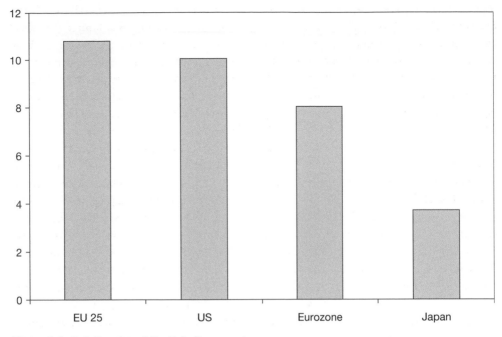

Figure 1.1 Relative size of the 'triad' economies

Source: Eurostat online.

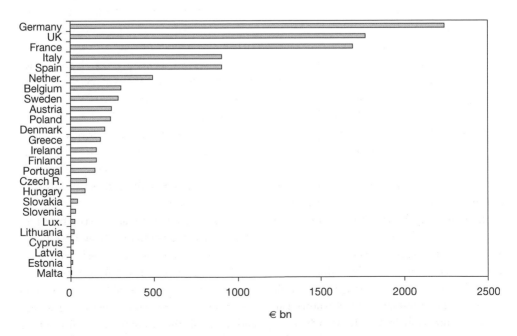

Figure 1.2 Relative size of EU economies, 2005

Source: Eurostat online.

performance, the US retains a big advantage over the EU. The final column of Table 1.1 sets out labour productivity per person employed for individual EU member states and for Japan and the United States. US productivity, an important measure of competitiveness, is more than 40 percentage points above the average of the EU-25 and outperforms all EU states apart from Luxembourg (see Case Study 3.1 for an alternative view of the relative performance of the EU and the US).

In order to understand European business and its environment, it is important to acknowledge the different units that make up this trading bloc – the individual nation states – which, although having much in common, also exhibit factors that give Europe significant diversity in terms of culture, organisation, tradition, history, economic structures and interests, etc. These can lead to major differences at EU level in relation to the determination of policy and the future direction of Europe. Moreover, diversity within Europe also continues to exercise an influence over the business environment. Thus, an abiding theme in the creation of modern Europe is the constant tension between convergence and divergence between the constituent member states of the EU.

In terms of convergence, Europe shares much in terms of a broad common history and intellectual traditions going back several centuries. More recently, there has been a convergence of political and economic ideology and of commercial structures. After the Second World War, economic policy in Western European states was based on Keynesian economics in which there was a clear role for the state in managing economic demand. The dominance of Keynesianism started to diminish in the 1970s when the simultaneous existence of high levels of inflation and unemployment began to undermine

its key assumptions. Neo-liberalism – that is, an economic ideology that limited the role of the state to more or less creating an environment in which market forces determine resource allocation – began to replace the demand management approach, albeit with more enthusiasm in some member states than others, and provided the underpinning economic philosophy of the SEM. Similarly, in the 1970s, the twin systems of political dictatorship and economic isolationism in Greece, Spain and Portugal gave way to convergence with Western European norms and, indeed, EU membership in the 1980s for all three countries. By 1989–90, it had become clear that the era of Soviet domination, both economically and politically, over CEE was rapidly drawing to a close. The former Soviet satellites, without exception, chose the model of democracy and market economics to guide their social, economic and political transformation (see Chapter 16). Moreover, the goal of EU accession required them to adopt the institutions of a market economy and all existing EU rules and regulations (the *acquis communautaire*) which essentially gave them a detailed road map to help them achieve their transition goals. In short, by the turn of the century, after over 50 years of division, Europe's nations had converged on a broad economic and political framework. However, many differences remained among Europe's nations in relation to the details of this framework (see below).

All European states are currently examples of mixed economies. Most have privatised some of their state-owned enterprises (SOE), although many still retain full or partial control of some SOEs, especially in the utility and transport sectors. The size and role of the welfare state also varies considerably within Europe (see Table 1.1 and section below on European economic

7

and social models). For example, as Table 1.1 shows, social protection expenditure (that is, expenditure on pensions, unemployment, disability payments, etc.) in Denmark, Germany, France and Sweden is above 30 per cent of gross domestic product (GDP) whereas it is below 20 per cent of GDP in Cyprus, Malta, Slovakia, Ireland and the Baltic states. Moreover, in 2003, spending on social protection in Denmark was essentially four times greater than in Slovakia. As well as reflecting differences in the ability of states to support such spending, these differences indicate different priorities in terms of the implicit bargain between the state and its citizens (see below). Moreover, given the ageing population (see Chapter 13), serious questions are currently being asked about the sustainability of European social models.

Trends in terms of economic structure are broadly similar in Europe. When the Treaty of Rome establishing the European Economic Community (EEC) was signed in 1957, agriculture's share of gross value-added and employment was much bigger than it is in the mid-2000s. Agriculture has subsequently declined in relative importance throughout Europe, comprising only 2 per cent of gross value-added GDP in the EU-25 in 2004 (see Table 1.2). Agriculture's share ranges from less than 1 per cent of value-added in Luxembourg and the UK to 6.4 per cent in Greece. In general, agriculture seems to make a bigger relative contribution to the economies of southern Europe and of the 2004 accession states. Industry has also declined in relative importance throughout the Union, accounting for 20 per cent of gross value-added in 2004 and ranging from 12 per cent in Cyprus to over 30 per cent in Ireland, Slovenia and the Czech Republic. Services dominate contemporary European economies and – for the majority of member states – contribute two-thirds to three-quarters of gross value-added. Table 1.2 gives some indication of the services strengths of individual countries. Financial intermediation and business services account for 46.7 per cent and 30 per cent of gross value-added in Luxembourg and the UK respectively whereas the contribution of distributive trades, hotels and restaurants, transport and communications is significantly above the EU average in Cyprus and Malta, two countries in which tourism is a major generator of income.

Member states are also subject to – and have to respond to – the same domestic and international challenges. They are, for example, all subject to the problems arising from an ageing population (see Chapter 13): the problem is more acute in some countries and the 2004 accession states, on the whole, are less subject to this problem than the EU-15 but essentially all countries will have to re-examine their welfare systems and their funding in the coming years. EU members are also subject to the same environmental imperatives and are vulnerable to energy supply insecurity. They are also facing increased competition from the emerging economies of Asia, are subject to international economic cycles, increased economic mobility and need to find a positive response to increasing economic interdependence or globalisation.

Despite the convergence in economic ideology, economic structure and the challenges facing European countries, significant differences remain which influence their response to these challenges and lead to different business and policy concerns. This diversity emerges from the interaction of economics, politics, history, social preferences and culture. Different organisational structures persist in European countries, whether of government (the Belgian and German states are organised along federal

Table 1.2 *Structure of European economies – composition of gross value-added, 2004 (% share of total value-added)*

	Agriculture, hunting, forestry, fishing	Industry	Construction	Distributive trades; hotels and restaurants; transport and communications	Financial intermediation; business services	Public administration and other services
EU-25	2.0	20.7	5.9	21.3	27.5	22.5
Austria	1.9	22.8	7.5	24.8	22.5	20.5
Belgium	1.4	19.6	4.9	20.6	29.0	24.5
Cyprus	3.8	11.9	8.0	27.7	24.1	24.5
Czech Rep.	3.0	30.7	6.7	25.7	16.7	17.1
Denmark	2.2	18.7	5.1	22.1	24.9	27.0
Estonia	4.3	22.2	6.7	28.2	20.7	18.0
Finland	3.1	24.8	5.4	23.0	21.0	22.7
France	2.5	15.8	5.9	19.1	31.0	25.8
Germany	1.1	25.1	4.0	18.1	29.1	22.6
Greece	6.4	13.7	8.6	28.6	20.9	21.9
Hungary[a]	3.3	25.5	4.9	20.8	21.4	24.2
Ireland[a]	2.7	33.0	8.2	17.6	21.4	17.2
Italy	2.5	21.4	5.2	23.2	27.7	20.0
Latvia	4.3	17.2	5.8	35.5	18.2	19.0
Lithuania	5.7	25.6	7.1	32.9	12.1	16.6
Luxembourg	0.5	10.6	5.5	20.4	46.7	16.4
Malta	2.5	20.1	4.5	27.7	19.3	26.0
Netherlands	2.3	18.6	5.9	21.2	26.9	25.1
Poland	2.9	26.6	5.5	28.4	16.4	20.1
Portugal	3.5	19.1	6.5	24.0	19.3	27.6
Slovakia	3.9	26.5	5.6	25.8	21.3	16.9
Slovenia[a]	2.6	30.2	5.7	21.0	20.2	20.4
Spain	3.5	18.5	10.8	25.9	20.8	20.5
Sweden	1.8	23.6	4.5	19.0	23.8	27.3
UK	0.9	18.5	6.2	22.2	30.0	22.1

Note:
a   Figures refer to 2003.

Source: Eurostat (2006) *European Business – Facts and Figures – Data 1995–2004.*

Table 1.3 Most specialised industrial activities by member state

Belgium
1 Chemicals
2 Recycling
3 Textiles

Czech Republic
1 Coal mining
2 Other non-metallic
   mineral products
3 Base metals

Denmark
1 Oil and gas
2 Furniture and other
   manufacturing
3 Other products

Germany
1 Motor vehicles
2 Electrical machinery
   and apparatus
3 Machinery and equipment

Estonia
1 Wood
2 Clothing
3 Textiles

Spain
1 Refined petroleum
2 Other non-metallic
   mineral products
3 Other mining and
   quarrying

France
1 Recycling
2 Office machinery and
   computers
3 Electricity, gas and hot
   water supply

Italy
1 Leather
2 Clothing
3 Textiles

Cyprus
1 Tobacco products
2 Mining and quarrying
3 Collection, purification
   and distillation of
   water

Latvia
1 Wood
2 Textiles
3 Electricity, gas and hot
   water supply

Lithuania
1 Clothing
2 Wood
3 Collection, purification
   and distillation of water

Luxembourg
1 Basic metals
2 Rubber and plastics
3 Textiles

Hungary
1 Refined petroleum
2 Radio, TV and communi-
   cation equipment
3 Electrical machinery and
   apparatus

Malta
1 Clothing
2 Furniture and other
   manufacturing
3 Textiles

Netherlands
1 Oil and gas
2 Publishing and printing
3 Recycling

Austria
1 Radio, TV and communi-
   cation equipment
2 Wood
3 Basic metals

Poland
1 Petroleum products
2 Collection, purification
   and distillation of water
3 Electricity, gas and hot
   water supply

Portugal
1 Clothing
2 Leather
3 Textiles

Slovenia
1 Clothing
2 Textiles
3 Wood

Slovakia
1 Basic metals
2 Electricity, gas and hot
   water supply
3 Leather

Finland
1 Radio, TV and
   communication equipment
2 Pulp and paper
3 Wood

Sweden
1 Mining of metal ores
2 Pulp and paper
3 Wood

UK
1 Oil and gas
2 Other transport equipment
3 Office machinery and
   computers

Note: This table refers to the three activities in which each member state is most specialised. Specialisation is defined as the proportion of value-added generated by each sector in relation to the same ratio for the EU-25 – a value of above 100% implies that the activity is relatively more important in the member state than for the EU-25 as a whole.

Source: Eurostat (2006) *European Business – Facts and Figures – Data 1995–2004.*

lines, for example, whereas the French state is highly centralised) or of legal and financial structures. As a result of the above, of varying geographical structures and of economic integration (a key outcome of which is increased specialisation), each member state has its own particular strengths. Table 1.3 sets out the most specialised industrial activities for most member states. In Table 1.3, specialisation is defined as the proportion of value-added generated by each sector in relation to the average for the EU-25. The higher the ratio is above 100 per cent, the relatively more important is the activity in the member states than in the EU-25 overall.

EUROPEAN SOCIAL MODELS

The development of competing European social models is a useful device to highlight similarities and differences among European countries. However, care needs to be taken in interpreting these models. First, the term 'social model' is misleading as the implications of the models stretch far beyond the social and into production, productivity and employment: that is, into areas that can have profound effects on growth, competitiveness and the ability to prosper within a more interdependent global economy. Second, the models themselves are stylised: in reality, individual countries will fit more or less with a particular model but on some criteria, they may show more elements of a different model.

Social models can be developed in a number of ways but one influential version, and one that has much in common with other models, has been developed by André Sapir. Sapir's analysis was presented to the Union's financial ministers at an informal meeting in September 2005 and is used here as an example of the classification of

Europe's economies. One drawback of Sapir's approach, as is the case with others, is that it is concerned with the EU-15 and does not yet incorporate the 2004 accession states. Their prime concern is to narrow the gap between themselves and the EU-15 and they do not have the finances to devote to social protection as the EU-15 (see Table 1.1).

Figure 1.3 provides an overall representation of the four social models identified by Sapir. The main characteristics of each model are:

1 *The Nordic model (Denmark, Finland, Sweden and the Netherlands)*: these countries have the highest levels of social protection and welfare in the EU. The protection offered to employment by legislation is rather muted but much emphasis is placed on active labour market policies to keep people in work and to ensure that those out of work can gain the necessary training and skills to get them back into work. Trade unions are strong and the range of incomes is relatively compressed. Political and economic decisions rely greatly on consensus and relations between the social partners are based on a high level of trust. High technology and the associated skills are regarded as key to future economic success with large

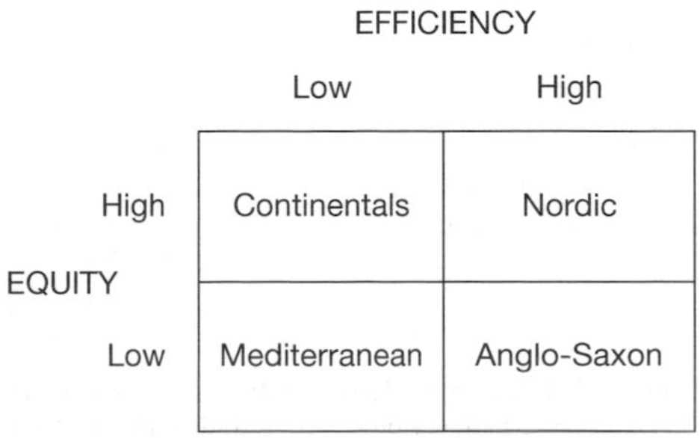

	EFFICIENCY	
	Low	High
High	Continentals	Nordic
EQUITY		
Low	Mediterranean	Anglo-Saxon

Figure 1.3 European social models
Source: Sapir (2005).

investments being made in education. Figures 1.4 and 1.5 illustrate this last point. According to Figure 1.4, Finland and Sweden are the only two EU member states that have achieved the Lisbon target of research and development (R&D) expenditure comprising 3 per cent and above of GDP. Moreover, in terms of patent applications per million of the labour force to the European Patent Office (EPO), Finland and Sweden take second place in the EU behind Germany, with Denmark also scoring creditably.

2 *The Anglo-Saxon model (the United Kingdom and Ireland)*: this is the most market-oriented model of the four with little employment protection afforded to the workforce. Social transfers tend to be smaller and more targeted than in other models and unions are generally weak. There tends to be a bigger pool of low-paid workers than in other models and

there is a wide spread of wages. In general, there is a preference for competition and deregulation.

3 *The Continental model (Austria, Belgium, France, Germany and Luxembourg)*: often categorised as the 'social market' economy in which the market was used as the major source of resource allocation but was regulated to attain socially acceptable outcomes, the continental model is coming under scrutiny because its emphasis on equity has derailed its quest for efficiency. This model relies heavily on insurance-based benefits, non-employment benefits and pensions. Although declining, the influence of unions remains strong and the social partners play an important role in industrial relations.

4 *The Mediterranean model (Greece, Italy, Portugal and Spain)*: social spending is traditionally relatively low with extensive family networks sharing the burden and

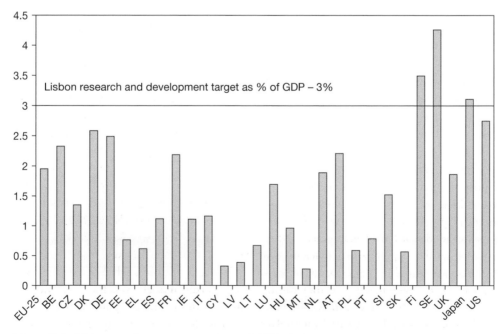

Figure 1.4 *R&D expenditure as a percentage of GDP, 2003*

Source: Eurostat (2006) *European Business – Facts and Figures – Data 1995–2004.*

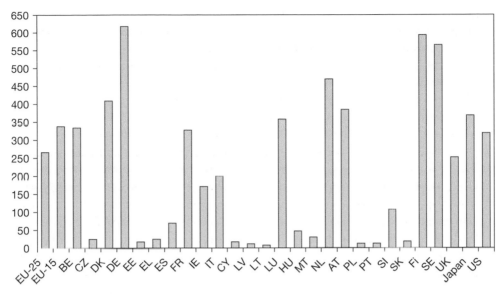

Figure 1.5 Patent applications to the EPO per million of the labour force, 2002

Source: Eurostat – *Statistics in Focus: Science and Technology – 2/2006.*

much of the expenditure is directed towards pensions. Employment protection tends to be strong in this model and early retirement has been used extensively to keep employment down. Figure 13.3 confirms how much needs to be done to meet the Lisbon target of a 50 per cent employment rate for the 55–64 age group. Collective bargaining determines wages and the wage structure is highly compressed.

Figure 1.3 places the four models in an equity/efficiency matrix. The ideal position to be in is that of the Nordic model – one of high equity and high efficiency. The worst position is that of the Mediterranean model which is neither equitable nor efficient. The Continental model is regarded as high on equity but low on efficiency. If they can increase their efficiency levels, the Continental model countries could well find themselves in the position where they can continue to fulfil their equity goals and perhaps even

improve their performance in this area. Without improved efficiency, however, it is clear that the sustainability of their high levels of equity will be undermined. The Anglo-Saxon model provides an efficient but inequitable system.

The Continental and Mediterranean models have become inefficient and reliance on strict employment protection laws has rendered their systems resistant to change, rigid and bad for overall employment levels. Figure 13.1 (see p. 304) shows that activity rates tend to be higher in the Nordic and Anglo-Saxon countries. Pressures from globalisation, ageing populations and low activity rates make these models unsustainable in the medium to long term and in serious need of reform. The Anglo-Saxon model is sustainable but is demonstrably less equitable than the Nordic model. Whether reform takes place in this model is a political matter.

The Nordic model appeared to be in serious trouble in the 1980s and early 1990s with serious doubts emerging about the long-term affordability of their generous welfare states. However, they have embraced elements of the Anglo-Saxon model to boost their growth rates: product markets have become as deregulated as those in Anglo-Saxon countries and labour markets are less heavily regulated than those in France and Germany. Increased labour market flexibility was matched by a serious emphasis on active labour market policies (see Box 13.1 p. 293) which help with re-skilling and strict fiscal prudence. Trust and consensus are important watchwords in the Nordic models. The Nordic countries have also emphasised technology, R&D, education and growth. This combination has, for example, facilitated the emergence of leading global telecommunications companies from within their midst. Although it is unlikely that other member states will be able to follow the example of the Nordic countries in all aspects because of different social bargains and different economic starting points, lessons can be learned from the Nordic experience in terms of securing a future that combines equity and efficiency. It is upon this basis that Europe can begin to address its competitiveness problems while not undermining its desire for social cohesion.

EUROPE'S COMPETITIVENESS PROBLEM

The assumptions surrounding the concept of competitiveness can be misleading, especially when they extend the basic principles of competitive advantage to the level of the state. The implication is that the same analytical principles can be applied to both the state and the firm. However, it would be misleading to extend the analogy of the 'state/region as a firm' too far. The notion of 'EU plc' is misleading as it makes certain

assumptions that can lead to misunderstandings about the different pressures on states and firms. Krugman (1994) disputes the notion that states — like firms — are in competition with each other due to the fact that:

- Firms are not like states: the firm is motivated by profit whereas the latter is motivated by broader social and political issues. Furthermore, firms can go out of business, states cannot.
- Trade is not a zero sum game: the metaphor of the state as a firm is based on the premise that the state will only prosper by winning market share from other states. However, trade liberalisation is expected to work to the benefit of all states. Thus, if the EU prospers in global markets, it may not necessarily be at another state's expense.

In addition, Krugman claims a complete lack of evidence to suggest that there is economic competition between states. While there is rivalry between states, the notion that the rise of China and India will decrease the importance of the EU and the US is of suspect validity. However, despite these criticisms, EU governments remain wedded to the concept of competitiveness. This raises the issue as to what exactly is the 'competitiveness' problem faced by the EU.

In part, the answer lies not at the macro level but at the micro level. The barometer of competitiveness is not how well the economy per se does but how well those firms located within that economy are performing. Thus, being competitive is based on the ability of the firm to preserve and enhance its presence within the globalising market place. What this means is that competitiveness is not about states or government but firms. As a consequence, firms must be the focus of policy. Thus, in the context of the EU, the notion of competitiveness is based upon the ability of all firms located within the region (both EU and non-EU owned) to thrive and prosper.

Porter (1990), while not taking an extreme view on the 'states as firms' perspective nonetheless believes that states do compete with each other. In this context, Porter argues that the competitiveness of nations is based on the characteristics of the domestic environment. It is the combination of a series of conditions (and their mutual reinforcement) within states that have a large influence upon the performance of business on both domestic and foreign stages. These determinants are:

- *Factor conditions*: all states have a combination of created and given factors of production: the former are generally regarded as more important than the latter. These factor conditions include infrastructure, skills, population, etc.
- *Demand conditions*: demand is important in understanding user needs and requirements, especially within the home market. The higher and more sophisticated the level of demand, the greater the scope for economies of scope and scale as well as assorted marketing skills that could be valuable in overseas markets.
- *Related and supporting industries*: these industries (if they are internationally competitive) when working close with firms are able to spur innovation and change.
- *Firm strategy, structure and rivalry*: how firms compete and are managed is influenced by the home environment. The education system, commercial cultures and competitive structures are just three factors that can influence the form and nature of firm behaviour within inter-

nationalising market places. As mentioned elsewhere, Porter places great emphasis on the intensity of competition as a driver of change.

Porter's framework for explaining national competitiveness sees the four above primary contributors supported by two other factors of secondary importance. These are chance (the potential for a random innovation or historical accident to create change) and government (the ability of government policy to influence outcomes via the primary determinants).

Over the last decade or so, Porter's framework for national competitiveness has become increasingly popular. In prescriptions for aiding the development of competitiveness, this framework has been widely adopted by national governments (Dicken 2003). While it can be criticised for its simplicity and the low priority given to the role of policy makers and multinational corporations (MNCs), the framework is a useful benchmark for addressing and examining issues of national and regional competitiveness. Taking each of the determinants in turn, it can be argued that the competitiveness problem is created by the interaction and mutual dependences between the primary factors identified by Porter.

Factor conditions

Historically, part of Europe's competitive strength has been derived from the natural factor endowments in terms of energy supply, raw materials, etc. which allowed these states to undergo a rapid burst of industrialisation. In the new economy, the factor conditions that the EU requires are markedly different. Indeed, over time, the created factors that are key to Europe's success have

15

been under-developed. In terms of labour, much blame has been heaped upon the prevailing social models in that they have led to a lack of labour market flexibility and created barriers to the redeployment and retraining of labour. Rigidities within labour markets mean that Europe could be rendered an uncompetitive place to invest in a globalising market. In addition, problems with the created skills of the workforce are evident in terms of the lack of scientists and researchers. The EU has produced far fewer Nobel prizes than the US and many of its better researchers tend to migrate towards more conducive and rewarding market places. These problems are compounded by an inability to create entrepreneurs in the numbers needed to generate change and speed up innovation across the EU's economy. Moreover, the absence of integrated capital markets inhibits the ability of EU firms to access the levels of capital needed for growth. Finally, these changes need to be supported by a supporting physical infrastructure. In Europe, this has developed in a fragmented manner (see Chapter 9) with the result that mobility across the EU is not as smooth is it needs to be to aid factor and product mobility.

Demand conditions

One of the motives behind the moves toward economic integration over the last two decades (see Chapter 4) was to move from a fragmented system of national markets to an integrated single market. A by-product of this process should be an increasing intensity of competition among EU firms that breeds excellence in product development, innovation, etc. However, despite the progress, this process remains incomplete as a large number of competitive distortions

remain. Many of these distortions arise from the sustained involvement of political forces within national economies which limit the necessity for some domestic firms to face up to the challenge of more intense competition. This is compounded by the actions of states that not only fail to meet their commitments in terms of implementing legislation but also go against the spirit, although not necessarily the substance, of EU law. Not only do these competitive distortions mean that an unlevel playing field for competition remains within the EU, but they limit the ability of firms to use the creation of a larger market as a platform for extra-EU strategies. Firms are limited as to their innovative potential and ability to improve their competitive advantage. In turn, such distortions limit the potential for entrepreneurship and signals fail to be sent to factor markets to adjust accordingly. In short, limiting the intensity of competition – while being politically expedient – may actually do long-term harm to the performance of the EU economy.

Related and supporting industries

One of the implications of the fragmentation of EU industrial structures and of the social model that prevailed within Europe is that it has hindered the forces for 'creative destruction' within the economy. In essence, one of the key problems facing Europe is that there is an absence of world-class supporting industries to aid the competitiveness of firms elsewhere within the EU economy. The dearth of such supporting industries is driven by factors such as the absence of entrepreneurialism, a limited advanced scientific research base and the lack of venture capital. The most evident example is the lack of an indigenous ICT sector within the EU. Across this industry value chain, the inter-linkages between hardware and software firms that drove the emergence of the US as a 'new economy' power are absent. This is despite the development and sourcing by Europeans of many of the core technologies within the new economy. In other cases, persistent regulations have hindered the development of supporting industries, as has been the case in aspects of logistics. This can be seen in other areas where small specialised manufacturers have been hindered by rising social costs. Overall, continued regulation has limited the intensity of competition, which has prevented the emergence of these supporting industries. This, in turn, has had a broader effect upon the performance of other businesses.

Firm strategy, structure and rivalry

Under pure market conditions, it would be expected that the intensity of rivalry will create a distinction between those firms that have successful strategies and those that do not. In these conditions, economies would be subject to the process of dynamic change causing a process of renewal both within firms and across industries as a whole. These pressures should breed excellence in products, services as well as innovation. However, within the EU, these forces have been curtailed as the intensity of competition has been limited by the actions of states. Driven by a suspicion of market forces and their ability to deliver socially optimal outcomes, governments have sought to limit the intensity of competition. The impact is that incentives are denied with the result that firms cannot use the benefits derived from intense competition in national markets to deliver

competitive advantage at the international level. The adherence to social models that keep competition at a distance, the persistence of protectionism as well as other constraints all curtail the freedom of business. In short, how can firms be expected to compete internationally when they are not allowed to compete domestically? This represents a failure of competition policy and of states to honour their commitment to key aspects of the integration process such as the SEM.

Of the supporting factors, government appears to have had an important facilitating role through its action and inaction to remove or create the impediments to competitiveness. The interest of politicians in the electoral cycle means that direct challenges to the prevailing social models or challenges to powerful vested interests can be an electoral liability if the positive effects of improving competitiveness do not coincide with elections or upswings in the trade cycle. As a consequence, there is a great incentive for political bodies to preserve the status quo.

Porter's perspective on competitiveness merely reflects a belief that it is the external environment that shapes a firm's competitive position and therefore enables an economy to prosper. The message is, get the environment right then competitiveness will result. However, this only represents one view of what enables firms to develop competitive advantage. Others suggest that competitiveness is based on the internal environment (see Fahy 2001). This is based on the interaction of firm- (finance, skills etc.) and country- (education systems, infrastructure, etc.) specific resources. The policy implications are that government should seek to ensure that country-specific resources are as valuable as possible to increase the differential provided by firm-specific resources. New theories suggest that competitiveness is based upon the institutional framework (Peng 2000). This perspective argues that the ability of firms to develop competitive advantage is derived from the form and nature of institutional constraints and freedoms created. These can be formal institutions such as laws, regulations etc., and informal institutions such as culture and ethics. Clearly, there is scope for overlap between these different views. However, for analytical purposes, much of the following analysis will draw on the framework and themes offered by Porter.

INTERNAL CHANGE AND THE LISBON STRATEGY

Launched in March 2000, the Lisbon Strategy is committed to making the EU the most competitive economy in the world by 2010. Expressed in terms of the above Porterian framework, the Lisbon Strategy was based on the development of a coherent plan to improve the above quartet of concerns to deliver a more competitive Europe. This overlap between the Lisbon Strategy and the Porterian framework is based on the fact that both are underpinned by the premise that the path to global competitiveness starts with competition at home. Consequently, the Strategy is focused on improving the quality of resources, fostering innovation, market reforms, etc. The emphasis of this Strategy was both on promoting a shift that was dynamic (i.e. open to change) and on the successful creation, dispersal and use of knowledge.

Reform within the Lisbon Strategy is about making Europe a good place to do business and generating positive spin-offs in terms of improving investment in capital and labour that will aid and enhance the competitive positioning of Europe. In Porterian terms, the Strategy is about reforming the social model to improve factor conditions, stimulating market-driven change, increasing the intensity of competition and aiding firm strategy and structure. With these conditions in place, the creation of a mutually supporting system to deliver competitiveness should be feasible.

The Strategy proposed a comprehensive but interdependent series of market-driven reforms that can be implemented without undermining a commitment to social models based around social cohesion, environmental protection and equity. National governments were requested to implement these reforms with the support of a supranational framework. The wide scope of the Lisbon Strategy made it necessary to establish a series of operational targets. However, the overarching objective is to raise growth and employment to cope with emergent challenges of international markets. The key areas for actions were as follows:

1 creating an effective internal market;
2 promoting free and fair trade within Europe and beyond;
3 better regulation that supports business while not undermining consumers;
4 improving European infrastructure to support mobility across Europe;
5 investing in R&D to promote change across the EU;
6 boosting innovation to help EU firms excel in product development;
7 creating a strong industrial base to ensure sustainable employment;
8 more and better jobs that offer better value-added and less insecurity;
9 an adaptable and mobile workforce that is not vulnerable to the negative effects of structural change;
10 better education and skills (linked to the above) to ensure that knowledge-based

work is embedded within the socio-economic system.

Cutting across one or more of these themes are the core objectives of stimulating more intense competition from both internal and external sources and aiding the onset of the knowledge economy.

The Lisbon Strategy was, in some sense, a watershed as it persuaded many sceptical governments of the need for reform through market-driven liberalisation. However, not long into the ten-year programme, it became evident that the proposal was massively over optimistic as governments failed to implement the reforms promised. Indeed, in key areas, Europe has started to move backward, for example, with regard to the Services Directive (see Chapter 4). It was evident that enthusiasm for the process of reform was waning as states backtracked on market opening and started to reintroduce market rigidities in key factor markets (such as labour).

This backtracking on reform can be explained by a combination of factors. First, those states that favoured the status quo were gaining the upper hand at EU summits. Second, the fast-track process to reform – which the Lisbon Strategy adopted – was undermined by governments who want to defend their strategic interests. Finally, a shifting economic outlook has also undermined the desire for reform. Many states needed to take difficult decisions regarding reform and market liberalisation at a time when the political cycle was turning towards elections and the economic cycle was less favourable.

The mid-term report for the Lisbon Strategy in 2005 pointed out that the failures the programme was meant to address remained. The only solution was for the EU and member states to try harder to implement reform. However, the failure of the Lisbon Strategy to really make a difference is more down to member states than the supranational institutions. All the EU can do is offer encouragement. In those cases where the EU does have power, it can often find its effectiveness undermined by reluctant states. As part of the Lisbon process, 84 directives were identified as needing to be transposed into national legislation to kick-start the process of change. The pattern of implementation of these directives is reflected in Table 1.4 and shows a very uneven transposition rate across the EU-25. Denmark (96.8 per cent) had the best record and Luxembourg (60 per cent) the worst.

One of the key problems for the Lisbon Strategy, which was initially motivated solely by reform and growth, is that it has been undermined by a gradual expansion of its remit to include other less growth-centred topics such as the environment, sustainable development and the protection of the social model. The focus of the Strategy, in short, has been lost by political compromise along the way. The programme consisted of a large number of targets in areas that sidetracked the fundamental premise of the strategy. Many of these targets (such as those for social inclusion) can often run counter to the core growth and reform themes of the Lisbon Strategy. Thus, it is argued the strategy

Table 1.4 Transposition of Lisbon Directives (state of play 1 June 2005)

	Percentage of directives transposed
EU-25	85.3
EU 15	81.7
EU-10	90.6

Source: European Commission.

needs to refocus on jobs and seek progress on ancillary goals at a later date.

Despite all this, reform is on the political agenda in most European states and even the most reluctant are beginning to embrace the notion that the current malaise (as represented by the stubbornly high unemployment rates) cannot go on forever and that change needs to be generated. In addition, some states are starting to push forward parts of the Lisbon Strategy. In one sense, Europe's problem is not the absence of change per se but the uneven nature with which it has been occurring across the continent.

National reform

As an indicator of the process of reform at the national level, the Commission has identified key gaps where member states need to focus domestic reform strategies. The following four actions are the measures – according to the Commission – that require the strongest political impetus and are those areas where there is the need for states to take the most immediate action.

R&D/innovation

As mentioned, the EU aims for states to invest 3 per cent of GDP in R&D by 2010. The focus on reform within this area is to encourage member states to improve the effectiveness of public sector support for research. This can be through direct means (such as direct subsidies) or indirect means (through the use of fiscal incentives). These are meant to support the prime mover behind research – the private sector. To support this private sector involvement, member states also need to incentivise the private sector to undertake this research and

innovation by fully implementing market-based reforms. The need for SEM development is especially pertinent in services where reform will ease access to capital to fund the research and innovation.

The pattern for the EU-25 with regard to the Lisbon Strategy is reflected in Figure 1.4 which indicates that only a few of these states are actually meeting the 3 per cent target. Approximately half of the EU-25 states use fiscal incentives to stimulate private sector R&D. The exact method of support varies across states. The Spanish and the Dutch have lowered taxes for R&D while others have developed specific measures aimed at increasing the number of researchers. For example, Germany has launched an excellence initiative to promote exceptional research at its universities. This pattern is being followed by Italy and other Mediterranean states that are developing designated centres of excellence. While these are merely some of the actions being undertaken by states, they do indicate the seriousness with which states are approaching the need to increase research and innovative activity. However, these more active measures have yet to be matched by passive actions to create incentives to innovate by further market liberalisation.

Improving the business environment

The EU business environment remains fragmented which hinders the ability of businesses to innovate and enjoy economies of scale and scope. In part, this sustained fragmentation has been driven by the lack of commitment by states to honour their obligations with regard to the SEM. In addition, the environment – through the legal and administrative systems – has also hindered the development of small and medium-sized enterprises (SMEs). To this end, the Commission has sought to ensure that member states – by the end of 2007 – have established effective support mechanisms for SMEs, and one-stop shops to allow these businesses to undertake all administrative tasks in one place. The Commission is also starting to encourage states to breed a more mature entrepreneurship culture via embedding the subject within the education system. In short, the environment has to be made easier for SMEs to be established, survive and prosper.

The most immediate measure taken by many states was to ensure that there are effective mechanisms for monitoring the implementation of SEM directives. In some cases, measures have been fast-tracked. In addition, e-government procedures have been improved, enabling the development of the aforementioned one-stop shop for business and citizen enquiries. This has begun to speed up the time it takes to start a business. For example, in Denmark, France, the Netherlands, Italy and Finland a business can now be started in less than two weeks. On top of this, the majority of states are undertaking an assessment of the administrative burden upon SMEs with some setting targets for cost reductions. Twelve states have established, or are establishing, simplification programmes to aid the comprehension of the administrative task for SMEs. Elsewhere, member states are undertaking piecemeal reform to open up the market for services.

Employment, financial sustainability and demography

An important driver of the Lisbon Strategy is to mitigate the economic effect of demographic changes, particularly the ageing population (see Chapter 13). Without action, the European workforce will shrink

from about 300 million employees in 2005 to about 250 million in 2050. A smaller workforce will reduce the potential growth rate of Europe's economy and, without reform, make current welfare systems unsustainable.

The Lisbon Strategy focuses on initiatives to improve productivity and increase employment. The intention is to draw more people into the workforce. The aim is to ensure that by 2007, every young person should be offered a job, apprenticeship, further training or some other form of employability measure within six months of leaving school. By 2010, this should occur within 100 days of leaving school. Financial incentives for SMEs to employ younger people are envisaged. Moreover, the aim is to increase female activity rates through gender policies, family-friendly policies and measures to reconcile issues of the work–life balance. These will include more flexible working arrangements, measures that will also help to keep older workers in the workforce by enabling them to combine part-time work and part-time retirement.

Overarching all the employment measures is the need to improve the adaptability of the work so that firms can more readily respond to the rapidly changing needs of global markets. This requires efforts to improve labour force quality with a greater emphasis on continuous training and lifelong learning. This will help workers already in the labour force and help entice the young, the old and female workers back into the workplace and improve productivity.

Some member states have travelled further along this path than others. The Nordic states, in particular, have followed the above prescriptions off their own initiative and with some success (see above). Other states have a lot of ground to make up and social and cultural factors to contend with which will make the introduction of such changes more difficult.

Energy and environmental technologies

Increased global demand for energy combined with tightening of supplies has thrust energy to the top of the EU's policy agenda where it is likely to remain (see Chapter 11). Europe's energy priorities are to ensure the availability of clean energy supplies at prices that do not undermine the competitiveness of its firms. As such, the Lisbon Strategy urges the deepening and strengthening of the internal energy market to promote competitiveness and security of supply. Chapter 11

demonstrates how difficult this has proved to achieve in practice and highlights the many obstacles that remain. Much will depend on the determination of the Commission to ensure that member states abide by the policy commitments they have made. Further progress on energy trans-European networks (TENs) will also help competitiveness and supply security. Exploitation of renewable energy sources and measures to improve energy efficiency will also play their part, as will a well-defined European-wide strategy for dealing with major energy producers. Many of the energy components of the Lisbon Strategy are contained in the 2006 Energy Green Paper which is discussed more fully in Chapter 11.

KEY POINTS

■ Europe is undergoing a process of economic integration within the context of a globalising world economy.

■ These processes pose challenges for Europe's social models.

■ Europe needs to adapt to sustain its competitive position within the global economy.

■ The policy response is engendered within the Lisbon Strategy.

ACTIVITIES

1   Research the Nordic model further, focusing on Sweden, Denmark or Finland. Exactly what have these countries done to transform their economic and social outlook? To what extent are they equipped to meet the twin challenges of globalisation and an ageing population? What can other member states learn from the Nordic model and to what extent can the Nordic experience be transferred to the rest of Europe?

2   Using the example of one state, identify the progress of national reform. Identify major successes and the problems encountered within the reform process.

3   Using one measure of the reform process identified within the Lisbon Strategy, assess the progress towards its realisation across all EU states.

QUESTIONS FOR DISCUSSION

1 What do you understand by the reform process? What does it seek to achieve?

2 Why is reform such a contentious issue?

3 Is reform inevitable or does the resistance to the process highlight the limits to globalisation?

4 What do you understand by innovation and why is it so important?

SUGGESTIONS FOR FURTHER READING

Aiginger, K. and Guger, A. (2006) 'The Ability to Adapt: Why it Differs between the Scandinavian and Continental European Models', *Inter-economics*, 41 (1), pp. 14–23.

Blyth, M. (2003) 'Same as it Never was? Typology and Temporality in the Varieties of Capitalism', *Comparative European Politics*, 1 (2), pp. 215–25.

Dicken, P. (2003) *Global Shift: Reshaping the Global Economic Map in the 21st Century*, 4th edn, London: Sage.

Esping-Andersen, G. (1990) *The Three Worlds of Welfare Capitalism*, Princeton, NJ: Princeton University Press.

Fahy, J. (2001) *The Role of Resources in Global Competition*, London: Routledge.

Hall, P. and Soskice, D. (2001) *Varieties of Capitalism*, Oxford: Oxford University Press.

Krugman, P. (1994) 'Competitiveness: A Dangerous Obsession', *Foreign Affairs*, 73 (2), pp. 28–44.

Peng, M. W. (2000) *Business Strategies in Transition Economies*, Thousand Oaks, CA: Sage.

Porter, M. E. (1990) *The Competitive Advantage of Nations*, Basingstoke: Macmillan.

Sapir, A. (2005) *Globalisation and the Reform of European Social Models*, background document for the presentation at the ECOFIN informal meeting in Manchester on 9 September 2005, available at www.bruegel.org, accessed September 2005.

Schmidt, V. (2002) *Futures of European Capitalism*, Oxford: Oxford University Press.

Werner, W. (2006) 'The European Social Model: Cause of or Solution to the Present Crisis of the European Union', *Intereconomics*, 41 (1), pp. 4–13.

Chapter 2

The integration imperative
Theory and practice

To understand Europe, you have to be a genius – or French.

Madeleine Albright, former US Secretary of State

This chapter will help you to understand:

- the characteristics of economic integration;
- why and how European integration has evolved;
- the role of the main EU institutions;
- the implications of European integration for business.

The extent to which the countries of Europe have striven to integrate their markets and to remove barriers to trade among themselves makes the European business environment unique. Indeed, European businesses and enterprises from non-European countries with European market aspirations have become increasingly affected by policies and programmes devised at the EU level. In other regions of the world, countries have also attempted to integrate and unite their markets but nowhere has the integrative thrust been as ambitious, as far reaching or as successful as in Europe. European integration with all its complexities and problems is worthy of study in its own right for its transformative impact on business, and acts as a benchmark and a learning opportunity for other regions.

This chapter explores the nature of European integration. It begins by providing an introduction to the theoretical aspects of integration, thereby setting the context for the second part of the chapter which outlines why and how European integration has developed in practice. This facilitates understanding of how individual policy measures such as the SEM and Economic and Monetary Union (EMU) have come about. The chapter then discusses the European institutions that have evolved to serve the integration process and whose activities determine the environment in which European business operates and, as a result, become a target for intensive business lobbying. The chapter concludes with general analysis of how European integration has transformed Europe's business environment.

WHAT IS ECONOMIC INTEGRATION?

The literal meaning of 'integration' is the act of combining parts to make them into a whole. Economic integration is based upon the removal of barriers that inhibit the flow of goods, services, labour, capital and communication between states or regions. In the context of the EU, this involves the removal of impediments to trade and mobility between member states so that the area, as interaction and interdependency increase, begins to transform itself into a single economic unit or market. In Europe, this process has evolved in response, in part, to the requirements of enterprises and other commercial and policy actors: the first stage was the creation of a customs union, followed by the creation of a single market and then, for some member states, by economic and monetary union.

Tinbergen (1965) identified two dimensions to integration. The first is negative integration. This refers to the removal of discrimination and restrictions on movement: that is, elimination of measures used by states to inhibit the free flow of resources across borders. The second is positive integration, which involves the modification of existing instruments and institutions to enable transnational markets to function more effectively. Negative integration is generally easier to achieve than positive integration, but has less far-reaching effects.

European integration has been a mixture of both types of integration.

European integration emerged as a consequence of processes within and, increasingly, external to the European economy. The initial themes and concerns of integration arose from the after effects of two world wars that devastated the European economy (see below) and highlighted the need to contain conflict. These initial objectives have increasingly been overtaken by a rationale in which consolidation as opposed to fragmentation is regarded as the most effective way of enabling Europe to sustain and enhance its economic and commercial standing in international markets. This became especially important for smaller European states that needed to re-define their commercial position within an increasingly internationalised economy. In short, at one level, the continuing push for an integrated European economy has become a response to the imperatives of globalisation (see Chapter 3).

Box 2.1 outlines the key stages of economic integration. There is no hard and fast rule that integration starts with a free trade area or customs union and inevitably concludes with EMU. The speed and depth of integration is determined by many factors such as the requirements of enterprises, levels of interaction across borders and the political willingness of elites to commit themselves to deeper forms of integration. Integration is, therefore, a pragmatic affair determined by the particularities of a specific area. Each stage implies a differing degree of commitment by states to the integration process and acceptance of the consequences for their freedom of action. Free trade areas generally require little constraint upon national policy actions whereas EMU implies a considerable loss of policy discretion. Other forms of economic integration lie somewhere in between.

BOX 2.1

FORMS OF ECONOMIC INTEGRATION

Form of integration	Characteristics
Free trade area	■ tariff and quota-free trade between member states ■ little ceding of sovereignty ■ no positive integration ■ persistence of non-tariff barriers between member states ■ retention of national tariffs with the rest of the world ■ problems of trade deflection (whereby commodities from third countries enter via the member state with the lowest tariff) overcome by rules of origin
Customs union	■ free trade in goods and services with a common external tariff to overcome problems of trade deflection ■ some positive integration ■ some common policies, especially in relation to trade with third countries
Single market	■ customs union enhanced by freer mobility of factors of production – notably, goods, services, capital and labour ■ more positive integration ■ fuller development of other common policies, such as competition and regional policy
Economic and monetary union (EMU)	■ measures to secure economic unification strengthened via enhanced coordination and, possibly, inter-state transfers ■ more intense positive integration ■ policy harmonisation to remove the remaining impediments to commodity and factor mobility ■ severe limits on the independent actions of states ■ monetary stability as an accompaniment to economic unification achieved via stabilised/fixed exchange rates or a single currency ■ more fulsome development of centralised supranational power, possibly within a federal context

In the EU, integration started with a customs union rather than a free trade area. Geographical proximity, shared historical experiences, cultural affinities, converging levels of economic development and rising levels of intra-industry trade have all combined to stimulate and enhance the integration process in Europe. Other regional blocs have seemingly little desire to move beyond the most dilute form of integration – the free trade area. However, this may alter as states reconsider their economic interests in the light of continuing globalisation.

An element of dynamism can operate within the integration process, resulting in the spillover of shallower integration into ever deeper integration. This dynamism is frequently born of commercial need: as enterprises exploit opportunities arising from one form of integration, the need for further freedoms emerges. For example, in exploiting the opportunities of a customs union, firms may find they need greater resource mobility to fully realise commercial gains, thereby creating pressure for a single market. Within weaker forms of economic integration, states can overcome problems derived from concerns over trade deflection by use of rules of origin, thereby removing the motive for a common external tariff and the need to develop a customs union. However, if closer trading links raise a demand for closer coordination of other internal policies, this process may be hard to resist.

Traditionally, economic integration has been examined within the bounds of static analysis in which the relative benefits and costs of integration are assessed in terms of trade creation and trade diversion. Briefly, the former refers to benefits from accessing cheaper resources and commodities from partner countries as opposed to their provision from more expensive indigenous production. The latter relates to increasing costs resulting from the replacement of imports of resources/commodities from third countries (which are now subject to a common external tariff) by relatively more expensive production from within the newly formed trading bloc. Such analysis offers an examination of theoretical welfare gains from integration but is often divorced from the process via which gains are realised.

The static nature of such analysis ignores the dynamic nature of the integration process. Integration is osmotic in nature, born of the adaptation strategies of actors to events within the political, economic and social sphere within which they operate and

which bring them into closer proximity with other actors in their own and related spheres. The integration process is complemented by a series of policy events that formalise the interactions and emerging interdependencies within the integrating unit. These policy events are best explained as decisions that often, via the legal, political or economic system, directly affect the actions and interests of operators. A classic example is provided by the SEM and its impact upon the strategies of organisations involved in the operation and development of the European economic space. The development of integration is, in part, explained by spillover where the establishment of one policy born of the integration process develops over time into a justification for further policy initiatives. Accordingly, integration from this perspective is the result of a series of events that are reflected in assorted policy initiatives pushing towards deeper integration.

Examining integration as a consecutive series of policy events underplays the deeper processes at work. There is no inevitability that the development of one policy will necessitate the development of further policy measures. Policy spillover will only occur if the interactions between operators are of sufficient intensity to warrant its development. This underscores a vital rationale for policy development: that is, it should be pragmatic and respond to the changing needs and requirements of those operators/actors directly affected by it. Policy is a phenomenon that can kick-start such processes but the outcome is very much a micro-phenomenon arising from the individual strategies and actions of each operator. For example, the SEM brought freedom of movement for factors of production but its effects were only as great as the willingness and ability of the individual actors to exploit the opportunities it created. Thus, policy events as formal expressions of economic integration are born of the ongoing processes that stimulated their initial development.

The process of integration is formalised within Figure 2.1. The three inter-related phases identified exhibit the following features and characteristics:

1 *Stage one: interactions*: interlinkages and inter-relationships across borders grow to a degree of intensity where the interests of each state become mutually defined, both formally and informally. In terms of the integration process, these links result from the operations of indigenous enterprises in the economies of partner states. Thus, the prosperity of the domestic economy starts to exhibit increasing reliance upon events and processes in other economies. Consequently, the intensity of interactions will be determined by phenomena such as intra-union foreign direct investment (FDI), resource movements between member states and trade links.

2 *Stage two: interdependence*: the mutuality of interest between actors (stimulated by the intensity of interactions) creates a degree of reliance in which the commercial interests of each party become mutually dependent. The result of such interdependence is a non-zero sum game for the states involved. Economic prosperity is mutually dependent to the extent that any independent action to secure advantages for domestic enterprises over foreign firms is likely to result in a commercial loss for all parties concerned. For example, levels of FDI between states can grow to such an extent that independent action to protect indigenous industry can be mutually damaging to all economies concerned.

3 *Stage three: integration*: the result of this process are policy events whereby the mutuality of interests reflected in the process is formalised. Integration need not be fully expressed as a policy event: it may be represented in economic terms by a series of formalised industrial or sectional reorganisations that reflect the preferences of economic operators operating within the larger economic space. Such integration reflects a response to the increased interactions and interdependence across space and may need to be sanctioned by policy measures or regulatory decisions.

In this context, the integration process reflects decisions made by enterprises and/or public sectors in response to interactions and interdependencies. Commercial operators exploiting changes in their operating environment are a powerful factor driving the process of economic integration. Operators working across borders may find limits upon their preferred level of interaction and require policies that further stimulate the integration process.

The emergence of the network economy is an example of the above process in action and promotes integration via the gradual

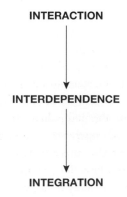

Figure 2.1 The nature of the integration process

expansion of networking relationships (see below). Networks are tools of transnational corporate strategy, enterprise value-added, market access and organisational efficiency. Such networks become ever more important for enterprise success on an international level and as wealth creation becomes more evidently tied into technology and intellectual investment.

Within the context of the network economy, Wallace (1990) offered a distinction between formal and informal integration that broadly mirrors the above analysis and which seeks to provide a formal statement of how, in practice, integration within the EU is likely to evolve. Informal integration arises from the interaction among market dynamics, technology and communications networks. In short, the emergence of informal integration is due to the practicalities of economics and commerce and not to any conscious political decisions. Generally, formal integration acts as a catalyst and facilitates the actions of commercial operators and public administrations and parallels the 'policy and event' analysis offered above. The osmotic tendency to policy (formal) integration is driven by processes derived from market behaviour. Such a stance perceives economics and enterprise functioning as the primary drivers behind the integration process to which politicians respond via a series of policy measures. Thus, political integration is a derivative of broader socio-economic integrative forces.

As economic integration has deepened, there has been pressure to complement it via closer political ties. Increasingly bigger political units are advocated to support the development of big business and as a complement to the coalescence of economic units. This is true of sectors where economies of scale are needed for the establishment of a global presence in specified sectors. Laffan (1992) distinguishes four aspects of political integration:

1 *institutional*: based upon collective decision making;
2 *policy*: based upon the transfer of policy developments to a higher level;
3 *attitudinal*: sources of support for the process among assorted communities;
4 *security*: non-violent inter-state relations.

Such political centralisation is frequently associated with dirigiste economic policies. In part, the desire to develop European champions as a replacement for national champions in the globalising economy offers a commercial rationale to some states for deeper political integration. Business, as a matter of routine, requires a policy (and therefore political) arena that best complements the needs and requirements of the environment within which it operates.

Policy initiatives that shape the development of the European business environment arise out of this process. The Treaties of Paris and Rome, which established the European Coal and Steel Community (ECSC) and the EEC (see below) were modest in what they prescribed in terms of necessary policy measures to complement their objectives. However, as these foundations have been built upon, the range and potency of transnational- or supranational-level policies have expanded. This is a response to policy spillovers in terms of resources and the effects of their consumption (for example, pollution), the need to address interdependencies in stabilisation policies (for example, the ability of competitive devaluations to distort intra-EU competition) and the need to compensate for the potentially negative side-effects of existing policy to complement further integration (for example, cohesion and convergence policies). It is through these

29

processes that policy starts to have an increasingly influential impact upon business.

EMERGENCE OF THE EEC

The idea of European unity pre-dates the establishment of the EEC by decades if not by centuries. However, it took the devastation of the Second World War before the first steps were taken to make this idea a reality. In the immediate post-war era, which coincided with the beginning of the cold war, Europe was preoccupied with economic and political reconstruction, the need to break the cycle of recurrent military conflict and assessment of the security threat from the Communist bloc.

In 1951, the first tentative steps in modern European integration were taken when Belgium, France, Italy, Luxembourg, the Netherlands and West Germany signed the Treaty of Paris establishing the ECSC. On one level, the ECSC was a technocratic organisation, intended to rationalise crucial coal and steel markets. On another level, it was much more than that. To some, it symbolised the first step in the construction of a European community that would gradually extend common policies to other activities. Coal and steel were merely the starting point: both products were central to industrial production and their surrender to supranational control made disintegration into military conflict much more difficult. The ECSC, therefore, provided a framework for the reintegration of Germany into the European mainstream and, in particular, for Franco-German reconciliation.

The ECSC was dirigiste in nature and was run by a strong supranational executive body, the High Authority. These characteristics reflected the backgrounds and aspirations of its architects, Jean Monnet and Robert Schumann, who sought a united Europe based on economic unity and strong, centralised supranational institutions. These ambitions were not wholly shared by participants in the 1955 Messina Conference which led to the negotiation of the Treaty of Rome establishing the EEC and the Euratom Treaty which set up the European Atomic Energy Community. Political unity, however, did not figure highly on the agenda: problems within the ECSC and failure to agree terms of a European Defence Community stymied more ambitious plans for European integration. Rather, the Treaty of Rome stressed economic integration and reflected the strong liberal philosophy of Germany and the Benelux countries who sought the development of a common market.

The Treaty of Rome made a commitment to an 'ever closer union', to economic and social progress 'by common action to eliminate the barriers which divide Europe' and to 'the constant improvement of the living and working conditions of their people'. The predominantly economic nature of the EEC was brought out by Article 2 which stated:

> The Community shall have as its task, by establishing a common market and progressively approximating the economic policies of Member States, to promote throughout the Community, a harmonious development of economic activities, a continuous and balanced expansion, an increase in stability, an accelerated rise in the standard of living and closer relations between the States belonging to it.

Apart from the Common Agricultural Policy (CAP), the prevailing philosophy of the Treaty of Rome was laissez-faire rather than interventionist, relying on benefits to materialise through the mechanisms of competition and interdependence – an approach

MILESTONES IN EUROPEAN INTEGRATION

BOX 2.2

1951	Treaty of Paris establishing the ECSC signed by Belgium, France, Italy, Luxembourg, the Netherlands and West Germany. The ECSC starts work under the leadership of Jean Monnet in 1952
1955	Messina Conference (Belgium, France, Italy, Luxembourg, the Netherlands and West Germany) establishes an intergovernmental committee to develop a framework for integration
1957	Belgium, France, Italy, Luxembourg, the Netherlands and West Germany sign treaties establishing the EEC (the Treaty of Rome) and Euratom (European Atomic Energy Community)
1958	Treaty of Rome comes into effect
1960	Austria, Denmark, Norway, Portugal, Sweden, Switzerland and the UK establish the European Free Trade Area (EFTA)
1961	Denmark, Ireland and the UK apply to join the EEC
1962	Norway applies to join the EEC
1963	President De Gaulle of France vetoes British membership
1965–66	Empty chair crisis → Luxembourg compromise and retention of national veto
1967	Denmark, Ireland, Norway and the UK make their second membership applications and Sweden its first
1968	Completion of the customs union
1969	Hague meeting of European Community (EC-6) leaders agrees to open membership negotiations with Denmark, Ireland, Norway and the UK and to phase in EMU by 1980.
1970	Council agreement to allocate 'own resources' to the EC
1972	Introduction of currency 'snake'
1972	Norway rejects EC membership in a referendum
1973	EC-6 becomes EC-9 with accession of Denmark, Ireland and the UK
1974	Heads of state or government agree to meet regularly as the European Council
1979	European Monetary System (EMS) established
1979	First direct elections to the European Parliament (EP)
1981	Greece becomes tenth EC member
1985	Commission presents White Paper on the single market
1986	Spain and Portugal become EC members
1987	Single European Act (SEA) in force
1987	Turkey applies to join the EC
1989	Presentation of the Delors Report on the creation of EMU
1990	Intergovernmental conferences (IGCs) on political union and EMU run in parallel from December
1990	Stage one of EMU begins
1990	Cyprus and Malta apply to join EC
1990	German re-unification – five eastern Länder become part of EC
1990	UK joins the Exchange Rate Mechanism (ERM)

1991	Sweden applies to join EC
1991	Maastricht Council reaches agreement on draft Treaty on European Union (TEU) → signing of the TEU in February 1992
1992	Portugal joins ERM and the UK and Italy leave it
1992	50.7 per cent of Danes vote against ratification of the TEU and 51 per cent of French vote in favour
1992	SEM deadline – majority of programme completed
1993	Second Danish referendum returns 56.8 per cent majority in favour of the TEU
1993	Currency crisis leads to widening of ERM bands from 2.25 to 15 per cent
1993	Maastricht Treaty (TEU) enters into force
1994	Stage two of EMU begins
1994	European Economic Area Treaty between EFTA and the EU in force – minus Switzerland
1994	First membership applications from CEE (Hungary and Poland) – other CEE applications follow in 1995–96
1995	EU-12 becomes EU-15 with the accession of Austria, Finland and Sweden Norway again rejects membership in a referendum
1996	IGC on review of Maastricht Treaty opens
1996	Dublin Council agrees stability and growth pact for EMU
1997	Amsterdam Council reaches agreement on 'Amsterdam Treaty'
1998	Enlargement negotiations begin with Poland, Hungary, Czech Republic, Estonia, Slovenia and Cyprus
1999	Stage three of EMU begins on 1 January – the single currency is born
1999	Amsterdam Treaty in force – 1 May
1999	European Commission resigns following report on fraud, mismanagement and nepotism
2000	Launch of Lisbon Agenda
2000	Nice European Council agrees text of Nice Treaty
2002	January 1 – euro notes and coins in circulation
2002	December – agreement that ten candidate countries will join the EU on 1 May 2004. Bulgaria and Romania scheduled for 2007. Turkey recognised as candidate country
2002–03	The Convention on the Future of Europe under the Chairmanship of former French President Valéry Giscard d'Estaing completes its work
2003	Nice Treaty in force – 1 February
2003–04	IGC draws up the draft constitutional treaty which is signed by member states in October 2004
2004	EU-15 becomes EU-25 with the accession of Cyprus, the Czech Republic, Estonia, Hungary, Latvia, Lithuania, Malta, Poland, Slovakia and Slovenia
2005	May–June referendum in France and the Netherlands reject the constitutional treaty, sending the ratification process into disarray
2005	October – accession negotiations begin with Turkey

that exactly matched the growing popularity of neo-liberal economics in Europe from the 1980s onwards.

THE TREATY OF ROME TO THE FIRST ENLARGEMENT

The trading credentials of the EEC were initially insufficient to attract the UK into the fold. The UK, always somewhat aloof from Europe and valuing its links with the Commonwealth and the US, preferred an arrangement that involved minimal surrender of national sovereignty. In 1960, this resulted in the creation of EFTA comprising the UK, Norway, Sweden, Denmark, Austria, Portugal, Iceland and Switzerland. EFTA dismantled tariffs barriers among member countries but left the tariffs of individual members vis-à-vis the rest of the world intact. Nevertheless, concerned about the possibility of growing economic and political isolation, the UK re-evaluated its position and applied for EEC membership in 1961. This was followed shortly afterwards by applications from Ireland, Denmark and Norway, which sought opportunities to extend the range of their markets. This initiative rapidly came to nought following veto of the British application by French President, Charles de Gaulle, in 1963, and again in 1967.

President de Gaulle was at the centre of another controversy which had a more long-lasting effect on the integration process. In 1965 the European Commission attempted to make the EEC self-financing. This was too much for de Gaulle who was very protective of national sovereignty, wary of supranationalism and who, accordingly, strongly resisted what he saw as the aggrandisement of supranational institutions, namely the Commission and the EP which would receive increased budgetary powers under the proposals. Failing to secure the support of other member states against the Commission, de Gaulle withdrew France from all involvement in EEC affairs – the so-called 'empty chair crisis'. In order to return business to normal, the other member states agreed to a number of concessions in what became known as 'the Luxembourg Compromise'. This was an informal agreement that when matters of national interest were under discussion, every effort should be made to reach a consensus. Failing this, each member state retained the right to veto policy if it adjudged its vital interests were at stake. As a result, unanimity in the Council became the norm and qualified majority voting (QMV) uncommon, thereby slowing down decision making, reducing ambitions and giving rise to a tendency for lowest common denominator policy formulation.

Although the first decade of the EEC had its successes (the customs union was achieved ahead of schedule, for example), the 1969 Hague Summit relaunched the integration process, giving it an ambitious new agenda which proposed:

- The opening of accession negotiations with the UK, Ireland, Denmark and Norway – the first three became members in 1973. Norway rejected membership in a referendum.
- A re-examination of the system of financing the EEC, which resulted in a shift from membership contributions to a system of Community own resources.
- The creation of a system of foreign policy cooperation known as 'European Political Cooperation' (EPC).
- The introduction of economic and monetary union to augment the common market by 1980 as set out in the 1970 Werner Report (see Chapter 8). In practice, the

implementation of EMU occurred almost 20 years after the Hague deadline.

POLITICAL STAGNATION AND ECONOMIC SCLEROSIS

Despite the Hague Summit's attempts to give integration greater momentum, the balance of success and failure was mixed by the late 1970s and early 1980s. On the positive side, the customs union was well established and accompanied by a common commercial policy. However, there was scant movement onto the next stage of integration – the creation of a common market – and many barriers to trade in goods, services, capital and labour remained firmly in place. The institutional structure of the Community, and the principle of unanimity in particular, were hampering further development.

In the early 1980s, European integration appeared becalmed and there was a fear that European competitiveness was falling behind that of the US and Japan, resulting in 'Eurosclerosis' – a period of lagging growth rates and rising unemployment. From 1979–84, the European Community was dominated by the efforts of the British Prime Minister Mrs Thatcher to achieve a permanent solution to what she viewed as the inequitable budgetary system. The only other policy measure that received any attention was the CAP, widely perceived to be badly in need of reform. The looming southern enlargement to include Greece (which took place in 1981) and Spain and Portugal (both 1986) also raised alarm bells about the need for political and institutional reform to offset the danger that the increased diversity resulting from the accession of these three states would paralyse decision making in the Community.

RENEWED VITALITY: FROM THE SINGLE EUROPEAN ACT TO THE TREATY ON EUROPEAN UNION

By the mid-1980s, several factors had come together to boost the integration process. The 1984 Fontainebleau Council reached a settlement on the budget issue and introduced measures to limit the growth of agricultural surpluses, thereby opening the way for enlargement. In the economic sphere, the old consensus around Keynesian economics was dead and a new one was emerging around supply side economics – that is, the introduction of a range of policies designed to enable competition to flourish and to remove barriers to trade. This approach had its most vocal adherents in the UK, but elements of supply side economics were creeping into contemporary Community policy documents and gaining influence in a number of member states. At the same time, large European firms were adopting an increasingly supranational perspective and, particularly through the European Roundtable of Industrialists (a lobby of the most influential entrepreneurs in Europe), added another powerful voice to the pressure for change.

In 1985, Jacques Delors became President of the European Commission. He pulled together and capitalised upon the above factors and, together with the Internal Market Commissioner, Lord Cockfield, developed the campaign to end the fragmentation of European markets – a major factor in Europe's continuing relatively poor economic performance. This revitalisation of European integration had two elements:

1 the 1985 White Paper *Completing the Internal Market*, which identified almost 300 obstacles which needed to be

removed to end Europe's market frag-mentation; and

2 the SEA, which introduced institutional changes to facilitate the implementation of the single market.

In the wave of Euro-enthusiasm that fol-lowed, the Community also adopted the Social Charter; pushed through the Merger Control Regulation (MCR) – a particularly timely achievement given the wave of cross-border mergers and acquisitions that accom-panied the single market programme; extended the reach of the SEM to previously excluded sectors such as energy and revived the drive towards EMU.

The Internal Market White Paper and the SEA represent a second, more successful relaunch of European integration. Within a short period, the apparent integration paralysis had been overcome and institu-tional obstacles to successful adoption of Community-level legislation had been removed, giving renewed momentum to integration. During this period, both within the SEM framework and through flanking policies (such as competition and social policy), EC activity spread into new areas: a doubling of the Structural Funds, intended in part to offset potential negative regional effects of the SEM, and a significant in-crease in budgetary resources, signalled the

---

KEY FEATURES OF THE SEA

BOX 2.3

The SEA, the first comprehensive revision of the EC treaties, was a response to the need to overhaul decision making in the light of the ambitious single market programme and the Iberian enlargement. Its key features were:

1 More qualified majority voting (QMV)
Article 100A enables the Council of Ministers to adopt most single market legislation by QMV and thus was a powerful weapon in the implementation of the SEM programme. Tax measures, workers' rights and the free movement of people remained subject to unanimity.

2 Increased role for the EP
The SEA introduced the cooperation procedure which enabled an absolute majority in the EP to reject a common position adopted by QMV in the Council of Ministers. In turn, the Council could only overrule the EP by acting unanimously. The cooperation procedure, which applied to most single market legislation, has subsequently been almost entirely replaced by the co-decision procedure.

3 Enhanced policy competence
The SEA formalised and clarified the EC's policy competence in environmental policy, research and technology and economic and social cohesion and codified the Community's role in foreign policy coordination.

4 Creation of a new court
The SEA created the Court of First Instance (CFI) to relieve some of the heavy burden on the European Court of Justice (ECJ).

willingness of member states to support greater integration.

Against this background, it is not surprising that EMU reappeared on the agenda. The 1988 Hanover Council established a committee under the chairmanship of President Delors to identify the actions needed to introduce EMU. This initiative led directly to the IGC that resulted in the TEU, commonly known as the 'Maastricht Treaty'.

The TEU, the most radical revision of the treaties to date, set the stage for EMU and extended the competencies of the Community into new areas. It defined itself as marking 'a new stage in the process of creating an ever closer union among the peoples of Europe' and set a number of objectives, including:

- the promotion of balanced and sustainable economic and social progress through the creation of an area without frontiers, greater social and economic cohesion and EMU;
- the assertion of identity in the international arena, particularly by the implementation of a Common Foreign and Security Policy (CFSP), including common defence;
- greater protection of individual rights through the introduction of Union citizenship;
- closer cooperation in justice and home affairs.

Negotiation of the Treaty was no easy matter. Notwithstanding the Euro-enthusiasm of the late 1980s, radically divergent views on the future of the Community were becoming apparent. Chief among the dissenters was the UK government. Under the leadership of Mrs Thatcher, the UK had been highly supportive of the SEM which both reinforced its own supply side agenda and

represented the ideal type of Community from the British point of view – an organisation based upon optimising market conditions but which does not require significant transfers of power from the national to the supranational level. Mrs Thatcher's resignation in 1990 did not lead to a significant change in the approach of the British government and John Major, her successor, negotiated opt-outs for the UK from the final stages of EMU and from the Social Agreement and Protocol. The UK was not alone in its reservations about further integration: Denmark also shared its preference for intergovernmentalism over supranationalism and enthusiasm appeared to be waning more generally for further integration even before the Maastricht negotiations were complete.

The radical step forward in integration which the TEU represented raised fears of loss of national sovereignty and identity and the rise of a European super-state. In order to prevent the Community acquiring too much power and influence at the expense of member states, the TEU formally introduced the notion of subsidiarity, which stated that:

In areas which do not fall within its exclusive competence, the Community shall take action, in accordance with the principle of subsidiarity, only if and in so far as the objectives of the proposed action cannot be sufficiently achieved by the Member states and can therefore, by the reason of the scale or effects of the proposed action, be better achieved by the Community. Any action by the Community shall not go beyond what is necessary to achieve the objectives of this Treaty.

(Article 3B of the Treaty on European Union)

The subsidiarity principle was introduced to ensure action was taken at Community

KEY FEATURES OF THE MAASTRICHT TREATY

BOX 2.4

The TEU is frequently compared to a temple supported by three pillars:

Pillar 1 The European Community

The first pillar represents the traditional '*acquis communautaire*' (the customs union, the single market, the CAP, Structural Policy, etc.) and new elements such as EMU and TENs. Policies under the first pillar are governed by Community institutions.

Pillars two and three are essentially intergovernmental in nature and are dealt with within the Council of Ministers as common policies agreed among independent states and not within the normal framework of Community institutions.

Pillar 2 Common Foreign and Security Policy (CFSP)

Pillar 2 specifies that the Union and its member states 'shall define and implement a common foreign and security policy . . . [which] shall include all questions related to the security of the Union, including the eventual framing of a common defence policy' [Articles J1 and J4].

Pillar 3 Cooperation in justice and home affairs

The third pillar requires member states to regard some justice and home affairs policies as matters of common interest. These include asylum policy, controls on external borders, immigration policy and residence rights of third country nationals, measures to combat drug addiction and international fraud, and customs and police cooperation.

1 Institutional changes

European Parliament (EP):

■ The TEU introduced a new legislative procedure – the co-decision procedure. Under the cooperation procedure, established by the SEA, the Council of Ministers can ignore the EP's wishes provided it acts unanimously. However, the co-decision procedure gives the EP a veto over legislative proposals and cannot be overruled. The TEU brought many measures designated as cooperation procedure measures under the co-decision procedures.

■ The EP gained the right to subject an incoming Commission to a vote of approval before its formal appointment.

■ The EP to appoint an Ombudsman to receive complaints from citizens about maladministration by Community institutions.

Council of Ministers:

■ Some extension of QMV.

European Court of Justice:

■ ECJ given power to impose fines on member states that fail to comply with its judgments or implement Community law.

Committee of Regions:

■ The Committee of Regions established to provide the Council and Commission with advice on matters of significance for the regions.

2 Policy competence

Community competence was extended in some areas and the Community was awarded new competencies in others:

- EMU: the TEU sets out the timetable, criteria and institutions required for the creation of EMU.
- new policies and policies that previously did not have an explicit treaty base were brought within the scope of the treaties, including consumer protection, development cooperation, public health, TENs, education and culture.
- The strengthening of policies areas first brought into the treaties by the SEA, including environmental policy, research and technological development and social and economic cohesion.
- the incorporation of the Social Charter into the legal framework of the Community in the form of the Social Agreement and the Social Protocol (see Chapter 13).

level only when it was clear that it was the most appropriate and effective level. The principle is difficult to apply in practice and, despite the development of guidelines to facilitate operationalisation of the subsidiarity principle, can give rise to argument about its implementation. In view of these problems, a Protocol on subsidiarity was attached to the Amsterdam Treaty, stating more precisely what it is and how it should be applied.

THE MAASTRICHT BACKLASH TO AMSTERDAM

Given the above reservations, ratification of the Maastricht Treaty was not a foregone conclusion. In July 1992, the Danish population voted against the Treaty in a referendum, technically sinking it forever. However, other member states continued with ratification in the expectation that some compromise would be reached to enable Denmark to change its mind. Ratification troubles rumbled on and the Treaty was even challenged, albeit unsuccessfully, in the German constitutional court. Although not

required under French law, President Mitterrand decided to hold a referendum on Maastricht, believing that an overwhelming 'yes' vote would put integration back on track. However, the referendum campaign became a popularity vote on his government and coincided with a second European currency crisis in a year. Thus, the outcome was an extremely narrow pro-Maastricht vote. However, ratification was able to proceed following minor concessions to Denmark which finally voted in favour of the Treaty, enabling it to come into force on 1 November 1993, one year later than planned.

Other factors also temporarily took the momentum out of European integration, including:

- the ambitious nature of the Maastricht Treaty: Europe's leaders were pushing ahead with integration too quickly for many European citizens, resulting in a lack of popular enthusiasm for, and even distrust of, the European project;
- the highly complex, technocratic and incomprehensible nature of the Treaty;

- the end of Soviet hegemony over CEE which necessitated a rethink of fundamental assumptions about Europe's political geography;
- German reunification;
- the timing of the Maastricht negotiations and ratification with economic recession: support for European integration has always been strongest when the economy is buoyant (early 1960s and late 1980s) and weakest when economic performance is sluggish (late 1970s and early 1980s);
- the currency crises of 1992 and 1993;
- the inability of member states to develop a common approach to the Yugoslav crisis.

In view of these setbacks and reservations, the European Commission which took office under Jacques Santer in 1995 continued the lower visibility, less proactive approach to European integration begun during the final years of the Delors Presidency. Nevertheless, there were some significant achievements during this period. Although not complete by the 1992 deadline and with implementation and enforcement issues outstanding, the SEM had still made significant progress. In addition, the most radical reform of the CAP to date and a significant overhaul of the Structural Funds took place in 1992. The accession of Austria, Finland and Sweden in 1995 went ahead smoothly, only one full year after the European Economic Area (EEA) agreement, which had given EFTA states access to the SEM, came into force. Moreover, the Community grasped the nettle of reassessing its links with CEE countries and later of preparing them for accession (see Chapter 16). Moreover, despite the apparent improbability at one stage of any member states apart from Luxembourg satisfying the convergence criteria, the EMU project became unstoppable

and was launched with the participation of 11 out of 15 member states in January 1999 (Greece was subsequently accepted for membership in 2001).

Article N of the TEU required a review of the Treaty in 1996. As 1996 approached, enthusiasm for the IGC was muted. The outcome was the low key Treaty of Amsterdam which came into force on 1 May 1999. This treaty's ratification occurred almost unnoticed and without the controversy that surrounded the ratification of Maastricht. This was more a symptom of the relatively modest and incremental achievements of the Amsterdam Treaty and the postponement of difficult decisions than of any renewed Euro-enthusiasm. The most significant changes brought about by Amsterdam were some extension of the EP's powers, inclusion of an Employment Chapter and changes to the third pillar (see Box 2.5). However, the IGC failed to undertake reform of the EU's institutions and decision-making processes in preparation for the eastern enlargement.

Amsterdam's relative failure left the way open almost immediately for another IGC and treaty revision. The resulting Nice Treaty was signed in 2001 and came into force in 2003. The driving force behind Nice was again the imperative to ensure that the creaking EU institutions could cope with the looming enlargement – the biggest ever. Once more, the Treaty negotiations soon became bogged down in controversy. This time, there was a significant gulf between the large and small states. The former had agreed to abandon their right to appoint a second Commissioner and the latter were concerned to ensure that all qualified majorities would have to include a majority of states. The main features of the Nice Treaty were:

- a decision to limit the number of Commissioners to one per country at the point

BOX 2.5

INNOVATIONS OF THE AMSTERDAM TREATY

The Amsterdam Treaty largely fell short of expectations but did contain the following important and innovatory elements:

■ Anti-discrimination became a key Community objective, opening the way for equal opportunity cases on the basis of gender, racial or ethnic origin, religion or belief, disability, age or sexual orientation.

■ Further enhancement of the EP's role, including significant and considerable extension of co-decision and the virtual disappearance of the cooperation procedure, except for some aspects of EMU.

■ Council of Ministers: QMV to apply to all new Treaty provisions but only extended to research framework programme among existing provisions.

■ Unanimity retained for all tax measures, for example.

■ European Commission: the Commission President gained rights to object to appointment of Commissioners and to allocate and reshuffle portfolios.

■ Flexible integration: Article K.15 allows those member states that wish to do so to push ahead with deeper integration provided the principles of the treaties are respected; a majority of member states are involved; the *acquis communautaire* is not affected; participation is open to all member states; and that this provision is used only as a last resort.

---

of the eastwards enlargement: when the number of Commissioners reaches 27 (likely to be in 2007 when Bulgaria and Romania accede to the Union), the maximum number of commissioners will be fixed by the Council (it must be fewer than 27) and their nationality will be determined by a rotation system to be agreed;

■ double majority voting: a qualified majority requires 72.3 per cent of weighted votes, a majority of member states plus the support of countries representing 62 per cent of the Union's population;

■ limited extension of QMV to industrial policy, the conclusion of international agreements on trade in services and commercial aspects of intellectual property, measures to facilitate the free movement of people, etc.;

■ flexibility: further refinement of the concept of 'flexible integration' introduced at Amsterdam. Eight countries or more are necessary for closer cooperation that does not include all member states. Previously, a majority of member states had been required. Thus, given the increase in the number of member states following enlargement, the conditions surrounding flexibility have eased considerably.

Despite an initial rejection of the Nice Treaty in a referendum in Ireland, a decision that was overturned in a second referendum, ratification proceeded in a relatively straightforward manner. However, questions continued to be asked on whether treaty reform had gone far enough. In December 2001, the Laeken Council concluded that it had not and launched the Convention on the Future of Europe which called for 'a deeper and wider debate about the future of the European Union'. The Convention was chaired by former French President, Valéry Giscard d'Estaing, assisted by former Italian and Belgian prime ministers, and comprised representatives of the governments of the EU-15 and of the candidate countries; representatives from the EP and national parliaments of current and future members and from the European Commission.

The Convention marked a new departure in EU reform. First, it started with a clean slate and all issues were potentially up for discussion. Second, the Laeken Declaration also set up a Forum for Civil Society to transmit ideas about Europe's future to the Convention from all areas of European society. Third, although the document that emerged from the Convention was not binding on the European Council, it did provide a draft text of a constitutional treaty that became the basis for the work of the subsequent IGC that sat from 2003–04. Many aspects of the Convention's work survived into the final text. In other words, the Convention represented a new, more transparent and inclusive way of agreeing treaty revisions.

The IGC completed its work in 2004 and the draft treaty was signed by member states in October 2004 with a view to ratification in 2006. However, the draft constitutional treaty marked a return to the controversy that dogged the Maastricht Treaty and its future is far from certain. Supporters and opponents of the Treaty cannot agree about what the Treaty means. British Prime Minister, Tony Blair, described the draft constitutional treaty as a 'tidying up exercise'. In other words, he sought to minimise the changes brought about by the Treaty, claiming it merely simplified the texts of the

treaties and brought them together into one document to make them more readable and accessible to the European citizen. In many senses, he was correct but the Treaty did other things as well.

Opponents of the Treaty claim it seeks to build a 'European Super-State' which gives more powers to the EU at the expense of member states. This claim is also difficult to substantiate if one looks at what the draft treaty actually says. For example, the Treaty confirms the principle of subsidiarity and, through the principles of conferral and proportionality, limits the EU to act within the limits of the competencies conferred upon it by member states and restrains the EU from taking action that goes beyond the objectives of the Constitution. In particular, the Constitution explicitly sets out the areas in which the EU has exclusive competence; in which it shares competence with member states; and where its competence is limited to supporting, coordinating or complementary action (see Box 2.6). In addition, for the first time, the Treaty gives national parliaments a role in the EU decision-making process and contains a clause outlining the procedures to be followed if a member state wishes to withdraw from the EU. In reality, the Treaty involves rather more than that implied by Tony Blair's tidying up statement but much less than that implied by the 'Super-statists' (see Box 2.7 for summary of main points).

In order for the Treaty to come into force, it must be ratified by all member states. The ratification process varies from state to state and depends on national practices and laws. In some countries, a referendum is necessary whereas in others approval by parliament is sufficient. Some countries chose to hold a referendum when there is no legal requirement for them to do so. This was the case in France and in the UK: the May 2005 referendum in France registered a

BOX 2.6

CLARIFICATION OF COMPETENCIES

Exclusive EU competence	Shared competence with member states	Supporting, coordinating or complementary action
Customs union	Aspects of social policy	Protection of human health
Competition (in relation to the SEM)	Economic, social and territorial cohesion	Industry
Monetary policy (for eurozone countries)	Agriculture and fisheries	Culture
Conservation of marine biological resources (i.e. fisheries)	Environmental protection	Tourism
Common commercial policy	Consumer protection	Education, youth, sport and vocational training
	Transport	Civil protection
	TENs	Administrative cooperation
	Energy	
	Areas of freedom, security and justice	
	Aspects of public health	
	Aspects of research, technology and space	
	Aspects of development cooperation and humanitarian aid	

BOX 2.7

KEY CHANGES IN THE DRAFT CONSTITUTIONAL TREATY

1 *European Council*
- President of the European Council to be elected by a qualified majority of European Council members for a two and a half year term (renewable once). Replaces the current six-month rotating presidency.
- Group of three countries to chair ministerial councils for 18 months under overall control of the new president but:
  - External Affairs Council to be chaired by new foreign minister;
  - Eurozone Finance Ministers Council to get new president for a two and a half year term.

2 European Minister of Foreign Affairs
- New post responsible for defence and security policy to be appointed by qualified majority of member states.

3 European Commission
- Until 2014, one Commissioner per member state.
- After 2014, number of Commissioners will be reduced to two-thirds of the number of member states (including its President and Foreign Affairs Minister)
- Commission to be chosen on the basis of equal rotation among member states.

4 EP
- Maximum number of seats raised to 750 (minimum of 6; maximum of 96 per country).
- 95 per cent of European laws to be adopted under co-decision procedure (to be renamed the 'ordinary legislative procedure').

5 QMV
- All but the most sensitive decisions to be taken by the 'double majority' system under which a proposal needs the support of 55 per cent of member countries, comprising at least 15 of them and representing 65 per cent of the Union's population. A blocking minority must include at least four members of the European Council.
- Unanimity will still apply to laws on own resources, the budget and future constitutional revisions, taxation and aspects of foreign, security and defence policy.

6 Exit clause
- For the first time, the constitution sets out the procedure for the withdrawal of a member state.

7 EMU
- Enhanced cooperation (a development of the flexibility of the Amsterdam and Nice Treaties) to become a possibility for the euro-group which will be able to adopt common tax policies via QMV.
- Members of euro area to have unified representation in international financial institutions.

8 Charter of Fundamental Rights
- Incorporated into the Treaty.

9 Greater transparency
- Council proceedings to be open to the public when the Council exercises its legislative function.
- National parliaments to be informed about all new Commission initiatives. A proposal must be reviewed if one-third of national parliaments consider it does not comply with the principle of subsidiarity.
- One million signatures by citizens from a significant number of member states can invite the Commission to submit a legislative proposal.

resounding rejection of the constitutional treaty and, as a result of the French vote and an even bigger rejection in the Netherlands shortly afterwards, the UK and other member states cancelled their plans to hold referendums (see Box 2.8).

Given the Dutch and French failures to ratify the Treaty, the draft constitution should fall. The referendum 'nos' in France and the Netherlands thrust the EU into disarray in the summer of 2005. Some member states still wished to push ahead with ratifica-

BOX 2.8

RATIFICATION OF EU CONSTITUTION – STATE OF PLAY, MAY 2006

	Ratified	Comments
Austria	Yes	Ratified by parliament – May 2005
Belgium	Yes	Ratified by parliament – February 2006
Cyprus	Yes	Ratified by parliament – June 2005
Czech Republic	No	Referendum scheduled for June 2006 put on hold
Denmark	No	September 2005 referendum cancelled
Estonia	Yes	Ratified by parliament – May 2006
Finland	No	Ratification scheduled for 2006
France	No	Treaty rejected by 55% of voters in May 2005 referendum
Germany	Yes	Ratified by parliament – May 2005
Greece	Yes	Ratified by parliament – April 2005
Hungary	Yes	Ratified by parliament – December 2004
Ireland	No	Referendum set for October 2005 – postponed indefinitely
Italy	Yes	Ratified by parliament – April 2005
Latvia	Yes	Ratified by parliament – June 2005
Lithuania	Yes	Ratified by parliament – November 2004
Luxembourg	Yes	56.5% in favour in July 2005 referendum
Malta	Yes	Ratified by parliament – July 2005
Netherlands	No	61.8% vote against Treaty in June 2005 referendum
Poland	No	Referendum scheduled for October 2005 put on hold
Portugal	No	Referendum scheduled for October 2005 put on hold
Slovakia	Yes	Ratified by parliament – May 2005
Slovenia	Yes	Ratified by parliament – February 2005
Spain	Yes	76.3% in favour in February 2005 referendum
Sweden	No	Decision to proceed with ratification delayed
UK	No	Plans to hold a referendum in 2006 cancelled

tion to confirm support for the EU whereas others, particularly those where ratification would be problematic, were pleased to suspend the process. The official position of the European Council, announced on 17 June 2005, was that there should be a period of reflection to enable further debate to take place on issues raised by the Constitution and its ratification. The Council proposes it should then return to the issue in the first half of 2006 to assess the situation and to decide how to proceed further.

The traditional way of dealing with referenda defeats in the past (for example, Denmark on the Maastricht Treaty and Ireland in relation to Nice) is to hold a second referendum following further negotiations to meet the needs of the reluctant country. This is unlikely to work in this case. First, the margin of defeat was more substantial than in previous cases and involves two member states traditionally at the heart of Europe. Second, referendum defeats are also probable in other member states. Third, analysis of the defeats indicates that the Constitution was rejected as a result of widespread, albeit non-specific, concerns about the direction in which Europe was moving and a reaction to the poor economic performance of the eurozone.

However, even if the draft constitution is never ratified, it is probable that elements of the Treaty will come into force by other means, either through the normal legislative process, as would be possible for some aspects of it, or through a less ambitious, revised treaty. Either way, the EU is entering turbulent times.

INSTITUTIONS OF THE EUROPEAN UNION

An understanding of European institutions and of their role in decision making is import-

ant for businesses when trying to ensure their views are heard. Businesses can try to influence decision makers directly or through national and/or European trade associations. They can target policy makers at national or at European level, notably the Commission and Parliament. The Council is not amenable to direct lobbying but companies and national interest groups do work to influence the position of their governments in Council negotiations. Once a directive has been passed, the lobbying of national governments will often continue as interested parties try to influence the way it is implemented.

The European Commission

The European Commission is the public face of the Community and, in many ways, is the glue that holds the Union together. The Commission also attracts heavy criticism from those of a more Euro-sceptic persuasion who tend to portray the Commission as a huge monolith, full of faceless bureaucrats circulating endless pieces of paper designed to tie companies and citizens down in a mass of regulation. The negative image was reinforced in 1999 when the whole Commission resigned following a report from the Court of Auditors on fraud, mismanagement and nepotism.

The reality of the Commission is more complex and it performs a range of tasks that give it no exact parallel in member states. It acts as guardian of the treaties and is engaged in policy formulation at all stages and levels: the nature of its involvement varies, ranging from policy broker to legislator in certain fields of secondary legislation. More specifically, the Commission performs the following tasks:

- *Initiator of legislation*: the Commission has the sole right to propose legislation under

Pillar 1 of the treaties and has resisted the EP's attempts to gain the right of initiation. This monopoly facilitates the achievement of a coherent and consistent body of legislation. The Council of Ministers can only take decisions based on Commission proposals, although it can and does ask the Commission to draw up proposals.

- *Legislator*: the Commission also has the power to legislate in its own right. Decisions on legislation involving major political issues or points of principle are taken by the Council of Ministers and the EP but their work would become bogged down if they were responsible for all decisions. Commission legislation, therefore, relieves the legislative burden by dealing with more detailed, technical legislation.
- *Administrator and monitor of EU laws*: the Commission monitors the application of Community law by member states. Failure to implement EU law properly can result in the Commission taking a member state to the European Court of Justice.
- *Representative of the Community in international fora and negotiator of trade agreements*: the Treaty empowers the Commission to act on behalf of the Community in aspects of international economic relations, such as the WTO, upon receipt of a negotiating mandate from the Council of Ministers.
- *Manager of the EU's finances*: the Commission draws up the Community's annual draft budget and plays a key role in management of its finances.
- *Broker and mediator*: in addition to bringing forward legislative proposals, the Commission plays a central, albeit informal, role in trying to reconcile differing views of member states about its proposals. This task calls for highly developed diplomatic

and political skills and can be made more complex because of divergent views within the Commission itself. For example, a proposal on energy taxes, controversial enough in itself, will receive input from at least three Directorate Generals (DGs), including DG Energy, DG Environment and DG Taxation, each of which approaches the proposal from a different perspective.

In 2005, the Commission is composed of 25 Commissioners, one from each member state. Many Commissioners have held high political office in their own member state. Since the 2004 enlargement, the bigger member states have lost their entitlement to two Commissioners. Once the number of member states reaches 27, expected to occur in 2007 with the accession of Bulgaria and Romania, the maximum number of Commissioners will be fixed below 27. Their nationality will be determined according to a rotation system to be agreed.

The Commission's term of office is for five years and begins in the autumn following elections to the EP. This enables the new parliament to approve the appointment of the Commission President-designate (chosen by the Council) and to scrutinise the suitability of the proposed new Commissioners. Member states, in discussion with the Commission President-designate, nominate the new Commissioners. Once appointed, the Treaty requires Commissioners to act totally independently: in other words, they must act in the Community interest and not as representatives of their own state. Each Commissioner has a portfolio of responsibilities corresponding to the Commission's areas of competence. The Commissioners are supported in their work by the Community's permanent civil service which is sub-divided into 26 Directorate Generals and several supporting services such as translation, interpreting and the statistical office.

Given the Commission's central role in the initiation and formulation of policy, businesses are assiduous in lobbying Brussels. Although the Commission could easily be overwhelmed by the number of interests wishing to gain its ear, particularly since the mushrooming of European interest groups and the siting of public affairs offices in Brussels by many companies and local and regional authorities following the SEM initiative, it remains open to technical policy inputs from specialised interests. Despite criticisms of its size, the number of European civil servants engaged in the development and monitoring of policy is less than those employed in national ministries of medium importance or even within a large regional authority. Indeed, shortages of in-house technical expertise create heavy Commission reliance on specialised committees and working parties made up of member state officials and independent experts. This brings needed technical expertise into the policy formation process but also opens the

Commission to criticism that it is working according to the narrow agenda of specific interest groups rather than in the broader interest. In addition, consultation of interested parties can smooth the way for the passage of legislation.

The Council of Ministers

The Council of Ministers performs elements of executive and legislative functions and remains the most important of the EU's decision-making bodies, despite being required to share its legislative powers more equally with the EP since the introduction of the co-decision procedure. Whereas the Commission and the EP are charged with representing European interests, it is in the Council of Ministers that the balance of national interests among member states is worked out and, consequently, where the big political battles are fought and compromises forged.

The Council itself is composed of ministerial representatives from member states.

TYPES OF EU LEGISLATION

■ *Regulation*: a regulation has general application and is binding and takes effect directly in all member states. The MCR is an example of this. The draft constitutional treaty proposes to rename regulations as 'European laws'.

■ *Directives*: directives are binding in terms of the results and objectives to be achieved but rely upon member states to implement them through their own national parliaments. This approach confers upon member states the ability to meet agreed objectives in ways that respect their own traditions and conditions. The draft constitutional treaty proposes to rename directives as 'framework laws'.

■ *Decisions*: decisions are binding upon those to whom they are addressed, which can be individual member states or even companies.

■ *Recommendations and opinions*: these instruments have no binding legal force.

BOX 2.9

Its membership is fluid as ministers attend the Council according to the subject under discussion: agriculture ministers, for example, attend the Agriculture Council whereas transport ministers will be present at Transport Councils. Member states take it in turn to act as President of the Council for a six-month period. The Council Presidency sets the agenda, within constraints, for its period of office, coordinates the Union's business and, along with the Commission, acts as a broker to find agreement between states at odds with each other. The Presidency, sometimes as part of the 'troika' (the immediate past, present and future Council Presidents) also acts as Council representative in relation to other institutions such as the EP and to third countries.

In addition, at least once during each Presidency, the European Council, which is composed of heads of government or state, meets to debate broader and wide-ranging issues surrounding European integration. Although the Council of Ministers was accounted for within the Treaty of Rome, the European Council was formalised in 1974 and was only incorporated into the Treaties under the SEA.

Another less public, but vital part of the Council network is Coreper (the Committee of Permanent Representatives) which is composed of national officials of ambassadorial rank, supported by lower ranking national officials. Coreper carries out much of the preparation for Council meetings and works out the more detailed and technical aspects of legislation, thereby leaving the elected representatives of member states in the Council free to take the more strategic and political decisions.

The history of the Council of Ministers has been dogged by controversies surrounding its voting procedures. The first concerns the debate over qualified majority and unanimous voting. Over time, QMV has been extended to more and more issues. In a Union of 25 states, the widespread retention of unanimous voting would paralyse decision making. Consequently, it is only on certain key issues, such as taxation, that unanimous voting prevails.

The second voting issue relates to the allocation of votes within the Council (see Table 2.1 for current weightings). In order for a qualified majority to be reached a minimum of 232 out of the 321 votes available are required. Moreover, a majority of two-thirds of member states must approve the decision and any member state can ask for confirmation that the votes cast in favour represent at least 62 per cent of the total EU population. Despite the fiercely fought battles over the weighting of the votes, in practice the Council, wherever possible, takes decisions by consensus.

Table 2.1 Weighting of votes under qualified majority voting (from 1 May 2004)

Austria	10	Latvia	4
Belgium	12	Lithuania	7
Cyprus	4	Luxembourg	4
Czech Republic	12	Malta	3
Denmark	7	Netherlands	13
Estonia	4	Poland	27
Finland	7	Portugal	12
France	29	Slovakia	7
Germany	29	Slovenia	4
Greece	12	Spain	27
Hungary	12	Sweden	10
Ireland	7	United Kingdom	29
Italy	29		

OTHER EU INSTITUTIONS

BOX 2.10

In addition to the four main European institutions – the European Commission, the Council of Ministers, the EP and the ECJ – several other institutions play an important role in the work of the EU, including:

The Economic and Social Committee (ESC)
The ESC was established by the Treaty of Rome to involve representatives of employers, workers and other interest groups in the creation of the common market. The main role of its 317 members is to draw up opinions on matters referred to it by the Commission and the Council of Ministers. In some cases, consultation is mandatory and in others it is optional, but other institutions are under no obligation to take heed of its findings.

The Committee of the Regions (CoR)
The Maastricht Treaty established the Committee of the Regions (CoR) as an institution to be consulted on the impact of EU policy at the local and regional levels. It is composed of 317 appointed members who are elected officials at local and regional level in their own member state. The CoR must be consulted on matters relating to TENs, public health, education, youth, culture and economic and social cohesion. It can also, on its own initiative, give its opinion on other issues affecting regions such as agriculture and environmental protection. There is no obligation on other institutions to take heed of CoR opinions.

The Court of Auditors
The Court of Auditors scrutinises the EU's accounts to ensure that spending takes place in line with the Union's budgetary rules and for the purposes for which it was intended. The Court has the power to carry out on-the-spot audits into EU spending wherever it takes place, including programmes managed outside the Community. The Court publishes an annual general report on Community finances and also reports back on individual cases of errors, mismanagement, irregularities, potential fraud, and flaws in systems and procedures that allow irregularities to take place. It was a Court of Auditor's report that ultimately led to the Commission's resignation in 1999.

The European Investment Bank (EIB)
The EIB provides long-term loans for capital investment to promote EU development and integration and works closely with other sources of Community finance such as the Structural and Cohesion Funds. The Bank's lending supports:

- economic progress in disadvantaged regions;
- construction of TENs;
- the enhancement of industrial competitiveness, integration at a European level and support for SMEs;
- protection of the environment, quality of life and Europe's architectural heritage;
- securing energy supplies.

In addition, the Bank lends outside the EU in support of the Community's cooperation policies.

The European Investment Fund (EIF)
The EIF was set up as a cooperative joint venture between the EIB, the EU and several dozen commercial banks as part of the European Growth initiative. Venture capital and loan guarantees to support the activities of European SMEs comprise its two main activities.

The Ombudsman
Since the coming into force of the Maastricht Treaty, all European citizens have had the right to apply to the European Ombudsman if they are the victim of maladministration by a Community institution or organisation.

The European Parliament

Long disregarded by many commentators as a talking shop of little consequence, the EP has, particularly since its democratic legitimacy was established by the first direct elections in 1979, gradually secured an enhanced role in the EU's policy-making process. This transformation has been slow and incremental and the EP is still a long way from fulfilling the same functions as national parliaments. However, the EP has been the major beneficiary of treaty reforms.

Since 2004, the European Parliament has consisted of 732 members (MEPs), organised into seven political groups along transnational rather than national lines. Once a month, the Parliament meets in plenary session in Strasbourg. A further week is set aside for meetings of transnational political groupings. Two weeks every month, the EP's committees sit and work in Brussels. In order to expedite Parliament's work during plenary sessions, there are 20 standing committees of the EP, each of which specialises in a particular area. In addition, the EP sets up temporary committees to deal with particular problems or committees of inquiry.

The EP's three basic functions are:

1 *Legislation*: after years in which the EP's only right was to be consulted on European legislation, it gradually gained powers to amend legislation (although this could be overturned by the Council of Ministers acting unanimously) and now has the power to reject many items of legislation in their entirety. After the Amsterdam Treaty came into force, there were three possible procedures by which the EP engaged in the legislative process (the cooperation procedure was retained only for certain aspects of EMU):

■ *The consultation procedure* (one reading): the EP's opinion must be obtained before a legislative proposal from the Commission is adopted by the Council. However, there is no obligation upon the Council to act upon Parliament's views. This was the dominant procedure in earlier years but has become less important as subsequent Treaty revisions have given the EP greater powers.

■ *The co-decision procedure*: this has become the dominant legislative procedure and has moved the EP towards greater parity with the Council of Ministers. Under co-decision, Parliament can prevent the adoption of a proposal if it believes the Council has failed to take sufficient account of its views. Moreover, if Parliament decides to reject a proposal, it cannot be adopted by the Council. If deadlock is looming, a Conciliation Committee of Representatives of Parliament, the Council and the Commission will try to resolve differences before the third reading of legislation. The draft constitutional treaty proposes renaming codecision as the 'ordinary legislative procedure'.

■ *The assent procedure*: the EP must give assent for the accession of new member states, association agreements, matters relating to citizenship, the Structural and Cohesion Funds and the tasks and powers of the European Central Bank (ECB). The Parliament can block decisions under this procedure but it cannot amend them.

2 *Scrutiny of the executive*: this is a key function of democratic parliaments worldwide and the executive is frequently drawn from the legislature itself. However, this is not the case in the EU and the problems of executing this task are made even more complex by the unusual blurring of executive roles between the Commission and the Council. Scrutiny of the Commission takes many forms, including approval of members of the Commission and the ultimate power of passing a censure motion on the Commission that would lead to its resignation. In relation to the day-to-day work of the Commission, MEPs receive and examine regular reports from the Commission, submit written or oral questions to it and question Commissioners directly in committees or plenary sessions.

3 *Budget*: approval of the Community's budget by the EP is needed. Its power to amend the budget is restricted to noncompulsory items within certain expenditure limits. Compulsory expenditure applies mostly to agriculture.

As the EP grows in stature, so its importance to the business community increases. There are a number of ways in which enterprises can realistically and legitimately engage with MEPs. As in national parliaments, a business can lobby its own MEP. Membership of European pressure groups and more informal networks bring business into contact with MEPs from multiple member states. MEPs on key standing committees can also be a useful channel of influence for business. Expert witnesses, including senior executives from major European companies, are also frequently invited to give evidence in front of parliamentary committees.

The European Court of Justice

Often neglected in discussions regarding EU institutions, the ECJ has nevertheless played a major role in the development of the EU (see Box 2.11) and its interpretation of EU regulations and directives has frequently had a significant impact on business. This is the case in issues of competition policy, pension law, employment law, etc. The Court itself is based in Luxembourg and comprises 25 judges and eight advocates-general who deliver opinions on cases brought before the Court to assist the judges in their deliberations. Since 1989, the overburdened ECJ has been assisted in its tasks by the CFI.

The fundamental role of the ECJ is to ensure that the treaties and Community legislation are respected. More specifically, the Court has jurisdiction in the following areas:

■ *Failure to fulfil an obligation*: these actions enable the ECJ to determine whether a member state has fulfilled its obligations under Community law. For example, the Commission has frequently taken member states to the ECJ for failure to comply with environmental regulations and instituted proceedings against France for refusal to comply with a Commission directive to accept British beef following the end of the BSE crisis.

■ *Proceedings for annulment*: member states, the Commission, the Council and, in certain circumstances, the EP, individuals and companies may apply to the ECJ for annulment of all or part of an item of Community legislation or decision if it conflicts with the treaties. For example, in 2000 the ECJ annulled the 1998 Tobacco Advertising Directive which was designed to phase out all tobacco advertising, including promotion and sponsorship by 2006. The Court ruled against the directive on the grounds that it had been introduced on spurious single market grounds under Article 100A when it was, for all intents and purposes, a public health measure that went beyond the Community's competence.

■ *Proceedings for failure to act*: the Court may review the legality of a failure to act by a Community institution. Such cases are unusual. The most renowned example was the 1985 decision which upheld the action brought by the EP that the Council of Ministers had failed to fulfil its obliga-

tions within the Treaty of Rome to develop the Common Transport Policy (CTP).

■ *Actions for damages*: the ECJ rules on the liability of the Community for damage caused by its institutions or employees in the performance of their duties.

■ *Appeals*: the Court hears appeals on points of law against judgments given by the CFI.

■ *Preliminary rulings*: national courts, when doubtful of the validity or interpretation of an item of Community law may, and in some cases must, request a preliminary ruling on the relevant questions from the ECJ. In addition, individuals may seek clarification of Community law which affects them. Preliminary rulings, which must be accepted and applied by the national court that made the original request for a ruling, form a major part of the work of the ECJ and promote consistency of application and interpretation of Community law across member states.

Over the years the Court has made a number of landmark decisions that have clarified the governance structure of the Community, especially on the relative balance of power between Community institutions and member states, or have had a profound impact on policy within the Community (see Box 2.11).

BOX 2.11

LANDMARK ECJ DECISIONS

The cases discussed below established important principles that have had a fundamental effect on the way in which the Community operates.

1 The supremacy of Community law (Costa v ENEL)
In this 1962 judgment, the Court ruled that by virtue of joining the Community, member states had voluntarily 'limited their sovereign rights, albeit within limited fields [that is, those allowed within the framework of the treaties]' and effected a permanent transfer of power to Community institutions. In other words, where there was a clash between treaty

obligations or legislation derived from the treaties and national laws, Community law was supreme. In fact, the supremacy of Community law is essential to make the Community workable as, without it, member states would be able to pick and choose which pieces of Community legislation they applied, thereby rendering achievement of treaty objectives unattainable.

2 The principle of direct effect (van Gend en Loos)

The 1964 van Gend en Loos case established the principle that certain provisions of the treaty have direct legal effect, enabling individuals and companies to claim treaty-based rights in national courts when there was conflict with national rules. This ruling has been of great practical importance as treaty-based rights prevail over national law even if there is no Community legislation to operationalise these rights. The Court has subsequently ruled on direct effect in relation to many treaty articles including Article 30 (free movement of goods), Article 48 (free movement of workers), Article 52 (right of establishment) and Articles 59–60 (free movement of services).

In one of the most famous ECJ rulings of recent years, professional footballer, Jean-Marc Bosman, challenged the system of demanding transfer fees for players even after the expiry of their contract which he claimed breached his right of freedom of movement as a worker within the EU. He won his case and the 1995 Bosman ruling has transformed business practices within Europe's multi-million euro football industry.

The treaties have enabled the Court to attack discrimination on the grounds of gender in the workplace. Article 119 establishes the principle of 'equal pay for equal work'. In the *Defrenne v SABENA* case, the ECJ ruled that 'the elimination of discrimination based on sex' is a fundamental right based on general principles of Community law which the Court had a duty to uphold. The Court, therefore, determined that Article 119 was in part directly effective, enabling women to claim their right to equal pay in any national court and that equal pay provisions were applicable to both public- and private-sector employees.

3 Principle of mutual recognition (Cassis de Dijon)

In this 1979 case, the ECJ ruled that national standards could not be used to prevent the free circulation of goods (in this case, blackcurrant liqueur) except on grounds of public health, fiscal supervision and consumer protection. The judgment firmly established the principle of mutual recognition which stated that if a product was lawfully sold and marketed in one member state, it must be allowed to circulate freely throughout the Community. This principle greatly simplified the principle of building the SEM by reducing the need to harmonise technical standards and was utilised not only in the case of goods, but also in service sectors and to help secure free movement of workers through the mutual recognition of qualifications.

4 State liability for damage arising from failure to meet obligations under Community law

The 1991 Francovich judgment made member states liable to pay damages for failure to observe its treaty obligations. The decision arose when Italian workers were unable to claim back pay from a guarantee fund for bankrupt enterprises because the Italian government had failed to establish such a fund in line with a Community directive.

THE BUSINESS ENVIRONMENT AND EUROPEAN INTEGRATION

Businesses have been among the strongest advocates of European integration, even if they differ about how deep the process should go. Pressure from the European Roundtable of Industrialists, for example, was an important factor in the launch of the single market, EMU and TENs. Generally, larger enterprises have a stronger preference for deeper integration than SMEs. This may be because the latter tend to operate within a localised market base whereas the former seeks to exploit the network economy. Clearly integration, as Box 2.12 shows, offers many commercial opportunities and challenges to business through easier access to other European markets and enhanced competition in their domestic markets.

Businesses require integration to deliver a regulatory, economic, legal and political environment that creates opportunities, consistency, certainty, clarity and transparency.

This includes smooth and predictable decision making as well as opportunities arising from the opening of national markets. Such issues render it important that businesses are aware of where political power lies within the European business environment, especially with regard to decisions that will affect their strategy and commercial performance. The need to address a number of policy authorities when developing a strategy is both time consuming and costly and is, therefore, something enterprises wish to avoid. In seeking policy approval for actions/strategies (where required) a 'one-stop shop' is almost always preferred. It is these primary concerns that influence the position of business with regard to European integration. The attainment of such objectives is hindered by fragmentation and a lack of credibility over policy formation and decision making.

Cross-border strategies, notably via the emergence of networking relationships, have been a key factor in the shaping of the process of economic integration by commer-

---

BOX 2.12

TYPICAL BUSINESS CHALLENGES AND OPPORTUNITIES FROM INTEGRATION

- enhanced value-added from more diverse sourcing opportunities
- greater intensity of competition within domestic markets
- stimulus to product innovation
- greater opportunities within foreign markets
- reorganisation of production and distribution systems on a transnational basis
- pressure upon costs and prices
- operational efficiencies derived from economies of scale
- exploitation of the international division of labour
- greater price transparency
- rationalisation of product lines
- development of networking relationships
- possible harmonisation of labour conditions
- financing opportunities through integrated capital markets

cial actors. Policies developed at national, supranational and, to an extent, at global levels have worked to support such corporate strategies. Many of these relationships are interactions based upon the emergence of a series of networks to develop positioning within selected markets. This corporate dynamism is a key factor in pushing the integration process and is symptomatic of the emerging network economy.

These transnational networks offer advantages to enterprises in terms of lower transaction costs when accessing new markets or developing new products. They can also produce efficiencies in terms of the division of labour and other aspects of resource usage. Because of the way in which they are formed (as an arena for firm participation) and the struggle for resources which is often the raison d'être for their development, these networks are also political organisations. Enterprise strategy, in view of the integration process and improved market access, will increasingly be based upon the nature and form of the links that it establishes and on the transnational networks to which it belongs. In this context, integration arises out of a network of inter- and intra-firm networks across the European space. These find an expression in transnational joint ventures, mergers, alliances, subsidiaries, etc. These networks are both a reactive and proactive force in the integration process. They are a commercial response to the changing economic environment within which enterprises find themselves and which, by its very nature, is an expression of the growing interdependence between states.

Within this context, policy becomes a tool to promote, control and harness networks as a complement to the integration process and thus as a means of ensuring Europe's commercial success. Competition, industrial, transport and R&D policies,

among others, are some of the clearest expressions of the way in which policy has a direct bearing upon the development of the network economy. This network management role of policy seeks to establish and foster links and to ensure that maximum value-added is derived from them and that activities of enterprises in exploiting these new freedoms do not run counter to the objectives of the regional bloc (for example, by establishing transnational cartels).

Enterprises will seek to use the opportunities created by the process of regional integration to maximise market share, profits or sales. Thus, strategy will seek to organise production or inter- and intra-firm trade to attain these objectives. This not only implies the international reallocation of resources but may also change the location of production to ensure the minimisation of tax commitments, for example. In turn, resource allocations by an enterprise may simply be reactive to the strategies of major rivals. The exact response of transnational corporations (TNCs) to the process of economic integration depends upon the nature of the barriers facing these enterprises. In simplistic terms, enterprises have tended to respond via investment creation or investment diversion. In the former strategy, FDI is stimulated by the need to circumvent barriers created by the development of the regional bloc. This applies to non-EU companies striving to service a market from which they would otherwise be excluded. For EU enterprises, investment diversion is more important as they reorganise production to exploit specialisation and economies of scale. Notably, firms in an integration context undertake investment designed to:

- protect market share in response to the increased competition stimulated by regional integration;

55

- reorganise themselves along transnational lines;
- enhance market share in new and existing markets;
- reflect the competitive advantages of different parts of the economic grouping.

As a result, two changes to industrial structure are anticipated:

- a reduction in horizontal integration as firms eradicate duplication across states and concentrate production in one or two key plants;
- increased vertical integration as firms seek to minimise the transaction costs involved in serving a more integrated market.

In practice, the benefits for business from the development of integration have, in part, been retarded by the extent of political and economic diversity within Europe. Such problems have limited the coherence of the process and have thereby limited the commercial opportunities from integration.

KEY POINTS

- An understanding of the evolution of the EU and of its institutions helps business understand the context of individual policies and how they can influence the decision-making process.

- Businesses can attempt to influence the formation of EU policy at both national and European levels directly or through national and European trade associations.

- The ECJ has had a major, and underrated, impact on forging the European business environment.

- Reform of the EU and its institutions is reactive and lags behind economic and market realities.

- The objectives of integration have changed. It is a complex process that is increasingly driven by the needs of business. Policy responses at national and EU level can slow down or accelerate the process, depending on the willingness of the politicians to act.

- Integration, in turn, results in industrial restructuring as companies seek to position themselves in line with new market realities.

 ## ACTIVITIES

1 Identify and research two decisions of the ECJ that have had implications for business. Be prepared to explain these implications in a presentation to your fellow students.

2 Choose an industrial or services sector and research how and where the industry trade association(s) lobby to try to influence policy. Note: there is likely to be both a national and a European/international dimension to this lobbying.

QUESTIONS FOR DISCUSSION

1   What were the main reasons behind the establishment of the EC? To what extent are they still relevant today? Are there any new developments that reinforce the rationale for European integration?

2   Why do businesses active in Europe need to understand the role of the EU and how it works?

3   What are the main implications of European integration for business?

4   The EU has grown from six members in 1958 to 25 in 2004 and is set to expand further. What does this mean for:

   ■ institutions and decision making;

   ■ business?

5   What is the significance of the problems concerning the ratification of the draft constitutional treaty for the future direction of the EU?

SUGGESTIONS FOR FURTHER READING

Beach, D. (2005) *The Dynamics of European Integration: Why and When European Institutions Matter*, Basingstoke: Palgrave Macmillan.

Bomberg, E. and Stubb, A. (2003) *The European Union: How Does it Work?*, Oxford: Oxford University Press.

Dinan, D. (2004) *European Recast: A History of European Union*, Basingstoke: Palgrave Macmillan.

George, S. and Bache, I. (2001) *Politics in the European Union*, Oxford: Oxford University Press.

Gillingham, J. (2003) *European Integration 1950–2003: Supranational State or New Market Economy*, Cambridge: Cambridge University Press.

Laffan, B. (1992) *Integration and Co-operation in Europe*, London: Routledge/University Association of Contemporary European Studies.

Middlemas, K. (1995) *Orchestrating Europe: The Informal Politics of the European Union 1973–1995*, London: Fontana.

Rittberger, B. (2005) *Building Europe's Parliament: Democratic Representation Beyond the Nation State*, Oxford: Oxford University Press.

Robson, P. (1998) *The Economics of International Integration*, 4th edn, London: Routledge.

Tinbergen, J. (1965) *International Economic Integration*, Amsterdam: Elsevier.

Tsoukalis, L. (2003) *What Kind of Europe?*, Oxford: Oxford University Press.

Urwin, D. W. (1995) *The Community of Europe: A History of European Integration since 1945*, 2nd edn, London and New York: Longman.

Wallace, H., Wallace, W. and Pollack, M. (eds) (2005) *Policy-making in the European Union*, 5th edn, Oxford: Oxford University Press, Chapters 1–3.

Wallace, W. (ed.) (1990) *The Dynamics of European Integration*, London: Royal Institute for International Affairs/Pinter.

Chapter 3

European business in a global context

It has been said that arguing against globalization is like arguing against the laws of gravity.

Kofi Annan, seventh Secretary-General of the United Nations

This chapter will enable you to:

- identify the key drivers of the globalisation of markets;
- demonstrate the commercial importance of the EU to the global market place;
- understand the role of European MNCs in international markets;
- explain corporate restructuring in the face of international competition;
- analyse the rise of economic nationalism.

Assessment of the role of the EU in the global economy requires examination of how European business is both affecting and affected by the process of globalisation. Much of Chapter 1 has highlighted how the onset of globalisation is altering prevailing models of economic and political management, especially at member state level. This chapter looks at the flipside of this question and analyses the importance of the EU and the activities of European business to the development of the global economy. The chapter initially discusses the globalisation process before moving on to examine the performance of the European economy and its businesses in the context of the broader international economic environment. An assessment of the impact of European business is then undertaken within the context of emerging economic nationalism – a threat to the internationalisation of markets.

THE FORM AND NATURE OF GLOBALISATION

There are many strands to the concept of globalisation but the unifying theme is one of interdependence. This phenomenon has arisen because of the successive removal of obstacles to the movement of factors of production. This has resulted in the blurring of national boundaries ultimately leading to the creation of what Ohmae (1990) called 'the borderless world'. This variation of globalisation results in a totally interdependent world economy in which market forces dominate and national borders become increasingly meaningless to the corporate sector. In the mid-1990s, the International Monetary Fund's (IMF) World Economic Outlook defined globalisation as: 'the growing interdependence of countries worldwide through the increasing volume and variety of cross-border transactions in goods and services and of international capital flows, and also through the more rapid and widespread diffusion of technology.'

This definition is a useful starting point, highlighting (the aforementioned) interdependence, the increasing number and range of cross-border transactions and the important role played by technology. However, it is incredibly difficult to define such a multilayered and complex phenomenon as globalisation or to reflect the significance of the different elements of the definition in one sentence.

From the corporate standpoint, globalisation results in the intensification of competition, within both domestic and export markets, requiring increasingly rapid adjustments to changes in business operating environments. Responses and strategies can vary but the forces alluded to above encourage the growth of the truly stateless enterprise which plans according to the dictates of the market and regards national borders as an increasing irrelevance. The characteristics of such strategies include a global conception of markets and a striving for critical mass, or size, as both a defensive and offensive

response to intensified competition. A typical strategy would be a renewed search for agreements, alliances and joint ventures both to help companies share the burdens of a range of costs and to confer upon them valuable 'insider' status in markets outside their home base.

In order to understand globalisation in terms of its deeper meaning and significance for business, it is essential to analyse the key, closely linked drivers behind the globalisation process.

The changing economic paradigm

The growing interdependence of economies referred to in the above definition of globalisation has only taken place because of the growing acceptance of economic liberalism as the preferred method of 'managing economies'. Indeed, the idea of managing economies is a contradiction in terms in the context of neo-liberalism. This approach is based on limiting the role of government to the provision of an environment in which businesses can flourish and which relies heavily on unleashing the forces of competition. The extension of competitive liberalism has increased the complexity of interdependence and deepened the globalisation that has taken place with significant implications for corporate strategies and behaviour. At one level, changing regulations and attitudes create additional and more secure investment opportunities, not only through traditional market entry modes such as mergers and acquisitions and joint ventures but also, increasingly, through participation in privatisation programmes in developed countries, newly industrialised economies, transitional economies and in many developing countries. At a deeper level, the greater openness arising from the spread of liberal ideas and

59

policies encourages the emergence of a mindset and a strategy that operates beyond traditional national market boundaries.

The spread of international governance and regulation

As economic liberal ideas were more widely adopted and barriers to cross-border business were eroded, questions came to be asked about the most appropriate location of policies to regulate the business environment. Increasingly, such policies were formulated at a regional level by organisations such as the EU and/or at international level. In itself, this development is a manifestation of the globalisation trend and originated with the progressive reduction of tariff barriers among WTO members. As integration through trade developed, other barriers to integration were thrown into the regulatory spotlight resulting in the emergence of a trade agenda with both a broader (for example, the Uruguay Round incorporated agriculture and services trade) and deeper scope. Technological developments, particularly the emergence of e-commerce, also pose new challenges to traditional governance structures. These factors combined are shifting the global economy from 'shallow' integration (trade-led integration brought about by tariff reductions) to deep integration (the need to harmonise or at least approximate domestic regulations). This shift is more evident at the regional as opposed to the international level. In the case of the EU, which has experienced the deepest integration of all regional organisations, much of what is perceived as domestic policy, at least in market regulation terms, has already shifted from the nation state to the regional level by way of the SEM (see Chapter 4). Moreover, the spectre of a shift

to a higher level of governance on a number of erstwhile domestic issues has strengthened the argument that integrative trends are blurring national boundaries and eroding the sovereignty of nation states.

Finance and capital spread

The additional trade and investment generated by globalisation requires parallel movements of capital and finance. Deregulation, liberalisation and technological change have, indeed, combined in recent decades to transform the finance sector to support the growing number of transnational transactions. Traditionally, finance was always a heavily regulated and hence geographically fragmented activity. Since the 1960s, the combination of more open markets with the adoption of new information and communications technologies (ICTs) has transformed international capital movements. In principle, capital can now be transferred around the world in an instant. In practice, although significantly reduced, regulatory barriers continue to prevent the full collapse of time and space for financial transactions. However, the potential for instantaneous financial transactions spanning the globe remains and is moving nearer to realisation. Although more mobile capital is clearly needed to support a more integrated international economic system and all parts of the production chain within multinationals, this mobility also brings with it more volatility.

The spread of information and communication technology

Technological innovation and its diffusion have clearly played a significant role in the globalisation process reducing both transaction and operational costs. For companies in many sectors, the development of new technology and/or its exploitation makes the difference between success and failure. This is increasingly the case not only in explicitly technological sectors but also, with the advent of e-commerce, in traditionally less technologically sensitive sectors such as retailing. However, technology's precise significance in the globalisation process is a subject of some controversy. Technological determinists argue that technology is the prime mover of change and that it makes globalisation inevitable and irreversible. A more eclectic approach maintains that technological developments, although central to the transformation of intra- and inter-state and enterprise relationships, are not sufficient to bring about such change on their own account. Other social, political and economic factors such as the spread of neo-liberal economic philosophy with its themes of liberalisation, deregulation and open markets, are also needed. In other words, technology is an important facilitator of change rather than its primary mover.

Social and cultural convergence

A consequence of greater liberalisation and the spread of global communications technology is a degree of social and cultural convergence, in itself a pre-condition for globalisation. This does not imply that a global culture has replaced, or is replacing, the diversity of local and national cultures in the world. The range and deep-rootedness of beliefs, values, experience and symbols is too extensive for that. Social and cultural convergence across boundaries is only possible when there is no clash with more profoundly held cultural beliefs specific to a particular place or grouping, such as religion. The

emergence of a global consumer, or at least consumers with common preferences across a significant part of the globe, creates opportunities for the creation of global products – that is, homogeneous products that can be sold throughout the world on the basis of global marketing and advertising campaigns. Truly global products are relatively few and far between but where their existence is possible, they increase the viability and desirability of developing international production systems and value chains, with all the potential gains in terms of scale economies and utilisation of different comparative advantages.

ECONOMIC INTEGRATION AND THE INTERNATIONAL BUSINESS ENVIRONMENT

Overall, the impact of globalisation on an economy can judged and assessed according to its impact across the following issues:

- *the scope of its impact*: in terms of the reach across a number of states as indicated by the diffusion of technology, growth of trade and FDI;
- *the intensity of its effects*: in terms of the depth, embeddedness and extensiveness of the integration that has taken place, both between countries and within firms;
- *the sensitivity of economies*: this represents the degree to which events in one part of the global system transmit themselves to other parts of the system.

In the case of the EU, the interaction of these three concerns has had a tangible impact not least upon the form and nature of the integration process. As globalisation has progressed so the rationale behind integration has changed to meet the requirements of internationalising markets. Increasingly, European integration is evolving to meet

61

the requirements of enterprises within this context.

Although the need to improve Europe's economic performance in relation to its main competitors, Japan and the US, was a significant factor behind the renewed drive towards European integration in the mid-1980s, the resulting focus on the creation of one 'economic space' paradoxically encouraged a concentration on the dynamics of internal processes, resulting in an almost total neglect of external impacts. However, policy makers, academics, journalists and other commentators simultaneously adopted the word 'globalisation' which is frequently used both to explain the economic ills besetting the advanced industrial economies, such as the return of mass unemployment and the apparent lack of affordability of welfare states, and to justify the policy inertia of governments in the face of these ills. These trends have justified actions by certain states to isolate and protect indigenous industries and populations from these impacts (see below). Underpinning this is an inbuilt suspicion of the internationalisation process and a belief in trade as a zero sum game.

The term 'globalisation' is often used loosely, with some limited agreement on its meaning but with scant consensus on whether the world economy is actually in the process of going global or on what stage it has reached. This creates problems for politicians in developing responses to the undoubted changes under way in the world economy. This is not the place to tackle these issues directly, but it is crucial to remember that European integration takes place within a much broader world context and that what happens outside Europe's borders (if, in fact, these borders still matter, which pure globalists would deny) has a significant and increasing impact on the formulation of EU policy and on the strategies of European firms.

One effect of this globalisation process upon the performance of Europe has been stimulating the reform of the level of state activity and the challenge to the prevailing social model (see Chapter 1). The shift in the balance of power away from the state and towards the private sector means that market-driven finance will move away from these locations that counter their interests. The core challenge is the extent to which these changes are acceptable to the electorate. The growing unease at the implications of globalisation and the most effective means of finding an appropriate solution to the challenge are at the heart of many popular political and economic debates.

However, as indicated, the impact of globalisation has been felt more strongly at the European level than at the global level per se. Europe's trade relations with developing states have been weakening and the form and the nature of regional trade agreements have shifted. While EU businesses are overwhelmingly focused on selling to, and investing in, other EU states (see below), it is important to stress that this 'psychic proximity' is part of a broader picture of the positioning of EU states and business on a global stage. Market integration could in theory aid the international/global competitiveness of EU business in a number of inter-related ways, including:

- the promotion of consolidated market structures to realise scale and scope economies;
- the creation of a single, more homogeneous home market;
- the sharing of best practice across firms of all sizes;
- the creation of a more focused effort on research and innovation;
- more efficient capital and labour markets.

While many of these benefits might appear speculative, it is nevertheless important to view the process as a platform to attack and/or consolidate positioning in the global economy. Thus, the process of the creation of a common economic base is important in establishing a means for these 25 relatively small states to compete within the global economy.

The impact of internationalisation upon European business is both reactive and proactive. The latest figures suggest that nearly 70 per cent of the trade of European business is with businesses in other EU states and the majority of EU FDI is also intra-European. This suggests that one challenge of internationalisation is to secure this market position from both internal and external threats. This means that EU business operations in international markets have multiple facets. First, a European firm must seek to prevent erosion of its competitive position within its domestic market. Second, a European business must seek to protect, preserve and, where possible, enhance its position within those international markets where it operates. Third (and perhaps most challengingly), the European firm seeks to create new and sustainable positions within emerging segments and new market places. The key to delivering on these proactive and reactive strategic challenges is reflected within the competitive positioning of the EU economy vis-à-vis its major competitors: both current and emerging.

THE EUROPEAN ECONOMY: COMPARATIVE PERFORMANCE

As highlighted above and in Chapter 1, the most pressing concern for European business and the environment within which it oper-ates is its ability to cope with the process of globalisation and what it means for both firms and national economies as well as for the health of the European economy gener-ally. The debate emerging within the European institutions and among European policy makers has centred upon the poor rel-ative performance of European economies and of EU businesses within the context of globalising markets (see Chapter 1).

The competitiveness of the EU economy is a reflection of its performance vis-à-vis its major rivals. This competitiveness is a reflec-tion of the ability of the EU economy (as well as the firms within it) to win market share and be successful in both export and dom-estic markets. While this may smack of mercantilism and suggest that trade is a zero sum affair, competitiveness is important in terms of generating sustainable employment and long-term growth. Thus barometers of competitiveness are based on whether an economic framework is sufficiently beneficial to business to facilitate job creation through nurturing an environment in which busi-nesses (irrespective of nationality or owner-ship) can thrive and prosper. In many ways, competitiveness as a concept almost seeks to apply the notion of strategic performance to policy environments.

A running theme of this text is the relative under-performance of the EU economy. An explanation of this proffered within Chapter 1 is the inability of the environment to encourage and promote business perform-ance and creation. As much of the Chapter 1 stresses, many place the blame for Europe's relatively poor performance on the existing social models and the way that these increase cost of production without any direct increases in productivity for firms. In this context, the Lisbon Agenda is about remov-ing such inconsistencies through a gradual process of reform.

As a region, the poor performance of the EU has been driven by the lack of competitiveness of the largest economies (notably France, Germany and Italy). While there are evident supply side problems, a major short-term problem is based on the inability of the economy to generate domestic demand to push growth forward. The World Competitiveness Report lists the 60 top nations ranked in terms of competitiveness. The resulting league table is shown in Table 3.1.

The best EU performers are the Nordic states who have been able to combine good social provision with a competitive environment (see Chapter 1). For states such as Italy and Spain, their competitiveness ranking is poor and lags behind that of many smaller states. In blunt terms, the conclusion has to be drawn that many EU states are simply not very good places to do business. The result is that these economies risk getting caught in a vicious cycle of declining competitiveness and sustained erosion of their share of trade and inward FDI.

However, despite this competitive threat to the EU, the commercial power of its con-stituent economies should not be under-stated. In crude statistical terms, the EU's role in trade and FDI is, perhaps, the highest profile evidence of the sustained importance of EU business to the global economy (see below).

Trade

The importance of the EU as a trading entity within the global system is reflected in the share of the EU-25 in both import and export markets for goods (merchandise trade). In 2003, the EU-25 was the single biggest trader of goods (measured by the sum of imports and exports) within the global economy, accounting for 18.4 per cent of total merchandise trade. This is just slightly ahead of the share of the US which had 17.7 per cent of global trade in goods, while China and Japan accounted for 7.1 and 7.3 per cent respectively. This importance of the EU in global product markets is also apparent in services markets where the EU-25 comprised 25.8 per cent of total global trade in services. This is some way ahead of the US which had an 18.7 per cent share. The rest of the market was highly splintered among a large number of states.

The EU's major import and export partners are reflected in Table 3.2. In 2004, the EU ran a trade deficit with the rest of the world of over €65 billion. The US was both the single largest exporter to, and importer from, the EU. The majority of this trade was in manufactured goods which comprised around 66 per cent of imports and around 85 per cent of exports. The EU is also a large net importer of energy which comprised nearly 18 per cent of imports and only 3 per cent of exports. Agricultural products comprise around 8 per cent and 7 per cent of imports and exports respectively. The remainder of

Table 3.1 World competitiveness scoreboard

Rank	Country	Rank	Country
1	USA	12	Ireland
2	Hong Kong	13	Netherlands
3	Singapore	14	Sweden
4	Iceland	17	Austria
5	Canada	22	UK
6	Finland	23	Germany
7	Denmark	30	France
8	Switzerland	38	Spain
9	Australia	53	Italy
10	Luxembourg	57	Poland

Source: World Competitiveness Report/IMD.

the EU's trade in goods consists of other primary products which comprise 9.1 per cent of imports and 6.5 per cent of exports. The EU's trade in services registers only substantive flows between the EU and the US.

As Table 3.2 indicates, the majority of the EU's trade is with developed states. However, an increasing proportion of EU trade (as Chapter 16 shows) is with developing states. Indeed, in 2003, the EU represented the single largest export market for developing economies, representing nearly 60 per cent of their total market. These imports tend to be focused in three main areas: energy, agriculture and textiles.

Table 3.3 highlights one of the core challenges facing the EU. Despite the expansion of the EU to include ten new members, the EU share of the global market place is declining; falling by 0.6 percentage points during 1995–2004. While it can be argued that to some degree this is a natural consequence of the emergence of China and India, the fact that the US has been able to sustain and even enhance its share of the global market raises concerns. These issues are dealt with in greater depth in succeeding chapters. However, despite this erosion of its market share, the EU's overall trade flows have been

rising. Figures 3.1 and 3.2 indicate the rise in European trade flows in both goods and services. These graphs show a deficit in merchandise trade and a surplus in service trade.

FDI

The importance of the EU to the international trading system extends into FDI. For the period 2001–03, the EU was the largest global source of both inward and outward FDI. Together the EU states represented 29 per cent of total global inflows of FDI. The US and China accounted for 20 per cent and 12 per cent respectively. The US is

Table 3.3 Share of world trade (excluding intra-EU-25 trade) (%)

State	1995	2004
EU-25 (excluding intra-EU trade)	19.1	18.5
US	16.5	17.1
Japan	9.5	7.1
China	3.4	8.4
India	0.8	1.2

Table 3.2 The EU's major trading partners, 2004

Imports				Exports			
Rank	Partners	Mio euro	%	Rank	Partner	Mio euro	%
	World	1,027,580	100		World	1,070,760	100
1	US		15.3	1	US		24.3
2	China		12.3	2	Switzerland		7.8
3	Russia		7.8	3	China		5.0
4	Japan		7.2	4	Russia		4.7
5	Switzerland		6.0	5	Japan		4.5

Source: Eurostat.

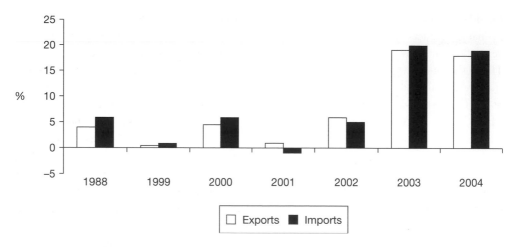

Figure 3.1 *European merchandise trade, 1998–2004 (annual percentage change in value)*
Source: WTO.

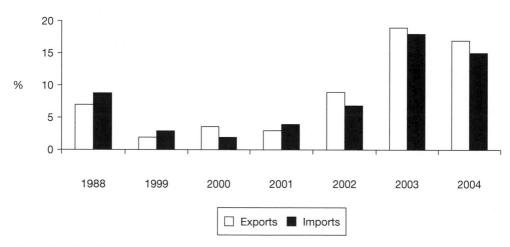

Figure 3.2 *Trade in commercial services, 1998–2004 (annual percentage change in value)*
Source: WTO.

the single biggest contributor of extra-EU inflows of FDI comprising 43.9 per cent of inward investment. Japan and Canada contributed 5.8 and 4.8 respectively. In terms of outward flows of FDI, the EU represents some 42.1 per cent of global outflows of FDI with the US representing 31.8 per cent. The US is the single biggest recipient of EU FDI outflows. It receives 34.1 per cent of total EU overseas direct investment while China receives 1.6 per cent, Japan, 0.3 per cent and Canada 2 per cent. These are reflected in Figures 3.3 and 3.4.

This pattern of EU FDI reflects the presence of a large number of MNCs on European territory as both inward and

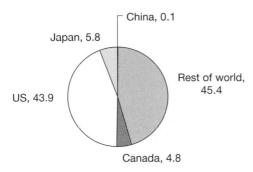

Figure 3.3 *EU FDI inflows, 2001–03 (%)*

Source: European Commission.

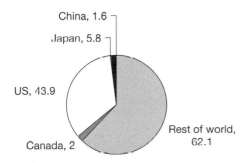

Figure 3.4 *EU FDI outflows, 2001–03 (%)*

Source: European Commission.

outward investors. In 2003, the EU-15 was home to 30,709 parent corporations and 64,464 foreign affiliates. The 2004 expansion increased the number of parent companies only marginally by 1,171 but the number of foreign affiliates increased substantially by over 124,000. These inward investment patterns reflect the substantial increase of intra-EU FDI since the launch of the SEM. Generally, intra-EU FDI accounts for around three-quarters of total EU FDI, though this has fallen from over 80 per cent in 1999–2000.

For the EU-15, the share of services-based FDI (as a percentage of total FDI) has increased substantially between 1990 and 2002, rising from around 55 per cent to nearly two-thirds. However, this hides big variations between states, with the services FDI representing over 80 per cent of total FDI in the UK, Germany and Austria. Export-oriented FDI projects tend to focus on call centres and IT services. This rise is reflected within Figure 3.5.

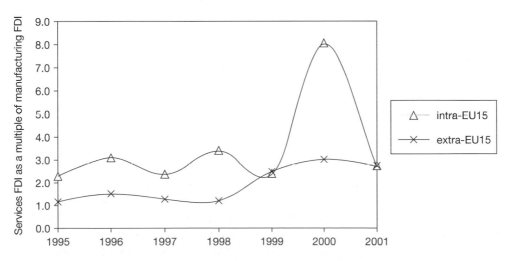

Figure 3.5 *The rise of services within EU FDI*

Source: European Commission (2005).

67

BOX 3.1

IS THE US REALLY THAT FAR AHEAD?

Many within the EU look towards the US as the benchmark for their economies. At first sight, the performance of the US economy has indeed been impressive. In the ten years to 2003, US economic growth has outpaced the EU's by an average of over 1.2 per cent per annum. In addition, there are other areas where the US has outperformed Europe, not least in terms of innovation and new business creation. However, GDP on its own is only a crude measurement of relative performance. Most notably, comparison of the relative prosperity of the US and the EU by GDP growth figures alone ignores the extent to which the former's population has been growing faster than Europe's. Thus, when GDP per capita is measured, the growth differential between the EU and US narrows sharply to just 0.3 per cent per annum.

Furthermore, much of Europe's underperformance can be explained by slow growth in France and, to a greater extent, Germany; which represents one-third of eurozone GDP. If Germany is taken out of the calculations, then Europe's growth more than matches that of the US. In addition, other anomalies tend to understate Europe's performance. For example, Europe's figures on labour productivity include the low-growth public sector which is excluded from US figures. Strip out the EU public-sector figures and labour productivity begins to draw level with that of the US.

It is also widely assumed that the US has done especially well at job creation compared to the EU. However, in the decade to 2003, employment in the US expanded only 0.3 per cent more than in the euro area. If Germany is excluded, then these growth rates were matched by the eurozone. Furthermore, between 1997 and 2003, job creation in the eurozone has risen by 8 per cent compared to 6 per cent in the US. While productivity growth has slowed within Europe, this has, paradoxically, been the result of successful economic reform. This reform has tended to take place at the lower skilled end of the labour market, thus as more unskilled enter the workforce as a result of these reforms, average productivity is bound to slip. This may only be a short-term phenomenon, as the re-skilling of this segment of the labour force is likely to raise productivity over the longer term. This is also reflected in the return on capital which has been broadly the same across the US and Europe despite the popular perception that the US has been powering ahead.

Differences in the way that growth is measured can also inflate/deflate figures to give misleading impressions. For example, the US counts information technology (IT) expenditure as investment, which inflates GDP. The EU counts such expenditure as an expense and thus excludes it from such figures. In addition, Europe does not include improvements in the quality of IT in the figures so any improvement in IT capabilities is excluded. In the US, if the processing capability of a computer doubles while the price stays the same, then the price is said to have halved. This difference matters when the price deflator (a measure of changes in prices over a defined period) is used to convert growth in nominal spending on IT into real terms. Again, this overstates US growth.

Despite all this, the average European in the eurozone is still 30 per cent poorer than the average US citizen and this has changed little over the past three decades. However, this may simply reflect a broader trade-off whereby the average European may prefer a more favourable work–life balance. As the EU economy has grown, so the average European has decided to exchange increases in productivity for more leisure time rather than more pay. While productivity has grown and caught up with the US, it has not been reflected in GDP per income as workers have chosen to work less. Thus, while the US has higher GDP, it arguably comes at the cost of higher economic welfare. In addition, US GDP is also inflated by idiosyncrasies in terms of climate, crime etc. which means that more has to be spent on these areas. While these increase GDP, they do little to improve US welfare. Inclusion of such factors narrows the gap between EU and US living standards to as low as 10 per cent.

However, while it may appear that US performance over the EU has been exaggerated, the EU still has to face many issues regarding its prevailing social models, the ageing population and its inability to create jobs in sufficient numbers. Thus, if the EU does not want to slip further with regard to its performance vis-à-vis the US, its workers may have to work longer hours.

THE GLOBAL PRESENCE AND ROLE OF EUROPEAN BUSINESS

One of the key features of the role of European business within the global economy is the pre-eminence of European MNCs across international markets. Alongside issues raised by the 'triad-led' development of the global economy (see Chapter 17), it is evident that these firms make a significant impact on the global economy. While the United Nations Conference for Trade and Development (UNCTAD) estimates that there are 70,000 MNCs globally, the largest 500 are the most significant players. The Global Fortune 500 represents the world's largest MNCs and dominates international business. These firms, measured by sales, account for 90 per cent of all FDI and nearly 50 per cent of world trade. Figures for the EU's MNCs highlight the consistent impact that these firms have had upon world trade and investment. The breakdown by state/regions is reflected in Table 3.4 and shows that over the past 20 years, European MNCs

Table 3.4 *The breakdown of the Global Fortune 500 (by region/state)*

Country	1981	1986	1996	2001	2005
US	242	157	162	197	176
EU	141	134	155	143	159
Japan	62	119	126	88	81
Canada	–	9	6	16	13
South Korea	–	13	13	12	11
China	–	–	3	11	16
Switzerland	–	10	14	11	11
Australia	–	9	5	6	9
Brazil	–	1	5	4	3
Others	55	48	11	12	21

Source: Fortune.

Table 3.5 *The largest European multinational companies (by sales), 2005*

Rank	Global 500 rank	Company	Country	Revenue ($m)	Rank	Global 500 rank	Company	Country	Revenue ($m)
1	2	BP	UK	285,059	26	58	Royal Bank of Scotland	UK	59,750
2	4	Royal Dutch/Shell Group	UK/Netherlands	268,690	27	59	Zurich Financial Services	Switzerland	59,678
3	6	Daimler-Chrysler	Germany	176,687.5	28	60	Crédit Agricole	France	59,053.8
4	10	Total	France	152,609.5	29	61	Crédit Suisse	Switzerland	58,825
5	13	AXA	France	121,606.3	30	63	France Telecom	France	58,652.1
6	14	Allianz	Germany	118,937.2	31	64	Électricité de France	France	58,367.2
7	15	Volkswagen	Germany	110,648.7	32	66	UBS	Switzerland	56,917.8
8	17	ING Group	Netherlands	105,886.4	33	68	Deutsche Bank	Germany	55,669.5
9	21	Siemens	Germany	91,493.2	34	69	E.ON	Germany	55,652.1
10	22	Carrefour	France	90,381.7	35	70	Deutsche Post	Germany	55,388.4
11	24	Assicurazioni Generali	Italy	83,267.3	36	71	BMW	Germany	55,142.2
12	30	Fortis	Belgium/Netherlands	75,518.1	37	78	RWE	Germany	50,951.9
13	33	Eni	Italy	74,227.7	38	79	Suez	France	50,670.1
14	35	Avivia	UK	73,025.2	39	80	Renault	France	50,639.7
15	36	HSBC Holdings	UK	72,550	40	81	Unilever	UK/Netherlands	49,960.7
16	37	Deutsche Telekom	Germany	71,998.9	41	83	Robert Bosch	Germany	49,759.2
17	41	Peugeot	France	70,641.9	42	85	ThyssenKrupp	Germany	48,756.1
18	42	Metro	Germany	70,159.3	43	87	HBOS	UK	47,755.7
19	43	Nestlé	Switzerland	69,825.7	44	89	Prudential	UK	47,055.8
20	45	BNP Paribas	France	68,654.4	45	91	BASF	Germany	46,686.6
21	49	Royal Ahold	Netherlands	64,675.6	46	93	Enel	Italy	45,530.4
22	53	Vodafone	UK	62,971.5	47	95	Statoil	Norway	45,440
23	54	Tesco	UK	62,458.7	48	97	Repsol YPF	Spain	44,857.5
24	55	Munich Re Group	Germany	60,705.5	49	101	ABN Amro	Netherlands	42,319
25	57	Fiat	Italy	59,972.9	50	106	Saint Gobain	France	39,831.5

Source: Fortune.

have been consistently among the largest firms in the global economy. Their number has grown as the EU has expanded. The largest 50 European firms are shown in Table 3.5.

As the figures in Table 3.4 indicate the majority of the world's largest MNCs are based in the triad of the US, Asia-Pacific and the EU. Rugman's (2005) analysis of European MNCs and where they generate sales concludes that these businesses are overwhelmingly focused on Europe. Of the firms for which information was available, nearly three-quarters were focused on their home region with relatively little involvement outside this area. Where there were strong external sales, they tended to be focused on North America. The states with the highest intra-regional sales were Luxembourg and Denmark, though these figures cannot be given too much scientific credibility given the limited number of firms surveyed. However, Rugman's work can be criticised in terms of the portrait that it presents of the form and nature of internationalisation. Basing a measurement of the degree and extent of internationalisation on sales alone can misrepresent and underplay the process. For example, these statistics say little with regard to the dispersion of R&D and other value-adding activities which are increasingly dispersed throughout the global economy.

As highlighted in Table 3.6, the distribution of MNCs across Europe is very uneven. Unsurprisingly, the majority of these firms are located within the larger states of the EU. Seventy per cent of European MNCs are from three countries – Germany, France and the UK. However, some smaller states have a larger number of MNCs than bigger states. For example, the Netherlands has 14 companies in the Fortune 500 compared to eight for both Spain and Italy. However, the fact that these firms are in the Fortune 500 should

Table 3.6 European companies in the Fortune 500 (no. of companies by state)

Member state	Number of companies in the Fortune 500
Belgium	3
Belgium/Netherlands	1
UK	35
UK/Netherlands	1
Denmark	2
Finland	3
France	39
Germany	37
Ireland	1
Italy	8
Luxembourg	1
Netherlands	14
Spain	8
Sweden	7

Source. Fortune.

not overplay the degree of internationality as many of these firms have a strong domestic focus.

There are other indicators that underline the importance of European MNCs to the global economy. UNCTAD figures for the 100 largest non-financial MNCs, indicate the spread of businesses from the EU (2002). For France, which has 14 of the top 100 firms spread across 38 states, the Network Spread Index (NSI) is 19.49; for Germany 13 firms spread across 45 states has an NSI (that is, the ratio of number of host economies to the number of potential host economies) of 22.84; the Netherlands has five firms across 41 states and has an NSI of 20.092. This small sample highlights the degree of spread of these firms throughout the global economy. The location of investment (for the top 1,000 non-financial MNCs) is focused on the US, Japan and

Canada (see above) although the figures are also high for intra-regional FDI.

The importance of Europe's MNCs on the global arena is underpinned by their merger and acquisition activity. During 1987–2003, 77 of the top 100 deals involved business from Europe. Of these, 28 per cent were intra-European with 36 per cent involving the merger or acquisition of a US-based business by a European business. Only 10 per cent were based an acquisition of a European-based business by a firm from another developed state. Not only was Europe pre-eminent in terms of the number of deals but it was also focal in terms of the size of the deals, with 87 per cent of the value generated by those involving European businesses.

Looking further at the top 100 non-financial TNCs, European MNCs have extensive network spread. Companies such as Deutsche Post World Net, Shell and Astra Zeneca have extensive holdings across a number of hosts. Indeed, according to UNCTAD figures, Deutsche Post World Net is the most extensive MNC globally with a presence in 97 states. The Transnationality Index (TNI) of Europe's top ten MNCs is reflected in Table 3.7.

EU firms are also dominant among the top 100 TNCs ranked by foreign assets. As shown in Table 3.7, EU states have a higher spread than other states. In terms of assets, sales and employment, European firms as a whole tend to be more spread than firms from other locations, though it is likely that this is heavily influenced by the SEM. This relatively high foreign spread does not just reflect overseas sales but also how European MNCs use networks to build and establish positions within overseas markets. When spread is used as a measure of internationality, the regional breakdown of global MNCs starts to reflect a different pattern from that exhibited within the Global Fortune 500 list. The regional/state breakdown by spread is shown in Table 3.8.

Table 3.7 *The relative spread of the top ten MNCs (as ranked by foreign assets, %)*

EU company (state)	TNI[a]	Non-EU company (state)	TNI
Vodafone (UK)	84.5	General Electric (US)	40.6
BP (UK)	81.3	Ford Motor Company (US)	84.5
Royal Dutch/Shell Group (UK/Netherlands)	62.4	General Motors (US)	27.9
Total Fina (France)	74.9	Toyota Motor Corporation (Japan)	45.7
France Telecom (France)	49.6	Exxon Mobil (US)	65.1
Volkswagen (Germany)	57.1	Chevron Texaco (US)	58.2
E.ON (Germany)	40.2	Hutchison Whompoa (Hong Kong,China)	71.1
RWE Group (Germany)	43.4	Honda Motor (Japan)	70.5
Vivendi (France)	65.7	News Corp. (Australia)	91

Note
a Transnationality Index (TNI) is the average of three ratios: foreign assets to total assets, foreign sales to total sales, foreign employment to total employment.

Source: UNCTAD.

Table 3.8 *Breakdown of world top 100*
non-financial MNCs (as ranked
by spread of foreign assets)

EU	52
US	26
Japan	7
Switzerland	5
Canada	4
Australia	2
HK/China	1
Singapore	1
Mexico	1
Korea	1

Source: UNCTAD.

The reach of European MNCs extends beyond sales and markets and into R&D. While it is well known that MNCs account for the major share of global R&D, it is evident that European MNCs are also involved in the globalisation of the research process. It is estimated that the largest 700 MNCs account for 69 per cent of global research. Over 80 per cent of the research is done by five states: the UK, Germany, the US, Japan and France. Of the top 700 research-active firms, 187 are EU-based compared to 296 for the US and 154 for Japan. In addition, it is estimated that around 40 per cent of European R&D takes place outside this home region. Furthermore, EU states are also becoming the hosts for internationalised MNC R&D. This is especially evident in the newer member states of CEE. For example, in Hungary between 1995 and 2003, there was a sharp rise in investment by MNCs for research purposes. By 2002, the EU-15 was the host location for nearly 60 per cent of overseas investment in R&D undertaken by US MNCs. In addition, the EU was host to 20 per cent of Japanese overseas R&D bases.

However, the ability of European business to create credible positions in overseas markets is limited by what is perceived to be a 'liability of foreignness'. This is not only driven by the power of the incumbent but also by the cultural differences between markets. For example, in the US, many are deceived of the difficulty in entering new markets by the perceived cultural proximity. Many EU businesses have tried to establish a credible foothold in the US only to fail. Many do so on the basis that entry into the US market will make the firm a global player. Many not only pay over the odds for assets but fail to understand the sheer intensity of competition. The cultural elements that can create differences are based around issues such as legal differences, the high risk/high reward culture in the US. However, despite such difficulties, the US will remain attractive to EU business.

CORPORATE-DRIVEN CHANGE IN EUROPEAN BUSINESS

As highlighted within Chapter 1, one of the core debates within Europe has been the process of national economic reform as politicians are pressed to make decisions regarding the future competitive position of Europe through action at both national and supranational levels. However, a strong under-current within this process is that reform is already under way at the corporate level as business leaders take action to secure the long-term survival of their operations. That corporate action has been more evident should come as little surprise given the nature of these firms as growth-seeking entities as well as their accountability to a narrower set of stakeholders than politicians.

Already across the European corporate landscape, businesses are cutting costs to

73

Case Study 3.1

FIAT: A TROUBLED EUROPEAN CAR GIANT

Despite intense competition and a declining market share, the automotive industry remains very important to the European economy. It represents 6 per cent of European manufacturing employment and 7 per cent of manufacturing output. While it contributes less than 2 per cent to total employment, the automotive industry's significance is derived from its linkages into the international economy. Thus, in securing the position of the European economy in a global setting, the automotive industry remains very important. Within the EU, domestic brands tend to dominate home markets with Fiat relying for a high proportion of its automobile sales on Italy. However, while domestic brands remain strong within Italy, this dominance is on the decline. In 2004, domestic brands had fallen to around 30 per cent of sales; down from 56 per cent in 1990.

However, Fiat's commercial troubles are based on more than a declining domestic market share. In an industry increasingly dominated by size, Fiat has neither the scale nor the products to operate as an effective competitor alongside the large US and Japanese manufacturers. By 2000, Fiat Auto was producing just 2.5 million cars, less than 50 per cent of Volkswagen's output. In 2000 Fiat formed a partnership with General Motors (GM) to rectify this problem. This joint venture implicitly recognised that Fiat could no longer compete on its own. As part of the agreement, the partners were to channel 80 per cent of their total car production costs into the venture. The aim was to save around €1 billion in the process. GM took a 20 per cent stake in Fiat with the latter taking a 6 per cent stake in the former. The agreement included a clause to allow Fiat to sell its car division to GM between 2004 and July 2009.

Such an agreement could not rectify the consequences of Fiat's past mistakes. Fiat's first mistake was that it spent only US$45 billion on R&D between 1995 and 2001. Its rivals spent more than double this amount with Volkswagen spending almost five times more than Fiat. The result was emerging gaps in Fiat's product portfolio and a failure by the company to move itself away from being solely a maker of small cars. Most notable was Fiat's failure to capitalise on the rising sales in mid-sized cars and people carriers in its core Western Europe market. Its belated attempts to move into other product segments met with spectacular failure, in part because Fiat was slow to increase the quality of its products. Furthermore, Fiat attempted to rely less upon the Italian market by moving into Latin America, Poland and Turkey with the aim of gearing up its production systems in an attempt to achieve global scale outside the US. The move into Latin America occurred at the same time as the two largest Latin American economies – Brazil and Argentina – started to encounter economic troubles and its efforts to be successful in CEE were undermined by cheaper imports from the Far East.

These actions have only compounded the underlying problems at Fiat, most notably its low margins on small cars, its slow adjustment to shorter product life cycles and its failure to reduce excess capacity. In 2001, it launched a plan to take costs out of the business by reducing the number of factories. This was needed as its factories were operating at only 75 per cent of capacity when they needed to operate at 80 per cent capacity to make a profit. To support this process, GM worked to integrate Fiat into its European operations to increase its scale and efficiency. The turnaround strategy saw the company cut its capacity from 2.6 million cars to 1.9 million per annum. However, Fiat's ability to restore its commercial fortunes was hampered by involvement of the government which feared a knock-on effect on its own popularity if restructuring went ahead. It was also important for Fiat to turn the business around to ensure that it would be attractive enough for GM to buy the rest of the company. By late 2002, GM had written down the value of its investment from US$2.4 billion to just US$222 million. The Italian government also became concerned about the possibility of selling a core Italian company to GM, regarding the retention of this industry in Italian hands as a core strategic asset. The cost reductions and redundancies that followed led to widespread protest and direct intervention from the government.

By 2003, it was evident that Fiat's route to salvation via a GM purchase was doubtful as the US partner was looking increasingly reluctant to purchase such a cash draining business. This reluctance was compounded by GM's own dubious financial position. To entice the Americans, Fiat began to sell off assorted parts of its businesses to support its core automobile businesses. The cash was used to support the development of new markets to overcome the weakness arising from Fiat's failure to carry out facelifts during a model's conventional seven-year cycle. This resulted in the rapid fading of certain models. Fiat has reversed this strategy and now regularly undertakes facelifts on existing models. In addition, it developed a range of Alfa Romeo cars to support its aggressive entry into the US market.

The problems at Fiat underline the problems with Italy's industrial system, in particular the problems inherent with the large family-owned companies at the cornerstone of its post-war economic development. These businesses now face generational turnover and increased overseas competition. Fiat was closely allied with the government which was instrumental to its post-war economic recovery and which enabled Fiat to shelter from international competition.

Case questions

1 What are the underlying problems facing Fiat's car division?

2 How strong is Fiat's brand in the EU market place?

3 How should Fiat position its car division?

4 What does the experience of Fiat's alliance with GM tell you about the use of such arrangements for positioning within international markets?

generate competitive advantage and engage with the global market. In Germany, companies such as Volkswagen and Daimler-Chrysler have been aggressive in cost-cutting – almost in complete contrast to the inertia witnessed at the political level. Such restructurings are part of a larger trend and UK, Dutch and Swedish businesses have been especially aggressive. However, the emergence of this trend among German businesses is important as Germany has been one of the strongest adherents of the consensual social model. The trend is also evident in France where many of the larger businesses, such as Peugeot, are undergoing restructuring – again, in spite of an apparent resistance to undertake such change by politicians. Across Europe these moves by businesses have been a mix of both pre-emptive and defensive actions.

Unilever – one of Europe's largest MNCs – was typical of these restructuring plans as it undertook a radical reform under its 'Path to Growth' programme. The aim was to transform itself from a sprawling conglomerate into a more focused business built around a more limited number of products. Since 2000, it has cut over 50,000 jobs and closed or sold over 130 factories. Similarly, Renault has been aggressive in closing factories in France and has sought substantial costs savings in the manufacturing process. In Germany, Karstadt Quelle (a retailer) has shed non-core operations and closed unprofitable stores as well as repositioning its remaining stores.

The internationalisation of capital has started to pose challenges for managers. Financial intermediaries can insist that if existing managers do not restructure the business, they will either get somebody else to do it for them or sell the business and somebody else will do it anyway. In part, this reflects how globalisation has created a more

Anglo-Saxon mindset among managers who have to be more responsive to shareholders and their need for corporate profits, healthy balance sheets and long-term growth. While much of this consolidation has been undertaken in many EU states, it has remained under-developed in states such as Germany where the potential for restructuring remains vast.

However, national restrictions do limit the ability of foreign capital to enter the corporate landscape of many states. Thus, despite an emerging global capital market, national regulations, non-market strategies and politicised relationships can limit the impact of foreign capital. In many EU states, there is a commitment to retain national control of strategic industries. This is especially true in the larger states where the home market can sustain the business. In the smaller states, this advantage does not exist and thus many have been more radical in promoting change. A good example is the different approach taken by states to airlines. In the Netherlands, there was no real controversy in allowing the national airline KLM to be taken over by Air France. In other states, such a move would have created a popular outcry.

EUROPEAN BUSINESS AND THE THREAT OF ECONOMIC NATIONALISM

One of the driving forces behind the integration process has been the desire to drive and develop a more competitive industry structure. One of the key implications of this objective is a more consolidated industry structure as the amalgamation of national economic bases reduces the necessity for a fragmented economic system. The consolidation of industries across a number of sectors is seen as aiding competitiveness through giving EU firms scale to compete on both a European and global scale. However, as the forces of consolidation gather pace as the process of international integration (at both regional and global levels) matures so there has been a growing suspicion among some member states of the longer term impact of liberalising forces.

This suspicion has seen its most potent expression in the rise of economic nationalism as states seek to sustain domestic ownership of key industries/firms in the face of global consolidating pressures. What the rise of economic nationalism has demonstrated is that integration and consolidation is by no means a one-way process or a foregone conclusion. States still have a degree of discretion should they feel that their 'strategic interests' are being undermined. Clearly, the rise of economic nationalism runs counter to the liberalising instincts of the SEM programme and is driven by a reluctance to accept consolidation when it involves the foreign acquisition of domestic assets.

In practice, cross-border mergers are a direct symptom of the success of the SEM and its ability to generate market structures that are less fragmented and more able to cope with the threat of international competition. Businesses seeking to generate long-term growth are using the freedoms created by the SEM to assert themselves as a force for consolidation and integration across Europe. Such a process implies the offensive strategies of the consolidator will need to be counteracted by the consolidated. Thus, in these terms, economic nationalism is in part driven by the intimacy between many of the target businesses (in areas such as energy) where there is a strong link between the regulated and the regulator. This allows for the development of aggressive non-market strategies by target businesses to use government struc-

tures and processes to seek to block or delay consolidation. In many instances, this reflects a desire by some states (notably France and Germany) to limit the ability of the market for corporate control to act effectively. These are the states that are often slowest in transposing single market directives. The SEM was meant to work with the Commission in deciding whether a cross-border merger/takeover posed a competitive threat and with financial markets in deciding whether a merger was a good idea in practice. Economic nationalism runs counter to this process.

Thus, it is important to see that such nationalism is about defending the status quo and a belief that the SEM is an à la carte process. Across the EU, there have been a number of instances in the mid-2000s where states have intervened to flout market processes to serve national aims. These include:

- intervention by the French government to merge Gaz de France and Suez (two French energy companies) to prevent acquisition of the latter by an Italian company;
- French attempts to put 11 sectors beyond the reach of foreign companies;
- the Spanish government's attempts to block a German utility's (E.ON) bid for Endesa;
- the Polish government hindering a takeover of a German bank by an Italian company because the former had extensive Polish subsidiaries;
- the French and Luxembourg governments' resistance to the takeover of a domestic steel producer – Accor – by the Indian firm Mittal.

The rise of economic nationalism shows that the nationality of ownership still matters. In some cases this is based on an implicit assumption that foreign firms could become agents of overseas governments. However, there is no empirical evidence for this. These events are not so much about the rise of economic nationalism per se but more about the ongoing battle between protectionism and economic nationalism (driven by governments and unions) and restructuring and globalisation (driven by business). The lasting impact is difficult to determine and depends on any retaliation undertaken by states in response to these actions. On the other hand, economic nationalism could simply be a phase driven by politicians wishing to appear solid to electorates in the face of the uncertainty generated by globalisation. Thus, these examples should not merely be seen as testament to the past success of the liberalisation process as they have often arisen from the uncertainty as to how far the process has gone both at the European and at the global level, especially given the rise of China and the 2004 enlargement. In this sense, these actions represent the expression and embedding of anti-globalisation measures within domestic political processes.

These conflicts are symptomatic of the interaction between market opening and market closing instincts. While the latter is rising, the former is embedded within business systems and remains strong. In addition, the market closing instincts across Europe are both uneven and not especially strong. Not only is the Commission liberal in its approach to markets but also many governments have also realised that any move to explicit protection would be counterproductive. Other than offering short-term political capital, there is no long-term interest in a return to autarky. On the other hand, the forces driving European business global are strong and getting stronger. Slow growth in Europe has led many businesses to seek efficiencies and has pushed many across

borders. In the context of this struggle between government and business, Germany represents a telling case as despite half-hearted and sporadic government attempts at reform, German business has undertaken radical restructuring (see above). However, relying on business alone to reform unilaterally may not be enough to promote the wholesale change needed to promote European competitiveness.

The rise of economic nationalism may, in practice, prove to be temporary but what it does show is that the forces of fragmentation of European industry are still alive and well. The ability of states to reflect vested interests to resist free market forces when the outcomes are not to their liking reflects a constraint upon European business, both internally and externally to the EU. However – as many chapters of this book show – the rise of economic nationalism is not so much a failure of the process of integration but is, in fact, more a reflection that it has gone so far that it is starting to encroach on the more politically sensitive areas of a state's economic base. The rise of economic nationalism is by no means confined to the EU as similar processes are evident within the US. In many ways, this trend is symptomatic of an emergent fear of globalisation. The 'no' votes by French and Dutch voters have been interpreted as 'no' votes against globalisation rather than European integration. However, the rise of economic nationalism has the potential to do a lot of damage as the SEM has been weakened by states failing to meet their commitments and the slowing down of the growth of intra-EU trade compared to extra-EU trade.

CONCLUSIONS

Despite evident competitiveness problems, European business plays a prominent role within the global economy. The global opening of markets has created challenges for European business as they seek both to defend existing market positions as well as to create a presence in non-EU markets. In terms of trade and FDI, the EU represents the world's single largest trading and investment entity. In addition, European MNCs are actively seeking a presence in global markets and constitute some of the world's biggest firms. The need for these firms to compete on the global stage means that many are undertaking the necessary corporate restructuring and reform that appears to be largely absent at the political level. However, this does not preclude the potential for governments to intervene if they fear that national interests are being compromised by these firms involvement in international markets.

KEY POINTS

- The impact of European business to globalisation is both practive and reactive.

- Europe is a key trade and investment component to the global economy.

- Europe's businesses play a significant role in the commercial life of the global economy.

ACTIVITIES

1 As a group, assess how and in what ways globalisation has impacted upon European business.

2 Research one European MNC and identify how it has approached operating within global market places.

3 Research one of Europe's major competitive rivals and assess Europe's relative competitive advantages and disadvantages to this state.

4 Find examples (other than those mentioned in the text) of European MNCs undergoing corporate restructuring.

QUESTIONS FOR DISCUSSION

1 What do you understand by the term globalisation? What has driven it?

2 How do you explain the global prominence of European business?

3 How do you explain why European business has been more proactive in pursuing reform than domestic governments?

4 Does economic nationalism represent a credible threat to globalisation?

SUGGESTIONS FOR FURTHER READING

Balanya, B., Doherty, A., Hoedeman, O., Adam Ma'anit, A. and Wesselius, E. (2003) *Europe Inc.: Regional and Global Restructuring and the Rise of Corporate Power*, London: Pluto Press.

Dicken, P. (2003) *Global Shift: Reshaping the Global Economic Map in the 21st Century*, London: Guilford Press.

Ohmae, K. (1990) *The Borderless World*, London: HarperCollins.

Ravenhill, J. (2006) *Global Political Economy*, Oxford: Oxford University Press.

Rugman, A. (2005) *The Regional Multinationals: MNEs and Global Strategic Management*, Cambridge: Random House.

Tsoukalis, L. (2003) *What Kind of Europe?*, Oxford: Oxford University Press.

Key websites

Eurostat: www.ec.europa.eu/eurostat

United Nations Trade and Development Organisation: www.unctad.org

World Trade Organisation: www.wto.org

Part II

Market integration

From a business perspective, the most important dimensions of European integration are the various initiatives that seek to end the fragmentation of the European market. This market integration, which is intended to help European businesses take advantage of economies of scale and scope to improve their competitiveness in the international sphere, is the theme of the chapters in Part II.

Chapters in Part II cover the horizontal policies, such as the SEM and EMU, which establish the broad integration framework that cuts across all sectors. Part II also includes two policies – competition policy and TENs – for which a major role is to support the core integrating initiative – the single market. Competition policy ensures that the removal of public barriers to trade in the EU is not replaced by the actions of private companies aimed at restricting market access. TENs parallel the legal market access granted by single market measures in physical terms: in other words, TENs provides the physical means by which the increased commercial interactions brought about by the creation of the single market can take place. The remaining two chapters in Part II – industrial policy and entrepreneurship – are also non-sector specific and are explicitly about helping European business improve its competitiveness.

Market Integration

Chapter 4

The Single European Market

The bedrock of European integration

You can't fall in love with the single market.

> Jacques Delors, former European Commission President

This chapter will help you to understand:

- the concept and major provisions of the SEM;
- the key implications and opportunities created for European business by the move towards the SEM;
- how customers are affected by the development of the SEM;
- the concept of the SEM as an evolutionary phenomenon based on a series of moving targets;
- the major external implications of the creation of the SEM.

The initial SEM programme, covering the years 1985–92, was limited (if not minimalist) in the efforts it made towards the realisation of its stated objective. Much of the programme was about catching up with lapsed priorities espoused within the founding treaties of the EC. Indeed, the Commission always marketed its Single Market initiative as merely the first phase of moves towards the establishment of an SEM. A true SEM will only exist when all goods, services and factors of production that can be traded and moved are freely tradable and movable.

This means that the creation of the SEM extends beyond the priorities outlined within the initial programme and will need to be adjusted as internationalisation creeps into more and more product, service and factor markets.

The initial section of this chapter explains the importance of, and opportunities afforded to, European business from the development of the SEM. After exploring the aims and intentions of the initial programme, an assessment of its impact in micro- and macro-economic terms is offered. Thereafter, how the SEM has been, and is being, extended to other sectors as well as further strategies to counter delays, deferrals and omissions in the realisation of the SEM are addressed. The external dimension of the programme is explored before the conclusion of the chapter.

EUROPEAN BUSINESS AND THE SINGLE MARKET

At its heart, the SEM is about improving the performance of European enterprises as a precursor to broader industrial success within international markets. Such success is pivotal in securing the greater levels of employment and investment that are increasingly the core focus of policy makers. Surveys prior to the initial SEM programme suggested that, across a number of sectors, the fragmentation of the European market was inhibiting indigenous business success on the global stage. For a market of a similar size, the US had considerably more efficient and rationalised market structures with fewer firms within core internationally traded sectors (for example, white goods and motor vehicles).

Opportunities from the SEM for business come from a number of areas, not least from the possibilities of the reorganisation of production offered by producing a single product for a single market instead of the multitude previously required by different national laws and regulations. Most analysts believe the advantages to European business from the SEM are derived from:

- wider availability of economies of scale in the production process;
- the effects of more intense competition;
- lower barriers to entry.

In combination, these advantages allow EU-based businesses a stronger platform from which to compete within both international and indigenous markets. Over time, this enhanced position will lead to greater levels of employment and investment. These benefits will be accentuated by higher levels of product innovation and a greater attention to non-price factors in the production process (for example, through enhanced product quality and design).

Many of the cost effects of the SEM are derived from alterations in the mode and manner in which firms alter their logistics chain. For many enterprises, this means re-establishing a new network of suppliers and distributors across the continent both as a means of entering new markets and as a more direct cost-reduction measure. Benefits to the enterprise's logistical chain are derived from:

- *suppliers*: sourcing from new suppliers that offer lower prices and/or better quality inputs to the enterprise;
- *production systems*: developing new locations to enter new markets with lower entry costs;
- *distribution systems*: competition in services to the firm (in areas such as transport, warehousing and retailing systems) can further increase efficiencies.

These cost-reduction measures will be complemented by new or renewed marketing efforts and promotional systems at the end of the logistics chain (that is, the consumer).

Naturally, how such efficiencies are realised comes down to the individual enterprise, its requirements and strategy. The response of many enterprises has been to seek the development of more pronounced transnational networks as a means of rationalising the production process and of providing an entry point into other markets. Porter (1990) disputes this as the most effective mechanism for realising the competitive gains from the SEM. Porter believes that if enterprises respond to competition by seeking to limit the intensity of rivalry, then they could limit the competitive benefits of the SEM to the economy as a whole. However, given the need for rationalisation of production, some consolidation is necessary. The issue is one of whether this emerges via a process of 'natural selection' (as Porter suggests) or through agreement/cooperation. One of the features of the SEM was the rise in the number of cross-border mergers and acquisitions (M&A) within services and manufacturing across the EU as firms consolidated as part of their strategy to enter new markets and to sustain competitiveness within this integrating market. This trend weakened during the recession of the early 1990s but the annual M&A trend has settled at a much higher level than in pre-SEM days.

The Lisbon Agenda (see Chapter 1) reinforced the strategic importance of the completion of the SEM to the future commercial success of the EU. The product and factor market reform – that is integral to the SEM process – is anticipated to act as a platform for broader economic reform across all aspects of the European market place. This reinforces the underlying principle that there is nothing better for competitiveness than competition itself. The ongoing development of the SEM is linked to many other aspects of the competitiveness agenda. There is a perceived link between the SEM process and improvement of the technological and innovative capabilities of Europe, the improved performance and prominence of SMEs, the emergence of knowledge industries and higher levels of employment.

The process of reform within Europe has been driven more by business than by politi-cians (see Chapter 3). This trend has been accelerated by the introduction of the euro, privatisation, the rise of IT and the spread of the Internet. As markets open, businesses are developing and pushing forward deals that open the market further and further promote its integration. However, this commercial drive has to be matched by political commitment if the effects of legislation are to feed through into tangible benefits to the European economy. In part, the inability to translate commitments into cast iron policy reflects differences between Anglo-Saxon and the more rational form of continental capitalism. However, the ongoing impact of the introduction of the euro may stimulate many of the reforms needed to push the process of European competitiveness forward.

THE INITIAL SEM PROGRAMME: INTENTIONS AND OBJECTIVES

Initially, the promotion of the SEM was the Community's response to the problems that were evident throughout the European economy in the late 1970s and early 1980s (that is, rising unemployment and slow growth: so-called 'Eurosclerosis'). The 1985 White Paper *Completing the Internal Market* proposed nearly 300 measures to push the development of the SEM. The programme was formalised in the SEA which was ratified in 1987. Importantly, the SEA set a deadline for the implementation of the initial measures – the end of 1992. It also reformed the decision-making procedure to speed up the implementation of SEM-related legislation. The central theme of these measures was to remove the remaining non-tariff barriers (NTBs) which fragmented the EU market (see Box 4.1). At its most basic, the SEM programme was an exercise in deregulation.

BOX 4.1

BARRIERS TO BE REMOVED IN THE SEM

The White Paper *Completing the Internal Market* argued that the fragmentation of the European market was sustained by a number of barriers that inhibited factor movements and trade as well as directly imposing costs upon business. Broadly these barriers, which varied in importance on a sector-by-sector or even on a firm-by-firm basis, were categorised as follows:

- *physical barriers*: these include border stoppages, customs barriers and other time-delaying and cost-increasing measures involved in mobility between states;
- *technical barriers*: these include the absence of common standards across the EU which means developing different versions of the same product for each market; also included are public procurement practices, technical regulations and differing business laws and practices (such as a culture of state support);
- *fiscal barriers*: these include differentials in the levels of VAT and excise duties among the states.

At the core of the SEM was the legislative programme and the implementation of the necessary supporting legal framework which consists of:

- rules set out in the treaty;
- rulings of the ECJ;
- secondary legislation, mainly directives which have to be implemented into national law.

This framework was underpinned by the core underlying legal principle of the SEM – 'mutual recognition' – according to which, a member state could not exclude the product of another member state from its market on the grounds that it did not meet the host's national standards. In short, if the product was assumed safe and reliable and could legally be sold in one EU state then it was considered saleable in any other. The establishment of this principle was important as it released the EU from the logjam created by decision making based on harmonisation of

national standards. It meant decisions could be made speedily and be applied promptly within the context of a readily understood framework. Since 1992, the total body of directives linked to the completion of the SEM has risen from 1,291 in 1995 to 1,475 in 2002.

The prioritising of the SEM by the EU has implications for other core complementary, or 'flanking', policies, notably:

- the requirement for the EU's competition policy to ensure a level playing field for the business community (see Chapter 5);
- a more effective regional policy to counter any regional imbalances that result from the advent of the SEM;
- the development of an appropriate social dimension to prevent any erosion of social rights that may arise from the development of the SEM (see Chapter 13).

In addition, the regulatory framework for the SEM has to be consistent with economic

reform and the delivery of a more competitive European economy. Overall, it is
important to recognise that the SEM will not
be realised by Community legislation alone.
It was evident that some form of alignment
will need to take place within national legal
structures and administrations, attitudes and
behaviour of market participants and (as
suggested above) the adjustment of complementary policies at both Community and
member state levels.

THE COMMERCIAL EFFECTS OF THE INITIAL SEM PROGRAMME

The 1988 Cecchini Report estimated substantial gains from the creation of the SEM
both within individual sectors and the
economy as a whole. In terms of the sectoral
effects (derived from the removal of barriers
to trade, economies of scale, competition
and other barriers limiting production),
Cecchini estimated that the SEM would add
4.3–6.8 per cent to the Community's GDP.
In terms of the broader economic picture, it
was estimated that the SEM would create
nearly two million extra jobs and have positive effects on fiscal and external balances
as well as inflation. Overall, the impact of
market integration is difficult to judge.
Inevitably, the impact of the SEM is directly
related to the extent to which the legislation
has actually been implemented (see Table
4.1). However, after nearly two decades, it
is apparent that the SEM can be felt on both
a micro- and macro-economic level.

Micro-economic effects

The full effects of the SEM are difficult to
gauge as many of the benefits are dynamic
and will occur over a protracted period of
time as industry responds to the new freedoms granted and opportunities created by
the process. Broad evidence suggests that
both trade and cross-border investment
have increased since 1992 (see Figures 4.1

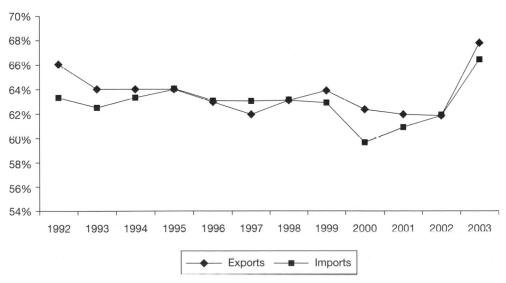

Figure 4.1 Intra-EU exports and imports, 1992–2003 (as percentage of total trade)
Source: European Commission.

and 4.2). However, there is limited evidence that these rising interactions have generated price convergence: an anticipated major benefit of the creation of the SEM. In theory, the process of economic integration should, under the law of one price, lead to similar if not the same prices across the EU. The extent to which prices have converged is, therefore, seen as a good indicator of the progress of market integration. Evidence presented in 2004 suggests that the process of convergence is by no means complete. Within the 14 largest states, prices still vary markedly. The reason for this incomplete nature of price convergence can be attributed to different competitive conditions across the EU, the mix of retail outlets, different distribution systems, and market separation and consumer preferences. There has as yet been little evidence that the euro has added any impetus to the process of price convergence within the EU (see below).

This trend towards limited price convergence is supported by evidence from individual product groupings. For fresh foods,

significant variations remain. In this segment, prices can be almost twice as high in the higher- than in the lower cost states. These gaps are smaller for consumer electronics with (based on the EU average of 100) the cheapest being 81 per cent of the EU average and the most expensive being 126 per cent. Furthermore, there is no one state that is cheaper than another. This is supported by evidence for supermarket goods where price differentials between states are larger than those between different locations within states. These can be explained by a combination of market size, consumer tastes, landscape and climate as well as brand differentials between EU states. These will continue to exist despite a maturing SEM. However, the EU believes that such price differentials are greater than can reasonably be explained by these 'natural' factors driven by differences in elements such as transport costs.

While the single market/single price rule is a very crude indicator of the degree of market integration, it is nonetheless an

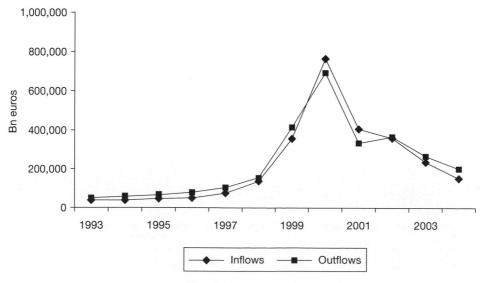

Figure 4.2 *Intra-EU FDI, 1993–2004 (€bn)*

Source: European Commission.

important barometer of the impact of inter-actions and emerging commercial freedom. However, Figure 4.3 indicates that there has been little progress in price convergence with some evidence of increased divergence since 2000. This runs counter to the expectations that the euro's introduction would reinforce the process of convergence.

The transparency afforded by the introduction of the euro should in theory stimulate price harmonisation. The theory suggests that savvy customers will look across Europe and note where prices are lowest. Then they will either purchase the good in that location (engaging in arbitrage) or they will use the information to prevail upon the local provider to reduce the cost of the product. Thus, the effect should be deflationary as both businesses and consumers seek to bid down the price of products. However, once again there is limited evidence that this has been occurring. The increased transparency has not (so current evidence suggests) stimulated an intensity of interactions between states to drive a process of convergence. This is partly because transparency is still difficult due to sustained market fragmentation which makes ready price comparisons difficult, the complexity of the trading system in Europe and the incentives given by suppliers to retailers to sell their products meaning that the true cost of a product is difficult to ascertain.

This absence of significant price convergence underlines the continuing importance of national borders in Europe despite the trends towards economic integration. National borders are discontinuities and run so deep that they cannot be overcome by a single development such as the introduction of the single currency. Such discontinuities caused by borders exist in areas such as:

- administrative rules and standards;
- social and religious phenomena;
- capabilities including geography and natural resources;
- economic development and infrastructure;
- information differences such as language.

These all influence the commercial environment. Thus, while the introduction of the euro will eliminate those barriers created by

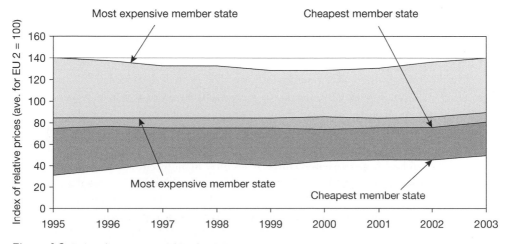

Figure 4.3 *Price divergence within the EU-25*
Source: Eurostat & Commission Services.

differences in currencies, it is likely to have little direct impact upon these broader concerns. Though price transparency will be more evident with the introduction of the euro, the impact upon price convergence will be more apparent than real. The euro was introduced into an environment that was very heterogeneous in terms of customer preferences regarding tastes, labels etc. This suggests that there has to be a convergence of customers before there is a convergence of prices. Thus, price convergence will only occur as part of a broader trend towards homogeneity across the EU.

This suggests that the process of convergence will be more gradual than was originally supposed. Moreover, convergence will be more evident in those areas where the cost to consumers of making a mistake is low. That is, big ticket items will be the last thing to actually converge. In areas such as pharmaceuticals, big price differentials will be exposed. In the long term this could lead to reform of the social systems but over the short term leads to a reform of a complex system of healthcare procurement. The size of the market within the EU has worked to stimulate the development of parallel imports. This industry is based on buying drugs where they are cheap and selling them to states where they are expensive and undercutting local suppliers in the process. This has brought inevitable resentment from drug companies who have sought to control the supply of drugs in cheap states. However, prices may take time to converge because the majority of drugs are purchased through national healthcare systems. Different national systems inhibit the ability to generate price harmonisation. The drug companies are resisting pressure to harmonise, fearing the price harmonisation and lower prices will limit further innovation. Thus, the fragmented systems work to their

benefit. Pricing strategies of drug companies reflects local demand and local procurement systems.

Macro-economic effects

The economic effects of the SEM have, according to the European Commission, been marked. It estimated that by 2002, the SEM had added 1.8 per cent to EU GDP and 1.46 per cent to total employment. The European Commission suggested that the SEM has increased manufacturing output by 1.4 per cent and accounted for 80 per cent of the increase in employment. In the network sectors, there is some evidence that the SEM has reduced the price cost margin: this has been most marked in telecommunications but has also been evident within the electricity sector. These benefits are derived from the following sources:

- *allocative efficiency*: as prices are reduced due to increased competition;
- *productive efficiencies*: derived from scale economies;
- *dynamic efficiencies*: derived from innovation and change.

These trends – when linked to the SEM – can explain at least part of the rise in productive growth between 1985 and 1998, especially in more sensitive sectors. This is supported by evidence that the SEM was mainly trade creating through stimulating cost efficiencies across the most sensitive sectors. In addition, research has found that price competition has increased and margins have shrunk. This was supported by other research which noted that in those sectors most exposed to the effects of the SEM, there was a more evident reduction in market power. However, much of this research has focused on manufacturing and not on service provision where little evidence has been forthcoming.

THE OPINION OF BUSINESS

Much of the aforementioned impact of the SEM relates to the performance of business and to the utilisation of changes associated with this legislative programme to push forward the competitive positioning of Europe. While it is clear that the SEM has impacted upon the development of business within Europe, there is the need for policy to work with business to ensure it has an impact in the desired areas. To ascertain these effects, the European Commission has undertaken extensive survey work to assess the impact upon business. This research points to the fact that manufacturing firms have a more positive outlook towards the SEM than service-based businesses. This is probably due to the fact that barriers to trade in this sector have been more surmountable than in the service sector (see below). In addition, firms within sectors most affected by NTBs (such as food) see the SEM as being the most effective.

Many large-scale enterprises (LSEs) are especially positive regarding the integrative elements of the SEM given that the programme has eliminated many obstacles to EU trade. This opinion is less strong among small businesses. Generally SMEs tend to be less positive towards the SEM than LSEs. This may be due to their more regional or national scope of operations. In short, the bigger the firm, the more positive they tend to be about the impact of the SEM. SMEs are particularly resentful about compliance costs and lack the same capability to deal with such administrative tasks as LSEs.

The most positive response among businesses regarding the SEM relates to the removal of the administrative tasks associated with customs control and VAT-related procedures. However, most businesses do not discern any great impact upon sales arising from the SEM programme. This lack of perception of impact is also evident in terms of how the SEM has changed the strategies of companies. The most tangible impact has been upon pricing and procurement policies within the EU. Furthermore, evidence of a positive effect on unit costs is again difficult to ascertain. In other areas, many businesses felt that the SEM is incomplete. This was especially in relation to labour mobility. There is also a consensus among businesses that they would like to see a further harmonisation of regulation while ensuring fair competition, though taxation is seen as a particularly troublesome issue. However, it is unlikely that politicians would want to cede much sovereignty upon taxation to the supranational level as these systems go to the heart of national sovereignty.

Survey work by the European Commission highlights that over 80 per cent of businesses would like to see the functioning of the SEM developed into the future. The aim would be to not only develop new policies but also to ensure existing commitments are adhered to. This desire is uniform across both small and large firms. However, this is not a commitment by firms to broader trends in European integration but merely an expression of a desire to ensure that trade within the EU is made easier.

THE EFFECT ON CONSUMERS

An important element of the SEM inception is that the programme works for the benefit of EU citizens as much as it does for business. Consumers can benefit through lower prices, increased choice, extension of legal rights, health and safety etc. However, the major impacts to date relate to:

- *Free movement*: this right gives the ability to live, work and study in another part of the EU. The aim has been to ensure a level playing ground for workers wherever they may be within the EU. Thus, mobility should not undermine the basic rights of workers. Over time, there is evidence to suggest that this mobility has been exploited with intra-EC migration increasing markedly especially into those states that allowed full mobility after the 2004 accession (see Chapter 13).
- *Social policy*: while outright harmonisation is not an objective, the SEM has worked to ensure that social systems complement the right of mobility. There is also a desire to avoid the negative consequence of free trade and investment by limiting the potential for social dumping (see Chapter 13).
- *Consumer interests* (see Chapter 15): along with wider choice consumers need to have their rights guaranteed across political borders. While, as mentioned, price convergence has proved inconclusive, there is evidence that consumers are benefiting from wider choice. What is more, this wider choice has not been at the expense of a decline in the rights of consumers. The SEM has put consumer safety before free trade. Thus, trade was allowed on the precondition of convergence of conformity assessment systems.
- *Environmental protection* (see Chapter 14): while it is too early to make a definitive assessment, the SEM and environmental policy are interlinked as the impact of the former in sectors such as energy will have a tangible effect upon the latter. These effects are also likely to be evident in transport which – if trade is stimulated as

a result of the SEM – is likely to increase. Thus, the EU sees a need for increased trade to take place in a manner that is consistent with the broad aim of the EU's environmental policies.

Thus, the EU has been able, through the SEM, to offer consumer rights that are secured within the broader context of European integration. Figures from the EU suggest that these rights of mobility have been exploited. Since 1993, up to 15 million citizens have moved to another state with 5 million currently residing in a partner state. In addition, around 40,000 qualified professionals have sought and obtained recognition of their qualification in another state. One notable trend has been the number of retirees from the UK and Germany moving to Spain and Italy. The latest figures (2004) suggest that there are nearly 200,000 retirees in these locations. Figures from the EU suggest that such mobility is not a true reflection of the desire to move. However, social ties and linguistic issues, for example, raise too many barriers to this mobility.

DEVELOPING THE SEM: TOWARDS A NEW STRATEGY

The initial programme highlighted above was, as suggested, merely the first stage in an ongoing process. The priorities for the second phase of SEM development focus upon:

- delays in the initial SEM programme, such as the uneven implementation of legislation;
- deferrals in the initial SEM programme, including issues, such as taxation, that were politically and economically difficult to achieve and were therefore shelved in order to promote work in those areas where agreement was possible;

■ omissions from the original programme: that is, to extend SEM opportunities to more actors (such as SMEs) and to more sectors (such as energy) as well as establishing a series of facilitatory measures.

The aim is to give the process of the creation of the SEM (which is essential to the development and proper functioning of economic and monetary union) an extra political and commercial impetus. This requires all states to renew their commitment to the SEM. The strategy does not require a new White Paper but a series of practical non-legislative measures.

The SEM was always a moving target that extended beyond the initial priorities established within the formative programme. It is a truism to state that Europe will not be a single market until all goods and services that can be freely and fairly traded can be and all factors of production that are able and willing to move face no impediments. Thus, despite initial successes barriers still remain to the full completion of the SEM. At the conclusion of the Dublin Summit in 1997, the Commission launched an Action Plan to seek to cement and build upon the gains made within the initial programme. In truth, this was the latest in a long line of initiatives that sought to maintain progress towards the SEM through building on past successes.

Through this programme, the Commission aimed to improve the functioning of the SEM by the beginning of 1999 in preparation for the introduction of the euro. To monitor developments, this Action Plan established a range of instruments (such as a scoreboard, an annual survey and dialogue with business and citizens). Most within the Commission feel that the Action Plan was a success, facilitating clarity over progress and demonstrating relevance to all parties affected by it. Indeed, the measures within the Action Plan

were key in generating a renewed political commitment to the process based on establishing fixed priorities, an established agreed time frame and regular monitoring. However, it was felt that these only went so far in meeting the longer term objectives for the SEM.

For the European Commission, the SEM has now to move away from being a legislative programme to become a more integrated programme that feeds into the broader long-term strategic objectives of the EU. Thus, synergies need to be recognised between the SEM and other policies, most notably competitiveness, and it should offer improvements in the quality of life of its citizens. To this extent the current strategy for the SEM has four key components.

1 Improving the quality of life of its citizens
In addition to the benefits noted above, the Commission seeks to ensure that the SEM is compatible with the sustainable development of the EU, adequate protection of consumer interests, protection of employment and social protection, ensuring that citizens are able to make full use of their rights and ensuring that freedom and security as basic rights are respected. These broadly stated objectives are intended to demonstrate the relevance of the SEM (and of the work of the EU generally) to European citizens. While European citizenship offers rights of mobility and settlement, it also confers political, civil rights. There is a need to ensure that citizens are able, through the SEM, to make informed choices and that consumer rights are respected. These measures are to be implemented and enforced by an active legislative programme.

2 Enhancing the efficiency of markets
This component represents a continuation of existing themes and recognises that the

existing programme has only gone so far in its objectives. Importantly, it frames the efficiency of market operation into the broad competitiveness objectives of the EU. As a precondition, existing rules need to be fully implemented and adapted where necessary to changing conditions. Thus, the aim of this theme is to promote economic reform as a precursor to market efficiency. This efficiency objective aims to ensure that financial services are able to deliver their full potential to the SEM. This requires the completion of the legislative framework supported by an active commitment to the process and its enforcement, the elimination of existing obstacles and improvements in the application of the principle of mutual recognition, promoting the liberalisation of the network sectors and ensuring the protection of intellectual property rights (IPR). These measures, in combination, have the aim of completing and securing the development of the SEM. The key idea is that not only should the programme be flexible to the demands placed upon it but also that it is adaptable to changing market conditions.

3 Improving the business environment
The business environment has to be compatible with the desire to implement the SEM programme in a manner that will enable European business to use these advantages for their commercial advantage. This requires that anti-competitive practices that inhibit the creation of a level playing field for business are removed. In this area, the objectives are to eliminate anti-competitive practices, remove remaining tax barriers and reduce the regulatory burden upon businesses. These are important in ensuring competition policy is able to cope with these demands but also that an interface is created with enterprise policy to ensure the ability of SMEs to participate in the SEM is not undermined by a high cost of regulatory compliance.

4 Exploiting the achievement of the SEM in a changing world
The SEM programme has the longer term strategic objective of helping secure the competitive position of the European economy in the modern global economy. Thus, actions have to be viewed within this broader context. The SEM has to consider two key components; first, to work within the emerging set of multilateral rules governing global trade and, second, to enable the SEM to contribute to the enlargement process. The SEM can be used as a means of establishing a consensus between states when seeking to develop global trading rules.

To assess progress towards the realisation of these objectives, the EU is building upon the initial Action Plan and has sought to establish an annual monitoring process. This raises awareness of the work that needs to be done, monitors and gives feedback on the effects of efforts to date and facilitates policy development and adjustment.

PROGRESS TOWARDS THE COMPLETION OF THE SEM

Integral to the adoption of the strategy was a reporting mechanism to underline the progress that has been made towards achieving the objectives. These reports underline that it is up to the member states to implement the SEM not the European Commission. The problems in meeting the objectives of the SEM have been compounded by a period of slow growth within the EU. This has made trade more difficult and slowed down price convergence (see above). Indeed, in 2003, intra-EU trade fell back after years of growth. These trends were compounded by an increasingly volatile performance of FDI, the majority of which is in the service sector but the integration of the EU's services markets has proved problematic (see below). However, the importance of the SEM has risen up the agenda of states, leading to a speedier implementation of directives. Where narrow national interests counteract with the needs of the SEM, policy tends to get shunted aside. There have been notable failures in areas such as industrial and public procurement, professional qualifications, industrial and intellectual property and taxation.

The SEM implementation scoreboard points to patchy implementation across the EU (see Table 4.1). The transposition deficit (the number of directives not yet fully transposed as a percentage of those that should have been transposed) increased to 3.6 per cent in 2005, more than double the target of 1.5 per cent. For the EU-15, the figure is 2.9 per cent. Of all the SEM directives 27 per cent or 427 directives had still to be fully implemented in 2005 in at least one state. This deterioration in the transposition figure has been brought about by the enlargement process and the performance of the EU-15 has worsened markedly since the enlargement. This suggests that despite the commitment made to economic reform at the Lisbon Summit, member states are at best paying lukewarm attention to it. The SEM strategy aimed for a 50 per cent reduction in infringements by 2006, although many states are not enforcing compliance among domestic businesses.

However, the big barrier to achieving the full benefits of the SEM is further liberalisation of services (see below). Despite progress in air and telecommunications,

Table 4.1 The transposition of SEM directives by states, 2005

State	Transposition deficit (%)	Number of directives not notified	State	Transposition deficit (%)	Number of directives not notified
Lithuania	0.7	11	Ireland	1.6	26
Hungary	0.7	12	Poland	1.7	27
Slovenia	0.7	13	Cyprus	1.7	28
Denmark	0.8	13	Austria	1.8	29
Finland	0.8	13	France	2.4	38
Malta	1.2	19	Belgium	2.4	38
Slovakia	1.4	22	Estonia	2.4	39
Sweden	1.4	22	Latvia	2.5	40
Germany	1.4	22	Portugal	3.4	54
Spain	1.4	22	Czech Republic	3.6	57
UK	1.4	22	Greece	4.7	59
Netherlands	1.6	25	Luxembourg	4.0	64
			Italy	4.1	66

Source: European Commission.

other aspects of service liberalisation remain incomplete. The economic slowdown within the EU has led to states stalling upon commitments already made. There are evident gaps in completing the SEM:

- *Energy*: market opening has been persistently frustrated, especially by the French – a phenomenon that has attracted the attention of the EU's competition authorities (see Chapter 11).
- *Financial services*: the implementation of liberalisation proposals for financial services has been held up by turf wars and technical battles. Resistance to these measures has come from both the EP and from member states.
- *Takeovers*: this measure was held up by the Germans who feared that golden shares (a nominal share that gives the right of decisive vote) held by the state makes them less vulnerable to takeover. These shares effectively give the state a veto on any takeover. Some states defend them as a necessary measure to prevent foreign ownership of key national resources.
- *A European patent*: most member states remain wedded to their own national preferences.

In practice, the European Commission has very little power to achieve compliance from states. Its most effective weapon is to name and shame those states that are not meeting their commitments as well as they might. This underlines the importance of the commitment offered by states to the realisation of the SEM. To ensure compliance, there are 'problem-solving' mechanisms for dispute resolution involving both formal (infringement procedures) and informal (cooperative agreements) arrangements for overcoming disputes. These operate on both a bilateral and multilateral basis. Member states have to provide contact points to allow their own citizens to monitor and question SEM enforcement within their own state.

To aid effective transposition, the European Commission has made a determined effort to simplify EU legislation under the Simpler Legislation for the Internal Market (SLIM) programme. The aim is to develop a simpler legislative environment within which the SEM can be realised. This applies to national as much as to EU legislation. The simplification of legislation was also driven by a desire for effective legislation that did not impose additional costs upon business. This was of special importance for enabling SMEs to realise the benefits of the SEM. To date, it has had some success in achieving the stated objective as teams of experts examine legislation to ensure its simplicity and easy comprehension.

The above underlines that the entire process of legislating for the development of the SEM requires close coordination between national and supranational administrations. These administrations essentially have a market surveillance role to determine the effectiveness of SEM measures at the sectoral level. This can ensure that measures are monitored and reviewed and therefore respond adequately to the concerns of business and consumers. This is especially important given that SEM legislation is implemented at the national level. This requires national bodies to oversee the implementation of legislation and report back to national and supranational administrations. The issue of surveillance is especially important in the area of technical standards where failure to implement product conformity sustains discrepancies and limits market development and integration. In these cases, it is up to national bodies on the ground to inform and press for these standards to be met. If this is to be effective, businesses and consumers need to be aware of how to complain. For many states, such bodies are only embryonic. These are enhanced by the Commission's Citizens First programme to inform consumers of their rights in the evolving SEM.

The Services Directive

The aim of this directive is to create a free market for the services sector and remove the remaining NTBs across the constituent sectors. The Commission claims that the directive will create 600,000 jobs as well as boost economic growth. Indeed, it is estimated that the directive could increase FDI in services by up to 35 per cent across an industry that accounts for 50 per cent of EU GDP and for 60 per cent of employment. The sectors included are those that are already open to competition. Thus the proposal does not require any extra liberalisation. The directive covers different types of services provision where:

■ the provider establishes in another state;
■ the provider moves temporarily into the state where the customers is located;
■ the provider offers services at a distance from its country of establishment (for example, through marketing, the Internet etc.;
■ the provider offers services in its home state to a customer who has travelled from another member state.

The proposal does not cover those services that are non-economic in nature – that is, those provided by the state as part of their public service obligations (such as healthcare) nor does it cover financial services or transport. Electronic services are only covered to the extent they are not dealt with

by the Electronic Communications Framework (see Chapter 12). However, the directive does seek to liberalise services in one fell swoop rather than to proceed on a sector-by-sector basis.

The approach under the Services Directive was novel in terms of:

■ coverage – which addresses the common features of services in a horizontal manner rather than dealing with sector-specific issues;
■ administrative simplification to allow business clarity over participation across multiple markets;
■ the removal of remaining obstacles outlawed by the ECJ such as those restricting establishment;
■ cooperative and consultative processes between member states;
■ the spread of best practice;
■ the promotion of information exchange between all parties;
■ the creation of partnerships between member states;
■ securing the rights of recipients of services through, for example, ensuring the right of non-discrimination.

As mentioned, the directive covers all services that correspond to an economic activity and consists of two proposals. The first grants a right to open a subsidiary in another EU state without lengthy, complex and discriminatory administrative procedures. Second is the 'country of origin principle', which states that so long as a business follows the law of its home state, it has the right to provide services in all other member states. Business has argued for the directive, believing it to potentially provide the biggest boost to the EU economy and competitiveness since the launch of the SEM programme in 1985. This is not only important for

97

EU-owned business but is also likely to be an important factor for those non-EU services businesses that invest heavily in the EU. The proposal allows for the removal of the need for the duplication of activities created by existing rules thus allowing for synergy in service delivery. In addition, it is expected that the directive would be a big boost to SMEs that are predominant within the services industry.

Despite the perceived benefits from the directive, it has proved very controversial in practice. The principal opponents were on the left of the political spectrum, notably trade unions who saw the directive as a direct challenge to the European social model and focused their opposition on the 'country of origin principle'. To its opponents, this principle will encourage social dumping as competition from lower cost states will drive down wages and social standards in the richer states. Thus, many see the Services Directive as creating a 'race to the bottom' and resistance to the Service Directive was very much about protecting existing social models.

The Commission believes that many of these concerns were covered within the directive as it stated that posted workers would be subject to local social and labour legislation wherever they are working. Thus, it would be illegal to undercut a local minimum wage or health and safety legislation. In addition, sensitive public services were already excluded. However, in a watered down proposal, many of the restrictions that the proposal was designed to remove have been re-introduced. While this was supported by the EP, it removed many of the features of the directive that would have benefited SMEs, especially in terms of the country of origin principle. Under the new watered down agreement, states retained the rights to curb foreign service providers in areas of public policy, security or protection of health, safety and the environment. In effect, this principle has been dropped in favour of continued adherence to the laws of the state in which they are operating. In addition, employment conditions laid down by union and employers will also be unaffected.

THE EXTERNAL DIMENSION OF THE SEM

The logic behind the development of the SEM was that ultimately the increased intensity of intra-EU competition would improve the competitive positioning of EU enterprises in the global market place. However, the intensity of competition was not solely an indigenous phenomenon as competition from foreign-based enterprises stimulated the process of adjustment and increased levels of competition within the European market place. It was an oft-mentioned concern that the development of the SEM would lead to a more inward looking EU that would seek to exclude non-EU enterprises from access to its markets. This so-called 'Fortress Europe' scenario was a real and genuine concern for non-EU states. In practice, such fears were to prove unfounded even though Europe remains, at best, a flawed trading partner (see Chapters 17 and 18).

The fact that the Uruguay Round of multilateral trade talks existed alongside the establishment of the SEM meant that moves to liberalise Europe internally were being matched by less vigorous action to liberalise its trade with non-members. Indeed, the acceptance of the global move towards liberalisation may, in part, have been fuelled by the success that Europe was having in the process of internal liberalisation. To European firms, the reorganisation stimulated by the SEM could now be exploited to

Case Study 4.1

FINANCIAL MARKET INTEGRATION

The EU has been trying to build a single market in financial services since 1973. The financial service sector is characterised by a plethora of national restrictions on investment opportunities which inhibit the ability of investors to seek the highest return and of borrowers to seek access to funds at the most attractive rate. Efforts to create a unified market in this segment of the EU economy have been given extra impetus given the perceived link between EU competitiveness and the liberalisation of financial services. The move towards an integrated capital market is especially important for the EU to be able to create an aggressive venture capital market. This should reduce the cost of capital, facilitate innovation, aid the development of new technology start-ups and enhance productivity within the EU economy. This is central to the EU for bridging the gap between itself and the US. The following illustrate the core problem:

1   the average US investment fund is six times bigger than its EU equivalent;
2   venture capital per head in the EU is 20 per cent of US levels;
3   the average real return on pension funds within the US was nearly 4 per cent higher than in the EU.

The Commission estimates that the absence of a single market in financial services costs both business and consumers around 1.1 per cent of EU GDP, that is, around €130 bn over the decade from 2004. At the Lisbon Summit in 2000, the EU committed itself to realising a number of key objectives such as better access to investment capital, elimination of barriers to pension fund investment and more consultation between governments on timetables for issuing debt as a means of integrating EU government bond markets more effectively. However, as with other aspects of the EU economy, Europe's financial markets are still very fragmented with 33 stock exchanges (compared to two in the US) and 11 cross-border payment systems (compared to one in the US). These problems are compounded by the need for regulators to keep up with the pace of change within financial markets, notably the ongoing consolidation between these separate exchanges – a process speeded up by the introduction of the euro.

To aid with this process of consolidation, the Commission launched the Financial Services Action Plan (FSAP) in 1999. This comprises a set of 42 directives to create the necessary financial system to complement and enhance the SEM. The FSAP aimed to create a single market for banking and saving products by 2005. However, the process of rapid technological and commercial change has made the aim a moving target. This is compounded by the time it takes to agree and implement a directive. For example, it takes on average three years to agree a regulation or a directive, which frequently then faces protracted delays in the implementation process across all states. These problems reflect the sheer complexity of the exercise. There are widely different market structures, legal traditions, ways of conducting business and attitudes to investment and savings across states. This makes an integrated financial market more difficult to achieve than a single currency and the FSAP has been criticised by many because of the up-front costs of regulatory change.

However, once again member states failed to hit the 2005 deadline. Since the FSAP was launched in 1999, 34 out of the 42 measures have been agreed by governments and the EP (including agreements on laws relating to insider trading and the raising of extra finance across the EU). In some cases, states have implemented less than 50 per cent of the legislation. In many cases, national champions are often still dominant in key segments, especially retailing. Benelux and the Nordic markets are exceptions to this. However, in other areas, banks complain that moves to integrate markets have actually resulted in new bureaucratic burdens.

In its review of the FSAP in 2005, the EU sought to refine the policy to limit the need for business to adjust to new regulations. The emphasis is to make existing policy work better rather than to impose new rules on financial institutions. The financial strategy for the five years from 2005 takes a less ambitious route seeking to consolidate existing progress, drive better regulation into all areas of policy making, enhance supervisory convergence, create more competition between service providers and extend Europe's influence into globalising capital markets. However, the starting point is to recognise that progress has been intermittent and thus there is not much new within the programme (in terms of legislation). The focus is on the practical implementation of policy.

Case questions

1 Discuss why the creation of a single financial area is important to the process of economic integration.

2 How can the forces of financial integration aid the position of European business within international markets?

3 What are the major barriers to the integration of financial markets?

gain market share within broader international markets. The impact of the SEM upon non-EU enterprises is derived not only from its impact upon external access but also from its effects upon FDI flows. Both of these have been integral to the European Commission's examination of the impact of the SEM.

External access to the EU market was helped by the fact that the SEM removed a plethora of national restrictions that had impeded non-EU access to the European market. In general, these were replaced with a common EU-wide approach to external competition. The clothing and textiles sector was especially prone to this method of national control. These barriers were a problem when there were differences between states in the danger posed to domestic producers from particular types or sources of imports (such as textiles and clothing from China). Thus, some states would let the goods in; others would seek to impair their access. It is felt that if the SEM has had an adverse impact upon trade, it is in the area of technical harmonisation especially where

EU-wide agreements may have raised the height of some barriers. This reflects the fact that technical barriers are the most important barriers for third-party products. In other areas, improvements to the business environment stimulated by the development of the SEM (in areas such as service provision, business law and taxation) have had as great and as positive an impact upon foreign firms as they have had upon EU enterprises. However, given the diverse product ranges it is not easy to assess the full impact of these changes.

Most of the FDI stimulated by the advent of the SEM were flows between EU states. However, there was a tangible impact upon extra-EU FDI (see Chapter 17). Inward investment by Japan and the US had been primarily market seeking. In the former case, FDI was frequently based around greenfield development whereas the latter favoured M&A. FDI (especially from Japan) tended to be stimulated more by factors such as market growth than by the SEM. Most of this Japan/EU FDI tended to flow into the EU rather than out of it. EU/US FDI exhibited more equal bilateral flows. Some states have been traditionally hostile to FDI, fearing foreign ownership of core strategic resources or that indigenous operators would be undermined by such flows. However, as the EU economy slowed so EU states became more hospitable and even began to compete for these flows.

CONCLUSION

The SEM is at the cornerstone of the process of European integration and links into many of the grander schemes relating to the EU project. The SEM provides the platform for EMU as well as for the broad-based competitiveness theme that is becoming embedded within many policies. However, progress towards the completion of the SEM has been chequered. This is especially so as it starts to move into more politically salient issues for member states. While there have been benefits for the EU, there is a growing fear of what globalisation means for states and the SEM could become a casualty of this process.

KEY POINTS

- The SEM programme seeks to unify the fragmented national markets into an integrated whole.

- The initial programme only had limited success in achieving its stated aims.

- The EU will only truly be an SEM when all goods and services that can be traded are traded across Europe.

- While progress has been made in the SEM programme, key problems remain.

ACTIVITIES

1 Research one sector and assess how it has been affected by the development of the SEM.

2 Using group research, assess how either the postal service or the energy sector would be affected by the SEM.

3 Using the example of one non-EU European state, assess how they have been affected by the development of the SEM.

QUESTIONS FOR DISCUSSION

1 How do you believe the advent of the SEM has affected the process of European integration?

2 Explore with examples how the SEM has changed firm behaviour within the European economy.

3 What needs to be done to complete the SEM?

4 Should the EU be worried about the rise of economic nationalism?

SUGGESTIONS FOR FURTHER READING

Barnard, C. and Scott, J. (eds) (2002) *The Law of the Single European Market: Unpacking the Premises*, Oxford: Hart Publishing.

European Commission (2002) *The Internal Market – Ten Years without Frontiers*, www.ec.europa.eu/internal_market/index_en.htm.

European Commission (2004) 'Internal Market Strategy Priorities', COM (2005) 11.

European Commission (2005) *Internal Market Scoreboard*, Brussels, www.ec.europa.eu/internal_market/index_en.htm.

Gallup Europe (2002) *Internal Market Business Survey*, Brussels: The Gallup Organisation.

Gallup Europe (2003) *Single Market Survey*, Brussels: The Gallup Organisation.

Grin, G. (2003) *The Battle of the Single European Market: Achievements and Economic Thought 1945–2000*, London: Kegan Paul.

Menz, G. (2005) *Varieties of Capitalism and Europeanization: National Response Strategies to the Single European Market*, Oxford: Oxford University Press.

Porter, M. E.(1990) *The Competitive Advantage of Nations*, Basingstoke: Macmillan.

Chapter 5

European competition policy

The guardian of integrated markets

> Competition is a painful thing, but it produces great results.
>
> Jerry Flint, in *Forbes*

This chapter will help you to:

- appreciate the importance of competition for the competitive positioning of European business;
- identify the main competition provisions of the EU treaties;
- understand the form and nature of the reform of EU competition policy;
- identify new and emergent themes in the management of competition within the EU;
- comprehend the international aspects of EU competition policy.

A prevailing belief within modern capitalism is that nothing is better for competitiveness than competition itself. Despite this, policy makers find themselves in the paradoxical situation that many of the beneficiaries of competition are doing their utmost to undermine its intensity. Even the earliest writers on modern economies noted the tendency for competition to self-destruct if left to its own devices. For this reason, competition policy is integral to states' involvement in the economy. States use competition policy to preserve the desired intensity of competition by establishing a series of rules and regulations that limit the ability of enterprises to operate in a manner that is contrary to this objective. The initial focus of this chapter is to examine the perceived benefits of competition. This will look initially at traditional economic thinking before moving on to examine the role and shape of competition policy. Thereafter, the themes and form of competition policy within the EU are explored. The chapter then examines the processes of change that are affecting competition policy development within the EU, notably trends towards European and global integration.

THE BASIS AND FORM OF COMPETITION POLICY

Economic theory presents competition as a social good and its maintenance is regarded as pivotal in ensuring efficiency gains, within both enterprises and the economy as a whole. This improved efficiency is expressed in many ways: first, in terms of prices, which are expected to fall as competition intensifies; second, from the pressure for greater cost efficiency within enterprises; and third, from the greater choice of goods and services that arises as more firms enter a particular market.

While policy seeks to increase the intensity of rivalry between enterprises, it also recognises that too much competition may be detrimental to the performance of European business. Uncertainty induced by excessive competition may limit investment, increase commercial risks and, consequently, result in retarded economic development. This is especially true of actions that are deemed pre-competitive, such as R&D. Policy makers may also decide to limit the extent to which certain sectors face competition for social or political reasons. This may be the case when excessive exposure to competitive forces in the short term results in detrimental employment consequences – this is a common fear within many of the 'old economy' industries such as coal, steel, etc.

Traditionally, competition policy has been based upon the notion that the larger the number of firms in a market, the greater the benefits to the economy concerned. This stance was inevitably corrupted as the state started to play an increasingly prominent role within the economy. This traditional viewpoint was based upon the premise that, aside from state control, monopolies are always and everywhere bad. Thus, where monopolies were deemed to be 'natural',

as was the case for many of the network sectors, there was a strong case for state ownership. This position has been increasingly challenged as policy makers have started to realise that monopolies are not necessarily detrimental if they are not accompanied or supported by insurmountable barriers to entry. This is important, for it implies potential competition has as big a role to play within market structures as actual competition. Knowing that other firms have the right and ability to enter the market should act as a constraint upon the actions of incumbents even if they hold a monopoly position. This challenge to the traditional policy stance has been supported by the gradual erosion of the notion of 'natural monopoly' (see Chapter 11 for the example of the electricity sector). Competition is increasingly possible and prevalent within sectors previously regarded as naturally monopolistic, whether it is through bidding for a franchise (as in the case of the UK rail sector) or where services are provided in a competitive manner over a commonly owned infrastructure (as witnessed in many of the network sectors).

In line with the structure–conduct–performance (SCP) paradigm that has dominated industrial economics since the 1980s, the ability of policy to influence the performance of business comes from measures that alter market structure or amend firm behaviour. In either case, the effect should be an impact on firm performance that works to the benefit of the economy. As a consequence, there are two broad types of competition policy:

- *form-based*: where the analysis of competition is based on an examination of objective, often quantitative, criteria such as market share or structure;

- *effects-based*: where the examination of competition is based upon the effects of the actions of enterprises within the sector concerned.

THE CORE FEATURES OF EU COMPETITION POLICY

Competition policy in the EU takes effect at both national and supranational levels. EU policy is only relevant when the actions of economic actors impede or distort trade between significant parts of the EU. As the SEM has increased interaction across borders so the pertinence of EU competition policy has increased. As more firms seek to move into other markets, the activities of incumbent enterprises (and of states) start to have a greater negative impact upon the functioning of the European market place. Clearly, EU measures have little relevance in highly local/regional or niche markets where national competition policy will come to the fore.

The need for common rules is based upon a desire to maintain the level playing field at the heart of the SEM (see Chapter 4). The intention is that all firms should face the same sets of rules and conditions with a simultaneous limit upon the discretion available to the member states insofar as their actions undermine this objective. The administration of rules from a single body will also lead to greater consistency and predictability in the outcome of policy. Integration and the increased interaction of firms across borders also have implications for the development of national policy and the way it is administered. Firms crave consistency and efficiency for the policy framework in their markets. Frequently, this requires policy implementation by a single body. To have many different decisions taken by a multitude of competition authorities is both time consuming and a waste of resources for both businesses (in compliance) and for the regulators (in administering).

Measures within the EU's competition policy reflect, in both a reactive and proactive manner, the dynamic inherent within the integration process. These rules seek to ensure that the actions of all operators, whether publicly owned/controlled enterprises or private businesses, are compatible with the objectives of the free and fair competition encapsulated within the SEM programme. Thus policy (as identified in Box 5.1) has the ability to liberalise protected markets, to remove competitive distortions sourced from the state and to curtail the activities of enterprises that abuse dominance or seek, via collaboration, to limit the intensity of competition.

Within the context of the Treaty of Rome, EU competition policy was an instrument to achieve the specified objectives of balanced development, free trade and harmonious growth. The Treaty on European Union has broadened these objectives to include social and environmental concerns as well as the evolving priorities of the EU's industrial strategy (see Chapter 6). In terms of meeting these objectives, competition policy seeks consistency with other policy areas. If there is a clash in policies (as there has been between competition and industrial policies), it is more often due to the nature of the policies followed by the member state(s). Clashes between EU industrial and competition policies are gradually being alleviated as the former starts to stress open and competitive markets. As a complement to the broad pro-market themes stressed by industrial policy, competition policy has emphasised the following themes:

- *State aid*: direct support is designed to push the managed, market-led decline of

BOX 5.1

EU COMPETITION POLICY INSTRUMENTS

Apart from the Merger Control Regulation, EU policy instruments are based upon Articles in the Treaty of Rome (subsequently renumbered in the Treaty of Amsterdam).

Article 81 prohibits any collusion between undertakings that restrict competition to the extent that it has an effect upon trade between states and therefore inhibits the development of a single market. Activities that are typically illegal under this Article include price fixing, quantitative restrictions on production, market sharing and the tying of supplementary conditions to sales. Such agreements may be allowed if they are able to fulfil the following conditions simultaneously:

- the agreement helps improve production and/or distribution and promotes technical or economic progress;
- there are significant benefits to consumers;
- restrictions are avoided that are not indispensable to the attainment of the above conditions;
- the agreement does not preclude competition in a substantial part of the market for the product in question.

Article 82 prohibits undertakings with a dominant position from abusing this advantage to the extent that their actions preclude competition within the single market or at least a significant part of it. Measures considered 'abusive' include predatory pricing, unfair trading conditions and discrimination between consumers or suppliers. There is no exemption clause so any conflict between scale efficiencies and competition is deemed not to exist due to the ease of market access.

Article 86 applies the conditions of Articles 81 and 82 to state-owned enterprises or firms that have been given special or exclusive rights. Thus, despite being neutral on property rights, the treaty maintains that state ownership does not imply a right to distort competition. Member states are allowed to grant special or exclusive rights for certain 'legitimate national objectives' but they should not contravene the rules of competition. If the application of competition rules threatens to undermine essential public service elements of these enterprises then these special or exclusive rights are exempt.

Article 87 specifies that any assistance given by the state which distorts or threatens to distort competition by favouring certain undertakings or the production of certain goods, insofar as such action distorts trade, is incompatible with the common market. Aid is assessed according to the 'market economy investor principle' which means aid is compatible with the SEM if the parties can prove a commercial investor would have behaved in a similar manner. If aid promotes technological or economic development, provides advantages to consumers, enables the relief of natural disasters or of a serious disturbance within the economy of a member state then it is permissible under EU law.

The Merger Control Regulation (MCR) seeks to prevent undertakings from creating or strengthening a dominant position on the market by acquiring control of another enterprise. Only mergers with a clear community dimension are caught by the regulation leaving member states considerable scope for discretion in this area of policy. As mentioned below, this aspect of policy has been significantly reformed.

the 'old economy' industries (such as steel) and to lower their use in those sectors where market forces are gradually being extended. Direct support is put forward in other sectors to meet the concerns of technological and regional development (for example, to attract FDI).

■ *Liberalisation*: this extends the benefits of the SEM to consumers by lowering prices in key, previously protected, services such as telecommunications and energy. The process also seeks to extend and enhance infrastructure quality and capacity as a means of delivering an improvement in the quality of services.

■ *Cooperation*: this allows for inter-firm cooperation in pre-competitive actions such as R&D or in areas where the market is global in nature (such as aerospace).

The above are in addition to the themes of protecting competition engendered within Articles 81 and 82 (see Box 5.1). The desire is to draw a distinction between the activities of firms that seek to progress and restructure European industry and those activities that partition markets (thereby denying the realisation of the SEM) and delay the onset of structural adjustment. Thus, competition policy, in line with the objectives of industrial policy, seeks to establish the conditions under which enterprises can be successful on a global basis.

REFORM OF COMPETITION POLICY

A new era of EU competition policy was ushered in on 1 May 2004 as new methods were introduced to enforce Articles 81 and 82. These changes were driven by evident flaws and emergent problems in the administration and effectiveness of EU competition

law, notably the failure of the previous system to catch hardcore cartels. In addition, limits on the extent of national action in the area of competition policy increased the workload of the Commission to the degree that speedy and effective decision making was affected. These concerns were compounded by the impending enlargement of the EU. In effect, these moves represent a reassessment of the nature of the integration process and the effective management of competition within Europe.

The core change in the policy regime centred on the fact that companies no longer needed to notify their cooperative agreements for routine clearance. This shift in policy was designed to work to the benefit of both parties. It would free business from this regulatory requirement and enable the European Commission to focus on those enterprises that actually violate competition law and represent the most cogent barriers to market integration. Furthermore, the enforcement process is shared by both the European Commission and the 'network' of national competition authorities. To support the necessary cooperation between these bodies, the EU has established a European Competition Network (ECN) to ensure all bodies are kept up to date with developments at their respective levels. This renationalisation of competition policy – where no cross-border issues are evident – is designed to work to a speedier resolution of disputes.

This decentralisation has been complemented by harmonisation of the substantive competition rules. For agreements on concerted practices, full harmonisation has taken place. Therefore, national courts cannot apply domestic laws if the result would be different from that derived by applying European rules. Thus, national law can no longer be stricter than European law. The

107

only exception is where there is no appreciable effect on trade. For unilateral conduct, harmonisation is less far reaching with only minimum standards being agreed. Thus, stricter rules can be applied as long as they do not fall beneath the standards set by Article 82. This has obvious benefits for business as it will be subject to increasingly uniform rules and need not adjust actions for every jurisdiction within which it operates. This should satisfy firms about a key requirement of competition law, namely certainty of application and jurisdiction as well as the reduction of compliance costs. To aid this process, the Commission has established an umbrella block exemption to reduce the need for individual notifications. The new approach, introduced in late 2001, offered increased flexibility and developed an economics-based approach (agreements would be assessed on market power) and the potential for self-assessment.

These reforms not only sought to clear up long-standing difficulties in enforcement but also to enable the Commission to cope with the expected increase in workload associated with the 2004 enlargement. However, by devolving decisions down to the nation state, the EU has opened up the question of whether many of the newer states will be able to cope, especially where there is a culture of supporting national champions. Furthermore, there is uncertainty whether some of the older members (such as Austria, Finland and Portugal) will be able to cope with the demands of the new regime given their relative newness to competition policy. For example, some states may struggle to identify whether agreements have an intra-EU effect. These are some of the problems the ECN was designed to remove. While an argument remains for developing an independent European competence in competition law, there is also a concern that it would

simply not have the capability to act as pan-European watchdog. Thus, if a European cartel body were to emerge, its caseload would be highly specific and limited to cases with a clear community dimension.

Overall, it is hoped that the reform will increase the effectiveness of EU competition policy by (Nicolaides 2002):

- raising the number of enforcers of EU competition policy;
- refocusing Commission resources;
- increasing the powers of investigation of the Commission;
- reducing bureaucracy through the removal of prior notification;
- increasing certainty for business.

However, there are problems: firms will tend to stray away from the tighter regimes and, in some cases, face increased costs derived from multiple compliances. Furthermore, the passing down of rules to the national authorities raises the question of whether these rules will be interpreted differently by the separate national authorities. If so, this undermines the notion of a level playing field and a coherent set of policies for business. It also moves business away from the benefits of the one-stop shop but the Commission denies this.

These changes have been supported by reform of the EU's merger control regulation. The new regulation also introduces greater flexibility into the system, especially regarding timeframes. The reform also helps avoid multiple filings by giving the firm the right to a Commission hearing if it has to file in three or more states. The reform also ensures that all mergers with an anti-competitive effect are caught and not just those that increase or support dominance. This makes policy more effects-based and offers more scope for deals to be referred back to national authorities. This has brought accusations that the Commission has dropped one of the more attractive elements of the merger regime (the 'one-stop shop' process of assessment) and fears that such powers will remove the benefits to business from the old MCR. In connection with this, the Merger Taskforce has been disbanded and distributed around the Competition Directorate.

The modernisation process has also been extended to state aid (see Case Study 5.1). The Commission has not only reaffirmed its priority to reduce the levels of state aid but it has also emphasised increased transparency and efficiency in their treatment and assessment. The Commission has made attempts to codify the principles developed within case law as well as enhancing its power. The Commission is growing increasingly reluctant to grant aid to large companies where it is sought on the basis of rescue or restructuring. However, the Commission is trying to exhibit greater flexibility in the aid measures, especially when it is given to support SMEs. To this extent, it has granted block exemptions with regard to risk capital, SMEs, training and employment and R&D for SMEs. The Commission reviewed state aid in 2006 in the light of an enlarged Europe and of the need to respond to competitiveness issues. The aim is to direct aid towards providing invectives for business rather than merely supporting firms because they are in less developed regions of the EU. Thus, the aim is to encourage more self-help than direct assistance. The reform is part of a larger plan to target projects that aid growth rather than merely support 'dying' industries.

These trends highlight that the increasing power for the Commission in competition policy as a legacy of the integration process is by no means inevitable. There has been considerable effort by member states to limit the scope and range of its existing powers and they have persistently tested the Commission and arguably undermined its authority and credibility as a regulator of competition. The credibility of the Commission as an effective guardian of the treaty provisions on competition has also been undermined by high-profile cases, notably the preferential tax schemes offered by the Netherlands, Belgium, Luxembourg and Ireland which were granted as a political compromise. The Commission has also seen key decisions on mergers (Schneider/Legrand, Sidel/Tetra-Laval and Airtours/First Choice) overturned by the European Court in 2002. The Airtours decision by the European Court of First Instance undermined its hostile stance to mergers and questioned much of the Commission's analysis. The conclusions were especially brutal, criticising both the method and analysis of investigation. Thus judgment precipitated a basic reassessment of the competition rules and procedures to deflect criticisms over its lack of rigour in its use of economics and of evidence.

NEW THEMES IN COMPETITION POLICY

The above reforms are part of an overall attempt to link competition policy (and its management/administration) to the longer-term goals of creating a more competitive Europe. To this end, the European Commission launched a more proactive policy framework. The aim is for competition policy to play a more substantive role in enhancing European competitiveness through:

■ improving the regulatory framework for business, thereby enabling enhanced competition, a more entrepreneurial culture and better deal for consumers (see below);

Case Study 5.1

FRANCE TELECOM AND STATE AIDS

One of the fundamental objectives of the recent reforms of the EU competition policy was to attack more effectively the state aid given by national governments to local or national strategically important businesses. Such assistance contravenes the requirements of the SEM. Over the past two decades, the French government has found itself in almost perpetual conflict with the European Commission over the level of support it offers to its 'strategically important' industries. In many ways, this reflects a strong tradition of intervention based on a culture of 'Colbertism' where the state is perceived as having a legitimate role in the 'direction' of industry. This desire to intervene has not been dimmed by the progressive liberalisation of the economy or by the gradual transfer of state assets out of public control. This desire to secure key domestic businesses from the excesses of corporate markets was evident again in the early years of the new millennium as the French government sought to support France Telecom (FT) in the face of a deteriorating and unstable commercial environment.

Up to the end of 2002, the French government granted FT an exemption from business tax. This exemption was given to financially support a business that had run up debts of over €70 billion following an aggressive acquisition spree. Such debts were not unique to FT as other of Europe's leading incumbent operators had also undertaken similarly aggressive expansionist strategies. Initially, the French government sought to inject €9 billion into FT – to support immediate financial difficulties in 2002 – via a state-controlled investment fund. As the French state is still a major shareholder, attempts were made to disguise this support as normal shareholder assistance. Thus, under the market economy investor principle, the support would be compatible with EU law. The money was to be repaid once turnaround was complete.

In response to complaints from other European states, the European Commission investigated the agreement. The European Commission felt that as the support offered was not matched by private-sector money, there were questions over its legality. This was compounded by allegations – after raids upon FT by the Commission – over illicit practices that inhibited the development of rivals within its domestic market. There were particular concerns that the regulatory body granted too many favours to FT. However, the case against the €9 billion injection was dropped and some argued that it never actually existed. The Commission suspects that although the aid was never used, the potential of support had a psychological impact upon perceptions of the future of the company resulting in higher share prices and credit ratings via the effect on investor confidence. Thus, the Commission could not ask for the monies to be repaid.

In 2004, the Commission launched another investigation over benefits received by FT in 2002. The Commission believes that between 1994 and 2003, FT was offered favourable rates and thresholds for a business tax (known as the *taxe professionelle*). The benefits were estimated to be around €1.1 billion. In July 2004, FT was ordered to repay this aid – the largest repayment ever ordered by the Commission. FT countered that since it had overpaid taxes between 1991 and 2001, it should not be liable for the sums and, in fact, the support was actually a repayment. Such disputes continue at the time of writing (2006).

The new rules that clamp down on aid allow for less discretion in policy and ensure that the 'one-time, last time' principle applies for ten years and that aid has to be paid back once the firm has recovered. However, taking action against the French desire to support ailing firms has been a constant challenge to the Commission. The French Government repeatedly supported its firms such as Crédit Lyonnais and Air France in the 1990s. Throughout the 1990s, the Commission has taken an increasingly aggressive stance with regard to state aid although it has had to compromise on many cases (such as Alstom). The new policy should, in theory, limit future challenges to the competition law by the French. However, improvements to policy cannot occur without the support of member states.

Case questions

1 Under what circumstances is state aid to firms justified?

2 Outline how state aid can distort the competitive process within the EU market place.

3 Outline the case for continued state support for key industries.

- an enforcement process that is focused upon removing barriers to entry that directly limit the competition of the SEM (see above).

This shifting stance reflects a growing perception of interdependence between competition and other policies that seek to enhance the competitive position of the EU. This position reflects the perspective – outlined at the beginning of the chapter – that there is nothing better for competitiveness than competition and that competition policy has to be more active in supporting the goals of the SEM rather than being merely a reactive policy process. Thus, policy has to directly tackle market impediments rather than wait for complaints to emerge. This is reflected in the reforms to the policy (mentioned above) that seek to rid the Commission of the duty of sanctioning all consolidations, cartels and other agreements even when there is clearly no intra-European dimension. Thus, the reform frees up the Commission to focus on those agreements that clearly impede the development of the SEM. A further aspect of the reform was to focus on an assessment method based on economic analysis. Thus, policy will concentrate on the effects of firms' actions, not on their potential impact. This means SMEs will not need to notify the Commission if they receive aid or seek limited inter-company agreements. These actions are supported by improved enforcement procedures.

The EU has adopted a competition policy that is based on a more liberal model. Thus, the aim is to make the competitive arena as intense as it is in the US to provide Europe with a base for its future competitive success. This is, in part, due to a more deliberately liberal line in policy management taken by successive Commissions.

Consumers

During 2003, the European Commission made a determined attempt to integrate its consumer protection (see Chapter 15) and competition policies. The main aim is to increase the direct dialogue between consumer groups (the main beneficiaries of effective competition) and the policy-making bodies. It is based on a recognition that competition authorities need to develop a more effective method of dealing with consumer complaints. The consumer is assumed to be an implicit and indirect beneficiary of many of the changes associated with a more proactive competition policy. Therefore, the priority is to develop better information for consumers about their rights with regard to their interests and the emergence of fair competition. Microsoft (see Case Study 5.2) is a classic example where the European Commission claims it is working directly in consumer interests through providing a direct link between consumer bodies and the competition authorities.

One of the aims of devolving decisions to the national courts and authorities (as part of the aforementioned reform process) is to give consumers better access to these bodies. The consideration of consumer interests has always been a theme within competition policy, notably in regard to ensuring that consumers benefit from any restrictive agreement approved. The aim is also to increase the transparency of policy to make consumers more familiar with these policies. Thus, the EU has implemented 'Competition days' where the Commission presents details about the policy to non-specialists, notably consumer bodies and associations. Consumers are key to the EU's proactive policy. Consumer complaints will be a key way for restrictive agreements and other competitive distortions to come to the Commission's attention.

The new economy

A key theme of the Lisbon Agenda is to push Europe towards what is loosely called the 'new economy' (see Chapter 12). In many ways, by providing customers with increased transparency, lower transaction costs, more integrated markets and better information, the new economy is a key contributor to the objective of increasing the intensity of competition within the EU. Much of this policy priority consists of spreading the usage of information and communication technologies throughout Europe's socio-economic strata. This requires persistent vigilance of competition policy to create a virtuous cycle of network usage of key technologies, most notably broadband. Traditionally these sectors were regulated rather than subject to generic competition policy. As competition has matured, this is changing. Competition law will be applied alongside direct regulation to ensure the priorities are met. For example, Article 82 will be applied alongside regulation to push for providing access to the local loop – a key requirement of achieving access to broadband (see Chapter 12). The EU has also been active in reducing international roaming charges for mobile telephony in Europe.

Already a number of mergers covering the Internet backbone (for example, MCI-WorldCom), mobile infrastructure and content have come before the Commission to assess their competitive effects. These have been driven by the desire to maintain access to the network and to content within the system. Without this, the new economy will be stillborn. The blockage of the WorldCom–Sprint merger was done on the basis that it would have too much influence over Internet connections. Business has increasingly argued that old economy rules based on market share do not always apply in the new economy where barriers to entry are more surmountable. Thus, simply using market share as a guide can be misleading about the state of competition within a sector (see Microsoft, Case Study 5.2, p. 118). This poses a challenge for regulators as the fast-moving nature of the new competitive environment means what looked like the correct decision could rapidly turn out to be incorrect.

THE INTERNATIONAL DIMENSION OF EU COMPETITION POLICY

As economics globalise, so competition policy becomes ever more important as the rules of competition — though not uniform in both form and structure — are pivotal in determining mutual access to markets. As a result, these rules need to be applied consistently and fairly to support the globalisation process by ensuring the equal treatment of indigenous and foreign companies. The certainty and fairness of competition policy is also important in attracting FDI as protection for local operators will deter such flows. Globalisation will affect EU competition policy in a number of ways:

- the global strategies of EU enterprises can potentially alter the definition of the relevant market;
- competition from imports increases internal competition (a fact reflected within the MCR);
- EU competition is affected by external factors.

The results of such problems are jurisdictional complexities and transnational spillovers in terms of respective policy domains. This suggests a need for cooperation to increase the efficiency of global markets, to improve the credibility of the global trading system and to create greater

certainty for enterprises. There is also a need for competition authorities to be better informed about each others' policies and how they will affect enterprise operations. These benefits are compounded by a desire by business for speedier proceedings and more legal certainty when dealing with different competition authorities.

The international dimension of EU competition policy has a number of overlapping themes: cooperation in lieu of enlargement; bilateral cooperation and multilateral cooperation. The aim of such cooperation is to assist enforcement agencies to focus on the most relevant issues as well as ensuring consistency across regimes.

Enlargement

Before states can join the EU, they have to demonstrate that not only do they have a proper functioning market economy but that domestic firms can also cope with competitive pressures and respond to market forces (see Chapter 16). Prospective members have to ensure that the legislative framework is in place for all competition provisions, that there is the capacity to effectively administer this policy and that they have a credible record of compliance with the *acquis communautaire*. These conditions have to be met well before the date of accession. To ensure this process is successful, there is technical assistance available for the creation of competition authorities as a means of promoting a more mature 'competition culture' within these states. This extra-territorial dimension of policy is essentially temporary as Europe works beyond its borders to ensure the smooth integration of new member states into the regulatory regime of the EU and to ensure that these states develop an effective competition policy for the first time.

113

Some of the problems of ensuring competition rules are met prior to enlargement were highlighted by the 2004 accession. In the 2004 accession states, there was uneven progress in the implementation of competition policy (notably with regard to state aid policy). The reasons for this were derived from:

■ incomplete understanding of competition policy based on a lack of administrative capacity and competence;
■ the staffing of competition authorities by members of the former Communist regimes who see their role as limiting the excesses of competition rather than actively promoting it;
■ the political sensitivity of removing state aids in key sectors.

Such problems require (again, especially with relevance to the problems of state aid) agreement between states upon balancing the desire for flexibility within a common framework and developing an effective monitoring system to ensure compliance with any agreed framework. A start has been made to secure the effective monitoring of aid via the establishment of aid-monitoring authorities. To support compliance, the Commission uses technical assistance through the ECN (see above). This advice has proved central to institution building. While the EU did not finish accession negotiations with the ten new members until December 2002, it did conclude a series of transitional agreements on state aid to assist restructuring and the gradual phasing out of tax aid regimes designed to attract FDI.

With the completion of the 2004 accession, the focus has shifted to the next set of candidates: Romania, Bulgaria and Turkey. Negotiations are more advanced with the first two states, which are aiming for membership by 2007. Bulgaria's and Romania's achievements are more advanced in relation to antitrust and mergers but state aid is, again, proving to be a sticking point, especially with unsatisfactory enforcement. Given support from the EU – in the form of education, training and technical assistance – adjustment to EU rules is anticipated.

Bilateral cooperation

The EU has concluded bilateral cooperation agreements with the US, Canada and Japan. In all such agreements, cooperation tends to be based on information sharing and coordination of enforcement activities as well as the exchange of non-confidential information. The 1995 recommendation of the Organisation for Economic Cooperation and Development (OECD) (see below) forms the basis of these cooperation agreements. These bilateral relations have also been extended to Latin America and other OECD states, for example, but cooperation tends not to be as intense in these instances as it is with other G8 members.

The existing bilateral agreements between states seek to iron out inconsistencies in the established mechanisms for the exchange of information as well as to encourage consultation on issues of common concern. In general, cooperation includes one or more of the following:

■ exchange of information on general issues related to the implementation of competition rules;
■ cooperation and coordination of the actions of both parties' competition authorities;
■ a 'traditional comity' procedure by which each party takes into account the interests of the other party;

■ a 'positive comity procedure' whereby one country can ask the other to act in those instances where the actions under consideration fall within one jurisdiction but affect another's interests.

This bilateral cooperation has had its most potent expression in the EU's dealings with the US. The EU–US cooperation agreement was concluded in 1991 and approved in 1995 with the positive comity agreement coming into force in 1998. Overall, the cooperation on mergers has been productive. Close cooperation has been evident on a number of mergers including AOL/Time Warner and MCI WorldCom/Sprint. Although, there have been differences, notably over the General Electric/Honeywell merger, which the Commission blocked after the US authorities had approved it. To the European Commission, such high-profile cases underplay the degree of convergence between US and EU competition policies. This is most evident in that both base their assessment upon economic analysis. However, there are clear differences, notably over state aid as highlighted by the Airbus/Boeing Case (see Chapter 17). This long-running dispute entered a new phase when the US registered a formal complaint to the WTO over the 'unfair subsidies' offered to Airbus. The EU then filed a counter-claim.

The rivalry and disputes among competition bodies have intensified since 2000, particularly over the aforementioned GE–Honeywell case in which the EU believed that US concerns were more likely to lodge a complaint in the belief that they would get a more favourable hearing. These disputes were also evident in the Microsoft case (see Case Study 5.2, p. 118). Part of the reason is not merely a change in personnel at the head of the US bodies but also institutional. The Commission has more power to attach conditions to merger approvals than the US bodies. Other sources of conflict include the EU use of market dominance based on industry structure rather than upon performance. In addition, the EU became involved in 'portfolio effects' where – as in the case of GE–Honeywell – a merger could allow a situation of dominance across a range of industries to emerge. This is often impossible in US courts. Furthermore, the increasingly litigious nature of the US legal system means that offended bodies have other sources of outlets for redress. The EU has limited scope for third-party enforcement. However, underlying these differences were clear ideological differences between the Bush team and the European Commission, with the former tending to be distrustful of government intervention. The EU points out that there have been deals that the EU has approved but which the US has blocked, notably the purchase by Air Liquide of the UK's BOC.

Bilateralism also extends to the European Economic Agreement states (Iceland, Norway and Liechtenstein) which are subject to rules identical to the EU Treaty, to secondary legislation as well as to ECJ decisions. This has been extended to generic agreements signed with third countries which include competition agreements (for example, Israel, Morocco and Tunisia) and is enhanced by informal channels of cooperation with many other states.

Multilateral cooperation

Multilateral cooperation between states is born of the oft-mentioned forces of globalisation. The aim is to establish a pluralistic agreement between industrialised states with similar competition rules and cultures. In short, these agreements consist of a common set of rules and mechanisms for dispute settlement. The European Commission has been pushing for an international body within the framework of the WTO to act as a forum for such action. Both UNCTAD and the OECD have made efforts to develop closer cooperation between states. A 1986 OECD recommendation has been used as a reference point for the negotiation of several bilateral agreements but these are fairly weak with no legal basis.

The European Commission report 'Competition Policy and the New World Trade Order' (published in 1995) argued that these flirtations with cooperation between leading industrialised states need to be strengthened due to:

- the conclusion of the Uruguay Round which has resulted in a progressive reduction in the role of state-imposed trade barriers – these could be replaced by other obstacles that could re-impose the division between world markets (see below);
- increased contradiction between international markets and the scope of competition policy.

Prior to this report, there had been little cooperation between states because there was often disagreement about the objectives of competition policy and the nature of competition policy frequently precluded cooperation. In its aftermath, the European Commission called for a stronger international framework for competition policy. The vision is for the WTO to adopt common proposals around which all states involved in trade negotiations would establish their own rules. The WTO does not have any competition laws although the promotion of market access is its fundamental objective.

Giving the WTO a more active role in the development of a multilateral agreement on rules to govern global competition has proved controversial. Not only is it unlikely that, on a multilateral basis, states would be able to agree on much but this is compounded by the fact nearly half the WTO's members have no competition policy. In addition, some states feel that the WTO has a general lack of expertise and resources to deal effectively with the issues concerned. Thus, over the short to medium term, the WTO is likely to play a minimal role and the international aspects of competition will be covered by a web of bilateral deals (see above).

The EU has more recently coordinated its ambitions for a reform of competition policy on a global basis by supporting, along with Japan, Canada and the US, the development of a study group upon this issue. This 'Quadrilateral Group' has attempted to put the issue of reform upon the WTO agenda, arguing that the development of a multilateral framework requires the following four elements to be in place:

- the exchange of information between competition agencies;
- a 'positive comity instrument' whereby one competition body can ask another to investigate and act, if necessary, against certain practices that are against its interests yet outside its jurisdiction;
- a set of substantive rules that counteract actions that have anti-competitive effects;
- a dispute settlement system containing safeguards to ensure strict compliance.

In many cases, the issue is one of consistency between trade and competition policies. To this end, the EU has placed itself among a network of interlinking organisations seeking to develop a multilateral framework for competition. Generally, such cooperation occurs within the context of the

WTO (see below), the OECD, UNCTAD and the international cooperation framework. Within the OECD and UNCTAD, the EU works with other bodies to review and assess competition policy. UNCTAD, for example, is responsible for 'Multilaterally Agreed Equitable Principles and Rules for the Control of Restrictive Business Practices' which provides a model law for competition. In each forum, the EU acts in a consultative role. The impact of these bodies upon the development of a more competitive environment tends to be more passive than active. UNCTAD has proved useful for smaller and developing states to garner experience of operating competition policy. It is through such fora that the EU offers technical assistance. This has been supported by the creation of the International Competition Network (ICN).

The ICN acts as an informal forum in which competition authorities from around the globe can meet to discuss the practicalities of policy and exchange best practice. It has had some important achievements, notably in terms of identifying key principles that authorities should respect when analysing mergers that cross jurisdictions. The ICN works closely with the OECD, the WTO and UNCTAD as well as with industry and consumer groups to develop a more consistent and coherent approach to competition policy. The group actively seeks convergence on key issues such as cross-border merger control and the advocacy role of competition authorities (that is, the role of authorities in preventing and curing competitive distortion created by public intervention). The ICN is proving especially important for the 'younger' competition authorities to learn and understand best practices in the management of competition. Membership has already reached 80 different authorities (2003).

Since the 1996 WTO Ministerial in Singapore, competition has been a major issue for the WTO. These negotiations began on the basis of the Van Miert report which proposed that the WTO should establish a working group to examine the issue. At the Doha meeting in 2001, the case for a multilateral framework was formally recognised. Such developments took place against a broad agreement to support competences and administrative capabilities to build and manage an effective competition policy at the nation state level. However, at the Cancun meeting in 2003, no formal negotiations were launched. According to the Commission any agreement on competition has to be based on:

- developing domestic legislative frameworks based on the principle of non-discrimination;
- effective cooperation between competition authorities;
- ensuring that the development dimension in competition policy is accounted for.

In any policy developments:

- sectoral actions and product exclusion should be treated in a pragmatic manner;
- developing states and others that have only recently implemented a competition policy should benefit from such a global arrangement;
- there should be increased and sustained transparency regarding laws, regulations etc.;
- there should be guarantees relating to the fairness of policy;
- judicial review of competition decisions should be possible.

However, the Commission is clear that as a precursor to such an agreement there has to

Case Study 5.2

THE EU AND MICROSOFT

The case against Microsoft was launched in 1998 after complaints from its rivals (notably Sun Microsystems) that the enterprise – via its Windows product – enjoyed a dominant position in the PC operating systems market. Indeed, the Commission estimated that Microsoft controlled 90–95 per cent of this market. Furthermore – as required by Article 82 – there was evidence that Microsoft had abused this dominant position by requiring that certain software for network computing had to be compatible with its own operating system (the software that runs PCs). This interoperability issue was later joined by further complaints that Microsoft's bundling of its media player into its latest software limited the ability of rival media players to compete. This was derived from an inability of competitors to access the information needed to develop compatible products and by Microsoft's insistence that licences would only be granted to users if they accepted the media player. This latter investigation brought the EU case closer to the one launched by the US authorities.

Given the rapidity of change in the IT sector, it is a wonder that Microsoft has been able to sustain its dominance. Rivals allege that it has been able to do this due to two key business practices. The first is the linking of the Windows PC system to Microsoft software running on other systems. This led – according to the Commission – to Microsoft extending its desktop dominance of workgroup services (such as file, print, e-mail and web servers). Microsoft sought to do this by keeping to itself protocols that enabled its desktop and server products to talk to each other. To Microsoft, this is a natural benefit of networked computing. To its rivals, it inhibits their ability to develop Windows-compatible products thereby creating interoperability problems. The second practice lies in Microsoft's habit of bundling new software features into Windows that are offered as separate products elsewhere.

While Microsoft had managed to fight off the conclusion of a US judge that it had used its monopoly power to block competition (and negotiated a far milder punishment), the EU had been developing a separate case to challenge the apparent abuse of monopoly power identified by the European Commission (see above). The European case is important as it focuses in on the firm's behaviour since the US decision – which is widely believed to have had little effect. In August 2000, the Commission sent a formal statement of objections to Microsoft outlining its complaints and asking the firm to comment. The power of the Commission to fine a firm up to 10 per cent of its annual revenues (US$2.5 billion in 2003) meant that Microsoft (and its shareholders) could not afford to ignore this action. Furthermore, constraints on its ability to bundle activities would not only consume management time but would also limit its ability to translate its dominance on the desktop into new and emerging electronic devices.

Microsoft signalled that – in the aftermath of its victory over the US antitrust authorities – it was unwilling to make major concessions beyond those that it had made to reach agreement with the US bodies. It was especially reluctant to remove the media player from its suite of services. For Microsoft, the US agreement was the basis for any agreement with the EU. However, by 2002, tiny concessions were made to allow limited access for rivals to the necessary technical information and it agreed to support three rival media programmes on PCs. Though this was unsatisfactory to its rivals, Microsoft argued that the demands for interoperability between servers went too far; that exposing the source code would impinge on its intellectual property and that the extra features were a response to user demands and not an extension of its market power. Furthermore, Microsoft argued that the Commission had defined the relevant market too narrowly, thereby overstating its degree of dominance.

After the initial complaints were made, Microsoft and the European Commission entered a period of negotiation but they could not agree on limits to the future actions by Microsoft, most notably in terms of limits to bundling. After this failure to agree, the EU launched the biggest antitrust case in its history. Microsoft agreed to allow limited access and licensing of its software to create enhanced interoperability as was agreed at the end of the US case. Bundling, however, has proved more controversial.

The problem with bundling is that – short of breaking up the company (as the US authorities initially proposed) – there is no real solution. Separating out the media player from Windows for European customers would result in them having access to an inferior product and create a grey market as the full version of Windows spreads because of imports from elsewhere. Furthermore, if Microsoft were compelled to carry other products exactly what products would it pick? In deciding to fight the Commission, Microsoft initially embarked upon a protracted war of attrition as it had with the US authorities. However, given the degree of change in the market, there is an unwillingness to allow the firm to be diverted from product innovations.

However, other parts of the Commission – notably the Single Market Directorate – were keen to ensure that any decision by the EU does not infringe Microsoft's IPR. In March 2004, the Commission ordered Microsoft to share interface information with its competitors and to offer a version of its Windows products without the media player. In addition, the company was fined €497 million – fairly irrelevant to a firm that has over €50 billion in cash reserves. Microsoft's immediate response was to stall by going to appeal through the European Courts. Furthermore, Microsoft alleged that the decision infringed its IPR. The appeal could take up to five years. Meanwhile, Microsoft has launched a separate application to have the two remedies frozen until the main case is decided.

A solution to this dispute is important not only for the credibility of the regulator and for the future fortunes of the company but also because of the state of the fast-evolving software market. Microsoft is aware that a defeat could lead to a free-for-all in examining all aspects of its competitive behaviour, something that is to be avoided at all costs in these rapidly evolving markets. A negative result on appeal would pose a core challenge to its business model. Microsoft has a lot of enemies and many would like nothing better than to see its dominance curtailed. Microsoft feels that the remedies go further than needed and pose a real threat to the company.

Attempts by the EU to change the competitive behaviour of Microsoft go far beyond what was demanded of the company by the US antitrust bodies. In pursuing Microsoft, the EU has kept the US authorities informed of its actions. This was despite a previous incumbent of the US Department of Justice criticising the economic analysis underpinning the EU's case. While the US supported Microsoft's assertion that its own decision provides a framework for the EU's case, it did not directly challenge any of the actions undertaken by the EU though neither did it fully support them. However, the Microsoft case provides further evidence of an increasing divergence between the two competition policy regimes. US law identifies competition and consumer benefit as the priority. In the EU, the emphasis is upon competitor welfare. In the US, lawyers and economists have found no harm in bundling. The EU clearly disagrees. However, Europe has to strike a balance between protecting IPR and ensuring fair competition in network industries.

In December 2004, the ECJ upheld the sanctions imposed by the European Commission. The ECJ felt that there was no proven case for an appeal by Microsoft which had argued not only that the sanctions would cause 'serious and irreparable damage' but that they would also make it increasingly difficult to add new functions to its Windows system. Thus, not only was Microsoft guilty of abusing its dominant position and fined accordingly (a record €497 million) but it also had to offer a version of Windows without the media player and make it easier for rivals to offer Windows-compatible products. The ruling has the potential to set a strong precedent, allowing the Commission to move more quickly against any future abusive behaviour.

By mid-2005, Microsoft was showing reluctant flexibility in its dealing with the Commission. Microsoft launched Windows XP Home Edition N to comply with the rulings. This version is without the media player; though consumers can still buy the full version at the same price. In addition, Microsoft accepted the critical area of the decision that it shares parts of its operating code with rivals. The Commission wanted 26 areas of its activities amended: the company easily consented to 20 of these and there has been significant progress on the remaining six. However, the company does not like allowing access to open source developers and the open source developers remain unhappy with the degree of access granted and the licence fees.

Case questions

1 What is the source of Microsoft's competitive advantage?

2 Outline the European Commission's case against Microsoft.

3 Do you think the case against Microsoft was justified?

4 Will technological change undermine the competitive threat of Microsoft?

be sustained cooperation and technical assistance to guide convergence of policy. Moves towards reaching agreement took a positive turn in July 2001 when the US agreed to support the EU's proposals.

Given its broad membership and ability to enforce rules, the Commission believes that the WTO is best suited to developing and implementing an international agreement on competition rules. Cooperation is seen as the most effective method of dealing with those anti-competitive agreements and combinations that affect global trade. It is also important that the notion of fair competition works to the benefit of all parties, thus there have to be efforts within any competition agreement to enable developing states to participate and benefit from any such agreement. For the Commission, the Doha declaration on competition policy was an important watershed as it:

- created a recognition among states of the need for such an agreement;
- created a clear commitment to begin negotiations on such a policy;
- enshrined the Commission proposals on global competition within the agreement;
- promoted the adoption and enforcement of domestic competition regimes;
- enhanced cooperation between antitrust bodies;
- facilitated effective combating of anti-competitive actions;
- operated as a base upon which pre-negotiation could begin.

CONCLUSION

Competition policy is integral to the internationalisation of the European economy. It defines the rules of entry and play within the game of competition. Clearly, competition policy is both reactive and proactive to the integration process but as internationalisation proceeds, the former is becoming more evident. However, the recent reforms have recognised that there are practical limits to the ability of the EU bodies to handle the volume of cases that emerge from an integrating Europe. The resulting renationalisation of policy requires a greater degree of harmony from states with regard to the form and substance of policy. However, some member states are not retreating from their, by now traditional, reticence to apply EU law vigorously where it affects 'strategic interests'. This is a clear impediment to the uniformity of competition management that is central to the SEM. On top of this, further challenges are emerging as the internationalisation of economies requires further bilateral and multilateral agreements. At the time of writing, these agreements are still evolving and – as the Microsoft case (see Case Study 5.2) has demonstrated – are still prone to dispute.

KEY POINTS

- Competition policy seeks to maintain the intensity of competition in order to sustain the objectives of the EU.

- Competition policy has extensive powers to regulate the activities of enterprises to the extent that these activities contravene treaty objectives.

- Policy is reacting to the process of integration via a gradual extension of policy scope and of new powers.

- Globalisation also requires a re-examination of the EU's competition policy.

ACTIVITIES

1 Take one recent competition decision by the EU and research how the form and nature of a competitive threat was established.

2 Using the example of one sector with which you are familiar, analyse the impact of competition on (a) market structure, (b) competitors and (c) consumers.

3 Research the GE–Honeywell case. What does this tell you about the different approaches to competition between the EU and the US?

4 Research the efforts by the WTO to develop provisions on competition policy. How warranted are such actions?

QUESTIONS FOR DISCUSSION

1 Why do states need competition policy?

2 What is the nature of the interface between economic integration and EU competition policy?

3 Why is the removal of state aids so important? Why is their removal so difficult?

4 What was the justification for the recent reforms of EU competition policy?

5 What are the major difficulties in developing a global competition policy?

SUGGESTIONS FOR FURTHER READING

Albors-Llorens, A. (2002) 'The Changing Face of EC Competition Law: Reform or Revolution', *European Business Journal*, 14 (1), pp. 31–9.

Albors-Llorens, A. (2002) *EC Competition Law and Policy*, Cullompton, Devon: Willan Publishing.

Dutilh, N. (2004) *Dealing with Dominance: The Experience of National Competition Authorities*, The Hague: Kluwer Law International.

European Commission (2004) 'Annual Report of Competition Policy'.

European Commission (2004) 'A Pro-active Competition Policy for Europe', COM (2004) 293.

Kahn, A. (1988) *The Economics of Regulation: Principles and Institutions*, Cambridge, MA: The MIT Press.

Kleit, A. (ed.) (2005) *Antitrust and Competition Policy*, Cheltenham: Edward Elgar.

Motta, M. (2004) *Competition Policy: Theory and Practice*, Cambridge: Cambridge University Press.

Neven, D. (1998) *Trawling for Minnows: European Competition Policy and Agreements Between Firms*, London: Centre for Economic Policy Research.

Nicolaides, P. (2002) 'Development of a System for Decentralized Enforcement of EC Competition Policy', *Intereconomics*, 37 (1), pp. 41–51.

Porter, M. (1990) *The Competitive Advantage of Nations*, Basingstoke: Macmillan.

Roger, B. and MacCulloch, A. (2004) *Competition Law and Policy in the EC and UK: An Introduction to Practice and Policy*, London: Cavendish.

Slo, P. (2004) 'A View From the Mountain: 40 Years of Developments in EC Competition Law', *Common Market Law Review*, 41, pp. 443–73.

Van Bergeijk, P. and Kloosterhuis, E. (eds) (2005) *Modelling European Mergers: Theory, Competition Policy and Case Studies*, Cheltenham: Edward Elgar.

Wijckmans, F. (2003) 'Internationalisation of Competition Policy: Observations from a European Practitioner's Perspective', *Antitrust Bulletin*, 48 (4), pp. 1037–44.

Chapter 6

European industrial policy
Meeting the challenges of international competitiveness

Lost wealth may be replaced by industry, lost knowledge by study, lost health by temperance or medicine, but lost time is gone forever.

Samuel Smiles (1812–1904), British political reformer

This chapter will help you to:

- understand the importance of international competitiveness;
- comprehend the nature of the competitive challenge faced by European business;
- identify and understand the role of industrial policy within modern internationalised economies;
- appreciate the key tools and devices employed by the EU to make the European economy more competitive.

Industrial policy has a pivotal influence over the development of the European business environment through establishing the framework within which other policies influence the performance of enterprise. The internationalisation of economies means that this framework is increasingly market oriented with emphasis away from direct state involvement in the economy towards one of state passivity. This chapter begins by examining the role of industrial policy within integrating and internationalising economies in achieving the core policy goal of inter-national competitiveness. Thereafter, the role of globalisation in increasing the prominence of supranational policy and the shift in the form and nature of the policy actions are explored. Finally, the policy measures used to promote the international positioning of European-based enterprises are examined.

THE CHANGING NATURE OF EUROPEAN INDUSTRY

The success of European industry lies at the heart of EU prosperity. European business performance in increasingly global markets is central to the EU achieving its objectives of generating sustainable long-term employment and overcoming deficiencies in Europe's ability to compete on the global stage (see Chapters 1 and 2). However, the nature and role of industry is changing as Europe relies for an increased proportion of its wealth upon services and less on manufacturing. With increased globalisation and deindustrialisation, pressure is increasing upon European business to develop new sources of competitive advantage. To this end, industrial policy has emerged as a means of providing direction and support for such change.

A steady structural shift has been under way within the European economy for some time. Since the 1970s, the contribution of manufacturing to total EU output has declined from 30 per cent (1979) to 18 per cent (2004) while the contribution of ser-

vices has increased from 52 to 71 per cent over the same period. Figure 6.1 reflects the falling contribution by manufacturing to overall value-added between 1979 and 2003. Traditionally, a strong manufacturing sector has underpinned the EU's international competitiveness. Under pressure from increased international competition, this traditional strength has been replaced by growing commercial advantage in the service sector in many 'mature' industrialised economies. Economists are divided over the impact of this trend but many doubt services can be as tradable and productive as manufacturing output.

This shifting competitive advantage of EU states is derived from the pervasive and combined impact of technology and freer trade on the global business environment. Thus, the richer states will have to rely upon the service sector and knowledge-based or capital-intensive industries to sustain and

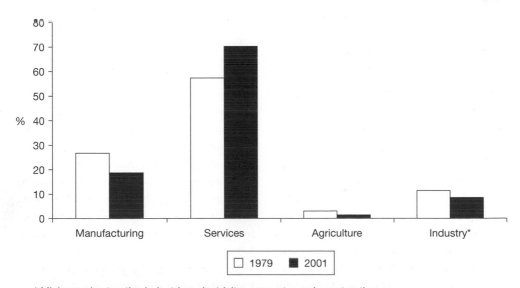

* Mining and extractive industries, electricity, gas, water and construction

Figure 6.1 *The breakdown of value-added within the EU-15*
Source: Eurostat (2003).

enhance their position within the global economy. Thus, the quality of an economy's factor base is an important determinant of competitiveness. This is especially pertinent for labour, which is the only factor of production that cannot be easily or quickly duplicated across the global economy.

In some states, this shift has brought little policy response given a belief that the manufacturing sector no longer matters in the knowledge/service sector economy. However, much of this shift has been driven by enhanced productivity growth in the manufacturing and industry sectors which has caused a transfer of jobs to the service sector. Thus, while sectors such as chemicals and aerospace have shed jobs, they have also experienced sharp increases in productivity. While such a shift represents a reallocation of resources and is not to be discouraged, it is also causes adjustment problems. This shift also reflects increases in wealth which have driven increases in household-oriented and/or personal services.

However, the continuing importance of manufacturing to the European economy should not be underestimated. In 2005, manufacturing still provided 20 per cent of employment (around 34 million jobs); received 80 per cent of all research and technological development (RTD) spending and generated 75 per cent of exports. Manufacturing is also important within the SME sector (which includes 99 per cent of manufacturing firms and 58 per cent of manufacturing employment) and in terms of its ability to spill over into wealth creation elsewhere within the European economy. While some sectors of European manufacturing (such as chemical and mechanical engineering) still compete in the global economy, there is a concern that much of this segment of industry is using medium-high technologies with intermediate labour skills. This

undermines the ability of the EU to compete on the non-price factors that are often central to market positioning.

The interdependence between service and manufacturing sectors has increased over time as the latter has outsourced activities to the former. Such a shift is symptomatic of the growing importance of knowledge as a differentiating factor in the global marketplace. Applications of knowledge are at the core of the increases in productivity growth and – ultimately – at the heart of the competitive challenge. To many, the growing complexity of knowledge has directly led to the growth in outsourcing and to the emergence of the service sector as a key wealth generator. This is compounded by the fact that industrial products have an increasingly high knowledge and/or service component which further integrates these two sectors.

If such changes are predicted, they can work to the benefit of the economy. However, this is rarely the case due to limited knowledge and political pressures to limit the effect of these changes. These shifts reflect changes in the EU's competitive advantage at the international level. In general (and in response to intensifying global competitive pressure) most of Europe's competitive sectors have made substantial efforts to adjust to the new environment. Many have upgraded their production infrastructures and implemented new forms of organisation. Many sectors considered medium-to-low technology (such as textiles, food processing and retailing) have increased technological capability. This has led to a change in labour demand in favour of higher skilled employees. This confirms that the competitiveness of European business depends upon human capital and investment in employee capability (see Chapter 13), although the EU continues to lag behind both

Japan and the US in investment in education and training.

Despite more intense competition on the global stage, European business remains a dominant manufacturing force (see Chapter 3). However, this must not hide the key competitive problems facing the EU. These undermine the competitive position of the EU business, especially within high-technology sectors: the EU is failing to compete not only in the high value-added end of the market (such as electronics and office machinery) but also in the medium- to high-technology sectors in which the EU specialises and in mature capital-intensive sectors where the take-up of ICTs has been slow. Low productivity growth in these sectors and their overall importance to the EU economy mean that the EU faces a real competitiveness problem. Reasons for this poor performance have been attributed to:

- great difficulties in accessing private research finance for RTD in Europe;
- a culture that is too risk averse;
- insufficient collaboration between public research bodies and the private sector;
- a much lower proportion of researchers in the population.

These concerns have been highlighted by the emergence of new economic powerhouses in the shape of India and China (see Chapter 18). China has shifted away from a focus on labour-intensive activities towards those that rely on increased technological specialisation. As these states develop further, they will act as a magnet to global business and potentially undermine investment in the EU and hinder its ability to grow. In the short term, Chinese growth has had an immediate effect on the cost-sensitive sectors of the EU economy, a trend that could spread to other sectors.

THE NATURE OF INDUSTRIAL POLICY AND INTERNATIONAL COMPETITIVENESS

In the context of such market-driven challenges, the role of industrial policy is to divert resources towards sectors that are more likely to generate sustained economic growth and promote long-term employment opportunities. Underpinning such a policy is the creation of a set of industries that are able to compete successfully on the global stage. In Europe's case, the challenge is often set in the context of reallocating resources to:

- manage the rise of growing and emerging industries;
- manage the performance of declining and/or poorly performing strategic industries.

Such resource reallocation needs to minimise its negative socio-economic as well as political impacts. Increasingly, therefore, industrial policy attempts to manage the consequences of structural change to ensure that such changes have an overall positive impact upon the economy. This implies that changes occur with no large transitional costs in terms of output or employment. Thus, ideally, resources no longer required in declining sectors can readily be absorbed into growing or emerging areas of the economy.

The reallocation of resources can occur through one or more of the following set of policy measures:

- *Generic policy*: generic policies apply equally to all sectors and include measures such as education, healthcare and others that improve the general economic environment at both a micro- and macro-economic level.
- *Selective policy*: selective policies apply to particular sectors.

127

The latter tend to be more activist than the former but, in practice, industrial policy tends to exist as a hybrid of both sets of policies. Within this context, policy can be differentiated between negative and positive actions. The former seek to slow down the process of change (for example, by protecting declining sectors from international competition); the latter seek to accelerate transition within a framework of pre-established socio-economic priorities. In a global economy, the domination of positive actions should come as little surprise.

The rationale behind such action is the creation of a sustainable competitive economy. However, what is actually meant by 'competitiveness' can be somewhat opaque. Factors such as costs of production, technological development or exchange rates are all used as indicators of competitiveness. In practice, competitiveness is a hybrid of all these phenomena: each will determine to varying degrees, businesses' abilities to successfully sustain a presence within their respective markets. Over the medium to long term, sustenance within markets requires a constant reappraisal and renewal of labour skills and capital. In other words, it is enterprises not states that compete and it is within this context that the role of national and supranational policy needs to be reassessed.

Conventionally, industrial policy is justified on the basis of the inability of the market to deliver outcomes that reflect the broad socio-economic interest of the commercial body. However, justifying policy on this basis has led to counter-accusations of government failure. Intervention based on poor knowledge/information and political bias, for example, can lead to inefficient outcomes. Despite a shift away from activist policies during the 1980–90s, the emergence of 'strategic trade policy' (STP) offered a renewed justification for direct involvement.

STP was based on the premise that – in the presence of imperfect competition – the development of strategic industries (via direct intervention) would lead to higher returns. Thus, to retain these profits within their borders, states have a direct incentive to create national champions through the artificial creation of a dominant position. This has been supported by activism to help new industries and to ensure national and/or regional support standards are adopted as the global norm, thereby creating a competitive advantage for indigenous companies.

However, despite this theoretical rationale for a return to activism, there has been a sea change in industrial policy across most industrialised states as they actively seek to promote structural change rather than limit it. Thus, instead of working in spite of or even against markets, policy is increasingly complementing the changes associated with these forces. Consequently, the aim is to harness market forces to improve competitive positioning of industry to secure growth and provide sustainable employment. The traditional role of industrial policy as a device to maximise the interests of nationally owned corporations is out of date, a concept that is disappearing as a result of the increased interactions between states. International competitiveness is no longer simply an issue for indigenous firms but for all enterprises located within an economy. An economy's success within international markets is dependent upon the competitiveness of all enterprises that source or locate themselves within it.

As a consequence, Foreman-Peck and Federico (1999) argue that within a globalising environment industrial policy has to be active on three levels, by:

1 creating a landscape (the legal and institutional framework);

Case Study 6.1

AEROSPACE – BOEING vs AIRBUS

The European aerospace industry is a high-technology industry based on the mutually dependent twin pillars of output comprising civil (64 per cent) and military (36 per cent) aircraft. In 2003, the European industry directly employed 415,000 and had an annual turnover of more than €74 billion. In 2004, the sector exported more than 50 per cent of its output as European companies continued to make inroads into the traditional high global market share enjoyed by the dominant US concern – Boeing. Indeed, the global market share of US companies had fallen to 44 per cent in 2003 as EU market share continued to rise. Historically the dominance of the US was aided by its large domestic market. However, the EU has challenged this advantage by integrating its aerospace industry within a single operation – Airbus.

The global aerospace industry is characterised by industry structures dominated by economies of scale. In civil aircraft, the global market structure is a duopoly based on a US (Boeing) and an EU (Airbus) supplier. Over recent years, Boeing has been losing market share in the civil aviation market to Airbus. In five of the six years up to the end of 2005, Boeing had been outsold by Airbus in terms of new orders (see Figure 6.2). Indeed, in 2003, Airbus delivered more commercial aircraft than Boeing for the first time in its history. In 2004, Airbus delivered 53 per cent of all commercial aircraft over 100 seats compared to 32 per cent in 1999. At the beginning of 2005, Airbus held an order backlog of 1,500 aircraft compared to 1,097 for Boeing. This rising market share took place against a backdrop of a trade dispute between the US and the EU over the extent to which this market share has shifted on the back of alleged illegal subsidies (see Case Study 17.1).

After successive years of market erosion, Boeing started to fight back with a change in its product portfolio and more aggressive sales tactics. The focus of the battle has moved to the mid-range market as Boeing takes on the popular Airbus A330-220 with its new 787.

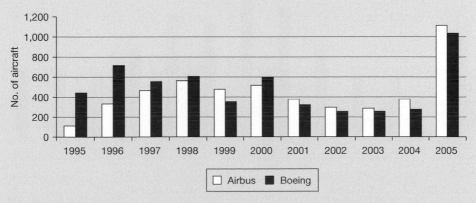

Figure 6.2 Orders for civil aircraft, 1995–2005

Source: Airbus/Boeing Annual Report.

129

While Boeing has been winning new orders, Airbus has responded with new comparable products, notably the A350. However, for both businesses, this is of secondary importance to the launch of the A380 – Airbus's long-haul product – which will challenge the monopoly of the Boeing 747 for the first time since its launch nearly 40 years ago. With the launch of the A380, Airbus finally has the range of products to compete with Boeing across all market segments. While many customers see the A380 as changing the dynamics of the industry towards low costs on long-haul flight, Boeing sees it as a white elephant targeting a declining market. Airbus believes the market for aircraft of this size is from around 1,250 up to 2,023; Boeing believes the market is less than 900. Boeing sees the air market as rising but fragmenting given the growing passenger preference for point-to-point services rather than the currently dominant hub-and-spoke model.

These successive product launches highlight the strategy of Airbus which has been both innovative and cost cutting. The accusation against Boeing is that it became complacent and lost its innovative nerve in the face of shareholder pressure. However, Airbus has faced a number of challenges: it has had to cope with the logistics of increasing production of the A380 while increasing production of its other models; the decline of the dollar which may require further assaults on its cost base; and a change in management that could undermine its strategy. By the end of 2005, it was evident that Airbus was still outselling Boeing. Despite trailing behind its US rival for most of the year, by the end of 2005, Airbus had gained an extra 1,111 aircraft compared to 1,029 for Boeing. This amounted to 52 per cent of the market by sales though the US business won 55 per cent of the market by value (reflecting its success in long-haul aircraft). The rising orders for these businesses reflect the fact that operators are looking to new technology to deliver greater efficiencies in the face of rising fuel costs.

Airbus represents an important feature of the European commercial environment. It is, in effect, a European champion that has worked to challenge the dominance of the large

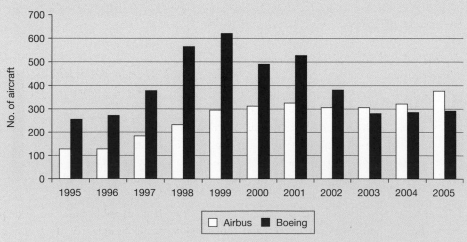

Figure 6.3 Deliveries of civil aircraft, 1995–2005
Source: Airbus/Boeing Annual Report.

US-based supplier. While there are ongoing disputes as to how it managed to achieve this objective, its ability to win market share has been impressive. However, this does not, and should not, signal the green light for the creation of other 'European champions' as its emergence was derived from a set of sector-specific factors that justified this strategic approach.

Case questions

1 Was the creation of a European 'champion' in aerospace justified?

2 Can the rise of Airbus explain all Boeing's commercial problems?

3 Why is a need to account for shareholders important to Boeing?

2 modifying the ecological environment (the technology and the market inputs and output);
3 changing the fauna (the relative importance of each firm).

These issues are reflected within the emerging framework to stimulate the EU's international competitiveness which is based on the views that:

■ intangible factors (such as education) are more powerful drivers of medium-term competitiveness than tangible factors (such as state subsidies);
■ innovation and intellectual property are the strongest drivers of the competitive environment;
■ relative costs and productivity affect growth and profits – though 'capital deepening' (that is high levels of capital intensity within enterprise operations) tends to be counter-productive in terms of both profits and employment.

This new agenda places belief in market forces as the main method of structural and strategic adjustment. However, the addiction to intervention in some states remains strong. In many instances, this is derived

from a long-standing mistrust of the role and the benefits of market forces. It also reflects the intimacy of state–business relations within some states where intervention is often desired by enterprises to enhance and support their international positioning. This has had its most vivid expression in the durability of the national champions' policy followed by certain member states. In these cases, the national prestige attached to these enterprises is little more than economic nationalism and a thinly veiled form of protectionism. Moreover, the ability of states to pick winners has proved to be extremely flawed.

THE EVOLVING SUPRANATIONAL POLICY: THEMES AND ISSUES

Community interest (see below) as a justification for strengthening the EU role in industrial policy tends to be defined in an uncontentious manner, partially as a result of the desire of European states to ensure industrial policy is compatible with the principle of subsidiarity. Consequently, the Community interest is identified by common concerns and issues, such as the legacy of industrial change. Importantly, it should not be taken

131

as proof of a convergence between states in the substance of policy: it may simply reflect areas of mutual concern. Where there is a convergence of policies, there is debate as to whether this is driven by the EU or is a natural consequence of the process of business interaction across borders. The case for a European industrial policy has to be based upon a prima facie case for supranational industrial policy and the erosion of the viability of national policies by spillover. There is little point in shifting the jurisdiction of policy beyond the national domain if the degree of market internationalisation is not that apparent. Thus, policy needs to be conducted at as local a level as possible to benefit from the levels of knowledge and complexity of industry that can otherwise undermine broad policy actions.

It is currently difficult to imagine that industrial policy at the supranational level will ever replace national initiatives in terms of importance. However, the integration of markets is breeding a degree of convergence between national policies that is broadly in line with measures being established at the supranational level. The power of European industrial policy is a direct derivative of the powers granted to the Commission by the member states. To date, this has in practice meant sanctioning national/intergovernmental industrial policy actions as compatible with EU law and establishing broad generic frameworks for promoting the industrial competitiveness of European-based business. To this end, the contribution of the EU to industrial policy is threefold and works through:

1 establishing the boundaries within which industry and small businesses can pursue their ambitions; to this end, policy aims to establish a predictable legal framework which can be adapted to needs;

2 establishing the necessary conditions to enable industry to be successful and to realise its competitive potential.
3 ensuring that the frameworks, institutions and instruments necessary for a vibrant business and industrial environment are in place and work effectively.

The EU's industrial policy takes the position that structural change is not an issue for the state but for the agents of change themselves – that is, enterprises. Policy actions are merely the catalyst of competitiveness by stimulating change via developing clear and predictable conditions for enterprises. This means policy needs to eliminate inefficiencies derived from competing policies; to reduce the unfairness derived from the unequal allocation of resources between EU states; to reduce the potential and incentives for a 'beggar-thy-neighbour' scenario; to account for policy spillovers; have the correct analysis and information regarding common problems; and to develop a consensus between states and implement policy in a coherent and transparent manner. This broad, market-driven policy is reflected within the Maastricht Treaty's provision on industry.

Trends within European industrial policy reflect the pressures upon the European economy resulting from the process of globalisation. Globalisation requires new solutions for international competitiveness. The targeting of specific industries and other active policy measures become increasingly difficult to establish with any great effect within such an environment. Policy reflects a belief that the European economy needs to exploit world markets to prosper. The ability to export depends upon developing a portfolio of goods and services that are in demand in the global market place. This implies that change must not be deterred and

---

INDUSTRY COMPETENCIES OUTLINED IN THE EUROPEAN TREATIES

BOX 6.1

Article 157

1   The Community and the Member States shall ensure that the conditions necessary for the competitiveness of the Community's industry exist.

  For that purpose, in accordance with a system of open and competitive markets, their action shall be aimed at:

- speeding up the adjustment of industry to structural changes;
- encouraging an environment favourable to initiative and to the development of undertakings throughout the Community, particularly small and medium-sized undertakings;
- encouraging an environment favourable to cooperation between undertakings;
- fostering better exploitation of the industrial potential of policies of innovation, research and technological development.

2   The Member States shall consult each other in liaison with the Commission and, where necessary, shall coordinate their action. The Commission may take any useful initiative to promote such coordination.

3   The Community shall contribute to the achievement of the objectives set out in paragraph 1 through the policies and activities it pursues under other provisions of this Treaty. The Council, acting in accordance with the procedure referred to in Article 251 and after consulting the Economic and Social Committee, may decide on specific measures in support of action taken in the Member States to achieve the objectives set out in paragraph 1.

  This title shall not provide a basis for the introduction by the Community of any measure which could lead to a distortion of competition or contains tax provisions or provisions relating to the rights and interests of employed persons.

---

that new and emerging sectors must be stimulated. The challenge is to find new solutions. There can be no protectionism, no massive government expenditure, no direct competition in terms of labour costs and no decline in the treatment of labour. This issue reflects the key concern of how Europe is to compete in a global economy where there are vast differentials in wage rates.

A policy that seeks to promote national or European champions is missing an important facet of the global economy. In a world of multinational companies, the development

of 'champions' is increasingly irrelevant. Thus, policy needs to complement the strategies of all firms that invest in the European economy, irrespective of ultimate ownership. Consequently, establishing the prerequisites under which these firms can be successful is essential and this has become the pivotal theme in European industrial policy and largely mirrors events going on elsewhere in the global economy, notably in the US.

In facilitating the process of strategic change, the EU requires all policies to be mutually supporting to deliver a more competitive economy. Thus, industrial competitiveness is not merely within the domain of what would conventionally be considered 'industrial policy' but has to take into account:

- a 'better lawmaking' approach that will continue to give industry the benefit of a market that is integrated and ensures that any regulatory burden is not too cumbersome;
- the mobilisation of all community policies that aid competitiveness;
- the specific needs of various industrial sectors within these policies.

Thus, not only must regulation create the freedoms for business to emerge and prosper, but where policy is needed it should not undermine the competitive positioning of these businesses. Finally, there is a need to be pragmatic in the application of these rules. This underlines the need for consistency between industrial policy and the demands and priorities of other policies.

The form and nature of these actions reflects the need to develop a generic framework that will lead to policy actions that cover the entire market within which particular enterprises are operating. These actions work alongside national measures as not all issues that affect international competitiveness of Europe can be developed or implemented at the supranational level. National policy is only dispensable when the economic market exceeds national boundaries. Consequently, there must be realism in terms of national policy and how it responds to the integration process. European policy is a complement to – not a replacement of – national policies. It is at best a coordination device to enable national states to achieve as many of their goals as possible.

TOWARDS AN INTEGRATED APPROACH TO INDUSTRIAL POLICY

In 1998, the Commission identified that globalisation was posing challenges to European businesses to which they were simply not responding. This started the debate that ultimately led to the Lisbon Agenda. The Lisbon Agenda (whose recommendations are discussed in several chapters) sets a broad scene for industrial competitiveness based on an integrated approach to the European policy environment linked to the stability provided by the euro. In reinforcing the market-led agenda of European industrial policy, the Lisbon Agenda pursues a programme that sees knowledge creation and utilisation as key to determining competitiveness. Thus, the passivity of industrial policy in this context is underlined. Policy is limited to merely creating, securing and enhancing an environment where firms are able to achieve their goals with limited government support. Importantly, this implies a recommitment by states to many current policies, most notably the SEM and its flanking policies.

The recent emphasis in EU industrial policy has stressed enhanced synergy between the different policy domains that can affect the competitive performance of EU business on a global stage. The aim is to promote permanent and continuing adaptation to industrial change within the context of open and competitive markets. Thus, while competitiveness depends upon the actions and strategies of firms, public authorities need to ensure that the environment is compatible with these objectives. To ensure that policies are mutually supporting towards this objective, the intention is to make the analytical foundations of these policies consistent and adequate. This stance revisits many ongoing themes within EU policy, notably macro-economic stability, TENs and the SEM. This re-emphasis is, in part, a reflection to the failure of past policy efforts. However, a clear change of emphasis is related to improving the environment for entrepreneurship and enhancing the spread of ICTs across the EU.

This approach reinforces the position that it is the state of competition within the EU that will be the basis for the success of EU firms on a bigger stage. Thus, the EU focuses on framework conditions that counteract evident system failures in the ability of Europe to compete. This framework is based upon:

- rules that establish the relevant market framework;
- rules that address specific categories of products;
- market enabling institutions;
- broad generic conditions (such as the macro-economic framework and societal conditions) whose direct impact is difficult to assess.

As other chapters highlight (see Chapters 4 and 11, for example), these rules are still incomplete, notably in areas such as the SEM and corporate governance. The EU is trying to ensure the implementation of these rules so that their absence does not act as an impediment to the success of European business. Regulation is limited to broad requirements, not to minutiae, and is directed towards easy and rapid adoption of core market standards.

The new policy is focused on Europe's relatively poor performance across key barometers, notably productivity and innovation (see Chapter 1). Thus, the emphasis is upon developing policy measures that overcome these problems and can be used as a basis for competitiveness. These include the promotion of:

- *innovation, knowledge and research*: largely through indirect means such as regulatory change in areas such as IPR and competition;
- *entrepreneurship*: to remove impediments to a vibrant SME sector as well as to provide support during the start-up phase (see Chapter 7);
- *a sustainable structure for industrial production*: growth has to be compatible with the broader sustainability objectives of the EU (see Chapter 14).

These themes are reflected within the generic framework for the new industrial policy identified in Box 6.2.

The common theme is identification of the strengths and weaknesses of the European economy as a basis for policy direction. It is these strengths that are perceived as necessary for securing the success of the European economy on a global stage. All businesses located within the EU, irrespective of the nationality of ownership, are to be the focus of policy measures. Consequently, these factors are needed to ensure not only that indigenous industry has the basis for global success but also that the European economy is an attractive location for FDI. Increasingly, the EU believes that the development of indigenous industry requires the development of more fulsome alliances (often with non-EU companies) to assist in the rationalisation of production among European enterprises as well as in promoting the dispersal of 'know-how' throughout the entire economy.

The first clear emerging theme is the need for 'joined-up thinking' in those policy domains where the effective creation and usage of information and knowledge will

BOX 6.2

THE EU'S NEW INTEGRATED INDUSTRIAL POLICY

Generic action	Sector-specific action
IPR/counterfeiting: to aid positioning in the new economy measures are being proposed to improve protection.	*Pharmaceutical fora*: engage with industry to establish necessary measures to aid competitive positioning.
High-level group on competitiveness, energy and the environment: the aim is to ensure coherence between these inter-related areas to promote sustainable competitiveness.	*Biotechnology strategy*: work with industry to identify key impediments to growth in EU.
External aspects of competitiveness and market access: a common strategy to be developed regarding the tackling of trade barriers with third parties.	*High-level groups on chemical and defence*: to consider key issues on development of these sectors on EU and global scale.
New legislative simplification programme: to ensure legislation is understood and aids competitive positioning.	*European space programme*: to establish a common platform for the activities of the European Space Agency.
Improving sectoral skills: to address skill shortages in key areas through identifying skills gaps etc.	*Taskforce on ICT competitiveness:* identify the main barriers to the take-up of ICTs across the EU as well as limits to developing a competitive ICT sector.
Managing structural change in manufacturing: the aim is to manage and engage with sectors affected by change to aid a smooth transition.	*Mechanical engineering policy dialogue*: to identify key weaknesses and strengths in the context of the global market.
Integrated approach to R&D: to aid the effectiveness of R&D support through less overlap and improved focus on key areas.	*Series of competitiveness studies for assorted sectors*: an assessment of key challenges for core sectors (such as shoes, fashion design etc.) to form the basis of policy.

benefit business. Thus, action in areas of research and technology policy, innovation strategy, social policy (notably in terms of investing in human capital), competition policy and ICT diffusion policies needs to be coordinated so that all aid and support the spread and usage of knowledge. Also, measures to create and enhance innovation must go hand-in-hand with measures that aid its dispersion throughout the EU and with those that directly facilitate its effective usage at the human level.

The second theme in this integrated approach is the improved operation of markets. Inevitably this means continued work to ensure that the commitments in the SEM are met and extended to all relevant areas of the economy (see Chapter 4). Policy has to secure the objective of the free movement of goods and services as a means of ensuring that European businesses can access the high-quality services and products needed to support their international position. These measures are based on the assumption that the active promotion of competition (from both internal and external sources) is a catalyst in stimulating international competitiveness. These catalysts are not enough on their own as they need to be complemented and supported to ensure that when firms do make decisions, it is the European economy that receives the benefits. Thus, prerequisites such as education, training and infrastructure networks need to accompany such a strategy. Furthermore, to ensure that these catalysts have an ongoing impact, they need to be accompanied by a series of accelerators that will spread and enhance the positive effects of competition and extend the benefits of liberalisation to SMEs. Key to this objective is the removal of remaining fiscal barriers, notably in terms of the simplification of VAT arrangements. This must be supported by a more proactive competition policy which aids speedier decision making for businesses (see Chapter 6). The new policy framework for competition will also allow the EU to focus more directly upon those actions that directly impede trade. This is compounded by new rules on state aid aimed at adding velocity to the restructuring process. Overlaps are also evident in terms of energy policy, security of supply and the opening of markets to competition in this segment. This has to be reconciled with the commitments that the EU makes in terms of its international obligations with regard to energy usage.

Third, the EU's cohesion policies are increasingly targeted towards supporting the impact of, and accelerating, structural change. To this end, policies are directed at enhancing innovation in regions adversely affected by these processes: this direct support is compatible with the broader, long-term objectives of the EU's competitiveness strategy. For example, the European

employment strategy is directly targeted at human capital, learning etc. This will be supported by TENs to reduce the distance of remote and poorer regions from the core markets.

Fourth, the move towards a more competitive economy must be reconciled with demands for sustainable development. The aim is to enhance productivity with fewer resources, by promoting clean energies and technologies as well as by encouraging social dialogue. Thus, competitiveness is directed not merely at economic growth at all costs but also at the quality of life.

Fifth, allowing businesses to develop internationally means that the competitiveness strategy must interact with trade policy to ensure European firms are able to access markets outside the EU. As a complement to these measures, EU policy-making bodies are working towards commonly agreed standards and regulations in areas such as the protection of IPR. In support of this, the EU acts as guardian of existing agreements to ensure that signatories of past global trade agreements comply with their obligations, and supports the extension of competition beyond the borders of the EU by seeking to extend SEM measures into neighbouring states.

The integrated approach sees national industrial policies as important: there is a need for each state to learn from each other in terms of how to adjust to globalisation, economic integration, structural adjustments and the technological revolution. The largely passive nature of European industrial policy mirrors the relative lack of power of central supranational institutions in industrial policy development. These measures are not the exclusive preserve of the EU and need to find a translation in national economies. Some states are reluctant to accept anything that

BOX 6.3

THE EUROPEAN INSTITUTE OF TECHNOLOGY

In early 2006, the Commission proposed the foundation of a European Institute of Technology (EIT) to operate as a flagship for research and knowledge creation within the EU. The central idea is that the EIT operates as a focus for allowing the best ideas and practices to be disseminated throughout the EU. The proposal is very much within the context of the Lisbon Strategy and its perceived failings in terms of altering Europe's comparatively weak position in terms of R&D (see Chapter 1).

The EIT will concentrate upon the three sides of the 'knowledge triangle' – education, research and innovation. The aim will be to exploit links between these areas through a network of partners. The EIT will in some senses have a virtual structure as it will consist of a governing board supported by a network of knowledge centres. Financially, the EIT will be supported by a combination of the EU, member states and the business sector. The EIT will seek to attract the best and most talented researchers within Europe and beyond. Working alongside businesses, the aim is to use this forum to generate and enhance the innovative potential of the EU.

The aim is to establish the EIT by 2009. To make research successful, it is widely recognised that the institute needs a broad funding base, performance-based payments, a highly selective admission policy, competition in research funding and focus on research. This will require a fundamental cultural change in the form and method with which research is undertaken. Thus, it may be misplaced to rely on building an EIT based upon existing formats of centrally funded institutions. Such networks are alleged to have too many vested interests and too little will to cooperate. In addition, past efforts to use a network of universities have delivered few tangible benefits as the funds are dispersed across a large number of participants. To make a difference, research needs to be focused and concerted on a limited number of bodies. Thus a physical format is likely to be more successful than a virtual format.

In this case, the EIT will establish a new format from day one. However, the proposal has come under a great deal of criticism: many feel the existing structures can deliver the necessary innovation and research if they are allowed to do so. Thus, the fault is not with the absence of an institution such as the EIT but with an environment that is bereft of competition, too political and an insufficient focus on the elite European institutions that are most able to deliver the research.

may mean the creation of jobs at the price of moving to US-style uncertainty. Over time, the EU may have little choice but to accept some hybrid of EU/US models as the information society and more intense international competition start to become a reality for more and more enterprises.

SECTORAL ISSUES IN INTERNATIONAL COMPETITIVENESS

The new policy statement on industrial policy reflects the priority of horizontal measures over sectoral measures. Thus, all sectors are expected to benefit from the successful establishment of a generic framework. However, there are sectors that have particular characteristics that require different policy prescriptions. In the context of the aforementioned framework, the EU seeks to work towards a more market-driven approach to sectoral support to ensure that measures respond more fully to the needs of business. Thus, within the more knowledge-intensive sectors such as pharmaceuticals and biotechnology, the aim is to ensure the needs of the sector are addressed within the generic policy framework. In these areas (and within the context of a more integrated approach to industrial policy), the aim is to provide a stable regulatory environment and provide the means – both direct and indirect – to enhance their innovative capability and capacity. For 'new economy' sectors, reconciling the unique problems faced by these industries within the generic framework is relatively straightforward.

Box 6.2 identifies the core sector-specific measures to be undertaken by the Commission within this new industrial policy. These measures are in addition to actions being undertaken for declining and restructuring industries. These sector-specific measures are based on working with industry to address the exact needs of the sector to aid their international competitiveness. Thus, sector specificity is born not out of protectionism but of the uniqueness of the problems faced. These measures will be generally pro-market, addressing market and regulatory impediments to the growth and development of these sectors across Europe and beyond. They will be supported by targeted market-distant support through R&D programmes.

In the 'old economy' sectors, reconciling market-driven policy with the needs of these industries becomes more problematic due to inbuilt political, social and economic issues. As a result, policy towards these old economy industries (such as steel and textiles) has tended to be more direct. In textiles, the EU aims to develop measures to strengthen its competitiveness. The aim of any sector-specific measures is to speed up the sector's adjustment to the impact of increasingly intense global competition within declining (which tend to involve primary production) and restructuring sectors (these tend to be manufacturing based and frequently suffer from excess capacity).

Many declining sectors are given support on the basis that it is needed to overcome the consequences of employment decline or regional imbalance. Such a decline is often derived from rising costs of production and/or the inability to face the consequences of more competition within global markets. Many European shipbuilders and steel producers (see Case Study 6.2) have faced declining market shares and coal has been hit by a decline in economically viable resources. Many of these enterprises would not survive without the support given or sanctioned by the EU. States differ on the validity of such support. Northern European states such as the Netherlands and the UK are hostile whereas France and Spain are more amenable to these methods of support. In many of these sectors, there have been attempts to coordinate the removal of over-capacity in the EU. In practice, this has proved very difficult. The steel sector was a case where such agreements proved difficult largely because the employment consequences were equally unpalatable for many states. The EU has made attempts to limit the forms of anti-competitive aid but states have proved themselves adept at circumventing such controls.

The 'restructuring sectors' tend to have substantial overcapacity but their political

Case Study 6.2

THE STEEL SECTOR

After China, the EU is the world's second biggest producer of steel – around 20 per cent of total global production – and is the market leader in terms of quality. The annual turnover of European steel manufacturers is around €70 billion (2001) and the industry continues to employ around a quarter of a million people. Despite the structural shifts within the European economy, steel continues to play a key strategic role. This is derived not just from its employment and market positioning (as a supplier of quality steels) but also from its role as a key supplier to many of Europe's most internationally oriented sectors, such as construction, vehicles, etc. However, the steel sector has been in a state of seemingly perpetual crisis since the 1970s given its limited exposure to foreign competition and its 'strategic importance' gaining it special exemption and protection by the EU. The 1980s' recession compounded by deep cuts in manufacturing, led to the Davignon plan whereby subsidies were given to firms based on their ability to offer cuts in production.

Since the mid-1990s, the sector has undergone a more fundamental restructuring. With EU guidance and support, steel enterprises have been gradually seeking to solve the fundamental overcapacity problem that has dogged the sector for decades. Due to its relatively high degree of labour intensity, the steel sector was always seen as something of a sacred cow by each of the major states. Consequently, getting states to agree to cuts was a highly charged political issue. The problem was compounded by the unevenness of the need to undertake reform across EU states. By the mid-1990s, there was a clear division between EU states over the progress of restructuring and the exposure of domestic steel businesses to competition. In the UK and France, the state had removed subsidies and had, in some cases, privatised their operations. However, in Germany, Spain and Italy, subsidies and massive overcapacity remained. This created problems as many of the unsupported businesses felt that the supported businesses should undertake their fair share of restructuring. To the unaided businesses, continuing state aid for many steelmakers was a direct contravention of the objectives of the EU. As more enterprises grew free of state control, they started to reduce capacity further and markedly increase their efficiency. However, this led to direct conflict with the subsidies sanctioned by the EU to other European producers. In 1994, 80 per cent of European steel protection was in state hands: five years later, this had fallen to less than 20 per cent.

It was becoming increasingly evident that the EU steel sector would be unable to escape its periodic crises unless reform was undertaken in a credible and confident manner across the EU. The more liberal European Commission needed to stand up to the steelmakers and counteract their political power. The Commission believes that every time the steel industry has been granted protection, it has merely been used to delay reform rather than to cut capacity or aid. Ultimately, the Commission was coming round to the view that reform was inevitable. If subsidies were allowed to remain, the efficient firms would suffer first. In constantly giving way to the demands of the sector, the EU lacked both credibility and effectiveness in view of the clear need to stimulate restructuring of the sector.

However, the Commission has started to be effective as the merger referee and is start-ing to allow steel mergers where such agreements are tied to capacity cuts. This has con-solidated the industry and led to a market structure characterised by a limited number of large suppliers and a small number of specialist suppliers. The late 1990s saw a raft of consolidation as Germany's Thyssen and Krupp merged, France's Usinor took over the Belgian Cockerill Sambre, the UK's Ispat bought parts of the Thyssen and Usinor group and the Luxembourg operator Arbed took a stake in the Spanish concern, Aceralia. More recently, British Steel merged with the Dutch concern Hoogovens. While competition and reduced prices are a key factor forcing consolidation, the euro and the price transparency it introduced have had an impact. The Hoogovens–British Steel merger, however, was driven less by a survival need than by a determination to consolidate the position of strength of these operators. By 2000, Europe had six of the world's ten biggest steel companies – though they still account for less than 20 per cent of total production. This change in fortune has been driven by consolidation and by moves into new markets overseas, most notably Latin America. However, the continued fragmentation of the steel industry on a global scale means that no one firm has the capability to push for the scale needed to counteract any changes in the economic cycle. This suggests that consolidation still has some way to go.

By 2005, the top five firms accounted for over 60 per cent of EU production. In effect, consolidation has been a key barometer of structural reform within the sector. This process has been driven not merely by synergies but also by recognition that scale was needed to enable these firms to sustain and maintain their positioning in what is an increasingly com-petitive global steel market. The consolidation of the sector had – through market forces – achieved what decades of political wrangling had failed to achieve – namely, restructuring. The consolidation of the sector has seen the EU steel industry close down 50 million tonnes of excess capacity and cut manpower by nearly 75 per cent. While steel production has remained constant, it is now produced by significantly fewer people. If the steel industry were going to survive it needed to create the capability to develop new technology. This could only be done by reducing capacity.

Over time, the European Commission has managed to reduce steel subsidies substantially. In the 1980–85 period, €36.5 billion in aid was granted. In 1999, aid was down to just €180 million per annum and has fallen further since. Support to the sector is governed by the steel aid code which ties support to environmental protection, aid for R&D and social measures linked with closure. Thus, aid will not be allowed for restructuring, rescue or regional purposes. However, while the EU has reduced levels of support for the EU-15, the accession of the CEE states has brought in states with a more liberal approach to subsidies (see Chapter 5). The support given by these states to their respective steel sectors was a constant cause for concern in the accession process.

However, the problems of the EU steel sector now have to be translated to the global level where chronic overcapacity remains. In 2003, there was surplus capacity of nearly 80 million tonnes. However, in Europe there have been concerns that the consolidation of the sector has led to price increases as these firms start to exercise their market power. The problem is seen as especially acute at the specialty end of the steel market where consolidation has led to concentration at the expense of customers. However, the global market is subdued by excess capacity, especially within the US, a position that the US attempted to safeguard by an unsuccessful attempt to impose tariffs on steel imports.

To maintain its competitive positioning in a highly competitive global steel sector, EU firms focus on upgrading to the latest technology and R&D. This is key to their ability to compete in the higher value, quality, tailor-made end of the steel market. With limited cost flexibility, the EU has little choice but to move into this segment of the market place. Profitability, however, will still be determined by highly volatile prices. In 2004–05, the European steel sector benefited from rising prices. The 2004 enlargement made further restructuring necessary as firms from the accession states are less efficient and produce lower quality steel and need to undergo the restructuring that has already taken place across the rest of Europe. Thus, the restructuring of Europe's steel sector is far from complete.

Case questions

1 What caused the decline of the European steel sector?

2 What are the remaining fundamental problems facing the European steel sector?

3 How has the emergence of China and India helped the EU steel industry?

4 Outline how the major EU companies seek to compete within the global steel market.

and economic importance often hinders the rationalisation process. The problems are generally similar to those experienced within the steel sector. The Commission seeks cooperative solutions to these rationalisation problems. In the aviation sector, this has been typified by the development of Airbus Industry (see Case Study 6.1). Action in this area is justified by the fact that the market under concern is global not European and that cooperation stimulates a more efficient allocation of resources and eliminates destabilising competition. The transport sector has also been an area where methods to distort competition have been evident. There are numerous cases where the EU has sought to curtail the subsidies given to airlines: an area where there is evident surplus capacity. The car industry is also protected but growing international competition has made the companies face up to these challenges. In any case, given the globalisa-

tion of car production, such protection seems increasingly anachronistic. Indeed, many of Europe's car manufacturers are in the process of undergoing radical restructuring in response to the global threat. Despite the unwillingness of governments to undertake the needed reforms, EU car producers have been aggressive in slashing production, globalising manufacturing and radically altering their product portfolios (see Case Study 3.1).

CONCLUSION

At the heart of the EU's industrial policy is the pursuit of the international competitiveness needed to secure growth and higher levels of employment. The actions of the EU itself tend to be very passive with the states taking the primary role in the policy process. EU measures amount to very little more than establishing a generic framework within which national policies can be developed. Where the EU does have treaty-based powers, it often finds itself under challenge from the member states. The policy itself is very liberal and is based on the belief that more intense competition is the only feasible, long-term route for Europe. While many states agree with this stance, their support is tempered by a desire to offer certain companies and sectors specific support despite the fact that this goes against the grain of what commercial investors would do. Thus, the EU finds itself with a hybrid policy. Despite the EU's desire for more liberal competition, the hostility of certain states means it cannot make consistent efforts in this direction.

KEY POINTS

- Industrial policy seeks to manage the decline of old and the emergence of new industries.

- There is a shift away from active (interventionist) towards passive industrial policies throughout Europe.

- Supranational policy has a dual focus of offering both generic and sector-specific support to European industry.

ACTIVITIES

1   Undertake research in one 'old economy' sector. Identify the nature of the economic transformation needed to make it globally competitive.

2   As a group, assess in what industrial sectors you believe Europe will be able to establish a competitive advantage. On what basis have you made such a decision?

3   Identify one EU-based firm and research how it has approached the issue of commercial transformation. Assess what, if anything, could have been done differently.

4   Divide into two groups and assess the case for and against active involvement in the EU economy.

QUESTIONS FOR DISCUSSION

1   What do you understand by the term 'competitiveness'?

2   Why do states have industrial policies and what function do they perform?

3   What do you understand to be the differences between active and passive industrial policy?

4   To what extent is an integrated approach to industrial policy required?

SUGGESTIONS FOR FURTHER READING

Bianchi, P. (1997) *Industrial Policies and Economic Integration: Learning from European Experiences*, London: Routledge.

Boltho, A. (ed.) (1996) 'The Assessment: International Competitiveness', *Oxford Review of Economic Policy*, 12 (3), pp. 1–16.

Davies, S. and Lyons, B. (1999) *Industrial Organization in the European Union: Structure, Strategy and the Competitive Mechanism*, Oxford: Clarendon Press.

European Commission (1998) 'The Competitiveness of European Enterprises in the Face of Globalisation – How Can it be Encouraged?', COM (1998) 718.

European Commission (2002) 'Industrial Policy in an Enlarged Europe', COM (2002) 714.

European Commission (2003) 'Some Key Issues in Europe's Competitiveness: Towards an Integrated Approach', COM (2003) 704.

Foreman-Peck, J. and Federico, G. (eds) (1999) *European Industrial Policy: The Twentieth Century Experience*, Oxford: Oxford University Press.

Hayward, J. (ed.) (1995) *Industrial Enterprise and European Integration: From National to International Champions in Western Europe*, Oxford: Oxford University Press.

Joao Rodrigues, M. (ed.) (2003) *European Policies for a Knowledge Economy*, Cheltenham: Edward Elgar.

Kassim, H. and Menon A. (eds) (1996) *The European Union and National Industrial Policy*, London: Routledge.

Navarro, L. (2003) 'Industrial Policy in the Economic Literature: Recent Theoretical Developments and Implications for EU Policy', Enterprise Papers No. 12, Brussels: European Commission, DG Enterprise.

Sauter, W. (1997) *Competition Law and Industrial Policy in the EU*, Oxford: Clarendon Press.

Wilson, J. (ed.) (2005) *Industrial Organization: Competition, Strategy, Policy*, Harlow: FT Prentice Hall.

Chapter 7

Developing small businesses and entrepreneurship within Europe

Innovation is the specific instrument of entrepreneurship . . . the act that endows resources with a new capacity to create wealth.

Peter Drucker (1909–2005), *Innovation and Entrepreneurship*, 1985

This chapter will help you to:

- appreciate the importance of SMEs to the European economy;
- identify and understand the major features of entrepreneurship;
- recognise the major impediments to SME formation and entrepreneurship within the EU;
- understand why entrepreneurship is pivotal to the EU's economic performance;
- identify the major themes and trends within EU policy towards SMEs and entrepreneurship.

SMEs are seen as central to the development of the European economy. They are among the most dynamic enterprises in Europe and are crucial in creating and sustaining the EU's competitive position. In terms of innovation, job creation and other key issues, SMEs are becoming more and more important. As a consequence, it is becoming increasingly important to recognise and, where necessary, support and aid the contribution that SMEs make to the European economy. However, Europe has historically had a problem in that, relative to its major competitors, it does not create enough entrepreneurs. This is important if the forces of 'creative destruction' that are pivotal to economic self-renewal are allowed to gather pace within the EU. This chapter opens with an exploration of the importance of SMEs to the European economy by describing how these enterprises contribute to its development. The chapter then moves on to examine the rising political and commercial importance of entrepreneurship. More

145

particularly, the chapter focuses on the hurdles to the creation of a more entrepreneurial culture within the EU. Finally, the chapter addresses the policy response to entrepreneurship and small business survival and success as well as the challenge of internationalisation to these businesses.

THE ROLE OF SMEs IN THE MODERN ECONOMY

Conventionally, SMEs were regarded as enterprises that were less efficient, paid lower wages and offered lower innovative potential than LSEs. As a consequence, this form of enterprise was widely seen as in decline. Thus, SMEs were marginal businesses, luxuries that undermined efficiency. This attitude was based on the premise that many factors in the global economy (such as access to capital, knowledge development, internationalisation, etc.) favoured LSEs. Traditional theory suggested that the more fragmented a country's economic base, the more growth is retarded. Thus in the postwar era, economic success was linked to scale and this was reflected in policy.

The ability of entrepreneurship to generate renewal and sustain change within economies is an increasingly important factor generating competitiveness. From the 1970s onwards, the attitude favouring scale had shifted as the interaction of technological, commercial and political change created an environment in which SMEs could begin to emerge and grow. Audretsch (2002) accounted for the rising significance of SMEs by the increased importance of globalisation which has shifted comparative advantage towards knowledge-based economic activity. This has placed an increased emphasis on marketing and technological innovation. Despite the common assumption that such

forces would work to the detriment of SMEs, when knowledge started to become increasingly valuable in its own right, an individual has the incentive to use this facility to their own advantage and establish their own business. This is based on the ability of the entrepreneur to stimulate change through innovation and to offer a unique value proposition that differentiates the firm in the global market.

Markets are fluid phenomena: firms enter and leave and new products and methods are always emerging. Most research indicates an evolutionary perspective of SME development based on a process of gradual growth. Generally, the impact of SMEs is felt through three key areas:

- *knowledge*: through knowledge spillovers SMEs can extend growth throughout the socio-economic body;
- *effect on competition*: increased competition generated by SMEs has an effect on innovation and the spread of new ideas throughout an economy;
- *effect on variety*: as each business creates a new approach, it can aid the process of growth.

This underlines the importance of SMEs as an agent of change within the knowledge economy.

A few simple statistics underline the importance of SMEs to the EU economy. According to the EU, in 2003, there were 19.3 million SMEs in Europe (including the EEA and Switzerland) providing employment for 140 million people. Ninety-two per cent of SMEs employed less than ten people (the so-called 'micro-enterprises') with small businesses (those employing between ten and 49 people) comprising 7 per cent of SMEs and medium-sized business (those employing between 50 and 249) representing just 1 per cent of SMEs. This pattern is reflected in employment figures, according to which 56 per cent of employment by SMEs is under-taken by micro-enterprises.

The figures in Table 7.1 reflect the dominance of SMEs in the European economy. The average European business employs just seven people with the average SME employing just five. These statistics hide variations in the patterns across states: Greek SMEs have an average of two employees while in the Netherlands SMEs employ an average of 12. Indeed, nearly 50 per cent of all businesses have no employees at all, indicating that they provide employment to the self-employed and family members only. In the 15 years to 2003, there has been a sustained increase in the levels of employment by SMEs whereas LSE employment has tended to decline. However, LSEs have used reductions in employment to increase their efficiency while SMEs tend to be prevalent in areas characterised by low levels of productivity such as the retail sector. This is supported by the fact that real turnover and value-added growth has been higher in SMEs than in LSEs.

The new member states and the candidate states broadly reflect the same patterns of the EU-15. This is reflected in Table 7.2. However, large differences are evident

Table 7.1 Basic facts about SMEs and LSEs in Europe-19, 2003

	SME	LSE	Total
Number of enterprises (1,000)	19,270	40	19,310
Employment (1,000)	97,420	42,300	139,720
Occupied persons per enterprise	5	1,052	7
Turnover per enterprise (€m)	0.9	319	1.6
Share of exports in turnover (%)	12	23	17
Value-added per occupied person (€1,000)	55	120	75
Share of labour costs in value-added (%)	56	47	52

Source: European Commission.

Table 7.2 Comparative SME size between the EU-15 and the ten new member states

	SME				LSE	Total
	Micro	Small	Medium-sized	Total		
Accession countries (2001)						
Enterprises (1,000)	5,670	230	50	5,950	10	5,970
Occupied persons (1,000)	10,210	4,970	5,350	20,530	10,150	30,670
Occupied persons/enterprise	2	22	107	3	919	5
Size class dominance					Small/medium-sized	
Europe-19						
Enterprises (1,000)	17,820	1,260	180	1,970	40	19,310
Occupied persons (1,000)	55,040	24,280	18,100	97,420	42,300	139,710
Occupied persons/enterprise	3	19	98	5	1,052	7
Size class dominance					Micro	

Note: totals have been rounded.
Source: European Commission.

between accession and candidate countries. The Mediterranean states tend to have low occupied person per enterprise (i.e. those employed) with those SMEs in CEE being larger.

The importance of SMEs to the functioning of modern economies is underscored by their sustained prominence in all major economies, notably the EU's major competitor states of Japan and the US. While the number of SMEs within the EU may be broadly similar to the number of SMEs in the US, they account for a lower share of employment in the US because many US SMEs are sole proprietors (around 80 per cent). This structure of SMEs may be due to the higher number of start-ups in the US based on a larger integrated market. Key differences are identified in Table 7.3. In terms of longer term trends, however, it is evident that in the EU there is a negative correlation of employment growth and firm size whereas in the US there is a positive correlation with LSEs increasing employment faster than SMEs.

There is evidence from the European Commission regarding the increasingly important commercial role played by SMEs within the European economy. This is based on SMEs:

■ acting as a vehicle for knowledge spillovers which can be accessed by LSEs;

■ creating an increased degree of competition in the input market;

■ increasing the degree of diversity within the market place.

These phenomena demonstrate that the impact of SMEs upon the European economy is not restricted to the SME sector. Their effects can be felt throughout the economy, including on larger businesses.

The impact of SMEs is not uniform across all of Europe's sectors. Enterprise size varies markedly across the respective sectors, mainly as a result of the production processes within these industries. The greater the benefit from economies of scale and scope, the larger firms will tend to be within the sector. For example, there is a tendency towards larger firms within the extractive industries. This is also true for the transportation and communication sectors, although there is a need to differentiate between large-scale broad activities on one hand and niche service provision on the other. In the latter case, there is scope for small firms to exist and thrive. Smaller firms tend to be more common in construction, trade, hotels and personal services.

SMEs have been characterised as having a low propensity to export (see below). Only within the wholesale trade is the percentage of turnover represented by exports

Table 7.3 *Comparative SME size across the Europe-19, the US and Japan*

	Europe-19 (2003)	US (2000)	Japan (2001)
Occupied person per enterprise	7	6	8
SMEs (1,000)	19,270	21,164	4,690
Micro	17,820	19,988	n/a
Small	1,260	1,009	n/a
Medium	180	167	n/a
LSEs	40	59	13

Source: European Commission.

comparable to the levels in LSEs. This lack of desire or inability to export has been a major reason in the 15 years to 2003 for the growth of SMEs to lag behind that of LSEs. As export growth has tended to increase faster than domestic sales, so LSEs have been able to increase their rate of growth. A further reason for this difference in growth is that SMEs have tended to raise prices faster than LSEs. Indeed, it is this rather than exports that explains a large proportion of the differences in growth between LSEs and SMEs. The reason for such a differential in terms of pricing behaviour is due to costs relative to productivity growth. One explanation for this is that as wages grow faster in LSEs than SMEs, the former have an increased incentive (and ability) to replace labour with capital.

Although SMEs play a prominent role in the EU's prosperity, developing common conclusions as to their impact and importance can be difficult due to the sheer heterogeneity of the firms involved. Clearly, not all firms are motivated by the desire to become big. Evidence from the European Commission suggests that only one-third are striving for growth. Over 40 per cent are merely struggling to survive or are seeking to consolidate the business. This is especially true for micro enterprises. Thus, in focusing upon how SMEs aid competitiveness, there is a need to focus on creating and encouraging entrepreneurship to enable businesses to become high-growth businesses.

CREATING A MORE ENTREPRENEURIAL CULTURE WITHIN EUROPE

The perceived link between scale and economic growth resulted in the neglect of SMEs in the policy process. However, this link broke down as knowledge became more important in commercial success. Thus, entrepreneurs with superior knowledge have an incentive to leave the employment of an incumbent firm and utilise this knowledge for their own commercial benefit. A key theme within the Lisbon Strategy was the creation of an environment that was compatible with allowing SMEs to flourish. SMEs are seen as important not merely to job creation and competitiveness but also in unlocking personal potential and adding to the broad social well-being of the EU economy. Thus, there was a need for policy to support the growth and development of SMEs and to maximise their contribution to the development of the European economy. Key to achieving this objective is the fostering of an enhanced culture of enterprise throughout Europe, a process that is long term and has to begin with education. Entrepreneurship is seen as a major driver of innovation as well as of competitiveness and growth. Yet, Europe is failing to produce enough entrepreneurs. As an illustration, in the US it took 20 years to replace one-third of the Fortune 500 companies listed in the 1960s against four years for those listed in 1998. Furthermore, eight out of the 25 largest firms in the US did not exist or were very small in 1960. In the EU, all of the largest firms in 1998 were already large in 1960.

The impact of entrepreneurship depends upon the context of the business. If it is out of necessity (i.e. in the absence of any other alternative) – as it is in many developed states – the effects will tend to be negligible. If it is done out of choice and opportunity it offers greater opportunity for growth. In Europe, entrepreneurship tends to be opportunistic as firms seek to create new niches and are more likely to grow and create new forms of employment. Overall, entrepreneurship involves a number of key elements:

149

- *Exploitation of creativity and/or innovation*: entrepreneurship is a mindset covering the ability of an individual to spot an opportunity and exploit it. To compete in a new market, the firm has to be based around innovation or creativity to change and create a new market. These traits need to be supported by sound management.
- *Entrepreneurs*: there has to be a capability to undertake and understand risk for the construction of new businesses. These entrepreneurs value independence and self-realisation.
- *Applications of entrepreneurship*: this can occur across any sector or type of business. It applies to all self-employed and to firms of any size.

The above emphasises that the function of enterprise is to change the nature and pattern of the modern economy by promoting change through technology, innovation or new practice. The key word is change and how change is linked to new enterprises stimulating a new commercial agenda.

In Europe, there is a weaker entrepreneurial culture than in the US. There are several reasons for this weakness: Europeans tend to be more risk averse and less willing to accept the uncertainties connected with self-employment. In addition, there are few entrepreneurial role-models for young people. Generally entrepreneurs are male and more prevalent among the younger sections of the population. Lower levels of entrepreneurship are also derived from the difficulties in starting and operating a business. This is, in part, a derivative of the past commercial experience of the EU and its ability to create effective social support mechanisms.

According to the Eurobarometer (2003) less than 20 per cent of the nearly 50 per cent of employees that are said to favour self-employment actually move towards establishing their own business. Furthermore, this research indicates that less than 4 per cent of Europeans are becoming entrepreneurs or state an intention to do so in the foreseeable future. This is just a third of the number of US citizens who express a similar desire. While nearly a third of SMEs state that growth is their major objective, only a small proportion of SMEs actually achieve it. European SMEs frequently suffer from low expansion rates in the years immediately after start-up. It is often claimed that new entrepreneurs in the EU face too many questions regarding viability before start-up compared to US businesses. Thus, whereas the latter are able to test the market and expand rapidly, EU start-ups often face inbuilt bias and cynicism. This is derived from an increased fear of risk and failure in the EU than in the US. Thus, in Europe, it is evident that the average European prefers to be an employee over self-employment. Nearly half of Europeans agreed with the sentiment that they would not start a business if there were a risk it might fail. These problems are compounded by an ageing population within Europe as the segment of the population that start up businesses (between the ages of 25–34) decreases in size and by a withdrawal from the market by entrepreneurs (mainly those running family businesses) who are expecting to stop running these operations over the coming decade. This will affect over 600,000 firms and nearly 2.5 million workers every year.

According to the Commission, SME growth has been hindered by aspects of the business environment that work to their detriment. Most SMEs found that a lack of purchasing power by customers was the major constraint. The smaller the firms, the more important this constraint was upon firm performance. In other areas, a lack of skills and an inability to access the finance needed for growth also proved to be key problems. The latter was especially important for medium-sized businesses. In securing access to finance, there is a problem in both access to equity and debt. The latter is an especially important form of finance for SMEs. This is unlikely to change in the near future as short-term financing will remain of prime importance. In terms of bank loans, the experience is generally positive: as many as 76 per cent of SMEs who applied for a loan were successful, although both banks and SMEs require greater transparency from each other. For around 10 per cent of enterprises, the administrative burden was considered to be the major impediment to growth. Many have indicated that it directly affects their desire and ability to recruit. These problems do not always emerge from administrative procedures per se (such as form filling, delivery of requested information and contacts with authorities, etc.) but from preparatory work, information collection and employment legislation. Compliance costs for SMEs in 2003 were 2.6 per cent of turnover compared to 0.02 per cent for LSEs.

In some instances, the reasons for risk aversion might be perfectly rational given the higher risks and lower rewards available within Europe. Rewards are lower because of relatively higher taxes. The risk is also higher because of European bankruptcy laws. In the EU, these laws are generally designed to protect banks rather than give the bankrupt a second chance as is the case in the US. In the US, business failure can be a positive thing in the minds of investors if entrepreneurs can demonstrate they have learnt from the experience. In the EU, a person in a similar position will find it difficult to start again. The issue, then, is of allowing honest bankrupts to make a fresh start. In treating all

bankrupts the same, the law does not distinguish between the reason for bankruptcy (for example, between the fraudulent and the unlucky). The result is that honest bankrupts can be stigmatised. However, as venture capital markets start to mature, this problem could be overcome. Stricter bankruptcy laws tend to occur in locations where there is an absence of venture capital and where lending is by commercial banks.

While SMEs offer tremendous potential, they do face specific problems. The European Commission's own figures suggest that over half of SMEs fail within five years of start-up. The Commission identifies five factors to explain this relative weakness:

- the increasingly intricate legal, fiscal and administrative environment which is particularly burdensome for SMEs;
- an inability to access research programmes and exploit their results;
- relatively inadequate management and training capabilities;
- additional borrowing costs arising from the higher risk attached to lending to SMEs;
- scale impediments in accessing new markets.

These problems are compounded by more generic problems related to their relatively poor productivity (when compared to larger enterprises) as well as lower returns to scale and poorer labour/working conditions.

THE EMERGING CHALLENGES FOR EUROPE'S SMEs: THE INTERNATIONALISATION OF MARKETS

Traditionally, international markets were seen as the preserve of large businesses. However, a recent strand in strategy

Case Study 7.1

THE EUROPE 500 LIST

The Europe 500 list identifies the 500 most successful job-creating small businesses across 28 European states (the EU-25 plus Iceland, Norway and Switzerland). The Europe 500 are identified by their aggressive strategies and high growth rates from inception which is sustained though their transition from a micro- to a medium-sized enterprise. In the three years to the end of 2004, the top 500 SMEs within these states increased their employment and turnover by over 48 per cent annually. The annual growth rate for these firms was 14 per cent. While there has been a slow down since the turn of the millennium, the Europe 500 have created an average of 259 jobs each over three years to the end of 2004: an average of 89 per year.

By the end of 2004, Germany has the most representatives (111) in the top 500, followed by the UK (106). France boasted two companies in the top five, Germany had six and the UK seven in the top 20. In total, the Europe 500 have created almost 130,000 jobs in the three-year period to the end of 2004 with their total employment being 397,810. The rate of employment creation was highest in Ireland and Iceland with higher than average growth rates also witnessed in the UK, Denmark and Austria. The relative growth of employment (that is, the extra employment as a percentage of total employment at the end of the previous period) was 48 per cent per annum. The smaller the company, the higher the relative growth rate.

In 2005, the Europe 500 consisted of 328 (66 per cent) medium-sized businesses where there are more than 100 but fewer than 1,000 employees. Only 12 per cent were small (that is, less than 100 employees). This was a marked change since 2004 when 38 per cent were small and half were medium-sized. These aggressive growth rates were also signalled by the exceptional financial performance of these businesses as they saw turnover increase by an average of €19.2 million, an increase of over €6 million from the previous period. In addition, these companies generated €88 billion in sales. The highest growth rates in turnover were evident in Iceland, Norway and the UK.

The Europe 500 is focused on the emergent new economy with IT services representing 22 per cent of the highest growth companies. Firms within manufacturing also demonstrated high growth with 18 per cent of companies within the Europe 500 sourced from this market segment. Interestingly, the highest absolute rate of job creation was in agriculture and mining with 656 jobs per company created over the three years to 2004. This was some way ahead of the next highest which was management services (448 average new jobs), though it was transport and logistics that demonstrated the average highest growth rate of employment at 28 per cent.

Across the Europe 500, there was a high degree of continuity as 51 per cent of firms were included in the 2004 listing. This means that they were able to sustain growth for at least four years. Indeed, many of these had been growing for even longer: 102 companies had been on the list since 1999, 80 since 1996 and 51 since 1995. Three had been included since inception of the rankings in 1991.

The success of these businesses seems to fly in the face of the convention that European business is dominated by LSEs whose size is seen as a precondition for global success. In addition, it highlights the potential of SMEs should the ever-present barriers to growth – created by high taxes, rigid rules and an inability to access capital – be removed. The top ranked company in 2005 was Assystem – a French consulting business selling designing and engineering know-how. Assystem is typical of many high-growth businesses that operate within knowledge-based industries and utilise skilled labour and research capabilities. This is true both across services and manufacturing where the emphasis is upon knowledge to create market niches and upon establishing a competitive differential with low-cost suppliers. In these businesses, innovation is the key to longevity and to a sustained growth rate especially in the 'older' economy businesses. In other areas, these firms have focused on improving efficiency. Some companies have generated growth by investing in state-of-the-art facilities to produce at lower cost.

Case questions

1 What factors underpin the growth of these high-growth enterprises?

2 Despite the emergence of China and India as low-cost bases of production, how can small firms compete?

3 What can be done to enhance the performances of these businesses?

literature has started to stress the importance of the internationalisation of the small business. For a long time, there was a consensus based around the idea that to be able to compete and be active in international markets, a firm had to be big. Certain factors, such as the fixed costs of learning about foreign governments, communicating over long distances and negotiating with overseas partners, all tended to count against small business internationalisation. Due to their heterogeneous nature, there was generally an absence of any overarching theory to explain the emergence of the international SMEs. The traditional explanations of the internationalisation process stress the importance of the learning process. Thus, as firms gain more experience of internationalisation, the more they become involved in the international environment. Under this process,

there were inevitable barriers to SME internationalisation derived from knowledge and financial deficiencies. However, a new breed of 'born global' and micro-nationals has started to challenge this perspective.

The rapid internationalisation of SMEs is driven by the nature of their management and the knowledge they possess. As a result, these firms may not need to undergo the learning process as assumed by more conventional process theories of internationalisation. These firms have managers that have a more developed global mindset, higher levels of global experience and a higher risk tolerance than other SMEs. These firms tend to operate within fast-moving environments and will position themselves within international networks to achieve the desired levels of reach and levels of policy assistance needed to support their move into

153

international arenas. These firms base their internationalisation on learning through networks. In short, the move towards 'born global' is a result of both push and pull factors, such as the maturity of the domestic market, technological capabilities and the attractiveness of overseas locations.

Thus, for SMEs the internationalisation process comes down to the characteristics of the decision maker in terms of knowledge, attitudes and motivation. These can be a mix of environmental and/or internal drivers that stimulate the move into new geographic markets. The move towards international markets is based on a number of factors, namely a manager's beliefs about the firm's competitive advantage; the risks associated with such a strategy and the internal and external barriers to such a strategy. Clearly, one of the biggest barriers is the lack of knowledge by SMEs when they initially seek to internationalise. This is influenced by the level of education of the entrepreneur, their experience and cultural familiarity with targeted markets.

The exploitation of international markets is not a concern for all SMEs. On a global level, the OECD estimates (for the manufacturing sector) that internationalised SMEs account for 25–35 per cent of world manufactured exports with, it is estimated, only 1 per cent of SMEs being truly global. Another 5–10 per cent show an extensive degree of internationalisation while a further 10–20 per cent draw between 10–40 per cent of their turnover from international activity. Thus, only a third of European enterprises (assuming a straight extrapolation of the figures) is likely to be affected to any great extent by the internationalisation process.

Within the EU, SMEs' exports represent only around 17 per cent of turnover with micro-businesses (not surprisingly) exporting a mere 9 per cent. These patterns are apparent across all markets and segments indicating that SMEs tend to focus on local and regional markets. Despite this, evidence from the OECD suggests that those EU SMEs with the highest degree of internationalisation represent some of the fastest growing enterprises within the European economy – growing by as much as two to three times the average enterprise growth rate. These SMEs tend to operate in narrow niche markets that enable them to exploit their specialist skills and market positioning more effectively. Evidence suggests that European SMEs are not seriously concerned about the competitive threat from the Pacific Rim or, indeed, from the US: although the latter is feared more than the former. This reflects the core issue that, for the majority of European SMEs, internationalisation means Europe, more particularly developing a strategy in response to increasing levels of intra-EU competition.

The SMEs' share of international trade is growing faster than that of larger enterprises. As suggested above, SMEs tend to export more to neighbouring countries than to the broader global trading environment, a situation that is aided by similarities in commercial culture and common trade regulations with members of the same regional group. Their ability to exploit the potential of the network economy, to develop new customer–supplier linkages and to enter new markets is dependent upon the quantity and quality of available information and the manner in which the enterprise utilises it. This is especially important given that many SMEs are based in single locations and thus face considerable spatial barriers in developing an international strategy and in establishing cross-border networking. This increases the prominence of ICTs within this group of enterprises as much as it does for larger firms (see below).

An EU survey of the interaction between SMEs and the international environment highlighted that the most common form of internationalisation was through the firm having a foreign supplier (30 per cent). Nearly 20 per cent had an export role only and 6 per cent were actively integrating into the network economy to support their internationalisation through collaboration or through a subsidiary or joint venture abroad. However, these figures reflect the fact that nearly two-thirds have non-internationalisation strategies. In this broader context, the following was evident:

- 18 per cent of internationalised SMEs are foreign supplier only;
- 6 per cent are export only;

- those that have a subsidiary abroad or a joint venture or use more than one form of internationalisation was 13 per cent.

These are still lower levels of internationalisation when compared to larger firms. Across SMEs, micro-enterprise tends to be less internationalised than either small or medium-sized enterprises.

THE EVOLUTION OF EUROPE'S ENTERPRISE POLICY

According to the prevailing attitude in the 1960s and 1970s, the interface between the firm and public policy was based on the aforementioned notion that the bigger the

---

DEFINITION OF SMEs

BOX 7.1

Member states have traditionally employed differing definitions of what constitutes an SME. However, in order to operate a common policy for SMEs and to provide an appropriate focus for policy, a single definition of SMEs was required. The Commission has, therefore, adopted a definition (see below) that is applied to all Community programmes for better targeting of policy initiatives.

Table 7.4 Criteria for SMEs

	Medium-sized	Small	Micro-enterprise
Maximum number of employees	<250	<50	<10
Maximum turnover (mn ECU)	40	7	–
Maximum balance sheet (mn ECU)	27	5	–

Source: European Commission.

To be classified as an SME, and therefore to benefit from EU Enterprise Policy, a firm has to satisfy the employees measure and one of the financial criteria. In addition, the firm must be independent: in other words less than 25 per cent of the enterprise is owned by another enterprise or group of firms.

firm, the better it was for an economy's performance. This was expressed through a number of measures such as public ownership, competition policy and regulation. This obsession with scale as a key determinant of international competitiveness lasted well into the 1980s. There were no specific policies for SMEs at the EU level until the mid-1980s, although many more generic EU policies affected the development of these enterprises to varying degrees.

Traditionally, the EU as a policy-making body was regarded as potentially damaging to SMEs. In particular, the plethora of regulations emanating from Brussels are frequently criticised for imposing unnecessary costs upon SMEs. There is, therefore, a need for the EU to balance the promotion of free trade (which is generally good for SMEs) alongside the need for regulation (which is potentially costly for these enterprises). As integration progressed, the lack of an EU policy framework for SMEs became an increasingly glaring omission. This changed in 1989 when a separate Directorate General for SMEs (DG XXIII) was created within the European Commission. The role of DG XXIII, now known as 'DG Enterprise', was to administer a series of SME-focused measures (which formed the embryo of the EU's Enterprise Policy) which sought to:

- safeguard and improve the environment for business during the completion of the internal market and beyond;
- develop policies that enable SMEs to exploit the opportunities created by the internal market;
- ensure consistency between enterprise policy and other EU policies.

Enterprise policy is a wide-ranging domain covering diverse areas and policy actions. The initial measures for a Community Enterprise Policy were reflected in the year for small and medium-sized enterprises in 1983 and were established on the basis of Article 235. There were two initial stages in the development: first, the setting up of an SME Task Force in 1986 and, second, the decision to provide enterprise policy with increased resources in the wake of the SEA. This facilitated the creation of the aforementioned DG XXIII to provide a primary focus for SME development. In order to achieve its objectives, EU policy focuses upon regenerating the institutional framework, stimulating information diffusion and reinforcing human capabilities.

Thus, a specific policy framework for enterprise and entrepreneurship is relatively new. Importantly, policies for SMEs and entrepreneurship are different. The former is a set of policy measures directed at promoting SMEs with the focus on the existing stock of small businesses, whereas entrepreneurship policies are much broader and are concerned with stimulating entrepreneurial behaviour. Thus, there are two main differences between SME and entrepreneurship policy. The first concerns the breadth of the policy measures. Whereas SME policy is focused on existing businesses, entrepreneurship is focused more on the broader process of change. Entrepreneurship policy needs to focus on broad environmental issues whereas SME focuses on the organisation. Second, SME policy is given more consideration within policy than entrepreneurship. Often, SME policy has a government agency directed at its promotion. In the case of entrepreneurship, this is rarely the case.

At the Lisbon European Council (2000), a new multi-annual programme for Enterprise and entrepreneurship was launched. The aim is for SMEs to complement the broader objectives of a European economy based on innovation and knowledge. An initial outcome of this conference was the European Charter for SMEs. The charter calls for actions by the member states in ten areas:

1 education and training for entrepreneurship;
2 cheaper and faster start-up;
3 better legislation and regulation;
4 availability of skills;
5 improving online access;
6 getting more out of the single market;
7 taxation and financial matters;
8 enhancing the technological capacity of small business;
9 successful e-business models and top-class small business support;
10 more effective representation at the EU and national levels.

These actions represent a broad set of both positive and negative measures designed not only to promote SMEs but also to free them from impediments to growth. The aim is to focus attention on the needs of SMEs. Five years into the plan, there is still a lot of policy action that needs to be undertaken at the national level to support the development of SMEs. The mid-term Kok Report highlighted, for example, that the administrative burden remained a considerable barrier.

Continuing on from the previous programmes, SME support is to be integrated with other policies to ensure that the objectives of the Lisbon Council are met. These new measures follow on and support the longer term forms of support offered by the EU. These have worked on both environmental and support measures. Typical measures offered include:

■ the BEST Programme which sought to bring together all the measures that aim to simplify the commercial environment of business;
■ the Euro-info centre network, which offers advice and support when dealing

with Europe and the legislation that emerges from this level of government;
■ improving access to finance through assorted forms of finance such as regional aid, credit and financing;
■ the establishment of the European Technology Facility which aims to improve finance to more advanced SMEs;
■ an SME guarantee facility to offer loans and other financial support;
■ the Joint European venture programme which aids access to venture capital markets;
■ structural funds which offer financial support for SMEs in eligible regions;
■ research and technical programmes which seek to offer support for SMEs to become involved in EU research programmes;
■ vocational training support from the European Social Fund (ESF) to support human capital development.

In response to the demands of the Lisbon Council, the EU has put forward new measures in areas such as benchmarking for best practice in start-up and has adopted the better regulation package which seeks to alter the manner in which policy is formulated. Increased consultation aims to improve the effectiveness of policy without making new actions an impediment to the start-up or performance of business. To support the finance of business, the EU is currently moving towards the Risk Capital Action Plan to support access to this source of finance. The latest RTD action plan has also sought to raise the importance of SMEs by offering increased levels of funding.

Entrepreneurship actions

The rationale for action on entrepreneurship is based on three market failures. The first is the need to exploit the advantages derived from network externalities. These are advantages gained from geographical proximity to complementary firms and which enable the firm to access knowledge spillovers. Thus, the value of entrepreneurs is increased when they are located near other entrepreneurs and so policy has sought to create clusters of SMEs. Market failure is based on the failure of these clusters to emerge. The second market failure concerns the existence of knowledge externalities: if SMEs are to benefit from the knowledge created by other parties, there is a need to be close to them. Thus, even if a firm fails, their experience needs to be registered with other firms. Finally, the prevalence of learning or demonstration effects is important in those locations where enterprise has been absent. Where a business starts up, others may seek to learn from its experience in creating their own concern.

In seeking to stimulate entrepreneurship, SMEs felt it was of paramount importance to reduce administrative and regulatory burdens. However, this is as true for the existing stock of SMEs as it is a disincentive for those seeking to build a business. With regards to entrepreneurship, in particular, a survey of businesses found that policy makers needed to create a more favourable attitude towards entrepreneurship; to present a more realistic image of entrepreneurship and to encourage its inclusion on the school curriculum. Many of the policy measures designed to promote enterprise are also of generic importance to existing SMEs. Thus, to a degree, EU entrepreneurship policy is directed as much towards promoting enterprise within existing SMEs as towards creating new businesses.

Likewise, for entrepreneurship, the EU has developed a series of actions to promote a broader entrepreneurial mindset across the EU. The 2004 Action Plan established a broad strategic framework for boosting entrepreneurship across Europe. On the basis of public consultation five broad policy areas were identified:

1 *Fuelling the entrepreneurial mindset*: through the use of role models and highlighting the positive contribution that SMEs make to the socio-economic system. There is a need to demonstrate the assorted ways by which people can become entrepreneurs. The Commission has been active in promoting entrepreneurship education and ensuring that all have access to this form of training and education.

2 *Encouraging more people to become entrepreneurs*: the key element is to reduce the administrative burden in start-ups. The EU has also made efforts to amend bankruptcy laws to reduce the stigma of failure. This will be coordinated among national bodies.

3 *Gearing entrepreneurs for growth and competitiveness*: this involves support to SMEs to enable them to grow. This can be through efforts to support internationalisation and to integrate entrepreneurs into the evolving knowledge economy.

4 *Improving the flow of finance*: as mentioned above, the EU has developed assorted devices to improve the flow of funds into small business and to allow ideas to become real.

5 *Creating an SME-friendly regulatory and administrative framework*: the reduction of red tape and of time-consuming paperwork involved in starting up and running a small business. In 2002, the EU launched a campaign to improve European governance to assess the proper role and relevance of decisions. These efforts are linked into the completion of the SEM which will enable businesses to develop cross-border interactions more easily.

It is apparent that creating a more entrepreneurial EU means coordination among all parties involved in developing policy that supports their development and emergence, just at the EU level but also at member state level. There also needs to be learning from the best in terms of what makes enterprises successful and of the positive role that they can play in the modern economy. This must be supported by more positive attitudes toward entrepreneurs within the economy. While it has no formal powers to harmonise laws, the European Commission has been lobbying for change as it believes that EU laws are basically outdated in two main areas: first, in terms of the legal restrictions placed on bankrupt companies, including restrictions on starting up the new business and, second, in terms of the discharge period (the timeframe over which an entrepreneur is liable for repayment of debts). In some states, the period of discharge is as long as six to seven years.

Policy to aid SME internationalisation

To overcome the traditional impediments to the integration of SMEs into international markets, the EU has acted in a number of ways. Though constrained by its limited budget, the EU has set up (as mentioned above) a number of specialist information centres to overcome deficiencies with regard to knowledge and financing in foreign markets. It has also sought to develop measures within multilateral fora to:

- aid network development to share best practice;
- assist foreign investment;
- offer training for improvements in the quality of management within firms;

- support enterprises that exhibit the highest growth potential;
- improve access to SME-supporting services;
- alleviate trade barriers with third countries.

Pragmatism is essential in this environment in enabling SMEs to exploit the opportunities afforded by the SEM as well as in meeting the challenges posed by the emerging internationalisation of markets on a broader scale.

To promote internationalisation, actions by policy makers cover many different areas. These have mainly focused upon the provision of information, financial support, counselling and inward investment support. Across 19 Western Europe states, just over half have deliberate SME-based internationalisation policies whereas the remainder focus on enterprises generally in their policy actions. The generic aim of these policies is to reduce the risk that SMEs face in the internationalisation process through measures such as export insurance and credits systems. There is a trend within some states to increase the degree of customisation of support. The lack of support in some states for SMEs may be driven by an assumption of these businesses that policy needs to be based upon a stages approach to internationalisation. Thus, many feel that support for co-operation etc. would not be as forthcoming. This needs to be corrected. The EU has indicated that the following factors need to be in place to secure the success of SME policy:

1 Policy (given the limited time and capacity of managers) should seek to perform some of the practical tasks on behalf of the manager, especially when they have no international experience.
2 SMEs often need targeted support with the result that policy should focus on the specific needs of the business.

159

3 Policy should recognise that SME internationalisation is more than just about exporting. Thus, policy needs to be multi-faceted in terms of the support that it offers.

4 All SMEs, no matter how they engage with the international environment, identify the same problems. This suggests that policy needs to be targeted in a broad manner.

CONCLUSIONS

SMEs are central to the commercial development of the EU and to its continuing commercial success. However, there are a plethora of problems to overcome to ensure their impact is fully realised. On one level, there is the need to aid the success of the existing stock of SMEs and to focus on areas where practical engagement can aid their success. On another level, instruments are needed to support emergent businesses through support for entrepreneurship. If policy is to enable these enterprises to both emerge and grow, then it needs to pinpoint those areas where its action can have the greatest impact. Policy studies indicate that targeted policies are likely to be the most effective but policy must still be hands-off as the success of an SME depends upon the skills and strategies within the enterprise itself and not upon those of policy makers, however laudable their intentions.

KEY POINTS

- SMEs form the vast majority of enterprises within the EU.

- A core policy objective is to help SMEs expand into international markets.

- Internationalisation is, however, only relevant to a select group of SMEs.

- Much of the policy effort centres upon developing a regulatory and administrative environment that is cost-minimal to SMEs.

ACTIVITIES

1 Research a local SME and identify the major impediments to their growth.

2 Identify the relative advantages and disadvantages of SMEs vis-à-vis LSEs.

3 Find examples of entrepreneurs and assess the key elements in their emergence.

QUESTIONS FOR DISCUSSION

1 How do you account for the commercial importance of SMEs?

2 To what extent is it fair to argue that economies of scale are being undermined as a source of competitive advantage?

3 How can Europe best overcome its relative inability to create enough entrepreneurs?

4 Should entrepreneurialism be taught in schools?

5 How do you explain the rise of the international SME?

SUGGESTIONS FOR FURTHER READING

Audretsch, D. (2002) *Entrepreneurship: A Survey of the Literature*, a report prepared for the European Commission, Brussels.

Chetty, S. and Holm, D. (2000) 'Internationalisation of Small Manufacturing Firms: A Network Approach', *International Business Review*, 9, pp. 73–93.

European Commission (2000) *Towards Enterprise Europe*, SEC (2000) 771.

European Commission (2003) 'Creating an Entrepreneurial Europe: The Activities of the European Union for Small and Medium-Sized Enterprises', COM (2003) 58.

European Commission (2003) 'Green Paper: Entrepreneurship in Europe', COM (2003) 27.

European Commission (2004) 'Action Plan: The European Agenda for Entrepreneurship', COM (2004) 70.

European Commission (2004) 'Benchmarking Enterprise Policy: Results From the 2004 Scoreboard', SEC (2004) 1427.

Hitchens, D. (ed.) (2003) *Small and Medium Sized Companies in Europe: Environmental Performance, Competitiveness and Management: International EU Case Studies*, Berlin and Heidelberg: Springer Verlag.

Jones, O. and Tilley, F. (eds) (2003) *Competitive Advantage in SME's: Organising for Innovation and Change*, Chichester: John Wiley & Sons.

Chapter 8

Economic and monetary union

An unfinished project

> I want the whole of Europe to have one currency; it will make trading much easier.
> Napoleon, in a letter to his brother, Louis, dated 6 May 1807

 This chapter will help you understand:

- how and why the single currency came into existence;
- the nature of EMU and the risks and benefits associated with it;
- the conditions which EMU requires to work and why these require fundamental reforms by eurozone members;
- the impact of the eurozone on the European business environment;
- why the UK, Denmark and Sweden remain outside the eurozone;
- the status and strategy of the 2004 accession states in relation to EMU.

In January 2002, euro notes and coins entered circulation and the single currency became a reality. This event represented the final stage in a long journey and the realisation of one of the 'big ideas' of European integration. The journey has not been without incident. It got off to a false start via the thwarted plans of the 1970 Werner Report which had envisaged full EMU by 1980. Attempts to forge closer monetary links subsequently encountered severe difficulties in the early 1990s with the crises in the ERM, EMU's predecessor. Although its

launch has largely been successful, EMU and the single currency continue to face many challenges, including the need for eurozone members to undertake economic reforms to enable the currency to operate smoothly; the management of relations with EU members outside the eurozone and the absorption of new members, especially from 2004 accession states.

This chapter addresses the above challenges by first exploring the nature of EMU and the single currency and the conditions that need to be met for it to succeed. Second,

162

the chapter briefly sets out how the EU arrived at its advanced stage of monetary integration, followed by an explanation of why it embarked upon such an ambitious path and of the risks attached to such a course of action. This process also reveals how EMU and the single currency have changed the business environment. The chapter then discusses the challenges facing the single currency. It concludes by drawing together the various strands in a tentative outlook for the project.

WHAT IS EMU?

A key part of the Treaty of Rome was the creation of a common market but it contained no explicit commitment to the objective of economic and monetary union. However, EMU is the possible, albeit not inevitable, next stage of integration after a common or single market (see Chapter 2). Indeed, the existence of separate national currencies is regarded by some as one of the remaining barriers to the attainment of a barrier-free single market. Moreover, as interdependence increases with the free movement of goods, services, capital and labour so the logic of increased common rules in areas such as competition policy and greater economic coordination and cooperation increases to the extent that separate economies and markets are melded together. Furthermore, in a highly interdependent market, the logic for monetary union increases to ward off the possibility of divergent monetary policies distorting and undermining the benefits of interdependence or of competitive policies setting off inflationary pressure.

EMU, therefore, embraces the following characteristics:

- policy harmonisation to remove obstacles to factor mobility. This corresponds to the achievement of the four freedoms (mobility of capital, services, goods and labour) – the heart of the SEM and of Stage one of EMU (see below);
- a more marked and wider range of common policies, especially in relation to macro-economic policy;
- irrevocably fixed exchange rates or, as in the case of the EU, a single currency;
- a common monetary policy – that is, one interest rate and exchange rate policy determined by a single central bank;
- some pooling of foreign exchange reserves;
- possible inter-state transfers to offset economic distortions arising from EMU.

The above characteristics are essentially technocratic and economic in nature but EMU also has a highly controversial political dimension. At a minimum, EMU implies a surrendering, or pooling, of sovereignty in certain areas of policy making, namely the national determination of interest rates and of exchange rate policies and the acceptance of constraints in the exercise of macro-economic policy. It also requires politicians to undertake the frequently unpopular policies needed to qualify for membership of EMU and, in the longer term, to introduce the structural reforms needed to ensure that their economies can thrive within EMU and that EMU itself runs smoothly. Although many current eurozone members showed tremendous political commitment in meeting the eligibility criteria for eurozone membership by restraining public spending and other deflationary measures, for example, it is the reluctance of some of the larger member states, in particular, to embark upon more fundamental structural reforms in their economies that is potentially building up serious problems for EMU (see below). Moreover, EMU inevitably gives rise to a broader political debate about how far economic and monetary union spills over into the need for greater political unity among its members, the future role and nature of the EU in general or, indeed, whether political union should precede monetary union for EMU to work. These questions underpin some of the British population's concerns about the euro – despite the efforts of pro-euro campaigners at least to keep it as an essentially economic issue (see Case Study 8.1, p. 180).

The above factors may characterise EMU but they do not in themselves determine whether the EU is a suitable grouping for launching EMU. The theory of optimum currency areas (OCAs) sets out the conditions that should prevail if two or more countries are to give up their separate currencies and replace them with a single currency. A high level of interdependence through trade and capital flows is clearly necessary but according to Robert Mundell, the originator of OCA theory, three further conditions must be satisfied for a common currency to be beneficial:

1 There should be an absence, as far as possible, of asymmetric shocks – that is, external economic shocks that affect individual members of the EMU in a differential manner. The greater the degree of economic convergence among participating states, so the likelihood of asymmetric shocks diminishes. Such shocks become a problem within EMU systems because of the centralisation of interest rate and exchange rate policies.
2 A high degree of labour mobility and wage flexibility is needed. so that when shocks do occur, individual economies within the union are able to adjust via labour migration or changes in wages

given they can no longer rely on changes in autonomous national monetary policy to correct for economic imbalances between countries.
3 A centralised fiscal policy which can redistribute resources to member countries performing poorly should be in place.

This raises the question of whether the eurozone meets the criteria of an OCA. The process of European integration prior to EMU has increased cultural, economic and political links among European countries but significant differences remain (see Chapter 1). There are strong regional sub-groupings within the EU: Finland, for example, has more in common and greater linkages with its Nordic and Baltic neighbours than with the countries of Southern Europe and vice versa. The 2004 generation of member states that are striving to meet the eligibility criteria of EMU may also find themselves in an asymmetric conundrum. Their long-term major economic objective is to ensure macro-economic convergence with older member states. In order to achieve this, their economies must grow substantially more quickly than those already in the eurozone. In order to meet the Maastricht convergence criteria (see below), deflationary measures may be necessary to contain their budgetary deficits and the inflation their buoyant economies may unleash but which is not necessarily a serious problem at their stage of development. Once in the eurozone, these constraints will persist. Despite this potential for asymmetries among EMU members, the more closely the countries integrate, through the SEM and other policies, including EMU, the greater the level of interdependence and synchronisation of business cycles which, although not totally removing the possibility of asymmetric shocks, significantly reduces their power to undermine EMU.

The eurozone scores less well in terms of labour mobility and wage flexibility. Although the SEM has played its part in reducing barriers, obstacles to the free movement of labour, including high cultural and language barriers, remain. Labour markets in some member states remain highly regulated and generally inhibit the ability of labour markets to adjust to compensate for the absence of differentiated monetary policy. Moreover, although OCA theory emphasises the need for labour market flexibility as an adjustment tool, the mobility of goods, service and capital plus the SEM also generally facilitate the workings of EMU. Capital is highly mobile throughout the EU and the single market in most goods and services, although far from perfect (see Chapter 4), has made significant progress in the 1990s.

The EU also lacks any strong central redistributive element to compensate for tensions within the eurozone. Its budget is tiny compared to those of member states and, although the Cohesion and Structural Funds are intended to bring about some degree of redistribution, member state resistance to increasing the EU budget and to its tax-raising powers means the prospect of the EU taking on this role in any meaningful way remains distant.

In short, on a theoretical level at least, the prospects for EMU within Europe do not appear bright. However, the political commitment of member states to launch EMU was underestimated by many and, having made that commitment, presumably the will to make it work should not be underestimated either. However, there are signs that some member states are shying away from the unpopular reforms needed in their economies to make EMU work, potentially causing problems for the project in the long term (see below).

THE ROAD TO EMU

The final realisation of the single currency in 2002 – when euro notes and coins came into circulation – was the third modern-day attempt at European monetary integration. The first began in 1969 when the Hague Summit strove to relaunch the process of European integration by, among other things, introducing EMU by 1980. This objective was reinforced by the Werner Report, adopted by the EU in 1971, and resulted, in 1972, in the 'snake in the tunnel' – an adjustable fixed exchange rate system in which member currencies fluctuated within a margin of ±2.25 per cent against the US dollar in a system administered by the European Monetary Cooperation Fund (EMCF). The upheaval in international financial markets that led to the end of the post-war Bretton Woods financial agreement and to inflation and high unemployment in the industrial world dealt a fatal blow to any serious attempts to meet the 1980 EMU deadline.

The second attempt at European monetary integration was the EMS, which was established in 1979 and formed the backbone of European monetary arrangements until the creation of EMU. The EMS was not intended to lead to EMU but to create a 'zone of monetary stability' – that is, to act as an anti-inflationary anchor in a world increasingly beset by inflationary problems. The ERM was a key part of the EMS: participation in the ERM required members to maintain their currency within specified fluctuation margins of ±2.25 per cent either side of the ecu central rates. Higher inflation countries such as Italy were permitted fluctuations of ±15 per cent. The ecu, or European currency unit, was a basket of currencies participating in the ERM, with each currency weighted according to its role in intra-EU trade.

165

BOX 8.1

MILESTONES IN THE DEVELOPMENT OF THE SINGLE CURRENCY

1969	Hague Council calls for EMU by 1980
1970	Werner Report endorses the goal of EMU by 1980
Mar. 1972	Currency snake launched
April 1973	European Monetary Cooperation Fund (EMCF) established to provide financial support to maintain stable exchange rates
1979	EMS, including the ERM, founded to create a 'zone of monetary stability' within Europe
1989	Delors Report proposes a three-stage approach to EMU and is adopted by the Madrid Council in June
July 1990	Stage one of EMU begins
Oct. 1990	UK joins ERM
Dec. 1991	European Council approves the Maastricht Treaty which establishes a three-stage timetable to achieve EMU. The UK and Denmark secure an 'opt-out' from Stage three
Sept. 1992	'Black Wednesday' – UK sterling and the Italian lira suspend membership of the ERM following massive speculation
Aug. 1993	Normal fluctuation band widened from 2.25 per cent to 15 per cent either side of the central parity of currencies within the ERM
Jan. 1994	Stage two of EMU begins with the establishment of the European Monetary Institute (EMI) – successor to the EMCF and forerunner of the ECB
Dec. 1995	Madrid Council confirms 1 January 1999 as the start of Stage three of EMU
Dec. 1996	Dublin Council agrees the terms of the Stability and Growth Pact
Oct. 1997	UK Chancellor of the Exchequer, Gordon Brown, commits the UK 'in principle' to eurozone membership and sets out five economic tests that must be satisfied before Britain joins
May 1998	Brussels Council decides 11 member states (Belgium, Germany, Spain, France, Ireland, Italy, Luxembourg, the Netherlands, Austria, Portugal and Finland) are eligible for adoption of the euro
Jan. 1999	Stage three of EMU begins with the 'irrevocable fixing' of the conversion rates between participating currencies. The European System of Central Banks (ESCB) starts to conduct a single monetary and foreign exchange policy and electronic trading in euros begins
Sept. 2000	The Danish people vote against joining the euro by 53.1 to 46.9 per cent
Jan. 2001	Greece joins the euro
Jan. 2002	Euro notes and coins enter circulation in 12 member states. Initially in 'dual circulation' alongside national currencies, the euro becomes the sole currency by the end of February
June 2003	Gordon Brown announces that the UK only passes one of his five economic tests and rules out UK membership for the foreseeable future
Sept. 2003	Sweden votes in referendum against joining the euro by 56.2 per cent to 41.8 per cent

Nov. 2003	Effective suspension of the Stability and Growth Pact (SGP) following persistent breaches of the budget rules by France and Germany
June 2004	Estonia, Lithuania and Slovenia join ERM II
Mar. 2005	Terms of the revised SGP agreed
April 2005	Cyprus, Latvia and Malta join ERM II
Nov. 2005	Slovakia joins ERM II

Currency realignments were permitted to reduce tension in the system. In the ERM's initial phase, states persistently devalued within the system and its ability to act as a disciplinary device to promote convergence in terms of key monetary indicators (that is, inflation and interest rates) was severely curtailed. By the mid- to late 1980s, the ERM had become more credible as a means of delivering convergence as member states showed a greater commitment to its rules and procedures. Consequently, inflation and interest rates converged and membership of the ERM expanded to include all EU states bar Greece. However, as the ERM expanded, tensions within the system grew: as the effects of the early 1990s' recession and German reunification took hold, the policy requirements and preferences of states started to diverge. Typically, some states had unemployment problems whereas others had inflationary difficulties. Such differences could not be sustained within the ERM framework and, in September 1992, the UK and Italy left the ERM. Instability continued with the Spanish, Portuguese, Irish and French currencies proving particularly vulnerable and in August 1993, the fluctuation bands were widened to ±15 per cent where they have remained.

The timing of the crisis was unfortunate as the EU had just committed itself in the Maastricht Treaty to a progressive move to EMU by the end of the decade. For the more

sceptical states, the crisis reinforced a belief that moves towards EMU were premature whereas, for the more Europhile states, the crisis confirmed their view that, in a world of free capital movements, a single currency was the best way to achieve the desired currency stability. Economic problems were compounded by political uncertainty arising from the rejection of the treaty by the Danish referendum and the unwillingness of the British to sign. The upshot was opt-out clauses for both the UK and Denmark which allowed both countries to refrain indefinitely from adoption of the single currency.

The Maastricht Treaty resulted from the resurgence of the integration begun by the SEM campaign. By 1988, a committee had been established under Commission President Jacques Delors to consider the issue of EMU and the steps needed to achieve it. The result was the 1989 Delors Report which fed directly into the Maastricht Treaty. The treaty, among other things, set out the timetable, the eligibility criteria for EMU membership and details of the institutions and framework of rules for EMU. The timetable comprised three stages:

- *Stage one*, which began on 1 July 1990, required the removal of all remaining obstacles to capital flows; the participation of all member states' currencies in the ERM and greater policy coordination and convergence of economic performance.

167

- *Stage two*, which began on 1 January 1994, involved the creation of the EMI, a transitional institution intended to prepare the EU for Stage three when it would be replaced by the ECB. During this stage, any central bank that was not already independent of its national government, was to become independent.
- *Stage three* (to begin either on 1 January 1997 or 1 January 1999) began with the irrevocable fixing of participating currencies. The ESCB, composed of the ECB and independent national banks, took over responsibility for monetary and exchange rate policy.

In practice, insufficient member states were adjudged to be ready for EMU by 1997. In May 1998, amid some degree of cynicism and accusations of creative accounting, the European Commission declared that 11 states met the necessary conditions to adopt the euro on 1 January 1999. It was clear that not all states would meet a strict interpretation of the nominal criteria outlined within the treaty. However, the Commission decided that as long as the criteria, especially those for public finances, were moving in the right direction, then membership could go ahead. Only Greece was excluded for economic reasons. The others – Denmark, the UK and Sweden – remained outside EMU, largely for political reasons.

The decision to maximise the number of states within the initial moves towards EMU, despite their apparent deviation from the Maastricht targets, derives largely from political expediency (notably so in the case of Italy) and recognition that the level of benefits from EMU are directly linked to the size of membership. In addition, an improving general economic environment would, according to the Commission, eventually

eliminate deviations from the targets. Moreover, Greece made strenuous efforts to reduce inflation and its budget deficit and joined the eurozone in 2001 – in time for the entry of notes and coins into circulation. Within three years, it became apparent that Greece's last-minute qualification for eurozone membership was due more to an imaginative interpretation of key economic statistics rather than a sudden conversion to monetary and fiscal discipline. This disclosure, although overshadowed by the SGP controversies (see below), could become an embarrassment when it comes to assessing the preparedness of the 2004 accession states for eurozone membership.

In addition to establishing a timetable for EMU, the Maastricht Treaty set out the conditions (generally known as the 'convergence criteria') with which member states must comply to be considered eligible for eurozone membership. The ultimate success of EMU depends upon convergence between member states in terms of economic development and performance. The endpoint of the convergence process is a state of 'cohesion' between states. This does not imply uniform economic development and performance – merely harmonious economic conditions. Convergence comprises three distinct, yet ultimately related, processes – nominal, real and institutional convergence:

1 *Nominal convergence.* This is convergence in terms of macro-economic performance as indicated by core fiscal and monetary variables and is the form of convergence referred to within the Maastricht Treaty. In practice, there is little economic rationale for the Maastricht criteria other than to prove that states can live with, and are committed to, what are essentially criteria for sustaining price stability. Thus entry into EMU requires states to meet the following criteria:

- budget deficits must be no more than 3 per cent of GDP;
- government debt must be no more than 60 per cent of GDP;
- interest rates must be no more than two percentage points above the average of the three 'best' performing states;
- inflation rates must be no more than 1.5 percentage points above the average of the three best performing states;
- states must demonstrate exchange rate stability by maintaining their currency within the normal band of the ERM for at least two years prior to entry.

Although Stage three has been launched, these convergence criteria remain important for two reasons. First, the budget and debt criteria remain at the heart of the SGP which is intended to provide the framework for continued fiscal discipline once EMU is operational. Second, EU members outside the eurozone wishing to become members of the eurozone must also meet the convergence criteria. Given that the first incarnation of the ERM effectively disappeared upon the launch of Stage three, ERM II was set up as an exchange rate waiting room for prospective EMU entrants. Within one year of accession, six out of the ten new member states had become members of ERM II, raising the possibility of adoption of the euro by 2007 by some of them at least.

2 *Real convergence.* Eligibility for EMU membership rests entirely on compliance with the conditions for nominal convergence. However, in the longer term, it is the degree of real convergence that will determine the success of the eurozone. Real convergence implies that levels of unemployment and industrial and economic development between states should broadly approximate. While there are no set criteria, certain core indicators need to converge to ensure that

harmony can be established within the management of a single currency. For example, vast differences in unemployment between states could imply differing policy priorities between constituent parts of EMU. The EU sought to strengthen real convergence by including provisions for a Cohesion Fund within the Treaty upon European Union but the burden for achieving real convergence falls mainly on the willingness of individual member states to undertake often unpopular structural reforms, particularly in the field of labour market flexibility.

3 *Institutional convergence.* The move towards EMU also implies increasing uniformity in terms of economic management. The most obvious form is to achieve a consensus between states around the priorities of economic policy (namely, low and stable inflation). As part of the commitment towards this policy objective, potential members also have to guarantee the independence of the national central bank.

Achieving nominal convergence by 1999 was a core political objective for many member states. The monetary criteria did not pose much of a problem as they had been provided for within the existing framework provided by the ERM. The fiscal policy criteria proved more problematic. In the short term, the fiscal retrenchment necessitated by efforts to meet the criteria magnified Europe's unemployment problem and created a fear that the nominal convergence criteria could lock Europe into permanent mass unemployment.

BENEFITS AND RISKS OF EMU

Given the difficulties involved in establishing eligibility for eurozone membership, it is pertinent to ask why 12 EU members went ahead with the project and why the ten 2004 accession states are striving to follow suit. The potential benefits of eurozone membership and the potential costs/risks associated with the eurozone are set out in Box 8.2. Many of these are difficult to quantify. Where they have been assessed, the gains do not appear to be particularly great. In the case of transactions costs, for example, it is estimated that EMU saves some 0.5 per cent of the EU's GDP. These relatively small benefits are also unevenly spread: smaller states with a higher dependence upon intra-EU trade will benefit the most. In practice, many of the gains from EMU will only be realised over the medium to long term (for example, through greater price stability stimulating higher levels of investment).

These effects are also unevenly spread across businesses. The biggest beneficiaries are those enterprises that derive the highest proportion of their revenues from foreign markets. Thus, larger enterprises are expected to benefit more from EMU.

These benefits will extend to large non-EU companies with extensive investments throughout the EU. However, not all large companies will benefit. Enterprises with a strong domestic market (such as utilities) will seemingly gain little until their markets start to exhibit a greater degree of internationalisation. For SMEs, the impact is difficult to predict. Although many SMEs have a strong tendency to serve local markets, there are a number with a high export focus (such as IT companies) which can expect to benefit from the introduction of the euro.

Despite nearly a decade of the SEM, there still remain large price differentials for many products between states (see Chapter 4). For many businesses, EMU should speed up price convergence through enabling consumers to compare prices across member states more easily because of enhanced price transparency. This transparency will extend to wages and other labour costs which some trade unions hope will lead to EU-wide collective bargaining – a hope which, as yet, remains

---

BOX 8.2

THE COSTS AND BENEFITS OF EMU

Costs
- short-term deflation
- loss of the exchange rate as a tool of national economic policy
- potential problems related to a lack of 'real' convergence and potential policy conflicts
- the inappropriateness of one monetary policy for so many states

Benefits
- elimination of transaction costs in intra-EU trade
- lower interest rates
- removal of exchange rate uncertainty in intra-EMU trade
- aids development of a genuine SEM by increasing price transparency and promoting international specialisation
- removes the option of competitive devaluations between EU states
- creates a new international currency to represent the EU's combined economic weight

largely unfulfilled. Price transparency could also change supply patterns as the elimination of exchange risk and greater transparency within the euro area will make it easier for firms to optimise their sourcing. Price transparency should also lead to price convergence within sectors such as banking, financial services, cars, chemicals and pharmaceuticals. However, complete price convergence will not occur because of continuing differences in transport costs, spatial variations in tastes and preferences, the costs of cross-border shopping, local cost differences and different competitive situations. Overall, however, the EU market should exhibit less fragmentation with internationalisation of markets affecting an increasing number of enterprises (regardless of size) as each is more able to sell its goods to a more geographically dispersed market. This process will be enhanced as inter-state direct mail and e-commerce become more widespread.

In practice, many of the positive and negative aspects of EMU will only manifest themselves over the medium to long term. Advocates of the process play up the fact that the benefits of EMU are directly linked to its size. As EMU membership expands, so the benefits to European business will grow. Opponents regard EMU as primarily a political exercise with negligible economic benefits. However, the core concern has to come down to whether the states are sufficiently similar for them to co-exist with a common currency.

Further problems could limit the ability to sustain convergence, including the perception that not all EMU states are at the same stage of the trade cycle – a major reason given for the UK's delayed entry into the EMU (see Case Study 8.1). A classic example is Ireland. At the time of its accession in 1973, Ireland was the poorest of all Community members in per capita terms.

However, its dynamic growth in the 1990s and beyond has meant that its GDP per head is among the highest in Europe in the mid-2000s and, in the early years of the single currency, a more restrictive monetary policy and higher interest rates than those preferred by Italy and Germany, both struggling with disappointing growth and unemployment, would have been more suitable for Ireland. In short, it is a legitimate question to ask whether one monetary policy *can* fit all. The implication of a single monetary policy is that, unless economies are perfectly aligned (which does not happen within let alone between states) some countries will have an inappropriate interest rate. Thus, attention needs to be paid to how economies can boost their factor mobility to balance out such differences and to whether closer integration will help bring these cycles into closer alignment.

A lack of real convergence between states represents the most potentially serious problem facing the fledgling EMU. If there is insufficient real convergence, EMU will be subject to asymmetric shocks whereby different parts of the zone will be affected by external shocks in markedly different ways (for example, some states could see unemployment rise, others could see inflation increase). If this is the case, a single monetary and exchange rate policy becomes difficult, if not impossible, to sustain. Only if shocks are symmetric or if there is an adequate response mechanism (in terms of fiscal transfers or resource mobility and flexibility) to compensate for such effects will an EMU work. As none of these conditions exists in the EU, EMU should, in theory, be a non-starter for this group of states. Despite this being a theoretical extreme (all states are themselves subject to asymmetric shocks or have inadequate resource mobility or flexibility to compensate for such effects: for example, most states have regional variations in unemployment), it does imply that EMU needs to be accompanied by structural reform of labour markets.

The move towards EMU highlighted new challenges for policy makers in complementing the competitiveness of indigenous enterprises. The option of a competitive devaluation to secure competitiveness in foreign markets is explicitly ruled out in terms of trade with other EU states. This places emphasis upon firms to alter costs and exhibit greater flexibility if they are to compete successfully in both European and global markets. Flexibility requires governments to free up market forces within the European economy in both factor and product markets (see Chapter 13).

THE EARLY YEARS OF EMU AND LOOMING CHALLENGES

The introduction of the euro went relatively smoothly. There were complaints from consumers in some countries that businesses took advantage of the changeover to round up prices (see Chapter 15). Although this undoubtedly took place in some instances, there was no overall significant impact on inflation in the eurozone.

When the euro was introduced in January 1999, the trend was for a weakening of the currency against the dollar (see Figure 8.1) and other currencies. This gave some ammunition to Euro sceptics who dismissed the euro as a weak currency. However, this was missing the point. During the first three years of its existence, the euro did not have the full functionality of a currency, given that notes and coins did not come into circulation until January 2002, and was therefore unlikely to operate as a full-blown currency. Moreover, the euro is a floating currency and its value can be expected to fluctuate in line with underlying economic fundamentals. From the beginning of 2002, the euro steadily strengthened to reach levels against the dollar that were above those prevailing at the time of the euro's launch. This pattern stemmed

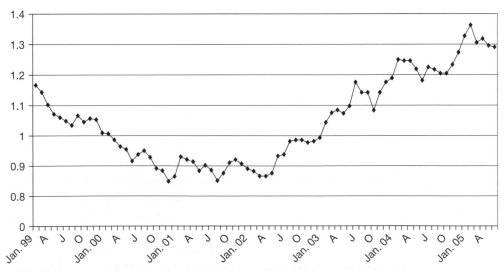

Figure 8.1 €/US$ exchange rate, January 1999 to May 2005

Source: European Central Bank.

from an inherent weakness in the dollar. However, there is nothing inherently desirable about having either a weak or a strong currency: the former can foment inflation and the latter makes life more difficult for exporters. From the trade and investment perspective, the best that can be hoped for from a currency is that it is neither seriously over- nor under-valued and that it remains relatively stable. It is excessive volatility that creates unpredictability and uncertainty and inhibits trade and investment. This uncertainty has so far been removed in the eurozone and there is no evidence that the floating euro is any more volatile than the predecessor national currencies.

... within the Eurozone

In terms of the transition to the euro and the performance of the currency since its introduction, there is nothing untoward to worry about. However, fundamental problems are arising from two linked factors:

1 the ineffectiveness of the SGP as a bulwark against fiscal profligacy;
2 the unwillingness of some member states to take the necessary reform measures to ensure they can compensate for the loss of national monetary policy as the main policy instrument used to correct competitiveness problems. In other words, some key economies are putting off unpopular reforms that would help their markets operate more efficiently in line with the OCA criteria outlined above.

The Stability and Growth Pact (SGP)

The move to EMU was based around a consensus that low inflation is the primary goal of economic policy. To ensure this priority is not diluted within EMU (and thus that states keep to pre-EMU commitments), in December 1996, upon the insistence of the German government, agreement was reached to sustain the Maastricht fiscal convergence criteria after the launch of EMU. That is, budget deficits should remain below 3 per cent of GDP and the national debt should be below 60 per cent of GDP after the launch of the single currency. Persistent failure to comply with the SGP could result in heavy financial penalties, including fines up to 0.5 per cent of GDP.

The SGP was considered necessary because if countries within a monetary union run large fiscal deficits, the single capital market means that financing of this debt will lead to higher interest rates for the whole union. Indeed, monetary union may even encourage expansionary fiscal policies if member states perceive that the cost of financing their debt is spread over more countries (this would, of course, only be a rational course of action, if other countries did not behave in a similar fashion). Moreover, large fiscal deficits can tempt politicians to place pressure on monetary authorities, even supposedly independent monetary authorities, to keep interest rates low – a strategy that would ultimately threaten the price stability goal of monetary union.

That fiscal discipline is needed in monetary union is uncontroversial. Some argued that the political capital locked up by respective member states in EMU would be sufficient to sustain convergence but experience and the dangers of free riders resulted in rejection of this option and adoption of the SGP. However, the SGP regime was regarded by many as too inflexible from the beginning. For example, the choice of 3 per cent and 60 per cent for the budget deficit and debt limits respectively was purely arbitrary. The SGP required member states to keep their spending within limits at all times despite the strong case for allowing members to vary government borrowing as a percentage of GDP throughout the stages of the trade cycle. In EMU, fiscal policy is the one macro-economic weapon left to states to manage their economies. If constraints are imposed upon this, then the automatic stabilisers could be severely affected. That is, it is part of the normal corrective process for deficits to increase during economic slow-downs in line with decreasing tax revenue and increasing expenditure on unemploy-ment and other social benefits, whereas budget deficits fall when economies prosper given rising tax revenues and falling social spending. In other words, to try to keep deficits below an arbitrary 3 per cent of GDP when the economy is in trouble will only increase deflationary pressure. The imposi-tion of fines in such circumstances will also only exacerbate the problems. Such prob-lems could be countered by a stronger central fiscal and redistributive policy but this is something that member states will clearly not countenance.

The above concerns about the potential for problems with the SGP were quickly borne out, even causing the then Commis-sion President Romano Prodi to call the pact 'stupid'. Fiscal deficits in Portugal, France and, ironically, Germany, the architect of the SGP, rapidly breached the 3 per cent limit. The imposition of penalties on the two biggest countries in the eurozone was politi-cally difficult and, indeed, the SGP was effec-tively suspended in November 2003 when sufficient members (excluding Spain, the Netherlands, Austria and Belgium) agreed not to proceed further against France and Germany. Despite the European Commis-sion's victory in July 2004 in its subsequent case at the ECJ against the finance ministers, the SGP's shortcomings had been exposed.

The problems with the SGP undermined the general credibility of EMU. It created tension within the eurozone itself by em-phasising the small–large country divide. The Netherlands and Austria, for example, were angry that they had taken difficult decisions in their attempts to comply with the terms of the SGP whereas France and Germany appeared to get away with ignoring it. It also sent contradictory signals to the new member states striving to comply with the Maastricht criteria ahead of adoption of the euro and who will thereafter be subject to the SGP.

In March 2005, the heads of government reached agreement on revisions to the SGP (see Box 8.3). In general, the changes result in greater flexibility in the system. The jury is out, however, on whether the relaxation has gone too far and undermined confidence in the fiscal framework of EMU and the sustainability of public finances in eurozone countries. It is the lack of clarity and the extensive range of 'relevant factors' that member states can invoke to avoid the excessive deficit procedure that brings in the greatest flexibility – or, in the view of its critics, significantly weakens the pact through its numerous exceptions, greater complexity and reduced transparency, all of which will make the pact harder to imple-ment. In the short term, the agreement should reduce the embarrassing political rows surrounding the deficits of key EMU members like France and Germany but in the longer term, it remains unclear whether the revised SGP has become so 'flexible' that it has effectively become meaningless.

Economic reform within the eurozone

One of the conditions for a successful EMU is flexible labour and product markets. In the absence of the devaluation option as the,

THE REVISED STABILITY AND GROWTH PACT

BOX 8.3

The revisions in the SGP agreed by heads of government in March 2005 were intended to make the pact more flexible. The main conditions of the agreement were:

- *Thresholds*: the 3 per cent ceiling for the budget deficit and the 60 per cent limit for national debt remained unchanged.
- *'Relevant factors' enabling countries to avoid an excessive deficit procedure*: member states in danger of breaching the deficit will be able to invoke a range of 'relevant factors' to avoid the imposition of penalties. Such factors include potential growth, the economic cycle, structural reforms (for example, in social security and pensions), R&D policies, public investment etc. The agreement does not establish an exhaustive list of factors but rather sets out chapter headings that establish general principles around which member states will be able to argue their case.
- *Extension of deadlines*: instead of one year, countries will have two in which to correct an excessive deficit. This can be extended further in the case of 'unexpected and adverse economic events'.

albeit temporary, solution to competitive pressures, flexible markets should be able to take the burden of adjustment. However, the record of European countries in reducing structural rigidities in their economies is mixed. Unfortunately for EMU, its three biggest members — Italy, Germany and France — suffer from excessive labour and product market inflexibilities and costly, swollen pension, welfare and health systems which make it difficult to meet both the fiscal requirements of EMU and the need for freely functioning markets. In all three cases, political leaders have attempted to push through reforms to address these issues but the reforms have not gone far enough and/or have been amended in the face of their general unpopularity or looming local or national elections.

Each of the big three has its own problems. Italy, for example, depends disproportionately on small, specialist manufacturing firms in sectors such as textiles, furniture, machine tools, food processing and white goods. These industries are relatively low tech and low skilled, need a low cost base to sustain their competitiveness and, as such, are particularly vulnerable to competition from CEE and Asia, notably China. Other competitiveness problems stem from poor infrastructure in the south, relatively high energy costs, low levels of R&D spending, a lack of large companies and a preponderance of small, family-owned companies with limited tendencies to merge. Italy traditionally maintained its competitiveness by devaluing the lira. Since 1999, this option has no longer been available and the need for structural reform was no longer hidden.

Political pressures have made reform difficult and they will not become any easier. Nevertheless, the government has made some reform efforts. In July 2004, parliament passed some pension reforms. Italy has a particularly acute problem in relation to its ageing population given its low fertility rates, increasing life expectancy and low labour force participation (see Chapter 13). The 2004 reforms included an increase in the contribution period for entitlement to retire on full pension, incentives to workers to extend their working lives and measures to promote private pensions. In May 2005, competitiveness reforms, including incentives to encourage mergers among SMEs, bankruptcy reforms and some welfare streamlining, were pushed through parliament. Although welcome, these reforms need to be taken much further to achieve sustained competitiveness.

Indeed, Italy could become a test case for the revised SGP. The European Commission has also made known its intention to hold Italy to account for failure to meet the terms of the revised SGP. Such a move, important to the Commission to preserve any lingering credibility of the SGP, could bolster calls by Italy's Welfare Minister, Roberto Maroni, immediately after the French and Dutch referendum rejections of the constitutional treaty in May/June 2005 to reintroduce the lira. Although not a proposition to be taken seriously at the time it was made, particularly as the reintroduction of a depreciating lira would cause Italy's debt service payments to spiral, there remains the possibility that such calls could gain momentum if more substantial reforms are not taken to address Italy's deep-rooted economic problems and the eurozone becomes a scapegoat for these problems.

Germany, too, has its structural problems which, by exacerbating the country's unemployment problems also make its budgetary problems worse, and inhibit its ability to adjust to increased competitive pressures in the absence of national monetary policy. Germany's problems stem, in large part, from its high wage and non-wage costs (see Figure 16.7), high taxes and generous

welfare state (see Chapter 13). In 2003, the government brought forward Agenda 2010, a moderately ambitious set of proposals for structural reforms in public pensions, healthcare and social benefits and the so-called Hartz labour market reforms which, among other things, were designed to end generous benefits for the long-term unemployed, to make it less easy for the unemployed to reject job offers, to put shorter limits on entitlements to unemployment benefit and to rein in the trend to earlier retirements.

Again, domestic political constraints and pressures caused a softening of the proposals and complaints by some that the reforms bring hardship without any benefits, whereas others say the reforms do not go far enough. The 2005 general election brought the more liberal-minded Angela Merkel to power. The full extent of her liberalism will not become clear until she has been in power for some time and she will have to work within the constraints imposed upon her by her coalition partners. Meanwhile, against the background of the threat of possible relocation abroad, several large German companies have negotiated deals with unions that have cut wage costs by forcing wages down, freezing wages or by persuading workers to work longer hours for the same pay.

France, one of the most enthusiastic proponents of the single currency, has also shown an unwillingness to free up its markets and generally deregulate its labour and products markets as implied by the logic of the single currency. Workers, for example, are protected by a high minimum wage, security from lay-offs and a short working week. Consequently, France has also been dogged by fiscal problems and stubbornly high rates of unemployment. The government has partially addressed some of the issues but overall there is an unwillingness to tackle the issues head on and raise the possibility of social conflict. This became apparent in spring 2006 when government attempts to make it easier for employers to hire and fire younger workers met with fierce opposition including large-scale street demonstrations. Indeed, the negative result of the 2005 French referendum on the constitutional treaty has been interpreted by many commentators as a rejection by the French population of the deregulation and liberalisation that has marked the latest phase of European integration and a preference for more protectionism – or 'economic nationalism' – a preference that is at odds with the market integration ideology of the single currency (see Chapter 2).

That reform is possible has been shown by the UK and the Netherlands in the 1980s and by Denmark and Sweden in the 1990s. The short-term impact is frequently painful and consequently carries political risks for the political party introducing reform. However, reform does hold out the possibility for longer term gains. Without reform, the rigidities in the eurozone's biggest economies will get worse, putting greater strain on the system. The danger is that the single currency gets the blame for these problems when, in fact, they have been building up for a number of years and would have come to the forefront even without the existence of the single currency, albeit probably not so quickly. Moreover, the absence of a single currency would not remove the need for reform in a world economy that is rapidly becoming more interdependent and globalised and nor would any attempt to insulate these economies from globalisation result in anything but deteriorating prosperity. In short, the eurozone is suffering from a political failure to implement the policies needed to make it work and needs national politicians with the courage to take these measures.

. . . within EU outsiders

Old outsiders

Three of the EU-15 – Denmark, Sweden and the UK – did not participate in the launch of the single currency. Denmark and the UK have a legal right to opt out of EMU under the TEU. Sweden, which acceded to the EU after the signing of the TEU and therefore was required to accept the *acquis communautaire* at the time, including a commitment to EMU, has no such right but was excluded from the euro on the technical grounds that it was not a member of the ERM. This was politically expedient as the Swedish government felt its population was not ready for EMU.

In all three cases, as Figure 8.2 demonstrates, levels of popular support for the euro are much lower than in the eurozone members. This helps to explain both why the countries were reluctant to join and why their adoption of the euro is not imminent. In September 2000, Denmark held a referendum in which 53 per cent voted against Denmark adopting the euro. In September 2003, 56 per cent of the votes in a Swedish referendum on the single currency were against membership. Consequently, euro membership is off the agenda in both countries for some time. Even though euro approval ratings in Denmark in particular have increased since the referendum, further efforts by the generally pro-euro political elites to take Denmark into the single currency are not likely for some time as the previous referendum itself showed that the possibility of gain was outweighed by the risk of failure.

Each country has its own reasons for not joining but, in general, public debate about the euro in these three countries has expressed concerns about loss of sovereignty,

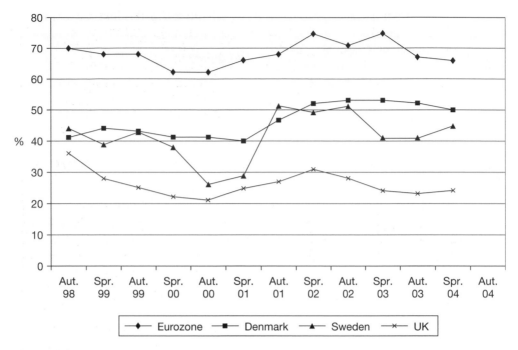

Figure 8.2 *Support for the single currency, 1998–2004*

Source: Eurobarometer.

especially in relation to the loss of monetary policy as a major economic policy instrument, loss of identity and doubts about whether it is possible for one interest rate to suit so many countries. On the other side, in addition to the usual general pro-euro arguments, the outsider countries also have to consider whether their continuing standing aside from the final stage of EMU will ultimately lead to their increasing marginalisation from core EU business.

However, even if the governments of Denmark, Sweden and the UK chose to try to take their countries into the eurozone, they would find it difficult to sell it to their respective populations given the poorer performance of the eurozone economies relative to their own. As the graphs in Figure 8.3 show, GDP growth in the outsider countries

has outstripped that of the eurozone; GDP per head in the outsider countries is above the average for most eurozone countries; the outsiders' unemployment performance is generally much better and inflation is below that of the eurozone. In these circumstances, especially given the tendency of the political elites in the outsider countries to talk up the economic side of the euro and downplay its political dimension, it would be difficult to convince the electorate that there is anything to gain by voting for the euro. There is a view that a sustained period of economic performance significantly below that of the eurozone countries is needed before euro referendums can be won in the outsider countries. Given the problems inherent in the eurozone area (see above), this scenario is unlikely in the short to medium term.

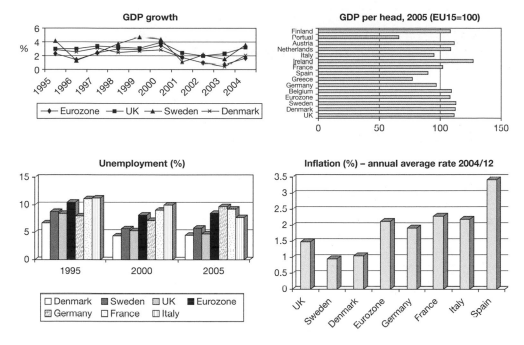

Figure 8.3 Comparative economic performance inside and outside the eurozone
Source: Eurostat.

New outsiders

On 1 May 2004, ten countries joined the EU. All new members accepted the *acquis communautaire*, including participation in the third stage of EMU with a derogation regarding adoption of the single currency. Moreover, the populations of the new member states have implicitly given their consent to eurozone membership by virtue of their 'yes' votes in the 2003 accession referendums as commitment to join the single currency was part of the bargain for joining. Opinion polls confirmed this: as accession approached, according to Eurobarometer, 58 per cent of the population of the new member states were in favour of single currency membership, ranging from 46 per cent in Estonia to 81 per cent in Slovenia.

The new member states have announced their intention to join the single currency as

soon as possible. The key issue for them is not *if* they join but *when*. In order to join, the new members must meet the Maastricht convergence criteria, including a minimum of two years in ERM II. It is likely there will be two waves of eurozone entry. The first will involve the smaller new members: Estonia, Lithuania and Slovenia joined ERM II in June 2004 and Cyprus, Latvia and Malta followed suit in April 2005. Assuming the absence of any major currency upheavals in the two years following their ERM entry, the first new member states could adopt the euro by 2007.

The second wave of new country entrants will comprise the larger new member states – Poland, Hungary and the Czech and Slovak Republics. These countries are bedevilled by persistent fiscal problems and the associated social welfare costs and political problems arising from attempts to resolve these

Case Study 8.1

OPTING OUT OF EMU: THE CASE OF THE UK

The UK's decision to opt out of the initial moves to EMU is significant given that it is the world's fourth largest economy and the EU's second largest. Moreover, the UK is not only the headquarters and primary EU location for many major multinational companies but is also, through the City of London, Europe's major European financial centre. In addition to the standard arguments made against single currency membership (loss of sovereignty, one monetary policy cannot fit all, etc.), several arguments specific to the UK are often made against UK membership. These include:

■ *Trade*: the UK has a lower level of intra-EU trade than other member states so is more vulnerable to external shocks. While it is certainly true that the UK has the lowest level of intra-EU trade in the EU, the majority of its trade (56 per cent) is still with other EU members, only three percentage points behind Italy and eight behind Germany. In short, this argument can be overstated.

■ *Personal sector*: the UK has one of the highest percentages of home owners in the EU and British mortgage holders are more dependent on variable rate mortgages than in other EU countries, making UK interest rates much more responsive to housing markets than is the case elsewhere in the EU.

■ *Oil*: the UK's position as an oil producer and exporter means the UK is affected differently by oil price movements, making asymmetric shocks more probable in a eurozone including the EU. The power of this argument is declining in line with the depletion of North Sea oil and the gradual transition of the UK from being a net energy exporter to a net energy importer.

That the UK opted out of EMU came as no surprise given the lack of public and political support for the project. The low level of public support is demonstrated in Figure 8.2. However, it is worth noting that for the majority of the British public, the single currency does not rank very highly as an important issue, raising questions about the depth of anti-euro feeling among the UK populace.

Business in the UK has tended to hold less polarised views. Foreign investors are the most 'pro-euro', especially if they view their investment as a platform for access to the SEM. Indeed, several foreign investors in the UK have warned that the UK's continuing absence from the eurozone will lead to mainland Europe rather than the UK being the first choice destination for future investment. Figure 8.4 shows the trend of inward investment in the EU since the early 1990s when the UK, along with France, was the main destination for inward FDI. The UK was even more dominant towards the end of the 1990s. Since then, the UK has been overtaken as a source of FDI by several EU countries. Although this is far from conclusive evidence that concerns about inward FDI if the UK stayed outside the eurozone were justified, the early indications are that the UK has lost its position as the major destination for inward investment in the EU, and it is likely that a major part of this loss is down to non-participation in the eurozone.

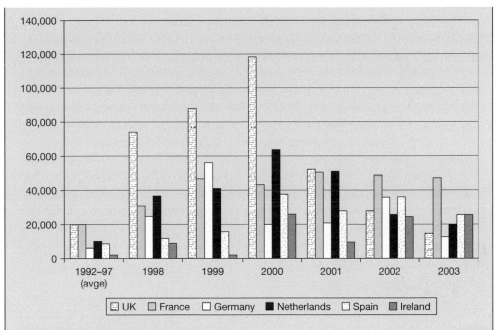

Figure 8.4 Inward FDI (US$m)

Source: UNCTAD, *World Investment Report.*

Larger UK companies, on the whole, have tended to be pro- rather than anti-euro, although there are several high-profile contrary examples. Smaller UK companies have a greater tendency to be anti-euro but, again, there are many exceptions to this.

Even with the UK outside the single currency area, British business cannot ignore the euro. A number of big EU groups active in the UK, as well as major UK enterprises, shifted their accounting to the euro from 1999. Once multinationals alter their business processes to account for the euro so the pressures upon SMEs to alter their processes grow. Despite the fact that operating dual currency systems is expensive, this cost is more than out-weighed by potential losses from ignoring the euro. Whatever their opinions upon EMU, UK businesses cannot ignore it as non-membership can act as a constraint upon their competitiveness within core EU markets.

Concerns have also been highlighted about the potential relative decline of the City of London as Europe's main financial centre if the UK decides to sustain its exclusion from the euro. The impact upon employment within the City depends upon its ability to capture a share of the market for euro securities. The fear is that new investment and the focus of banks could shift towards Frankfurt at the expense of London. Others doubt this, noting that the UK is a centre for international, not just European, business. Thus global, rather than intra-European, competition is more of a threat. Some feel that the presence of skilled workers and the ability of the City of London to be innovative and exist in 'unofficial markets' as well as global markets means that EMU may deliver more benefits than costs.

British political parties are also divided. The Liberal Democrats are the most enthusiastic Europeans and single currency supporters. The Conservative Party, torn apart by its divisions on Europe during its final years in government in the 1990s, contains a wide range of Euro sceptics, from a minority advocating total withdrawal to those arguing that integration should go as far as the SEM and no further. A small, but nonetheless deeply committed, minority support euro membership. The ruling Labour Party equally provides a home for all sides of the euro debate but European divisions have not inflicted fundamental damage on the party as is the case with the Conservatives. However, the overwhelming stance of Labour is supportive of Europe and the euro, a major turnaround from the early 1980s when the official policy was withdrawal. The official position of the government is that it is 'in principle' supportive of the idea of UK adoption of the euro but it will not entertain UK membership until the time is right economically. In order to determine when this will be, and in addition to the Maastricht criteria, the UK government has set out the following five economic tests or questions that must be satisfactorily answered before it takes the UK into the eurozone:

1 *Convergence*: are business cycles and economic structures compatible with European interest rates on a permanent basis?
2 *Flexibility*: if problems emerge, is there sufficient flexibility to deal with them?
3 *Investment*: would membership of the eurozone create better conditions for firms making long-term decisions to invest in the UK?
4 *Financial services*: what impact does joining the eurozone have on the UK's financial services industry?
5 *Growth, stability and employment*: will joining the euro promote higher growth, stability and a lasting increase in jobs?

In June 2003, Chancellor Gordon Brown concluded that, although progress had been made towards satisfying the five tests, only the test on financial services had been passed and therefore it was not in the economic interests for the UK to join at that point. During the 2005 election campaign, Prime Minister Tony Blair appeared to rule out UK adoption of the euro for the foreseeable future. Indeed, given the UK's better all-round economic performance than the eurozone (see Figure 8.3) and the problems in the eurozone, business pressure to join has eased off and in the mid-2000s, UK membership of the single currency appears much lower on the political agenda than it has been for some time. In short, for now at least, the euro has become a non-issue in Britain.

Case questions

1 In the mid-2000s, UK adoption of the euro is further away than ever. Why might this be the case?
2 How might UK business be damaged by continuing exclusion from the eurozone?
3 What benefits might continuing exclusion from the eurozone bring to UK business?
4 Discuss the political and economic role of the 'five tests' in determining whether the UK should join the eurozone.
5 To what extent does the 'distinctiveness' of the UK economy justify its continuing absence from the eurozone?

problems. Accordingly, their dates for potential euro membership have been retreating. In mid-May 2004, for example, Hungary announced postponement of the target date of euro entry from 2008 to 2010 as a result of its higher than forecast inflation and budget deficit. The Czech and Slovak Republics are looking at 2009–10 and 2008–10 respectively as their target entry dates, and Poland is unlikely to be ready before then.

In short, there will be a minimum of five to six years for the larger countries between EU accession and adoption of the single currency. This period could be longer if these countries shy away from difficult political decisions regarding fiscal reform. In the interim, there is sufficient time for any gap between expectations of EU membership and the reality to become apparent to the populace of these countries, thereby creating the conditions for a backlash against eurozone membership and a divergence between elite and popular support for eurozone membership. Moreover, the longer the gap between accession referendum and a serious attempt to join the single currency, the more the euro legitimacy of the accession referenda will fade, possibly leading to demands for a euro-specific poll.

In terms of the nominal Maastricht convergence criteria, the new member states are differentially placed. As stated above, the larger states have greater problems meeting the fiscal criteria and, in general, inflation accelerated somewhat in 2004, creating problems for some countries where previously there was none. However, the inflation problems were created by higher oil prices (which affect all European countries to a degree and thus do not necessarily represent a deterioration in the relative position of the new member states vis-à-vis current eurozone members) and by one-off accession-related tax reforms and other price increases that will drop out of the inflation figures within a year.

With regard to real convergence, the new member states are growing significantly more quickly than the older member states (see Chapter 16) and, indeed, need to do so for many years before their economic levels are broadly comparable. Given the massive economic reform processes that the majority of new member states have gone through since 1989, several of them have better credentials regarding product market flexibility and liberalisation and deregulation generally than older member states. They do tend to suffer from labour market inflexibility and high levels of unemployment. The former have not been helped by the transition periods imposed on free movement by most old member states. By the mid-2000s, unemployment remained high in many cases despite rapid economic growth. This is because growth has taken place within a context of ongoing structural reform with the result that job creation was often offset by the loss of jobs in sectors undergoing reform. Moreover, growth has been accompanied by productivity improvements originating from restructuring. Although bad for employment in the short term, improved productivity performance is essential for the long-term competitiveness of these countries and will ultimately help them compete in the eurozone and beyond.

The entry of the new member states into the eurozone depends on their compliance with the convergence criteria but it may also be affected by factors such as how the existing eurozone members respond to their current challenges. For example, how meaningful will the revised SGP be? Will eurozone growth remain fitful and below that of its main economic competitors? If it does, will the attractiveness of the eurozone as a way of boosting growth, trade and investment diminish and undermine efforts to take the countries into the area? Will the predominantly pro-European government coalitions in the new member states be replaced by governments with less enthusiasm for the European project? So, although the prospects for these countries to become eurozone members looked promising at the time of their accession, there are several factors that could derail euro adoption for at least some of them.

OUTLOOK

The early years of the single currency were largely successful. However, fiscal indiscipline, the persistent poor performance of the eurozone's biggest economies and their slowness/failure to undertake the necessary structural reforms to improve their competitiveness and to create the optimal environment for EMU coupled with the blow dealt to the whole European project by the French and Dutch rejection of the constitutional treaty in mid-2005 have raised a question mark, albeit as yet a small one, over the long-term health of the eurozone.

The ratification failure of the constitutional treaty should not, in itself, damage EMU. The business of the EU will continue as usual. The threat from the rejection of the treaty stems from doubts and differences about the long-term future of the EU and from the interpretation of the treaty rebuff as a revolt, at least on the part of France, against the liberalising, open market approach of much EU policy to date. This links to the most urgent challenge to EMU – the resolution of the competitive problems of key eurozone economies via painful but needed micro-economic reform in terms of labour and product markets. Failure to do this will, eventually, put intolerable strains on the single currency area. Appropriate action by the member states concerned is certainly probable: they showed tremendous political commitment to get EMU off the ground in the first place and failure to carry the project through would carry extremely high costs as well.

In the shorter to more medium term, it is unlikely that the 'old' EMU outsiders – Denmark, Sweden and the UK – will take any significant steps to adopt the single currency. There is no immediate incentive for them to do so. In the longer term, if their relative economic positions vis-à-vis the current EMU members change, or if they find themselves increasingly marginalised from EU business, their single currency membership cannot be ruled out. The 'new' outsiders (that is, the ten 2004 accession states) have, without exception, expressed their intention to join the eurozone as soon as possible and their commitment remains strong.

KEY POINTS

■ From a business perspective, EMU facilitates trade and investment and generally reinforces the market integration theme of earlier integration initiatives.

■ Reform of the SGP has taken place but the jury is out on whether its credibility has been irreversibly undermined.

■ Improvements in labour and product market flexibility are required in several euro members if EMU is to succeed. Some of the bigger states, in particular, are finding it politically difficult to introduce the needed reforms.

■ In the mid-2000s, adoption of the single currency does not appear to be an option in the short to medium term for Denmark, Sweden and the UK.

■ Adoption of the euro looks a real possibility within two to three years of accession for the smaller 2004 accession states whereas the larger new member states will have to wait longer.

ACTIVITIES

1 Choose one of the ten 2004 accession states and research their preparations for, and potential gains from, EMU membership. Also identify the risks that EU membership exposes them to.

2 In a classroom, organise a debate in which one side puts forward the case for UK adoption of the euro and the other puts the case against.

3 Choose France, Italy or Germany and research their efforts to pursue key economic reforms. Although it can be argued, the need for economic reforms existed before the euro and are needed for broader competitiveness reasons, consider how and why the reforms are also linked to the success of EMU.

4 Research a European company and consider how the existence of the euro might have an influence upon its strategy and operations. Companies ranging from global multinationals to SMEs based either in or outside the eurozone are suitable for this exercise as they will all be affected in some way, albeit differently. In a classroom context, individual students or groups of students can be allocated a different company and asked to present their findings to the class. Their findings can then be compared and contrasted to pull out the similarities and differences. Note: issues to look at include location in or out of the eurozone; location of suppliers and markets; characteristics of the sector; relative share of activities in the eurozone. For non-eurozone companies, to what extent do they utilise the euro? etc., etc.

185

QUESTIONS FOR DISCUSSION

1 'Present policies, institutional arrangements and political attitudes are incompatible with a sustainable economic and monetary union in the long run' (*FT* 8 June 2005, p. 17).

   Explain and comment upon this statement in the light of the challenges currently facing the eurozone.

2 'The reform of the Stability and Growth Pact has rendered it useless as a mechanism for fiscal discipline within the single currency area.' Explain why this statement may have been made. Do you agree with it (make sure you justify your answer)? What do events since the 2005 reform tell us about its success or failure?

3 In what way has EMU changed Europe's business environment?

4 What are the main dangers to the long-term success of the single currency?

5 'EMU is as much a political as an economic project.' Do you agree? Explain your answer.

SUGGESTIONS FOR FURTHER READING

Ardy, B., Begg, I., Hodson, D., Mahe, I. and Mayes, D. (eds) (2005) *Adjustment to EMU: One Europe or Several?*, Basingstoke: Palgrave Macmillan.

Backé, P., Thimann, C., Arratibel, O., Calvo-Gonzalez, O., Mehl A. and Nehrlich, C. (2004) 'The Acceding Countries' Strategies towards ERM II and the Adoption of the Euro: An Analytical Review', ECB Occasional Paper Series, No. 10. Frankfurt: European Central Bank, http://www.ecb.int/pub/.

Brown, B. (2004) 'Exiting EMU', *The International Economy*, 18 (2), pp. 57–60.

Commission of the European Communities (2004) 'EMU after Five Years', *European Economy*, Special Report, Number 1/2004, http://europa.eu.int/comm/economy_finance/publications/european_economy/2004/eesp104en.pdf.

De Grauwe, P. (2002) 'Challenges for Monetary Policy in Euroland', *Journal of Common Market Studies*, 40 (4), pp. 693–718.

De Grauwe, P. (2005) *The Economics of Monetary Union*, 6th edn, Oxford: Oxford University Press.

De Grauwe, P. and Kouretos, G. (2004) 'EMU: Current State and Future Prospects', *Journal of Common Market Studies*, 42 (4), pp. 679–89.

De Grauwe, P. and Schnabl, G. (2004) 'EMU Entry Strategies for the New Member States', *Intereconomics*, 39 (5), pp. 241–7.

Duckenfield, M. (2006) *Business and the Euro: Business Groups and the Politics of EMU in Britain and Germany*, Basingstoke: Palgrave Macmillan.

European Central Bank (2004) *European Central Banks: History, Role and Functions*, http://www.ecb.int/pub/pdf/other/ecbhistoryrolefunctions2004en.pdf.

Feuerstein, S. and Grimm, O. (2004) 'The Road to Adopting the Euro', *Intereconomics*, 39 (2), pp. 76–83.

Gabel, M. and Hix, S. (2005) 'Understanding Public Support for British Membership of the Single Currency', *Political Studies*, 53 (1), pp. 65–81.

Hayo, B. (2003) 'European Monetary Policy: Institutional Design and Policy Experience', *Intereconomics*, 38 (4), pp. 209–18.

Hermann, S. and Jochem, A. (2003) 'Real and Nominal Convergence in the Central and East European Accession Countries', *Intereconomics*, 38 (6), pp. 323–7.

Intereconomics (2003) 38 (1) – four articles on the Stability and Growth Pact.

Intereconomics (2004) 39 (5) – three articles on the eastwards enlargement of the eurozone.

Intereconomics (2005) 40 (1) – four articles on reform of the Stability and Growth Pact.

Journal of Common Market Studies (2000) *Taking Stock of EMU*, whole issue, 38 (4).

Journal of European Integration (2005) 27 (1) – whole issue on EU members outside the eurozone.

Louis, J. (2004) 'The Economic and Monetary Union: Law and Institutions', *Common Market Law Review*, 4 (2), pp. 575–608.

Schwartz, A. (2004) 'Risks to the Long Term Stability of the Euro', *Atlantic Economic Journal*, 32 (1), pp. 1–10.

Tanzi, V. (2004) 'The Stability and Growth Pact: Its Role and Future', *Cato Journal*, 24 (1/2), pp. 57–69.

Tavlas, G. (2004) 'Benefits and Costs of Entering the Eurozone', *Cato Journal*, 24 (1/2), pp. 89–106.

Trichet, J.-C. (2001) 'The Euro after Two Years', *Journal of Common Market Studies*, 39 (1), pp. 1–13.

Yeager, L. (2004) 'The Euro Facing Other Moneys', *Cato Journal*, 24 (1/2), pp. 27–40.

Key websites

There are many sites on EMU – the following is merely a selection.

The Commission's EMU website: http://europa.eu.int/comm/economy_finance/index_en.htm

The European Central Bank's website: www.ecb.int

The website of the *Financial Times*: http://specials.ft.com/euro/index.html

Chapter 9

Trans-European networks

Building an infrastructure for Europe

> When you don't invest in infrastructure, you are going to pay sooner or later.
>
> Mike Parker, former Assistant US Secretary of the Army for
> Civil Works, speaking in 2005 after Hurricane Katrina

This chapter will help you to:

- understand the concept of TENs;
- understand the importance of supporting infrastructures to the process of European integration;
- identify the major policy themes and priorities within the TENs programme;
- appreciate the changing policy shifts within the TENs programme over the past decade;
- identify the major achievements and problems within the TENs programme.

Throughout the early to mid-1990s, TENs were very much the EU's 'big' idea. Against a background of high and rising unemployment, TENs offered a way both to generate short-term employment and to boost the competitive positioning of businesses within the EU. The ultimate rationale was that if mobility was to work to the benefit of European business, then the rights of mobility guaranteed in law under the SEM had to be matched in practice via series of infrastructures across the transport, telecom-munications and energy sectors. Securing mobility via infrastructure required the transitional development and orientation of three inter-related network components:

- *Nodes/hubs*: geographically fixed points on a network infrastructure that allow for the collection, coordination and distribution of tangible and intangible products around the network. Examples of nodes are power stations, telephone exchanges, rail stations, airports, etc.

- *Links*: the physical pathways/means of moving materials or providing services between hubs/nodes or between hubs/nodes and the end user. Links are differentiated between fixed links (such as gas pipelines, electricity transmission lines, road and rail links, etc.) and flexible links (such as rolling stock, etc.).
- *Services*: much of the value to business from a network derives directly from the services delivered across the network to the end user. These include transport services, natural gas and electricity supply and all forms of telecommunication services.

As individual network sectors are dealt within in more detail elsewhere (see Chapters 10, 11 and 12), the aim of this chapter is to underline the importance of infrastructure for the development of European business. It offers a political and economic rationale for the development of a coherent policy for the development of pan-European infrastructure under the TENs programme. While an examination of the key network sectors is undertaken, the emphasis is upon common themes and problems inherent in the development of these infrastructures.

THE COMMERCIAL IMPORTANCE OF NETWORK INFRASTRUCTURE

Infrastructure evolution has been pivotal in defining the form and nature of the commercial development of the European economy. As the European economy has evolved, so the supporting infrastructure has had to adapt to changing requirements in terms of mobility and accessibility. Different stages of economic development placed unique demands upon the supporting infrastructure. Four such broad periods can be identified:

- *the Hanseatic Period*: (from the thirteenth to the sixteenth century) based upon inland and coastal waterways connecting cities along rivers and coastal areas in Northern and Western Europe;
- *the Golden Age*: (from the sixteenth to the eighteenth century) based upon big improvements in maritime transport systems;
- *the Industrial Revolution:* (from the middle of the nineteenth century to the First World War) in which the invention of the steam engine revolutionised transport systems;
- *the Information Revolution*: (from the 1970s onwards) in which the development of advanced telecommunications infrastructure has promoted new industries and growth.

Through these transformations, the link between economic development and infrastructure has become well understood by policy makers and has provided the rationale for infrastructure policy and state involvement in its development.

At the firm, industry and economy levels, the core benefits from infrastructure are derived from the quality and quantity of the service provided over it. The key function of infrastructure is to compress space in terms of both cost and time through the provision of network services between physically separate locations. This function rationalises policy formation to stimulate increased investment in the provision of infrastructure to support the more efficient delivery of network services through spatially dispersed markets. Overall, policy makers see a direct link between infrastructure, service quality and industrial performance.

Figure 9.1 offers a value chain perspective of the role of networks. In this context, infrastructure networks are pivotal to firm operations through the ease with which inputs, outputs and internal resource mobility (especially important when a business is located over several sites) are supported. The interlinkages with other firms and resource flows between them grow ever more complex when analysis starts to focus in on value networks.

The realisation of cost and performance benefits from the development of TENs is closely related to the progressive liberalisation of service provision within the network sectors. This underlines that infrastructure provision alone is not sufficient to deliver the benefits expected from its development. This concern is especially notable in Europe as the EU seeks to move from a fragmented infrastructure system to one that reflects the following concerns:

■ *the volume effect*: the need for infrastructure to support the anticipated increases in trade associated with liberalisation;

■ *the interoperability requirement*: the need for physical and technical network compatibility of networks to ensure interoperability;

■ *the dimension effect*: the recognition, within national planning systems, that the development of infrastructure has effects beyond the borders of the nation state concerned;

■ *the quality requirement*: TENs are needed to ensure the quality of network services to sustain the competitive position of European business;

■ *the cohesion effect*: the impact of infrastructure provision upon attempts to promote more even business development across the European economic space.

Concerns in network development reflect the need for enterprises to take advantage of the opportunities for efficient transnational production, to exploit the international division of labour and to facilitate just-in-time production techniques. This is, of course, in addition to the fact that these networks are a representation of the physical mobility and

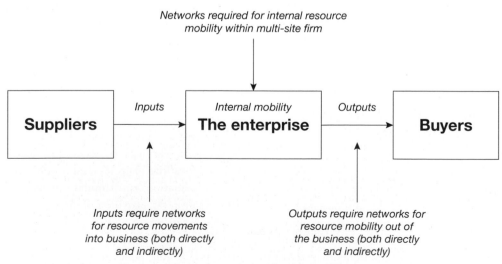

Figure 9.1 A value chain representation of the importance of networks

Source: Derived from Johnson and Turner 1997.

Case Study 9.1

THE LOGISTICS OF THE AIRBUS 380

There is, perhaps, no better example of the importance of infrastructure to the commercial development of Europe than the Airbus 380. The Airbus 380 is the world's largest passenger aircraft and is able to carry up to 555 passengers on a 14,800 km journey. The aircraft is manufactured by 6,000 Airbus employees throughout Europe at 15 different sites across four states with much of the manufacturing taking place at purpose-built sites. The breakdown of construction by nation is as follows:

France: the nose is made at Saint Nazaire; the fuselage and cockpit sub-assemblies are
    constructed at Méaulte and the final assembly occurs in Toulouse.
Spain: the horizontal stabilisers with the rudder are made in Puerto Real and the
    horizontal tail plane is made in Getafe.
UK: the wings and associated components are made in Broughton, Wales.
Germany: seven facilities are responsible for manufacturing and assembling fuselage parts,
    for cabin installation, painting (Hamburg) and the tailfin (Stade).

The dispersed manufacturing system is organised around the assembly of large modules already equipped with wiring, hydraulic and fuel systems, and air conditioning brought in from multiple locations. Each location has a centre of excellence reflecting the need to share work around the Airbus consortium members and to tap into government support.

Given this dispersal and the focus on assembly in Toulouse, Airbus faces the logistical problem of moving large sections of the plane around Europe to converge on a single location at a given time. Consequently, not only does work across locations need to be closely synchronised but components need to be moved around Europe to coincide with the assembly schedule. This places different demands upon infrastructure. In the construction of components, the sheer scale of the A380 necessitated the development of specific facilities within each of the above locations. However, moving components places even larger demands on local and transnational infrastructure. Prior to the Airbus 380, the company moved components around the construction and assembly plants via its own Beluga aircraft. However, the size of the A380 and its components made a new logistical system necessary as only the tail assemblies were transportable by air.

The logistical process takes a number of discrete steps from manufacturing to assembly. First of all, the fuselage section is taken by ship from Hamburg to Mostyn in Wales where a set of wings is taken on board. In each location, special port facilities had to be constructed to cope with the scale of the operation. Thereafter, the ship heads to St Nazaire which acts as a de facto ante-chamber to the full assembly. At St Nazaire, the forward section of the nose fuselage is constructed and joined to the rear part of the section sent from Hamburg and Wales. In addition, other components built in France (such as the wing box in Nantes) and the components manufactured in Spain are transported to St Nazaire. These components are assembled and then transferred to specially constructed roll on/roll off barges for an inland waterway trip to Langon. A total of four barge journeys is required to transport the six very large sections needed to produce an A380. These journeys will increase from 30 in 2004 to around 200 a year in 2008 when one aircraft will be produced a week. The sections are then trucked the last 200 kilometres to Toulouse. Some sections of the road had to be re-built at the cost of €171 million to enable the extra-wide trailers to pass: 43 per cent of the finance came from the French state and the rest from Airbus. This final journey takes three days and takes place at night to avoid local traffic.

However, the infrastructure pressures of the A380 do not stop at assembly. Many airports simply do not have the runways to cope with the A380. This should be solved in time but an issue remains regarding the ability of hub facilities to cope with the logistics of handling the A380. First, many do not have the space to park the A380. Moreover, the A380 has two entrances to handle the smooth access of passengers to and from the plane and needs two gangways extending from the same terminal. Only a few airports currently have this facility. In addition, given passenger capacity of the A380, facilities to cope with checkin and security could prove problematic. Indeed, if two or more A380s land at the same time, it could take almost a day to process passengers and find their luggage.

Case questions

1   What does the experience of Airbus indicate about the need to develop transnational infrastructure?

2   How does the case reflect interdependencies between national infrastructure systems?

3   Are there any lessons from this case for the broader development of TENs?

accessibility required by the legal changes resulting from the SEM.

Potential benefits from the development of TENs in terms of enterprise performance explain why the issue rose up the EU's agenda. These networks are powerful factors in promoting the economic convergence associated with the development of a more capacious, efficient and evenly developed series of infrastructure networks. The issue of even development is important given that the services delivered by these infrastructures are of generic interest across the socio-economic spectrum: communication, mobility and access to energy are necessities for modern-day living. These public interest concerns can, and do, operate as a constraint upon the liberalisation of network services

and have the potential to undermine the competitive benefit to enterprises derived from the development of these advanced infrastructures. However, these concerns have, to some degree, been allayed by the Services of General Interest Directive which seeks to ensure that such services are provided in a market-driven framework.

THE EMERGENCE OF TENs

As stated above, the emergence of TENs was a derivative of the moves within Europe towards the creation of the SEM. Indeed, meeting the concerns of enterprises to exploit the opportunities of the internationalising markets was initially very much the dominant theme of the EU's infrastructure strategy. Explicit powers to develop these networks were formally given within Title XII of the TEU (also known as 'the Maastricht Treaty') (see Box 9.1).

The TEU provides a legal basis for TENs. Under the terms of Chapter XV of the Treaty (Articles 154, 155 and 156), the EU must aim to promote the development of TENs as a key element in the creation of the Internal Market and in the reinforcement of economic and social cohesion. This development includes the interconnection and interoperability of national networks as well as access to such networks. To realise these objectives, the Community has developed guidelines covering the priorities, identification of projects of common interest and broad lines of measures for the three sectors concerned (transport, energy and telecommunications). The EP and the Council must approve these guidelines after consulting the ESC and the Committee of the Regions.

The emphasis of TENs extends beyond meeting the requirements of the SEM to become a more all-embracing policy that directly complements and involves other themes of integration. More importantly, TENs has become a key feature of the EU's

strategy for competitiveness insofar as they enable firms to derive greater value-added from infrastructure. The adaptation of the underpinning rationale for TENs is born of the osmotic process of interaction between national infrastructures. Increased user demand (largely driven by increased freedom of movement) for national and transnational infrastructure has created a situation in which commercial interest in the condition of a state's infrastructure is not solely the concern of indigenous enterprises. Such spillovers highlight the need for movement towards a set of integrated infrastructures that aid mobility and accessibility in a broader context than previously defined: that is, national infrastructures become mere sub-groups of a broader international network of networks.

While Europe has recognised the interdependencies between national infrastructures, national planners need to take a broader perspective of the development of domestic infrastructures (see below). The lack of a transnational dimension is reflected in a number of deficiencies across networks:

- *Nodes (such as airports)*: these are usually developed to meet national needs and access to them is often impeded by

---

TITLE XII – TRANS-EUROPEAN NETWORKS

BOX 9.1

Article 154, paragraph 2

This title outlines not only the role of the Commission in the development of TENs but also the priorities of such networks, namely that:

- their development should be market led and financed;
- these networks should be physically integrated;
- the networks should, even where not interconnected, be compatible with each other to facilitate future integration;
- access to these networks should be as broad as possible to ensure the aims of economic and social cohesion.

national laws and regulations. This is compounded by the inability of certain nodes to deal with the rising interactions across space.

- *Links (such as pipelines and roads)*: many of the links needed to meet the requirements of the SEM either do not exist or are inadequate to meet the demands placed upon them. Within many states, networks tend to be based upon a national core–periphery model radiating from capital cities and declining in quality and intensity as frontiers approach. This is inadequate as cross-border interaction increases.
- *Services (such as passenger and freight movements)*: a lack of compatibility between networks hinders the functionality and value-added derived from the network. The value to businesses from network services will be complemented by the liberalisation of service provision.

Within the market-driven framework established by the TEU, the Commission outlined a range of priority projects to alleviate bottlenecks in core regions and to bring peripheral areas more closely into the hub of the European economy. While these themes are very much linked to the benefits of physical mobility derived from TENs, policy has also evolved to stress the economic and social benefits from infrastructure linked to the emergence of the knowledge economy. Policy has started to emphasise the importance of intangible mobility as a priority recognising its broad impact across a range of EU policies. However, such a shift in policy also reflects a more realistic TENs policy as the introduction of the euro and enlargement has left the EU otherwise engaged. Over time, the EU has moved away from grand initiatives towards the more practical task of making existing integration plans work.

In framing TENs in the context of the Lisbon Strategy, solutions at the EU level towards the development of TENs were considerably curtailed. In this case, policy sought to focus on pushing for more open markets in all network services, on developing market-based charging mechanisms for infrastructure, on seeking to address remaining inconsistencies and fragmentation (such as in air traffic control) and on utilising existing infrastructure better. Thus the policy is more focused, a lot less of a 'grand idea' and considerably more pragmatic. Of especial note is that the financing offered by the EU is more concentrated than under previous programmes with a focus on 30 priority projects.

THE NETWORK SECTORS: GENERIC THEMES AND POLICIES

Unlike most industrial companies, utilities have, to date, tended to remain nationally focused with an emphasis upon meeting domestic demand. This approach has been compounded by regulatory structures that have governed network management and reinforced this national focus. However, this national focus is changing as liberalisation across these sectors becomes more prevalent. As enterprises start to operate internationally and as utilities begin to exercise rights of entry in other markets so the interdependencies between national networks (see Figure 9.1, p. 190) become more evident.

Most of the priorities within the TENs programme have focused upon strengthening links as opposed to upgrading nodes. This is due to:

- the spatial fixation of TENs;
- the greater ability of nodes to attract commercial funding;

- concerns that EU intervention may distort inter-nodal competition.

Across the network sectors involved in the development of TENs, a number of themes and generic concerns were apparent within the priorities established by the European Commission.

Transport

The needs of transport infrastructure cut across diverse modes to contribute to the goal of sustainable mobility, implying that each of the networks (road, rail, inland waterways, coastal shipping, airlines and integrated transport) should complement each other (see Chapter 10). Indeed, to help transport flows, these networks were also aided by developments in other network sectors, most notably by efforts to apply telecommunications technology to traffic management.

Priority projects within the transport sector reflect a political compromise among member states (which are keen to get hold of Commission funding to develop domestic infrastructure), thereby highlighting the national as opposed to transnational basis of the plans. Priority projects also need to be compatible with the objectives of a more environmentally friendly transport system: this is reflected in the relative priority given to rail over road infrastructure in terms of Commission funding. The aim is to reduce the dependence on roads for the bulk of freight and passenger traffic (see Chapter 10): a dominance that has been accentuated by the increased provision of better roads within the core regions of the EU.

The Essen Council identified 14 priority projects and invited states to take the steps needed for their realisation in terms of administration, regulation and legislation.

Generally, the priority projects fall into two broad categories:

- those designed to relieve congestion in the core of the EU such as the Paris–Brussels–Cologne–Amsterdam–London high-speed rail network;
- those intended to lessen the isolation of peripheral regions.

Decision 1692/96/EC set a completion date of 2010 for the priority projects. By 2003, only three of the Essen projects had been completed with a further five expected to be finished by 2010. However, it is anticipated that substantial sub-sections of the six remaining projects will be complete.

In 2003, the High Level Group reporting on Transport TENs reported that effective transport was not solely about building infrastructure but also about more effective usage. The group selected a restricted number of projects across the expanded EU for support. It afforded such projects the label of 'priority project' to create more effective and coordinated financial support. To this end, it has identified 22 new priority projects proposed by states up to 2020. The main priorities are to:

- improve use of existing networks through the use of the Galileo project to aid satellite navigation;
- sustained focus on rail;
- aid cross-border movement and overcome physical obstacles such as the Alps.

To add impetus to their development, the group proposed that coordinators be appointed on certain projects.

Energy

The central theme of energy TENs is to ensure the security of supply at a reasonable cost for European business (see Chapter 11). The aim is to broaden the supply of energy in some member states (for example, by extending gas to Portugal and Greece – one of the first achievements of energy TENs) and to ensure that all areas have access to a diverse array of energy sources. The development of this network is also closely linked with the liberalisation of energy markets to ensure that rights of access and transit are facilitated. However, the liberalisation process has developed intermittently across the EU (see Chapter 11).

The development of the energy TENs sector is related to the interconnection of gas and electricity networks and to increased competition within these sectors. Generally, the core themes are to integrate national infrastructure and to extend networks to ensure a diverse and secure energy supply throughout the EU. The specific themes within each sector are outlined below.

Electricity: the concern here is interconnection between areas ensuring that all parts of the area can be supplied from anywhere else within the EU. This underlines the apparent close linkages between liberalisation and the notion of security of supply. Furthermore, the EU wishes to ensure access to energy sources by the more remote areas, an essential prerequisite for any business wishing to locate in these areas, and integration of European electricity networks with external networks. The most recent guidelines sought to extend these concerns by looking to integrate the new Eastern European states into the electricity grid. The programmes are built around a number of axes where interconnection is inadequate. These axes are designed to remove congestion and secure the security of supply.

Gas: a major concern about gas are the growing imports of gas from external sources such as North Africa and Russia. Thus, a key aim of energy TENs is to enhance energy supply security for the EU. Other objectives of priority projects are to provide access to gas to those peripheral areas that are without it and to connect isolated networks into the main network. In addition to project-related actions, a series of horizontal measures have also been undertaken to identify, manage and control key elements of the emerging energy infrastructure to make them compatible with the objectives of the TENs programme and with the broader industrial strategy.

Telecommunications

Priorities for the development of the telecommunications networks are closely linked to the development of the information society within the EU (see Chapter 12). Information infrastructure is becoming an increasingly important factor in determining the competitiveness of the economy and will have a pervasive effect on the quality of factors of production and markedly alter the cost, time and spatial aspects associated with the emerging global market place.

Initial actions within the TENs programme were designed to meet the information requirements (in areas such as customs, etc.) of administrations in attempting to manage the effects of the SEM. The market-led strategy for the development of networks was based upon achieving a critical mass for these technologies by utilising a core of commercial and semi-commercial applications. The intention was that the success of these applications would lead to the development of services of generic appeal across a broad range of users.

The programme has shifted away from the deployment of infrastructure towards offering support for the roll out of services that contribute to the socially inclusive development of the information society. Thus, there is the desire to push for the development of e-learning etc. Among the plethora of policies developed to support the development of the information society within Europe, the Telecom-TENs programme is focused on 'roll out' issues in areas of evident market failure. As in other sectors, the aim is to undertake a degree of commercial risk to see the programme through to viability. Thus, it takes the generic market failure approach of other sectors within the context of a sector where competition is relatively mature.

THE FINANCING OF TENs

The financing required for infrastructure in the EU is vast. The priority transport projects selected by the EU represent an estimated funding of €235 billion between 2003 and 2020. Of this, nearly €112 billion is required for the initial Essen projects yet to be completed. These sums, if anything, underestimate the scale of the investment needed in EU infrastructure if it is to meet the requirements of the European economy. Indeed, it is estimated that for all projects more than €600 billion needs to be spent (a figure that is exclusive of maintenance costs).

The role of business in the development of TENs is not only as user of network services but increasingly as a provider of the networks themselves. The desire of the EU to involve the private sector in developing infrastructure, when combined with the scale of the resources required, represents the biggest impediment to the realisation of TENs, especially within transport. This is partly driven by the practicalities of an environment where the public sector is retreating (due to fiscal retrenchment, the requirements of EMU, etc.) and does not possess the funding levels required to develop TENs in the manner envisaged within the EU's plans. The problems of attracting commercial investment are not uniform across the sectors involved in the development of TENs:

Telecommunications: this sector has already received substantial investment in infrastructure derived from the onset of competition within the sector. Any financing problems arise from the desire of the public sector to meet, over the short term, the broad socio-economic requirements of the information society (see Chapter 12). Investments in infrastructures to meet the needs of business have little trouble attracting funding.

Energy: in the case of energy, problems of meeting TENs objective arise more from planning and administrative problems than from the inadequacy of financial resources. The private sector has considerable experience of investment in energy TENs.

Transport: this is the sector with the most evident financing problem. The problem of attracting private-sector financing into transport infrastructure is compounded by the commercial risks that developers face, namely:

- in the promotion and preparation stage of the project, there is still no guarantee that the project will take place;
- the high-risk construction phase due to the likelihood of cost overruns throughout the lifetime of the project;
- the uncertain revenues once a project starts operating and the potential for policy changes to undermine the viability of the project.

This situation is compounded by a commercial culture that is not, for the most part, accustomed to investment in large-scale infrastructure projects over the long term and does not readily accept the scale of investment required by transport infrastructure. The banking system has already proved reluctant to offer financing on the scale required and especially over the time horizon (frequently 20 years plus) needed for commercial return from infrastructure. This position is compounded by variations in the ability and experience of banks to finance these projects over the lifespan of the trade cycle. These, and other market failures, have meant that the public sector cannot abrogate responsibility for the development of infrastructure. Consequently, much of the development of transport networks is expected to take place within the context of public private partnerships (PPPs).

Generally, the role of PPPs is to share risk between the public and private sectors, to ensure that the anti-competitive effects of network development are precluded and to sustain a public-service element within network development. This confirms that public-sector support is not only important in terms of finance but is also essential in political terms. For example, regulatory uncertainty can also undermine the viability of a project. The form of the PPP will vary on a case-by-case basis along with the commercial viability of a project. Thus, PPPs need to be developed pragmatically and the nature of public involvement in the development of TENs varies according to:

- the extent to which the developers are state owned;
- the attitude of the state to infrastructure;
- the attitude of the state to commercial investment in infrastructure;

- the opportunity cost of resources devoted to infrastructure;
- the willingness of the private sector to invest in infrastructure;
- the perceived risks of the project;
- the externalities associated with a project.

The PPP represents a balancing issue that revolves around the injection of sufficient public-sector resources into a project to lower risks sufficiently to stimulate the desired levels of private-sector investment. If the public sector does not plough in enough resources or fails to offer other ways of lowering commercial risk, then TENs will not be realised as desired. Such a problem has already been evident throughout the TENs initiative.

THE ROLE OF THE EU

The role of the EU in the development of TENs is defined by the terms of the TEU (see Box 9.1, p. 193) and is very much based upon complementing rather than directly assisting their realisation. Thus, in order to achieve the TENs objectives the EU may, according to the treaty:

- establish a series of guidelines covering the development of TENs of common interest;
- establish measures to achieve the interoperability of networks;
- support the financing of these projects.

There are a number of supranational funding sources for the development of TENs, namely, the Cohesion Fund, the TENs budgetary line and the Structural Funds.

These are complemented by other supranational sources (not directly linked to EU funds), notably:

- the European Investment Fund (EIF);
- the European Investment Bank (EIB).

These sources will not cover the full cost of the development of TENs projects and, as such, merely seek to supplement existing financing, whether from the private or the national public sector.

Any EU financial support is given upon the precondition that the projects are commercially and technologically feasible. The Cohesion Fund and the Structural Funds are directed towards the attainment of a specific objective, namely the promotion of even development within the EU. The most specific measures relate to the TENs budgetary line. The support has to work with commercial operators in the development of projects: hence the conditions of commercial and technological feasibility. This finance is generally used to support and overcome initial uncertainties derived from factors such as an absence of feasibility studies for the prioritised projects. Up to 2006, €700 million was given to TENs via this dedicated budgetary line. It is proposed that this figure be increased for the period 2007–13 to over €20 billion. In addition, it is proposed to increase the co-financing rate from 20 to 30 per cent and, in exceptional cases, 50 per cent where there is a strong cross-border element.

As noted, this finance is merely incidental to the overall levels of funding required for the development of TENs: amounting to around 0.3 per cent of the total needed. Thus, the Commission finds its direct efforts to support TENs severely limited. To maximise its impact, the EU has promoted the Quick Start Programme (QSP) of target funding on projects that are of declared European interest. This is in combination with the increased scope for co-financing. The aim is to kick-start TENs by targeted funding. In line with this objective, the EU has scaled back the number of priority projects deemed to be of European interest. The QSP is focused upon 30 sections of infrastructure that are estimated to cost €38 billion. The aim of the increased focus is to give added certainty to projects and to provide a more solid foundation for PPPs.

In response to the successive EU initiatives identifying TENs in the EU-25 and the remaining accession states, the EIB has scaled up its already heavy involvement in the financing of TENs. The EIB is paying particular attention to the TENs-related part of the QSP, part of the European Action for Growth. Up to €25 billion will be made available in the period 2004–06 for transport TENs, particularly for projects under the QSP. In special cases it will be possible for loans to be granted for up to 75 per cent of the investment costs and for periods of up to 35 years, with flexible repayment terms. In 2004, signed loans in support of TEN projects within the enlarged EU totalled €7.9 billion, of which €6.6 billion were for transport and €1.3 billion for energy projects.

The money to develop TENs does exist within the EU economy: the challenge lies in attracting this finance into the development of these infrastructures. Existing methods are unable to achieve this objective with large gaps in financing remaining. The easy solution to these problems would be to offer more public money. But this is only part of the problem. There still needs to be a clearer regulatory environment for private operators. The insistence of many member states on strong public service commitments within network sectors will inevitably deter commercial involvement. The statement of services of general economic interest should offer some legal certainty to this dilemma. Whatever the problem, the development of these networks requires greater commitment from member states whether in terms of finance, administrative or regulatory support.

The new, more focused efforts by the EU represents a step away from a grand project for TENs and towards a more pragmatic approach based on experience and the fact that the EU is living with the legacy of both enlargement and the introduction of the euro. Given past failures of TENs, the new scheme is less ambitious. The experience of telecoms has shown a link between liberalisation and private financing and infrastructure, a trend that is also evident in energy TENs. The big problem remains transport where even seemingly high-demand projects (such as the Channel Tunnel) have struggled to generate the revenue to justify private-sector finance. In transport, core problems with regard to committing long-term funding with projects with high sunk costs and uncertain traffic flows are evident.

Case Study 9.2

SHORT SEA SHIPPING AND 'MOTORWAYS OF THE SEA'

Under current trends, it is estimated that internal freight movements within the EU-15 will increase by 70 per cent by 2020. This rise is expected to be even sharper in the new member states where they are expected to increase by 95 per cent. Accompanying this trend has been a sharp rise in the rate of growth in short sea shipping which is growing as fast as road freight and increased by 25 per cent during the period 1995–2002. By 2005, short sea shipping carried 41 per cent of tonne kilometres moved in the EU compared to road freight which accounted for 45 per cent. However, the efficiency of road freight is being undermined as congestion continues to rise. Such problems are not apparent in short sea shipping. To support these trends, there is a perceived need to increase the usage of Europe's sea resources to provide a means to by-pass natural barriers such as the Alps and the Pyrenees as well as providing quicker routes between remote regions and by-pass emergent congestion problems.

Consequently, an emerging theme within the TENs programme has been the focus upon 'motorways of the sea' as a means of making better usage of Europe's transport resources. The aim of this programme is to support the concentration of flows of freight on sea routes and divert traffic away from motorways, thereby reducing road congestion as well as improving access to the more remote and difficult to access parts of the EU. Thus, the aim is to create a new intermodal maritime-based logistics chain to support the floating infrastructures of the European seas. The programme targets both facilities and infrastructure concerning at least two ports in two different member states and seeks to influence some element of passenger traffic, although freight remains the dominant focus of supported projects.

The scheme targets four major maritime corridors or 'motorways':

1 *the Baltic Sea Corridor*: linking Nordic states with CEE;
2 *Western Europe*: linking the Iberian Peninsula via the Atlantic to the North and Irish Seas;

3 *south-east Europe*: connecting the Adriatic to the Ionian Sea and the eastern
  Mediterranean;
4 *south-west Europe*: focusing on the western Mediterranean to connect the Southern
  European states and islands via a linking system of ports.

To benefit from Commission support, any initiative to promote investment in one or more
of the constituent parts of these respective corridors has to demonstrate that it promotes
cohesion and/or modal shift. There is also a need to ensure – as a means of securing supranational investment – that the projects are subject to the normal commercial viability tests.
However, it is also important to ensure that any investment to support a facility will not lead
to a distortion of competition either across modes and/or between locations.
  The programme supports key aspects of the motorways of the sea, namely:

■ *infrastructures* – port infrastructures, infrastructures for direct land access and sea
  access as well as access from waterway and canal infrastructures;
■ *facilities* – including electronic logistics management systems, safety, security,
  administrative and custom facilities as well as facilities for ice breaking and dredging
  operations.

For each project, there are a number of conditions that must be met, such as choice regarding ports and intermodal services and corridors, an explicit commitment by all parties to
these projects and the need to stress quality of service to attract users. The aim is to make
the targeted motorways flagships of integrated short sea shipping services that will generate
a critical mass for further investment within and beyond these corridors. As with other TENs
programmes, this requires a PPP to ensure the planning and investment. This is based on
the need to integrate logistics value chains. The partners work together to target key ports
where attaining critical mass is more likely.
  As the motorways of the sea concept is focused upon breaking down the barriers between
transport modes and making better use of existing transport resources, the programme does
not require massive investment but the interaction between assorted stakeholders to agree
on priorities. This has to be complemented by a broader programme to support and more
effectively market short sea shipping. Despite its growth, it does face a number of obstacles
such as an old-fashioned image, an absence of door-to-door modality, the complexity of
administrative procedures and the inefficiency of ports.

Case questions

1 How do you account for the rising importance of sea freight in European logistical
  systems?

2 Explain and examine the link between the motorways of the sea programme and the
  broader objectives of the EU.

3 What are the major problems to be addressed in stimulating increased usage of short
  sea shipping?

FURTHER ISSUES IN THE DEVELOPMENT OF TENs

While the financing problem is undoubtedly the greatest barrier to the development of TENs, it is by no means the only one. Across all TENs sectors, further problems exist which are related largely to administrative and regulatory hurdles. The nature of these problems is largely idiosyncratic to each TENs sector. Within telecommunications, there is a need to balance the liberalisation of the sector with the desire for a socially inclusive information society. This has become increasingly salient as the sector deals with the aftermath of the sharp increase in investment in the mid- to late 1990s and the consequent crash. Within the energy sector, problems are more related to administrative and legal constraints than to finance per se. These constraints stem from a number of causes but the expression of environmental concerns has excited local opposition against the development of energy infrastructures. Such factors make the authorisation procedure long and cumbersome; a feature that increases the overall cost of projects and limits the ability of operators to respond to market conditions. Liberalisation problems (see Chapter 11) also undermine the creation of energy TENs.

The problems for each of the network sectors are also compounded by the desire of a number of states to maintain a high public service dimension in the development of networks. This offers an apparent contradiction with the desire of the EU to involve the private sector and other commercial operators in their development. This public-service element has held up liberalisation across a number of sectors. In telecommunications, the liberalisation of the sector has gone hand in hand with attempts by operators to define a minimum 'universal service obligation'. This is an uncertain concept that will evolve with technology. Similar efforts are being made elsewhere, usually by offering state subsidy to sustain levels of service in otherwise unprofitable activities. In 2004, the Commission defined its policy for the development of 'services of general economic interest' and their sustenance in an increasingly competitive environment. It stresses the role of national, regional and local authorities in defining, organising, financing and monitoring services of general interest. In this area, the Commission has moved away from developing an enveloping framework towards treating each sector on a stand-alone basis. Such arguments are often used by incumbents to delay the opening of a market to competitors. To aid the financing of these services, the EU has proposed that companies can receive state aid to support their provision.

Despite the supranational nature of these projects, there are still many challenges for their development facing member states. These challenges stem from a change in the nature of the culture of infrastructure provision. As economies integrate, there is likely to be a greater spillover between states in terms of network development. Such integration and externalities could lead to an impasse as some states may benefit from the development of infrastructure for which they do not pay. This is evidently still a problem due to the state maintaining a large role in infrastructure finance. Clearly states may be reluctant to invest in the network when other states may clearly benefit from its provision without having contributed to its development. A way to remove such an impasse is to promote mutual investment in networks.

Getting national planners to recognise the European element in infrastructure development is also proving problematic. Planners within member states traditionally developed infrastructure to meet national and local requirements. In this context, the European element of infrastructure planning was an afterthought: in an integrated European business environment this can no longer be the case. There also needs to be speedier decision making within member states based upon a realisation that the national network is a mere sub-network of a larger European series of networks. There also needs to be a realisation that prolonged administrative procedures have a spillover effect upon other member states and are potentially damaging to indigenous enterprises. Therefore, there has to be an appeal to the broader economic interests of the states based upon a recognition that isolation in network development is anachronistic and commercially damaging. Thus, integration will be driven by economics not compulsion. Consequently, a short term role for the EU is coordination of national infrastructure policies to create a 'virtual single network' via the interconnection and interoperability of national sub-systems.

An interrelated issue is attempts by member states to control the power of the Commission via the application of the principle of subsidiarity to the development of TENs. Thus, Title XII of the TEU provides the EU with a mere coordination role with member states taking the primary role. Individual network guidelines set the parameters for the application of the principle of subsidiarity to each network. The guidelines conclude that the development of networks falls between member states and the EU. For example, the development of guidelines is a Community role: but the details, timing and their implementation are a job for member states. In practice, subsidiarity reflects the political and economic realities of TENs development. The EU has developed a facilitator role for itself in which TENs develop in response to need and via the coordination of national policies.

THE EXPANDING DIMENSIONS OF TENs

The TEU highlights the desire to develop and extend TENs to new members and to third countries, both on the European continent and beyond. The desire for international interoperability of networks reflects:

- the need for networks to reflect the internationalisation of markets;
- the desire to extend TENs to account for the expansion of the EU;
- the potential for economic success of the EU beyond its own political borders.

The major new development in the TENs programme is to include the new member states of CEE in the initiative. Within the broad context of political change within these states, the inclusion of projects integral to these states increases their degree of integration with the older members of the EU to facilitate trade. This is driven by the factor/resource endowment of this region and by the desire to enter new markets and to provide incentives for these regions to continue with the adjustment process. Eastern European infrastructure needs to reflect changing trade patterns and not the old political objectives that frequently motivated the former Communist regimes. However, this is not necessarily a major innovation as many of these states were included in the development of TENs from the beginning as part of a broader political agenda in the run up to enlargement. However, the fact of enlargement has given a greater imperative to the upgrade of Eastern European infrastructure to fully engage these states in the process of European integration.

Many of the transport links to Eastern Europe were in a state of chronic disrepair at the onset of transition: as economic ties strengthen and trade grows, so these crucial arteries threaten to clog up totally. To overcome this potential problem, links to – and within – this region have been included in the list of priority projects. These links are targeted on both north–south and east–west transport routes. The accession agreements highlighted that approximately 20,000 km of roads and 30, 000 km of rail (as well as ports and airports) need to be built or upgraded to make them compatible with the objectives of infrastructure specified within the TENs programme. The cost of this investment is estimated by the Commission to be somewhere in the region of €100 billion – which is a vast amount of resource compared to the national income of these states. The theme of transport has led to the establishment of a five-point plan to build a European-wide transport network via:

■ establishing pan-European corridors and areas as a framework for ensuring efficient transport systems within the European continent;
■ preparations to extend TENs to other states as a prerequisite of accession;
■ a common approach to transport technology;
■ the encouragement of intelligent transport technology;
■ closer cooperation on research and technology.

The need to develop the necessary corridors to enable fuller integration with the new member states has been a driving factor behind the rethink of TENs undergone over recent years. The poor state of infrastructure

within – and between – these states is seen as a key retardant to their full integration into the EU. In the run up to enlargement support was offered from the European Bank for Reconstruction and Development (EBRD) and the EU via its Phare programme to aid the development of infrastructure within CEE. This support was not just financial but was also intended to help these states develop the necessary legal framework to support the involvement of the private sector in the development of networks.

In the light of these developments the EU has looked to develop closer transportation links with Mediterranean states. With the strengthening of the partnership between the north and south of the Mediterranean through the Euro-Mediterranean partnership, the aim is to develop a new corridor to support the closer interactions that result. These links are already evident in the external dimension of energy. Trade and tourism is increasing among states in the Mediterranean basin. This need to develop closer links between all parts of the Mediterranean also reflects a political imperative to stem labour flows etc. and a desire by the EU to create new hubs in Southern Europe. The EU supports the development of two key transport corridors:

■ *the trans-Mahgreb multimodal corridor*: focusing on major urban areas in Algeria, Morocco and Tunisia with maritime and air links to the northern shore;
■ *the double corridor of the eastern Mediterranean*: focusing on states on the east of the Mediterranean and comprising the arc of states from Bulgaria through to Egypt.

Importance will be given to short sea shipping within the programme and will fit into the TENs priority of creating motorways of the sea (see Case Study 9.2, p. 200).

Typically, funding for infrastructure in many of the Mediterranean states has not sought to develop internal networks with strong external links. In recognition of the limited resources available to these states, the EU seeks to develop PPPs to develop this infrastructure. To aid its development, a new Facility for Euro-Mediterranean Investment and Partnership (FEMIP) has been established within the framework of the EIB. FEMIP seeks to increase funding in infrastructure within this sub-region by up to €2 billion per annum by the end of 2006. Given the limited funds, such programmes would merely act as catalysts for the development of PPPs.

The energy sector has external connections beyond the European continent. Indeed, the development of networks in these areas extends to North Africa. Again the reason for the development of these networks essentially concerns the security of supply. Despite this, there are concerns about the political stability of these states which could endanger the EU's primary concerns in extending networks to these regions. This north–south corridor is also supported by an east–west corridor to secure supplies from Russia into Western Europe.

The development of telecommunication networks has the strongest global element. The globalisation of trade and the emerging information society has bred a desire to ensure that development of Europe's advanced infrastructure is interconnected and interoperable with global networks. Therefore, much of the work to standardise networks in Europe is set within the context of global requirements. The G8 initiative on the development of the information society reflects the desire for interoperability in many key TEN initiatives as part of developing Global Information Infrastructures. This has been further enhanced by the

number of European (as well as US and Japanese) network operators that have become involved in alliances to develop global enterprise networks to meet the unique communication requirements of multinational enterprises (MNEs).

PROGRESS TOWARDS TENs

The QSP will not only be a highly targeted policy strategy but also will allow the EU to commit extra funds to these projects with a clear cross-border dimension. In line with increased funding, the Commission is seeking to appoint a number of officials with highly specialised knowledge to aid the implementation of their development. If such a range of staff is not available to the Commission, they will seek to develop an executive agency to which the Commission would delegate extra staff. These staff will act as project coordinators for the priority projects to ensure the full coordination of projects that have a clear cross-border dimension. These coordinators seek to overcome administrative and regulatory hurdles by bringing states together to create effective coordination in project development. By 2005, the EU had appointed six coordinators for six priority axes. Several of the coordinators are ex-Commissioners who have the authority and political know-how, in theory, to move the projects along.

The development of energy TENs is proving more successful and over half the priority projects are on their way to completion. This has happened despite slow progress towards liberalisation within this sector. There have been delays in the development of projects in the electricity sector which have run into local/regional impediments due to environmental and other concerns. Once these are out of the way, the

Commission aims to start funding for further projects of common interest for which it has agreed to partially fund feasibility projects.

As a later chapter indicates (see Chapter 12), the development of a supporting infrastructure to support the mobility of communications has by and large been achieved. However, there are still issues with regard to infrastructure in the local loop and with the development of more advanced mobile infrastructure. Therefore, the emphasis of policy has shifted away from infrastructure towards service delivery. In this case, the progress has been more focused on developing applications and rolling out services. In this case, there has been more limited progress. Service and application development have been driven more by mass market needs than by the public sector and socially inclusive applications. The thinking is that as mass markets mature, so the viability of the socially inclusive programmes will increase.

The legal framework for TENs has been hindered by disagreements between member states and the EP. Part of this is derived from a continued reluctance of member states to adapt national priorities to build TENs. The administrative procedures are also ill-suited to the commercial provision of infrastructure across borders. The EU has sought to help by developing a help desk to smooth the process of administration of evolving projects. When looking at the TENs programme, it is still evident that many of the priorities have been driven by the interests of member states rather than by the broader needs of an integrating Europe.

CONCLUSION

TENs are an important complement to the ability of enterprises to function successfully within the integrating European economy. Despite this, TENs are still very much at an embryonic stage within the EU. This is partially due to the uneven state of liberalisation within the TENs sectors themselves. However, for many priority projects across all areas, the private sector is still unwilling to commit the funds needed to secure their development. Nevertheless, there is considerable private-sector involvement within both telecommunications and energy sectors. Future private-sector involvement in the transport sector will increasingly rely upon greater levels of public-sector involvement to support the strategies of commercial operators more fully. This greater public-sector support is by no means guaranteed.

KEY POINTS

■ TENs were born of the desire to complement the mobility and accessibility requirements of the SEM. This objective has been expanded to include the desire to achieve sustained economic growth.

■ The sectors involved are transport, energy and telecommunications, though much of the policy effort is directed at transport.

- The realisation of TENs is to be largely through PPPs though few, to date, have proved successful.

- Progress has been varied across the sectors with each facing its own unique challenges. Transport TENs, in particular, face huge financial problems.

ACTIVITIES

1 Research the efforts to create the Channel Tunnel. What does this experience indicate regarding the private finance of infrastructure?

2 As a group, explore the instances where you have used transnational infrastructure networks.

3 Dividing into two groups, assess the relative merits of private versus state provision of infrastructure.

QUESTIONS FOR DISCUSSION

1 Why is infrastructure so important to economic development?

2 To what extent are TENs needed?

3 What are the major barriers to the creation of TENs across the EU?

4 Explore and explain the link between liberalisation of network services and increased provision of physical infrastructure. Is the Commission right to have confidence in this link?

SUGGESTIONS FOR FURTHER READING

European (2003) *High-level Group on Trans-European Transport Network* (Van Miert Report), http://europa.eu.int/comm/ten/transport/revision/index_en.htm.

Helm, D. (ed.) (2001) 'The Assessment: European Networks – Competition, Interconnection, and Regulation', *Oxford Review of Economic Policy*, 17 (3), pp. 297–312.

Henry, C. (ed.) (2001) *Regulation of Network Utilities: The European Experience*, Oxford: Oxford University Press.

Johnson, D. and Turner, C. (1997) *Trans-European Networks: The Political Economy of Integrating Europe's Infrastructure'*, Basingstoke: Macmillan.

Kessides, I. (2004) 'Reforming Infrastructure: Privatization, Regulation and Competition', *World Bank Policy Research Reports*, Washington, DC: World Bank.

Nijkamp, P., Vleugel, J., Maggi, R. and Masser, I. (1994) *Missing Transport Networks in Europe*, Aldershot: Avebury.

Part III

Inputs and factors of production

The broad framework for economic integration is set out in Part II. However, for many businesses, particularly those that were the most heavily regulated when the SEM was launched, the broad generic policies outlined in Part II were insufficient by themselves to end the market fragmentation that was the goal of the SEM. Part III performs a number of roles. First, it presents examples of how the integration imperative has impacted on individual sectors, such as energy and transport, and takes into account the sector-specific efforts to create internal energy and transport markets, for example. Second, the sectors under examination, such as energy and transport, are also important inputs into other sectors. Information and labour are also key inputs and factors of production, and environmental concerns also impact on the resources available to firms across all sectors and markets. Third, together with labour and consumer issues, the environment also highlights issues of corporate social responsibility (CSR). These issues are important not only in their own right and for CSR reasons but also to ensure that the European population, as citizens, consumers and employees, do not become alienated from the process of economic integration.

Chapter 10

Transport policy

Towards efficient and effective mobility

The introduction of so powerful an agent as steam to a carriage on wheels will make a great change to the situation of man.

Thomas Jefferson, 1802

This chapter will help you understand:

- major trends in European transport and how they affect the business environment;
- major trends in European transport and how they feed through into transport policy;
- the link between market integration and an efficient transport system;
- how the SEM has influenced Europe's transport system and industry;
- the impact of Europe's transport policy on business.

Efficient transportation systems are essential for the competitiveness of European business and to the process of economic integration. The Community's founders signalled the importance of transport by according it its own title within the Treaty of Rome (Articles 74–84 – later to become Articles 70–80), the only sector apart from agriculture to be treated in this way. Why does transport merit such special treatment? The answers are various and relate to the characteristics of the sector itself, its role in fostering European integration and to the way in which transport has evolved throughout Europe.

The first section explores the contribution of Europe's transport sector to Europe's corporate and economic well-being and is followed by a summary of long-term European transport trends. The following section traces the evolution of the EU's transport policy, drawing out some of its key features and its interaction with market developments. The final three sections deal with the evolution of policy in three key transport sectors – road haulage, air and rail – and the impact of this policy on both transport suppliers and consumers.

THE IMPORTANCE OF TRANSPORT TO EUROPEAN BUSINESS

Transport is an important sector in its own right. In 2001, there were almost one million enterprises in Europe's transport services sector, ranging from owner-driver haulage companies to international airlines and including transport ancillary services such as travel agencies, tour operators, cargo handling and storage. The transport sector of the EU-15 also employed 6.2 million people, a figure that increases to 7.4 million when ten 2004 accession states are included. Transport services accounted for €308 billion of value-added, almost 30 per cent of EU energy consumption and about 40 per cent of public investment throughout the EU. Regardless of any other considerations, of which there are many, the well-being of such a major sector must be of concern to policy makers.

An efficient transport system supports and promotes all other economic activities. Transport is an important cost factor for most sectors and efforts to control these costs have major spillovers for competitiveness. In particular, transport and related costs form a high share of the costs of high-volume, low-value-added goods such as construction materials and liquid products, and initiatives to control their transportation costs effectively extends the market of such sectors. Transport and logistics costs of around 10 per cent of total revenue are commonplace in many sectors. Such costs include not only transportation but also warehousing, administration and the carrying of inventories, all of which are affected by

the efficiency of the transport system. Efficient transport services also reduce the time taken for supplies and components to reach manufacturers, thereby enhancing the viability of just-in-time management, and the time needed for a product to reach its market – an important factor in time-sensitive sectors, such as the food industry. In short, not only is an efficient and competitive transport sector an important element in cost control and the development of competitiveness but it also provides a general stimulus to growth and brings more firms into direct competition with each other with secondary effects for competitiveness.

Transport also plays an important role within the context of European integration. By facilitating and encouraging trade, an efficient transport sector and integrated transport network enables European business to take maximum advantage of the SEM. Indeed, the absence of an efficient European-wide transport system jeopardises the achievement of a genuine SEM by limiting cross-border trade within Europe. The 2004 enlargement has accentuated the need for a genuinely pan-European transport policy and system as the countries of CEE seek to overcome the dual legacy of a generally poor standard of physical infrastructure and the eastward facing configuration of their transnational infrastructure. The realisation of SEM benefits for both old and new members depends upon the liberalisation of Europe's transport sectors and upon the construction of genuine trans-European transport networks (see Chapter 9).

The state of European transport services has great significance for other policies, particularly for energy consumption and the environment. Transport also has implications for public health and safety: increased vehicle usage pollutes the atmosphere with adverse consequences for respiratory disease and almost 50,000 people are killed and 1.3–1.4 million injured each year on the EU's roads. The promotion of social and economic cohesion through regional development is also a primary Community objective in which transport plays a key role. The Maastricht Treaty gives the Community the power to develop trans-European transport networks to satisfy the 'need to link island, landlocked and peripheral regions with the central regions of the Community' — a reflection of the view that there is a direct correlation between the level of economic development and the quantity and quality of infrastructure. Transport policy also has implications for external commercial policy, for example, in the negotiation of transit rights and in the Commission's attempts to gain the right to negotiate airline agreements with third parties (see Case Study 17.1) to protect the integrity of the SEM (see below and Case Study 10.1).

LONG-TERM EUROPEAN TRANSPORT TRENDS

Pressures for a more positive EU approach towards transport policy emerged from the logic of European integration and from the dynamics of long-term transport trends. According to the European Commission (European Commission 2001), personal mobility has more than doubled from 17 km a day in 1970 to 38 km in the late 1990s. Moreover, this mobility is increasingly seen as a right, making it difficult for policy makers to introduce measures to reduce congestion or to enforce the polluter pays principle (PPP) (see Chapter 14) which would require individuals to pay more for their motoring, for example.

Road transport is Europe's dominant transport mode and its dominance continues to grow. A few figures illustrate this point. Private car ownership in the EU-15 increased from 232 per thousand in 1975 to 469 per thousand in 2000 and continues to grow. Moreover, the distance travelled by all road vehicles has tripled over the same period. The strong growth in road transport has been the case in both the passenger and freight sectors as Figures 10.1 and 10.2 show. Road's share of the passenger market has risen from 73 per cent in 1970 to 83 per cent in 2002 at the expense of both rail (a drop from 11 to 7 per cent) and bus and coach transport (a fall from 13 to 9 per cent). Road freight has increased its share of inland transport from 52 per cent in 1970 to 75 per cent in 2002. All other freight sectors experienced a declining share but the biggest loser was rail whose share of freight transport in the EU-15 fell from 30 to 13 per cent over the period.

This growing dominance of road transport, whose attraction arises from its door-to-door flexibility, has resulted in a transport crisis in terms of both efficiency and the environment. Efficiency problems arise from bottlenecks, growing congestion and delays. The 2001 Transport White Paper estimates that 10 per cent of Europe's road network is affected by daily traffic jams, increasing fuel consumption by about 6 per cent. Moreover, the White Paper quotes a study that the external costs of road congestion are equivalent to 0.5 per cent of GDP and that, without measures to tackle congestion, its costs will rise to 1 per cent of GDP. Road transport is also one of the most environmentally damaging transport modes in relation to emissions and land usage. As a result, a major thrust of European transport policy (and the closely linked TENs policy) is to bring about a modal shift from road towards rail transport, an objective that will be immensely difficult to achieve. Policy makers will have

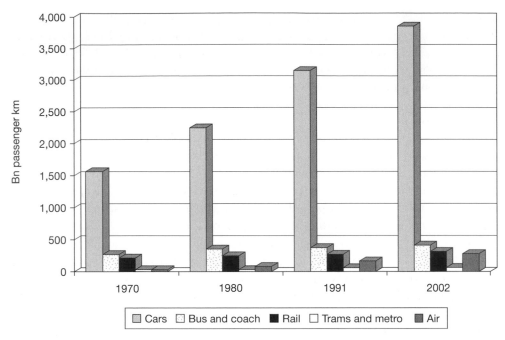

Figure 10.1 Modal performance for passenger transport, EU-15 (bn passenger km)

Source: European Commission, *Energy and Transport in Figures, 2005*.

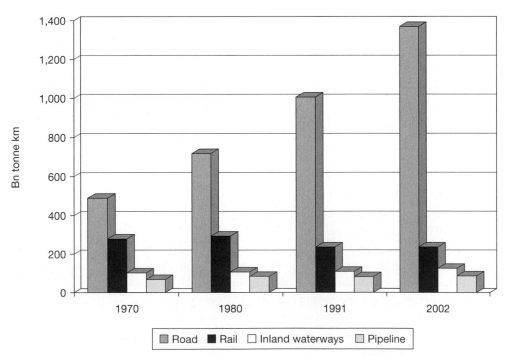

Figure 10.2 Modal performance for freight transport, EU-15 (bn tonne km)

Source: European Commission, *Energy and Transport in Figures, 2005*.

to overcome a wide range of vested interests, change basic attitudes towards mobility and establish an environment in which investment in the rail sector is forthcoming.

Figure 10.3 demonstrates that the freight modal split varies significantly among member states, a factor that feeds into European plans to create a modal shift. In particular, it is striking how much more significant rail freight is in several of the CEE accession states, particularly, but not only, in the Baltic states. Moreover, inland waterways make an overall minor contribution to inland freight transport within the EU (7 per cent of the total) but its contribution, for geographical reasons, is much more significant in northern Europe. The Netherlands utilises inland waterways for over 40 per cent of its inland freight needs and in Germany, for example, inland waterways account for about 12 per cent of freight, almost as much

as that carried by the rail network. There is potential, with some investment to remove bottlenecks in the inland waterway system, to increase the usage of this transport mode heading eastwards.

EVOLUTION OF THE COMMON TRANSPORT POLICY

Although its translation into practical measures was limited for many years, the legal basis for the CTP has been in existence since 1958. The guidance given by the treaty to the Council of Ministers on the development of the CTP was relatively vague and applied only to rail, road and inland waterways. The inclusion of air and sea transport was only confirmed later following a decision by the ECJ. More specifically, Article 71 empowered the Council of Ministers to formulate:

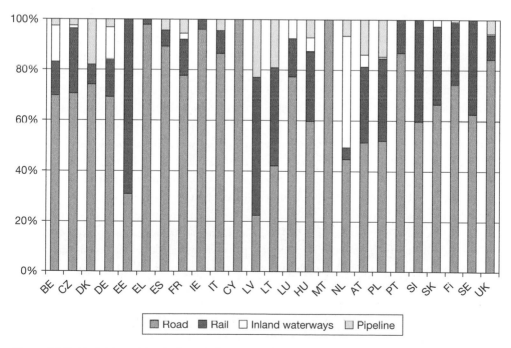

Figure 10.3 Freight modal split by member state, 2002 (tonne km)

Source: European Commission, *Energy and Transport in Figures, 2005.*

1 common rules applicable to international transport to or from the territory of a member state or passing across the territory of one or more member states;

2 the conditions under which non-resident carriers may operate transport services within a member state;

3 any other appropriate provisions.

Certain derogations are allowed under specified circumstances for the protection of living standards and employment. State aids are also sanctioned 'when they meet the needs of coordination of transport or if they represent reimbursement for the discharge of certain obligations inherent in the concept of public service' (Article 73).

In 1961, the European Commission published the Schaus Memorandum, which represented the first attempt to establish comprehensive and specific objectives and principles to enable the Commission to operationalise the CTP. The main thrust of the Memorandum lies in the need to introduce more competition in the Community's transport markets, but it does presage the later TENs initiative by alluding to the need for coordination of investments and the integration of transport systems (see Chapter 9). The Memorandum identified the following three key principles for the CTP which are entirely consistent with the subsequent evolution of the CTP and the TENs programme from the 1980s and beyond:

1 *The elimination of difficulties in the general implementation of the common market arising from national transport regulations*: this principle underpins later attempts to liberalise individual transport sectors as part of the SEM initiative (discussed more fully below in relation to road haulage, airlines and rail).

2 *The integration of transport throughout the Community*: the originators of the CTP intended to establish common rules for transport between member states and to admit non-resident EU carriers to the markets of fellow member states. In later years, this integration increasingly referred to physical integration of transport systems through the TENs programme as much as to the creation of common rules, the impact of which would be jeopardised without physical integration.

3 *The organisation of the transport system*: this was initially interpreted to mean the introduction of a more competitive transport system. It also came to imply organisation of transport according to European rather than national requirements, both via regulations and by the development of a trans-European transport network.

Despite the early flurry of activity shown in Box 10.1, implementation of these CTP principles was limited for some time. For nearly 30 years, the transport provisions of the Treaty of Rome were interpreted to mean harmonisation of conditions, particularly of technical and social standards, but progress was slow. Forging the CTP was made more difficult by the high and varying levels of state intervention and regulation in all transport sectors. In the road haulage sector, for example, cabotage restrictions and bilateral trade quotas were in operation; prices were regulated via compulsory tariffs; entry to the road haulage sector was strictly controlled by licensing systems and the range of taxation systems meant that competition was far from a level playing field. Controls on price, quantity and market entry were also endemic in other transport sectors. State ownership, particularly in the rail and airline

MILESTONES IN THE COMMON TRANSPORT POLICY

BOX 10.1

1957   CTP accorded its own section within the Treaty of Rome

1961   Schaus Memorandum establishes comprehensive principles and objectives for the CTP

1982   EP takes the Council of Ministers to the ECJ for failure to introduce the CTP in line with its treaty obligations

1985   The ECJ supports the EP and requires the Council to table measures to liberalise transport services

1985   Single Market White Paper contains transport liberalisation measures

1987   Agreement on first airline package

1989   Transition agreement on the lifting of road haulage cabotage restrictions

1990   Agreement on second airline package

1991   Directive 91/440 – the first attempt to introduce market opening to the rail sector

1992   Agreement on third airline package

1993   Removal of most short sea coastal cabotage restrictions

1993   Maastricht Treaty gives the Community the legal base to develop TENs

1997   All airline cabotage restrictions lifted

1998   Full cabotage liberalisation: road haulage

2002   ECJ confirms Community powers to develop and negotiate an external aviation policy. Ends the negotiation of bilateral agreements between individual member states and third countries

2003   First rail package in force

2003   Negotiations between the EU and the US on a Joint Aviation Agreement (known as 'Single Skies') under way

2004   Second rail package in force

2004   Commission adopts third rail package – goes forward to Council and EP

2005   Legislation on air passengers' rights in force – ECJ decision in January 2006 rejects a legal challenge to the legislation by key airline groups

2005   The EU signs its first international aviation agreements: the first is with Chile; the second is with Ukraine. Successful negotiations with 18 other countries await signature or Council approval

sectors also resulted in high levels of state aid. In short, for a variety of reasons, member states had seen fit for many years to protect their transport industries and to isolate them from the forces of competition – a situation that was clearly at odds with the principles of the Schaus Memorandum and the SEM.

Further complicating factors in the development of the CTP were the diversity of transport structures, national policies and modal preferences within the member states themselves. France, for example, followed a long-term policy of developing the rail sector and maritime transport was not as important for the EC-6 as it was for later entrants such

BOX 10.2

KEY TRANSPORT TERMS

Cabotage: the transportation of goods or passengers wholly within the territory of one country by lorries, vessels or aircraft owned by nationals of another country. Restrictions on cabotage operated in the road haulage, short sea shipping, inland waterway and aviation sectors until the SEM campaign succeeded in lifting such restrictions. A limited agreement on reducing road haulage cabotage restrictions was reached in 1989 and established the principle of ending cabotage constraints. This agreement paved the way for full cabotage liberalisation, not only in road haulage but also in other sectors – a central factor in the opening of transport markets to competition.

Fifth freedom: the right of an airline from one country to land in another country, to pick up passengers there and carry them to a third country. For example, with fifth freedom rights, British Airways has the right to fly from London to Rome, to pick up passengers in Rome and carry them on to Athens. The EU's three airline liberalisation packages have granted authorised EU airlines full fifth freedom rights.

as the UK and Greece. Member states have also often invested their transport policy with a significant regional policy role and have imposed tight public service obligations on different transport modes. The need to serve its island communities, for example, made Greece resistant to the lifting of cabotage restrictions in short sea shipping.

The emergence of a more concerted attempt at developing the CTP received further impetus from the EP which, concerned at the apparent stagnation in transport policy, took the Council of Ministers to the ECJ in 1982 for failing to fulfil its treaty obligations. In May 1985, the ECJ supported the EP's position and required the Council to bring forward measures to liberalise transport services 'within a reasonable time'.

The ECJ judgment preceded wider developments that were to result in important breakthroughs in European transport policy. The British peer, Lord Bethell, had been lobbying for a number of years for the opening of Europe's airline markets. His campaign was helped by the spread of economic liberalism and supply side economics that emphasise the benefits of competition, deregulation and liberalisation. The 1985 White Paper *Completing the Internal Market* was essentially about removing NTBs to trade (barriers which, as shown above, were rife in transport) and is an example of the growing reliance on the market as the guardian of competitiveness.

The SEM was the key to the substantial changes that have taken place in the transport sector since the mid-1980s and which, as shown below, have resulted in significant corporate restructuring, particularly of production and distribution networks. In 1988 the Cecchini Report estimated that failure to liberalise Community transport systems would result in costs to business that were 2 per cent higher than they would otherwise be. The additional trade flows and prosperity anticipated from the dynamics of the SEM would lead to higher demand for transport services and would be jeopardised by the fragmentation and inadequacy of Europe's transport systems.

These factors resulted in a two-pronged attack on Europe's transport problems:

- programmes to liberalise systematically all traffic modes within Europe;
- a campaign to develop trans-European transport infrastructure (see Chapter 9).

DEVELOPING THE CTP: THE CASE OF ROAD HAULAGE

The EU has introduced a wide range of single market measures that directly affect the road haulage industry. These are roughly divided into liberalisation and harmonisation measures. The former increase market access and were intended to increase competition throughout the EU market. Harmonisation measures were intended to ensure that increased competition between road hauliers from different member states is fair. Safety and technical measures, for example, are designed to prevent road hauliers gaining a competitive advantage from compliance with lower national standards – a requirement that could place undesirable downward pressure on safety standards throughout the EU in an open market. In practice, rather than adopt common standards, which represent absolute harmonisation, the Union has frequently opted for minimum standards.

The main single market measures include:

- market access measures, such as establishing criteria for admission to the profession of road haulier; the mutual recognition of qualifications; the removal of quotas on the carriage of goods by road between member states and the final lifting of restrictions on cabotage, which occurred in 1998;
- tax measures, including actions on vehicle taxes, excise duties on fuel and user charges for infrastructure. Infrastructure charging potentially requires users to pay the full costs of their activities and further development of these ideas is undergoing a lot of scrutiny as a way of bringing about intermodal shift – that is the encouragement of rail transport to reduce the congestion and other pollution effects of road transport;
- safety and social measures regarding driving hours and the transport of dangerous goods, for example;
- customs controls and regulation, including the abolition of frontier checks and the reduction of formalities and documentary requirements at borders;
- environmental regulations concerning noise and other emissions from commercial vehicles;
- technical harmonisation in relation to the dimensions, weights and technical characteristics of commercial vehicles.

Other related measures are important for the road haulage sector. The TENs initiative, for example, could have a major impact on road transport efficiency and result in modal shifts; third country relations have implications for transit rights and environmental initiatives will continue to exercise their influence on road haulage.

Road haulage provides the fastest and most flexible option for door-to-door carriage of goods and contributes more than 2 per cent to EU GDP. The majority of road freight traffic in the Community is domestic with cross-border trade accounting for approximately 3 per cent of road freight transport in tonnage terms. However, given the greater average distance travelled in international haulage, the share of cross-border business in terms of tonne kilometres is much greater at almost 20 per cent of the total.

219

The emergence of logistics as a distinct business function since the 1970s is both a response to the changes in the external business environment (such as internationalisation and the emergence of integrated trading blocs) and a cause of the changes themselves. The holistic approach of logistics to the management of product movement and broader changes in manufacturing has helped change the nature of transport demand. Just-in-time management techniques and shorter product life cycles, for example, have increased demand for transport and reduced the average size of individual consignments, thereby increasing the number of journeys and placing a greater premium on reliability. Transport companies that can supply a range of integrated logistical services on a cross-border, or even a world-wide, basis are well placed to serve these shippers.

In view of these changes, shippers have correspondingly rationalised their carriers and are basing their transport and logistics strategies on Europe as a whole, or on significant sub-regions of it, rather than on individual national markets. This has both made business harder to come by for carriers and has extended the distance over which goods are transported. The greatest beneficiaries of these trends are the larger hauliers with a strong regional and/or logistics speciality and which have the financial clout to invest in the necessary equipment and information technology (crucial for tracking and tracing shipments) and to develop distribution centres. These companies are also increasingly contracting out the physical transport side of their logistics business to smaller companies – an attractive option, given that it is the sub-contractor who has to bear the cost of compliance with national and EU regulations. The contractor simply has to choose the most competitive bid.

The SEM and enlargement have encouraged companies to search for the holy grail of a pan-European distribution strategy, using a single hub as their basis for the whole of Europe. The increased geographical extent of the single market has made it more practical for companies to set up one, two or three main distribution centres to serve sub-regions of the SEM, sometimes with satellite centres performing the final distribution. In 2000, Parker, a leading supplier of components to the motor industry, consolidated its network of 75 local warehouses across Europe into two sites – one in Germany to serve its Northern European markets and one in Italy to do the same for its Southern clients. The main motivation behind the creation of these European distribution centres was to centralise stocks, enabling the company to reduce its total inventory while increasing the availability of parts and offering shorter lead-times. In the process, the company claims to have reduced its storage and transport costs and has introduced automated ordering systems to make buying from Parker easier and to bring together various logistics functions.

In the longer term, these changes could have a substantial transformational effect in the spatial distribution of economic activity throughout Europe, particularly if the result is a clustering and concentration of major production and distribution sites around key nodes and along main trans-European transport corridors. At one level, the emergence of large pan-European logistics providers, often engaged in strategic alliances with shippers who are integrating and rationalising their activities across Europe, parallels the physical development of TENs (see Chapter 9). The logistics networks that are being developed, like the physical infrastructure itself, are based on the control of distance through time (achieved by organisation and physical networks), accessibility and optimal network management.

DEVELOPING THE CTP: THE CASE OF AIRLINES

The European airline sector has been transformed since the early 1990s. Although European liberalisation cannot take all the credit for this, the restructuring, which continues in the first decade of the twenty-first century, would not have been possible without the lifting of the most restrictive barriers to intra-EU airline activity. Indeed, prior to the implementation of the three airline packages in the late 1980s and early 1990s, the airline sector was one of Europe's most heavily regulated sectors. At the beginning of the liberalisation process, most airlines were large, state monopolies; fares were subject to state approval; access to routes and airport slots was tightly controlled to the benefit of incumbents, and cabotage restrictions and other constraints on routeing effectively prevented airlines flying in and out of any state apart from their own. In short, airlines, even if they wanted to (and most incumbents were happy with the status quo), were inhibited from operating on a commercial basis. Not surprisingly, the lack of competition reduced the incentive to become more efficient and in the 1980s, the majority of Europe's airlines were operating at a loss.

In its 1994 Report, *Expanding Horizons*, the Comité des Sages, an independent group of experts set up by the European Commission, concluded that 'European airlines pay a heavy price for the fragmentation of their market in Europe . . .. In concrete economic terms, the structure of the European airline industry is still very much oriented towards outdated national boundaries.' The

result was significantly poorer productivity, lower profitability and higher operating costs than US airlines. In other words, a number of obstacles over and above those included in the three airline packages needed to be removed before the full benefits of airline deregulation could be felt. The roots of these further obstacles were in politics (state aids) and lack of capacity (congestion, air traffic control, slot allocation, inadequate infrastructure).

The first and major steps in opening Europe's airline sector were the three airline packages, introduced between 1987 and 1992, which gradually chipped away at the most blatant obstacles to competition. These reforms gave European airlines the freedom to set fares on both scheduled and charter services and opened all intra-EU routes to EU operators.

The three packages detailed in Box 10.3 provided the central part of the liberalisation of Europe's airline industry but several other changes were necessary to ensure that access and competition in the sector was free and non-discriminatory:

State aids were widespread in the airline sector for many years. Intense political lobbying by member states regarding the survival of their national flag carriers had long defied the European Commission's attempts to eradicate this assistance. State aids seriously undermined the integrity of the single aviation market, allowing recipient airlines to distort trade and escape commercial pressures, thereby significantly reducing incentives to improve efficiency and putting non-recipient competitors at a serious disadvantage. In 1994, the Commission established guidelines for the evaluation of state aids in the airline sector which operated on the market economy investment principle. In essence, if the Commission's investigations

BOX 10.3

THE THREE AIRLINE PACKAGES

The First Package (1987) reformed capacity sharing practices so that member states were no longer able to insist that 50 per cent of traffic on a particular route be reserved for the national airline; introduced more flexible procedures for fare approval and removed single-designation provisions.

The Second Package (1990) built on the liberalisation measures in the First Package, increasing the flexibility to set fares and granted third and fourth freedom rights to all Community carriers (that is, the right for European carriers to carry passengers to and from their home countries to other EU members). This package also included fuller fifth freedom rights (see Box 10.2). The above provisions initially related to passenger traffic only but were extended to freight in 1990.

The Third Package (1992) completed the liberalisation process. It included the common licensing of carriers. Holders of a community licence were allowed to serve any international route within Europe. From April 1997, full cabotage rights were granted to licensed EU operators – that is, an airline from one member state was given the right to operate a route wholly within another member state (see Box 10.2). Domestic markets were fully open by 1997 and member states are required to grant charter services access on the same basis as scheduled services. In short, European airlines were granted access to all inter-European routes and, as a result of another part of the third package, became free to charge almost whatever fares they wished.

into public assistance conclude that no private investor would have invested a similar amount into an airline, this assistance is considered to be state aid. The aid may still be approved if it is part of a comprehensive restructuring programme of limited duration and must be self-contained – that is, no further aid will be necessary (the 'one-time, last time' principle). The assistance must also include capacity reduction if necessary and must not involve expansions. There must also be no government interference in the operation of the company which must be run along commercial lines. The Commission has reported that since 1991, seven airlines have received state aid for restructuring (Sabena, Iberia, Aer Lingus, TAP, Air France, Olympic Airways and Alitalia) and that the restructuring needed to prepare

Europe's airlines for competition is complete. Although it is premature to say the state aid problem has been solved, it is certainly the case that it rarely hits the headlines in the mid-2000s as it did during the first half of the 1990s.

Congestion results from a variety of sources, including too few landing and take-off slots; shortage of terminal and runway capacity and aircraft stands; inadequate surface access to airports and air traffic management systems which fail to keep pace with the demand. Further congestion is anticipated as a result of current trends in air traffic growth and additional growth resulting from airline liberalisation. Congestion at airports and in the skies will prevent the full exploitation of market opportunities offered by the airline liberalisation packages and acts as a market entry barrier. Solutions to congestion in which the EU has a role include:

- *Physical infrastructure*: improvement of airport infrastructure falls within the remit of the TENs initiative (see Chapter 9) but airports have not loomed large on the list of priority projects. In short, although there is a growing crisis in the provision of key airport infrastructure, the solution will not, in the short term at least, come from the EU. Although some EU funding will be available for airports in peripheral regions, the biggest boost to airport investment will come from the current wave of airport privatisations throughout Europe.
- *Air traffic control*: European air traffic control costs are frequently ten or more times greater than in the US and provide a good example of the damage caused to European airlines by excessive market fragmentation. European air traffic control is run from over 50 centres, causing complex and unnecessary management problems that add to costs and congestion. However, member states are proving reluctant to create a single air traffic management system in Europe.
- *Slot allocation*: given the infrastructure and capacity problems faced by many European airports, the allocation of take-off and landing slots has become an acute problem. The provision of additional capacity or the improvement of operating conditions is the best way to deal with the problem of slot allocation but this will not occur in the short term.

Airlines: the global market place

Airlines account for by far the biggest share of passenger traffic between the EU and third countries. The indivisibility of the global and European markets resulted in a fierce battle between the Commission and member states over who should have the responsibility for conducting airline diplomacy with third countries. The European Commission frequently restated its claim to exercise exclusive competency in the negotiation of airline agreements with third countries, thereby ending the practice of bilateral negotiations between individual member states and third countries, but for many years member states resisted the EU's attempt to gain competence in this area.

The case for EU competence in this area was strong. Bilateral agreements undermine the principles of the single aviation market. The Commission argued that anti-competitive practices on non-EU routes also allow carriers potentially to cross-subsidise unprofitable intra-EU routes. Furthermore, bilateral talks tipped the balance of the negotiations in favour of the US. Negotiations conducted on the basis of two large internal markets would result in more parity between the negotiating partners and a greater likelihood of opening the US market to European airlines on equal terms. However, a fixed determination to guard national negotiating rights within the EU, for a long time placed European airlines at a competitive disadvantage compared to their US counterparts and fragmented the internal market. Moreover, ownership restrictions on non-US nationals are much stricter in the US than for US carriers in Europe and cabotage is a concept that is not entertained by the US authorities.

Following a successful legal challenge to the status quo at the ECJ in 2002, the European Commission eventually gained the right to negotiate international airline deals on behalf of the EU as a whole. Consequently, in the mid-2000s, talks are under way between the EU and the US to create a liberal transatlantic airline regime (see Case Study 17.1, p. 401 for further details).

Changes in Europe's airline sector

As a result of the single market in air transport, European carriers gained almost total freedom to choose their routes, schedules, capacities and fares without the intervention of governments. Access to the European market was open to all who qualified for a Community licence. In short, commercial rather than political factors became the key determinants of fares, routeing and capacity. However, market opening occurred at a time when most European airlines, particularly national flag carriers, were making losses or minimal profits. This made it doubly difficult, but essential, for them to meet the new challenges of competition. The preliberalisation constraints on competition had removed incentives for the constant efficiency gains sought by firms in competitive markets and so there were many opportunities in the new liberalised world for those airlines that could spot them. Indeed, the single aviation market created a whole new industry sub-sector – the 'low-cost' or 'budget airlines' which quickly recognised and moved to take advantage of the new opportunities open to them (see Case Study 10.1). There has also been the rise of the niche operator at the other end of the market. Companies such as Eos have focused on business fliers only. Thus, the impact of the single aviation market was market segmentation.

Europe's civilian passenger airline sector currently has four main sub-sections:

1 *Full-service scheduled airlines*: These are primarily made up of traditional 'flag' carriers with one or two additions such as BMI and Virgin Atlantic. The financial performance of these airlines has been poor: as a group, they made sustained losses in the 1980s and early 1990s, experienced four years of profitability from 1995–98 before returning to a loss-making situation. They typically operate a range of destinations and offer a wide range of services such as in-flight meals and entertainment, frequent flyer programmes, premium cabins and airport lounges. They operate in both short-haul and long-haul sectors and are increasingly encountering competition from low-cost carriers on the former routes. Many of these airlines are members of strategic alliances, which enables them to offer a greater choice of routes to their passengers.

2 *Low-cost airlines*: based on the North American model which developed following the deregulation of US airlines, these airlines currently operate on short-haul flights within Europe and offer simple, no-frills scheduled services. By squeezing every aspect of their cost base they are able to offer previously unimaginable low fares (see Case Study 10.1).

3 *Regional airlines*: these provide scheduled services within a European sub-region. They include operators such as Tyrolean Airways, Aegean Airways and Air Dolomiti and tend to operate with smaller aircrafts on less dense routes. Some regional airlines are subsidiaries of full-service airlines whereas others are independently owned.

4 *Holiday charter airlines*: these exist to carry leisure passengers to and from their package holiday destinations. The biggest charter airlines are owned by large tour operators (for example, Britannia Airways and First Choice Airways); some are independently owned (Monarch Airlines) and others are owned by scheduled airlines or have multiple shareholdings.

Important as the regulatory framework is, the airline industry is also affected by political, economic and other events. The long-term trend of steady upward passenger growth stuttered in the early 2000s under the combined effect of the terrorist attack on the World Trade Center in New York in 2001, the subsequent war in Iraq and the outbreak of SARS (severe acute respiratory syndrome) in Asia. These factors particularly hit long-haul flights to and from Europe and, consequently, hurt traditional scheduled airlines the most.

The scheduled airlines have developed a range of strategies to improve their ability to compete in the changing business environment and industrial structure, including:

1 *The purchase of small airlines in other European countries*: these airlines are then used as feeder services to connect passengers with more profitable long-haul services. Examples include Air UK (renamed KLM UK) which flies from regional UK airports to Amsterdam Schipol, KLM's hub, where passengers then feed into flights to other European destinations or into KLM's extensive range of long-haul flights. Similarly, SAS and Lufthansa own 20 and 30 per cent respectively of BMI (formerly British Midland) whose services consequently complement those of its major shareholders and which has been integrated into the Star Alliance along with its major shareholders.

2 *Merger with other national airlines*: one response to increased competition is to merge with or acquire one or more companies in the sector. This brings economies of scale in many aspects of the business and gives a certain critical mass to enable a company to compete successfully (with the proviso that size by itself is far from sufficient to deal with competitive challenges). The most notable example of this so far is the deal between Air France and KLM, finalised in May 2004, which effectively made KLM part of Air France. KLM will fly under its own distinct brand identity for five years but the operations of the two will be increasingly integrated.

3 *Change the business model*: although the traditional–low-cost airline divide in Europe accurately reflects the structure of Europe's airline markets (see Table 10.1), some blurring of the boundaries between the sectors is occurring as some of the full-service scheduled airlines adopt aspects of the low-cost model. Case Study 10.1 identifies how ticketing practices of full-service airlines are changing as a result of the low-cost example. Aer Lingus, the Irish national flag carrier, is going a stage further and is aiming to compete directly with the low-cost airlines. In order to do so, it has dispensed with business class on its short-haul flights. It is also considering introducing, where possible, low-cost practices onto its long-haul flights.

4 *Membership of a strategic alliance*: these alliances, which became commonplace in the 1990s, are an international rather than a European phenomenon but they enhance the capability of members (scheduled airlines) to compete on European as much as on long-haul flights. Initially starting as code-sharing agreements which gave passengers access to all routes within the alliance, other cost savings and benefits quickly became apparent. These include the sharing of the costs of sales offices, maintenance facilities and operational facilities such as catering. Lower costs also help reduce fares and give passengers greater choice and optimised transfers between flights and carriers. Potential problems occur if alliances eliminate

225

Case Study 10.1

LOW-COST AIRLINES – THE MAIN BENEFICIARIES OF THE SINGLE AIRLINE MARKET

Prior to the liberalisation of European airlines brought about by the three airline packages, Europe's airline industry was dominated by national, mostly state-owned, flag carriers that were largely shielded from the forces of competition by restrictions on market access, fares and other regulations alluded to above. Liberalisation changed all that. European carriers were granted the freedom to choose their routes, schedules and fares with only minimal government interference (usually on public-service grounds). Commercial considerations became the primary motive for new routes and for changes to fares and to capacity. As a result of the new opportunities, a whole new segment of the European airline sector – the low-cost or budget airlines – was born, a segment that could not have possibly existed under the previously highly regulated system.

The first budget airline to emerge in Europe was Ryanair and it remains a leader in this field. Ryanair began operating in the mid-1980s, benefiting from the early liberalisation of UK–Irish routes. The early years were difficult but the airline persevered. By 1995, Ryanair had overtaken Aer Lingus and British Airways to carry the most passengers on the London–Dublin route. By 1997, Ryanair had launched its first routes into continental Europe and carried 3.7 million passengers. Having established a number of continental European bases and acquired and integrated Buzz, KLM's loss-making, low-cost subsidiary, Ryanair carried 27.6 million passengers on its extensive European network in financial year 2004–05.

The other dominant budget airline in Europe is easyJet, founded in 1995 when it carried a total of 30,000 passengers. By 2005, easyJet was carrying almost 29.6 million passengers a year on 224 routes involving 67 European cities in the UK, France, Spain, Sweden, the Netherlands, Denmark, Italy, Greece, Germany and Portugal. It had a fleet of 109 aircraft and had acquired British Airway's low-cost subsidiary, Go. Further route expansions, especially to Eastern Europe, and aircraft acquisitions are in the pipeline.

By the mid-2000s, over 80 low-cost carriers were active in Europe. The total number of passengers carried by these carriers had increased from 13 million in 1999 to an estimated 80 million in 2004. The most developed market for low-cost services is the UK, one of the leaders in the campaign to open up Europe's airline markets. By mid-2003, low-cost airlines accounted for over 20 per cent of intra-EU scheduled activity but their market share reached 40 per cent for services touching the UK. As the success of the low-cost model has become apparent, it is spreading throughout the territory of the EU with the emergence, and often demise, of new carriers.

The low-cost model was originally developed in the US in the late 1970s following the deregulation of the airline sector there. The original low-cost airline was Southwest Airlines which transformed itself from a regional into a low-cost carrier operating from a secondary airport in Dallas, Texas. By the mid-2000s, Southwest was carrying over 70 million passengers a year on low fares and at a profit – a performance that many of the more traditionally run and troubled scheduled US airlines have found difficult to match. Southwest pioneered many aspects of the low-cost model used by European low-cost operators, who have subsequently taken the model further to take advantage of developments in IT and other technologies.

The low-cost airline business model is based on driving each aspect of an airline's costs down as far as possible. This enables the successful low-cost operator to lower its fares, attract more passengers and, ultimately, increase revenues and profits. Low-cost airlines typically offer direct flights on short-haul routes from secondary and regional airports located near major population centres. They do not operate a hub-and-spoke service like some of the conventional scheduled airlines. Although hub-and-spoke can offer more destinations, point-to-point flying avoids the costs of through services, including baggage transfer and passenger assistance costs. Secondary and regional airports are also less congested than major international airports, thereby offering greater punctuality, faster aircraft turnaround times (enabling carriers to utilise their assets more intensively) and do not have the slot restrictions that can limit services from other airports. General airport fees and other related costs tend to be lower at secondary and regional airports.

Table 10.1 Comparison of airline business models

Low cost airlines	Traditional scheduled airlines
Direct sales channels – reliance on Internet ticket sales. No sales commissions	Multiple sales channels including travel agents
'No frills' – all extras (e.g. catering, etc.) paid for. Reduces staff numbers and costs	Full-service – entertainment, catering, business and first class, lounges, etc.
Higher plane utilisation because of quick turnaround times (c.20–25 minutes) – helped by simpler boarding procedures	More time spent on ground – slower turnaround time (c.45 minutes)
Use of regional and secondary airports – lower airport fees and quicker turnaround	Use of international airports – higher airport fees and slower turnaround time
Standardised fleet – reduces costs of maintenance, training, stockholding, greater simplicity	Wide range of aircraft types – increases attendant maintenance costs
Higher seating density	Lower seating density
Direct flights, short haul, no transfers	Long and short haul with transfers Greater complexity
Staff incentives (higher percentage of variable wage costs) – keeps unit wage costs down	High basic wage costs with little staff incentives

From the first contact with the customer, the emphasis of the low-budget airline is on cost reduction. In the case of both Ryanair and easyJet, for example, around 95 per cent of tickets are sold via the Internet. When booking online, easyJet passengers receive an e-mail with their travel details and a booking reference that acts in lieu of a conventional ticket. This eliminates the significant costs of issuing and distributing millions of tickets each year. Services are eliminated or kept as simple as possible to keep costs down. Hence, low-cost airlines do not offer free in-flight meals (passengers are charged if they want a meal, for example) and seats are not pre-assigned.

Fares are structured to fill the aircraft and will vary significantly on the same flight, although even the most expensive seats tend to compare favourably with those on traditional scheduled services. Low fares are intended to stimulate demand, especially from leisure and cost-conscious business travellers who may not travel, or perhaps would have used alternatives such as the train, without the promise of lower fares. Fares are set according to demand for a particular flight and with reference to the period remaining to departure. Higher fares are charged on flights with higher levels of demand for bookings made nearer departure. However, fares can be as low as €0.99 (excluding taxes) on certain routes or key promotions.

Moreover, low-cost airlines offer the passenger greater flexibility with their fares. For example, tickets are sold on a one-way basis, eliminating the need for minimum periods of stay or to stay over a Saturday night. This has started to affect the practices of traditional scheduled airlines. By the early 2000s, many had dropped the minimum stay of one Saturday night rule for their cheaper tickets. Increasingly, scheduled airlines are selling one-way tickets and dropping the practice whereby a single ticket costs significantly more than a return fare. BMI, for example, has adopted this policy on most of its routes and, although not offering this flexibility across all its networks, British Airways is following suit on many European routes. Given the concentration of low-cost airlines on UK-related routes, it is not surprising that UK scheduled airlines are changing their practices but, as competition from low-cost operators spreads throughout Europe, it is to be expected that many more scheduled airlines will follow suit.

What is the overall impact of the budget airlines on Europe's passenger airline sector and more generally? The intensification of competition is obvious, both with other sectors of the airline industry and within the low-cost sub-sector itself. Indeed, the intensity of competition will lead to a rapid turnover in companies with many new entrants finding it difficult to establish themselves and survive in such a cut-throat environment. However, analysis of the demand for low-cost services indicates that the majority of passengers of low-cost airlines are new passengers rather than those that have been 'poached' from the traditional scheduled airlines. This is borne out by the continuing long-term growth trend of all major airline sub-sectors (although none is as buoyant as the low-cost sector). Moreover, a survey conducted in 2002 suggests that less than 30 per cent of the demand from the low-cost carriers represented a shift within the airline market. Of the remaining new demand, 70 per cent was from passengers who would not have travelled at all without the low fares and 30 per cent was from passengers who would have travelled by other means in the absence of such fares.

The greater competition created by liberalisation in general and by the low-cost airlines in particular has forced all airlines to pay more attention to efficiency, especially the national flag carriers which, in pre-liberalisation days, were immune from normal commercial pressures. Many flag carriers are changing key practices as a result of the low-cost airlines (see above for changing BMI and British Airways ticketing practices) or even adopting wider aspects of their business model, such as Aer Lingus. Intensified competition has resulted in improvements in punctuality, less lost luggage, more responsiveness to consumer complaints and generally greater attention to consumer service throughout the sector. The low-cost airlines have also created more competition between airports, forcing them to grow more efficient and have helped ease congestion at Europe's major airports.

In more general terms, the emergence of low-cost airlines has met the objectives of the EU liberalisation package and supported the creation of the SEM by facilitating free movement around the EU, offering greater consumer choice and generally simplifying travel. The low cost airlines have also had a positive effect on regions, creating jobs at regional airports and in related aviation activities. The boost to regional airports stimulates inward investment and tourism, boosting the local economy and creating jobs beyond the aviation sector. In terms of the environment, low-cost airlines claim that their high levels of capacity utilisation and greater density of seats per plane reduce the amount of pollution per passenger. On the other hand, the total of flights is higher because of the low-cost sector with all the attendant environmental implications.

Case questions

1   Explain why liberalisation of the airline markets was necessary in order for the low-cost budget airlines to develop and prosper.

2   What have been the main impacts of the phenomenal growth of budget airlines in Europe since the implementation of the EU's three airline packages?

3   Changes in airline regulation have led to both entries into and exits out of the low-cost sector. Investigate why some companies have left.

4   How sustainable is the low-cost model in the long term? What factors might make it difficult to sustain?

competition on particular routes. Given the frequently shifting membership of key alliances and general routeing changes, the competition implications of such alliances can quickly change.

In the mid-2000s, the three biggest alliances carry an estimated 54 per cent of the world's airline passengers a year. They are:

■   the Star Alliance (21 per cent of the world market): members include Air Canada, Air New Zealand, ANA, Asiana Airlines, Austrian, BMI, LOT, Lufthansa, SAS, Singapore Airlines, Spanair, TAP, Thai Airlines, United Airlines, US Airways and Varig;

■   One World (14 per cent of the world market): members include Aer Lingus, American Airlines, British Airways, Cathay Pacific, Finnair, Iberia, Lan, Qantas;

■   Skyteam Alliance: Aeroméxico, Air France-KLM, Alitalia, Continental, CSA Czech Airlines, Delta, Korean Air and Northwest.

Overall, the new regulatory framework for airlines in Europe has transformed the industry in many ways and has overturned conventional ways of thinking about the industry. For example, in 2001 the Belgian flag carrier, SABENA, went into liquidation as a result of recession and of large debts owed to it by Swissair which itself had gone out of business shortly beforehand. The Air France KLM merger means that the Netherlands no longer has a national flag carrier. These developments would have been inconceivable a few years previously as the existence of a national flag carrier was regarded as essential to a nation for prestige and strategic reasons. In a more liberal market place, it is likely that there will be further shakeouts of the industry and that a few large European airlines will emerge and compete on a global stage with a number of smaller airlines focusing on niche or regional routes. A comprehensive EU–US airline agreement will create new opportunities and contribute to more industrial restructuring.

DEVELOPING THE CTP: THE CASE OF RAIL

The SEM is, among other things, about promoting commercial exchanges between member states and it needs an interconnected transport system to support this. As the previous two sections demonstrate, the road haulage and airline sectors have been given the single market treatment and have also exploited the opportunities offered by the reduction of boundaries. This has not been the case for the rail sector which continues to be constrained by national boundaries while the market for its services has become increasingly transnational.

Moreover, Europe's rail sector is characterised by heavily subsidised and indebted state monopolies. In 2000, for example, the Commission estimated that state subsidies for rail infrastructure approached €25 billion

and that the compensation for public service obligations was almost €10 billion. The combination of these factors has contributed substantially to rail's falling share of freight traffic throughout Europe.

The 2001 Transport White Paper sees rail as having great potential to relieve congestion and wishes to bring about a modal shift in favour of the rail sector. The priority transport TENs projects are also weighted heavily towards developing the rail network. However, in order for these objectives to be met, progress needs to be made in two main policy areas – market access and interoperability.

The Community's first attempts to open the rail markets (Directive 91/440) seemed significant at the time but in retrospect, did little to change the status quo. By requiring the separation of accounts for infrastructure and via provisions regarding autonomy, it did at least set the foundations for later initiatives to open international markets. The next attempt to do this occurred in 1995 but got nowhere because of lack of support in the Council.

Attempts to open up the rail markets were helped by the Treaty of Amsterdam which made transport subject to co-decision, thereby conferring a greater role in the formation of transport policy to the EP, an institution that was anxious to push European transport policy further. In 1998, the Commission tabled three proposals on rail infrastructure (commonly referred to as the 'first rail package') and, following a long and controversial debate during which the package was considerably strengthened as a result of EP interventions, the three directives eventually came into force on 15 March 2003. In essence, international freight became open to competition on a significant part of the Union's network. This market opening had to overcome the power of the incumbent operators. The directives sought to do this by separating out 'essential functions' to ensure transparent and non-discriminatory access to the infrastructure including, most importantly, separation of control over the track and the services that operate over the track. In order to monitor developments and to provide an efficient appeals system, member states were also required to set up an independent regulatory body to rule on complaints.

In 2002, the Commission brought forward its second rail package with a view to taking the construction of an integrated rail network further. This package contained five proposals designed to improve safety, interoperability and the extension of market opening to domestic rail freight, including the introduction of cabotage. Moreover, the package proposed the establishment of a European Rail Agency, subsequently set up in Valenciennes in France, to direct work on safety and interoperability. The second package came into force in April 2004, causing the then Transport Commissioner Loyola de Palacio to declare:

> This is the end of the physical and technical barriers in European freight railway transport: this new context will change radically the picture for rail transport and will really boost it. It will also contribute to the fight against road congestion. This is a revolution which represents a genuine European rail transport integration.
>
> (Commission Press Release, 22 April 2004)

In 2004, the Commission took things a stage further when it tabled proposals for its third rail package. The main thrust of the third package's measures is to open the market for rail passenger services by 2010; to protect the rights of international passengers; to introduce minimum quality clauses in rail freight contracts, and measures to attest to the qualifications and standards of locomotive drivers. Significant progress was made in December 2005 when the Transport Council reached a political agreement on the measures in the package.

CONCLUSION: THE FUTURE OF THE CTP

The CTP has passed through several distinct phases. It experienced almost three decades of inactivity which only ended after the Council was successfully taken to the ECJ for failure to meet its treaty obligations to develop a CTP. The court case coincided with a phase from the mid-1980s in which major strides were made in the liberalisation of road haulage and airline transport as part of the SEM programme. Liberalisation of these sectors was regarded as an important development in its own right but also increasingly as a necessary support to underpin the increased interdependence and trade between member states. In other words, along with transport TENs, the CTP has assumed considerable importance as a way of ensuring, among other things, the efficient functioning of the SEM.

Following the market opening progress in the road haulage and aviation sectors, the Community's attentions have turned to other sectors, notably short sea shipping ('the motorways of the sea' – see Case Study 9.2, p. 200), ports and railways. The opening of these markets comes much later and is not as advanced as that in the early liberalisers. However, much rests on their success, including an easing of congestion and a reduction in environmental degradation resulting from a modal shift from road to rail, in particular. The market access and

231

interoperability measures being taken by the Community in relation to rail transport are certainly necessary but also not sufficient to bring about this shift. Rail's share of freight transport, in particular, has fallen steadily for several decades and it is likely to take more than a few directives at European level to achieve a steadying and then a reversal of these trends. Moreover, the 2004 accession has made the overcoming of problems that inhibit the development of transnational rail services in Europe even more important. The countries of CEE transport a much greater proportion of their freight by rail, although this has been declining quickly since the onset of transition. However, the potential of rail is demonstrated by the US where approximately 40 per cent of freight is carried by rail.

KEY POINTS

- Efficient and effective transport services underpin all forms of economic activity and enable European business to maximise their benefits from the SEM.

- Development of the CTP has been slow but the legal framework is now largely in place.

- The SEM has encouraged the reconfiguration of business activity across boundaries, requiring and receiving an appropriate response from individual transport sectors.

- Transport liberalisation has transformed transport supply and related sectors: for example, it has facilitated the growth of low-cost airlines and helped transform logistics practices within the EU.

- Liberalisation and infrastructure development were the overriding CTP themes of the 1990s and will continue to guide policy. Other priorities for the twenty-first century include quality, sustainable development and external aspects of transport policy.

- Reversal of the decline in the rail sector to ease congestion and for environmental reasons is a key theme of contemporary European transport policy.

ACTIVITIES

1 Identify the main transport policies of individual member states. How do these priorities vary (factors behind this variation could include geography, history, etc.)? How might differences within member states affect the formation of policy at European level?

2 This chapter identifies mergers as one possible strategy for European airlines to help them deal with the intensification of competition. Air France and KLM have gone down that route. Research the Air France–KLM deal. What were the expectations of this deal? Has it lived up to expectations so far? If not, what are the problematic areas? How has the deal changed the

way both parties operate? Are there any general lessons to be learned for Europe's airlines as a result of the Air France–KLM experience?

3 The chapter refers to the new distribution strategy of auto component supplier, Parker. Identify other companies that have changed their European distribution strategy. What factors underpin this change?

4 The opening up of Europe's rail sector occurred after the liberalisation of other sectors. Research the sector and consider whether the Commissioner was right to refer to one of the rail packages as 'a revolution which represents a genuine European real transport integration'. What factors might inhibit this 'revolution' and how might they do so? What are the benefits (to both the rail sector and to business generally) of a successful rail liberalisation?

QUESTIONS FOR DISCUSSION

1 How realistic are the European Commission's aspirations to engineer a modal shift towards rail?

2 Can the tension between an apparently incessant demand for more mobility in Europe and increasing congestion and pollution be reconciled?

3 How and why have logistics strategies evolved in Europe?

4 How would an effective transport policy contribute to overarching EU objectives?

SUGGESTIONS FOR FURTHER READING

Button, K. (2004) *Wings across Europe: Towards an Efficient European Air Transport System*, Aldershot: Ashgate.

Chlomoudis, C. and Pallis, A. (2002) *EU Port Policy: The Movement towards a Long-term Strategy*, Cheltenham: Edward Elgar.

Creaton, S. (2004) *Ryanair: How a Small Irish Airline Conquered Europe*, London: Aurum Press.

Dorrenbacher, C. (2003) *Corporate Reorganisation in the European Transport and Logistics Sector in the 1990s: Diversification, Internationalisation and Integration*, Münster: LIT Verlag.

European Commission (1992) 'White Paper: The Future Development of the Common Transport Policy – A Global Approach to the Construction of a Community Framework for Sustainable Mobility', COM (92) 494.

European Commission (2001) 'White Paper – European Transport Policy for 2010: Time to Decide', COM (2001) 370.

OECD (2006) *Trends in the Transport Sector*, Paris: OECD.

Stevens, H. (2004) *Transport Policy in the European Union*, Basingstoke: Palgrave Macmillan.

Chapter 11

Energy policy

Developing competitive, clean and secure energy supplies

Nos numeros sumus et fruges consumere nati (We are just statistics, born to consume resources).

Horace, Roman poet, 65–8 BC, Epistles bk 1, no. 2 1.27

This chapter will help you to:

- appreciate the links between energy and other policy areas at European level;
- understand the main themes of European energy policy – sustainability, competition and security of supply – and how they interact with each other;
- assess the current problems facing electricity market liberalisation;
- identify and assess the energy policy options facing Europe in relation to the environment and security of supply;
- identify the issues shaping the strategies of utilities in the European market place.

Modern economies cannot function without energy and the search to secure reliable energy supplies at an affordable price is one of the most important quests for European business. In the absence of a crisis, the wider business and policy-making community tends to demonstrate complacency about energy markets. However, it takes only the threat of disruption for energy to move up the policy agenda. This was apparent in January 2006 when the row over gas supplies between Russia and Ukraine threatened to spill over and disrupt gas supplies to the EU as a result of their transit through Ukraine. This incident placed energy in the spotlight once more. It could well remain there for some time given ongoing high energy prices and greater competition for supplies in international markets: the US, for example, increasingly needs to fulfil its energy needs through imports given the depletion of its domestic supplies, and emerging markets such as China and India seek to fuel their continuing high levels of growth.

In reality, energy is always important. European oil, gas and electricity companies account for a significant part of EU value-added and are important economic actors in their own right. Moreover, without their output, the rest of the economy could not function – mobility and production would grind to a halt and the modern way of life would be untenable. The centrality of energy to Europe's well-being was recognised by the fact that two out of the three founding treaties of the European Community – the Treaty of Paris and the Euratom Treaty – were organised around energy. Despite this, energy has not always been a major preoccupation of European institutions and, when it has featured strongly, it has done so around one of the following three main themes, or pillars, of energy policy:

- competition and the integration of markets;
- environmental protection;
- security of energy supply.

The chapter opens with a brief discussion of Europe's energy situation and the interaction of the three main pillars of energy policy. It then discusses each of the three pillars of energy policy in turn and concludes by analysing the corporate response to the major policy-induced changes in their operating environment.

BACKGROUND TO EU ENERGY POLICY

Europe's energy sector encompasses some of Europe's largest corporations and poses a wide range of significant policy challenges that demonstrate several recurring themes in relation to the EU's interactions with business and which overlap with several other distinct areas of policy making (see Figure 11.1). These themes and policy overlaps include liberalisation and deregulation, tax harmonisation, public service obligations, environmental issues, enlargement and the development of constructive sectoral relationships with third countries and regions – a process that takes on an additional dimension for energy in view of the demands of security of supply (that is, ensuring that the EU always has good-quality, reliable sources of energy available). Not only are these themes central to the development of strategy in Europe's energy producers but they are also significant for Europe's commercial and industrial energy consumers for whom energy can be a major cost component.

Energy policy does not emerge from a vacuum. Its starting point is the prevailing energy situation in the EU – and this is made up of the varying supply and demand situations across member states. Thus, while all member states support in principle the three pillars of EU energy policy, the significance attached to each pillar varies from state to state, depending on individual supply and demand situations and diverse ownership and market structures. Figure 11.2 shows the consumption profile of member states: this snapshot yields significant differences between member states. Malta and Cyprus, both small island states, rely entirely on oil for their energy needs. Others, such as the Czech Republic, Estonia and Poland rely more heavily on solid fuel, notably coal, than the EU average (indeed, EU reliance on coal fell in the 1990s from almost 30 per cent of total energy consumption at the beginning of the decade to 18.5 per cent in 2000) (Figure 11.3). This implies a different approach to environmental matters, particularly to climate change, is appropriate for these coal-consuming countries compared to those with a lesser reliance on carbon-emitting fuels.

235

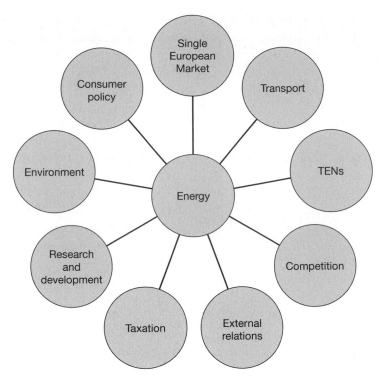

Figure 11.1 Integrated aspects of energy policy

Figure 11.3 shows that gas will increase in importance during the next decades whereas Figure 11.2 highlights those countries that were most reliant on gas in 2003. The UK, for example, has long been a gas producer, but the depletion of its supplies will make gas security a long-term policy preoccupation of the UK.

Moreover, as becomes apparent below, especially in the discussion about liberalisation, member states exhibit different approaches to their energy sectors. Some, such as the UK, have committed themselves fully to the opening of gas and electricity markets, whereas others, driven to a large extent by their own industrial policy traditions, are hanging onto the concept of the strategic nature of the energy industry which

they then justify to create or hold onto national champions (see below).

CONTINUITY OF EU ENERGY POLICY

The primary framework and principles of Europe's approach to energy have remained constant with the three pillars of energy policy – competition, environment and security of supply – providing the main policy focus. The relative importance of each pillar has varied in line with changes in global energy markets. For example, following the energy price hikes of 1973 and 1979, security of supply became the dominant energy policy concern. However, by the mid-1980s, the

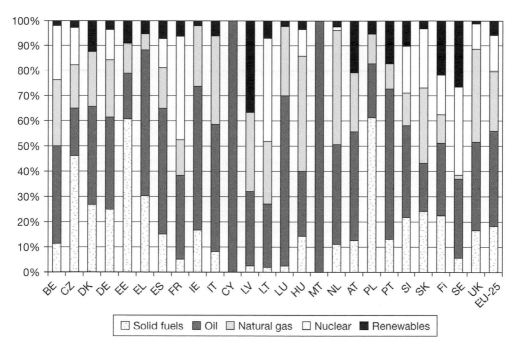

Figure 11.2 Gross inland energy consumption by member state, 2003

Source: European Commission, *Energy & Transport in Figures, 2005.*

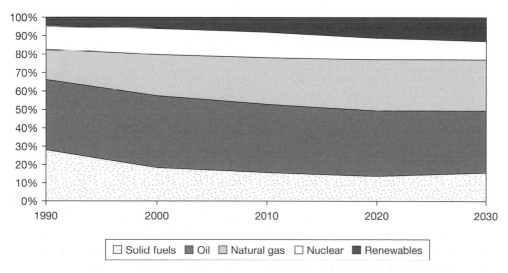

Figure 11.3 Share of energy sources in total energy consumption, EU-15

Source: European Commission (2006) Annex to the Green Paper.

237

return of real energy prices to below pre-crisis levels, the re-emergence of oil surpluses and the single market campaign pushed security of supply issues into the background and thrust competition to the forefront of energy policy priorities. There was also the additional complication that environmental protection issues had become increasingly prominent. The competition and environmental pillars continued to exercise strong influences over EU energy policy throughout the 1990s. However, security of supply issues slowly began to move back up the agenda as indigenous energy supplies started to decline and international energy markets tightened. The key challenge for EU energy policy in the early years of the twenty-first century is to ensure these three objectives work in concert and not in conflict with each other.

These pillars are not independent and frequently interact with each other, sometimes in a supportive and sometimes in a conflicting way. The promotion of energy efficiency, for example, improves both environmental protection and energy supply security by reducing energy demand and the need for energy imports. However, competition measures that lower energy costs to consumers may weaken incentives to enhance energy efficiency and increase demand and, therefore, could have negative security of supply and environmental effects. On the other hand, competition and open markets end the isolation of individual markets and enhance their security.

Support for technological R&D is also aimed at making renewable resources more competitive with conventional resources. Promoting Europe as a 'centre of excellence' for energy efficiency technologies will yield benefits in global terms as countries outside the EU become increasingly committed to improving their own efficiency, environ-mental protection and supply security levels. Energy efficiency represents a potentially huge export market for European technology and services, a factor that is reflected in energy trade diplomacy.

The energy TENs initiative is a prime example of a policy that incorporates all three pillars (see Chapter 9). There is a strong link between the Internal Energy Market (IEM) which removes legal barriers to energy trade, and energy TENs which remove physical barriers to energy trade. Without the physical means to take advantage of the IEM, the benefits of increased competition, greater efficiency, lower costs, greater competitiveness and economies of scale will remain theoretical and elusive. Energy TENs also serve security of supply by improving the efficiency and reliability of existing supplies and by diversifying supply sources and routes. The environmental pillar benefits from increased access to natural gas supplies which emit lower levels of carbon dioxide than other fossil fuels.

The continuity of the European approach to energy policy was reaffirmed in March 2006 with the publication by the European Commission of a Green Paper, *A European Strategy for Sustainable, Competitive and Secure Energy*. European-wide consultation on the Green Paper will be used to develop a tighter, more transparent approach to energy policy. Although the Green Paper suggests new individual energy proposals, these proposals all sit comfortably within the framework of the three energy policy pillars – indeed, the full title of the Green Paper (see above) confirms this. The Green Paper concludes that the three main objectives of European energy policy should be sustainability, competitiveness and security of supply, stressing that although member states have their own energy choices to make, energy policy must have a European dimension in a

THE 2006 ENERGY GREEN PAPER AND THE THREE PILLARS OF ENERGY POLICY

BOX 11.1

Sustainability

Europe needs to:

- develop competitive, renewable sources of energy and other low carbon emitting fuels, especially in transport;
- curb European energy demand;
- exercise a leadership role in global efforts to halt climate change and improve air quality.

Competitiveness

In addition to completing the IEM and improving interconnections, Europe needs to:

- ensure energy market opening benefits consumers and the economy as a whole and stimulates investment in clean energy production;
- mitigate the impact of higher international energy prices on the EU economy and citizens;
- keep Europe at the cutting edge of energy technologies.

Security of supply

Europe needs to:

- reduce demand and diversify the EU's energy mix and sources and routes of imported energy;
- create a framework that stimulates sufficient investment to meet growing energy demands;
- better equip the EU to cope with emergencies;
- improve the conditions for European companies seeking access to global resources;
- ensure that all European citizens and businesses have access to energy.

Source: European Commission (2006) *Green Paper: A European Strategy for Sustainable, Competitive and Secure Energy.*

world of global interdependence. Box 11.1 sets out how the Green Paper proposes to address the three energy policy pillars.

THE COMPETITION PILLAR

The competition pillar has been a constant, often dominant, theme in EU energy policy

since the 1950s. During the 1960s, the emphasis was on determining the broad principles of energy policy and on trying to coordinate a common approach to energy policy among the ECSC, Euratom and the EEC. Specific energy actions were limited but policy statements consistently emphasised the gradual creation of a market with the lowest possible prices, the widest

239

possible consumer choice and the free movement of goods in line with the principles of the Treaty of Rome.

The 1973 and 1979 oil price hikes substituted security of supply for competition as the pre-eminent theme of EU energy policy for a while. However, the re-emergence of oil surpluses and the return of low real oil prices resulted in the return of competition to the top of the energy policy agenda by the mid-1980s. The re-emergence of competition was also encouraged by the growing popularity of supply side policies, both at member state level, led by the UK, and at Community level following the 1985 White Paper, *Completing the Single Market*.

The application of SEM philosophy to the energy markets required a fundamental transformation of nationally based energy markets with a large degree of administrative price setting and central planning into a European-wide market with significant cross-border trade and prices that are responsive to market forces. In other words, the aim was to forge isolated or semi-isolated national markets into a functioning, integrated 'whole' operating on market-based, cost-driven pricing via the provision of a

---

BOX 11.2

MILESTONES IN EU ENERGY POLICY

1951	Treaty of Paris establishes the European Coal and Steel Community (ECSC)
1958	European Atomic Energy Community (Euratom) comes into existence
1968	Guidelines for Community energy policy give priority to competition and consumer interests
1973	Yom Kippur War – oil prices quadrupled
1974	International Energy Agency established to coordinate the OECD response to crisis. France declines to join
1979	Iranian revolution – further oil price hike
1988	Commission publishes inventory of energy trade barriers – the IEM
1990	Electricity Transit Directive adopted
1991	Gas Transit Directive adopted
1991	Gas and Electricity Price Transparency Directives in force
1994	Hydrocarbon Licensing Directive in force
1996	Directive establishing 33 per cent opening of the EU electricity market by 2003 adopted
1998	Adoption of a directive to open a minimum of one-third of the EU's gas markets within ten years
2003	Second Electricity Directive requires 100 per cent opening of the market by 2007
2006	Commission publishes a Green Paper on Energy – to be used as a basis for consultation on energy policy and on eventual formulation of new strategic EU energy policy
2006	Commission starts legal proceedings against 17 member states for failure to open up their gas and electricity markets as required

'level playing field' on which energy companies from one member state could compete equally with those from another.

Or at least, that was the plan. At one level, the introduction of competition into energy markets merely represented the application of economic liberalism to the energy sector in the same way as it has been applied to other sectors. However, certain perceived characteristics of the energy sector made the process more problematic. Energy liberalisation began from a situation in which most gas and electricity utilities were structured as either national monopolies (for example, France, Italy and pre-privatisation UK) or as regional monopolies (for example, Germany). The common perception of energy was that it was a strategic good and a natural monopoly which made it unsuitable for the type of changes being undertaken elsewhere in the single market.

Unsurprisingly, therefore, the 1985 Single Market White Paper contained no explicit reference to the creation of an IEM. Although, general treaty provisions, such as those relating to competition and free movement, applied to energy in the same way as to other sectors.

However, treaty provisions were insufficient in themselves to address the many energy-specific barriers within Europe. In preparation for removing these considerable obstacles, in May 1988 the European Commission published an inventory of barriers in the form of a Working Paper, *The Internal Energy Market*. This formed the base of subsequent proposals to free up the Community's energy markets – a task that has proven much more problematic than originally contemplated.

Given the international integration of oil markets; the large number of players (multinationals, state companies and smaller independents); oil price transparency and the

alternatives to line-bound transportation, the oil sector is considerably more open to competition than other energy industries and has taken a relatively low profile in relation to creation of the IEM. That is not to say that the oil sector has been entirely without trade barriers. Widespread barriers persisted in the upstream activities of exploration and production where most oil-producing states reserved some or all exploration and production rights to national companies. This resulted in the Hydrocarbon Licensing Directive which brought these activities into line with single market principles through ensuring non-discriminatory access to exploration and production.

Gas and electricity were another matter, however. Initially, it was anticipated that gas and electricity markets would be fully open by 1996. However, by 1996 it had only proved possible to attain agreement that member states would open up one-third of their electricity markets to competition by 2003 (see Table 11.1). In 2003, a second Electricity Directive was adopted, committing member states to a 100 per cent opening of their electricity markets by 2007. Negotiations on gas market access proved more difficult but the directive that opened the gas markets, paralleling the one in the electricity sector, was formally adopted in 1998.

The Electricity Directives continued the work of the Price Transparency and the Electricity Transit Directives adopted in 1990. Prior to the transparency directive, gas and electricity prices for large industrial consumers were unpublished and subject to negotiation and wide variations. The Price Transparency Directive required member states to inform the Commission of the prices and terms of sale of gas and electricity to industrial end users. It contributed to the IEM by increasing the market information

241

Table 11.1 *Evolution of rules governing Europe's electricity markets*

	Prior to 1996	1996 Directive	2003 Directive
Generation	Monopoly (public/private and/or regional/national)	Authorisation tendering	Authorisation*
Transmission and distribution	Monopoly	Regulated TPA Negotiated TPA Single buyer model	Regulated TPA
Unbundling	Not required	Accounts	Legal
Customers	No choice of supplier	Choice for eligible customers (33%)	Choice of supplier for: all commercial customers (2004); all customers (2007)
Regulation	National ministries	Not specified in directive	Independent regulatory authority to be established by each member state

* Tendering still possible if insufficient capacity to ensure supply security or to promote new technology in the cause of environmental protection.

available to consumers, thereby enabling them to make more informed choices about the sourcing of energy supplies and became more important when the gas and electricity markets are totally open. The Directives on electricity and gas transit mirror each other almost exactly. They require member states to take the necessary measures to facilitate the transit of electricity between high-voltage grids and of natural gas between high-pressure transmission grids.

Although an important milestone in the prising open of the Community's gas and electricity markets, the transparency and transit Directives were merely appetisers to the main course of energy liberalisation – the opening of the markets of member states to competition, both domestically and from other member states. Nevertheless, progress in this area was slow because of:

■ the reluctance of some member states, particularly those lacking indigenous energy resources, to relinquish control of their energy utilities to market forces;

■ the perceived need to control 'naturally monopolistic' enterprises such as gas and electricity utilities via national, regional or municipal government;

■ fears of national energy monopolies about the erosion of their market control and level of protection;

■ the fear of national energy monopolies that they will be left holding their public service obligations (PSOs) while new market entrants would be able to 'cherry pick' the most lucrative parts of the business, unburdened by PSOs;

■ expectations that greater competition would spell the end of long-term contracts without which major infrastructure investments are regarded as too risky.

The traditional view of Europe's gas and electricity utilities as naturally monopolistic implied that effective competition could not be developed for line-bound utilities, thereby creating potential for abuse of market power in the form of artificially high prices and 'monopoly profits'. Given the central and sensitive economic role of these utilities, they had long been controlled by public institutions at central, regional or local government level to ensure social obligations were observed and wide energy planning objectives (for example, priority for the consumption of domestically produced coal) were taken into account. The bundling of social obligations (for example, universal service, uniform pricing, social pricing, etc.) onto monopolistic publicly owned gas and electricity utilities in return for protection from competition is often referred to as the 'regulatory bargain'.

However, several member states increasingly moved towards liberalisation of their gas and electricity markets, including the partial or complete privatisation of state utilities. Problems raised by the 'regulatory bargain' were among the most difficult to resolve in this process. As some member states have found, problems of creating a competitive environment only begin with the transfer of a publicly owned monopoly into private ownership. Where 'natural monopolies' are no longer under state ownership, a publicly accountable, yet politically independent, regulator tries to provide the same economic signals to the monopolist as those within more competitive markets, with the purpose of contributing to greater efficiency, lower costs, and greater attractiveness to private investors.

In recent years, however, there has been a marked change in the perception of electricity and gas industries as 'natural monopolies' – a change that is the result of the disaggregation of the activities of utilities and of the realisation that all but one of these activities are individually amenable to the introduction of competition. These activities cover:

■ *generation*: that is, the actual production of energy;

■ *transmission*: long-distance transportation of electricity and gas through high-voltage grids and high-pressure pipelines respectively;

■ *distribution*: the physical transportation of energy from the grid to the end user through low-voltage grids and low-pressure pipelines;

■ *supply*: a trading rather than a physical function which includes sales and metering and invoicing and which has both wholesale and retail elements.

While transportation or grid functions such as transmission and distribution are, to some extent, still considered as 'naturally monopolistic', other functions such as generation, wholesale and retail sales, metering and billing were increasingly regarded as prime candidates for competition. Furthermore, devices such as open-access regimes and third-party access (TPA) have promoted the view that even 'naturally monopolistic' infrastructures such as transmission and distribution systems can be made more open to competition. The result of this more relaxed view towards the electricity and gas sectors was the compromise reached on the Electricity Directive in June 1996 and which was taken further by the 2003 Electricity Directive. Major features of the 1996 Directive were:

Competition in generation: member states were free to adopt authorisation or tendering procedures for new generation capacity. The authorisation procedure allows generators to build and operate new plants subject to certain technical criteria (such as safety standards, energy efficiency standards, etc.). This procedure is largely driven by commercial criteria, rather than by centralised energy planning. Under the tendering procedure, planning for new plant capacity is in the hands of a central planning authority. Under the 2003 Directive, the authorisation procedure was made the sole option.

Transmission and distribution: under the 1996 Electricity Directive, member states were able to chose between TPA (negotiated or regulated) and the Single Buyer Model (SBM). Under negotiated TPA, grid owners on the one hand and competitive suppliers or customers on the other negotiate conditions of access to the grid. Grid access charges must be published annually to enhance their transparency. Under regulated TPA, grid access charges must be non-discriminatory and published. Under the SBM, a 'Single Buyer' is appointed by the government and functions as the sole purchaser of electricity. The competitive element of the SBM comes from the differential between the price at which competitive suppliers can buy the original electricity from the generator and the resale price at which they can sell to the Single Buyer. Regulated TPA is the most competition-friendly way to increase market access and was made the only permitted market access regime in the 2003 Electricity Directive.

The 1996 Electricity Directive guaranteed open-access only to consumers requiring over 100 GWh/per year and 33 per cent of the market had to be opened by 2003. The 2003 Electricity Directive took things further and required 100 per cent market opening in stages by 2007.

In line with the principle of subsidiarity, the 1996 Electricity Directive set the broad parameters and principles of electricity liberalisation but left the details of implementation to member states. For example, irrespective of whether a member state chose TPA or SBM, the Electricity Directive

clearly defined the level of market opening required to ensure comparable degrees of competition. The Electricity Directive also did not establish exhaustive technical specifications for operation of the EU's post-liberalisation electricity supply industry (ESI). The only proviso was that any technical arrangements must conform to competitive principles and not create discriminatory barriers to market entrants nor 'tilt the level playing field in favour of the home team'.

Given the time that it took to reach agreement on the 1996 Electricity Directive, it was understandable that the parties to the negotiations felt a sense of relief and achievement in concluding the deal. However, in another sense its achievements were less remarkable, considering that it required the opening of only one-third of the market. Certainly, the directive was rather modest and unambitious compared to the original proposals which urged full liberalisation by 1996. This was, in part, due to diversity within the EU's energy sectors. When decisions are made which affect crucially important economic aspects of member states such as the performance of their electricity utilities, agreements are inevitably reached according to the lowest common denominator. This is especially so when the energy circumstances of individual members are characterised by a wide diversity of resources, policies and historical development. The directive represented a major shift in policy and was responsible for a spate of reforms and changes in member states as they prepared for the impact of power market opening in the EU. It also gave leeway to member states to adapt to the directive in line with their existing practices.

However, the passage of the 1996 Directive established the principle of electricity market liberalisation and the 2003 Electricity

Directive provided for the complete opening of electricity markets and restricted the options available to member states when opening their markets. In each case the option chosen – authorisation, regulated TPA, legal unbundling – is the one that is most akin to the liberalisation spirit (see Table 11.1).

In 2004, the European Commission set out its vision for Europe's electricity supply industry in which it spoke of:

seeking to create a competitive market for electricity for an enlarged EU, not only where customers have choice of supplier, but also where all unnecessary impediments to cross border exchanges are removed. Electricity should, as far as possible, flow between Member States as easily as it flows within Member States.

In theory, many of the legislative building blocks are in place to make the above vision a reality but, in practice, there is much evidence to show that, in the mid-2000s, this remains a distant prospect. Key features of the liberalisation programme are designed to foster competition and increase market access. The extent to which this has occurred can be done in a number of ways. Table 11.2 sets out the degree of market concentration in Europe's ESI. Although it does not tell the whole story about competition and access, it does indicate potential problems which can then be confirmed or otherwise by other indicators. For example, there appears to be a high degree of concentration in several member states. In France, one generator, Electricité de France, accounts for 85 per cent of generating capacity. On the supply side in France, there is only one supplier with a market share over 5 per cent, yet the top three suppliers have a market share of 88 per cent, implying a very high market share for the one company. Moreover, foreign sup-

pliers have only a 9 per cent share of the market. All these factors together, plus other concerns relating to the French market (see below) suggest that competition and access in the French market is restricted. Conversely, market concentration in both the generation and supply sides of the UK market is much lower: for example, the largest generator has only a 20 per cent share of the UK market and foreign companies have a 50 per cent share on the supply side. This confirms the general perception about the openness of the UK markets.

The degree of market integration can be measured by the amount of cross-border trade (see Figure 11.4) and by the level of import capacity as a percentage of installed capacity (see Figure 11.5). The 2004 accession states from CEE tend to have the highest degree of trade. At the other extreme, the island status and smallness of Malta and Cyprus have kept them unconnected from the rest of the grid. In many other cases, the level of cross-border trade is insufficient to provide any significant competition to dominant generators in individual markets. For example, the competitive impacts of the high levels of market concentration in France referred to above would be offset to some extent if there were a high level of electricity imports into France. However, France is essentially an exporter rather than an importer of electricity.

One of the causes of the low level of cross-border electricity trade is the insufficient degree of cross-border high-voltage links and the reservation of capacity on those links that occur as a result of pre-liberalisation agreements. The TENs initiative (see Chapter 9) was one way of attempting to overcome these problems. Although some progress has been made in developing energy TENs, problems have arisen in the electricity sector from the diversity of authorisation

Table 11.2 Degree of market concentration in Europe's electricity supply sector

	Generation		Suppliers		
	Largest producer by share of capacity (%)	3 largest producers by share of capacity (%)	Number with market share > 5%	Share of top 3 suppliers (%)	Market share of foreign-owned suppliers (%)
Austria	45	75	4	67	2
Belgium	30	70	2	90	10
Czech R.	65	75	–	–	
Denmark	–	–	5	67	Not known
Estonia	–	–	1	–	3
Finland	–	–	6	30	25
France	85	95	1	88	9
Germany	30	70	3	50	20
Greece	100	100	1	100	0
Hungary	30	65	7	56	97
Ireland	85	90	4	88	12
Italy	55	75	6	35	Not known
Latvia	95	100	1	99	0
Lithuania	50	80	1	100	0
Luxembourg	n.a	n.a	2	100	0
Netherlands	25	80	3	88	18
Poland	15	35	3	32	17
Portugal	65	80	3	99	33
Slovakia	75	85	4	84	28
Slovenia	70	95	6	71	20
Spain	40	80	5	85	8
Sweden	15	40	4	70	39
UK	20	40	6	60	50

Source: Derived from European Commission (2005) *Technical Annexes to the Report from the Commission on the Implementation of the Gas and Electricity Internal Market,* SEC (2004) 1720.

procedures within the Union and from environmental protests about the construction of high-voltage lines. Not only is the physical construction of these networks a concern but so is the management of the traffic across the networks which requires greater coordination and harmonisation than has been achieved by the mid-2000s, although some improvements have been made in this direction. In order to achieve greater competition and access among member states, the 2002 Barcelona Council set a target of 'a level of electricity interconnections equivalent to at least 10 per cent of

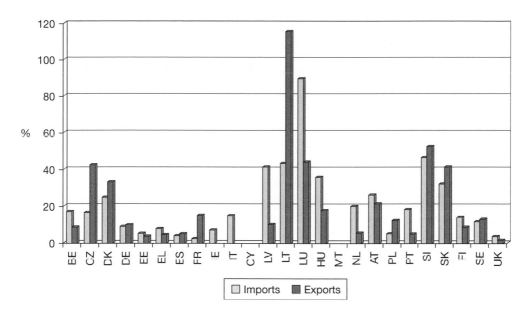

Figure 11.4 Imports and exports as percentage of electricity consumption, 2004

Source: Eurostat (2005) *Electricity Statistics: Provisional Data for 2004–5/2005.*

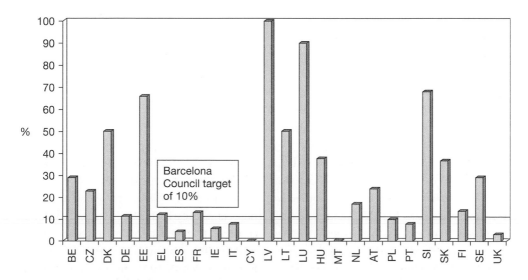

Figure 11.5 Import capacity as percentage of installed capacity

Source: European Commission (2005) *Technical Annexes to the Report from the Commission on the Implementation of the Gas and Electricity Internal Market,* SEC (2004) 1720.

their installed production capacity by 2005' (Presidency Conclusions 2002). Figure 11.5 shows that the majority of member states meet the Barcelona target but this, in itself, is not enough to increase cross-border trade.

Vertical integration is widespread in Europe's power and gas sectors, a factor which, despite unbundling and strengthening of regulation, dilutes the impact of liberalisation and increases the market power of incumbents. It involves the control by one firm of all stages of the utility supply chain from generation/production, through transmission, distribution and eventual supply to the consumer. From the perspective of individual utilities, vertical integration offers synergistic possibilities as a result of collaboration between different segments of the value chain and allows for compensation for market fluctuations at one stage of the value chain by fluctuation elsewhere. Case Study 11.1 on pp. 256–58 shows how RWE (Europe's third biggest power utility) has taken vertical integration on board. However, from a wider market perspective, vertical integration has the potential to make many types of anti-competitive behaviour possible, including cross-subsidy of activities or making access to networks for new entrants difficult or even impossible. Unbundling (namely, the separation of production and supply from transmission and distribution) and regulation to ensure the transmission grid is open to all in a non-discriminatory environment can help prevent this. Given that the unbundling that is in the Electricity Directives has not led to the desired results, EU Competition Commissioner Neelie Kroes has made it known that unless existing unbundling requirements are fully implemented 'not just in their letter but also in their spirit', the option of full structural unbundling (that is, the separation of the supply and retail businesses from

monopoly infrastructures) will have to be considered. Any further action will occur after the Commission's enquiry into the apparent lack of competition in energy markets and consultation on the Energy Green Paper is complete.

Further evidence about the discrepancy between the vision of a common electricity market and the reality emerged in early 2006 from the actions of individual member states more concerned with bolstering the position of national champions than with creating a single electricity market. For example, E.ON of Germany has made a bid for Spanish electricity utility Endesa but the Spanish government has introduced legislative changes to prevent this happening, claiming that energy is a strategic good that needs protection. France has been accused of blocking the takeover of the Franco-Belgian utility, Suez, by Italy's ENEL and of promoting the merger of Suez with Gaz de France instead. Moreover, Italy, the victim of the assertion of 'economic nationalism' in the previous example, has reportedly given itself the power of veto regarding the takeover of Italy's largest gas distribution company. In all these cases, the actions of the member states in question run contrary to the objective of the creation of pan-European energy markets.

In addition to new legislation and greater efforts to implement existing legislation, the Commission can use the courts to open up the markets, an approach that it used with some success in relation to telecommunications in the early 1990s. In April 2006, it appeared that the Commission has decided to go down this route in a big way when it sent formal warnings to 17 member states for failure to implement the gas and electricity directives in full. The areas that have caused concern for the Commission are:

- price discrimination that favours pre-liberalisation customers;
- insufficient legal unbundling and management separation between electricity and gas transmission and distribution operators;
- preferential access to networks for historical customers;
- insufficient transparency in tariffs;
- little or no free choice of supplier;
- weak national regulators or regulators that are not independent.

Member states have two months in which to make a formal response. Failure to do so could lead to a second formal warning and, ultimately, to a law suit filed at the ECJ. The Commission is also studying the energy laws in Hungary and Portugal to ascertain whether they comply with EU laws. In addition, the Commission has opened legal proceedings at the ECJ against Spain for failure to dispense with laws on voting rights in the energy sector (a 1999 law limits the voting rights of state-owned companies that buy stakes in Spanish energy firms to 3 per cent or less). The Commission has also requested Italy to do away with a similar law, threatening it with a similar court case if it fails to do so.

Energy is under the spotlight given high prices and threats to supply. Moreover, policy is lagging at a time when the need to fulfil Europe's energy policy objectives is greater than ever. Further directives and policy initiatives are, therefore, very likely but the Commission, unusually, seems prepared to grasp the political nettle and put pressure on member states to fulfil their existing legal obligations. This is a high-risk strategy but, if successful, could transform the business environment for energy utilities as the original IEM proposals intended.

THE ENVIRONMENTAL PILLAR

The link between the environment and energy is a key consideration in the formation of energy policy. This has not always been the case. The prime objectives of EU energy policy during its first 25 to 30 years, when environmental awareness was rudimentary, fluctuated between common market and security of supply issues. This only began to change in the 1980s with the emergence of concerns in Scandinavia and Germany about acid rain. By the end of the decade, global warming had moved into the political mainstream, further strengthening the link between environmental and energy issues. Policy initiatives aimed at tackling the climate change problem were bound to have an impact on the energy sector which is subject to the general tenets and principles of EU environment policy within the framework of the Sixth Environmental Action Programme (EAP) (see Box 14.4, p. 326).

The 2006 Green Paper on Energy Strategy confirms the centrality of environmental concerns to energy policy. Not only are environmental issues important in themselves, but they also make a positive contribution to other energy policy objectives. For example, an essential part of its environmental dimension is to reduce consumption through strategies to increase efficiency. Initiatives that reduce energy consumption also serve the goal of enhancing security by reducing the need for energy imports.

The Green Paper stresses the urgent need to address climate change and alludes to the following initiatives and themes:

The Emissions Trading Scheme: this encourages the adoption of more climate-friendly energy production technology and also promotes Europe's technological leadership in an increasingly important area (see Chapter 14).

249

The promotion of energy efficiency: the Commission estimated that up to 20 per cent of Europe's energy consumption could be saved. In addition to contributing to environmental objectives, such consumption reductions would lead to €60 billion less spent on energy, make a major contribution to energy security and create jobs. Accordingly, while recognising that many of the tools to realise enhanced energy efficiency lie in the hands of member states in the forms of grants and tax incentives, the Commission proposes to publish an Action Plan on Energy Efficiency. Possible actions, among others, include initiatives to improve energy efficiency in buildings and transport, especially urban public transport and a greater focus on the rating and display of the energy performance of major energy-consuming products, such as household appliances, vehicles and industrial equipment. The Green Paper also floats the idea of proposing and promoting an international agreement on energy efficiency so that it becomes a global priority.

Increased use of renewable energy sources (see Box 11.3): the renewable energy market in the EU has an annual turnover of €15 billion, half the world market. While renewable energies may have some negative environmental impacts they contribute much less to climate change than the use of fossil fuels and, given the EU's already dominant presence in this sector, open up the possibility of a global leadership role in renewables for European business (see Chapter 14 – section on ecological modernisation, pp. 316–21).

Carbon capture and storage: this technology literally involves the capture of carbon dioxide from power generation and its storage underground. More R&D and economic incentives are needed before this technology can become widely adopted.

Innovation – a strategic European energy technology plan: the development of new energy technologies across a range of applications is seen as important to sustainability, security of supply and industrial competitiveness. The EU's Seventh Framework Programme for Research, which runs from 2007–13, covers renewable energy technologies, clean coal, carbon capture and sequestration, biofuels for transport, fuel cells, energy efficiency, etc. In the Green Paper, the Commission expresses its preference for a strategic energy technology plan that not only seeks to accelerate the development of energy technologies but which also helps bring the technologies to the market and which promotes research into areas of high energy use. It envisages a role for the proposed EIT (see Chapter 6) in this.

THE SECURITY OF SUPPLY PILLAR (THE INTERNATIONAL DIMENSION)

The EU is a major net energy-importing region. This import dependence increasingly relates not only to oil but also to coal and gas (see Table 11.3, p. 253), two fuels in which there is expected to be a dramatic increase in import shares in the first three decades of the twenty-first century. The increasing reliance on energy imports results from a combination of increasing consumption and declining indigenous energy production and, unless current trends are reversed, Europe's dependency on energy imports could rise from around 50 per cent in the mid-2000s to over two-thirds by 2030.

This growing gap between EU domestic energy production and consumption requires greater attention to security of supply issues. The concentration of reserves in relatively few locations, especially gas (about half of

RENEWABLE ENERGY – A SOLUTION TO EUROPE'S ENERGY PROBLEMS?

BOX 11.3

Renewable energy sources cover a variety of technologies, including wind, solar power, hydroelectricity, biomass, energy from landfill, biogas and sewage treatment gas, geothermal energy and wave and tidal energy. Some of these technologies are already exploited to near maximum potential (large-scale hydroelectricity); the exploitation of others has grown rapidly in the 1990s and 2000s (wind power) whereas others remain largely unexploited (wave energy) and/or too expensive to compete with other energy sources in most circumstances (forms of solar power). Moreover, although most renewables do not contribute to greenhouse gas emissions, they are not neutral in their environmental impact: the construction of dams for hydroelectric power generation, for example, clearly has significant effects on the landscape as can wind farms. Proposals to develop the latter frequently result in strong opposition to their construction from local communities.

Nevertheless, renewable energy sources can help limit the emission of greenhouse gases and, in the process, displace imports and thereby help improve the supply security situation. Accordingly, the Commission has set two renewable energy targets. These are to:

- double the share of renewable energy from 6 per cent of Europe's gross inland energy consumption in the early 2000s to 12 per cent by 2010;
- increase the share of electricity generated from renewable sources to 22 per cent in 2010; the corresponding figure for the EU-25 in 2004 was nearly 14 per cent.

Figure 11.6 shows how much needs to be done to reach the first target. Sweden, Portugal, Finland and Austria already easily exceed the 12 per cent target and have done so for some time. This has been possible because hydroelectric power is a significant part of their generating portfolio. This option is not available to all member states as not all possess suitable locations. What is also apparent from Figure 11.6 is that the increase in the contribution of renewables between 1990 and 2003 was marginal (about one percentage point). The task of reaching the 2010 target, therefore requires an acceleration in the contribution of renewables that is hitherto unknown.

Figure 11.7 tells a similar story for the use of renewables in the power sector. In the seven years between 1997 and 2004, the contribution of renewables to power generation only increased from 12.8 to 13.7 per cent in the EU-25. Yet the target requires a leap from 13.7 per cent to 22 per cent within six years. Countries that generate hydropower, or wind power in the case of Denmark, already exceed the target. The 2010 figures on the graph represent the targets set for individual member states. These targets take into account the starting point and renewable potential for each country: in 2004, for example, renewables only accounted for 3.7 per cent of UK power generation. A 22 per cent target would have been completely unrealistic for the UK which, instead, has a target of 10 per cent for 2010 – in itself, this represents an ambitious 2.7 times increase in the share of electricity generated by renewables.

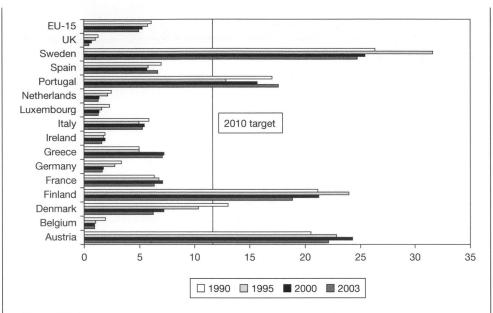

Figure 11.6 Renewable energy as a percentage of gross inland energy consumption, EU-15

Source: Eurostat.

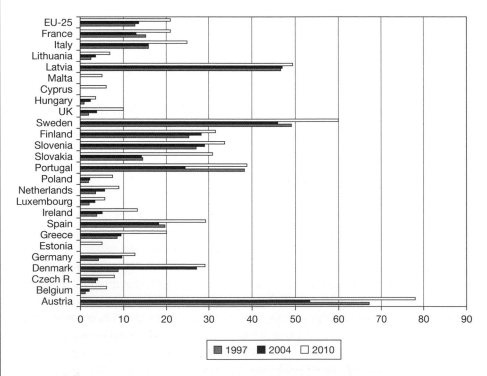

Figure 11.7 Share of electricity generated from renewable sources

Source: Eurostat online.

Overall, the renewables example demonstrates that there is not one simple magic solution that will resolve Europe's energy problems. Ambitious targets, which look certain to be missed, have been set for the contribution of renewables to Europe's energy economy. Even if these targets were to be met, renewables would still only account for 12 per cent of Europe's energy consumption. In other words, there would be a further 88 per cent that needs to be sourced and whose environmental impact needs to be minimised. This does not mean that the development of renewables is not worth pursuing but it does imply that they are not a panacea for environmental and supply security problems and that energy policy, whether in its environmental, competitive or security of supply dimension – or all three – needs to wrestle with a wide range of policies and issues.

Table 11.3 Import dependency in the EU-25 (%)

	1990	2000	2010	2020	2030
Solid fuels – e.g. coal	17.4	30.1	37.4	50.8	65.7
Liquid fuels – e.g. oil and oil products	80.9	76.5	81.4	86.1	88.5
Natural gas	47.6	49.5	61.4	75.3	81.4
Total	44.8	47.1	53.3	62.1	67.5

Source: European Commission: DG Tren – *Energy and Transport Outlook to 2030.*

the EU's gas consumption comes from only three countries – Russia, Norway and Algeria) and the location of significant reserves of oil and gas in politically volatile areas, including the Middle East, raises concerns about Europe's supply security. Europe is increasingly sourcing its energy supplies in markets that are subject to increasing demands from rapidly growing emerging markets (see Chapter 18).

In view of the above, the Green Paper sets out the need to establish an external energy policy with the following goals and instruments:

■ *A policy on securing and diversifying energy supplies, especially gas*: this entails the clear identification of priorities for the upgrad-ing and construction of related infrastructure, especially gas pipelines and liquefied natural gas (LNG) terminals (see Chapter 9) with emphasis on building up gas procurement from the Caspian, North Africa and the Middle East. A recent EU–Africa strategy anticipates the interconnection of European–African energy systems to help diversification of sources.

■ *Energy partnerships with producers, transit countries and others*: this process has already started via energy dialogues with Russia, Norway, the Gulf Cooperation Council, Ukraine and Mediterranean countries. The Green Paper envisages a role for energy dialogues with major consumers such as the US, China and India and perhaps through the G8.

253

- *Development of a pan-European Energy Community*: through its European Neighbourhood Policy, the EU has been trying to widen its energy markets to include its neighbours and to bring them closer to the IEM. Ultimately, this implies developing common trade, transit and environmental regulations as well as market integration. It is hoped that the resulting predictability and transparency would stimulate investment, growth and supply security. TENs have an important role in drawing in supplies from – or which transit through – North Africa, the Caspian and South East Europe, including Turkey and Ukraine.
- *Effective reaction to external crises*: the Green Paper suggests the development of a more formal, targeted instrument to cover emergency external supply crises, perhaps involving an early warning system.
- *The integration of energy into other policies with an external dimension*: this involves giving a greater focus in discussions with consumer countries facing similar energy and environmental challenges to the EU (for example, the US, Japan, China and India) on climate change, energy efficiency and renewable energy plus better use of multilateral institutions such as the UN, the International Energy Agency and G8.

In short, as with the environmental pillar, the enhancement of Europe's energy security depends on a variety of actions, including: reducing demand through increased energy efficiency; diversifying energy demand through greater use of renewables, for example, and through the use of a wider network of suppliers (to be achieved by energy diplomacy and by promoting the development of the necessary infrastructure); and better mechanisms for dealing with crises.

CORPORATE RESPONSES TO EU ENERGY POLICY

Liberalisation and the possibilities it creates have transformed the business environment in which gas and electricity utilities operate and have thus introduced new strategic considerations and tools. Prior to liberalisation, competitiveness was not an issue: rather, the main concern for utilities was to guarantee supply and to satisfy other public-service obligations facing them. The senior management of the energy utilities was dominated by engineers whose main concern generally was to attain the best technical answer to problems rather than to seek the most cost-effective solution. Traditional planning methods incorporating large-scale models, simulation and forecast of the overall markets were used to prepare for the future. In some senses, the industries took on some of the characteristics of central planning utilised by the Soviet system as they strove to meet targets and objectives set by governments rather than by responding to a captive market.

In a more liberal scenario, utilities must become more responsive to changes in the environment, which occur more quickly. They also have to take into account factors that were previously irrelevant: the only competition these utilities encountered in bygone days was competition between gas and electricity in limited applications. There was no competition within individual sectors and thus little heed was paid to issues of consumer choice or the creation and management of brands. Key stakeholders were the government, taxpayers and employees. Private shareholders in many, albeit not all, European countries did not exist and thus concerns about shareholder value also were non-existent. Since liberalisation, all these factors have been turned on their heads, requiring new approaches to all types of commercial risk and the utilisation of business models and strategic tools that are commonplace in the rest of the business world. This shift from monopoly to market requires a complete change of corporate culture and structural reorganisation – a process that is more developed in some countries than others.

Although the impact of the environmental and security of supply pillars of EU energy policy should not be underestimated, it is the deregulation of markets that will have the most profound long-term effect on business practices and strategies and, ultimately, on market organisation in Europe. The ramifications of the reforms will take many years to materialise fully but some are already becoming apparent, including:

Changes in purchasing practices: the introduction of a choice of supplier is important for purchasing practices and patterns of major industrial consumers and transfers an element of the commercial risk from the buyer to the seller. The reforms imply a shift from a long-term, stable relationship between buyer and seller to a wholesale market for energy similar to that for any other product. Large industrial consumers have, indeed, shifted suppliers in search of lowest cost supplies but the degree of switching varies considerably between member states, implying different degrees of competition within individual member states. Another rational response for large industrial energy consumers is the appointment of a single buyer for the whole group. Previously, each site within a bigger group would have purchased electricity from the monopoly supplier, of which there could have been several depending on the location of the sites. However, group purchasing of energy, and indeed of other utilities, offers the possibility of obtaining lower prices for bulk purchases. In addition, it enables enterprises to develop expertise in utility purchases, which requires market and technical knowledge.

Strategic flexibility: utilities have responded to the new European market situation by assessing their strategic positioning in the market. One option is the development of horizontal integration leading to the emergence of 'super-utilities' which bundle together not only gas and electricity sales but perhaps also water and telecommunications. This was one of the first responses of a number of European utilities to liberalisation but several have pulled back from this option. Vertical integration has also been adopted by several large utilities. Case Study 11.1 shows how and why RWE has gone about the vertical integration of its activities.

Geographic flexibility: geographical flexibility is closely allied to the concept of strategic flexibility. That is, with the extension of market boundaries, energy suppliers enter the utility markets of other member states, either on their own or through the development of joint ventures, strategic alliances or M&A. In some cases, they will also be driven to develop defensive alliances to protect their domestic markets and will be subject to predatory take-overs. As Case Study 11.1 shows, even the largest utilities at this relatively early stage in liberalisation are concentrating on regions rather than on the European market as a whole. However, as liberalisation proceeds and if the Commission is successful in its legal challenges to reluctant liberalisers at member state level, the geographical reach of the bigger utilities will spread further.

Although legally complete, the actual practical liberalisation of Europe's electricity

Case Study 11.1

RWE – FROM GERMAN TO EUROPEAN LEADER IN POWER SUPPLY?

Given the unprecedented and rapid changes in the business environment facing Europe's electricity utilities, how has their business strategy altered? The changes in question stem from liberalisation, environmental policy, a switch to gas for power generation, etc. They have resulted in intensification of competition, falling prices, sectoral restructuring, bigger markets with enhanced opportunities and the need for a new approach to risk. Many companies have moved from being a state or private monopoly to being one among several players in markets with reduced barriers to entry – a radical transformation indeed.

The response of individual companies to these changes has varied depending to a large extent on their pre-liberalisation market situation. In the Netherlands, for example, there were a number of small publicly owned suppliers: liberalisation put them on the defensive and their tendency was to seek critical mass through consolidation and mergers with others in their markets. Large state monopolies, such as EdF, that managed to come through liberalisation without being broken up, adopted an aggressive attitude to other markets and acquired some of their smaller counterparts as a bridgehead into new markets while maintaining dominance at home.

The German company, RWE, is a good example of a utility breaking out from a strong position in its national market to become one of the leaders in Europe's ESI. Prior to the liberalisation of the German industry, which occurred in 1998, one year before it was required by EU legislation, the German ESI comprised nine supra-regional monopolies which controlled about 80 per cent of generation, 100 per cent of transmission and about one-third of supply and distribution. The remainder of the industry comprised about 60 regional companies and 900 local companies that were responsible for the remaining generation, supply and distribution.

Although the German market is big enough to provide a platform for attacking the rest of the European market and to sustain emerging pan-European companies, some consolidation has taken place among both the smaller/medium-sized players as well as the bigger companies. Consequently, the post-liberalisation German ESI is dominated by an oligopoly of four regional monopolies formed, in large part, from the original nine with some foreign involvement. The companies in question are E.ON in Central Germany; RWE in the west, EnBW in south-western Germany and Vattenfall Europe in the new Länder and Berlin. In 2000, E.ON was formed from the merger of two of the supra-regional monopolies, Bayernwerk and Preussenelektra. Also in 2000, RWE acquired VEW, another of the erstwhile regional monopolies.

RWE's strategy in the newly liberalised world is to concentrate upon its core businesses and regions. RWE defines its core businesses as electricity and gas. Since 1990, it has divested itself of its interests in mining and raw materials, petroleum and chemicals, waste management and environmental services, mechanical and plant engineering, construction and telecommunications. In November 2005, it announced its intention to withdraw from the water industry in the UK and the US. The following elements lie at the heart of the strategy of this new, streamlined, multi-utility:

1 *Cost leadership*: the limiting of costs (and doing this more successfully than one's competitors – hence, cost leadership) potentially makes an important contribution to success in a liberalised European environment in which competition is intensified. During 2000–04, RWE successfully concluded a cost saving programme of €2.55 billion per annum. A second cost reduction programme has been launched for the period 2004–06 which targets annual savings of €700 million from Group reorganisation and the reaping of synergies from acquisitions.

2 *Vertical integration*: RWE has opted for vertical integration – that is, it maintains a presence at all stages of the utility supply chain from generation and production, through transmission, distribution and eventual supply to the consumer. Figure 11.8 shows how RWE achieves this. From the regulator's point of view, care needs to be taken to ensure that vertical integration (especially when a utility controls transmission as well as generation) does not result in cross-subsidy of activities or the blocking of access to the transmission system for competitors. It is for this reason that the EU's electricity directives required unbundling of the transmission from generation, initially through a minimum of the unbundling of accounts, and by the 2003 Directive, through legal unbundling.

3 *Multi-utility*: RWE adopted a multi-utility approach which originally encompassed electricity, gas and water. This raised the possibility of further synergies between activities in terms of customers, costs and competence. At the retail end of the business in particular, there is scope for economies of scale in terms of metering, billing and sales. Consumers can benefit from one-stop utility shopping and utilities can offer them lower prices if they sign up to more than one service. At the production end, RWE's involvement in gas production potentially extends the value chain from the wellhead to the light switch with some assurance of supply for generation and some guarantee of a

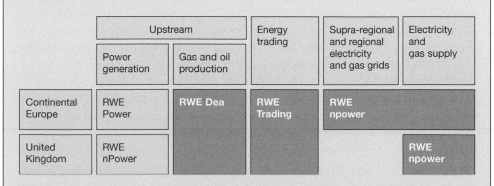

Figure 11.8 Vertical integration in the RWE Group

Source: *RWE Facts and Figures* (updated March 2006).

market for gas production, enabling further balancing of earnings. The November 2005 decision to withdraw from water in the UK and the US was because of insufficient synergies between these business and the core activities of gas and electricity.

4   *Regional focus*: RWE has decided to focus on four regions – Germany, the UK, CEE and North America. According to RWE, these represent high-quality markets in which it can establish a strong presence with a critical mass and in which there are no 'problem zones'. It also anticipates regional synergies, particularly relevant to the contiguous German and CEE regions. Although the markets are largely saturated and slow growing in Germany and the UK, this is balanced by much faster rates of growth in CEE, a market that RWE entered early and thus gained some first mover advantage. The company also compensates for this stable but low growth by its presence in more than one sector which facilitates cost savings and helps competitiveness. Moreover, a presence in multiple markets enables a utility to balance its risk. As Table 11.4 shows, RWE aims to take a leading position in whatever market it is in.

Table 11.4 *RWE's position in power and gas markets*

Electricity	Gas
Germany – No. 1	Germany – No. 2
The UK – No. 2	The UK – No. 4
Central and Eastern Europe • Hungary – No. 2 • Slovakia – No. 3 • Poland – a beachhead position	Central and Eastern Europe • Czech Republic – No. 1 • Hungary – leading position
Europe – No. 3	Europe – No. 6

Source: *RWE Facts and Figures* (updated March 2006).

In short, RWE's strategy has been tightly managed with the objective of creating a balanced portfolio which, to a large extent, cancels out cyclical variations. The restructuring of the 1990s and early 2000s, was intended to provide a focus on core businesses and regions and to generate growth organically and through ongoing cost and efficiency improvements. It is essentially a conservative, risk averse strategy designed for a mature market and for one in which there is no scope for differentiation of products resulting from product characteristics. It thus relies on cost savings and other efficiencies to yield success. This requires regional and cost leadership which, as shown above, RWE appears to have achieved. In the longer term, regional spread cannot be ruled out as the strategy continues to evolve along with the changing business environment. Any spread, however, will almost certainly have to satisfy the current acquisition criteria of market attractiveness in terms of growth potential, risk and market position, and offer high-quality management and assets and synergy with existing assets and regions. In the interim, further consolidation of RWE's position in current core markets remains a priority.

Case questions

1 Research another major European utility (for example, EdF, E.ON or Vattenfall) and compare and contrast its strategy for engaging with the European market with that of RWE.

2 What do you understand by the term 'multi-utility'? Why has it been an attractive concept for large utilities? Have these attractions been exaggerated?

3 What are the attractions of vertical integration for large utilities? In what ways might vertical integration conflict with the principles of the IEM?

4 Why has RWE chosen to focus its European activities on Germany, the UK and CEE? Should RWE consider entry into other parts of the European market? If so, which parts of the market should it consider and why? If not, why not?

industries has a long way to go. Consequently, the European utility landscape will be very different in a few years' time, assuming the apparent backlash against liberalisation in the form of economic nationalism is defeated.

KEY POINTS

■ The three pillars of energy policy can and do conflict. The challenge for energy policy is to balance the three objectives.

■ Re-evaluation of the concept of 'natural monopoly' finally made agreement on the key directives on common rules in the electricity and gas sectors possible. However, the power of incumbents and economic nationalism are threatening the attainment of fully open gas and power markets.

■ EU energy policy has had, and continues to exercise, a powerful influence on the corporate strategy of European energy companies.

■ Security of supply could become the dominant energy pillar once more. The combination of increasing consumption and declining indigenous production will increase dependency on the imports of major fuels in the coming decades.

■ There is no single solution to the environmental problems facing Europe. Europe must develop a range of policies to deal with these issues.

■ An emphasis on energy efficiency and the development of renewable energies could deliver Europe a competitive advantage.

ACTIVITIES

1 Analyse Figure 11.1 and find examples of how energy interacts with each of the policy areas in the figure. Draw up a similar diagram for another sector (for example, transport or telecommunications) and explain how your chosen sector interacts with other policy areas.

2 Research the renewable energy options available to Europe. Identify the environmental pros and cons of each option.

QUESTIONS FOR DISCUSSION

1 'A truly competitive single European electricity and gas market would bring down prices, improve security of supply and boost competitiveness. It would also help the environment, as companies react to competition by closing energy inefficient plant' (European Commission (2006) *Green Paper: A European Strategy for Sustainable, Competitive and Secure Energy*).

Explain the above statement. To what extent do you believe the above claims are justified?

2 The Green Paper suggests a number of environmental initiatives in relation to energy. To what extent do you agree that these proposals may be good for competitiveness and jobs? Note: see the discussion on ecological modernisation in Chapter 14.

3 Europe's looming problems in relation to security of supply will be long lasting, involve most fuels and have a demand component as a result of rapidly growing demands in international markets. How can Europe seek to ease the situation?

4 Will the European Commission's vision of a single gas and electricity market ever be realised? What obstacles stand in its way?

5 How has European energy policy and the environment facing European energy companies affected their behaviour and strategy?

SUGGESTIONS FOR FURTHER READING

Arentsen, M. and Kunneke, R. (eds) (2003) *National Reforms in European Gas*, Oxford: Elsevier.

European Commission (2004) *Medium Term Vision for the Internal Electricity Market*, DG Energy and Transport Working Paper, Brussels, 1 March 2004.

European Commission (2005) 'Commission Staff Working Document: Technical Annexes to the Report from the Commission on the Implementation of the Gas and Electricity Internal Market', SEC (2004) 1720, Brussels, 5 January 2005.

European Commission (2006) 'Green Paper: A European Strategy for Sustainable, Competitive and Secure Energy', COM (2006) 105.

European Commission (2006) 'Commission Staff Working Document: Annex to the Green Paper – A European Strategy for Sustainable, Competitive and Secure Energy. What is at Stake – Background Document', SEC (2006) 317/2.

European Renewable Energy Council (2004) *Renewable Energy in Europe: Building Markets and Capacity*, London: Earthscan Publications.

O'Dell, P. and Pinder, D. (2003) *European Energy Economy*, Harlow: Prentice Hall.

Peteri, G. and Horvath, T. (2004) *Navigation to the Market: Regulation and Competition of Public Utilities in Central and Eastern Europe*, Budapest: Central European University Press.

Chapter 12

Meeting the challenges of the European information economy

You can see computers everywhere – except in economic statistics.

Robert Solow

This chapter will help you to:

- appreciate the importance of information and communication technologies for business;
- understand the link between information, knowledge and international competitiveness;
- identify how and where ICTs have become increasingly prominent across the EU economy;
- recognise the form and nature of the EU's policy towards the creation of the information society;
- identify the major policy challenges faced by the EU in creating a socially inclusive information society.

Many of the actions to secure Europe's long-term competitive positioning within the global economy are linked to the development of the information economy. The development of the information economy, itself, is linked to the wider use of ICTs to create value and stimulate the emergence of new industries and skills. As manufacturing employment shifts towards locations where labour inputs are cheaper, so the value-added created in the European environment has to change. This solution increasingly lies in enhancing the mental capabilities of the workforce to generate, understand and utilise information. Furthermore, while information represents the raw material of the economy, longer term competitive strength lies in the ability to turn this resource into knowledge. Initially, this chapter discusses the form and nature of the information economy, before examining progress made towards its attainment within the EU. The chapter then examines the policy measures needed to stimulate its development in the EU.

THE INFORMATION REVOLUTION AND INTERNATIONAL COMPETITIVENESS

The trend towards globalisation has increased the salience among developed economies of undertaking the widescale economic transformation associated with the development and emergence of the information economy. If Europe is to create a competitive niche in a more intensely competitive global economy, then a new competitive paradigm needs to be developed around the management and utilisation of stocks and flows of information within and between businesses. This paradigm creates new demands, new industries, new opportunities and new challenges. It requires, first, the ability to create a competitive base in those industries that facilitate such flows (such as telecommunications). Second, it needs to enable users to handle, process and assimilate this information into useful knowledge. Third, it must offer the opportunity to renew the industrial base through stimulating information-intensive and knowledge-rich industries, such as biotechnology, pharmaceuticals, ICT, etc. Finally, the new paradigm offers opportunities for 'old economy industries' to create new sources of competitive advantage based on the increasing knowledge intensity of their products. In Europe's case, the paradigm needs to be shaped to take advantage of its competitive strengths of a developed education system and of a mature knowledge infrastructure, to generate economic renewal and to create new forms of competitive advantage.

The emergence of information intensity within 'older' and 'newer' industries will facilitate the emergence of new business models and strategies based on new value chains/networks created by increasing information and knowledge flows across borders. Thus, ICTs have the potential to raise the competitiveness of a generic range of industries through raising productivity in all industries and influencing the design, production and distribution of a large number of products and services. It will also facilitate new organisational forms such as outsourcing and increasingly tight linkages between industry and services. Thus, the effects of ICTs can offer a number of competitive improvements across a broad range of industries reflecting the development of the information economy as an interface between managerial and organisational techniques, a skilled labour force and the underpinning technology. The dynamic nature of the technology places an imperative upon states to constantly upgrade their skills base and stresses the importance of lifelong learning. Linked into the development of the information economy is the need to raise spending on RTD which contributes up to 40 per cent of increases in labour productivity.

Thus, not only are ICTs ubiquitous, but they also mirror a deeper source of change that renders information increasingly commercially salient. Moreover, the falling communication costs associated with the spread of ICTs are also increasing the commercial impact of globalisation. The shift towards more information-intensive activity within developed states reflects the fact that these states have limited labour and capital and need to seek new ways of increasing the value of their output. Thus, the impact is not merely across all sectors but also across all functions. This has been compounded by

263

sharp declines in the cost of processing of information.

Generally, the impact of information upon the competitiveness of an economy is dependent upon four 'permanent' factors, namely:

- how ICTs reinforce an enterprise's strategic vision and assist in effective and efficient decision making;
- how the utilisation of ICTs aids the rationalisation and optimisation of production;
- how the application of ICTs promotes increased reactivity and flexibility of organisations;
- how the use of ICTs stimulates further development of new technology and innovation.

The realisation of such competitive benefits is driven largely on an enterprise-by-enterprise basis in accordance with the desire to master uncertainty, to substitute a functional-based approach for a product-based approach, to develop complementary human resource systems and bring forth new and better technologies.

Consequently, the information society implies a growing and increasing interdependency between the productivity and flexibility of an economy and the quality and quantity of the information and communications environment. This trend is linked intensively into the process of globalisation. In general, ICTs facilitate globalisation by:

- making skills and know-how portable;
- facilitating a more rapid response to competitive pressures;
- eliminating barriers of distance;
- reducing the communication and transaction costs in trade.

A key building block in the development of the information society is accessibility to the information/telecommunication network. By offering universal access, these networks enable the anticipated economic effects to be reached. The basis of the network is a series of information infrastructures that have the physical capability to offer services and applications associated with the information society across the socio-economic spectrum. As the network economy develops, so these factors are likely to breed a virtuous cycle of integration within both European and global market places, a process fostered by more mature inter- and intra-firm networks.

Figure 12.1 defines the broad framework for the development of the information economy and establishes the context of the market-based actions of policy makers. The key aspects are:

- *users*: the people and organisations that access content via dedicated infrastructures;
- *infrastructures*: the technical medium through which the user accesses content;
- *environment*: industry and policy factors that drive the development of the information economy.

This framework highlights the interdependent nature of the development of the information economy. That is, the interaction users and industry with policy makers that facilitate this market-led development provides a core framework to analyse the development of the information economy.

Development of knowledge-based sectors within Europe has generally been poor. These industries are important not only in their own right, but also for their impact upon other sectors. By 2002, the ICT industries contributed 6.2 per cent of all manufacturing employment within the EU-15 (down 0.2 percentage points from 1990) but their con-

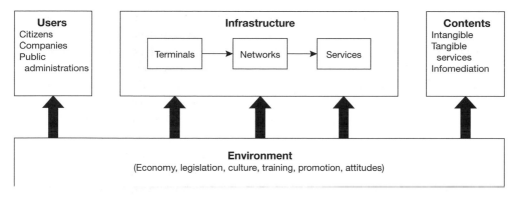

Figure 12.1 The framework for the development of the information economy

tributions to service employment had risen by 5.3 percentage points over the same period. In addition, value-added by ICTs in manufacturing fell by 0.3 percentage points between 1990 and 2002 but rose in services by nearly two percentage points over the same period. These trends suggest ICTs have had a greater impact on services than manufacturing. Moreover, between 1995 and 2002, there was no employment growth in the ICT sector but there was a 17 per cent rise in labour productivity. For services, over the same period, employment grew 4 per cent per annum, labour productivity 5.9 per cent per annum and value-added 9.5 per cent.

Evidence suggests that computers are often a catalyst for bigger changes: they not only provide a basis for the development of a fast-growing sector but also act as key enablers for an inclusive and dynamic information economy. Evidence from the OECD suggests that ICT investments up to 2004 had added 0.3–0.8 per cent to annual economic growth rates. In addition, an active ICT sector makes significant contributions to economic growth and can be the source of productivity improvements. The economic impact of ICTs has continued despite the 'bursting of the Internet bubble'.

A healthy ICT sector depends on the creation of a mature information culture. This not only generates the demand for ICT products but, more importantly, fosters the emergence of skilled professionals able to generate the needed innovations, etc. Over 30 per cent of the EU's working population is now engaged in the creation and diffusion of information across all industries. This is only likely to increase over the medium to longer term as the value-added within each stage becomes increasingly information sensitive. While the usage of ICTs is spreading, a core motivation behind policy is to help Europe catch up with the head start made by the US in the development of the information economy. While Europe may have more broadband connections etc., US businesses have proved more adept in using this technology for innovation and the development of products. When the new industrial policy was formulated in the late 1990s, EU ICT expenditure was less than half that of the US and Japan, the EU devoting only 18.9 per cent of RTD funds to ICTs. In other OECD states, the figure was as high as 30 per cent. In absolute amounts, the EU's investment in ICT research was only two-thirds of that of Japan and one-third that of the US.

Generally, only around 10 per cent of investment in ICTs is on the actual technology itself. The vast majority of investment is made up of new products, new marketing and training. Thus, if businesses can mitigate some of these costs through having a ready trained workforce that is able to adapt to new technologies, the burden on investment is reduced. This may stimulate new investment by existing firms and from FDI. In addition, the widespread use of this technology by many enterprises can lead to ways of reducing costs by placing increased pressure upon customers to undertake some of the processes themselves. However, there is said to be a productivity paradox within the development of the information economy: that is, despite the claims made by its advocates, there is limited evidence of ICTs offering any tangible improvement to the commercial performance of business.

PROGRESS TOWARDS THE INFORMATION SOCIETY

The development of the information economy was a key priority of the Lisbon Agenda: that is, the increased usage of ICTs throughout the socio-economic spectrum was targeted as a key driver of economic growth. The EU was looking to emulate the experience of the US which was closely linked to the rapid evolution of the information economy and which benefited from rapid growth as a result. This underlines the need to judge the development of the information economy in both absolute and relative terms. The majority of this section addresses the development of the EU information economy in absolute terms, addressing its relative performance where necessary. This analysis uses the framework offered in Figure 12.1.

A core building block of the information economy is the establishment of a common information area. This has its parallel in the SEM. In this case, free mobility is about information rather than the goods, services

and the traditional factors of production. Increasingly, information needs to be as mobile as any other commercial resource. This implies that the following are interconnected, interoperable and thus can move easily from one economic/social situation to another:

- *information*: this needs to be presented in a standard (that is, digital) format and be readily understood;
- *hardware, software and components*: (for example, PCs etc.) that are readily transferable between economies;
- *physical infrastructure*: developed in line with common standards that facilitate interconnection;
- *telecommunication services*: these need to be usable and accessible while possessing uniform functionality and availability across space;
- *applications*: where relevant these should exhibit standard format and functionality and be readily transferable;
- *users*: similar levels of awareness and familiarity with technology.

Users

As Figure 12.1 suggests, there are three types of users – citizens, companies and public administrations. There has been a rapid extension of the use of the Internet by EU citizens. In 1996, EU users represented just 15 per cent of total Internet users. By 2003, they represented almost 38 per cent. In 2001, Germany had the highest number of users but the general trend of a sharp rise in usage was common across all member states and the number of users in many smaller states rose by over 100 per cent annually. However, these figures are for broad availability and do not reflect access from the home. Eurostat figures suggest that by 2003, some 43 per cent of households had Internet access while many more accessed the Internet from their place of employment.

The EU is a relatively mature market: in the EU-15, the penetration of PCs was 31 per 100 inhabitants in 2003. In addition, there has been a significant rise in the number of Internet hosts which increased nearly eightfold between 1996 and 2003. By the end of 2003, nearly 40 per cent of the EU population were regular Internet users. This increasing information intensity is also highlighted by the rise of the mobile phone which had a penetration rate of nearly 80 per cent across the EU-15 in 2003.

Figure 12.2 shows the number of users as defined by individuals and business. By the end of 2003, nearly 50 per cent of Europe's population between the ages of 15 and 74 used the Internet. Internet usage was especially high in the Nordic states which had the highest levels of usage among both individuals and businesses. In addition, the majority of individual Internet users were male with higher levels of education. Unfortunately, Eurostat figures suggest that the usage gap between the better and less educated is

growing. There are also gender gaps in the use of the Internet with the Baltic states showing the lowest gap between males and female usage.

Figure 12.3 suggests that business access to the Internet is reaching saturation point. This is especially true among medium and large businesses. Thus, not surprisingly the main source of growth in business usage is in small-sized business (those with less than 50 employees). These businesses lag behind large business in use of the Internet for obvious reasons such as costs, management awareness, etc. Across European states, the smallest gap between small and large business usage is in the Nordic states.

In terms of enterprise usage, by 2003 only 30 per cent of all businesses were using the Internet for e-purchasing and 13 per cent for e-sales. The low rate of take up reflects continued concerns over security but logistical problems do not seem to be important at all. By the end of 2004, 48 per cent of large businesses had used the Internet for purchases but only 31 per cent of small businesses had done so. However, only 18 per cent of large businesses and 11 per cent of small businesses had received orders over the Internet.

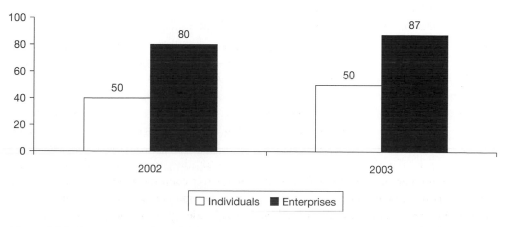

Figure 12.2 Internet usage by individuals and enterprises (%)
Source: Eurostat.

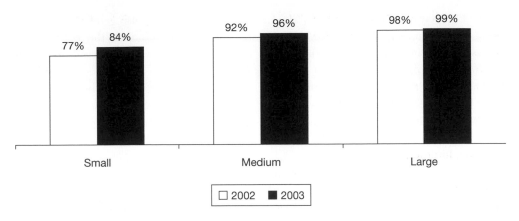

Figure 12.3 *Internet usage by all enterprises (%)*
Source: Eurostat.

The form and type of usage by business of the Internet is highlighted within Table 12.1.

In 2003, only an average of 9 per cent of European households had broadband access compared to 41 per cent of businesses. By 2003, employee use of computers was growing: over 60 per cent of all employees used them, the majority of which were Internet-enabled machines. Once again, the highest penetration rates were in the Nordic states. Eurostat estimates that 19 per cent of citizens have used the Internet for the purchasing or ordering of goods with only 5 per cent using it to sell goods. Thus, e-commerce remains unpopular with Europeans as a result of fears over trust etc. Indeed, in 2003, 60 per cent of Internet users in the EU-15 had admitted to never using the Internet for e-commerce. ICT usage is considerably lower in many of the newer member states – 35 per cent compared to 50 per cent for the EU-15. In candidate states, Internet usage was as low as 15 per cent (Bulgaria). These figures are mirrored in readiness for e-commerce (as assessed by adoption and usage) which suggests that there are three distinct categories among European states. The Nordic states have the highest state of readiness while Eastern European states (such as Bulgaria and Romania) are laggards. However, there is a gap between adoption and use as those that have adopted ICTs do not necessarily use it for e-commerce etc. Across the EU-15, 94 per cent of enterprises use ICTs with near universal adoption among large business.

Table 12.1 *Business usage of the Internet, 2003*

Usage	%
Have used Internet	81
Market monitoring	46
Receive digital products	36
Obtain after sales service	22
Market products	81
Possess a website	67
Access to product catalogues and price lists	44
Deliver digital products	8
After-sales support	29
Offer mobile Internet services	5

Source: Eurostat.

Across all 25 states, the EU's regular benchmarking highlights the progression of the information society, thus:

- 83 per cent of the population have access to mobile telephony, this rises to 87 per cent for the EU-15;
- 43 per cent of the population have access to the Internet;
- 89 per cent of businesses have access to the Internet;
- 87 per cent of large businesses, 71 per cent of medium-sized businesses and 52 per cent of small businesses have broadband access;
- 85 per cent of businesses in the EU-15 has broadband access compared to only 8.6 per cent for the 2004 accession states;
- 40 per cent of public services are available online with full interactivity.

Across the broader socio-economic spectrum, the spread of ICTs is also evident. While 93 per cent of schools had Internet access in the EU-15, only 53 per cent had an internal network. However, there were only 11 PCs per 100 pupils in EU schools. Further indicators of the state of the EU market indicate that computer professionals represented only 1.7 per cent of total employment in 2002, although most states reported a rise in numbers. Again, the Nordic states had the highest numbers of computer professionals. By early 2003, over 50 per cent of the active population was using a computer for professional purposes. Once again, these figures were especially high for the Nordic states where the figure was over 60 per cent.

In terms of the use of ICTs by public administrations, the benchmarking report in 2005 highlighted that over 90 per cent of public service providers have an online presence and that 40 per cent of basic services are fully interactive. The use of the Internet by

Table 12.2 Internet usage by individuals interacting with public authorities, 2004 (%)

Year	Obtaining information	Ordering forms	Returning filled forms
2002	12	7	4
2003	21	10	6

Source: Eurostat.

Table 12.3 Public administration and Internet usage by firms and citizens in EU-25, 2004 (%)

	Enterprises	Individuals
Obtaining information	45	22
Obtaining forms	41	10
Sending in filled forms	29	6

Source: Eurostat.

both business and citizens with regard to interaction with public administration is also rising. Now these services are available the objective is to move towards wider use of these services. Importantly, the gap between the EU-15 and the new member states was not especially large. The forms and types of Internet usage by business and individuals regarding public administration services are reflected in Tables 12.2 and 12.3 which show more widespread usage by enterprises than by individuals.

The ICT sector and market

A key spillover from the widespread usage of the ICTs is that it offers a framework for the development of the ICT sector throughout Europe. While on the demand side, there has been progress in matching its major rivals, Europe's ability to develop a progressive and thriving ICT sector that can rival the US and

269

Japan has yet to reach any degree of maturity. Across the industry environment, the spread of broadband and the Internet is transforming networks as is the development of digital television, etc. The maturing of these technologies in Europe should enable Europe's ICT players across telecoms, content and IT sectors to create credible competitive positions. Indeed, the foundations of a successful ICT sector are evident: Europe has large telecommunications operators, increasing broadband access, a large number of mobile users moving to more advanced services and strong investment in digital TV. In addition, new players are emerging in new technologies such as voice over the Internet.

Overall, the EU represents 32 per cent of the global ICT market, the US 29 per cent and Japan 14.5 per cent. In addition, the EU represents 31 per cent of the telecom market, the US 22 per cent and Japan around 15 per cent. In sum, in terms of the total global IT market, the US has 39 per cent, the EU 34 per cent and Japan 14 per cent. The pattern of growth in the EU's IT and telecommunications market is reflected in Figure 12.4. However, the relative growth of ICT in

Europe is low when compared to its major rivals. In Western Europe, ICT annual growth during 1995–2005 was around 3 per cent compared to around 4 per cent in the US. The figures for ICT market growth in Western Europe are shown in Figure 12.4.

Europe's ability to translate its lead in certain segments (such as mobile telecommunications) into a more mature information industry has been limited due to the absence of a large number of large IT companies, limited innovation and cooperation, limited growth in ICT demand from business and problems in developing pan-European initiatives to support such programmes. The adoption of digital technology is not feeding through into the development of this sector. This problem is compounded by structural weaknesses in the training and retention of researchers, patent applications, etc. In short, Europe has a number of key weaknesses within its knowledge base. The European IT sector contributes only 6 per cent to its GDP compared to 7.3 per cent in the US. In addition, Europe's IT investment lags US investment by nearly 2 per cent per annum. Thus, a core policy strategy is to increase the attractiveness of Europe to

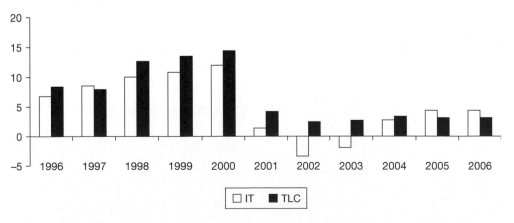

Figure 12.4 *Western European ICT market growth, 1996–2006 (per cent per annum)*
Source: EITO.

Case Study 12.1

NOKIA

Nokia is a rarity within European business – an EU-based firm that is doing well within the emerging information economy. Nokia has transformed itself from a sprawling timber firm into an electronics conglomerate that has become the world's leading maker of mobile phones and the world's largest seller of telecommunications equipment. In 2005, Nokia had around a third of the annual market for mobile phones. In addition, given the complexity of handsets in terms of software and cameras, Nokia can feasibly argue to be the world's largest computer and camera maker. Nokia's rise to prominence was aided by its insight that the mobile phone was becoming a fashion accessory. As a result Nokia placed a heavy emphasis upon design to enable users to tailor the handset to meet their individual needs and tastes. In short, the mobile phone was a classic case of mass customisation. In addition, its rise was also facilitated by the rise of the Global System for Mobile Communications (GSM) standard. GSM was adopted as the norm across Europe to aid mobility and roaming across these states. The US market, in contrast, was originally based around three to four separate standards. Finally, Nokia understood the challenges of implementing this standard. As its technology emerged as the dominant global standard, Nokia was able to achieve a strong market position and overtake Motorola as the market leader.

However, since 2003, Nokia's progress has been checked. Its market share has begun to erode as its sales have declined. The source of this trouble was widely blamed on its failure to innovate sufficiently to take account of the rising popularity of flip-phones or clamshell handsets. These are particularly popular in Asia and the US. This market development enabled Motorola (as well as emerging handset manufacturers such as Sony Ericsson, LG and Samsung) to catch up through the design of better and more popular products. Furthermore, when Nokia belatedly introduced a clamshell phone in 2004, it did so to mixed reviews. Nokia's design weakness was compounded by the fact that operators were becoming keener on operator-specific customised handsets. The result is that Nokia had to increase brand differentiation which often locked users into a specific network. However, as Nokia regards its customers (and not the operators) as the end users, the company was disinclined to get involved in these developments. This reflected the idiosyncrasies of the EU market where users are more loyal to handset manufacturers than operators. However, as others were willing to play along with operators, Nokia continued to lose market share. On top of this Nokia internally re-organised which preoccupied the company to the extent that it took its eye off shifting market dynamics.

Nokia's response to this challenge was to cut prices and to adjust its portfolio through more aggressive innovation. Furthermore, Nokia has shifted position on operator customisation as the firm has to offer tailored software and hardware to the major global operators. The immediate impact was that Nokia has started to consolidate its market share and in some segments is even beginning to reclaim old customers. However, Nokia still has to address the challenge of the commoditisation of mobile telephony, shorter product lifetimes and intense competition. Nokia's immediate response to the challenges has been to use its scale and prowess in logistics to keep ahead but it needs to combine these advantages with rapid adjustments in its portfolio to maintain its lead over its rivals.

Nokia was also relatively late in bringing latest advanced 3G phones to the market place. When it did bring these products to market, they offered limited functionality compared to rival offerings. However, Nokia is unworried by this as this technology is yet to be tried and tested and first mover advantage may not be strong as benefit can arise by delaying entry from maximising their impact and learning from other companies' mistakes. This aside, Nokia still has to identify new sources of growth. While it is doing well in emerging and developing economies, it has yet to convince users in mature developed markets to migrate to higher value devices, especially within the business user market.

Nokia is increasingly repositioning itself at the convergence of mobile telephony, software and media industries. In practice, this means transforming handsets from mobile phones into mini-computers with multiple channels to transmit voice and data. This convergence will enable the handset to support multiple applications for handling content. As a result, single application devices are becoming redundant. Convergence represents the latest phase of the development in the mobile phone industry that has gone from conception to commoditisation to convergence in little over ten years. By the end of 2005, Nokia had cemented its position as the world largest marker of both cameras (100 million camera phones) and MP3 players (40 million music handsets). The next frontier is mobile TV. Despite this, Nokia still makes the bulk of its revenue from the commodity product. However, the new smarter phones are seen as the way forward for the company. Thus, the future of Nokia rests on adjusting its product portfolio to develop and enhance its brand. This may mean refocusing the business away from benefits of scale based on integrated operations towards brand management. This implies moving much of the manufacturing out of the business to third-party suppliers.

Despite its initial success, the case of Nokia highlights the fluidity and rapidly changing market for information products. Its experience underlines the need for firms to constantly innovate and adjust product offerings to stay ahead of shifting industry forces. In part, this is a reflection of the intensity of competition faced by Nokia. The need to constantly pre-empt and respond to competitor actions has created a firm that has been able to stay industry leader despite the threat noted above. In developing a more mature information industry across other segments, the experience of Nokia is something upon which the EU states and businesses can draw.

Case questions

1 How did the emergence of GSM as a single standard for mobile phones across Europe aid the ability of Nokia to become a global leader?

2 What do Nokia's commercial troubles indicate about the strategies to be followed by market leaders?

3 What has driven the commoditisation of mobile telephony?

4 Is the strategy of moving towards 'brand management' by Nokia valid?

researchers. The development of the information economy is being driven by European consumers supplied by non-EU content providers. Furthermore, the market is driven by infotainment and not commercial applications.

THE EUROPEAN INFORMATION SOCIETY: GENERIC THEMES AND STRATEGY

The European model of the information society is based on a strong ethos of solidarity. The key preoccupation of this model is the creation of a socially inclusive information society that avoids cultural and economic isolationism across a broad range of socio-economic groupings. In this context, the EU's approach is to foster the creation of a knowledge-based society by focusing on market failures in the development of the emerging information economy. This means creating conditions for supply and, where necessary, stimulating demand to meets its broadly defined socio-economic objectives. According to Rodrigues (2003), policy towards the development of the information society within Europe must become more demand led to enable it to focus on job creation and to close existing disparities in digital usage across the EU. The attainment of these objectives is set within a market-driven framework. This framework is based on the transnational environment as the most effective arena in which these changes can be realised because:

- national markets are of insufficient size to realise the needed investment in advanced ICTs;
- many technologies are aimed at niche markets that are too small in any one state;
- the speed and ability of these new services

to offer multi-media could allow them to break through linguistic barriers.

Within the context of the transnational market place, public authorities throughout the EU are playing a largely market-creating function, seeking to push the market for information society services, applications and technologies towards a 'critical mass' and an environment in which:

- telecommunications and other communications technology should be affordable;
- user demands are adequately expressed;
- there is adequate awareness of ICTs in all parts of the European economy;
- education and training systems readily absorb the implications and dynamics of ICTs;
- new information products emerge that are useful, usable and affordable;
- supply conditions improve to the extent that greater economies are available in the production and supply of ICTs;
- there are commercial incentives to supply all parts of the European socio-economic body;
- state involvement is largely redundant.

This highlights the public sector's role as a catalyst, not as a primary driver, in efforts to develop the information society. A lack of financial power means that much public sector action seeks to bring together partners with a mutual interest in developing projects that actively contribute to the development of the information society.

Policy actions are set within a framework of creating a mature information market. This operates on both the supply and demand side as well as developing measures that cut across these market drivers (see Figure 12.5). The broad set of actions followed are as follows.

273

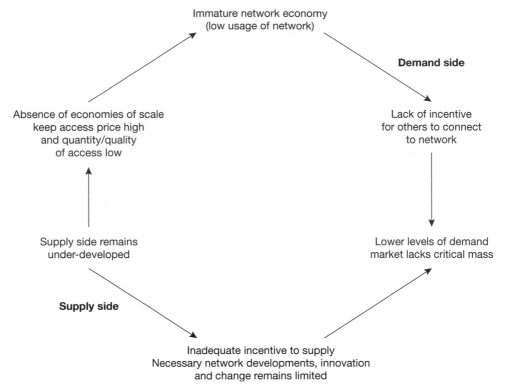

Figure 12.5 The strategic policy framework for the development of the EU information economy
Source: European Commission, 2005.

Developing a mature information industry

The EU has a large trade deficit in ICTs and past failures in seeking to target ICT champions (notably Bull in France and Olivetti in Italy) have pushed the EU into a much more market-led direction. Initial action towards strengthening the European ICT industry has focused on attaining a critical mass for information society-related technologies and services within Europe. The market for information is being developed within the context of the convergence of the telecommunications, computing and 'content' (for example, the broadcasting and software industries) sectors as the respective markets and technology used by each sector start to overlap. However, the development of an

information industry not only requires more commercial freedom but also greater autonomy from other constraining factors such as state ownership and its implications for resource availability.

Regulation

Changing the regulatory structure of the telecommunications sector is essential to stimulate the investment required for information society-related products and services. This process has been ongoing since 1987 and the final phase towards complete open markets began in 1998. The initial consequence of such actions will be to breed greater transparency and consistency in national regulations derived from the desire to extend the principles of the SEM to the telecommunications sector. The application of the SEM to this sector will not only speed up investment in the necessary networks but will also stimulate the needed innovation, improve the quality of communications and deliver lower tariffs (and thus stimulate the demand) for these technologies. These processes, in combination, are expected to have a positive impact upon the ability of EU-based enterprises to minimise their core operating costs associated with the network enterprise: a factor that will aid the ability of these businesses to compete successfully on a global basis.

In 2003, a new regulatory framework was launched to reflect the process of convergence between the telecoms, IT and content sectors. The structure builds upon the generic framework provided by competition law and thus is seen as temporary until competition matures. Once maturity is reached, the sector becomes subject to generic competition law not to sector-specific regulation. Thus, over the short term, the regulation seeks to ensure that new entrants are not disadvantaged vis-à-vis incumbents in the liberalisation process. There are a number of key principles underpinning the regime, namely:

- *cutting red tape*: including development of a general authorisation to enter markets as opposed to the need for individual licences;
- *light touch system of regulation*: based on competition – direct control needed where market power is evident though regulation is ultimately seen as temporary;
- *technological neutrality*: to reflect the process of convergence the framework treats all technologies in the same manner to create a common market for electronic communications. This gives the framework the flexibility to deal with the convergence process;
- *consistency across markets*: ensure the regulatory regime is consistent across markets.

In addition, the framework establishes new processes to allow for collaboration between national bodies to establish the necessary levels of coherence. The framework consists of six directives that deal with the generic framework, authorisation of generic licence, directive access and interconnection, universal services, e-privacy and data protection and competition and radio spectrum. The new process created by the directive will rely heavily upon the work of the independent national regulatory authorities (NRAs) in each state. At the member state level, action is based on a local analysis of key competitive roadblocks.

The Commission has an overseeing role to ensure the timely and effective implementation of the directive. When a member state is in breach of its commitments, the Commission can take that state to court. Member states were required to transpose the EU regulatory framework into national law by May 2004. Of the 25 states, 20 have completed the adoption of primary legislation. However, by the end of 2004 five states had yet to adopt the primary framework. In a further eight states, aspects of the secondary legislation had still to be implemented. In addition, the Commission is concerned that the NRAs are not as independent of decisions from the state as they should be. This is largely due to a residual shareholding by some governments in incumbent operators. In addition, the Commission feels that even where there are independent ministries, they have not always been forthcoming with the necessary market analysis.

Research

Support for the development of ICTs has been a recurrent theme within the EU's successive R&D programmes. However, there has been limited success in contributing to the development of the information society, given:

- the inadequate resources directed to the R&D effort;
- the relatively poor commitment to R&D compared to Europe's major competitors;
- the poor coordination of R&D at various levels;
- the inability to convert scientific and technological achievements into industrial and commercial successes.

One of the key objectives within the sixth framework (2002–06) was to bring universities, research institutes, SMEs, LSEs, government etc. together to create a critical mass in terms of research. Policy sought to overcome fragmentation in research through two new instruments – networks of excellence and integrated projects. Both of these were developed for the purpose of fostering collaborative research and to tie the research priorities into the Lisbon Agenda. Thus, the need to develop a competitive ICT sector was an influence over the direction of funds within the research programme. The objective of the research initiative is to secure Europe a lead within critical technologies that underpin the development of the information economy globally. To this end, the EU is focusing on a number of key building blocks, notably miniaturisation, broadband communications infrastructures and the user-friendly nature of the technology offered.

Deployment

The EU has developed successive programmes to overcome initial commercial uncertainty (notably over-demand) within a number of information society-related services and applications. The major thrust of the EU's efforts to create an information market from 1999 to 2005 was the eEurope initiative. The aims of this programme were broadly to:

- stimulate the deployment of the underlying infrastructure through the development of a secure broadband infrastructure;
- stimulate the development of advanced services such as e-government;
- promote the uptake of e-business.

Alongside these broad themes, the programme promoted the use of the Internet through investment in the human dimension of the information society.

The aim of these policies was to work passively on both demand and supply sides of the market to generate a virtuous cycle of growth in the usage and spread of ICTs. To meet this objective, all EU-15 states drew up national broadband plans to connect all public administrations and sought to remove any digital divides. Demand side initiatives included financial incentives to stimulate usage in under-served segments, increased usage via the public sector and the connecting of both public administrations and SMEs to the Internet. While progress had been made by the end of 2005 (notably in areas such as the deployment of government services, eHealth and eLearning), concerns remained over broadband deployment, especially in less favoured regions, and about the roadblocks provided by incumbents.

With the ending of the eEurope programme, the EU launched a new policy framework to support the development of the information economy. The new programme, i2000, is based on promoting the development of an open and competitive digital economy based on the following core priorities:

1   *The creation of Single Information Space*: that is, a framework that allows the harmonious development of the movement of information in all forms throughout Europe. This requires a common set of regulations that govern the supply of content and services and the operation of networks. These regulations (as per the regulatory framework) should be technologically neutral. Thus, existing regulations will be reassessed to take account of the new demands created by convergence. There is also action to create uniform security and rights management as well as efforts to support the creation and distribution of content.

2   *Research*: the programme aims to increase investment in European ICTs by 80 per cent by 2010. The 7th Framework for RTD is likely to double the funds available for ICT research. The Commission wants to use this programme to enhance the links between research and deployment.

3   *Inclusive Information Society*: in continuity with other programmes, the aim is to develop a policy framework that offers all citizens the ability to interact with the information economy. This will work via strategies that use ICT in services that all citizens access, such as healthcare and learning.

4   *To contribute to the new start for the Lisbon Strategy*: the EU is lagging in terms of many of the targets set by the Lisbon Agenda. The relaunch of the programme should provide an added impetus and commitment to speed up the development of the information economy.

The i2000 programme offers an integrated approach to the information society and audio-visual policy within the EU. The policy is an all-embracing strategy and includes all aspects of the EU's work in this area as well as the actions of member states whose own information society priorities run parallel to those developed by the EU. This integrated action plan will give more coherence and greater consistency to the EU's increasingly dispersed policy efforts. It is also important that these policy measures act as a supporting framework for national policy measures. Thus, the EU can act as a catalyst and benchmark for national policies by setting targets that can help to prioritise and align policy.

CHALLENGES TO THE CREATION OF THE EUROPEAN INFORMATION SOCIETY

Advanced mobile deployment

The deployment of mobile technologies is one area where the EU has been able to turn a technological lead into higher levels of employment. Between 1993 and 2003, the number of jobs in the mobile telephony sector increased from around 50,000 to almost 700,000. A key objective is to turn the lead in basic mobile technology into leadership in the new era of advanced mobile communications. This leadership was facilitated by the creation of a common European standard for mobile telephony (GSM) which was adopted globally. This standard was a direct legacy of EU-funded research which enabled suppliers to develop a common product for multiple markets, thereby facilitating interoperability and the creation of network effects to stimulate the further spread of the standard. Currently, there are over 1 billion users with a GSM-standard phone. The coordinated approach taken to GSM has worked to the EU's advantage and the EU has sought to sustain this strategy into the next generation of mobile telephony: third generation (3G). To this end the EU has agreed a new standard – Universal Mobile Telecommunications System (UMTS) – for the harmonisation of this next generation (3G) of mobile technologies.

However, flaws within the licensing regimes have limited the ability of operators to both build and deploy the necessary networks to support the development and deployment of new advanced mobile services. On top of a roll out process that was expected to cost €105 billion, operators paid governments €110–130 billion for licenses to provide these services. This led to a massive transfer of funds from private to public sectors and diverted market resources from the development of the information society. This problem was compounded by a range of other issues that slowed the development and deployment of advanced mobile services such as:

- delays arising from supply and demand as suppliers underestimated the time needed to develop hardware and overestimated demand for these advanced services;
- traffic forecasts fell when the dotcom bubble burst;
- the lack of a harmonised and stable regulatory framework for infrastructure-free competitors;
- differences in the licensing procedure between states which created different market conditions between states;
- uncertainties over the regulatory structure;

- environmental and health regulations, notably over the positioning of masts;
- an inadequate number of licences and allocation of spectrum;
- coverage obligations in licences which directly increased the costs of roll out.

According to the network operators, acceleration of the roll out of 3G would be helped by a regulatory framework that is more laissez-faire than previous regimes. The regulatory regime has to give operators greater freedom of cost increasing and reducing measures such as coverage requirements and infrastructure sharing. For example, in some states where coverage requirements are not met, operators face sanctions. Network operators also feel there is a need to extend licences.

By 2001, the German regulator had signalled that it was prepared to allow infrastructure sharing: a move that could save operators around €14 billion. However, although there are some concerns that these changes could limit competition and choice and raise prices, the European Commission did not anticipate competition concerns through infrastructure sharing, especially in areas with lower population densities. While conditions vary across Europe, sharing is allowed if the operator maintains full operational control of their network. Thus, the sharing of frequencies and the core network is not allowed. In the UK, sharing is limited to smaller cities. This reflects a need to both sustain competition and ensure that there is extensive coverage.

The Lisbon Agenda increased the political and economic importance of a rapid roll out of 3G. The difficult financial environment led to many firms refocusing their market strategies and seeking to alter the terms of licences and of the regulatory environment to make the roll out easier (see above). This was intended to appeal to the broad socio-political objectives of the political bodies to make market strategies less constrained. Roll out deadlines were extended when it became apparent that not only was equipment not available but the financial cost was – over the short term – prohibitive. The Commission was unsympathetic to the complaints of mobile operators. Indeed, the Commission has sustained the belief that the pre-eminent focus has to be on operators getting their market strategies right and that the regulatory framework is sufficiently flexible to adapt to changing conditions. However, its does acknowledge that there may be a need for greater coordination between states to ensure social inclusiveness in the process of roll out. The adaptation of the regulatory environment has been evident in terms of changes to roll out obligations; licence duration and fees and other payments as well the sharing of network infrastructure.

Employment

History has bred a suspicion of technological change given that every time a new form of technology is adopted by business, lower levels of employment result from changes in the ratio of capital to labour. Concerns about ICTs are particularly salient due to:

- the pervasiveness of ICTs across all sectors;
- the speed with which ICTs are being introduced;
- the high level of cross-border mobility brought about by ICTs.

The counter-argument is that while the evolution of the information society may destroy jobs, it is also expected to create new forms and types of employment – a natural consequence of any 'logistical / technological'

revolution. The conventional view implies that 'old' mundane and low-skilled jobs will be replaced with 'new' higher skilled occupations that deliver higher value-added.

However, it is likely that there will be a lag between the destruction of 'old economy' jobs and the creation of 'new economy' employment in sufficient quantities to absorb the surplus labour resulting from the transition. Minimisation of the length of this lag has to be a core policy priority. The application of ICTs will also change work patterns, work organisation and the functioning of labour markets. The adoption of ICTs is symptomatic of broader trends towards more flexible work forces (see Chapter 13), network enterprises and growing instability for less-skilled employment. The requirement of policy is to stimulate flexibility, thereby minimising the disruption within labour markets from the emerging information society. Policy is responding to such challenges by stressing the notion of lifelong learning to ensure that resources are sufficiently flexible to match the changes brought about by the development of the information society. The success of such strategies requires a more fundamental shift in the mentality of the labour force. Thus, it is not simply a case of policy makers taking ICTs to workers but also of workers being willing and able to participate in such changes.

Social cohesion

The major social fear from the advent of the information society is that it works to reinforce existing socio-economic divides. In a market-driven pattern of evolution, effective demand will determine access to information and ICTs. A lack of effective demand will retard the development of the information society within certain socio-economic

279

groups, especially the low skilled who are most likely to be adversely affected by the changes. An inability to obtain and access information risks creating 'information haves and have nots' and reinforcing existing social divisions and economic deprivation. For this reason, the Commission has attempted to define universality of access to certain core services as integral to the development of the information society. This needs to be coupled with the affordability of the necessary technologies.

A secondary concern is that the new work and leisure patterns facilitated by the information society could undermine sociability by confining people to an isolated existence. Consequently, there is a desire that these changes promote new forms of contact with people as well as with technology. For these reasons, the Commission intends that the development of the information society should be people centred. Thus, ICTs are to be utilised in people-centred services such as health and education. However, the consequences for social cohesion and ICTs are not totally understood.

A further concern is that the information society will lead to social homogeneity based upon the fact that the majority of the information will be largely US sourced. Member states have been keen to stem this 'cultural imperialism', in some cases limiting opportunities for US-sourced English-language content within the EU's emerging information market. Increasingly, European states are taking counteractive measures to resist potential cultural domination by trying to ensure that the information society reflects the diversity of Europe.

Regional cohesion

The Commission implicitly recognises that the development of the information society

will occur in an uneven manner across the EU. One of the key points of the European information economy is that it is primarily an urban phenomenon. One of the key legacies of a market-driven approach is the focus of infrastructure and service deployment on areas with the highest density of users. Thus, there is an assumption that areas of lower population density will tend to be underserved by these infrastructure and services. In the least developed (Objective 1) regions of the EU, Internet usage is 33 per cent compared to 57 per cent for other regions (2003).

As the information society becomes increasingly important for economic development such differences run counter to the EU's objective of economic cohesion. This is inevitable given that investment will naturally focus upon high-demand areas. The ability to utilise the information society as a tool for regional development is restricted by the relative immaturity of the local information culture and the provision of supporting infrastructure (both of which are especially lacking in the cohesion states). In practice, much of the development of the information society is occurring on a localised, regional basis and not necessarily in line with the priorities of the Structural Funds. The Commission has encouraged regional cooperation to overcome vicious cycles of under-development for these regions. There have already been a number of initiatives to speed up the deployment infrastructure in remote and rural regions. These have sought to create and aggregate demand to stimulate the market for these technologies in these areas. However, these actions are not designed to undermine the market place.

The European Initiative for Growth has increased the emphasis on the development of broadband coverage through the Digital

Divide 'Quick Start' project. The aim of this project is to accelerate the provision of broadband in under-served areas through a technologically neutral approach. This is supported through RTD programmes linked to 3G technology as a means of spreading the reach of broadband. As mentioned, as part of the eEurope programme, member states have been compelled to introduce their own broadband implementation programmes. One of the key aims of this is to manage the spread of broadband in rural areas. With a process of time/space and cost/space convergence, broadband opens up new opportunities to stimulate economic development and renewal. The aim of the policy is to achieve at least a 95 per cent coverage rate by 2008. This is a minimum requirement given the broad socio-economic changes under way within the EU and its competitor nations.

The choice of technology for access in rural areas is a function of the density of users. In sparsely populated areas (less than 20 users per square kilometre), the Commission is aiming for a pan-European initiative to aggregate demand from these regions to stimulate market-driven deployment. In areas with between 20–50 users per square kilometre, the policy seeks to create public private initiatives. In some states, municipal authorities have entered the broadband market by rolling out fibre optic networks which were designed to stimulate investment by the private sector. However, many have criticised the involvement of local government in this action as it could lead to policy failure and be a waste of money. In addition, action in the supply of capacity policy has also worked to aggregate demand for broadband. This is often done by interconnecting administrations, schools and health centres.

CONCLUSION

The information society is having an increasing influence over many aspects of European policy (from regional through to industrial policies). Its importance is driven by the need for Europe to re-position its competitive strengths within a global economy in which Europe's traditional employment-supporting activities are increasingly being undertaken by third countries. In spite of the need for Europe to catch up with its major rivals, there are clear areas where the EU is ahead of the US in terms of the development of the information economy, notably the penetration of broadband in the Nordic states. However, some claim that Europe has overstated its progress, especially when it has failed to close productivity gaps or given its inability to create a successful indigenous ICT sector. Nonetheless, the EU has been successful in creating an increased awareness of the role and potential of ICTs but ultimate success will depend upon securing the implementation of the necessary regulatory system.

KEY POINTS

- The creation of the information society is key to the future competitive positioning of the EU.

- To date, progress towards the development of the information society in Europe has been mixed as the EU lags behind the US and Japan in key segments.

281

- Policy has sought to overcome these lags through research, deployment and market development.

- Despite these policy actions, the EU still has to face evident problems in the creation of the information society.

ACTIVITIES

1 As a group, identify the key differences between 'old' and 'new' economy firms.

2 Research a leading ICT company and identify the reasons for its commercial success.

3 What are the reasons behind the US leadership of the development of the global information economy?

4 Find examples (other than those noted in the text) of leading European 'new economy' firms.

QUESTIONS FOR DISCUSSION

1 What is the difference between knowledge and information?

2 Identify how and in what ways information is affecting the nature and performance of business.

3 To what extent is the EU focus on a socially inclusive information society justified?

SUGGESTIONS FOR FURTHER READING

Botterman, M. (ed.) (2003) *Enabling the Information Society by Stimulating the Creation of a Broadband Environment in Europe: Analyses of Evolution Scenarios for Future Networking Technologies and Networks in Europe*, Leiden: RAND Corporation.

Buigues, P. and Patrick, R. (eds) (2004) *The Economics of Antitrust and Regulation in Telecommunications: Perspectives for the New European Regulatory Framework*, Cheltenham: Edward Elgar.

Dutta, S., Meyer, A., Jain, A. and Richter, G. (eds) (2006) *The Information Society in an Enlarged Europe*, Berlin and Heidelberg: Springer-Verlag.

European Commission (2003) *Information Society Statistics*, www.eu.int/information_society.

European Commission (2004) 'Connecting Europe at High Speeds: Recent Developments in the Sector of Electronic Communications', COM (2004) 61.

European Commission (2005) 'i2010 — A European Information Society for growth and Employment', SEC (2005) 717/2.

Jordana, J. (ed.) (2002) *Governing Telecommunications and the New Information Society in Europe*, Cheltenham: Edward Elgar.

Maldoom, D., Marsden, R., Sidak, S. and Singer, H. (2005) *Broadband in Europe: How Brussels Can Wire the Information Society*, New York: Springer-Verlag.

Rodrigues, M. (ed.) (2003) *European Policies for a Knowledge Economy*, Cheltenham: Edward Elgar.

Rutherford J., Gillespie, A. and Richardson, R. (2004) 'The Territoriality of Pan-European Backbone Networks', *Journal of Urban Technology*, 11 (3), pp. 1–34.

Servaes, J. (ed.) (2003) *The European Information Society: A Reality Check*, Bristol: Intellect Books.

Chapter 13

European labour markets
The search for flexibility

In a few years we will be faced with a shortage of labour, not with a shortage of jobs. We should break away from this artificial segregation of nation from nation. Who is going to pay for the old age pensions and social services unless we have an addition to our population, which only immigration can provide in the years to come?

James Callaghan, MP, British Prime Minister, 1976–79,
speaking in the House of Commons on 19 June 1946

This chapter will help you to:

- identify and interpret the meaning of key trends in European labour markets;
- understand the concept of labour market flexibility and its importance for European integration and for European business;
- understand how labour market policy has evolved in Europe and evaluate its implications for business;
- assess the potential role of labour market mobility and migration in addressing Europe's labour market problems;
- identify the challenges facing Europe's labour markets and assess how these challenges can be met by policy and by business.

European business needs a workforce that is skilled, well educated, flexible, plentiful, mobile and healthy. Fulfilment of these needs depends on a mixture of corporate action and policy at national and European levels. In response to these needs, the focus of European labour market policy has shifted away from workers' rights, the integrity of the SEM and the harmonisation of labour market regulations – which characterised the 1980s and early 1990s – towards the struggle against unemployment, efforts to improve labour market flexibility and the response to problems raised by an ageing population. The 1990s saw the growth of fears throughout Europe that unemployment had become a structural phenomenon as a result of the introduction of advanced technologies and the competitive consequences of globalisation. The response to these challenges has been varied, ranging from the relocation of firms overseas to national reforms, often fiercely resisted, and to European initiatives.

The chapter opens with a discussion of recent trends in European labour markets. These trends, together with the following discussion about the significance of labour market flexibility for European business, provide a context for later sections on policy. The chapter then traces the evolution of European labour market policy, concluding with a discussion on labour mobility within Europe.

TRENDS IN EU LABOUR MARKETS

Current European demographic and labour market trends are both a reflection of social and economic change and can themselves stimulate a change of policy or strategic direction. Consistently, one of the key drivers in labour market policy has been the evolution of unemployment (see Table 13.1). In the 1970s, with the exception of Ireland and Italy, unemployment was not a problem for the EU-15 for whom unemployment of below 3 per cent was the norm. Such low unemployment rates equate to frictional unemployment: that is, individuals that are in the process of moving between jobs. The international economic crisis in the 1970s, which resulted in high inflation and high unemployment, changed all this. Indeed, Table 13.1 demonstrates how by 1980, unemployment was several times

higher in many member states than in 1970 and how, by 1985, as Europe approached the end of a deep recession, jobless levels were even higher.

Since then the long-term trend has changed in some countries. Ireland, for example, has switched from being a country of seemingly permanent high unemployment and outward migration to a country with unemployment levels well below the EU average, largely as a result of many years of high growth. Spanish unemployment, helped by a combination of growth and economic reform which removed some of the more rigid labour market controls, halved between 1995 and 2005. In countries such as France, Germany and Greece, there has been little, if any improvement in unemployment which remains a major economic and social problem. The unemployment record in the new member states is mixed. In the Czech Republic and Slovenia, unemployment is around the EU average, whereas in Latvia and Estonia, for example, unemployment, although above the EU average, is gradually moving in the right direction. However, in Poland and Slovakia, despite slow downwards movement in unemployment since 2002, the joblessness rate remains over twice the EU average – which itself is significantly higher than in the EU's main developed country rivals – the US and Japan. Consequently, tackling the unemployment problem remains a major task for European policy makers.

The structure of EU labour markets and employment has undergone massive changes since the signing of the Treaty of Rome. As a consequence of the relative decline in agriculture and of deindustrialisation, services have become the EU's dominant economic sector (see Table 13.2). This is reflected in shifts in the structure of the labour force. In the mid-1960s, agricultural employment

285

Table 13.1 *Unemployment rates by member states, 1970–2005 (percentage of labour force)*

	1970	1980	1985	1990	1995	2000	2001	2002	2003	2004	2005
Austria	–	–	3.6	–	3.9	3.6	3.6	4.2	4.3	4.8	5.2
Belgium	2.2	9.1	13.6	6.6	9.7	6.9	6.6	7.5	8.2	8.4	8.4
Cyprus	–	–	–	–	–	4.8	3.9	3.6	4.1	4.7	5.3
Czech Rep.	–	–	–	–	4.1	8.7	8.0	7.3	7.8	8.3	7.9
Denmark	1.0	6.7	8.7	7.2	6.7	4.3	4.5	4.6	5.4	5.5	4.9
Estonia	–	–	–	–	–	12.8	12.4	10.3	10.0	9.7	7.8
Finland	–	–	5.1	3.2	15.4	9.8	9.1	9.1	9.0	8.8	8.4
France	1.3	6.4	10.3	8.5	11.1	9.1	8.4	8.9	9.5	9.6	9.5
Germany[a]	0.6	3.4	8.4	4.8	8.0	7.2	7.4	8.2	9.0	9.5	9.5
Greece	–	–	7.8	6.3	9.2	11.3	10.8	10.3	9.7	10.5	10.0
Hungary	–	–	–	–	10.4	6.4	5.7	5.8	5.9	6.1	7.1
Ireland	5.3	8.2	18.0	13.4	12.3	4.3	4.0	4.5	4.7	4.5	4.3
Italy	4.4	7.2	12.9	8.9	11.2	10.1	9.1	8.6	8.4	8.0	7.6
Latvia	–	–	–	–	–	13.7	12.9	12.2	10.5	10.4	9.0
Lithuania	–	–	–	–	–	16.4	16.5	13.5	12.4	11.4	8.2
Luxembourg	0.0	0.7	1.7	1.6	2.9	2.3	2.1	2.8	3.7	4.8	5.3
Malta	–	–	–	–	–	6.7	7.6	7.5	7.6	7.3	7.2
Netherlands	1.0	6.2	13.3	5.9	6.6	2.8	2.2	2.8	3.7	4.6	4.7
Poland	–	–	–	–	13.3	16.1	18.2	19.9	19.6	19.0	17.7
Portugal	2.8	8.4	8.6	4.8	7.3	4.0	4.0	5.0	6.3	6.7	7.6
Slovakia	–	–	–	–	13.1	18.8	19.3	18.7	17.6	18.2	16.4
Slovenia	–	–	–	–	–	9.8	9.1	9.1	9.0	8.8	8.4
Spain	1.2	12.0	21.9	13.1	18.8	11.4	10.8	11.5	11.5	11.0	9.2
Sweden	–	–	–	1.7	8.8	5.6	4.9	4.9	5.6	6.3	6.3
UK	2.5	6.0	12.0	6.9	8.5	5.4	5.0	5.1	4.9	4.7	4.6
Eurozone 12	–	–	–	–	10.5	8.1	7.9	8.3	8.7	8.9	8.6
EU-15	–	–	–	8.1	10.7	7.7	7.3	7.6	8.0	8.1	7.9
EU-25	–	–	–	–	–	8.6	8.4	8.8	9.0	9.1	8.7
Japan	1.1	2.0	2.6	2.1	3.1	4.7	5.0	5.4	5.3	4.7	4.4
US	4.9	7.0	7.2	5.6	5.6	4.0	4.8	5.8	6.0	5.5	5.1

a Prior to 1995, the figures for Germany refer to West Germany only. From 1995 onwards the figures refer to unified Germany.

Source: Eurostat.

Table 13.2 *Employment by economic activity and gender, 2000–02*

	Males as percentage of male employment			Females as percentage of female employment		
	Agriculture	Industry	Services	Agriculture	Industry	Services
Austria	5	43	52	6	14	80
Czech Rep.	6	50	44	3	28	68
Denmark	5	36	59	2	14	85
Estonia	10	42	48	4	23	73
Finland	7	40	53	4	14	82
France	2	34	64	1	13	86
Germany	3	44	52	2	18	80
Greece	15	30	56	18	12	70
Hungary	9	42	49	4	26	71
Ireland	11	39	50	2	14	83
Italy	6	39	55	5	20	75
Latvia	18	35	47	12	16	72
Lithuania	20	34	45	12	21	67
Netherlands	4	31	64	2	9	86
Poland	19	40	40	19	18	63
Portugal	12	44	44	14	23	63
Slovakia	8	48	44	4	26	71
Slovenia	10	46	43	10	29	61
Spain	8	42	51	5	15	81
Sweden	3	36	61	1	11	88
UK	2	36	62	1	11	88

Note: Data may not always add to 100 for each gender because of rounding and classification differences.

Source: World Bank: 2005 World Development Indicators.

as a share of total employment in the EU-15 ranged from 3 per cent in the United Kingdom to 47 per cent in Greece. In the mid-2000s, agriculture's share of male employment in the EU ranged from 2 per cent in the UK and France to 20 per cent in Lithuania.

The service sector already provided most employment in the EU-15 in the mid-1960s but its lead over industrial employment was marginal in most cases. By the mid-2000s, however, the dominance of service-sector employment was unambiguous. Services accounted for 40 per cent (Poland) to 64 per cent (France and the Netherlands) of total male employment in 2000–02 (see Table 13.2). The dominance of services in female employment in 2000–02 was particularly marked, ranging from 61 per cent in Slovenia to 88 per cent in Sweden and the UK. The gender differences in sectoral economic activity have a number of implications. The concentration of females in a narrow range of activities reduces economic efficiency by limiting the range of job opportunities and deployment of a significant section of the labour force. Although males have a greater range of employment opportunities and choices than females, they have been disproportionately hit by the loss of jobs in industry over the last decades.

The development of the service sector, in conjunction with the rise of the information society (see Chapter 12), is also changing the skills mix required by employers and contributing to the growing trend for active labour market policies to ensure Europe's labour force is more responsive to the competitive pressures from globalisation. These factors require a highly skilled and educated workforce to ensure commercial success. The 2004 accession states tend to be less service oriented than the EU-15 but their economic restructuring and transition has rapidly pushed them in the same direction.

The above trends have transformed Europe's labour force: no longer is it typically composed predominantly of male full-time workers employed in manufacturing but it is increasingly made up of female, part-time and short-term workers engaged in service-sector activity. The feminisation of Europe's workforce is demonstrated by Table 13.2. Indeed, there have been significant increases in female activity rates in the EU-15 since 1985. Female activity rates have long been over 60 per cent in Denmark, Finland and Sweden. Seven of the EU-15 – Austria, Belgium, Germany, Ireland, the Netherlands, Portugal and Spain – have seen female participation rates rise by well over ten percentage points or more between 1985 and 2005. This represents a major social change and a significant shift in the structure of the labour force. Historical figures for the 2004 accession states are not so readily available but their female activity rates in 2005 were, with the exception of Malta (37.1 per cent), Hungary (55 per cent) and Poland (57.6 per cent), between 60 and 70 per cent.

In recent years, there has been a slow but inexorable rise in the share of part-time jobs throughout Europe (see Table 13.3) and of temporary contracts. In the EU-15, for example, there were 35 per cent more jobs involving temporary contracts in 2005 than in 1996. There is a great deal of variation in the popularity of part-time work in member states. Although part-time jobs for the EU-25 comprise 18.5 per cent of total employment in the EU, their share ranges from 2.4 per cent in Slovakia to 46.2 per cent in the Netherlands. What is common throughout the EU, however, is the trend for a much higher proportion of female workers (32.6 per cent of the females in employment in the EU) than men (7.4 per cent) employed in part-time jobs. On the one hand, this offers flexibility to female workers who frequently bear the main burden of family commitments and to employers who can break away from traditional work organisation. On the other hand, part-time workers tend to lose out on career progression.

A side-effect of the demise of manufacturing and the rise of service industries, the feminisation of the workforce and changes in the organisation of work has been a general reduction in trade union membership as a percentage of Europe's workforce. The decline in unionisation has been a trend across the whole of Europe since the mid-1980s but unionisation, almost universal in Soviet times, has collapsed particularly dramatically in CEE: in Poland, for example, only 14 per cent of the labour force are members of trade unions. In 2006, approximately one-quarter of Europe's labour force is unionised and in only eight member states

Table 13.3 *Part-time work and work of limited duration in member states (% share in total employment)*

	Part-time employment				
	1995	2005	2005		2004
			Males in part-time employment	Females in part-time employment	Employees with contract of unlimited duration
Austria	13.9	21.0	5.9	39.0	9.6
Belgium	13.6	20.9	7.1	34.9	8.7
Cyprus	–	8.9	5.1	13.8	12.9
Czech Rep.	–	4.8	2.1	8.4	9.1
Denmark	21.6	22.0	12.8	32.7	9.5
Estonia	–	7.7	4.9	10.4	2.6
Finland	11.8	13.6	9.1	18.5	16.1
France	15.6	17.4	5.8	30.9	12.9
Germany	16.3	24.1	12.8	44.3	12.6
Greece	4.8	4.8	2.1	9.1	11.9
Hungary	–	4.4	2.9	6.1	6.8
Ireland	12.1	12.8	5.0	24.4	4.1
Italy	6.6	12.8	4.5	25.7	11.8
Latvia	–	9.6	7.6	11.6	9.5
Lithuania	–	6.5	4.6	8.5	6.3
Luxembourg[a]	7.9	17.8	2.4	40.2	4.9
Malta	–	9.2	4.7	19.3	3.9
Netherlands	37.3	46.2	22.6	75.3	14.8
Poland	–	10.6	7.7	14.2	22.7
Portugal	–	11.5	7.1	16.6	19.8
Slovakia	–	2.4	1.2	3.9	5.5
Slovenia	–	8.9	7.1	11.0	17.8
Spain	7.4	12.8	4.7	24.9	32.5
Sweden	26.2	25.0	11.8	39.9	15.5
UK	24.1	25.7	10.6	43.1	6.0
Eurozone	14.1	19.0	6.9	34.9	15.4
EU-25		18.5	7.4	32.6	13.7

a Luxembourg figures refer to 2004

Source: Eurostat.

are over half the labour force in unions. Unionisation remains strongest in the Nordic countries. The biggest member states all demonstrate low levels of unionisation by historical standards – Italy 30 per cent, the UK 29 per cent, Germany 27 per cent and France 9 per cent.

The single biggest demographic and labour market challenge facing Europe is the ageing of its population. Without exception, the demographic balance in EU member states is shifting towards the higher end of the age range. The reasons for this are numerous, including longer life expectancy and reduced fertility rates. Table 13.4 sets out the EU's forecasts for the evolution of the age dependency ratio for the EU and its current member states until 2050. In 2000 between four and five people of working age on average were needed to support one individual over the age of 65 in the EU-15. Given current demographic trends, there would be slightly fewer than two people to support each over 65-year-old by 2050. Each EU member state will experience an increase in its age dependency ratio but the extent of the increase varies considerably. In the case of Luxembourg, the ratio is anticipated to increase by only 14.5 points, from 21.4 to 36.1 in 2050 when there will still be almost three people of working age to every individual over the age of 65. However, in Spain and Italy, where fertility rates in particular are very low, the increase in the dependency ratio is around 40 points so that in both cases, there will only be about one and two-thirds individuals to support each pensioner.

The implications of this rapid ageing of the population are significant for both Europe's labour markets and, more broadly, for its welfare and social systems. There will be more people leaving than entering Europe's labour markets, giving rise to the likelihood of labour shortages. Moreover,

the financial burden of supporting a more aged population will increase not only in terms of pensions but also in terms of health and other social provision. These trends, therefore, require European nations to reconsider their approaches to migration and to their welfare systems generally. This process has started in some member states but is not proceeding quickly as politicians shy away from the difficult decisions that need to be made. The Lisbon and Stockholm Agendas also recognised the need to respond to these challenges and have set member states labour market targets that, it is hoped, will at least relieve member states of some of the burdens (see below).

LABOUR MARKET FLEXIBILITY

Labour market flexibility has become a key issue in contemporary debates about the European labour markets and the business environment. Improved labour market flexibility, for example, is widely regarded as crucial for a successful eurozone (see Chapter 8) as member states seek an alternative method of adjustment to macro-economic imbalances following the replacement of national interest rates by a eurozone-wide rate. More generally, efficient, smoothly operating labour markets are regarded as a key factor in competitiveness – but are an ideal against which many member states do not currently match up to that well.

A major problem surrounding labour market flexibility has been conflict about what the key components of labour market flexibility should be. In broad terms, there are two schools of thought about labour market flexibility. These are:

1 Success is based on lower costs arising from minimal regulation, market clearing wages and the freedom to hire and fire.

Table 13.4 Old age dependency ratio in EU member states

	2000	2010	2020	2030	2040	2050
Austria	22.9	26.3	30.3	40.8	50.4	53.2
Belgium	25.5	26.4	32.2	41.3	47.2	48.1
Cyprus	17.0	19.1	25.5	32.9	36.1	43.2
Czech Rep.	19.6	21.9	31.8	37.1	43.8	54.8
Denmark	22.2	24.8	31.2	37.1	42.1	40.0
Estonia	22.4	24.7	28.7	33.4	36.6	43.1
Finland	22.2	25.4	37.0	45.0	46.1	46.7
France	24.6	25.9	33.2	40.7	46.9	47.9
Germany	23.9	31.0	35.1	46.0	54.6	55.8
Greece	24.2	28.0	32.5	39.1	49.8	58.8
Hungary	22.0	24.3	31.2	35.1	40.3	48.3
Ireland	16.8	17.5	22.5	28.3	35.9	45.3
Italy	26.8	31.3	36.6	45.2	59.8	66.0
Latvia	22.1	25.2	28.0	33.4	37.4	44.1
Lithuania	20.8	23.4	26.0	33.4	39.3	44.9
Luxembourg	21.4	21.6	24.7	31.5	36.7	36.1
Malta	17.9	20.4	30.0	36.0	35.9	40.6
Netherlands	20.0	22.2	29.0	36.7	41.6	38.6
Poland	17.6	18.8	27.1	35.7	39.7	51.0
Portugal	23.7	26.5	31.5	39.0	48.9	58.1
Slovakia	16.6	16.9	23.5	31.7	38.1	50.6
Slovenia	19.8	23.6	30.8	40.4	47.7	55.6
Spain	24.5	26.4	30.0	38.9	54.3	67.5
Sweden	26.9	28.0	34.4	38.5	41.5	40.9
UK	23.9	25.1	30.3	37.4	43.8	45.3
EU-25	23.4	26.3	32.1	40.3	48.5	52.8

Note: The age dependency ratio is the ratio between the number of elderly economically inactive persons (normally aged 65 and over) and the number of persons of working age (from 15 to 64). A ratio of 33 implies that there are three persons of working age for every person over 65 whereas a ratio of 50 implies there are two persons of working age for every person over the age of 65. The higher the ratio, the fewer economically active people there will be to fund pensions, health, etc.

Source: Apart from 2000, the figures in this table are derived from Eurostat forecasts.

2 The 'flexible specialisation' approach in which a skilled workforce is viewed as a major resource and competitive success relies on multi-skilling, flexible labour deployment, cooperative rather than adversarial industrial relations and employee identification with the goals of the organisation.

The neo-classical approach regards regulation as an unjustifiable interference in the operation of the market. Its most purist proponents support only the most minimal forms of regulation, notably in the realm of health and safety. Regulation is regarded as a major factor in increasing costs and therefore in hindering competitiveness. Non-intervention, they argue, facilitates efficiency and enables employers to pay a market clearing wage and to compete with low-cost suppliers, particularly from Asia, the source of severe competitive pressures on European businesses. Many supporters of this view also argue for the rollback of the welfare state and social security benefits, which they claim raises the 'reservation wage', that is, the wage below which the unemployed will not seek employment. This model gives employers a high degree of flexibility in terms of hiring, dismissals and wages, encourages adversarial industrial relations and discourages internal organisational flexibility based on multi-skilling, goodwill and the higher levels of productivity resulting from greater investment in the workforce.

The term 'flexible specialisation' was coined by Piore and Sabel (1984) in response to the shift away from 'Fordist' production methods and 'Taylorist' traditions of work organisation which were too inflexible for the new demands for customised and high-quality products (see Box 13.1). The intensification of competition arising from globalisation also encouraged rapid changes in consumer tastes and necessitated more frequent product adaptations and shorter production runs, resulting in leaner production and greater emphasis on teamwork, multi-skilling, flexible deployment of labour and closer links between production and marketing. In other words, modern production techniques require a cooperative, skilled labour force that is both prepared and able to respond to rapidly changing consumer demands.

This version of labour market flexibility does not necessarily view regulation as inhibiting adjustment to changing markets but, rather, sees it as a way of providing opportunities to reconcile the legitimate claims of labour with efficiency. According to this view, labour market regulation exists to protect the workforce in terms of health and safety, job security and working conditions. Respect for workers' rights and welfare generates greater workplace flexibility by reducing the disillusion and alienation frequently present in the first model and by encouraging worker identification with the long-term well-being of the firm and generating trust between employer and employee. An emphasis on worker information and consultation and ongoing workplace training also accompanies this approach. Any rigidities in the model, it is claimed, are outweighed by long-run gains in terms of greater technical and organisational innovation. A downside of this approach is its potential exclusion of the low-skilled, long-term unemployed.

It is the flexible specialisation approach that is currently exerting the greatest influence on EU labour market policy, leading to a set of policy prescriptions based on active labour market policies and the creation of a more cooperative, less adversarial system of industrial relations. However, the two flexibility approaches may not prove to be

KEY LABOUR MARKET CONCEPTS

Taylorism and Fordism: Frederick Taylor was an engineer who aimed to improve the efficiency of production by breaking each task into small, repetitive tasks. This approach was incorporated into mass car production by Henry Ford. Taylorism, or 'scientific management', dominated industrial production until the 1980s. It lent itself to long production runs but was inherently inflexible and relied heavily on a relatively unskilled, plentiful labour force.

Passive and active labour market policies: passive labour market policies are directed towards management of unemployment through income support to the unemployed rather than through job creation or moving the unemployed into employment. Active labour market policies are more concerned with increasing employability, job creation and improving labour market flexibility and emphasise the acquisition of skills through education and vocational training programmes. The EU's focus on employability, entrepreneurship and adaptability represents a commitment to flexible specialisation and active labour market policies.

Social dumping: the practice of relocating to regions with lower costs as a result of disparities in labour market regulations. In a frontier-free world, in the absence of common standards, member states with high standards might be pressured to lower their standards in order to avoid job migration, resulting in a downward spiralling of the standards of social provision. It was the fear of social dumping that lay behind the negotiation of the Social Charter.

mutually exclusive. There is growing recognition in some member states that over-regulation may result in persistent labour market problems. France, for example, suffers from an unacceptably high level of youth unemployment (23 per cent for those under 26 years of age). In order to reduce it, the government is proposing a First Job Contract that gives employers the right to sack young workers within two years. This measure is intended to give employers greater freedom to hire and fire and it is hoped will encourage them to take on more young workers. However, the proposals have led to a series of protests and demonstrations during the month of March 2006, opinion polls that recorded opposition of 60 per cent of the French population to the changes and a partial national strike. This episode demonstrates the political challenges facing governments seeking to reform their labour markets.

EVOLUTION OF EU LABOUR MARKET POLICY

The Treaty of Rome contained a surprisingly extensive range of social policy provisions (see Box 13.2). The recitals and preamble included broad social objectives, speaking of 'economic and social progress' and 'an accelerated raising of the standard of living'. Some aspects of the treaty were ahead of their time, particularly Article 119 which established the principle 'that men and women should receive equal pay for equal work' – a seemingly remarkable inclusion in the treaty for the 1950s but which occurred because of

BOX 13.2

SOCIAL POLICY PROVISIONS OF THE TREATY OF ROME

Article

48–51   Free movement of workers – to be achieved by abolishing discrimination on nationality grounds in relation to employment, pay and other employment conditions.

52–58   Right of establishment for nationals, agencies, branches and subsidiaries of one member state in the territory of another.

59–66   Freedom to provide a service by nationals established in a member state different from the recipient of the service.

117–122   General social provisions, including:

- improved working conditions and living standards as a result of the common market and other provisions in the treaty (117);
- cooperation between member states on employment, labour law and working conditions; training; social security; health and safety; occupational hygiene; and the right of association and collective bargaining (118);
- men and women to receive equal pay for equal work (119);
- member states to maintain existing equivalences between paid holiday schemes (120);
- common measures regarding social security for migrant workers (121 and linked with Articles 48–51).

123–128   Establishment of the European Social Fund.

French concerns about the competitiveness of their textile industry.

The buoyant economic growth and low unemployment of the 1960s resulted in Community social policies that focused on the correction of mismatches between labour supply and demand through enhanced labour mobility; the mutual recognition of qualifications and the transferability of social security rights for migrant workers rather than on job creation. Some health and safety measures were also introduced during this period.

In the 1970s, social policy was given a fresh impetus with the adoption of the 1974 Social Action Programme (SAP) which launched initiatives in the field of employ-ment law, equal opportunities, industrial democracy, workplace health and safety and further development of the ESF. The 1970s was an important decade in Europe for equal opportunities legislation: in 1975, the Equal Pay Directive required member states to abolish pay discrimination and applied the principle of equal pay for work of equal value; the 1976 Equal Treatment Directive gave equal access for men and women to employment, promotion, vocational training and working conditions and in 1978 a direc-tive on equal treatment for men and women in state social security systems was adopted. A substantial body of case law on workplace gender issues has subsequently evolved.

MILESTONES IN EU LABOUR MARKET POLICY

BOX 13.3

1957   Treaty of Rome contains several articles relating to the labour market (see Box 13.2).

1974   SAP directed towards attainment of full employment, industrial democracy, health and safety, equal opportunities and a greater role for the ESF.

1987   SEA introduced qualified majority voting for health and safety measures and incorporates the Social Dialogue into the treaties.

1989   Social Charter signed by 11 out of 12 member states (excluding the UK).

1993   Social Protocol annexed to the TEU.

1994   European Works Council Directive adopted – first directive adopted under the Social Protocol.

1996   Parental Leave Directive adopted – second directive adopted under the Social Protocol.

1997   Following Labour election victory, the UK abandons the Social Protocol opt-out.

1997   Amsterdam Treaty: the Social Protocol brought into main body of treaties and the Employment Chapter included in the treaties for the first time.

2000   Launch of Lisbon Agenda – sets employment targets for 2010.

2000   Charter of Fundamental Rights signed at Nice Council – later incorporated into draft constitutional treaty.

2001   Stockholm Council – sets target for employment of older workers.

2005   Relaunch of the Lisbon process.

The 1980s began with further progress on health and safety issues and equal treatment for men and women but measures relating to worker information and consultation (the Fifth Company Law Directive and the Vredeling Directive) and to part-time and temporary work reached stalemate. However, fresh impetus was given to social policy via the campaign to create the SEM. Although not explicitly included in the 1985 Single Market White Paper, social policy was regarded as a 'flanking policy' of the SEM, that is, it was intended to provide support to broad SEM aims. The Commission had become increasingly concerned that the SEM was widely perceived as a programme to benefit business but that its success required the support of both employers and employees. Without a widening of its appeal, Commission President Jacques Delors believed the SEM programme would lose support.

Social policy received a major boost from the SEA, particularly from Article 118A which required member states to pay particular attention to harmonisation of workplace health and safety standards while maintaining improvements already made. In other words, member states were not to use the drive towards harmonisation of standards as an opportunity to lower them. At this time, differences in labour market regulations were often regarded as equivalent in effect to other NTBs scheduled for removal under the SEM. Member states with higher labour market standards were fearful that in a single market, companies would relocate to regions of the Community with lower standards and thus lower costs – the phenomenon of 'social dumping' (see Box 13.1). In this scenario, such member states would be faced with the choice of losing a significant number of jobs or giving in to pressure to lower standards.

Article 118A also introduced QMV for health and safety measures. This assumed great significance when the Commission put forward several labour market provisions under the guise of health and safety measures following the UK's opt-out from the Social Protocol, a tactic that was spectacularly successful for the Working Time Directive (see Case Study 13.1). Unanimity was still required for other measures relating to labour market policy, including free movement and other employment rights. Article 118B gave the Commission responsibility for encouraging dialogue between employers and employees at European level which it hoped would lead to formal agreements between both sides of industry.

The changes brought about by the SEA were, however, insufficient to dispel fears of social dumping. The Commission chose to combat these fears with the Community Charter of the Fundamental Social Rights of Workers, signed by 11 out of the then 12 member states (the exception being the UK) in December 1989. The Charter was not a legally binding document but a 'solemn declaration' that established basic minimum rights in the workplace in relation to freedom of movement; employment and remuneration; improvement of living and working conditions; social protection; freedom of association and collective bargaining; training; equal treatment of men and women; worker participation, information and consultation; workplace health and safety; protection of children and adolescents; the elderly; and the disabled.

These minimum rights both served as a defence against alleged social dumping and responded to concerns about an over-preoccupation with the priorities of business. In order to implement the principles of the Social Charter, the Commission introduced an SAP containing 47 proposals for directives and regulations.

Although many aspects of the Social Charter were largely symbolic (which employer, for example, would claim that they unfairly remunerated their workforce – which was contrary to the Charter?), the Social Charter encountered fierce opposition from the UK. In the early 1980s, Mrs Thatcher's government prided itself on limiting trade union powers and on reducing the number of restrictions on business in industrial relations. Mrs Thatcher was anxious to ensure that her government's reforms were not reversed by Brussels and vigorously opposed the Social Charter. This opposition was partly a reflection of a more voluntarist approach to labour market regulation than prevailed elsewhere in Europe. Although the majority of employers in the UK met most, if not all, of the requirements of the Social Charter, there was no legal requirement on them to do so unlike in other member states where many of the rights were already enshrined in law and, in some cases, in the constitution. In short, implementation of the Social Charter implied big changes in UK law, although not necessarily in the practices of all UK businesses. Moreover, given the unanimous and, indeed, enthusiastic support of all other member states, several of whom had centre-right governments, it is also difficult to give credence to Mrs Thatcher's argument that the Social Charter represented 'socialism through the back door'.

Case Study 13.1

WORKING HOURS – A TEST CASE FOR FLEXIBILITY

The topic of working hours has proved to be highly controversial, both at European and at nation state level. In essence, the controversy revolves around conflicting ideologies. On the one hand, there are those who urge restrictions on working hours to protect health and safety and to preserve the European social model. On the other hand, there are those who argue that too much labour market legislation, as represented by the EU's Working Time Directive, for example, reduces the flexibility of labour markets and damages Europe's competitiveness.

The original Working Time Directive was adopted in 1993. Its main provisions were that there should be:

- a minimum rest period of 11 consecutive hours a day;
- a rest break when the working day is longer than six hours;
- a minimum rest period of one day a week;
- a maximum working week of 48 hours, including overtime, averaged over a reference period;
- four weeks' annual paid holiday;
- a restriction on night working of no more than eight hours on average.

The Directive was originally intended to apply to all economic sectors and activities but the Council of Ministers decided to exclude certain sectors, namely 'air, rail, road, sea, inland waterway and lake transport, sea fishing, other work at sea and the activities of doctors in training'. The Commission estimated 5,630,000 employees were exempt from the directive. In an amendment agreed in 2000, the above workers were brought within the scope of the Directive. Member states were required to implement the amendment by 1 August 2003 (1 August 2004 for doctors in training). The only categories of workers currently excluded from the Directive are:

1 managing directors or others with autonomous decision-making powers;
2 family workers;
3 workers officiating at religious ceremonies in churches and religious communities.

When the Directive was originally passed, a review of its operations was envisaged after ten years. This review duly took place and the Commission brought forward a package of reforms that has sparked a return to the fierce debates that marked the initial introduction of the Directive. The three main reform proposals concern:

1 *The opt-out*: the opt-out was negotiated by the UK during the adoption of the 1993 Directive. Under the terms of the opt-out (which are not specific to the UK, although the UK is the only member state to make any significant use of its provisions), enterprises are allowed not to adhere to the 48-hour working week maximum, provided:

- the worker has agreed to work more than 48 hours per week;
- no worker is put at a disadvantage by deciding not to opt out;
- the employer keeps up-to-date records of all opting-out workers;
- the records must be made available to the competent authorities. They have the power to restrict working hours for health and safety reasons.

The review proposes to scrap the opt-out. The Commission claims the opt-out makes workers vulnerable to pressure from employers to sign an opt-out, particularly when they sign their contract, a view that is shared by trade unions. The UK Labour government has fought to keep the opt-out as fiercely as its Conservative predecessor fought, unsuccessfully, to defeat the original Working Time proposal and on the same grounds, that it represented an unwarranted interference in business activities and would increase costs and reduce competitiveness. Businesses unsurprisingly support its retention, arguing that it increases their flexibility and that any abuses of the opt-out (which they claim are relatively rare) should be dealt with individually and that the end of the opt-out would hit SMEs particularly hard.

In May 2005, the European Parliament voted in favour of removing the opt-out but in the two Employment Councils that have taken place (at the time of writing) subsequent to the EP vote, it has proved impossible for the Council to reach agreement. The British government has assembled a number of allies on this issue, including Germany, Poland, Slovakia, Cyprus and Malta, that argue for freedom of choice. Other member states are arguing that extension of the reference period for the calculation of weekly working hours will increase the flexibility of the Directive enough to make an end to the opt-out possible.

2 *On-call time*: following ECJ rulings in 2000 and 2003, time spent on-call by health professionals must be counted as working time if their physical presence is required at the workplace, even if they are resting, member states argued that the decision would require them to recruit thousands more doctors and nurses at great cost. The review suggests that time spent on call that is not worked should not count as working time but that it cannot be taken into account when calculating the 11 hours' daily rest or the 24 hours' weekly rest period. In other words, the review proposes that inactive parts of on-call time should be regarded as neither working time nor rest time for the above calculations.

3 *Extension of the reference period for calculating the maximum working week* from four to 12 months: this proposal gives greater flexibility to employers by allowing them to build seasonal and demand fluctuations into their calculations.

At the time of writing, the fate of the review is unresolved. Reaching an agreement will prove problematic given the big ideological divide represented by the opt-out. The initial inclusion of the opt-out was a compromise to satisfy the UK who opposed the Working Time Directive on the grounds, among others, that it represented over-regulation of business and reduced the flexibility of business to respond to the main competitive challenges facing it from less regulated regions.

Working time is causing controversy in member states as well as at European level. In Germany, high labour costs (see Figure 16.8, p. 380) necessitate outstanding levels of productivity growth, which have not been forthcoming in recent years. Agreements are being reached by employers and unions to rein back some of the more inflexible aspects of German working conditions in return for greater job security. In 2004, for example, the German Metalworkers Union (IG Metall) agreed with Siemens to increase weekly working hours from 35 to 40 at two mobile phone plants, without any increase in pay. Siemens claimed the deal would enable it to more easily adapt working time to changes in demand. Shortly before the deal was reached, Siemens had announced its intention to relocate at least 2,000 jobs from the two plants to Hungary, where wages are significantly lower, if the unions did not make concessions towards reducing labour costs. The Siemens deal is not isolated. Also, in 2004, Daimler-Chrysler announced that it was prepared to safeguard 6,000 jobs at its Baden-Württemberg plant (where terms and conditions were better than at its other German plants) until 2012 in return for agreement by the unions on wages (employees agreed to forgo a wage rise in 2006), on a gradual increase in working time to 39 hours per week and on other changes in working conditions. Daimler-Chrysler estimated that the package would save it an annual €500 million in wage costs. Without this agreement, the company had stated its intention to relocate the activities of the Baden-Württemberg plant to Bremen and South Africa.

During 1998–2000, the then Socialist French government phased in laws (also known as the 'Aubry laws' after the minister who introduced them) establishing a maximum 35-hour working week. The main aim of the law was to reduce employment with supplementary aspirations relating to adjustments in the work–life balance. Since the laws came into effect, French unemployment has remained stubbornly in the 9–10 per cent range. In the vast majority of cases, wages were not cut to reflect the reduction in working hours, thereby harming corporate competitiveness. Some employers have subsequently clawed back some of these losses by freezing wages but critics argue that the best way to reduce France's unemployment problem is to deregulate heavily protected markets. These restrictions vary by sector, and include complex training requirements and the apparent rationing of licences required to undertake certain activities. Others argue that France is suffering from a 'work deficit' that sees French employees working an average 15 per cent fewer hours than their counterparts in competing US businesses.

The centre-right government that came to power in 2002 is, unsurprisingly, opposed to the 35-hour week but recognises that scrapping the law will prove virtually impossible. President Chirac has acknowledged that the law is now regarded as a 'social right'. Nevertheless, the government has loosened the restrictions imposed by the law. It has managed, for example, to raise the overtime ceiling from 130 to 220 hours per year and has tried to make the law operate more flexibly for small business. The government has also promised workers in the private sector more freedom to work longer hours by choice if they can reach a collective agreement with their employers. The government would undoubtedly like to repeal the law in its entirety but has to tread carefully because of strong opposition from many quarters.

Case questions

1 The *Financial Times* described British lobbying of the EP against the end of the opt-out in the Working Time Directive as 'a strategic defence of the UK's liberal economic vision for Europe' (*FT*, 12 May 2005, p. 3). Explain and analyse this statement. How do you interpret this statement in terms of contrasting economic models in Europe (see Chapter 1) and of the debate over labour market flexibility?

2 At the time of writing, agreement on the review of the Working Time Directive has not been reached. Find out whether the review has been concluded. What does the struggle over the directive tell us about attitudes towards labour market flexibility?

3 The case refers to agreements concluded by German companies with their unions to increase working hours in an attempt to boost their competitiveness. Research this practice and assess how widespread it has become.

4 In your view, are the French laws on the 35-hour working week and other labour market regulations in France sustainable? What challenges does the French government face in attempting to reform these regulations? You may gain some insight into the second question by investigating the reaction in spring 2006 to the government's attempts to free up the regulations on hiring and firing young workers.

The Social Charter debate cut across the key labour market debate identified above – the need for and the nature of labour market flexibility. The UK argued vehemently that the Social Charter would inevitably increase the cost burdens on business with resultant losses in competitiveness. Exaggerated claims were made that the Social Charter would lead to harmonisation of social protection and to the introduction of a European-wide minimum wage. In fact, at no time was there any suggestion that the EU would harmonise social protection schemes (EU action on social protection has been limited to facilitation of the free movement of workers) nor was there any intention to introduce European legislation on a minimum wage. However, that is not to say that implementation of the Social Charter's principles were costless but, rather, that the alleged costs were frequently overestimated.

The Social Charter debate spilled over into negotiations on the Maastricht Treaty during which the 11 Charter signatories clearly stated their wish to incorporate the Charter into the treaties. UK opposition made this impossible and led to a unique compromise in which the Social Charter was essentially annexed to the treaty in the form of the Social Protocol. This enabled the Charter signatories to act on social policy matters without Britain. The Social Protocol resulted in two legal bases for social policy action within the EU. The first related to social policy provisions emanating from the Treaty of Rome and the SEA: these applied to the UK as much as to other member states and, wherever possible, social policy initiatives were introduced under this heading to include all member states. The second related to actions under the Social Protocol which introduced social policy in line with Social Charter principles.

One of the first acts of the new Labour government following the UK election in May 1997 was to sign the Social Charter. This move facilitated the incorporation of the Social Protocol into the main body of the Amsterdam Treaty. In practice, only two pieces of legislation were passed under the Social Protocol during the short life of the opt-out – the 1994 Works Council Directive and the 1996 Parental Leave Directive. The former required the establishment of works councils to act as a formal channel for information and consultation of employees in companies with over 1,000 workers or employing over 150 in two or more member states. In practice, many large UK companies with a presence in other member states chose to comply with the directive. The Parental Leave Directive entitled employees to three months' unpaid leave to look after children aged eight years or under.

The early 1990s saw recession throughout Europe with a consequent increase in unemployment and a policy shift from an emphasis on rights towards employment creation. Attempts to reduce unemployment coupled with increasing recognition of the need to reduce the budgetary burden of generous social welfare provision began to dominate policy making. Moreover, Europe experienced a crisis of confidence arising from globalisation and the spectre of increasing low-cost competition from Asia. The prospect of successfully meeting the low-cost challenge was made even more difficult because not only were Europe's direct wage costs higher than its low-cost competitors but its indirect costs (that is, statutory social security contributions, collectively agreed, contractual and voluntary social security contributions, direct social benefits, vocational training and other social costs) were much higher in Europe than elsewhere, representing one-quarter to one-third of total employment costs in several member states.

In response, the European Commission published its 1993 White Paper, *Growth, Competitiveness, Employment*, which placed job creation at the top of the EU policy agenda, and Green and White Papers on Social Policy. These documents were based on emerging social and labour market trends (see above), and highlighted the growing demographic, technological, fiscal, human and industrial pressures that required significant adaptation of existing policies. Technological change was causing shifts in employment patterns by creating demands for new skills and new work models such as teleworking. The growth of part-time and temporary work contracts was changing the role of work in society. Unemployment, population ageing, changes in family structure and growing poverty were placing the welfare state under extreme pressure. Issues of social justice, equality of opportunity, the role of education and training, changing workplace relationships and workers' and women's rights also figured highly in the policy deliberations.

The outcome of this debate was a greater concentration on the issues of labour market flexibility, albeit not necessarily in terms that would be understood by British Conservatives. The thrust of policy moved away from a focus on workers' rights, which have not been abandoned, towards measures that were intended to improve workplace adaptability; to shift the burden of taxes away from labour; to increase the quantity and quality of training; to develop new areas of employment; to encourage the development of self-employment and SMEs, a potentially important source of new jobs; and to develop local job creation initiatives.

301

AMSTERDAM AND BEYOND

The above debate culminated in the inclusion of an Employment Chapter and the incorporation of the Social Protocol and Social Agreement into the Amsterdam Treaty (see Box 13.4). Although of great symbolic importance, these changes, which confirm the importance of employment and social policy, did not confer major new powers on the EU. They did, however, mark the beginning of the 'Luxembourg process' (so-called after the 1997 Luxembourg Council) which initiated the European Employment Strategy, derived from the employment aspects of the Amsterdam Treaty, and which intended to coordinate and give direction to the employment policies of member states. In addition, the non-discrimination provisions of Amsterdam relating to age, religion and sexual orientation were of major importance.

Following the June 1997 Amsterdam Summit, a special Employment Summit was held in Luxembourg in November 1997

BOX 13.4

KEY SOCIAL AND EMPLOYMENT INITIATIVES IN THE AMSTERDAM TREATY

Preamble	A new recital confirms the EU's commitment to the principles of the Social Charter – made possible by the end of the British opt-out.
6A	Affirms the principle of non-discrimination and gives the Council of Ministers power to take action against discrimination based on gender, racial or ethnic origin, religion or belief, disability, age or sexual orientation. This Article has implications for member states where religion, age and sexuality do not figure in domestic legal regimes.
2 and 3	Gender equality is mainstreamed by insertion of the words 'equality between men and women' to the list of general principles to be promoted by the EU. Article 3 states that 'in all the activities referred to in this Article, the Community shall aim to eliminate inequalities, and to promote equality, between men and women'.

Employment Policy

B TEU	This Article has been extended to include 'a high level of employment' in the Union's objectives and additions to Article 3 establish a coordinated employment strategy as a Community objective.
109N	Member states and the Community required to develop 'a coordinated strategy for employment and particularly for promoting a skilled, trained and adaptable workforce and labour markets responsive to economic change'. Subsequent articles establish the procedures to be followed in the development of these employment strategies.

Social Policy

(A. 117–9)	Following the end of the UK opt-out, the Social Protocol and Social Agreement are integrated into the treaty (with a few amendments) in the form of a new Chapter on Social Policy.

which set about implementing and opera- tionalising the employment and social policy principles incorporated into the treaties at Amsterdam. In reality, the Summit, the sub- sequent Employment Guidelines and the SAP, published in spring 1998, contain nothing startling or new but represented a codifying, consolidation and stronger articu- lation of themes that had been increasingly stressed since the 1993 Competitiveness White Paper, the 1994 Essen Summit and the Green and White Papers on Social Policy. The SAP summarised current think- ing on labour markets and took as its main themes the need to enhance labour market flexibility and to place greater emphasis on active labour market measures. In order to promote these aspirations, the SAP identified four key areas for EU activity:

- job, skills and mobility;
- the changing world of work;
- an inclusive society;
- the external dimension.

The Nice Treaty did not fundamentally change the parameters of European labour policy but the Nice Council in 2000 signed the non-legally binding Charter of Funda- mental Rights which, among other things, asserted the rights of EU citizens to educa- tion and access to vocational and continuing training; the rights of workers and employers to negotiate collective agreements; and of workers to take collective action to defend their interests, including strikes; and the equality between men and women in all areas, including employment, work and pay. Aspirations to incorporate the Charter into the Nice Treaty were foiled but it has been incorporated into the draft constitutional treaty.

The Lisbon Council of 2000 launched the Lisbon Agenda and Process which was essen-

tially a response to continuing European competitiveness concerns. Its optimistic goal was to help Europe 'become the most com- petitive and dynamic knowledge-based economy in the world, capable of sustainable economic growth with more and better jobs and greater social cohesion' – by 2010. Indeed, after disappointing progress, the Lisbon Agenda was relaunched in 2005. The Lisbon Agenda was multi-dimensional, covering better implementation of EU legis- lation; completion of the single market; proactive application of competition rules to ensure markets have been properly opened; continued opening of markets at an inter- national level; and greater investment in R&D and innovation.

A central plank of Lisbon was the objec- tive of 'creating more and better jobs'. This involved bringing more people into employ- ment, improving labour adaptability and the flexibility of labour markets and greater investment in human capital through better education and skills. Employment targets for overall, and for female, activity rates were established at Lisbon. The Stockholm Council in 2001 set a target activity rate for employees in the 55–64 age group. The targets for 2010 are:

- an overall employment rate of 70 per cent;
- a female employment rate of 60 per cent;
- an employment rate of 50 per cent for workers between the ages of 55 and 64.

A number of initiatives at EU and member state levels are needed to achieve these targets, such as the introduction of greater incentives to enter the labour market by reducing the tax burden on the lowest paid or by improving childcare facilities, extending parental leave for fathers or improving the care facilities for the elderly and disabled. Achievement of the targets would, among other things, address some of the challenges being posed by the ageing population (see above). Enhanced activity rates for all sectors of the population would go some way to relieving the burden of pension and associated provision through increasing the revenue stream for governments through higher taxes, and by reducing spending on pensions and welfare.

Figures 13.1–3 demonstrate the size of the tasks facing member states if they are to achieve these targets. In 2004, four member states (Denmark, the Netherlands, Sweden and the UK) met the overall employment target (Figure 13.1). The target looks readily attainable for Cyprus, Austria, Portugal, Slovenia and Finland. Poland, Slovakia, Malta and Italy will have to deliver growth in employment at a much faster rate to meet the target. Thus, this target would appear to

be beyond them. More member states have already reached the female activity rate target of 60 per cent (see Figure 13.2). These are Denmark, Estonia, the Netherlands, Austria, Portugal, Slovenia, Finland, Sweden and the UK. A further six member states (France, Ireland, Cyprus, Latvia, Lithuania and the Czech Republic) are within touching distance. Below 50 per cent, and with a lot of catching up to do, are Greece, Spain, Italy, Malta and Poland. However, feminisation of the workforce is increasing in these member states but from a lower base.

Denmark, Estonia, Cyprus, Portugal, Finland, Sweden and the UK already reach the target of 50 per cent activity rates for workers in the 55 to 64 age group with Ireland virtually there as well (see Figure 13.3). However, Belgium, Italy, Luxembourg, Hungary, Malta, Austria, Poland, Slovakia and Slovenia are 20 percentage points or

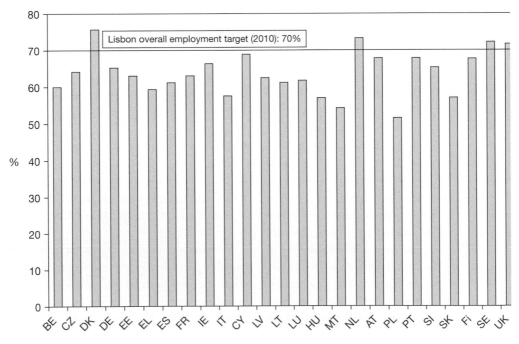

Figure 13.1 Overall employment rates, 2004 (%)

Source: Eurostat, *Labour Force Survey, 2004.*

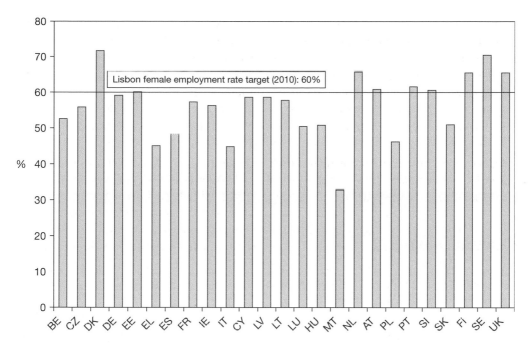

Figure 13.2 Female activity rates, 2004 (%)

Source: Eurostat, *Labour Force Survey, 2004.*

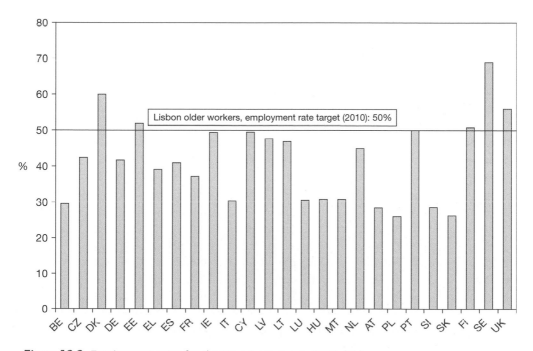

Figure 13.3 Employment rates for the 55–64 age group, 2004 (%)

Source: Eurostat, *Labour Force Survey, 2004.*

305

more below the target. Poland and Slovakia, which already have the highest unemployment rates in the EU, will find it particularly difficult to achieve this target. Moreover, a country such as Italy which has one of the most deteriorating age dependency ratios in the EU (see Table 13.4) needs more than most to boost its performance on all three targets. A culture of early retirement when activity rates are low and the population is ageing rapidly is not sustainable.

LABOUR MOBILITY

Free movement of labour is one of the key precepts of the EU. The freedom for Euro-pean workers to work anywhere within the EU is a basic right of European citizens and is important in the quest to increase labour market flexibility – an important part of which is labour mobility. Labour mobility implies that workers will move to areas where labour is in short supply and move away from regions where there is excess labour.

However, labour mobility in Europe is relatively limited. Table 13.5 shows that in 2005 only 0.4 per cent of the resident population of working age in the EU-15 was from the ten accession states. By far the biggest non-national share in the EU labour market was from outside the EU. Moving to live and work in another EU country often requires

Table 13.5 Resident working age (15–64) population by nationality in EU-15, 2005 (%)

	National	EU-15	EU-10	Non-EU
Austria	89.2	1.9	1.4	7.5
Belgium	91.3	5.8	0.2	2.8
Denmark	96.4	1.1	–	2.4
Finland	98.3	0.4	0.3	1.0
France	94.4	1.9	0.1	3.6
Germany	89.5	2.8	0.7	7.0
Greece	94.0	0.3	0.4	5.3
Ireland	92.3	3.0	2.0	2.8
Luxembourg	57.9	37.6	0.3	4.2
Netherlands	95.7	1.4	0.1	2.8
Portugal	97.0	0.4	–	2.6
Spain	90.5	1.2	0.2	8.1
Sweden	94.8	2.3	0.2	2.7
UK	93.8	1.7	0.4	4.1
EU-15	92.4	2.1	0.4	5.1
EU-10	98.4	0.2	0.2	1.2
EU-25	93.7	1.7	0.3	4.3

Notes:
– Implies data not reliable because of small sample size.
Italy excluded because it does not disaggregate by nationality.

Source: Eurostat data presented in *Report on the Functioning of the Transitional Arrangements set out in 2003 Accession Treaty (period 1 May 2004–30 April 2006)*, European Commission COM (2006) 48.

learning a new language and acclimatisation to different cultures, rules, regulations and administrative requirements. Other members of the immediate family also have to overcome language problems and can encounter difficulties finding a job. Compared to the US where employees move job and state much more readily than in Europe, the European labour market is relatively immobile.

Why does this relative European immobility matter? First, it represents labour market inflexibility which, as discussed above, hinders European competitiveness and the smooth functioning of the eurozone.

Second, despite ongoing unemployment problems in several member states, Europe is experiencing growing labour shortages in a number of sectors. Indeed, the co-existence of high levels of unemployment and labour shortages is, in itself, a symptom of labour market inflexibility. Shortages in IT workers are commonplace throughout the Union, but there are frequent reports of shortages of both unskilled labour and of more highly skilled, professional workers. Labour mobility is far from the total solution to this problem. More and better focused education and training must play its part and the home states of migrant workers will suffer if too many of their more skilled citizens opt to work outside their home state. However, labour mobility does have a part to play in ending the skills gap.

Third, the rising age dependency ratio has already been noted. In other words, Europe is heading for a situation in which there will be fewer workers available to support the retired population. One response to this dilemma is to raise activity rates generally and for specific groups of workers, such as women and older workers — key targets in the Lisbon Agenda (see above). Another, complementary approach,

FREE MOVEMENT OF LABOUR FOR THE 2004 ACCESSION STATES

BOX 13.5

As part of the accession treaties signed in 2003 prior to the 2004 enlargement, the EU-15 are able to impose restrictions on the free movement of workers from the new member states for a maximum of seven years. The restrictions were scheduled for review after two years and then after a further three and two years after that.

Initially, Ireland, the UK and Sweden, notably all member states with unemployment below the EU average, were the only member states not to apply restrictions. A European Commission Report published in February 2006 found that in the period since accession, workers from the EU-10 had helped relieve labour market shortages and had been integrated smoothly into labour markets. Labour flows from CEE to the EU-15 were lower than expected and there was scant evidence of the 'welfare tourism' anticipated by some. In view of this, and while recognising the legal right of member states to do so, the Commission urged member states to consider whether continuation of the transitional arrangements was necessary. Member states have until 30 April 2006 to inform the Commission of their intentions. By the end of March 2006, Spain, Portugal and Finland had expressed their intention to allow free movement of labour for the new member states, whereas Germany, Austria and Belgium have indicated they wish to continue with the transitional arrangements.

is to increase the number of migrant workers, an approach that is often politically difficult to implement but one that European countries might have to adopt. This increased migration is likely to incorporate both greater labour flows among member states and more inflows from outside the EU.

CONCLUSION

As part of a trend towards a growing consensus around modified economic liberalism, there has been a subtle but perceptible shift in the EU's social policy since the late 1980s and early 1990s, when workers' rights dominated the EU employment agenda, towards a greater emphasis on improving labour market flexibility. However, there is no move to remove these rights or reduce standards at European level (indeed, the review of the Working Time Directive confirms this – see Case Study 13.1, p. 297)

which are, in any case, relatively modest by the standards of most member states.

Demographic and labour market trends are also driving the EU's employment strategy. Although the rise in unemployment appears to have been stemmed throughout Europe, concerns about the ageing population, labour shortages and the need to improve the quality and adaptability of Europe's workforce so it can compete in an increasingly technological and knowledge-rich age are high. The need for flexibility is also increased by the demands of EMU, from the points of view both of limiting public expenditure and of improving factor mobility, which will assist in the adjustment of countries within the eurozone to internal economic pressures. The long-term solution to labour market problems, in this view, is in line with the needs of enterprises. Given increasing global competition and the changing demands placed on the workforce, business requires highly trained, adaptable and mobile workers.

KEY POINTS

- Europe's labour markets can no longer be characterised as predominantly composed of male full-time workers employed in manufacturing, and are increasingly made up of female workers on atypical contracts in the service sector.

- The age profile of Europe's population is becoming increasingly skewed towards the upper age ranges with serious implications for European labour markets and welfare systems.

- Improvements in European labour market flexibility are important tools in the battle to boost the competitiveness of European business in the face of globalisation and to ensure smooth economic adjustments in the eurozone.

- Attempts to reform labour markets are fraught with political difficulty.

- The emphasis of labour market policy has shifted from a concern for workers' rights to the battle against unemployment and towards improvements in labour market flexibility.

■ Increased labour mobility and migration can play an important role in the resolution of Europe's labour market problems.

ACTIVITIES

1 Research the efforts of either France or Germany to reform their labour markets. What problems have they encountered along the way?

2 Research labour mobility in the US and suggest reasons why labour mobility is much higher there than in Europe. What advantages does this give the US over Europe?

3 Identify how and where Europe suffers from labour shortages? Suggest ways in which they might be overcome.

4 Find examples of European firms relocating because of high labour costs.

5 The Amsterdam Treaty contained a clause banning discrimination based on gender, racial or ethnic origin, religion or belief, disability, age or sexual orientation. Research how this Amsterdam provision has affected employment practices in relation to one of the above forms of discrimination.

QUESTIONS FOR DISCUSSION

1 What are the most important problems facing Europe's labour markets? Identify and assess the responses of the EU, member states and business to these problems.

2 Labour markets in many European states suffer from both high unemployment and labour shortages. What factors have contributed to the emergence of this apparently contradictory situation?

3 What role can increased labour market mobility and migration play in providing an answer to at least some of Europe's employment problems? What obstacles might attempts to increase labour mobility encounter?

4 Consider the conflicting concepts of labour flexibility. To what extent can they be reconciled?

5 Consider ways in which business can respond to the ageing population in Europe.

6 Discuss the James Callaghan quotation at the head of the chapter. How relevant is it to contemporary Europe?

309

SUGGESTIONS FOR FURTHER READING

Ashiagbor, D. (2005) *The European Employment Strategy: Labour Market Regulation and New Governance*, Oxford: Oxford University Press.

Conaghan, J., Fischl, R. and Klare, K. (eds) (2004) *Labour Law in an Era of Globalization: Transformative Practices and Possibilities*, Oxford: Oxford University Press.

Eberwein, W., Tholen, J. and Schuster, J. (2002) *The Europeanisation of Industrial Relations: National and European Processes in Germany, the UK, Italy and France*, Aldershot: Ashgate.

European Commission (2005) 'Communication to the Spring European Council: Working Together for Growth and Jobs – Working Together for the Lisbon Strategy', COM (2005) 24.

European Foundation for the Improvement of Living and Working Conditions (2004) 'Ageing and Work in Europe', http://www.eurofound.eu.int/publications/files/EF0483EN.pdf, accessed March 2006.

Ottossen, J. and Magnusson, L. (eds) (2002) *Europe: One Labour Market?*, Brussels: European Interuniversity Press.

Pestieau, P. (2005) *The Welfare State in the European Union: Economic and Social Perspectives*, Oxford: Oxford University Press.

Piore, M. J. and Sabel, C. F. (1984) *The Second Industrial Divide*, New York: Basic Books.

Voom, B. de, Mirabile, M., Overleye, E. and Maltby, T. (eds) (2004) *Ageing and the Transition to Retirement: A Comparative Analysis of European Welfare States*, Aldershot: Ashgate.

Zeitlin, J. and Trubek, D. (eds) (2003) *Governing Work and Welfare in a New Economy: European and American Experiments*, Oxford: Oxford University Press.

Zimmermann, K. (2005) 'European Labour Mobility: Challenges and Potentials', *De Economist*, 153 (4), pp. 425–50.

Zimmermann, K. (2005) *European Migration: What do we Know?*, Oxford: Oxford University Press.

Chapter 14

Environment policy
Green light for competitiveness

The Earth belongs to each . . . generation during its course, fully and in its own right, no generation can contract debts greater than may be paid during the course of its own existence.

Thomas Jefferson, 1789

This chapter will help you to:

- explain the concept of ecological modernisation and its relevance to business;
- trace the evolution of EU environmental policy and identify the main influences on it;
- distinguish between different types of environmental policy and demonstrate how they can affect corporate behaviour;
- identify and evaluate examples of how an organisation's obligations rising from environmental legislation can impact on corporate performance;
- explain why European business is subject to national, European and international environmental policies.

In the early years of European integration, environmental issues barely appeared on the corporate or public policy agenda. In the first decade of the twenty-first century, the situation is completely different. European business is under constant pressure not only to improve, but to be seen to improve, its environmental performance. Part of this pressure stems from the need to comply with environmental regulations and policy, originating from the national, European and international levels. Sustainable develop-

ment has become a core objective of EU policy and over 300 directives, regulations and other initiatives are in place to support this objective. Moreover, many environmental laws of member states should be set in the context of EU policy and aspects of EU policy, such as climate change, are increasingly driven by, or linked to, international environmental imperatives.

The EU justifies its increasingly dominant environmental policy role by arguing that pollution is not bound by frontiers.

Moreover, the persistence of substantially different environmental policies throughout Europe creates potential to refragment the single market or for firms to relocate to member states where standards, and hence costs, are lower, thereby creating pressure on states with high standards to lower them.

Whatever the justification for EU environmental policy, businesses located in Europe have to take into account and comply with European environmental requirements. Given the range and scope of EU environmental initiatives, this is a complex and crucial undertaking. The chapter commences by highlighting the importance of EU environmental policy to European business with particular reference to the debate on the link between environmental policy and competitiveness. This debate has been transformed by the emergence of ecological modernisation ideas, ideas that have increasingly permeated EU environmental policy and corporate thinking. The following section traces the evolution of EU environment policy, looking in particular at the widening range of policy instruments used by the EU. The chapter then briefly considers the interaction between European and international environmental policy. Case studies are used to demonstrate the link between business and policy.

EUROPEAN BUSINESS AND THE ENVIRONMENT

For many years, companies complained about the cost and other burdens placed upon them by the growth of environmental regulation. These burdens, it was alleged, reduced their competitiveness, resulting in loss of jobs and investment. However, the movement of environmental measures into the policy mainstream, both at member state and at EU level, has meant that resistance to the general principle of environmental regulation has become pointless – although much debate remains about the detail of environmental policy. The real challenge for business is to secure policies that meet environmental objectives in a flexible manner. Therefore, environmental planning has become an important part of corporate strategy. Most major corporations now produce regular environmental reports and action plans to demonstrate their commitment to the principle of corporate environmental responsibility, to help them deal with the changing regulatory framework and to meet environmental objectives and obligations in a way that maximises benefits for the organisation.

European business has to comply with EU regulations that attempt to restrict pollution in a range of media. For example, several directives protect the environmental quality of water, including surface and underground water and bathing and drinking water. Other directives aim to limit airborne emissions from large combustion plants, especially power stations, and from motor vehicles. Action is increasingly taken to combat noise pollution and rules to limit pollution from the chemical industry are being revised (see Case Study 14.1). Several directives focus on the collection, disposal, recycling and processing of various categories of waste and are constantly being added to and tightened up. Initiatives, such as measures on environmental liability or environmental impact assessment, cut across individual sectors and others are voluntary including the Eco-Management and Audit Scheme (EMAS) and eco-labelling (see below). It is beyond the scope of this chapter to analyse all EU environmental initiatives and their impact on business. There are simply too many of them. However, examples of different types of EU initiative are discussed below.

Case Study 14.1

THE EUROPEAN CHEMICAL INDUSTRY AND THE ENVIRONMENT

In 2003, chemicals produced in the EU-25 represented one-third of world chemical sales and 15 of the world's top 30 chemical companies had their headquarters in the EU. During 1993–2003, the value of EU chemical production grew 5 per cent per annum whereas annual growth of extra-EU chemical exports was over 10 per cent. By 2003, Europe's chemical industry generated a trade surplus of €72.8 billion compared to €26.8 billion in 1993 and had the highest value-added per employee of all Europe's manufacturing sectors (€93,000 compared to an EU average of €51,000). Moreover, its labour productivity was 63 per cent above 1990 levels.

Europe's chemical industry is, therefore, a key contributor to Europe's economy and in drawing up any chemical-related environmental policy initiative, the EU must find a balance between environmental protection and economic growth. Indicators suggest that the industry's environmental performance has improved: in 2002, for example, chemical industry carbon dioxide (CO_2) emissions were about 90 per cent of 1990 levels which, given the rising production of the industry, represented CO_2 emissions at 60–65 per cent of 1990 levels in terms of per unit of production. Significant cuts in emissions of other pollutants such as nitrogen compounds, heavy metals, sulphur dioxide and volatile organic compounds were also registered over the same period.

Europe's chemical industry has responded to the environmental imperative in several ways. First, Europe's chemical associations have signed up to the voluntary industry-driven 'Responsible Care' initiative (see below). Second, the industry must comply with national and European environmental policy initiatives that apply to all industries. Third, it must comply with European policies specifically designed to meet the environmental challenges posed by the chemical industry. In 2003, for example, the European Commission brought forward proposals for a new system of chemicals management. The proposal, known as REACH (Registration, Evaluation and Authorisation of Chemicals), will replace 40 existing directives and regulations on chemicals. Its legal base is Article 95 of the EC Treaties in keeping with the objective of safeguarding the internal market while ensuring a high level of health, safety, consumer and environmental protection

Current legislation distinguishes between 'existing' and 'new' chemicals. 'Existing' chemicals are those chemicals, of which there are about 100,000, brought to the market before 1981. 'New' chemicals refer to chemicals introduced after 1981, of which there are about 3,000. New chemicals have to be notified and tested at production volumes as low as 10 kg per year and chemicals produced in volumes over one tonne require extensive testing. While the present system does not require testing for existing chemicals, the submission of information on high-volume existing substances is required. It is the public authorities that are responsible for identifying substances that need examining and then for conducting the work. However, this process is slow and cumbersome and since 1993, only 140 high-volume chemicals have undergone risk assessment.

The REACH proposals require manufacturers and importers to register all substances produced or imported in volumes of one tonne or more per year per manufacturer or importer. Significantly, REACH removes the distinction between existing and new substances, with the result that existing substances will be phased into the Union's chemical management programme in the 11 years following the entry into force of the REACH legislation. The Commission estimates that approximately 30,000 chemicals will need to be registered. In order to register, manufacturers and importers must provide information on the properties, hazards and uses of the substance, including information on how to manage it safely. This information will then be submitted to a central database administered by the newly formed European Chemicals Agency. If there is reason to believe a substance may damage human health or the environment, an evaluation of that substance will be carried out by competent authorities in member states. The Commission estimates that around 20 per cent, or 6,000, of the chemicals registered will require evaluation. If there are very high concerns about substances in particular uses, the European Commission itself will authorise use of the chemical, but only if the manufacturer or importer can show that the risks can be adequately controlled or that the socio-economic benefits of using the substance outweigh the risks. The Commission assesses that about 1,500 substances may be subject to authorisation. The Commission will also have the power to impose restrictions, including outright bans, on any substances deemed to pose unacceptable risks.

Comparison of REACH with the current system of chemical management

Current system	REACH
Gaps in knowledge about many chemicals on the European market.	Knowledge gap to be closed – covers existing as well as new chemicals.
'Burden of proof': on the authorities – they need to prove use of a chemical is unsafe before restrictions can be imposed.	'Burden of proof': on the industry – must be able to show a chemical can be used safely and how.
Notification for 'new substances' starts at a production level of 10 kg.	Registration required when production or import reaches one tonne.
Relatively costly to introduce new substances, thereby encouraging the continued use of 'existing' untested chemicals and inhibiting innovation.	Innovation of safer substances encouraged: more exemptions for R&D and lower registration costs for new substances.
Public authorities required to perform slow and cumbersome comprehensive risk assessments.	Industry is responsible for assessing the safety of identified uses. Public authorities able to focus on issues of serious concern.

The REACH proposals are highly significant in a number of ways. In particular, the proposal shifts the burden of proof and responsibility for assessing and managing chemical safety from public authorities to industry. This is consistent with the concept of making producers responsible for their products, a concept that is embodied in the polluter pays principle (PPP) (see Box 14.3) and in the concept of product and environmental liability – another area in which the European Commission has recently legislated (see below).

REACH has also unleashed a debate about competitiveness. The European Commission argues that the current chemicals management system acts a disincentive to innovation as companies continue to use existing untested substances to avoid the costs of testing new ones. The Commission maintains that REACH will improve incentives for innovation by ending the discrimination between new and existing substances and by introducing a much higher threshold for the registration of substances (one tonne as opposed to 10 kg). This will entail significantly lower registration costs and be much quicker than the existing system.

The industry itself is less optimistic about the impact of the measures on competitiveness, arguing that REACH imposes a heavy administrative burden, particularly on SMEs, and will cost many times more than the €2.8 5.2 billion estimates of the European Commission. REACH applies to imports, and so there should be no competitiveness effect within Europe, but the industry has warned that REACH will impose an additional cost that could put extra-EU exports at a disadvantage. The Commission has responded by pointing to the global nature of the chemical industry and by asserting that international trade in chemicals makes chemical safety an international issue. It points to international initiatives and to initiatives in other countries that address the same issues as REACH, implying that cooperation, and perhaps even integration, with some of these initiatives will eventually be on the agenda. Environmental non-governmental organisations (NGOs) claim that, by exaggerating the effects of REACH, the industry is simply scaremongering.

The proposals went through an extensive consultation phase before they were tabled and were scaled back somewhat, leading to accusations by some environmental groups that the EU had given in to industry pressure. Issues raised during consultation included the scope and cost of the proposed system; concerns about the administrative burden; calls for greater prioritisation; matters of commercial confidentiality and the need for publicly available data about chemical risk; and greater clarification about the role of the European Chemicals Agency.

The ultimate fate of the proposal is, at the time of writing, not yet finally determined. REACH is still wending its way through the Environment Council and the EP. Further amendments or outright rejection of the proposal cannot be ruled out (although the latter is unlikely). Meanwhile, Cefic, the chemical industry trade association, is to participate in SPORT (Strategic Partnership on Testing REACH), along with the Commission and other stakeholders, to assess the workability of REACH and to consider solutions to any problems identified.

The impact of European environmental policy varies, given the widely different propensities of sectors to pollute and the targeting of some policies towards specific sectors. Moreover, some environmental issues have no European dimension at all: planning issues, for example, are typically determined at a sub-European level. However, much national environmental legislation represents the implementation of EU directives. Directives allow member states to meet EU objectives in a manner that is best suited to their own specific environmental conditions. Conversely, international initiatives, particularly, but not only, those relating to climate change, are also increasingly shaping European environmental policy (see below). Case Study 14.1 identifies some of the environmental policy issues impacting upon Europe's chemical industry. Case studies of other industries would uncover different environmental concerns and priorities.

THE RISE OF ECOLOGICAL MODERNISATION

Since the early 1970s, when environmental issues made their first tentative steps into the political mainstream, conceptualisation of the relationship between economic growth and environmental protection has changed radically. Initially, there was a general assumption of incompatibility between continuing economic growth and environmental protection. This was symbolised in the title of the Club of Rome's influential 1972 report 'Limits to Growth' which warned that mankind could not afford to exploit the earth's resources indefinitely without dire consequences. Such an underlying philosophy resulted in inflexible command-and-control policies that sought to regulate and constrain the activities of business. Increasing knowledge about the environment and the growing complexity of the environmental debate challenged this conventional wisdom and caused reassessment of the link between economic growth and the environment. This change has given rise to a broader range of environmental policy instruments and to a more complex and positive attitude on the part of policy makers and business to environmental protection.

The emergence of the concept of ecological modernisation underpins this shift to a large extent. Ecological modernisation originated from Dutch and German social scientists in the early 1980s. It implies that environmental protection need not be a burden to business but can be a source of competitiveness and growth and is implicit in much contemporary debate about the environment.

The theoretical debate rapidly influenced policy. In a 1995 speech, for example, the then EU Environment Commissioner Ritt Bjerregaard gave a ringing endorsement for ecological modernisation ideas, urging 'respect for the environment must not be seen as a burden for industry, but as an opportunity to stimulate innovation and to reduce inefficiencies'. In other words, ecological modernisation represents a shift away from the perception of environmental policy as a threat to business in terms of increased compliance costs and reduced competitiveness, towards providing opportunities for future growth. This thinking has continued to influence EU thinking on the environment. The European Commission's 1999 *Global Assessment: Europe's Environment* claimed 'environmental action can generate benefits in the form of economic growth, employment and competitiveness'. The executive summary of the Sixth Environmental Action Programme (see Box 14.4, p. 326), the framework for European environmental policy in the early twenty-first century also asserted that 'high environmental standards are an engine for innovation and business opportunity'.

The key implications of ecological modernisation for business can be summarised as follows:

■ *The reconciliation of environmental and economic objectives*: in other words, economic growth and environmental protection are mutually beneficial. However, growth will be qualitatively different from the past given the incorporation of environmental features into technology. This integration of growth and environmental objectives results in a 'win-win-win' situation for the environment, the economy and business.

■ *Technocentrism*: that is, the emphasis on innovation and technology (modernism) to deliver both growth and environmental benefits. This is reflected in the so-called 'Porter hypothesis', which states that not only are growth and environmentalism compatible but also that competitiveness depends on this link. Accordingly, stricter environmental regulations and policies act not as a cost burden for industry but as an incentive to innovate and compete.

■ *The primacy of the market*: (albeit a market modified by state intervention to correct for market failures). This is marked by a movement away from the command-and-control regulations and standards used to regulate and constrain business activities in the early days of environmental policy activism. Such instruments proved to be inflexible and relatively ineffective. Instead, policy makers are increasingly seeking to use policy instruments that tap into market dynamics, such as taxation, eco-labelling and emission trading schemes. Indeed, this approach was central to the EU's Fifth Environmental Action Programme, although its success in introducing such policies was limited, and remains at the core of the Sixth Environmental Action Programme (see Box 14.4).

The most direct manifestation of the economy-boosting impact of environmentalism is the growth of eco-industries (see Box 14.1). These have developed as a response to the growing market for environmental goods and services and have generated billions of euros in revenue and thousands of new jobs, both in large companies and in SMEs. For example, the proliferation of recycling legislation that began in the 1980s, stimulated research, development and investment in recycling technology and created new markets. This was the case in the plastics sector. The plastics industry faced problems in the sorting and separation of individual resins, a process crucial to the economic viability of plastics recycling as the greater the homogeneity and purity of the resin recovered, the more suitable is the resulting recyclate for higher value-added applications. Development of this technology to deal with a wider range of plastic resins and products at greater speed requires substantial initial investment, but the potential returns for the companies that manage to establish themselves in this market are significant. It is in markets where recycling legislation is strongest that the incentive to develop such technology is greatest and participants can gain first mover advantages.

In short, it is increasingly accepted that possession of the proven technical and production capability to produce low-polluting goods acts as a significant competitive advantage. This manifests itself, for example, in the motor sector's attempts to develop cars with high levels of fuel efficiency and component recyclability (see Case Study 14.2). Not only does this generate marketing advantages in relation to increasingly environmentally sophisticated consumers (although the extent to which consumers will pay extra for less environmentally damaging products is probably limited), the constant effort to gain an environmental edge encourages innovation and can help companies build up important technological leads in increasingly competitive markets. In this respect, ecological modernisation is more appropriate to higher value-added sectors with a high technological content. Its application is likely to be less relevant to resource intensive and commodity-based activities. In addition, the negative competitive impact of environmental regulations can be offset in part by the promotion of incentives for R&D, support for infrastructure and a generally more favourable business environment.

317

BOX 14.1

THE RISE OF EUROPE'S ECO-INDUSTRIES

As the obligations on business to operate in a more environmentally responsible way have increased, so a wide range of eco-industries has developed to service the environmental needs of business and other organisations. According to the OECD, eco-industries engage in:

> activities which produce goods and services to measure, prevent, limit, minimise or correct environmental damage to water, air and soil, as well as problems related to waste, noise and eco-systems. This includes cleaner technologies, products and services that reduce environmental risk and minimise pollution and resource use.

Since 1994, total European expenditure on cleaner technologies and pollution management has grown by 5 per cent per annum, reaching €127 billion in 1999, 38 per cent of which was spent on waste water treatment, 37 per cent on solid waste management and 12 per cent on air pollution. A further €56 billion was spent on resource management, including €33 billion on water supply, €14 billion on recycled materials and €7 billion on nature protection.

Altogether, the turnover of the EU's eco-industries was equivalent to 2.3 per cent of GDP. Germany accounted for one-third of the market in 1999, followed by France (21 per cent), the UK (13 per cent), Italy (9 per cent), the Netherlands (5 per cent) and Austria (5 per cent). On a per capita basis, the member states with the largest expenditures were Denmark (€1,130), Austria (€1,100) and Luxembourg (€750), followed by Germany, France and the Netherlands. The lowest per capita expenditure was in Greece, Portugal and Spain (all of which spent the equivalent of €230 or less).

In 1999, direct employment from pollution management and resources management in the EU totalled over 2 million jobs. Since 1994, over 500,000 jobs have been created in pollution management alone. In Austria and Denmark, 2.3 per cent and 3 per cent of the labour force, respectively, is supported directly through environmental expenditure.

Environmental technology is a growing market at both European and world levels and covers a number of fields. These new markets often face trade barriers and reduction of these barriers has been an item of discussion in the ongoing Doha Round of trade talks. However, in part as a result of the need to comply with more stringent regulation than elsewhere, the European eco-industries have emerged as world leaders in several fields and hope to benefit from first mover advantages. Between 1994 and 1999, exports of environmental products from the EU increased by 63 per cent in real terms and Europe maintains a healthy trade surplus in these goods. North America is Europe's biggest market, a market that has shown considerable growth. Traditionally, South-East Asia was the EU's second biggest market but as accession and the need for compliance with the environmental *acquis* approached, the candidate countries knocked South-East Asia into third place.

Case Study 14.2

BMW

In developing its environmental strategy, the BMW Group has embraced the philosophy of ecological modernisation. Dr Helmut Panke, Chairman of the Board of Management, has said 'the experience of the BMW Group shows that economic efficiency and sustainability can be compatible with one another'.[1] Board member, Dr-Ing Burkhard Göschel, has commented that 'innovations create success and safeguard the future viability of companies. They are also essential for sustainable development.'[2]

At the end of 2003, the BMW Group operated 24 automobile production and assembly facilities in 15 countries worldwide. Although its international production network is developing quickly, the BMW Group retains a strong German and European flavour in relation to its sustainability policy and, as seen below, its point of reference for its environmental strategy is frequently European legislation or voluntary agreements.

The company has a policy of flexible capacity management in an integrated production network. For example, changes to a particular model can be made almost simultaneously throughout the world and production can be balanced across the Group by changing the output of individual production lines to different models, thereby enabling the Group to react swiftly, flexibly and efficiently to market requirements. This has become extremely important in view of the seemingly constantly shortening production cycles, greater technical complexity of the product and continuing internationalisation.

In order for this high degree of integration to work, since 1999 all BMW Group locations maintain uniform standards: quality and environmental standards are certified to ISO 9001 and 14001, respectively, and, in some cases, the European eco-audit system, EMAS II. By applying uniform standards to all its production facilities worldwide, the BMW Group meets the standard requirements of the *Charter for Sustainable Development* of the International Chamber of Commerce (ICC) and the *OECD Guidelines for MNEs*. BMW's strategy is also at odds with the anti-globalisation view that MNEs invest overseas to avoid more stringent environmental standards at home. The BMW Group complies with European standards, which tend to be higher than standards in several of its production locations because the commercial sense of seamless integration of its production network is much greater than reducing environmental compliance costs (themselves a very small part of total costs) in a limited part of its production network.

An increasingly common practice among vehicle and other manufacturing MNEs is to consider the quality and management systems in the selection of suppliers. In June 2003, 79 per cent of BMW's suppliers, for example, had 14001 certification, 11 per cent operated EMAS II systems; 4 per cent operated other management systems whereas only 6 per cent had none.

The BMW Group is engaged in many development projects that have an environmental dimension, too many to mention here. The following examples indicate the type of activities in which the group is engaged: some are voluntary, some are driven by voluntary agreement and some are a response to legislation:

- *Work on hydrogen-powered vehicles*: in order to eliminate CO_2 emissions and to move away from over-reliance on non-renewable hydrocarbons, BMW has begun work on hydrogen-powered drive for the BMW 7 series, on developing the tank for liquid hydrogen and is participating in a group testing the infrastructure required for the provision of hydrogen at public filling stations.
- *Driver management*: BMW maintains that changes in driving style offer potential for fuel savings of up to 20 per cent. Accordingly, it has developed SAM – a drive management system that constantly collects data on the route and the state of the car and recommends a driving style consistent with the most favourable fuel consumption.
- *Designing cars for recycling*: all BMW Group cars can be almost completely recycled and the Group is increasing the amount of recyclates in new vehicles (up to 15 per cent of current BMW models are made of recycled materials). In order to facilitate recycling, BMW is working on the greater use of recyclable plastics or composite materials; reducing the variety of materials used in its cars; developing suitable joining technologies; using quality recycled materials and the marking of components for separation into pure-grade materials during recycling.

In part, BMW is driven by EU legislation in this area: the EU Directive on End-of-Life Vehicles (ELV) requires manufacturers to prove during the development stage that a vehicle is recyclable. According to the directive, at least 85 per cent of the ELV weight must be reused or recycled from 2006 and only 5 per cent of the residual weight may be brought to landfill from 2015. The Directive also requires manufacturers to establish a network of take-back points for ELVs: BMW already operates such a network with selected partners in Germany and is setting up similar networks in other European countries.

Notes

[1] *The reduction of fuel consumption*: as part of a voluntary commitment by the Association of the German Automotive Industry (VDA), the BMW Group committed itself to reducing the fuel consumption of its fleet by 25 per cent between 1990 and 2005. This was achieved by 2002. The Group continues to work to fulfil its share of the commitment made by ACEA (the European Automobile Manufacturers Association) following voluntary agreement with the European Commission to reduce CO_2 emissions in the fleets of European manufacturers to an average of 140 kg per km by 2008.

[2] BMW Group *Sustainable Value Report, 2003–04*.

Although ecological modernisation is an important factor in changing the nature of contemporary environmental debate, resistance to environmental legislation on the grounds that it increases costs and therefore decreases competitiveness retains strong resonance. The challenge to the EU and to other environmental policy makers is to formulate policy in such a way that it meets environmental goals without damaging the EU's competitiveness at a time when unemployment is a major issue. In other words, there is a need to operationalise the principles of ecological modernisation. This can, for example, involve the use of a wider range of policy instruments and coordination of policy at international level, both of which the EU is trying to do with varying degrees of success.

EVOLUTION OF EU ENVIRONMENT POLICY

The Treaty of Rome contains no direct reference to environmental issues. Indeed, given the rudimentary environmental aware-ness of the 1950s, it would have been remarkable if the environment had been incorporated into the treaties. The preamble did speak of 'the constant improvement of living and working conditions', sometimes interpreted not only as a commitment to increase prosperity but also to improve the

quality of life. Article 2 refers to 'harmo-nious development of economic activities', also occasionally interpreted to include environmental issues. However, there is little evidence that this was the intention of the drafters of the treaty.

By the late 1960s, there was an upsurge in environmental debate, culminating in the influential United Nations Conference on the Human Environment in Stockholm in 1972. The Paris Summit of EC Heads of State and Government in October 1972 continued the work of the Stockholm Con-ference and instructed the European Com-mission to draw up a Community environ-mental policy. The result was the First Environmental Action Programme (EAP), the first of six EAPs to date.

MILESTONES IN EU ENVIRONMENT POLICY

BOX 14.2

1957	Treaty of Rome signed without explicit environmental reference
1972	United Nations Conference on the Human Environment, Stockholm
1972	Paris Summit instructs the European Commission to develop an environmental policy
1973–76	First Environmental Action Programme
1977–81	Second Environmental Action Programme
1982–86	Third Environmental Action Programme
1987	SEA explicitly incorporates the environment into the treaties
1987–92	Fourth Environmental Action Programme
1992	Rio Earth Summit commits industrial countries to return CO_2 emissions to 1990 levels by 2000
1993	Maastricht Treaty extends QMV to most aspects of environmental policy
1993–2000	Fifth Environmental Action Programme
1997	Amsterdam Treaty consolidates environmental gains of Maastricht
1997	Kyoto summit agrees an average 5.2 per cent reduction by 2010 in six greenhouse gases compared to 1990 levels in the major industrialised countries
2004	The Russian Parliament votes to ratify Kyoto, giving sufficient votes to enable the agreement to come into force in 2005
2001–10	Sixth Environmental Action Programme

The rationale for EU environmental policy grew during the 1980s as the campaign to develop the single market gathered pace and the potential for differences in national environmental regulation to perpetuate market fragmentation was recognised. Article 100 of the Treaty of Rome empowered the Council to pass directives to approximate laws that 'directly affect the establishment or functioning of the common market', thereby providing some justification for early environmental policy. Moreover, Article 235 enabled the Council to take actions that prove necessary to meet Community objectives where the 'Treaty has not provided the necessary powers', a useful catch-all article. It was also feared that in a more open market, different environmental standards would result in downward pressure on standards as higher-standard countries strove to prevent migration of investment to member states with lower standards. However, given the relatively small percentage of environmental compliance costs in total costs in most sectors, this 'race to the bottom' argument is contested.

BOX 14.3

KEY ENVIRONMENT POLICY PRINCIPLES EMBEDDED WITHIN THE TREATIES

The following policy principles are embedded in the EU treaties as a guide for the development of environmental policy. These principles also often find themselves alluded to in the consideration of national and international environmental initiatives.

The 'polluter pays' principle (PPP) stipulates that polluters should pay the full cost of the environmental damage they cause. Environmental costs are often referred to as 'externalities' (for example, damage to health, rivers, the air, etc. arising from economic activity) that are not incorporated into the costs of a product but are borne by society as a whole. By making the polluter pay the full cost of its activities, including externalities, the PPP provides an incentive to make products less polluting and/or to reduce the consumption of polluting goods. This internalisation of external costs can be met through the use of market-based policy instruments such as taxes or emission permits (see below).

The prevention principle involves changes to products and processes to prevent environmental damage occurring rather than relying on remedial action to repair damage after it has taken place. This implies the development of 'clean technologies'; minimal use of natural resources; minimal releases into the atmosphere, water and soil; and maximisation of the recyclability and lifespan of products.

The precautionary principle acknowledges that our understanding of ecology and environmental processes is, at best, incomplete and constantly evolving. Policy is therefore formulated against a background of uncertainty. However, lack of scientific knowledge should not be used to justify failure to introduce environmental policy. Indeed, even without conclusive scientific evidence about outcomes, precautionary action should be taken if the potential consequences of inaction are particularly serious or if the cost of action is not high.

The SEA removed the need for reliance on general treaty articles to justify environmental policy and gave the Community explicit powers in the environmental field for the first time. It established that Community environmental policies should preserve, protect and improve environmental quality; contribute towards human health; and ensure a prudent and rational use of natural resources. Four principles were to guide Community environmental action:

- prevention;
- the rectification of environmental damage at source;
- policy integration;
- 'polluter pays'.

It was in relation to the environment that the principle of subsidiarity was introduced into the treaties for the first time (a principle granted much wider application in the Maastricht Treaty). Article 130r of the SEA authorises the Community to take environmental action when its environmental objectives 'can be attained better at Community level than at the level of the individual Member States'. In practice, it can be argued that many environmental problems may be more appropriately dealt with at a supranational level as pollution is no respecter of borders. The ongoing discharge of waste into river systems and incidents such as the 1986 Chernobyl nuclear accident, demonstrate the transnational, transcontinental and, in the case of global warming, the global nature of many environmental problems. This same Article also acknowledges the competence of the Community to cooperate with third countries and international organisations in certain environmental matters while acknowledging the continuing scope for member state action.

Importantly for Northern member states, particularly Denmark, Germany and the Netherlands, which have been the leaders in many aspects of European environmental policy, the SEA allows member states to take stronger environmental measures than those advocated at Community level, provided they are compatible with other aspects of the treaty, such as the SEM and competition rules. These safeguards exist to inhibit fragmentation of the market arising from differential environmental standards.

The Maastricht Treaty took Community policy further. It confirmed the 'preventive', 'polluter pays' and 'rectification at source' principles and added another – the 'precautionary principle' (see Box 14.3). The treaty also made the promotion of 'measures at international level to deal with regional or world-wide environmental problems' an explicit Community objective and committed the Community to aim for a 'high level of protection'. However, the potentially most important change was the extension of QMV to all environmental matters, with the exception of measures:

- 'primarily of a fiscal nature' – i.e. environmental taxes;
- relating to town and country planning, land use and water resource management;
- affecting the choice between energy resources for member states and the general structure of their energy supply.

The Amsterdam Treaty consolidated the environmental gains of the Maastricht Treaty by giving them greater prominence and status. The commitment to sustainable development became a core EU objective and was incorporated into the preamble and Article 2 of the treaty. The integration of environmental policy into all aspects of Community policy was moved from the environmental title to Article 3c. The Commission also attached a declaration to the treaty committing it to incorporate environmental impact assessments into all proposals with significant environmental implications.

The Amsterdam Treaty also extended the co-decision procedure to all environmental measures, thereby increasing the role of the EP, the Community institution that has shown the greatest appetite for enhancing the EU's environmental role. However, proposals to extend qualified majority voting to all aspects of environmental policy (proposals strongly supported by Denmark, the Commission and environmental NGOs) were not accepted in the negotiations on the Amsterdam and the Nice Treaties. There is also no significant change in the role of environmental policy in the draft constitutional treaty.

THE EXPANDING RANGE OF EUROPEAN ENVIRONMENTAL POLICY

During the 1970s and 1980s, European environmental policy largely took the form of 'command-and-control' legislation – that is, a series of directives that aimed to limit the amount of emissions of particular pollutants from motor vehicles, industrial plant and agriculture, for example. Such standards were imposed in reaction to environmental problems and fall into the following categories:

■ *Process standards*: process standards are designed to control the production process and are intended to protect the health of workers and to minimise pollution from production. Their direct effects are largely domestic and do not have an impact on intra-Community trade or cause friction with trade policy generally. However, process standards can encourage a 'race to the bottom' by acting as an incentive for manufacturers to relocate where regulations are less strict.

■ *Product standards*: these standards are concerned with the composition and performance characteristics of a product. Examples include the directive on lawnmower noise or vehicle emission standards. The implementation of product standards stricter than normal Community product standards can fragment the single market as failure to meet stricter national environmental standards can keep products from another member state out of that market. However, safeguards introduced in the SEA were designed to avoid this.

■ *Environmental quality standards*: such standards establish the maximum amount of polluting substances that can be permitted in a particular environmental medium such as the soil, water or air. These standards allow a certain leeway to local conditions: identical behaviour in different eco-systems can result in substantially different outcomes, requiring different technological responses for the purposes of environmental control.

Since 1973, the broad parameters, principles and ambitions of European environmental policy have been set out in a series of EAPs. As knowledge about the environment and commitment to environmental objectives increased, the EAPs have progressively become more complex. Contrary to what their names suggest, the EAPs do not themselves comprise a list of proposed initiatives but, rather, establish general objectives that provide a platform and framework for subsequent specific proposals. For example, the general objective in the 6th EAP of an 8 per cent reduction in greenhouse gas emissions by 2008–12 compared to 1990 resulted in the 2003 directive on emissions trading.

Each EAP has built upon its predecessor, responding to its shortcomings and building upon its successes. In practice, the principles laid down in the various EAPs have often been ahead of actual achievements. The First EAP, for example, acknowledged the 'polluter pays principle', a principle that is still to be fully implemented, and highlighted the concept that decisions should be taken at the most appropriate geographical level – the subsidiarity requirement that was only formalised in the SEA and that still invites controversy about exactly where environmental policy responsibility should lie.

By the time the Fifth EAP came into force in 1992, the Community's approach towards the environment had become more integrated, programmatic and long term. The Fifth EAP differed from its predecessors by covering eight years instead of five – recognition of the long-term nature of many environmental problems and their solutions. The Sixth EAP has an even longer, ten-year, term (1 January 2001 to 31 December 2010). Continuity between the Fifth and Sixth EAPs was also apparent through the envisaged use of a wider range of environmental policy instruments (see below); greater integration of environmental policy with other policy domains to ensure they are not at odds with environmental policy objectives and greater cooperation with third countries.

The longer duration of EAPs necessitates, and also facilitates, a more fundamental appraisal of long-term economic and environmental trends that need to be taken into account in drawing up the programmes. The following trends, for example, threw down challenges to the authors of the Sixth EAP:

■ economic globalisation and the increasingly global nature of environmental issues: although preceding the Sixth EAP, globalisation generally, and the cross-border nature of many environmental issues in particular, became much more apparent during the 1990s;

■ the emergence of the e-economy which creates new business models;

■ the rise of modern communication technologies, especially the Internet, which facilitate dialogue between policy makers and stakeholders and also enhance the organisational capabilities of environmental NGOs, thereby transforming the political context in which environmental policy is formulated;

■ EU enlargement to 25 states in 2004 – with further enlargement to come: the extension and implementation of the environmental *acquis* to states that have suffered severe environmental degradation and lack financial resources to rectify this damage pose a major challenge;

■ improving the competitiveness of European business: the assumptions of the Sixth EAP are very much in line with the precepts of ecological modernisation. The competitiveness debate is no longer so much about whether environmental policy harms competitiveness (although this argument is still aired) but about which policy instruments provide the most scope for stimulating competitiveness. Not surprisingly, business tends to argue for more voluntary and fewer legislative initiatives on the grounds that they allow for greater flexibility in achieving environmental objectives.

The range of options and obligations facing European businesses when trying to manage their response to environmental challenges has broadened considerably and become significantly more complex. For many years, business faced legislation that

325

BOX 14.4

KEY FEATURES OF THE SIXTH EAP (2001–10)

The Sixth EAP sets out the EU's environmental policy objectives for ten years from 2001. The Programme was drawn up after a comprehensive review of the Fifth EAP. This review identified several successful areas, including lower toxic industrial emissions, such as lead and mercury, into the atmosphere; reduced pollution in many lakes and rivers resulting from better sewage and water treatment and big reductions in the acidification of forests and rivers as a result of lower sulphur dioxide emissions. The review also identified areas where improvement was needed, thereby providing the strategic context for the formulation of the Sixth EAP.

Four priorities have been identified:

1 *Climate change*: the EU is of the view that 'climate change is happening and that human activity is causing the increases in concentrations of greenhouse gases that are the cause of the problem'.[1] Although this view is contested, the EU has developed a raft of policies to reduce greenhouse gas (GHG) emissions, the main one concerning emissions of CO_2, methane and nitrous oxide. In line with the Kyoto Protocol, the EU has committed itself to reducing GHG emissions by 8 per cent in 2008–12 compared to 1990 levels. In the longer term, a global cut of 20–40 per cent is required by 2020 and 70 per cent beyond that. The Sixth EAP envisages the following in relation to climate change:

- better resource management – namely, energy efficiency and saving, greater use of renewable energies and market instruments and support for advanced technologies;
- integration of climate change objectives into sectoral policies such as transport, energy, industry, regional policy and agriculture – a continuation of the policy integration that was an important part of the Fifth EAP;
- cross-sectoral approaches such as an EU-wide emissions trading scheme and energy taxation (see below);
- research into innovative technologies and materials;
- improved information to citizens and business about climate change to help them contribute to GHG reductions.

2 *Protection of wildlife and nature*: i.e. ensuring that natural systems continue to function in the face of threats from human activity such as chemical leaks, over-fishing and destruction of the countryside. In this area, the Sixth EAP envisages strategies for soil protection, for greater integration of the environment into the Common Agricultural and Common Fisheries Policies and for marine protection.

3 *Environment and health issues*: in order to reduce the impact of man-made pollution on human health (for example, increasing incidence of allergies, infertility and cancer), the Sixth EAP proposes to:

- reinforce Community research;

- develop a new system for the testing, evaluation and risk management of new and existing chemicals (see Case Study 14.1, p.313);
- develop a strategy on the sustainable use of pesticides;
- develop a new strategy on air pollution;
- reinforce and enhance existing policies on water quality and noise pollution.

4 *Preservation of natural resources and the management of waste*: increased wealth has resulted in increased consumption of natural resources and more waste. The objective is to transform the link between resource use and economic growth into greater resource efficiency, dematerialisation of the economy and waste reduction and prevention. More specific objectives are to reduce waste, including hazardous waste, by 20 per cent by 2010 compared to 2000 and by 50 per cent in 2050. In order to achieve this, the Sixth EAP envisages:

- policies to identify hazardous substances with producer responsibility for collecting, treating and recycling waste products;
- a strategy on recycling complete with recycling targets;
- promotion of markets for recycled materials;
- a range of specific initiatives under an Integrated Product Policy (IPP) approach to promote the greening of products and processes.

In order to push these policy areas forward, five approaches have been highlighted as central to the Sixth EAP. Several stem from problems identified in the Fifth EAP and represent continuity with the predecessor programme:

1 *Putting legislation into practice*: the implementation and enforcement of EU environmental legislation has been a problem for many years and is not getting any better. A Commission survey found that in 2003, there were 88 instances in which environmental directives had not been transposed on time; 118 cases in which directives were not correctly transposed by member states; and 95 cases in which member states did not meet secondary obligations within directives. Moreover, more than a third of all complaints and ongoing infringement cases regarding non-compliance with EU law concerned the environmental sector, with over 500 new complaints being brought forward each year. France, Greece, Ireland, Italy and Spain were among the worst offenders whereas the Nordic countries and Portugal appeared to have fewer implementation and enforcement problems. Directives concerning water, waste, nature protection and environment impact assessment encountered the most problems. Full application, implementation and enforcement of existing environmental legislation is a strategic priority for the Sixth EAP. In addition to a continuation of legal procedures, the Commission also intends to pursue a 'name, shame and fame' strategy whereby both good and bad practice is publicised, in part through the development of an implementation scorecard.

2 *Putting the environment at the heart of policy making*: the Fifth EAP called for the integration of the environment into all policy areas and identified five priority sectors –

industry, energy, transport, agriculture and tourism – for such treatment. The Amsterdam Treaty made it a formal treaty requirement to integrate environmental issues into other Community policies. The Sixth EAP reaffirms its commitment to this approach and highlights the need for regular monitoring of the integration process.

3 *Encouraging the market to work with the environment*: this approach is in line with ecological modernisation philosophy (see above). The EU's approach to business and the environment has long depended upon the setting of standards and targets with which business has had to comply. Although standards and targets remain important to EU environmental policy, the Sixth EAP aims to use economic instruments to further its environmental objectives. Economic instruments comprise incentives for firms to change their behaviour, and include taxes, application of the concept of environmental liability and emissions trading, etc. (see below). Indeed, an aim of the Fifth EAP was to introduce more market-based measures and, although most member states use taxation as a key part of national environmental policy, the EU itself has not had much success with fiscal measures. However, prospects are much better for emissions trading, environmental liability, etc. (see below).

The other aspect of encouraging the market to work with the environment is to work with industry. This includes encouraging more businesses to assess their environmental performance (and thus to improve it) via the EU's EMAS; assistance to SMEs to help them understand and comply with EU policy; the introduction of environmental performance award schemes; the encouragement of voluntary schemes and the development of an IPP approach. An IPP approach seeks to 'green' products and processes via addressing the environmental performance of a product at all stages of its life cycle.

4 *Helping people make environmentally friendly choices*: the purpose of this approach is to introduce measures to improve the accessibility and quality of environmental information to citizens to help them develop more sustainable lifestyles.

5 *Better use of land*: the responsibility for planning decisions lies mostly at local, regional and, in some cases, at national level. There is a directive and a proposal that try to ensure the environmental implications of infrastructure projects and planning are properly addressed but, for the most part, the Union's role is limited to encouraging effective planning and policies through the promotion of benchmarking and best practice.

Enlargement and international cooperation

The 2004 enlargement brought a number of countries with serious environmental problems into the Union. During the Sixth EAP, there will be an emphasis on environmental assistance to these countries, plus ensuring that sustainable development is incorporated into all the EU's external relations. Moreover, the EU is keen to develop its leadership role in international environmental matters and to strengthen international environmental initiatives.

1 European Commission, 'Environment 2010: Our Future, Our Choice – the Sixth Environmental Action Programme', COM (2001) 31 final, p. 4.

not only set minimum environmental standards but also distorted innovation by, usually inadvertently, favouring one strand of technological development over another. In recent years, although minimum environment standards are still used, a much broader range of policy instruments are utilised in Europe. Therefore, although the diversity of environmental initiatives in use in Europe, both at a national and at supranational level, can seem bewildering from the corporate perspective, business can benefit from much greater flexibility in how they achieve these objectives. Policy initiatives fall into two distinct categories – voluntary and compulsory.

Voluntary schemes

Voluntary schemes take a number of forms. In general, they offer greater flexibility, and hence potentially greater cost-effectiveness, in meeting environmental objectives. Voluntary initiatives currently operating in Europe, include the following.

Own initiative schemes

Own initiatives schemes are devised and run by individual industrial sectors. One of the most well known is *Responsible Care*, a voluntary world-wide initiative on health, safety and the environment launched in 1985 by the Canadian Chemical Producers Association and adopted in 1989 by Cefic. Currently, *Responsible Care* covers the manufacture of over 85 per cent of the world's chemicals by volume. The scheme operates through national and regional trade associations and involves:

■ formal corporate commitment to a set of guiding principles;

■ a series of codes, guidance notes and checklists to help companies fulfil their commitments;

■ the development of indicators to help assess improved performance;

■ a continuing process of communication on health, safety and environmental matters with stakeholders inside and outside the industry;

■ forums in which companies can learn from the experiences of others in implementing the commitment;

■ systematic procedures to verify the implementation of the measurable elements of *Responsible Care* by corporate members.

In 2002, Cefic and the European Chemical Distributors' Association (FECC) jointly produced an important new guidance document on Product Stewardship for use in commercial agreements between chemical suppliers and distributors. The guidance gives information and advice on handling, storage, transport, product and packaging disposal, packaging, classification, labelling, etc. and represents extension of *Responsible Care* along the supply chain.

Cooperation

A long-term aspiration of the EU is to develop cooperation and shared responsibility on environmental matters between industry and regulators. Auto-Oil, a long-term programme intended to reduce emissions from road transport and involving extensive collaboration between the European Commission and the oil and automobile industries, is an example of this cooperation in action. The programme gives companies an opportunity to shape legislation and policy, ideally to make it more flexible, and gives the Commission access to a high level of technical expertise. Auto-Oil initially focused on emission reduction via improvements in fuel quality and vehicle technology and the extension of vehicle maintenance and inspection schedules. Critics of Auto-Oil point to a failure to consult independent experts and allege the close cooperation has resulted in the 'capture' of the Commission by motor and oil interests, resulting in unambitious proposals.

Eco-labelling

Many manufacturers claim their product is 'green' or 'environmentally friendly' without any external confirmation of their claims. Not surprisingly, these claims often lack credibility, are ill founded and/or lead to consumer confusion or suspicions. In order to allay these fears, eco-labelling schemes have sprung up in many countries. According to these schemes, companies earn the right to display an eco-label on their products and publicity material provided these products comply with ecological criteria laid down and verified by the independent label-awarding body.

Several European countries operate their own eco-labelling schemes. Among such schemes are the 'Nordic Swan' in Finland, Sweden, Denmark and Norway; the 'Milieukeur' in the Netherlands and 'Der blaue Engel' in Germany. These schemes operate wholly within national boundaries. Since 1992, a European eco-label scheme – 'the Flower' – has been in existence. The scheme has established separate environmental criteria for individual product groups such as paper products, textiles, detergents, paints, household appliances and services such as tourist accommodation. Significantly, the 'Flower' label can be used across the whole of the EU. In other words, this particular eco-label serves all markets and obviates the need for manufacturers, retailers and service providers to apply for an eco-label in each member state.

Success of such schemes depends on public recognition of, and trust in, the logo, which takes time to develop. By 2004, 198 companies throughout the EU had acquired the right to use the Flower on their products. The take-up of the scheme varied: it has proved most popular in Italy, France and Denmark but was almost unknown in the UK, Belgium and Finland and has yet to penetrate the new member states. Only six companies had applied for and qualified for the Flower in Germany, a country normally at the forefront of environmental initiatives. However, Germany's 'blue angel' has been in existence for over 25 years and covers over 3,000 products involving 700 label users. The success and recognition of the Blue Angel appears to be making it more difficult for the European scheme to take root in Germany. In short, although the number of Flower labels is increasing, the rate of progress is relatively slow and the label has to compete with other, more established labels throughout the Union.

Environmental management schemes

Environmental management schemes (EMS) provide organisations with tools and methods to manage their activities, products and services in a systematic way that helps them achieve their environmental obligations and goals. Since 1993, the EU has operated its own voluntary EMS – EMAS. Initially, registration under EMAS was available only to industrial sector companies but since 2001, EMAS has been open to all economic sectors, including public and private services. In 2004, over 4,000 organisations were registered under EMAS.

EMAS registration requires a company to:

1 carry out an environmental review covering all aspects of an organisation's activities, products and services, including existing environmental management and procedures;

2 establish an effective environmental management system to achieve the goals of the organisation's environmental policy. The resulting EMS must establish responsibilities, objectives, means, operational procedures, training requirements and monitoring and communication systems;

3 conduct an environmental audit assessing the EMS and its compliance with the organisation's own policy and all relevant environmental legislative obligations;

4 provide a statement of its environmental performance in relation to its policy objectives and outline action to be taken to improve the organisation's performance.

The review, audit and statement must all be improved by an accredited and independent EMAS verifier, thereby giving the scheme the transparency and accountability needed for the scheme to have credibility. Effective EMAS schemes enable companies to demonstrate their commitment to sustainability and to enhance their efficiency and profitability. These benefits can come from greater energy efficiency, waste reduction, a safer working environment and generally improved management of operations and demonstration of the benefits of ecological innovation. EMAS may also help firms reduce their liability for environmental damage given that an effective EMS helps reduce the exposure of organisations to environmental risk. This will be particularly helpful in view of the coming into force of the EU's Environmental Liability Directive in 2007 (see below).

Compulsory initiatives

European business remains subject to the old command-and-control legislation on minimum standards and licensing but increasingly policy is switching to a reliance on market-based or economic instruments such as environmental taxes, charges, tradable permits, deposit refunds and subsidies. These instruments use market forces and the price mechanism as an incentive to consumers and producers to change their polluting behaviour and to reduce the depletion of resources: an energy tax, for example, encourages greater investment in energy efficiency technology; restrains energy consumption; promotes fuel switching. Producers and consumers can determine the response they make to these incentives in relation to their own circumstances and needs whereas more regulatory approaches tend to be more inflexible and impose the same solution on all parties. Moreover, the newer policy instruments tend to reflect the polluter pays and precautionary principles set out in the treaties (see Box 14.3, p. 322). The following examples demonstrate how some of these policy instruments work in practice.

Environmental liability

The polluter pays principle (PPP) (see Box 14.3) is a key principle of EU environmental policy. In 2007, the Environmental Liability Directive, designed to operationalise this principle in its broadest sense, comes into force. The directive's basic objective is to ensure that those operators whose activities have caused environmental damage, rather than society as a whole, are held financially liable for remedying the damage. It is hoped that the possibility of being held liable will act as an incentive to companies to take greater care in preventing damage occurring

331

in the first place, thereby satisfying two other key principles of EU environmental policy – precaution and prevention.

Member states already have their own civil liability schemes but they tend to cover damage to persons and property rather than to the wider environment. Only a few member states, for example Sweden and Denmark, have a more general regime calling for compensation for damage to the environment. The damage covered by the directive includes damage to biodiversity (especially damage to protected species and natural habitats); damage to water resources; and soil contamination that carries a risk to human health. The remedial measures that can be demanded under the directive vary depending on the type of damage: soil, for example, can frequently be decontaminated whereas damage to water or to biodiversity can be more complex. In the latter case, the competent authorities have some scope in which to decide what measures needed to be taken. For example, if a damaged site cannot be restored, the authorities can demand that another nearby site of equivalent environmental value has to be enhanced.

The directive has been designed to complement, rather than overlap with, existing civil liability legislation in member states and international liability legislation. Traditional damage to people and property will continue to be dealt with by national civil liability legislation. The directive does not cover damage included in international liability schemes, namely maritime oil spillages and nuclear accidents, on the grounds that their scope is much greater and legally binds many more countries than those in the EU and/or their regime provides for additional guarantees such as compensation funds. The objectives of the EU directive are clear: the extent of its effectiveness will only become clear after it has been in force some time.

Emissions trading

On 1 January 2005, the EU's emission trading scheme (ETS) began operating as part of the EU's strategy of meeting its commitment under the 1997 Kyoto Protocol to reduce its GHG emissions by 8 per cent between 2008 and 2012 compared to 1990 levels. Initially sceptical of the efficacy of such schemes, the EU has rapidly developed one of the world's most ambitious ETSs.

The EU's ETS applies at installation level and participation is obligatory for thermal power plants over 20 MW, oil refineries, coke ovens, iron and steel plants and factories making cement, glass, lime, brick, ceramics and pulp and paper. Strong industrial lobbying resulted in the exclusion of the aluminium and chemical industries from the scheme. The Commission estimates that over 12,000 installations are covered by the directive in the EU-25: in larger member states, anywhere between 1,000–3,000 installations are covered by the scheme whereas in smaller states the number ranges from 50–400. Non-compliance will result in a fine of €40/tonne of excess CO_2 emissions during 2005–07, rising to €100/tonne from 2008 onwards.

The implementation of the ETS has not been straightforward. It requires identification of all the installations covered by the scheme and allocation of allowances to each installation. Allocation requires accurate figures on current emissions and the determination of appropriate principles by which to allocate the trading allowances. The responsibility for doing this lies with member states: they must draw up National Allocation Plans that determine the total number of CO_2 emissions granted to their companies. These plans are assessed by the Commission to ensure compliance with the directive. Non-submission of plans or rejection of a plan will deny access to the European-wide trading system to companies from non-compliant states.

Taxation

Environmental taxes are used extensively throughout the EU: in 2001, environmental tax revenue in the EU-15 totalled €238 billion or 6.5 per cent of all tax revenues.

This revenue derived almost entirely from taxes originating in individual member states: attempts to introduce European-wide taxes have fallen at the first hurdle. In 1991, for example, the European Commission proposed a 'carbon/energy tax' to be introduced in phases, reaching US$10 per barrel of oil equivalent by 2000. Although the proposal received some support, the requirement for unanimity on fiscal measures

---

WHAT IS EMISSIONS TRADING AND HOW DOES IT WORK?

BOX 14.5

Emissions trading enables emission targets to be reached at the lowest possible economic cost. Their success in achieving this depends on getting the details right, particularly the design, allocation of emission permits and monitoring of the scheme. Emissions trading schemes operate according to the following principles.

Assuming two companies emit 100,000 tonnes of CO_2 per year and each is given an emission allowance of 95,000 tonnes per year, neither is fully covered for their total emissions. They can either cover their shortfall by reducing their emissions by 5,000 tonnes or by buying allowances to cover the 5,000 tonne shortfall. Their choice of option will depend on the market price of the allowances relative to the cost of reducing their emissions by 5,000 tonnes.

If, for example, the market price of an allowance is €100 per tonne of CO_2 and Company A's cost of reducing its emissions is €50 per tonne whereas the emission reduction costs of Company B are €150 per tonne, then it is in Company A's interests to remain within its emission allowance by reducing its total emissions. It may even decide to reduce its emissions further (say, by 5,000 tonnes) and sell its unused emissions. However, it would be cheaper for Company B to buy additional allowances to the tune of 5,000 tonnes at the market price of €100 per tonne rather than physically reduce its emissions.

In the above scenario, Company A reduces its emissions by a total 10,000 tonnes at a cost of €500,000. However, it is able to completely offset its emission reduction costs by selling 5,000 tonnes of allowances at the market price of €100 which brings in revenue of €500,000. Without trading of emission allowances, a 5,000 tonne reduction in CO_2 would have cost Company A €250,000 (5,000 tonnes × €50 per tonne reduction cost). Company B meets its commitments under this emission trading scheme by buying 5,000 tonnes of allowances at a total cost of €500,000. Without the possibility of emissions trading, it would only have reached its emissions target of 95,000 tonnes by carrying out the physical reduction at a total cost of €750,000.

Under an appropriately designed emissions trading scheme, it is clear from this example that the cheapest reductions in emissions are made first, making this particular instrument one of the most cost-effective ways of meeting a given target.

(a situation that has not changed in subsequent treaty reforms and will be even more difficult to achieve with the expansion to 25 members), the fervour with which member states protect their tax raising prerogatives and the failure of the EU's main OECD competitors to adopt similar measures were enough to sink the proposal.

The Commission did not give up and in 1997 proposed to extend the scope of excise duties to natural gas, electricity and solid fuels on the grounds that the present excise system, which applies to mineral oils, distorts competition between fuels. In addition to these single market-related, fiscal harmonisation reasons, the proposal promotes environmental objectives by setting minimum rates of duty significantly higher than existing rates. Reaction to these proposals was also unenthusiastic and the major environmental impact from these measures hoped for by the Commission has not materialised.

Arguments levelled against environmental taxes tend to focus on the alleged negative impact on competitiveness if key competitors are not subject to similar charges. Indeed, some critics argue that such taxes merely result in loss of jobs in the taxing country by encouraging environmentally damaging activity to move elsewhere. The counter-argument has its roots in ecological modernisation and maintains that taxation gives incentives to improve efficiency and innovate, thereby improving competitiveness and possibly giving rise to first mover advantages if other countries and regions eventually adopt similar policies.

THE INTERNATIONAL DIMENSION OF ENVIRONMENTAL POLICY

Environmental issues have increasingly taken on an international perspective and feature prominently on the agenda of international organisations such as the UN, the WTO and the OECD. This is both because of growing awareness of the transboundary and even global nature of much pollution and because of trade liberalisation and the greater interdependence of the world economy which increases the relative importance of remaining regulatory differences, such as environmental policy. This focus on the environment stems from concern over the implications of the potential competitive disadvantage, particularly in relation to high compliance costs, experienced by firms located in countries that aim for higher levels of environmental protection.

This concern manifests itself in a number of ways. A common fear is that the existence of countries with lower process standards will act as 'pollution havens' – that is, in order to avoid the costs of complying with these standards in their current location, firms will relocate to countries where they do not incur such costs with consequent loss of jobs and investment in the country with higher standards. These higher standards would then, ironically, lead to greater environmental damage as firms are free from constraints in their new location. These developments will also lead to pressure to lower standards to prevent such migration occurring. Although these arguments have a certain logic, reality is more complex. The pull of pollution havens depends to a large extent on the overall share of environmental compliance costs in total costs. In general, such costs tend to be no more than 1 to 2 per cent of total costs and, as such, are only a relatively minor factor in a whole host of other locational factors. That is not to say that in certain cases the additional costs incurred as a result of environmental regulation will not be a determining factor in relocation or casting around more widely for location for new investment. The environmental cost factor will become more influential when profit margins are tight and the economic environment is generally unfavourable. Nevertheless, although there are examples of the pollution haven hypothesis in action, there is scant evidence to support it in any systematic way.

Responses to these concerns range from studies into the link between trade and the environment through to debate about the possibility of the use of trade barriers to offset the negative competitive impact of some environmental measures and of the formulation of international approaches to global environmental problems such as climate change. Increasing convergence and harmonisation of environmental policy would appear to be the most promising environmental approach to dealing with cross-border pollution issues. However, there are important environmental and economic limits to this approach arising from legitimate differences in process standards which stem from a diversity of environmental conditions and which, themselves, could be argued to be part of a country's comparative advantage.

KEY POINTS

- EU environmental policies are increasingly reflecting an 'ecological modernisation' approach. Nevertheless, conflict persists between those who view environmental policy as increasing cost and red tape burdens on industry and those who see environmental policy as providing opportunities to promote competitiveness.

- Over the years, the scope of EU environmental policies has expanded greatly and now encompasses many voluntary and compulsory initiatives. In particular, the most recent EAPs have promoted the use of economic instruments.

- Failure to implement environmental policy remains a problem and the accession of ten new member states in May 2004 highlights the issue of implementation and compliance still further.

- Much pollution is not contained with national or European borders and many environmental issues increasingly have an international dimension.

- In recent years, most major companies have developed their own environmental strategies. These developments and efforts to encourage greater industrial participation in policy formation will intensify.

ACTIVITIES

1   Case Study 14.1 outlines how the European chemical industry has been affected by, and has responded to, environmental challenges (or at least to some of them). Research another

335

European business sector and develop your own case study of how it has responded to these challenges. Note: the challenges vary considerably from sector to sector. Consider, for example, whether your chosen sector has any voluntary industry environmental codes and to what extent does it have to consider national, European or international environmental policy imperatives.

2   Case Study 14.2 outlines the BMW Group's response to the environmental challenges facing it as a European-based multinational. Research another European-based company (it may be active in one or more member states or on a global scale) and identify how it has responded to these challenges. Note: companies' strategies vary according to the sector and the reach of their production and marketing networks. Consider whether your company takes a national, European or international approach to environmental issues or does it use a combination of all three? What factors might have caused it to adopt its approach?

3   This chapter describes examples of different types of European environmental policy – it cannot describe all of them. Choose one of the following European environmental initiatives and research it further with a view to identify its implications for business:

- The Eco-Management and Audit Scheme (EMAS);
- End-of-Life Vehicles Directive (hint: impact of recycling targets for product design);
- Integrated Product Policy (hint: life-cycle analysis, 'cradle to grave' – raw materials → design → manufacture → use → disposal).

4   Transport has a major impact on the environment. What is the nature of the links between transport and the environment? Identify how the EU has so far integrated policy in these areas. Is there scope for further integration?

QUESTIONS FOR DISCUSSION

1   European businesses have to take national and EU environmental policy into account. Increasingly, international initiatives are also taking effect. Consider the rationale for the introduction of policy at all three levels and the potential impact of one level of policy on another (for example, EU member states are allowed to comply with national environmental legislation that is stricter than EU policy – but only under certain conditions).

2   Discuss the implications of ecological modernisation for business and for policy formulation.

3   Does European environmental policy stimulate or damage competitiveness? Where possible, provide examples and evidence to support your argument.

4   Policy integration is a central theme of EU environmental policy. Energy and environmental trends clearly interact with each other. However, issues of energy supply security and the single market also have a major impact on energy policy. Identify and discuss how these other policy objectives can clash with the environmental goals of energy policy.

5 Assess the relative benefits of voluntary compared to compulsory environmental schemes.

6 What are the implications of the 'polluter pays principle'? Identify examples of EU policies that implement this principle and how they affect business.

SUGGESTIONS FOR FURTHER READING

Barry, J., Baxter, B. and Dunphy, R. (eds) (2004) *Europe, Globalization and Sustainable Development*, London: Routledge.

Butzengeiger, S. and Michaelowa, A. (2004) 'Greenhouse Gas Emissions Trading in the EU – Background and Implementation of a "New" Climate Policy Instrument', *Intereconomics*, 39 (3), pp. 116–18.

Carmin, J. and VanDeever, S. (eds) (2004) *EU Enlargement and the Environment: Institutional Change and Environmental Policy in Central and Eastern Europe*, London: Routledge.

Environmental Policy (2004) Whole issue on EU enlargement and the environment, Vol. 13, No. 1.

Hussen, A. (2004) *Principles of Environmental Economics*, 2nd edn, London: Routledge.

Jackson, C. (2002) 'Where to Now? A Look at Likely New Developments in EU Policy and the Environment', *Intereconomics*, 37 (6), pp. 298–9.

Jeppesen, T. (2002) *Environmental Regulation in a Federal System: Framing Environmental Policy in the European Union*, Cheltenham: Edward Elgar.

Jordan, A. and Liefferink, D. (eds) (2004) *Environmental Policy in Europe: The Europeanization of National Environmental Policy*, London: Routledge.

Jordan, A., Wurzel, R. and Zito, A. (eds) (2003) *New Instruments of Environmental Governance: National Experiences and Prospects*, London: Frank Cass.

Mol, A. and Spaargaren, G. (2000) 'Ecological Modernisation Theory in Debate: A Review', *Environmental Politics*, 9 (1), pp. 17–49.

Porter, M. and Van der Linde, C. (1995) 'Green and Competitive – Ending the Stalemate', *Harvard Business Review*, 73 (5), pp. 120–34.

Turner, K., Pearce, D. and Bateman, I. (1994) *Environmental Economics: An Elementary Introduction*, Hemel Hempstead: Harvester Wheatsheaf.

Weale, A. (1992) 'The Politics of Ecological Modernisation', Chapter 3 in *The New Politics of Pollution*, Manchester: Manchester University Press.

Wurzel, R. (2002) *Environmental Policy Making in Britain, Germany and the European Union: The Europeanisation of Air and Water Control*, Manchester: Manchester University Press.

Young, S. (ed.) (2000) *The Emergence of Ecological Modernisation: Integrating the Environment and the Economy*, London: Routledge.

European Commission documents

'Environment 2010: Our Future, Our Choice – the Sixth Environmental Action Programme', COM (2001) 31 final, p. 4.

'Fifth Annual Survey on the Implementation and Enforcement of EU Environmental Law', SEC (2004) 1025, *Commission Working Paper*.

Chapter 15

Europe and the consumer

Taking the European consumer into account

People of the same trade seldom meet together but the conversation ends in a conspiracy against the public, or in some diversion to raise prices.

Adam Smith (1723–90)

This chapter will help you to:

- appreciate the importance of consumers to the European economy;
- understand how and in what ways the process of European integration can work to the benefit of consumers;
- appreciate the actual impact of the process of integration upon consumers;
- identify key policy frameworks and legal measures to support consumer involvement in the integration process.

Consumer policy is linked into two broad objectives of the EU: namely, improving the quality of life of its citizens and modernising the economy. This reflects the fact that many areas central to the development of the EU and the integration process in general have an impact on consumers. For many Europeans, the impact of the process of economic integration upon them as consumers is a major determinant of their levels of satisfaction with the process. Thus, while consumer policy focuses upon the interaction of consumers and suppliers, its political importance must not be ignored. The development of a Europe that works for the consumer means a broader commitment to liberalisation, an open Europe and an awareness of how broader global trends empower consumers.

This chapter examines the evolution of consumer policy within the EU. Initially, it focuses on the importance of consumers to the integration process. This rests on understanding how their transactions and interactions with non-domestic suppliers can influence the intensity of the process. Thereafter, the chapter moves on to examine actions undertaken by the European Commission to generate confidence in cross-border trade. The final section of the chapter examines specific measures in more detail.

THE IMPORTANCE OF CONSUMERS

There are 456 million inhabitants and thus 456 million consumers in the EU. Yet, during the development of economic integration, consumers' concerns have been given relatively little attention. Historically, the majority of the issues and decisions affecting consumers' interests have taken place at the national level. In focusing upon businesses, European integration has been underpinned by an assumption that consumers benefit only indirectly from the process through the by-products of more intense competition in the form of wider choice, product innovation, lower prices, better quality, etc. However, there is no guarantee that economic integration (and the intensified competition that results) will deliver these benefits. As a consequence, there is a need to ensure that consumers' rights are not compromised by an enlarged and more consolidated market place. A lack of confidence in consumer transactions across political borders has the potential to derail the process of economic integration.

Effective consumer protection is important to the functioning of the modern economy. The everyday expression of choice by individual consumers about what they buy creates strong competitive pressure within the economy. The more confident consumers are, the better it will be for European business. This can have a direct impact upon businesses: a demanding set of customers can compel businesses to offer products that (through adding value to customers) can deliver a tangible advantage on a broader stage. Thus, those businesses that offer the greatest bundle of customer benefits will progress further under market-based rules. Those that fail will suffer. For these forces to work to the benefit of the economy, the consumer has to be sufficiently informed to make the best choices for themselves. If this information is lacking, then there is a justifiable regulatory role to fill this gap to ensure a broad awareness is generated.

To fully support the development of the SEM, consumers have to play their role to the full. There must be confidence in the operation of the SEM and an understanding that it is relevant and beneficial to them. Inevitably, realising this objective means overcoming a natural reticence about purchasing goods from overseas: a problem heightened when cross-border shopping over the Internet is considered (see below). Thus, as much as businesses have driven the process of economic integration forward, consumers have been important in sustaining the process. Consumers, via their expressions of choice, have the potential to spread and intensify economic interaction across borders. The increased mobility of the individual and the spread of the Internet and electronic commerce are just two ways in which consumers contribute to the process of economic integration. As consumer awareness grows and empowerment rises, so consumers will start to become aware of the full potential of cross-border interactions as a means of enhancing their welfare and the value they derive from transactions. This power will be increased by the price transparency created by the euro (see Chapter 8) and by the mobility fostered by transport liberalisation (see Chapter 10). This underlines the close links between consumer empowerment and the achievement of broad quality of life objectives.

However, the ability of consumers to act as agents of change within Europe has to be based upon their ability to exercise informed choice about the goods and services they purchase. As markets become more complex, so consumers need to be given the necessary information to enable them to make purchase and consumption decisions from non-traditional locations in the most effective manner. If the consumer does not have faith in the single market to deliver and meet their expectations, it will be seen as a major failure. It is evident in a number of areas, such as automobiles, that cross-border consumption can have an effect upon trade. However, the ability to exploit this for the consumers' benefit is curtailed by a generic lack of knowledge regarding rights in cross-border transactions.

Table 15.1 indicates the differences across member states of the awareness of, and confidence in, consumer rights. Confidence in consumer rights is strongest in domestic markets where, across the EU-15, 56 per cent of consumers consider their rights well protected. Across the member states, confidence in rights remains marked and varied: 82 per cent of Finnish believe they are well protected while only 21 per cent in Greece and Portugal feel themselves similarly protected. These figures are even lower for cross-border trade where an average of just 31 per cent believes their rights are well protected. Ironically, Greeks (49 per cent) and Italians (56 per cent) feel the most protected, while the Germans (16 per cent) and the Swedes (20 per cent) feel the least protected. These figures indicate vast disparities across

Table 15.1 Consumer awareness across the EU-15, 2004 (%)

Consumers considering their rights to be well protected in	For a dispute within their own member state	With a supplier in another member state
Belgium	52	25
Denmark	64	24
Germany	59	16
Greece	21	49
Spain	38	32
France	58	28
Ireland	66	38
Italy	44	57
Luxembourg	53	25
Netherlands	66	23
Austria	69	33
Portugal	21	36
Finland	82	28
Sweden	68	20
United Kingdom	75	34
EU average	56	31

Source: European Commission.

the EU as to the awareness of, and confidence in, consumer rights generally. An improvement in this confidence is central to the EU objective of integration through interaction.

Research undertaken by Eurobarometer in 2002 presents a mixed picture of consumers' views of the benefits of the SEM. Overall, 80 per cent of those questioned felt that the SEM had increased choice and that the increased competition had been beneficial. This was in addition to benefits derived from increased travel and mobility. However, while over two-thirds felt that the quality of products was better, less than half had seen reductions in prices. In addition, less than half were aware of their rights: awareness was very mixed across Europe (see Table 15.1). On the positive side, just over half would consider going to another state to buy goods. These figures are highest for the UK and Luxembourg. In the former case, this is been driven by high taxation on alcoholic and other products. However, only 6 per cent have ever done so and 67 per cent have never even considered it. This reflects poor awareness of such opportunities but also the high costs often involved in undertaking cross-border purchases. The survey was based on 7,500 interviews across the EU-15.

THE EMERGENCE OF EU CONSUMER POLICY

The development of consumer policy was a natural spillover from the development of the SEM. If the SEM was going to stimulate transactions across states and allow consumers to act as a proactive force in the process of economic integration, they had to be assigned a number of fundamental rights. These were necessary to ensure the free mobility of goods and services through facilitating the ability of users to buy a good wherever they wanted and be certain of their rights when they did so. The implicit recognition is that consumers are no longer confined to their own state and that consumption has an increased transnational element. Thus, consumers can:

- purchase products overseas when travelling;
- purchase products from a firm established in another state;
- order and purchase products from another state online or through other distance selling methods;
- transfer money between states to make investments.

Consumer protection revolves around three issues. The first is a proper framework of rules that reflect the broad concerns of consumers and protect their interests. The second is an effective mechanism for applying these rules in a manner that is both fair and understood. The third is the empowerment of consumers themselves. Traditionally, consumer protection has taken place at the nation state level. In many states, this policy overlaps with a broadly defined competition law. The different methods used across states reflect different legal systems, social-cultural traditions as well as the broader political setting. As a result, the approach to ensuring consumer protection across states has varied between self-regulation and direct intervention from the state. There are also differences as to the scope of policy which, in some cases (such as agriculture), favours trade distortions over the supply of products.

When it began to emerge in the 1970s, supranational consumer policy action was low key. At this time, actions were based on health and safety, protection of economic interests, damages, information and education and representation. While there were a number of actions linked into generic EC policy such as agriculture, there was no real concerted action until the development of the SEM which introduced the notion of the consumer into the treaties through the SEA. This inclusion sought to afford them a 'high level of protection'. Moreover, Article 100a of the SEA operates as the foundation for the development of a consumer policy. The SEA also aided the development of consumer policy by relaxing the need for unanimity in areas related to consumer protection. Thus consumer policy became integral to the completion of the SEM. Initially, concerns were related to areas such as:

■ consumer protection;
■ information;
■ product safety;
■ transactions.

High-profile areas in which the SEM worked to protect consumer interests included toy safety, cross-border payments, distance selling and time shares. These actions arising from the SEA were supported by provisions in the Maastricht Treaty which allowed for action in financial services (see below), access to justice, food law etc. In many areas, the Commission sought to develop a consumer policy that was compatible with the broader policy and strategic priorities of the EU, notably in areas such as environmental protection. These efforts were given fresh impetus with the Treaty of Amsterdam which, under Article 129a, specified the need to protect the health, safety and economic interests of consumers. The article sought to give the consumers rights to information and education to safeguard their interests. In addition, all other

policies – where there is overlap – need to consider the consumer angle.

What underpins all this is the free movement of goods and services as well as consumers. Where the Commission acts, the ECJ has underlined that it has to demonstrate a clear cross-border dimension. To this end, consumer policy in the EU is based less on mutual recognition and more on harmonisation. There is, to the Commission, little benefit to the customer from such divergences. In initially developing an action plan for the EU, consumer policy was based upon three areas:

1 *Offering consumers a more powerful voice*: to this end, the EC offered financial and logistical support for meetings.
2 *Offering a high level of health and safety*: this priority was directly stimulated by food safety concerns.
3 *Full respect for the economic interests of consumers*: the needs of consumers needed to be reflected across all of the EU's actions.

In response to these concerns, EU consumer policy is based on the following:

A proper framework for consumer protection rules: many measures to support consumer protection are based on the *acquis* and cover a wide range of issues. These present the fundamental basis for consumer protection but are only one part of the emerging body of rules. Most notable are those related to services of general interest (telecoms, energy etc.) and the emerging body of rules in financial services and competition. Over the medium term, the EU is seeking to move towards a harmonised level of protection as a direct reflection of the increased interdependence between different national markets. This marks a break with the traditional strategy of seeking to base rules upon a minimum level with states free to increase protection as they desire. This move towards harmonisation does not imply prescription just a defined generic framework.

Proper application and respect for rules: this means that there has to be some method for coordination between policies as well as a method for effective monitoring. In addition, any measures have to be credible through an effective system of deterrence and resources to employ corrective sanctions. This relies upon the interaction of public bodies and consumers to create such a framework.

Consumer empowerment: this involves a direct input into the policy process by consumer representatives. An initial basis for this has to be support from public authorities to establish the credibility of these bodies in the minds of consumers as well as providing these groups with access to the required expertise. The Commission has offered financial support to consumer associations and has made active involvement by consumers in the development of policy a key priority. This is linked to a broader EU objective of better decision making.

THE STRATEGY FOR CONSUMERS

In 2004, the EU established ten basic principles for consumer protection:

1 Buy what you what when you want.
2 If it doesn't work send it back.
3 High safety standards for food and other consumer goods.
4 Know what you are eating.
5 Contracts should be fair to customers.
6 Sometimes consumers can change their mind.
7 Making it easier to compare prices.
8 Consumers should not be misled.
9 Protection while you are on holiday.
10 Effective redress for cross-border disputes.

These are broadly defined to encompass all the elements necessary for businesses to extend rights to consumers. Between 2002 and 2006, a new consumer strategy was implemented based around creating a rule-based system. The system needed to ensure that not only were rules developed but they were implemented, enforced and supported by enhanced awareness. This highlights a key focus of consumer policy: that is, consumers have a natural disadvantage with regard to business. There are more consumers than businesses and they are much more difficult to organise. Consumers have fewer resources to create an effective organisational framework to put forward their concerns. Consumers encounter evident information gaps regarding matters of complaint and redress. However, the EU, when pursuing these objectives, has to do so while balancing potentially conflicting needs of business and the consumer. In short, the commitment to consumer protection should not be so onerous that it undermines the commercial viability of businesses.

The policy, therefore, has to do no more than seek to give consumers the rights without necessarily being active in their promotion. This means not just direct policy measures with regard to consumers but also broader measures where the consumer is an indirect beneficiary. Thus, there is a key focus on knowledge creation among all parties to ensure there is an awareness of the role and importance of consumer protection. The strategy between 2002 and 2006 was developed within the context of a number of factors:

- the introduction of the euro;
- changes in usage of the technology;
- the maturing of the SEM;
- corporate governance reform;
- enlargement.

The strategy between 2002 and 2006 stressed the objectives and linked action in three areas (which stress the above themes):

A common high level of consumer protection: this means harmonising through the most appropriate means (framework, directive, standards and best practice) the safety of goods and all other measures that generate the confidence for consumers to undertake transactions anywhere within the SEM. To date, there has been action in this area on general product safety (see below) which reinforces rules, controls and recalls for all non-food products. The Commission has also launched a scheme to improve knowledge with regard to chemicals and their impact on health. There has also been action in the safety of services where there are gaps in comparable data. To protect consumer interests, the Commission has made efforts in areas of unfair commercial practices to promote better awareness of consumer credit terms and the long-term harmonisation of contract law. This is supported by non-legislative activities such as the promotion of consumer rights in schools and other educational settings. This has been supported by better guidance on food labelling.

Effective enforcement of consumer protection rules: the aim of giving consumers the same rights across the EU must be supported by deeper administrative cooperation between member states. To support enforcement, the Commission has established guidelines for enhanced cooperation between states to help surveillance, has approved a consumer

protection cooperation regulation and established a consumer network to offer help in seeking redress.

Involvement in consumer organisation in EU policy: there has to be a method through which consumers can express their wishes and desires within the policy process. This involves a commitment of resources from the Commission to aid their interaction. To this end, the Commission has increased the role of the European Consumer Committee as a means of increasing the effectiveness of their policy, and has supported training courses for staff from consumer organisations. This is an area where there has probably been the greatest progress. There is increased prominence given to consumer rights as awareness grows.

Through these methods, the aim is to harmonise consumer protection to create a more level playing field and legal certainty for both businesses and consumers. There is a general feeling that the fragmentation of the consumer protection system has worked to create uncertainty for all stakeholders. To support this, the EU proposed a supporting framework around which all actions related to consumer protection would be set. All directives would stem from the easily understood framework and would allow all to participate. The development of consumer policy has to be supported by effective enforcement but also has to ensure that the concerns of consumers are not isolated from broader policy developments, such as enlargement, the euro, etc. Indeed, there is a need to integrate consumer concerns within the Services of General Interest directive. This is especially relevant where concerns of universal service are apparent. This has to be complemented by effective coordination with competition policy to ensure consumer interests are accounted for in proceedings.

However, the benefits of this law to consumers have met with complaints from retailers, especially where the new level of consumer protection represented a marked increase. For example, the directive on the right to refund or replacement has met with dismay from UK retailers who feel that such a radical departure from UK practice will lead to increased prices as the right to a full refund or replacement within one year and free repairs if it goes wrong within two years will – within the context of a highly competitive environment – lead to increased costs. This will especially hurt those retailers who earn high profits from extended warranties. Under UK law, the burden of proof is on the consumer. The EU law reverses this. Retailers estimate that the directive will add as much as 2 per cent to costs. In other areas, there is a fear that meeting EU laws in consumer credit card cover could reduce protection. The UK is the only country that offers credit card protection should a company go bankrupt.

In 2005, the Commission launched a new programme to integrate consumer protection and health policies, reflecting synergies between the two areas. The aim is to bring the two areas together under a single framework. Both of these areas under Articles 152 and 153 of the treaties rely on the same type of actions, such as consultation, information, etc. The aim is to:

- protect citizens from risks and threats that are beyond the control of individuals and that cannot effectively be controlled by member states;
- increase the ability of citizens to make better decisions;
- integrate these concerns into all policies.

These joint actions will emerge in areas such as communication, participation, integration with other polices, expert advice, prodcut safety and international cooperation.

CONSUMERS AND THE EURO

Since 2002, consumers have been using euro notes and coins. In theory, the introduction of the euro was meant to make things easier for the average European consumer by reducing the transactions costs of undertaking purchases in another state and directly improving cross-border price transparency. However, the introduction of the euro has been controversial among Europe's consumers because of price increases as well as more practical problems.

With the introduction of the euro, national consumers lost their national currency reference which they used to assess the prices of goods and services. The result is that they have had to create a new personal scale of value related to the euro. Initially, consumers found it difficult to adjust, despite attempts by national and supranational bodies to create a familiarity with the euro prior to its launch. As it initially existed as merely a book currency, there was little opportunity for users to get used to the currency before it was in their pockets. In addition, the display of dual prices was only voluntary and did not help consumers gain a proper sense of the value of the euro. Consumer organisations lobbied for dual pricing to be mandatory but this did not happen.

However, the major controversy was the allegation that the introduction of the euro allowed firms to covertly increase prices. The problem for retailers was that the national currency did not convert nicely into a euro equivalent. In some ways, retailers

345

were in a lose-lose situation. If they rounded prices up, consumers would complain; if they rounded them down it would leave them out of pocket. Evidence from consumer groups suggested that retailers often used the introduction of the euro to hide unjustified price increases. A survey found that the price of dry cleaning in Germany increased by 25 per cent and a cup of coffee in Greece had increased in some cases by 46 per cent immediately after the introduction of the euro. These figures fail to highlight the fall in the price of some goods.

Across the EU, the pattern has proved extremely mixed:

- In Germany there have been reports of minor price increases due to the introduction of the euro.
- In Greece there have been price rises across the board.
- In Ireland and Italy there were more cases of rounding up than rounding down.
- In Luxembourg, the Netherlands and Portugal and Spain there have been limited prices increases.
- Price increases were also evident in Finland and France.

In some states, there were consumer boycotts and consumer complaints soared against what many saw as rampant profiteering by retailers. Little direct action was taken by the authorities as there was little they could do other than to increase transparency. Despite the fact that they were told the introduction of the euro was going to work to the consumer's benefit, there was little immediate suggestion that it would. Inevitably, over time as the euro became embedded, the number of complaints declined. However, many complaints overstated the extent to which prices had actually increased as price reductions were less newsworthy. In part,

these fears were driven by the lack of the anticipated price convergence. These prices increases have now tailed off and the initial effect on consumers has largely dissipated.

THE EUROPEAN FOOD SAFETY AGENCY

Driven by the strategic importance of the EU's agro-chemical sector as well as by the protection of the health of the consumer, the EU published a White Paper on food safety. In the aftermath of the BSE crisis (see Case Study 15.1) and the GM (genetically modified) food scare (see Box 15.1), there was a need by the EU to restore consumer confidence in the safety of food while ensuring that no damage was done to strategically important industries. The BSE and GM problems demonstrated that weaknesses in the supply system have had a deep-seated effect on food production and upon consumer confidence in it. The EU's food and drink industry is highly important, employing 2.6 million people in addition to the 7.5 million employed in agriculture with an annual turnover of over €600 billion and representing 15 per cent of EU manufacturing production. However, as the sector moved towards greater efficiency, higher technology competence and more intensive methods, there was a need to ensure that consumers were not only confident in these new methods but were also sure that the increasingly diverse sources of food production were also safe.

The European Commission White Paper on food safety sought to develop an integrated approach to this issue. In practice, this meant that all aspects of the food value chain need to be involved in the development of food safety. This is what the EU calls a 'farm-to-table' policy with all partners taking responsibility for their respective portion of

Case Study 15.1

THE BSE CRISIS

For over a century, sheep have suffered from scrapie: a form of mental deterioration in the species linked to their consumption of meat and bonemeal. Historically, this has not caused a problem for human health. The emergence of BSE (bovine spongiform encephalopathy) in cattle changed this as this disease jumped the species divide, mutating to cause a new variant of Creutzfeldt-Jakob disease (vCJD) in humans. This condition is linked to the mental and physical deterioration of humans who consume contaminated beef, especially tissue from the nervous system of infected cattle. The disease first emerged in the UK where the combination of intensive farming and a highly competitive bonemeal sector lead to infected bonemeal being fed to cattle. However, its emergence became a European-wide problem given the rights to free movement of products linked to the development of a single market in agricultural goods.

Under EU law, states are allowed to re-introduce (temporarily) trade barriers against other member states when they feel there is a risk to consumer health. As a consequence of the emergence of BSE in UK cattle, this is exactly what the other member states pushed for and achieved. By the beginning of 1996, ten (of the then 15 states) had quarantined British beef. The fear was not only linked to human health but also to the fear that the loss of confidence in the British product would lead to a collapse in beef prices as consumer confidence deteriorated. Supermarkets responded to the crisis by putting labels on meat to certify the state of origin. Resentment was also growing in member states as they felt that the Commission was putting the desire for free movement over the need to protect consumer health.

As an interim measure, the EU offered compensation to UK farms affected by the outbreak of BSE and implemented a global ban on British beef and its by-products. This was on the back of the Dutch government slaughtering the 64,000 British cattle in the Netherlands and the banning of UK beef products. In addition, it banned all cattle older than 30 months from the food chain. The UK was inevitably resentful of such measures, feeling that such moves were little more than protectionism in disguise and challenged the imposition of the world-wide ban as illegal. However, the EP accused the UK government of using such methods to deflect attention from its own mistakes and of neglecting to take countermeasures since 1988 when the scare first came to popular awareness. To the Parliament, this inaction was complemented by Commission inertia over its desire to put trade above health concerns. According to the Parliament's report, the UK government had effectively 'blackmailed' the Commission since the late 1980s, placing a lot of pressure upon the Community institutions to ignore the problem. In addition, the UK was accused of refusing to allow veterinary inspections and of using the UK officials that sat on the EU's scientific committee advising on the BSE crisis to swing decisions in its favour. Thus, it alleged the decisions made by the Commission were anything but impartial and the sharp rise in the export of UK animal-based feed, despite a national ban, was a failure to comply with the principle of cooperation that needed to exist between member states. Where scientists judged BSE to be a concern, the UK ignored them.

In the years immediately after the emergence of the BSE crisis, little effort was still being made to develop effective monitoring systems across the EU. Indeed, there was a sense that many states were in a state of denial about the true extent of the disease. There were especial concerns that the French, Irish, German and Dutch were understating its spread, either by accident or design. EU vets suggested that there could be as many as 1,700 cases in continental Europe and Eire while only 290 had been reported. However, this was still way below the UK where 165,000 cases had been reported. The lack of a uniform method of detecting BSE also meant that many of the figures could be understated. The UK was especially concerned as it could undermine its own efforts to eradicate the disease via its own reporting methods and the mass culling of infected cattle. Only four EU states (aside from the UK) insisted that the spinal cords and brains be removed from cattle (and sheep) before they enter the food chain. Given this and the continued export of both beef and cattle throughout the 1980s, there is a case for believing there was an under-reporting of the incidence of BSE. Indeed, Belgium was censured by the EU for knowingly allowing BSE-infected cattle to be rendered. This move infringed both national and EU regulations though the UK was still under charge through allowing the illegal export of beef.

Only from the late 1990s, was concrete action agreed and undertaken by the EU. The surveillance measures introduced by the EU were:

- a ban on meat and bonemeal from 1 April 1997;
- active surveillance from 1 May 1998;
- removal of high-risk material from cattle and sheep from 1 October 2000.

With the introduction of these measures, the EU had finally turned the corner. A common agreement had been reached and some sort of order could begin to be restored to both intra- and extra-EU export markets for beef and cattle.

By 1998, these measures were starting to have a tangible impact as the EU voted to lift the global ban on UK exports of beef. Prior to the ban, the UK was exporting £600 million of beef. The effort was now to win these markets back and restore confidence in the product. However, the effects of the crisis on beef consumption lasted beyond the short-term logistical impact and measures undertaken. Consumer confidence was clearly shaken. The effects were Europe-wide: for example, in Germany beef prices had fallen 36 per cent and consumption had halved by 2001. The result was a growing beef mountain. As prices and consumption fell, the effect on beef farmers was Europe-wide. One measure to restore balance to the market was to ban the feeding of meat-based meal to all farm animals: the measure was opposed by both Germany and Finland. The former felt it did not go far enough whereas the latter felt it went too far. The result is that governments had high stockpiles of beef and bonemeal which needed to be disposed of. However, the larger states were initially reluctant to open up their markets to younger UK-produced cattle due to sustained health scares. The cull mitigated some of the fall in consumption as it was accompanied by EU aid and the Commission wanted to apply the UK's strict measures across the EU.

In 2001, the crisis re-emerged due to a dip in consumer confidence as many felt governments were being too lax in cracking down on BSE. The problem is that some states (such as Greece) were still exhibiting their first cases of BSE despite the above EU-wide measures.

This was coupled by the fact that major export markets across Africa and Asia remained closed. However, customer confidence, both in the EU and beyond, was dented by the fact that new cases of BSE were emerging despite a commitment by states to take the necessary preventative measures. In Germany and Spain, where the incidence was very low, consumption fell very sharply. In the UK, where there was the highest incidence of disease, beef sales were rising. The result was a series of new measures from 1 January 2001, namely:

- suspension of the use of meat and bonemeal in feedstuffs for all animals;
- testing of all animals over 30 months;
- extension of the list of risk materials;
- a ban on mechanically recovered meat;
- heat treatment of fats to be included in animal feed;
- removal of the backbone from slaughtered cattle.

By 2002, the crisis was in decline as less than one case per 5,000 animals tested was uncovered. In addition, 40 per cent of all scrapie cases were now detected by monitoring. However, there is the need to prevent slippage. In addition, remaining intra-EU trade restraints upon beef trade were removed.

Direct consequences of the BSE crisis were the EU move to establish a Food Safety Agency (FSA) and a shift in the manner of food regulation. Traditionally, food regulation occurred on an ad hoc basis and/or developed within the jurisprudence of the ECJ. However, the BSE crisis showed that where political interests were involved, such an approach does not work as policy is prone to capture and manipulation. The Commission was involved in a process between 1990 and 1994 of disinformation as it sought to promote the market over consumer safety. This led to a number of reforms, notably, all relevant scientific committees were brought under the authority of DG XXIV as a means of avoiding conflict between economic interests and health protection. It also meant a new approach to consumer and health safety, moving away from merely focusing on food security to a broader remit including consumer health protection. BSE influenced the Treaty of Amsterdam, leading to Articles 95, 152 and 153 which reflect health and safety concerns.

Case questions

1 To what extent is intra-EU protection justified on health and safety concerns?

2 What lessons can be learned from the BSE case regarding consumer health and safety issues?

3 Is the creation of the FSA justified?

the value chain in ensuring that food standards are addressed. In addition, there has to be traceability for food and ingredients. Core to this is effective monitoring and surveillance, rapid alert systems and effective research and scientific cooperation. Often these aspects of food safety occur in an ad hoc manner. To overcome such challenges, the EU has proposed the creation of a food safety authority.

To the Commission, the creation of a European Food Safety Authority (EFSA) was a necessary and appropriate response to the emerging challenges. The authority would be trusted with a number of roles including:

- independent scientific advice;
- operation of rapid alert systems;
- networking with national agencies.

The EFSA will provide the European Commission with expert advice. The response to the analysis provided will be the role of the Commission. The setting up of this body will be accompanied by a wider range of other measures to bring coherence to the large range of legislation covering all aspects of food products. The White Paper has set up over 80 separate measures.

BOX 15.1

THE EU AND GENETICALLY MODIFIED (GM) FOODS

Over the last 30 or so years, there has been a rapid advancement in agricultural technology. One of the most notable advancements has been the creation of GM foods. These foods rely on genetic modification which is based on a technique whereby the genes from one organism are transferred to another organism. The aim is to use this mixture of genes to improve disease resistance, nutritional value, tolerance to herbicides/extreme weather and boost yields. The US has been the leader in this field of biotechnology and, by 2004, GM accounted for 75 per cent of soya bean and 34 per cent of corn production.

However, from the late 1990s emerging health and safety fears led the EU to start restricting access to these foods. In 1998, it established an unofficial moratorium according to which the EU did not allow the growth of new GM crops after October 1998. In addition, the EU restricted field trials of GM crops which fell by 90 per cent between 1998 and 2002 as a consequence. However, in 2003, such bans were challenged by the US, Argentina and Canada claiming that there was little scientific basis for these draconian actions. As a result the blanket ban was lifted in 2004 though a series of GM crops remained banned by individual states.

In early 2006, the WTO ruled against the EU, although its officials are seeking to limit the ban's effectiveness. The WTO decision was important as it reinforced the notion that such products are both safe and enable farmers to increase their productivity. In its defence, the EU said the decision referred to old rules and not the current regime. However, inbuilt suspicions remain. Indeed, eight states still have restrictions on these foods. European business supported the WTO decision arguing that there was no scientific basis to restrict their research into GM foods.

Ultimately, the choice of GM foods is down to the consumer. In many cases, the dispute between the EU and the US is not about food safety but about technological competition in biotechnology. However, the decision has a number of far-reaching implications. The first is that wider access to new technologies is important in building trust in the global trading system. Second, there needs to be greater harmony in regulatory practices. In GM foods, the risks were perceived as opposed to real. As a result, it was largely a political not a scientific issue. This also places pressure upon business to improve public knowledge about such technologies.

These include measures on animal feed, additives, flavourings, etc. These measures have to be developed alongside actions to improve customer information and international action to ensure that other suppliers from outside the EU do not subvert quality requirements.

The EFSA was formally established in January 2002 as a separate legal entity funded from the EU budget but operating independently of other EU institutions. The aim is for the advice given to be based on independent scientific research. Its remit covers all aspect of the food value chain and all issues that both directly and indirectly affect food quality and safety. Its aim is to prevent the emergence of new crises but also to create effective channels of communication to the public when such crises emerge. The intention is that this new infrastructure will negate the challenges posed by past crises for both industry and consumer.

EU CONSUMER PROTECTION LEGISLATION

There are a number of EU directives on consumer rights no matter where they shop within the EU. The rights within the EU are that:

- when the company makes contact with the consumer it should say who it is, where it is and what it is and state that it is trying to sell something (Distance Selling Directive and Ecommerce Directive);
- the selling price and/or price per unit must be clear (Directive on Price Indications);
- the consumer must be told how and where to cancel an order as well as being offered a 'cooling-off period';

- the consumer can appeal against unfair terms in a contract and/or advertising (Unfair Contract Term Directive/Misleading Advertising Directives);
- the right of the consumer to be aware of and stop unsolicited advertising e-mails (E-Commerce Directive);
- all products should be safe (General Product Safety Directive);
- consumers should be compensated where necessary (Product Liability Directive);
- the consumer has two years to identify faults that were present when a product was purchased. In these cases, if proved, suitable compensation should be arranged (Directive on Sale of Consumer Goods and Associated Guarantees);
- personal details may only be used if agreed to by the consumer (Data Processing Directive).

Two major directives of note are the General Product Safety Directive and the Product Liability Directive:

General Product Safety Directive (GPSD): this covers all products not included in single or sector-specific regulations and offers a safety net to ensure all products sold in the SEM can be considered safe. Foodstuffs were excluded from the directive as these were included in other directives. A new directive came into force in 2001: this represented an updated system based on changes in the socio-economic environment and driven by new technology products as well as the need to remove existing legal uncertainties. The new directive increased consumer rights in areas such as better information, focus on information for special groups of consumers, the recall of dangerous products, etc. In addition, the directive places an emphasis upon consumers to use the products in a normal way and for the purposes for which they were designated.

An immediate impact of the introduction of the directive in 2004 was a sharp increase in product recalls. In the year following the introduction of the directive, product recalls increased by 175 per cent with a rise in insurance claims anticipated. It is estimated that the advertising costs of a product recall can be as much as £10,000 with the final figure when including compensation etc. running into millions. In total, across the EU, 373 products were recalled between January 2005 and January 2006. In most cases, these products were recalled under the order of the regulator rather than by the voluntary action of the firm.

Liability for Defective Products: this seeks to ensure that manufacturers are responsible for products that harm. The directive deals with redress for the consequences of the deficiencies with the product. Though the GPSD deals with the product itself, the notion of 'defective' is based on an expectation of the safety of a product. It is manufacturers, not retailers, that are responsible for safety and the directive limits the burden of proof required so that expensive technical advice is no longer required. Again, the emphasis is upon the consumer to ensure that he or she was using it for the proper purpose in the first place.

THE INTERNET AND CONSUMER PROTECTION

By mid-2004, less than 20 per cent of Europeans used e-commerce even though it is expected to be a major growth area for trade in the coming decade. The main problem is that as consumers, Europeans have little confidence in e-commerce and their ability to protect their interests through this medium. To the European Commission, if the SEM is going to prove its value to the average European, then e-commerce has to mature. It is through this medium that consumers will be able to access the wider choice, lower prices and better quality associated with the integration process. In many cases, the lack of confidence in e-commerce is symptomatic of broader trends whereby consumers mistrust traders due to a feeling of inadequate protection when they engage in international transactions.

The emphasis is, therefore, upon commercial operators demonstrating to users that they can have confidence in the use of the Internet for the purposes of transactions. The EU can help by putting in place the necessary supporting regulatory structures. The Unfair Commercial Practice Directive established a means for protecting consumers by allowing for mutual recognition in security and trust procedures. This is supported by coordination between national bodies to track and prosecute rogue online traders. It is evident that there need to be measures to generate the necessary confidence. This can be aided by the demonstration of trust-marks and codes of conduct.

In addition to the trust in usage, there are issues related to confidence in payment systems. This is pivotal, for while many may surf the net, many ditch their 'virtual basket' before they reach the checkout. While there is good security technology, this benefit is not being felt through increased transactions by customers. It only takes one fraud to set back consumer confidence in this area substantially. Again, there is a need for some degree of self-regulation to help solve this problem to overcome this confidence gap. The Commission's e-confidence strategy aims to identify third parties that consumers can trust, especially when problems emerge, and to increase confidence in cross-border transactions. To support this, the Commission has launched a series of initia-

Case Study 15.2

AIRLINE COMPENSATION

In 2002, new regulations came into force compelling airlines to pay higher compensation to passengers left stranded by overbooking and flight cancellation. The rules work in a number of areas:

- In cases of denied boarding due to overbooking, the airline must pay compensation dependent on the length (in terms of kilometres) of the flight.
- In cases of cancellation, the airline must offer a choice of refund and a flight back to the original destination or another way of getting to destination. In addition, the airline must provide refreshments to passengers.
- These rules apply to any flight from or to an EU airport when the flight is operated by an EU airline.
- With regard to long delays, if passengers check in on time, the carrier must provide refreshments, hotels rooms etc. based on a sliding scale depending on the length of the delay.

Unsurprisingly, this regulation was challenged by the airlines especially by those based on the low-cost model. This is mainly because the system was not based on the original fare but on the length of the flight with the result that airlines be forced to make compensation payments many times the cost of the original fare. Thus, there is a large financial risk for low-cost businesses. The industry argues that this will result in higher fares and reduced choice for consumers. Thus, as a result, measures designed to make the consumer better off could end up eroding their welfare. The industry estimates that the extra cost to airlines would be around €560 million (£383 million) above what is currently paid out. It is estimated that for mid-sized airlines, this regulation could amount to as much as 20 per cent of operating profit. The major complaint, though, is that it makes airlines responsible for circumstances that are beyond their control. However, with the rejection of their complaints by the ECJ in January 2003, their ability to change these laws ended.

Case questions

1 To what extent are the compensation measures justified?

2 Outline the challenge to low-cost airlines from these regulatory measures. Are their concerns warranted?

tives to prevent problems arising by encouraging best practice (use of codes of conduct, trustmarks and credit card chargebacks), by seeking remedies other than redress to legal action and by enabling legal action where necessary. By 2001, a common standard for best practice was agreed between industry and consumer bodies. The scheme will enable consumers to identify which sites they can trust.

However, since the emergence of the Internet as an economic force for integration in the mid-1990s, the Commission has struggled to understand the best way to approach the development of e-commerce. This is especially true given differences between Europe and the US over key aspects of the development of the global information economy, especially in areas such as privacy and security. These disputes have also occurred between member states.

This area underlines links between consumer policy and the information society initiative as well as the internal market programme. In support of this measure, the EU has launched a legal framework for e-business that brings together all elements affecting the development of e-commerce under a single framework. One measure that has been transposed into national law which should aid consumer confidence in e-commerce is the Privacy Protection and Data Directive which controls the use to which data can be put when they are volunteered over the Internet. A 2003 survey indicated that the lack of confidence in e-commerce was compounded by lack of access to the Internet.

FINANCIAL SERVICES

Financial services are an area in which there is great deal of asymmetric information between providers and consumers with the result that it can be difficult for the latter to make confident, well-informed decisions. This is due to the:

■ complexity and intangible nature of the products offered;
■ fact that these purchases are made very rarely;
■ fact that the effect of the product may not be felt for many years.

In spite of this uncertainty, financial products have the potential to have a highly significant effect upon consumers' lives through, for example, the level of disposable income spent on outstanding consumer credit.

As a result of Article 153 – which establishes the requirement for a high degree of consumer protection as a necessary feature of the SEM – there are a number of specific directives for financial services. Many of these focus on regulating the competence and financial strength of the providers. In other areas, policy is designed to enable consumers to make more informed choices on the purchase of financial products. However, the EU market for financial services remains fragmented. The Commission attempted to remove this anomaly through its FSAP (see Chapter 4) but consumers have still found it difficult to enforce their rights, especially within the context of a patchwork of different bodies to whom they can turn for redress.

While the Commission has made consumer protection a high priority within financial services, there is a feeling that consumers still feel powerless with regard to financial bodies. This is especially true in relation to cross-border trade where information asymmetries are especially acute. Evidence from the European Commission suggests that not only have EU citizens failed to source financial services overseas but they are also reluctant to purchase any in the future. This is directly caused by lack of information and language barriers which prohibit confident buying of financial products across borders.

To help overcome such problems, the Commission has been working on a series of directives covering insurance and investment. These address areas of solvency, reliability and better information. Consumers, themselves, are also growing increasingly active. With the increasing movement of people across borders (especially within growing expatriate communities), the potential for cross-border selling has increased. Such a trend led to complaints by UK expatriates in Spain against mis-selling by UK-based companies. In these cases, expatriates have found the differences in rules have reduced protection. For example, by moving from the UK to Spain, consumers found they moved to a regime that was historically much less stringent.

The Commission tried to overcome uncertainty generated by different regimes by creating FinNet in 2001. This promoted cross-border complaints through a network of official arbitration bodies. However, in practice, the process was hindered by the different forms of product selling and financial advice that occur across the EU. While it is meant to stop disputes going to court, consumers still have the capability to take issues further.

CONCLUSION

Consumer policy has only been a recent issue in the development of EU policy. This was a glaring oversight as consumers are expected to be major beneficiaries of the process of economic integration. Action by the EU in the area of consumer policy has to be geared not merely to getting the message across of the opportunities created by the process of economic integration, but also to extend the necessary protection. Without awareness and security, users will lack confidence in the process of integration to the extent that the transactions that drive the process may be undermined.

KEY POINTS

■ Consumers are major beneficiaries of the process of economic integration within the EU.

■ EU consumer policy was a direct spillover from the creation of the SEM.

■ the EU has launched a consumer strategy to support consumer confidence in the integration process.

ACTIVITIES

1 Discuss how consumer confidence in e-commerce can best be achieved.

2 Divide into groups and assess the relative merits of allowing continued research into GM foods.

3 Assess the relative merits of extensive versus intensive food production.

QUESTIONS FOR DISCUSSION

1 How and in what ways have consumers benefited from the process of European integration?

2 To what extent is the development of EU policy towards consumers justified?

3 Why is consumer confidence in the SEM important for its development?

SUGGESTIONS FOR FURTHER READING

Bamford, R. (2004) 'Shopping Around: Dealing with Cross-border Complaints', *Consumer Policy Review*, 14 (4), pp. 108–12.

European Commission (2002) 'Consumer Policy Strategy 2002–2006' COM (2002) 208.

European Commission (2004) *Consumer Protection in the EU: Ten Basic Principles*, www.europa.eu.int/comm/consumers/.

Howells, G. and Wilhelmsson, T. (eds) (1997) *EC Consumer Law*, Aldershot: Dartmouth.

Stack, F. and Crampton, S. (2002) 'Making Europe Work Better', *Consumer Policy Review*, 12 (4), pp. 148–52.

Part IV

Europe and the rest of the world

Economic integration serves many purposes but a central purpose is to strengthen the competitive basis of European business to help it compete with the rest of the world. The three chapters of Part IV are about how European business relates to the rest of the world. The first chapter deals with Central and Eastern Europe (CEE). Although the 2004 accession has taken place and eight CEE states have been incorporated into the EU (with two more due to follow in 2007), a separate chapter on the CEE states was included, and in Part IV, because businesses from both Western and Eastern Europe have had to develop new strategies to contend with the new competitive environment, both within individual CEE states and the EU itself, resulting first from transition within CEE and, second, from accession to the EU. The chapter on Europe and the developed world, which contains the EU's main trading partners, is more orthodox in its approach. The final chapter of both Part IV and of the whole book deals with the increasing challenge to European business from the emerging economies of China, India and Russia. These economies have great potential and China and India, in particular, have begun in recent years to demonstrate what that potential can mean. Russia's economy has been more problematic but its energy resources make it an important partner for Europe. Thus, the final chapter is forward looking and addresses issues that will grow in importance as the years unfold.

Chapter 16

Central and Eastern Europe

Response to a new business environment

Capitalism is the exploitation of man by man. Communism is the reverse.

Anonymous Polish joke

This chapter will help you understand:

- how and why the most recent enlargement of the EU has taken place;
- changes in investment, trade and labour markets that have taken place during transition and the enlargement process;
- how transition and enlargement have helped shape the European business environment;
- how enlargement has played a part in the restructuring of some sectors;
- how enlargement has influenced corporate strategy for some companies in some sectors.

On 1 May 2004, ten countries entered the EU, increasing its membership from 15 to 25. This enlargement increased the population of the Union by 20 per cent to 457 million, expanded its area by 26 per cent and increased total GDP by 5 per cent or an amount roughly equal to the GDP of the Netherlands. This enlargement, to be followed by Bulgaria and Romania in 2007, and later by Croatia, Turkey and possibly others, presents a major challenge for the Union in terms of its functioning, economic and business environment and future direction.

Eight of the ten new member states in 2004 were from CEE, fresh from nearly 15 years of transition from Communism to liberal market economies. In order to establish the magnitude of the changes that have occurred in these countries in what is a relatively short time in their history, the chapter begins by examining the legacy of the Communist period. It then briefly discusses the process by which they became EU members before analysing their potential impact on the European economic and business environment given their new status as full members of the SEM.

359

THE LEGACY OF THE PAST

Since 1990 the countries of CEE have completely transformed their political, social and economic systems with knock-on effects for business both in CEE itself and in a wider Europe. In order to appreciate the extent of this transformation, which has also allowed these countries to join the EU, it is useful to dwell briefly on the situation of these countries at the onset of transition.

The period 1945–89 was one in which the USSR imposed its own political and economic system upon the countries of CEE. The Soviet bloc (that is, the USSR and its CEE satellites) presented a united face to the rest of the world and the cold war resulted in a permanent state of antagonism between East and West. This antagonism derived from competition between ideologically different political and economic systems – competition that affected all aspects of the international economic and political system. Indeed, part of the rationale for the creation of the European Community was to establish a political and economic framework in Western Europe to act as a counterweight to, and a defence against, the Soviet bloc. The status of the Soviet Union as one of the world's two 'superpowers' ensured that the Soviet bloc, with its alien ideology, was treated with a circumspection that further increased the psychological distance between Eastern and Western Europe.

More specifically, the defining characteristics of the period for the CEE countries were:

■ *Soviet domination*: CEE political and economic systems were formally modelled on those of the USSR. The CEE countries were also obliged to follow the USSR's foreign policy. This resulted in extremely limited contacts with the West. The only

exception was Romania which, under Nikolae Ceaucescu, was allowed to pursue a relatively independent foreign policy, largely because it followed hard-line Communist policy at home. Soviet domination also extended to military matters: the CEE countries were united through the Warsaw Pact in a unified military command structure under the guidance and control of the Soviet Union.

■ *Authoritarian, one-party political systems*: the CEE Communist parties were under the influence of the Communist Party of the Soviet Union and were formally committed to Marxism-Leninism. These parties wielded ultimate power via their tight control of the organs of the state and were inseparable from the state machinery. This control extended to national, regional and local bureaucracies, trade unions, the media and enterprise management. There was, in short, an absence of democratic institutions and processes, such as free elections and opposition parties and freedom of speech and the press, as normally understood in the West.

■ *Command or planned economies*: in a command system, allocation of resources is undertaken by the state, which also owns the means of production. The command system is thus the complete antithesis of a market economy and of the underlying philosophy of the SEM where competition and the price mechanism are dominant means of resource allocation. The command system by-passes the price mechanism and the basic laws of supply and demand: enterprises decide what and how much to produce according to targets established by state planning agencies. During the command economy era, the economic plans followed by the CEE countries were closely aligned to the preferences and interests of the USSR, resulting in neglect of the consumer sector and an economic structure skewed towards heavy industry and ill-prepared for integration into the SEM and the global economy. The rigid planning and isolation of the CEE economies from the rigours of the market resulted in uncompetitive enterprises with obsolete, decaying capital stock and from which the concepts of entrepreneurship and incentives for greater efficiency or innovation were almost completely absent. This was the case throughout CEE, although the New Economic Mechanism had introduced limited elements of the market into Hungary before 1989 and some private agriculture had been allowed in Poland and elsewhere.

The Soviet bloc was not without its problems. These came, in particular, from the intrinsic problems within the command system itself and became acute in the 1980s when economic stagnation and falling living standards took hold and the credibility of the regimes themselves was questioned. This is not the place to analyse the reasons and events behind the collapse of the Soviet system. However, once the process of change began, it became unstoppable. Change began under Soviet President Gorbachev who, faced with a stagnant economy, embarked upon limited market reform and restructuring (*perestroika*), accompanied by political reform under the heading of openness (*glasnost*), and a more positive relationship with the West. In CEE, the catalyst for change was the September 1989 opening of the border between Austria and Hungary. This was followed in November 1989 by the symbolic breaching of the Berlin Wall. The collapse of the Communist regimes of CEE was bloodless (almost), sudden, rapid and complete and by 1990, free elections had been held in all CEE countries.

RAPPROCHEMENT BETWEEN EAST AND WEST EUROPE

The old East–West divisions had inhibited the development of meaningful trade and commercial cooperation between the two blocs and limited formal contact to the bare minimum despite their geographical proximity. It was not until the joint June 1988 declaration between the EC and the Council for Mutual Economic Assistance (CMEA), the organisation that provided the framework for trade and economic relations among the CEE countries and the Soviet Union, that official relations between the countries of Eastern and Western Europe were established. By June 2004, eight former members of the Soviet bloc, including the three Baltic states – Estonia, Latvia and Lithuania – which had been, albeit unwillingly, part of the Soviet Union itself, had become members of the EU. In the interim, these eight countries (plus Bulgaria and Romania who will follow their neighbours into the EU by 2007) embarked upon a radical and often painful reform of their political and economic systems to bring them into line with the Western model and as a prerequisite for EU membership.

The events of 1989–90 required countries in both Eastern and Western Europe to reassess their basic assumptions about the internal and external policies of the CEE countries. For the CEE countries themselves, the events of 1989–90 represented total rejection of the previous past four decades and a reorientation towards the Western model of liberal democracy and market economics. The key consideration for them was not what they wanted to achieve (the goal of a free market, liberal democracy was almost unanimously taken for granted) but how they could achieve it, and was largely framed in terms of the pace

BOX 16.1

MILESTONES IN THE EU–CEE RELATIONSHIP

1988–89	EC signs trade and economic cooperation agreements with Poland and Hungary
Nov. 1989	Berlin Wall breached
Dec. 1989	Romanian uprising and execution of the Ceaucescus
1990	Free elections throughout CEE
Jan. 1990	Poland implements shock reform therapy
3 Oct. 1990	German unification
1991	CMEA and Warsaw Pact formally dissolved
26 Dec. 1991	USSR formally dissolved following Gorbachev's resignation the previous day
1992–93	EC interim trade agreements with Czechoslovakia, Hungary, Poland, Bulgaria and Romania
1993	Trade and economic cooperation agreements with Latvia, Estonia and Lithuania in force
1 Jan. 1993	Czechoslovakia split into Czech and Slovak republics
June 1993	Copenhagen Council sets out conditions for CEE membership of EU
1 Sept. 1993	Cooperation agreement with Slovenia in force
1 Feb. 1994	Europe Agreements with Poland and Hungary in force – within two months both countries apply for EU membership
Dec. 1994	Essen Council adopts pre-accession strategy – Europe agreements, 'structured dialogue', development of PHARE and alignment of single market legislation
1995	Slovakia, Bulgaria, Romania, Estonia, Latvia and Lithuania apply for EU membership
1 Jan. 1995	Free trade agreements with Estonia, Latvia and Lithuania in force
1 Feb. 1995	Europe Agreements with Czech and Slovak Republics, Romania and Bulgaria in force
12 June 1995	Europe Association Agreements signed with Estonia, Latvia and Lithuania
15 June 1995	Europe Agreement with Slovenia initialised
1996	Czech Republic and Slovenia apply for EU membership
July 1997	Agenda 2000 published, includes Commission Opinions on membership applications and recommends Czech Republic, Poland, Hungary, Slovenia, Estonia and Cyprus for first wave of next enlargement
31 Mar. 1998	Enlargement negotiations begin with Czech Republic, Poland, Hungary, Slovenia, Estonia and Cyprus
1999	Helsinki Council decides Turkey is a candidate for membership
2003	Croatia applies for EU membership
2003	Accession negotiations completed with Cyprus, Czech Republic, Estonia, Hungary, Latvia, Lithuania, Malta, Poland, Slovakia and Slovenia
2003	Membership referendums in nine out of ten acceding states all support accession. Cyprus ratifies accession treaty without referendum

March 2004	Former Yugoslav Republic of Macedonia (FYRM) applies for EU membership
1 May 2004	Cyprus, Czech Republic, Estonia, Hungary, Latvia, Lithuania, Malta, Poland, Slovakia and Slovenia become EU members
17 Mar. 2005	EU postpones start of Croatian accession negotiations because of Zagreb's failure to work with the UN War Crimes Tribunal
April 2005	Bulgaria and Romania sign accession Treaty with view to accession in 2007
3 Oct. 2005	Scheduled beginning of accession negotiations with Turkey

of reform – rapid and immediate with short-term pain but with long-term benefits, the 'big bang' approach as followed in Poland, or a more measured, gradual approach as adopted in Hungary.

Each CEE country quickly came to view membership of the EU as immensely desirable and as a crucial part of their transition into democratic, market economies. The requirements of bringing the CEE countries into line with the *acquis communautaire*, an essential part of the enlargement process, coincided with the tasks that are central to the transition process. In other words, enlargement required successful transition and transition received strong guidance from the necessities of enlargement. In short, although enlargement was not, in itself, a necessary condition for a successful transition, in practice, the linking of the two raised the stakes and made these processes highly interdependent on each other. In tandem, transition and the preparations for accession helped significantly transform the business environment in CEE for private enterprise, both domestic and foreign-owned. They also affected the wider business environment in Western Europe.

Once the CEE countries decided they wanted reintegration into an all-encompassing European economic and political space, they also had to develop strategies to engage with the internationalisation of markets. In other words, the CEE states, previously isolated behind the walls of CMEA, suddenly lost not only the security of belonging to a regional bloc, but were also immediately opened to strong international competitive forces. Membership of the EU, itself striving to respond to this competitive challenge, provides a better platform for the CEE states to respond both to the new global market place and to their own internal challenges.

The disintegration of the conventional wisdom about relationships between East and West extracted a complex reaction from the EU. Although the end of the cold war and the triumph of the democratic, liberal economic model on which the EU itself was firmly based were welcome, the transition of CEE created a number of other problems and dilemmas which, given their proximity to the EU, could not be ignored. The Communist regimes had, for example, kept tight control over their populations, enabling them to contain centuries-old ethnic rivalries. The consequences of the re-emergence of old rivalries became only too tragically apparent in former Yugoslavia (a country outside the Soviet bloc for most of the post-war period but which had maintained its own form of command economy). The Slovak

Republics, Bulgaria and Romania also contain sizeable ethnic minorities which have the potential, at least, to create significant political instability. In short, the possibility of superpower conflict as a result of East–West divisions gave way to fears about the possibility of 'Balkanisation' on the Union's eastern borders.

The EU's reassessment of its relationship with CEE countries extended beyond security issues. Although economic links had been minimal between the two for decades and real personal disposable income was low in CEE countries, the size and long-term potential of CEE markets was significant. Furthermore, the EU and its members had to decide precisely how close relationships with the CEE countries should become. There was, for example, serious concern that enlargement on such an unprecedented scale and involving countries with incomes so significantly below those of existing members would place an intolerable financial burden on the EU and jeopardise further integration. In light of the magnitude and suddenness of the transformations, the EU's initial reaction to the CEE changes was, unsurprisingly, piecemeal and ad hoc. Development of a commitment to CEE accession and a systematic accession strategy took longer.

The initial reaction of the EU to changes in CEE was to negotiate bilateral trade and cooperation agreements with them and by October 1990, such agreements had been reached with all CMEA's European members. These initial trade concessions were reinforced by the Phare programme of financial and technical assistance from 1989.

It quickly became apparent, however, that conventional forms of assistance would not suffice in these unprecedented circumstances and the EU quickly moved to negoti-

ate 'Association' or 'Europe' agreements with the CEE countries. These agreements were more far reaching than traditional trade agreements. In addition to enhanced trading arrangements, they included a political dialogue via regular high-level meetings and consultation on issues of common interest; provisions on supply of services and movement of capital; and a commitment by the Associate states to render their legislation compatible with EU laws, especially in the areas of competition policy, non-discriminatory procurement policy and IPR. The first Europe Agreements were in force with Poland and Hungary by February 1994. Although forming some of the most extensive agreements the EU had ever reached with third countries, the Agreements themselves fell short of making a direct link between Associate status and accession. However, they did acknowledge accession as the ultimate objective of the Associate states, an objective that was confirmed by Poland and Hungary, which both applied for full membership less than two months after their agreements came into force.

The EU was thus coming under increased pressure from the CEE countries to commit itself to further enlargement and, preferably, to establish a timetable for the process. Despite differing views on enlargement within member states, a major breakthrough was made at the June 1993 Copenhagen Council which spelt out the membership eligibility criteria more explicitly (see Box 16.2), concluding that:

the associated countries in CEE that so desire shall become members of the EU. Accession will take place as soon as an associated country is able to assume the obligations of membership by satisfying the economic and political conditions required.

BOX 16.2

MEMBERSHIP ELIGIBILITY AND THE COPENHAGEN CONDITIONS

Traditionally, a country was regarded as eligible for EU membership if it was European, democratic and operated accorded to market principles. The 1993 Copenhagen Council set out the following four conditions which CEE associates had to satisfy before accession could proceed:

- stable institutions that guarantee democracy, the rule of law, human rights and respect for, and protection of, minorities;
- a functioning market economy;
- the capacity to cope with competitive pressure and market forces within the Union;
- the ability to take on the obligations of membership including political, economic and monetary union.

In addition, the Council added a fifth condition which applied to the EU, stipulating that 'the Union's capacity to absorb new members, while maintaining the momentum of European integration, is also an important consideration in the general interest of both the Union and the candidate countries.'

The Copenhagen criteria provided the overriding principles by which preparedness for accession was judged. In the interim, numerous other more detailed measures to facilitate compliance with the criteria were developed. These include the 1995 White Paper which specified not only the measures needed to be taken in each sector to align the CEE countries with the SEM but also the sequence in which the approximation of measures – including competition, social and environmental policies – should take place. As such, the White Paper provided a road map for accession, and also transition itself, as the steps needed for accession coincided with the requirements of transition. The treaty revisions of Amsterdam and Nice were intended to facilitate reform of EU institutions in preparation for enlargement (see Chapter 2). Agenda 2000 established accession partnerships which set out the priorities for each applicant in meeting the *acquis*

communautaire and the financial resources to be made available for that purpose.

Accession negotiations themselves began with the majority of the applicants by 1998. A fundamental principle of applying to join the EU is that applicant states must accept the *acquis communautaire* – that is, the treaties and laws that govern the EU. In other words, new members agree to abide by the existing rules of the organisation that they are joining. The negotiations are, therefore, not about which bits of the *acquis* to accept but, rather, how the applicant states will adopt, implement and enforce the *acquis*. The negotiations are also concerned with the duration of any transition periods beyond the accession date agreed to allow new members longer to adapt to specific policies. The general principle is that transitions should be limited, both in number and duration. In relation to the 2004 enlargement, this principle was strictly adhered to with relatively few transitions allowed given the number of new members and the expansion of the *acquis* since previous enlargements. The most notable transition was that accorded to the existing member states which were given the option of restricting access to their labour markets to workers from the new member states for a limited period of time (see Chapter 13). The commitment to EU membership also entailed a commitment to adopt the single currency, albeit not on the accession date but once the convergence criteria were met.

Once the negotiations were complete in 2003, the existing and aspiring new member states signed the accession treaties, prior to their ratification. In the old member states, this took place through the parliamentary process, whereas nine out of ten of the new member states held referendums. As Table 16.1 shows, the referendum results were clearly or overwhelmingly in favour of accession. The only country in which the outcome was in any doubt was Malta where, significantly, the turnout in the referendum was much greater.

Table 16.1 Accession referendum results, 2003 (%)

	Yes	No	Turnout
Cyprus	No referendum		
Czech Republic	77.3	22.7	55.2
Estonia	66.9	33.1	64.0
Hungary	83.8	16.2	46.0
Latvia	67.0	32.3	72.5
Lithuania	91.0	9.0	63.3
Malta	53.7	46.4	90.9
Poland	77.4	22.6	58.9
Slovakia	93.7	6.3	52.2
Slovenia	89.6	10.4	60.2

Source: Authors.

Following successful ratification of the accession treaties, the EU's biggest ever enlargement took place on 1 May 2004.

WHAT DOES AN ENLARGED EUROPE MEAN?

The 2004 enlargement has far-reaching implications for the old and new member states, for their citizens; for the EU, its institutions and policies; and for businesses from the old and the new member states and even for businesses with their primary locations outside Europe. Many implications straddle all or several stakeholders: for example, enlargement-related labour market issues (see below) are relevant to workers and companies throughout the EU and to policy makers at both a national and supranational level.

A common concern regarding enlargement is not so much the scope of the enlargement but the big divergence in economic standards between old and new countries. These disparities, it is claimed, could lead to large-scale population movements as low-paid CEE workers seek a better life elsewhere, thereby depriving workers in old Europe of jobs, placing burdens on social infrastructure and depriving the country of origin of the brightest and the best. Others argue the disparities will lead to social dumping as Western European businesses migrate to Eastern Europe in search of lower cost labour. Others fear the disparities will overwhelm the EU budget and the decision-making process and loosen the ties between members, making a two- or multi-tier Europe more likely. Those of a more positive bent identify a multitude of business opportunities arising from enlargement.

Whatever one's views about the extent of the enlargement challenges, it is indisputable that the new member states have structurally and systemically travelled an extremely long way in a relatively short space of time. At the onset of transition, according to Vintrová (2004), the institutional framework of former Soviet satellites 'was diametrically opposed to the institutional framework established by developed market economies'. The requirements of accession, particularly the Copenhagen condition of establishing a stable democracy and the adoption of the *acquis communautaire*, accelerated institutional transformation and provided a solid and stable anchor for these changes. From a business perspective, this brings benefits in terms of predictable and enforceable contracts, lower transaction costs, initially from more transparent rules of conduct and subsequently from greater harmonisation of practices, and a business environment which is less liable to graft.

... for growth?

In economic terms the journey has frequently been painful. Although there are clear differences between the strategies adopted by individual countries (such as the Polish 'shock therapy' compared to the more gradual approach of Hungary) and, increasingly, between the economies themselves as they promote their own specific comparative advantages, the CEE economies have tended to follow a similar growth path (see Figure 16.1 a and b). In the early 1990s, as the old system collapsed and before the reforms began to take hold, these economies experienced precipitous falls in real GDP (with attendant problems for employment, etc.): in Central Europe, GDP falls of 10 per cent in one year alone were commonplace whereas in Baltic states, the worst year saw falls of 15 to 35 per cent. To put this into

perspective, any negative growth in the old member states is considered a serious problem and recessions in recent decades have tended to register short-term falls in GDP of no more than 1 or 2 per cent. Positive growth returned in 1993–94, and a little earlier in Poland and has remained positive ever since, with a slight dip in some countries in 1998–99 as a result of the international financial crisis that affected Russia and had some spillover effects for the CEE states. However, in the years immediately following the recession, growth accelerated once more and, by May 2004, the new member states were growing at two to three times the average rate of the old member states (see Figure 16.1 a and b), with the Baltic states, in particular, booming.

Despite the promising economic performance at the time of accession, several of the new member states from CEE had only reached the level of real GDP that had prevailed in 1989, immediately prior to the economic crash in the region, shortly before accession took place. In the case of Latvia and Lithuania, where the economic downturn had been particularly severe in the early 1990s, real GDP had still only reached around 80 per cent of 1989 levels the year before accession (see Figure 16.2). These factors, together with the low levels of GDP per head in the CEE states (see Figure 16.3), imply that these economies need to outstrip growth in the old member states for many years to come before they can be said to be at a similar level of development as the older member states.

... for trade?

Accession has not had a major impact on the geographical structure of CEE trade, largely because as a result of the Europe Agreements

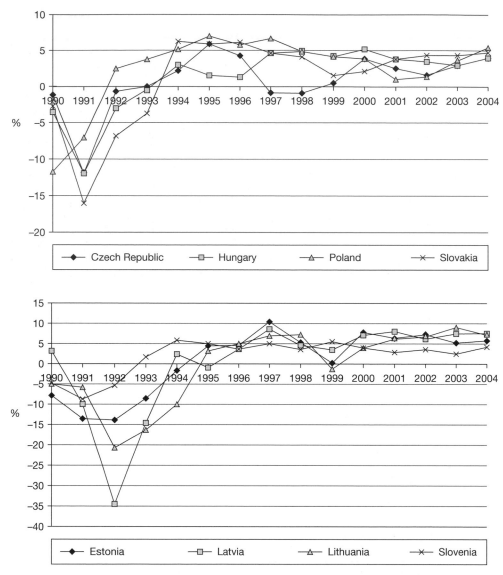

Figure 16.1 (a) Real GDP growth in Central Europe, 1990–2004; (b) Real GDP growth in the Baltic states and Slovenia, 1990–2004

Source: EBRD.

of the early to mid-1990s, the vast majority of CEE–EU trade had already been liberalised for some years. Indeed, following the collapse of the CMEA in 1991, the westward reorientation of CEE trade began almost simultaneously with transition and by the early 2000s, over 60 per cent of exports from CEE states, apart from Lithuania and Bulgaria, were destined for the EU states – and a level of intra-regional trade which is consistent with that in the EU-15. Similarly, CEE imports from the EU-15 have also increased correspondingly (see Figure 16.4).

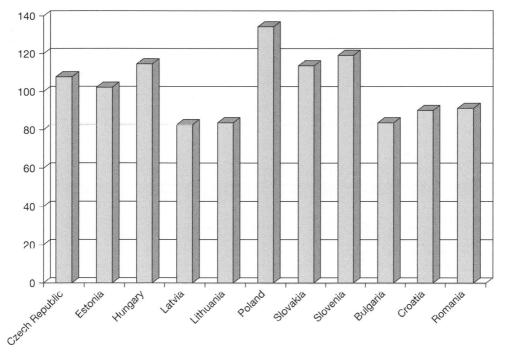

Figure 16.2 Real GDP, 2003 (1989 = 100)
Source: EBRD, *Transition Report, 2004.*

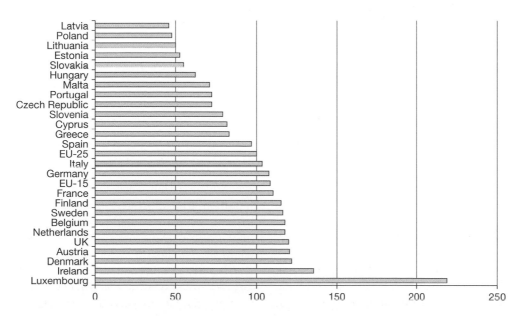

Figure 16.3 GDP per capita in purchasing power standards, 2005 (EU-25 = 100)
Source: Eurostat.

369

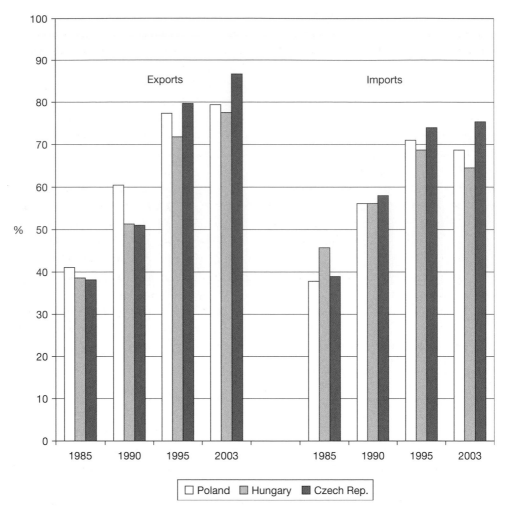

Figure 16.4 EU-25 shares of Central European imports and exports, 1985, 1990, 1995, 2003
Source: UNCTAD *Handbook of Statistics.*

The increasing trade shares of the EU-15 were largely at the expense of intra-CEE trade which plummeted from its pre-transition levels. In part, this was an inevitable consequence of the unnatural structural rigidities of the CMEA. However, some recovery of intra-regional CEE trade is to be expected, especially given the industrial restructuring and specialised clustering that is under way and is driving the increase in intra-industry trade within the region.

CEE trade has also undergone an important structural shift since the beginning of transition with a greater share of exports taken up by manufactured products. Significantly, prior to accession, the CEE states were also running a small trade surplus with the EU-15 in relation to services, signifying a growing ability to compete in tourism and financial and professional services. Manufactures comprised 90 per cent of Czech and Slovenian exports immediately prior to accession. In most cases, the share of manufactures increased at the expense of agricultural goods and metal products. This trend has not been so marked in Latvia and Lithuania where manufactured exports remained below 60 per cent.

The growing dominance of manufactures in both exports and imports in the majority of CEE states represents a growing shift towards intra-industry trade, particularly increasing specialisation and an ability to compete in the markets of the EU-15. Intra-industry trade can be divided into two types. The first is vertical trade which refers to trade in similar goods differentiated by product quality. The second is horizontal trade which refers to trade in similar goods differentiated by product characteristics. As a country moves up the value-added ladder, enterprises shift from producing lower quality versions of the same goods produced elsewhere to higher quality products with specific features that make them attractive to specific groups of consumers. The initial growth of intra-industry trade in the CEE states was of the vertical type. In 1997, a World Bank study found that the activity of MNEs in the first years of transition was directed towards establishing their subsidiaries in the region as manufacturing platforms for sub-premium exports. This trend is changing, at least in Hungary, the Czech Republic and Slovakia given their participation in intra-EU trade in motor components, office equipment, telecommunication and other specialised equipment, a testament to their growing integration into more technologically advanced transnational production networks and a progressive shift to horizontal intra-industry trade.

Two other trade changes occurred as a result of accession. First, all the EU's bilateral trade agreements were extended to the CEE states. In the majority of cases, this made little difference given that most of the EU's bilateral trade pacts were with countries with limited trade with CEE states. However, it was important in relation to the EU–Russia relationship as EU enlargement increased the EU's share of Russian trade from 35 to 50 per cent. This underlines the growing importance of the EU to Russia in trade and commercial terms.

Second, accession necessitated some realignment of CEE tariffs to align them with the EU's Common External Tariffs which average 3–4 per cent. In most cases, the adjustment was not significant. However, the average of tariffs on manufactured goods in Slovakia was 21 per cent, resulting in major liberalisation. Moreover, Estonia, where liberal trade reforms had resulted in almost total elimination of tariffs on manufactures, had to re-impose tariffs upon accession.

. . . for investment?

At the onset of transition, hopes were high in the CEE states that large inflows of FDI would facilitate their economic restructuring, improve the quality of their capital stock and increase their technology, quality and environmental levels. However, it was not until the mid-1990s that FDI began to flow to the region in any significant volumes (see Figure 16.5). That this should be the case is not surprising. Foreign investors look for a stable business environment and a transparent and effective regulatory and institutional framework to support and protect their interests. As seen above, the earliest transition years were ones of macroeconomic turmoil and instability and it took time before the semblance of a satisfactory legal environment took shape. As the CEE states progressed towards accession, so the requirements of adopting the *acquis* served to

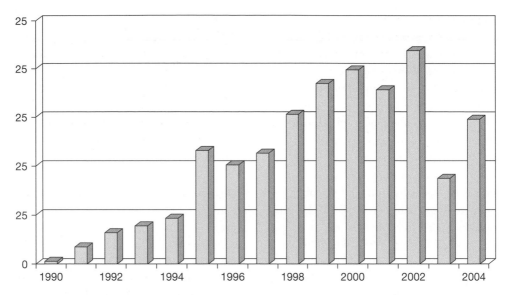

Figure 16.5 Net FDI inflows into Central and Eastern Europe (US$ bn)
Source: EBRD, 2004.

reassure investors about the region and FDI inflows continued on their upwards trend.

By the mid-1990s, FDI stocks in the region were ten times those at the beginning of the decade – in part, a reflection of the exceedingly low level of FDI at the beginning of transition. At this stage 85 per cent of FDI into the region had been directed towards the three most advanced transition countries, the Czech Republic, Hungary and Poland. Hungary, in particular, attracted the lion's share of investment as a result of its longer experience of elements of market economics; confidence in the reform programme; a skilled and educated labour force; proximity to Western European markets and the nature of the privatisation process, which emphasised the need to attract capital rather than to spread share ownership. By 1996, Poland, with its much bigger and more diversified economy, had overtaken Hungary as the most important destination for FDI in the region in absolute terms, with the Czech Republic attracting the most FDI on a per capita basis. Although far behind the big

three in absolute terms, the remaining CEE states have attracted increasing FDI inflows. Indeed, in terms of FDI stocks per capita, several exceed the total of Poland. However, the Czech Republic is way out in front on this measure (see Figure 16.6 a and b).

In terms of its composition, FDI in CEE, unlike other emerging economies such as China where FDI inflows are overwhelmingly in the manufacturing, or secondary, sector, the majority of inward FDI is in the service, or tertiary, sector (72 per cent of the total in 2001–02 according to UNCTAD). Individual sectors that have proved particularly attractive to inward FDI are wholesale and retail distribution, transport and communications, and finance. These sectors, in particular, are facing significant opportunities from the new logistical possibilities stemming from a seriously enlarged single market. Significant investment in distribution, communications and finance provides a solid base on which to build future investment in more advanced sectors which require a developed infrastructure and financial sector. Moreover, given

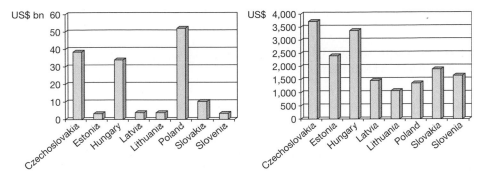

Figure 16.6 (a) Cumulative FDI, 1989–2003; (b) Cumulative FDI inflows per capita, 1989–2003
Source: EBRD.

the normalisation of West European commercial relations with the CEE states in the run up to accession, more investment from SMEs can be anticipated.

The EU is the major source of inward CEE FDI; over 50 per cent of FDI originates from there, and in the cases of the Czech Republic, Estonia, Hungary and Slovenia, over 80 per cent of inward FDI is from the EU-15. FDI from Asia is limited, coming mostly from Daewoo, Matsushita, Panasonic, Samsung, Suzuki and Toyota and accounting for no more than 2 per cent of inward FDI in all cases bar Poland (where the figure is nearer 5 per cent). North America's contribution is bigger, although way behind that of EU members, and is significant particularly in manufacturing. Moreover, US firms have demonstrated a preference for investment over trade in their commercial dealings with the region (imports from North America account for 1 to 3 per cent in individual CEE countries compared to 4 to 14 per cent in terms of inward FDI). The attractions appear to lie in cheap, skilled labour, greater proximity to big markets, access to the SEM and the possibility of using the region as a potential platform for export to the currently underdeveloped but potentially lucrative markets of Russia.

The motivations for investing in CEE vary. An obvious attraction of the CEE countries for foreign investors is the existence of a large, relatively untapped market for consumer and industrial goods. However, given the relatively low levels of GDP per head and the currently limited disposable income in these countries, profitable exploitation of these markets in many sectors will take time. Nevertheless, the rapid growth of recent years and the role that increased domestic demand has played in this growth does give the markets of this region some allure. Poland, given its position as by far the largest market in the region and its economic recovery since the early 2000s, has been particularly attractive to market seekers. Moreover, in view of their absorption into the SEM and their geographical proximity to Western Europe, FDI in CEE also acts as a platform for markets in the EU-15.

FDI in CEE is also resource seeking and efficiency seeking. The resources in question are cheap, skilled labour and, in certain regions, resources that can be developed for tourism. Efficiency-seeking investment occurs when investors seek to rationalise their value chains. This is particularly appropriate following the launch of regional integration initiatives as the opening of borders creates opportunities for investors to reap new economies of scale, to serve a number

373

Case Study 16.1

WHIRLPOOL IN CENTRAL EUROPE – AT THE HEART OF A GLOBAL STRATEGY

Whirlpool, the world's biggest manufacturer of large domestic appliances, was one of the first Western companies to manufacture in Central Europe. The beginning of the transition of the former Soviet bloc into modern market economies fortuitously coincided with the beginning of Whirlpool's globalisation strategy.

Established in 1911, Whirlpool's first 75 years were concentrated almost entirely on its domestic US market. By the mid-1980s, however, it was apparent that the US market was mature and highly competitive and that further strong growth could only take place outside North America. From this point, Whirlpool followed a strategy of global expansion through acquisition in key regions. Whirlpool entered the European market in 1989 through a joint venture arrangement with the Dutch company, NV Philips. Within two years, Whirlpool had taken over the Dutch part of the partnership and Whirlpool Europe became a wholly owned subsidiary of Whirlpool Corporation.

As well as marking the beginning of transformation in CEE, the early 1990s was a period of European recession. Whirlpool's strategy to cope with this was to develop strong pan-European brands and to seek cost savings through ongoing improvements in productivity, manufacturing and distribution. This fitted neatly into the company's global strategy of integrating its businesses and production globally to help with purchasing efficiency and to accelerate product development. In this scenario, Whirlpool production facilities world-wide share common parts and technologies but are able to tailor their products to the needs of individual regions in terms of design or energy efficiency, for example. Global procurement, production and information technology spreads innovation across regions, improves efficiency and helps keep costs down. Accordingly, the company established 'focused' factories to produce one product line for sale in multiple markets in order to gain competitive advantage through low-cost production which exploited economies of scale – a philosophy that was in harmony with that of the SEM.

Meanwhile, opportunities were opening up in Central Europe. Unlike Western Europe in the early 1990s, the market penetration levels of some domestic appliances were relatively low, or in the case of automatic washing machines, very low. At the time, Whirlpool was looking to establish itself in CEE, both to serve the domestic and regional market and, in the longer term, the Western European market. Uncertainty about the future in the early days of transition resulted in Whirlpool considering all options for market entry, including whether to focus on exporting, joint ventures, acquisitions or greenfield development and whether to choose partners from Poland, Hungary and/or Czechoslovakia as it then was.

In 1991, Whirlpool selected Tatramat as its joint venture partner in the region. Tatramat was a washing machine manufacturer located in the town of Poprad in what became Slovakia. In 1990–91, it employed about 2,300 people; produced 200,000 washing machines per annum; supplied about 88 per cent of the washing machines in Czechoslovakia and exported a relatively small proportion of its output, entirely to CEE. Poor productivity and quality, the bane of all appliance manufacturers in the region, plus production levels that were way below the optimum levels for minimising costs, rendered Tatramat uncompetitive in the new business environment. Tatramat's management, which had been given greater freedom to manoeuvre under the new regime, recognised the need to change products, increase production and quality and reduce costs per unit. The business was also badly hit by devaluation of the local currency (which increased costs), the collapse of CMEA and the depressed state of the domestic economy which accompanied the beginning of transition. Accordingly, they had also been looking for a Western joint venture partner to help resolve some of these issues.

In 1994, Whirlpool took a controlling interest in the joint venture. During its first 13 years in Slovakia, Whirlpool has increased capacity to about 2 million units per annum. The quality and productivity have become such that about 90 per cent of the plant's output is exported throughout Europe and some production has been diverted to Poprad from Whirlpool factories in France and Germany. Consequently, Poprad is Whirlpool's biggest factory in Europe and markets its output under the Whirlpool, Bauknecht, Ignis, Laden, Estabon de Lujo and Consul brands. Including suppliers, who continue to move to the site, about 3,000 jobs depend upon the Poprad plant and Whirlpool is credited with bringing a whole new business culture to the region, as well as technology and know-how.

In 2002, Whirlpool expanded its operations in CEE by acquiring the Brandt Group's Wroclaw factory in Poland. The plan was to develop the existing refrigerator and dishwater production, which it has done under the Whirlpool, Laden, Ignis and Bauknecht brands, and to install a new cooker production line. The particular location was chosen, according to Whirlpool spokesmen, because of the well-educated workforce, investment incentives offered by the Polish government and the strong support from local officials. The transformation of this acquisition has directly created 1,000 new jobs and hundreds of others via supplier networks.

At the time of accession, Whirlpool President, Jeff Fettig, outlined the following reasons for his company's investment in these two CEE states and why he hoped his company would rapidly expand there:

1 these countries represent attractive markets in their own right;
2 the favourable business climate, cost-base and educated and available workforce help Whirlpool to respond to the demands of retailers and customers for high quality and give it the flexibility and productivity needed to compete;
3 his company has detected 'a real appetite for US brands as a visible symbol for increasing choice, prosperity and lifestyle, that was not previously available to those consumers in those markets for a very long time'.

Moreover, he envisaged that the new member states would have a positive impact on the whole of Europe by pressing in Brussels for less regulation and bureaucracy in order to maintain their attractiveness for foreign investment. In other words, he is implying that the new member states from CEE have emerged from their transformation from the old command economies of the Soviet days into greater champions of neo-liberalism and competition than the older member states. This view is supported by Errico Biondi, the general director of

Whirlpool Slovakia, who claimed that the Poprad workforce was the most flexible in Whirlpool's European operations, adding:

> Of course labour is cheaper than Western Europe but we care more about productivity, flexibility and people's skills and quality. Here in Poprad all these are very good and, crucially, unlike in Western Europe flexibility is not restricted by trade unions.

To date, Whirlpool's ventures in CEE have been successful, although not without problems at times. Economic problems in 1997, for example, necessitated some caution and in April 2005, Whirlpool Slovakia announced planned cuts in output and the loss of 120 staff in Poprad because of economic problems stemming from appreciation of the Slovak currency and an increase in inflation. Such difficulties should prove temporary but, in the long term, its CEE operations will have to work hard to retain their competitiveness in the light of economic convergence with older EU states and increased competition from potentially new EU members and from emerging economies outside the EU.

Case questions

1 Explain how Whirlpool's global strategy and its involvement in Slovakia and Poland complement each other.

2 Why might Whirlpool have chosen to embark upon manufacturing in CEE through joint venture and eventual acquisition of existing operations instead of setting up its own greenfield operation? What potential drawbacks does its strategy have?

3 What implications do Whirlpool's activities, and those of other foreign investors, have for manufacturers and employees in Western Europe?

---

of markets and to reorganise their production and logistical functions in a way that reduces their costs and raises their overall efficiency. Accession has provided these opportunities in CEE. Investment in components for automobiles, telecommunications and other forms of technologically advanced equipment confirms the growing integration of the CEE states in trans-European production networks. Moreover, the trend towards greater intra-industry trade referred to above also confirms this trend.

There is, however, a finite amount of capital available and the CEE states are in a fiercely competitive market place for this capital. Although they benefit from lower wages, this benefit is not unique to them but is shared by emerging markets, especially in Asia. Wages are also likely to increase along with their relative level of development, thereby eroding this particular competitive advantage. Indeed, in certain areas, especially around capital cities, wages and other conditions pertinent to FDI are not that far removed from those prevailing further westwards in Europe. In the early 2000s, for example, real wage increases exceeded productivity growth in Hungary, leading to an increase in real unit labour costs and declining competitiveness. The result was outward

FDI migration in 2003 totalling US$1.6 billion, including the relocation of Hungarian plants of Flexitronics, IBM and Philips to China. Moreover, as the more developed countries of CEE experience some loss of attractiveness, FDI is being diverted to other countries in the region, such as Bulgaria and Romania. These trends do not necessarily mean the end of FDI in CEE, merely that the trend of wage convergence with the West, which over the region as a whole still has a long way to go, requires these countries to maximise their gains from their core assets, namely their human capital base and central location in the expanded pan-European market, to attract further high-quality investment.

... for labour markets?

A major competitive advantage of the CEE countries is their much lower level of labour costs relative to those in the rest of the EU. Figure 16.7 demonstrates this point quite dramatically. It sets out the total annual average labour costs (that is, pay plus a range of other costs and benefits) of employing a full-time male worker in the majority of EU countries and in key players in the global market place. On average, total labour costs in Western Europe are four times those in Eastern Europe. However, labour in the costliest EU countries is over ten times that in the cheapest EU countries. Moreover, this competitive advantage of CEE countries

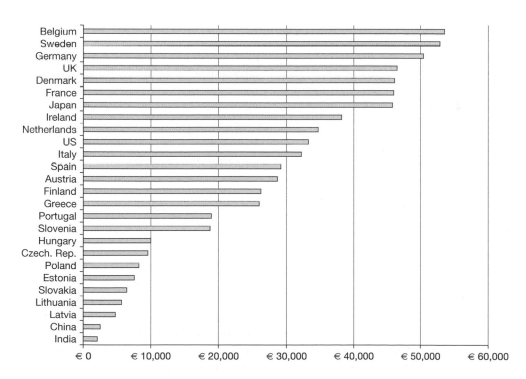

Figure 16.7 Comparison of employment costs – annual average full-time male

Note: Above employment costs are composed of pay + employers' social security costs + mandatory benefits + vountary benefits (i.e. the average cost of employee benefit plans that employers typically provide).

Source: Mercer Human Resource Consulting, Press Release, 4 April 2005.

377

over the older EU member states is made even stronger given that their education and skills levels are high relative to their costs. This places them in a strong position, not only relative to Western Europe but also to compete with low-cost competition from outside the EU.

Low labour costs in CEE have the following implications for European business. First, they enhance the attractiveness of CEE as a destination for foreign investment (see above), especially, but not only, investment in more labour-intensive industries.

Second, what employers view as low labour costs are seen as low wages by employees. In a genuine single market in which labour is as mobile as the other factors of production across borders, low wages would ordinarily encourage workers to search for better paid jobs elsewhere. However, as part of the accession process, old member states have been given the option of keeping restrictions on labour from the new member states for up to seven years after transition. Significantly, only Ireland, the UK and Sweden, member states that not only have employment levels below the EU average but which are also suffering labour shortages in some sectors, have chosen not to exercise this option. If the concerns about the level of post-accession free movement were justified, significant funnelling of migrant workers to these three member states is to be expected. One year after accession, although there has been some east to west movement, its scale has been more than manageable for the recipient countries (see Chapter 13). This is consistent with the Mediterranean enlargements of the 1980s when fears that there would be large-scale movements of workers from new member states to the more prosperous existing members proved to be unjustified. In part, this is explained by the relatively limited labour mobility within the new member states themselves, with the apparent reluctance of workers from relatively depressed regions in the new member states to move to more prosperous regions within the same country. A willingness to move even further afield to another country represents a step too far. Moreover, the new member states are, at last, experiencing a period of prolonged prosperity, thereby reducing the incentive to move. Assuming that the economies of the new member states continue to perform better than those of the old member states and increase their level of convergence with them, then the incentive to move for a higher standard of living will continue to fall.

Third, in an open market, low wage costs in CEE place downwards pressure on wages and associated costs elsewhere in the EU, especially in countries such as Germany where wage costs and unemployment are high. Germany's high level of regulation and high costs need to be tackled if Germany's competitiveness and economic performance are to be restored. However, measures needed to ensure this are politically unpopular. In the spring of 2005, the German government was reportedly considering measures to restrain downward movement of wages, especially in sectors that do use East European labour. Any measures to impose a floor on wages in specific sectors would be difficult to implement. Despite the transition period on the free movement of labour applied by Germany against the new member states, there is still scope for such workers to enter Germany. In 2004, for example, despite high levels of unemployment, Federal Labour Agencies issued 870,000 authorisations to companies, allowing them to fill vacancies that could not be filled by Germans, with foreign workers. Moreover, in sectors that are potentially mobile, unlike agriculture, any wage intervention would not

Case Study 16.2

EMERGENCE OF A NEW AUTOMOTIVE CLUSTER?

Europe's motor manufacturing industry has been operating on an integrated, transnational basis since long before the single market got off the ground. That is, research, development and production have been located across several countries and models developed with an eye to a European rather than a national market since the 1960s. In part, this is because the optimum production level for mass car production is, according to D. Garel Rhys, about 3 million units per annum, albeit lower if significant outsourcing takes place. In other words, manufacturers aim to reap economies of scale to bring their unit costs down. Transnational, integrated production facilitates this.

Since the beginning of transition in the early 1990s, the boundaries of the transnational European market have been stretched to incorporate the countries of CEE. Indeed, since 1990, the CEE states have been the destination for virtually all significant investment by car manufacturers in Europe, leading one commentator to claim there will be no more major car investments in Western Europe. Until 1989, nine independent companies in CEE produced over 3 million cars per annum for the local market. The quality of the cars made them unsuitable for export outside the region. With the onset of transition, these CEE producers found themselves the subject of takeovers or involved in joint ventures with Western partners.

The rise of the automobile industry in CEE has benefited in particular from:

1 *A qualified and low-cost labour force, bolstered by state support, especially for training*: the workforce in CEE generally has a level of skills usually associated with much higher wage levels. Figure 16.8 illustrates the scale of the difference, with hourly labour costs in the motor industry being ten times higher in Germany than in Romania and over five times greater than in Slovakia. Indeed, as Figure 16.7 shows, the pattern of relative labour costs in the motor industry is replicated across other sectors. Given the nature of the investment in CEE, the productivity advantage of the traditional motor manufacturers in Western Europe is not as great as it once was. However, real wage increases in the medium term could erode some of the labour cost advantage of the new member states which, accordingly, will lose some of their new-found competitive advantage unless the wage increases are offset to some extent by increased productivity.

The relative inflexibility of CEE labour markets, especially in terms of regional dispari-ties and labour immobility is already showing signs of creating problems, with reports that the TPCA (Toyota Peugeot Citroën Automobile) joint venture is encountering problems recruiting sufficient skilled staff for its new plant in the Czech Republic.

2 *Anticipated long-term strong regional demand*: the long-term potential of the domestic automotive markets in CEE is strong and has encouraged market-seeking investment. Car ownership rates are much lower in CEE states than in Western Europe: as a rule of thumb, there are approximately two people for every vehicle in Western Europe compared to over

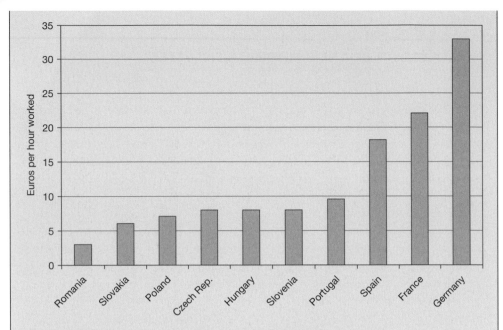

Figure 16.8 *Labour costs in the motor industry, end 2004*
Source: Derived from *Revue Elargissement*, Dossier 52, March 2005.

four people in Latvia, Slovakia and Bulgaria (see Figure 16.9). Moreover, the current stock of cars has an average age of 12–13 years in CEE compared to eight years in the EU-15. Assuming that real growth in CEE continues to outstrip that in the EU-15, car ownership levels will increase in CEE and the average age of cars will fall. Initially, demand is highest in the lower end models but as real GDP increases there will be an increase in demand for medium and higher range models. This process will inevitably be interrupted by cyclical effects but, in short, these trends will combine to create a much more dynamic market for cars in CEE than in the rest of Europe.

3 *Proximity to the major markets of Western Europe*: the proximity of CEE states to the markets of Western Europe and particularly their involvement in the SEM confers additional attractiveness to a Central European location for automobile manufacturers. Although the new car market has been relatively stagnant in the early part of the 2000s, the absolute size of the market makes it one that most car manufacturers cannot choose to ignore.

4 *Links with related industries*: investment in the CEE automobile production industry has been helped by the presence of competitive upstream industries in materials (for example, metals and plastics) and has stimulated the development of a components industry which, initially grew up to serve the CEE industry but quickly became globally competitive in its own right.

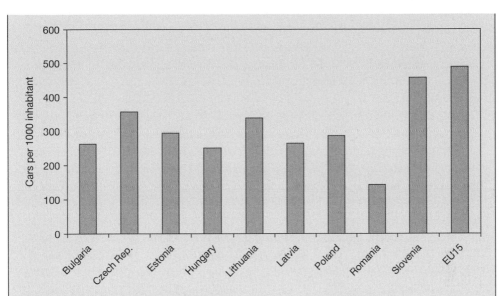

Figure 16.9 Car ownership levels, 2002

Source: Derived from *Revue Elargissement*, Dossier 52, March 2005.

Table 16.2 Car production by foreign investors in CEE

Country	Company	Output and planned output
Slovakia	VW	300,000 units
	PSA Peugeot-Citroën	300,000 units by 2006
	Hyundai Kia	200,000 units by 2006 with possible expansion to 300,000 if market conditions permit
Czech Republic	VW	450–500,000 units per annum
	TPCA Toyota Peugeot Citroën Automobile	Production began early 2005 and will rise to 300,000 vehicles per annum
Romania	Renault Dacia	95,000 units (2004), 200,000 by 2010
Hungary	Suzuki	95,000 units (2004), 200,000 by 2006 and later 270,000
	Audi	Engine plant and 55,000 vehicles
Slovenia	Renault	132,000 units in 2004
Poland	Fiat	360,000 units in 2004
	Opel	110,000 units in 2004 – planned to increase to 150,000

Slovakia

Before transition began, Slovakia possessed no car assembly capacity. By 2006, Slovakia will have the capacity to produce 850,000 cars per annum and will be the world's largest car producer in terms of cars produced per head of the population. Car production accounts for 20 per cent of industrial production, 17 per cent of GDP and 25 per cent of exports. The country's success in attracting inward investment in the motor industry stems from its location close to the heart of Europe, both in terms of the automotive market and the emerging cluster of assembly plants, power train factories and component suppliers that takes in the Czech Republic, Hungary, Poland and Slovenia. Slovakia's transport links are better than some in CEE and it has a highly skilled, low-cost workforce and a government that is supportive of new investment.

Three transnational companies are behind this transformation. First, Volkswagen which in 1991 took over a Bratislava plant producing parts for Škoda in the Czech Republic. VW gradually transformed the plant into an assembly plant and since 1998, VW Slovakia has been Slovakia's largest firm and exporter, employing 11,000 and helping the development of the associated supplier industry.

The second is PSA Peugeot Citroën which invested €730 million in a greenfield site at Trnava, 45 kilometres from Bratislava which opened in 2006 with a capacity to assemble 300,000 small cars. The central location, good transport links and the proximity of supplier parks were key inputs in the investment decision.

The third is Kia, part of the Hyundai Group, which announced the construction of a 200,000-unit plant to be completed by the end of 2006 with the possibility of expansion by a further 100,000 units if market conditions are favourable. The company will benefit from free land and other incentives equivalent to about 15 per cent of the investment costs and will initially create 2,800 jobs.

Czech Republic

In addition to its presence in Slovakia, VW is a major player in the Czech Republic, regularly accounting for 8–10 per cent of all Czech exports, taking up 50 per cent of the Czech domestic market and selling to more than 70 countries world-wide. In 1991, VW took a 30 per cent stake in Škoda, a stake that was increased to 70 per cent in the middle of the decade. In 2000, VW acquired the last of the government's stake in the company. In total, VW Škoda employs 24,000 people in three plants and makes 450–500,000 vehicles per annum. The investment has helped transform Škoda's erstwhile image for poor quality and unreliability by sharing VW technology at lower cost. The investment has also helped pull in many world-class suppliers to the extent that VW Škoda and its domestic supply chain employ about 4 per cent of the Czech workforce.

In 2002, as part of the TPCA joint venture, Toyota and PSA Peugeot-Citroën announced the start of construction of a new plant for the manufacture of small cars at Kolin, 60 kilometres east of Prague. Initially, BMW was bidding for the site but political pressure caused it to decide to invest in Eastern Germany. The €1.5 billion investment, the biggest ever green-field investment by a foreign multinational in the Czech Republic, began production in early 2005 and has a capacity of 300,000 vehicles per annum. Toyota's role is to manage development and production where Peugeot-Citroën is responsible for purchasing and logistics.

Romania

In 1999, Renault took a 51 per cent stake in the newly privatised local motor manufacturer, Dacia. Over the next five years, Renault invested €189 million and in 2004 raised its stake to 99.3 per cent. The company employs over 12,000 people and generated revenues of €570 million. Renault regards Dacia as its platform for an assault on the markets of CEE. Its main weapon in this campaign is the 'Logan', a €5,000 car developed in line with West European standards for sale in Romania and export to CEE and other emerging markets.

Renault's investment has been matched by inward investment by major component suppliers such as Valeo (France), Johnson Controls (US), Yazaki (Japan) and Siemens (Germany). Some have invested in Romania to service Dacia whereas others see Romania as a platform for supplying manufacturers elsewhere in the region.

Hungary

Two major foreign investors are active in Hungary. In the mid-2000s, Japan's Suzuki is in the process of tripling the capacity of its Hungarian assembly plant from 95,000 in 2004 to 150,000 in 2005, 200,000 in 2006 and, eventually, 270,000. The expansion includes two new models, one of which is a sports utility vehicle to be jointly developed with Fiat who will supply the engine. Suzuki accounts for about 20 per cent of the Hungarian market and sales revenue of US$1.6 billion is forecast for 2005.

The second is Audi, one of Hungary's biggest investors and exporters. In 1994, Audi opened an engine plant, investing €1.6 billion in the plant in the first ten years of its existence. In 1998, Audi began to assemble cars in Hungary and turns out 55,000 units each year.

Poland

Cumulative FDI in Poland's automotive sector reached over US$6.5 billion in 2003 and employed over 90,000 people, 55 per cent of whom were employed in supplier plants. Indeed, over 200 foreign-owned suppliers, including some of the world's biggest supplier names, are located in Poland. Moreover, Toyota has invested in two greenfield sites to produce gear boxes and engines for the PSA Toyota project at Kolln in particular.

In short, the motor industry is very important to Poland but it has lost out to other countries in the region when major investments have been considered. For example, Slovakia has been preferred by Kia, in part because of Slovakia's better quality infrastructure and the political uncertainties in Poland.

Nevertheless, three major car manufacturers are producing and assembling cars in Poland. Fiat, Poland's biggest exporter has invested US$1.8 billion in Poland and produced 360,000 cars there in 2004. Opel has transferred production of Astra II to Poland and in 2004 produced 110,000 units (Agila and Astra). Opel's output will eventually rise to 150,000 units. Daewoo FSO produced 60,000 units in 2004. VW is also involved in vehicle manufacture in Poland but produces vans rather than cars.

Slovenia

In February 2005, the two millionth car rolled off the Renault production line in Slovenia where Renault has been active since 1972. In 2004, Renault employed 2,500 in Slovenia and output was a record 132,000 vehicles, namely the Renault Clio.

Case activities and questions

1 The case focuses on the final production of motor vehicles. However, the investment in motor vehicles has spilled over into growth in both domestic- and foreign-owned components sector. Consider the impact of this development in terms of growth, trade, investment, jobs and industry structure. In particular, try to identify the extent to which such companies have become part of transnational production networks that stretch beyond the borders of CEE and even the EU.

2 Consider the extent to which the growth of the motor industry in CEE has the potential to encourage growth in vertical and horizontal intra-industry trade and to shift from vertical to horizontal trade.

3 Identify factors that threaten, or could threaten, CEE's pre-eminent position in new automobile investment in the EU.

4 Choose one of the motor manufacturers producing in CEE and research its strategy in the region since the beginning of transition. In particular, consider the form its investment took (e.g. joint venture, greenfield investment, etc.) and why a particular form was chosen. Why was CEE chosen as a location for investment and how and why has the firm's strategy evolved in the interim?

increase German employment but encourage movement of jobs eastwards.

In the longer term, the low labour cost advantage of CEE countries will be eroded as convergence proceeds and they find themselves subject to greater competition from their neighbours directly to the east in particular and from emerging countries such as India and China. Their longer term success will, therefore, depend on translating the investment that has taken place in CEE into higher productivity.

... for the EU?

Enlargement created a need to reform the EU's institutions to make them responsive to the demands of a much bigger organisation – a process only partially carried out by the Amsterdam and Nice Treaties and which the constitutional treaty was supposed to complete (see Chapter 2). The fifth Copenhagen condition also required the EU to absorb new members while continuing the momentum of integration. The most obvious policies requiring attention were those involving revenue and expenditure, namely, the budget, the CAP and the Structural Funds. However, enlargement placed pressure on, and had profound implications for, virtually all European policies, resulting in the following implications for business:

■ *The SEM*: the extension of the SEM was the single most important business-related change for the EU, resulting in shifting investment patterns (see above), enhanced competition and more consumer choice. Entry into the SEM required significant legislative and regulatory changes on the part of the acceding states to comply with the requirements for membership. Case Studies 16.1 and 16.2 show how SEM extension has affected the strategic perspective of an individual company (Whirlpool) and changed the dynamics of a major manufacturing sector (car manufacturing). Each company and sector experiences its own unique set of SEM-related effects upon enlargement, depending on their original starting point and upon key characteristics of their sector. Poor-quality infrastructure could reduce the enlargement benefits for some new member states (see Chapter 9 and 10), especially those located outside the Central European heartland.

■ *Competition policy*: the substance of competition policy has not been changed by enlargement but accession required the introduction of competition laws into countries in which they had been previously unknown and required significant technical assistance and training for their introduction.

■ *Environment policy*: the acceding countries suffered severe environmental degradation in most spheres. Accession necessitated adoption of EU environmental regulations, a costly process but one that should ultimately accelerate improvement of the environmental situation in CEE countries. Resolution of the region's environmental problems could create new markets for environmental products and tighter regulation reduces the likelihood of environmental dumping.

■ *Information society and telecommunications*: the CEE region is one of the world's most promising ICT markets and some of the new member states, notably Hungary and Estonia, have, as a result of FDI, developed a presence in ICT export markets.

■ *Transport*: the CTP involves application of the SEM to transport, the harmonisation of competition conditions and the development of infrastructure. In particular, there is an urgent need in new member states for investment and improvements in infrastructure (quality and quantity), safety and environment to enable full benefits of enlargement and SEM to be realised, thereby providing opportunities for construction firms, equipment manufacturers and related activities.

■ *Energy*: enlargement increases the EU's dependence on energy imports, especially of gas, from Russia. It also necessitates greater attention to network investment, nuclear safety, energy efficiency measures and environmental standards. In particular, the new member states are required to implement gas and electricity liberalisation measures. This provides market opportunities for utilities from Western Europe and, as the countries have also chosen to go down the privatisation route, investment opportunities as well.

■ *SMEs*: accession has placed great competitive pressure on CEE SMEs but they also benefit from increased economic activity brought about by enlargement. Moreover, accession and, before that, the prospect of accession, have increased the attractiveness of FDI in CEE for SMEs from outside the region by creating greater certainty about the business environment and reducing the perceived risk of investment there. The initial growth in FDI in the region was borne by larger firms who were in a better position to bear any risk but SME involvement in FDI in the region increased as accession became more secure.

■ *Economic and monetary union*: acceptance of the *acquis communautaire* included a commitment to participate in the third stage of EMU (that is, adoption of the single currency). This commitment did not take effect on 1 May 2004 but will do so when they meet the same convergence criteria as those faced by the existing eurozone members. Significantly, by April 2005, six out of the ten new member states had already joined ERM II, raising the possibility of the first of the new member states adopting the single currency some time in 2007 (see Chapter 8) for further details.

... for the old member states?

Given that the combined GDP of the new member states is equivalent to only 5 per cent of the GDP of the EU-25, their aggregate economic importance to the old member states is limited. Indeed, the consensus of several studies is that as a result of enlargement, GDP in the old member states will be only 0.2–0.3 per cent higher five years after enlargement takes place (Lammers 2004), taking into account static, dynamic and factor mobility effects. These studies show that the strongest income and welfare effects will take place in countries bordering the new member states, such as Austria, Germany and Finland, whereas the least positive impact will be on peripheral member states such as Spain, Portugal, Greece and Ireland, assuming some diversion of FDI and the loss of transfer payments on the FDI.

Given the labour-cost advantage of the new member states, the more labour-intensive industries of the old member states are those most likely to experience intense competitive pressure from the East. However, the low-cost advantages of CEE will increase the competitive pressure on most sectors in both the manufacturing and service sectors and increase the competition for investment. Although much FDI had already taken place prior to accession, further cost-related investments and relocations remain a serious possibility if flexibility and cost issues are not faced up to in the old member states, especially as relocation eastwards would still entail production near to major markets and involves relatively little cultural readjustment.

THE FUTURE

The May 2004 accession is one of the most significant events in EU history and it was inconceivable even as recently as 15 years beforehand. That it proceeded as smoothly as it did is testament to the willingness of the new member states themselves to embrace the imperatives of transition and the related necessities of accession, namely, the adoption of the *acquis communautaire*, and to the recognition by the old member states of the overriding political, economic and commercial benefits of ending the old divisions in Europe.

The enlargement process is not complete. In April 2005, Bulgaria and Romania, two countries for whom transition has taken a little longer, signed their accession treaties with a view to accession on 1 January 2007. Both treaties contain a 'safeguard clause' that could delay their entry until 2008 if they fail to comply with the *acquis* in the interim. Croatia applied for EU membership in 2003.

Accession negotiations with Croatia were due to begin in spring 2005 but the EU postponed them as a result of Zagreb's failure to work with the UN War Crimes Tribunal. In March 2004, the Former Yugoslav Republic of Macedonia (FYRM) formally applied for membership and other applications from South-east Europe and elsewhere are expected. Turkey's current application for membership was lodged in 1987. It was not until 1999 that Turkey was officially recognised as a candidate country and negotiations only began in 2005. Despite its status as a candidate country, Turkey's membership, for a host of political and economic reasons, remains controversial and its passage to membership is likely to be longer and more arduous than that of other countries.

KEY POINTS

- The combination of the requirements of transition and of enlargement provided a road map which accelerated the development of market institutions and practices in Central and Eastern Europe.

- CEE economies have been growing much faster than the economies of the EU-15 during the 2000s – and need to continue to do so for some time if economic catch-up is to occur.

- Cheap and skilled labour, market potential and proximity to bigger markets have made the CEE economies an attractive location for FDI.

- The EU has not yet reached its maximum size: the future challenge is for the absorption of states from South-east Europe.

ACTIVITIES

1 Case 16.1 describes the evolution of Whirlpool's involvement in the new member states. Research another foreign-owned company (either from the old member states or from outside the EU altogether) and trace its involvement in CEE. How and why has your chosen company elected to invest in the region and what is its strategy for the future?

2 Case 16.2 describes how and why the motor industry has expanded into CEE as a result of transition and EU enlargement. Research another business sector and develop your own case study of how its structure and performance has changed as a result of transition and enlargement. Each sector faces different challenges, depending on its fundamental characteristics and original starting position.

3 Research one of the new member states with a view to determining how its business environment has changed during the transition period. In particular, identify emerging areas of strength and why they are strong. Which sectors are struggling and why? What roles have government policy and FDI played in transition? What are the prospects for prosperity as an EU member? Note: at the onset of transition, each of the transit countries had broadly similar political and economic systems. As transition has progressed, their diversity has become more apparent. One way to highlight this diversity would be for students or group of students to research different countries and present their findings for discussion in class.

QUESTIONS FOR DISCUSSION

1 Why were the new member states so eager to join the EU? Why were the older member states willing to welcome them?

2 How has the 2004 enlargement changed the business environment in the EU?

3 What pressures does enlargement place upon the EU itself? What are the knock-on effects for business?

4 What limits are there or should there be to future EU enlargement?

5 Discuss how transition and enlargement has changed and is changing investment patterns in Europe?

SUGGESTIONS FOR FURTHER READING

Aslund, A. (2002) *Building Capitalism: The Transformation of the Former Soviet Bloc*, Cambridge: Cambridge University Press.

Balcerowicz, L. (2002) *Post-Communist Transition: Some Lessons*, London: Institute of Economic Affairs.

Barry, F. and Curran, D. (2004) 'Enlargement and the European Geography of the Information Technology Sector', *World Economy*, 27 (6), pp. 901–22.

European Bank for Reconstruction and Development, Transition Reports, annual publications which summarise the current economic performance and which focus on a specific issue, London: EBRD.

Hanzl-Weiss, D. (2004) 'Enlargement and the Textiles, Clothing and Footwear Industry', *World Economy*, 27 (6), pp. 932–45.

Hoekman, B., Djankov, S. and Aturupane, C. (1997) *Determinants of Intra-Industry trade between East and West Europe*, Washington, DC: World Bank.

Iankova, E. (2002) *Eastern European Capitalism in the Making*, New York: Cambridge University Press.

Lammers, K. (2004) 'How Will the Enlargement Affect the Old Members of the EU?', *Intereconomics*, 39 (3), pp. 132–41.

Marrow, T., Loane, S., Bell, J. and Wheeler, C. (eds) (2005) *International Business in an Enlarging Europe*, Basingstoke: Palgrave.

Okey, R. (2004) *The Demise of Communist East Europe: 1989 in Context*, London: Arnold.

Rhys, D. G. (2004) 'The Motor Industry in an Enlarged EU', *World Economy*, 27 (6), pp. 877–900.

Vintrová, R. (2004) 'The CEE Countries on the way into the EU – Adjustment Problems: Institutional Adjustments, Real and Nominal Convergence', *Europe-Asia Studies*, 56 (4), pp. 521–41.

Chapter 17

European business in a global context

The developed world

The case for trade is not just monetary, but moral. Economic freedom creates habits of liberty. And habits of liberty create expectations of democracy.

George W. Bush (1946–), speech, 19 November 1999

This chapter will help you to:

- recognise the importance of the EU to global trade via its position within the 'triad' of regions;
- highlight the interface between the EU and the WTO via its Common Commercial Policy;
- understand the form and nature of intra-industry trade;
- appreciate the EU's trade relations with its major trading partners – the US and Japan.

This chapter is focused on the concept of the triad (the EU, US and Asia) as the dominant force within the global economy and on the linkages and relations between the EU and the other parts of the triad. The dominance of these regions in the global economic system demonstrates that these other industrialised states are the EU's major competitors. Initially, this chapter examines the form and nature of the emerging triad. Thereafter, it analyses the trade relations between the EU and other triad members, particularly, for the purposes of simplicity, the higher-profile members of these regional groups – the US and Japan.

EUROPE AND THE TRIAD

In 1985, Ohmae used the term 'triad' to capture the broad macro-trends that were emerging in the global economy. This perspective argues – perhaps too simplistically – that the world economy is based around a tri-polar regional structure consisting of North America, East Asia and Europe. There is a great deal of anecdotal evidence to offer credence to this perspective. Dicken (2003) suggests that the popularity of this concept has been driven by the practicalities of modern business given that these regions dominate trade, production and FDI. If anything, since the 1980s the degree of interdependence between these regions has increased. This has been especially marked with the rise of China as an economic power (see Chapter 18).

According to Ohmae, the triad shares a number of common traits: low macroeconomic growth, similar technological infrastructure, the presence of large, capital- and knowledge-intensive firms in most industries, a relative homogenisation of demand and protectionist pressures. This supremacy is best indicated by the global dominance of triad-based MNEs (see Chapter 3). This underlines their importance to the development of the modern global economy. Interesting and pertinent as Ohmae's concept of the triad is, in many ways it has been overtaken by events. The extension of regional trading blocs around these three regions has enhanced their power and prominence within the global economy and fosters ever deeper intra-regional integration. Global trade is focused on these regions because of a combination of the ability of MNCs to overcome the liability of foreignness in their host region and the problems of achieving global reach with a global product. In addition, where there is a trade-off between responsiveness/integration and global strategy, the issue of regionalisation becomes attractive if it allows overlap between the two areas. Thus, at the regional level synergies in terms of product, marketing, uniform competitive moves, integrated value chains and uniformity of customer demands

This trend is important for the development of European business for both internal and external reasons. From the internal perspective, the EU is the focus of considerable activity by overseas MNEs (see Chapter 3). Thus, in terms of reorganising their value chains, many MNEs seek to utilise EU-specific resources and capabilities. In addition, overseas MNEs want to sell to and invest in EU states. From an external perspective, EU MNE activity has been, and will continue to be, focused on other parts of the triad. Again, their activity is expressed in terms of access to markets and resources.

More recently, there has been renewed interest in the triad concept, especially within the context of the vigour given to the study of international business since the mid-1990s. Authors, most notably Rugman (2000), argue that it is misleading to talk of a global economy, especially in terms of reach. In a study of the largest MNEs, he noticed that flows both within and between MNEs were greater at the regional level than the global level. This research, repeated a number of times across a number of sectors, highlighted not only the importance of intra-EU trade and investment by European MNEs but also the external focus of European MNEs on Japan and North America. This pattern was replicated by MNEs in other regions.

Despite the distance between the respective members of the triad, the similarities between them in terms of economic development etc. are stronger than the links between some members of the intra-regional groupings. For example, some European states may be more proximate to US levels of economic development than the US is to Mexico. Likewise, more developed European states have closer levels of economic development to the US than to some of the newer members of the EU. Thus, some states within the EU have more in common with states outside the club than with all states within it. Given this status and the possibility of policy heterogeneity, regionalisation might be open ended to stimulate global agreement.

However, Poon *et al.* (2000) suggest that evidence for the existence of the triad is weak and that trade and investment are much more complex than literature on the triad suggests. These authors present compelling evidence that within blocs, there is great deal of segmentation as trade flows within these regions tend to be stronger within rather than between sub-groups of states. For example, in Europe, trade and investment tends to be stronger within the sub-groups of Northern and Southern Europe than between them. While the triad might be a useful way of characterising trade flows, it does understate the complexity of these flows.

THE EU, THE WTO AND THE COMMON COMMERCIAL POLICY

The EU, due to its pre-eminent position within the global trading system, is an important member of the WTO. This multilateral forum is responsible for setting the rules that govern global trade. The WTO commits member states to honour the ground rules for global trade as well as promoting a commitment to market opening. All 25 EU states are represented by the European Commission at the WTO. The Commission acts on a negotiating mandate specified by the Council in WTO negotiations. While the Commission is the negotiator, it is the Council that decides whether to accept an agreement or not. In addition to multilateralism, the EU is also involved in bilateral negotiations with third parties to advance specific goals which complement (and do not conflict with) the WTO framework.

The EU has a common trade policy, known as the 'Common Commercial Policy' (CCP). Member states act as a single entity in trade matters, one of the few areas in which the EU has a genuinely common policy. The CCP comprises a number of instruments, such as the common external tariff, but its main strength is the common negotiating position. The role of the Commission, under instruction from the Council, is to ensure that the CCP remains compatible with fair trade as well as best representing the group's interests. This is not always possible. This combining of power suits the EU as it can leverage its collective weight to increase its influence over the global trading system. The EU has been at the forefront of the current Doha Round of multilateral trade talks which have been seeking to create a trading framework that is able to cope with the pervasiveness of globalisation and the increased importance of global issues. The EU is using its collective power through the CCP to push for further market opening, especially in services.

The commitment of the CCP is to both fair and free trade. This is intended to ensure that all states are treated equally and that competitive distortions can be counteracted. However, this notion of fairness does imply value judgements by the EU regarding other states' trade practices. Where the EU feels this fairness has been compromised, it has recourse to the WTO, a rule-based system which seeks to ensure that all members adopt the same standards for global trade. These rules were devised on the basis that some actions are unfair. In line with its membership of the WTO, the CCP comprises three interlinked trade policy elements:

The dispute settlement mechanism: a cornerstone of the WTO that offers states the confidence that all parties will meet their commitments.

Introduced in 1995, it acts as a forum for members to assert their trade rights under multilateral agreements. Instead of unilateral action against an infringement, the mechanism allows for redress via the multilateral framework. As a result, the mechanism protects small members from arbitrary acts by the stronger states. The emphasis is on settlement through consultation but the procedure also allows for discretionary sanctions should non-compliance be sustained.

Trade Policy Instruments: these include both trade defence instruments and the Trade Barriers Regulation (TBR). Under the former, states are allowed to use anti-dumping duties, countervailing subsidies or safeguards instruments against other WTO members where the other party has engaged in unfair competition. These measures are employed by states under the auspices of the WTO. According to the TBR, a piece of EU legislation, business has the right to lodge a complaint with the European Commission when it has good reason to believe that it is facing restrictive trade barriers. The TBR can also be used to assess whether there is evidence of violation of international trade rules. The TBR is an offensive aspect of the CCP (that is, it is primarily concerned with improving access to the markets of trading partners) as opposed to the defensive nature of the other trade instruments, which are concerned with the flow of the goods entering the EU market.

Monitoring of third-party commercial defence actions: with the support of industry and member states, the Commission is proactive in ensuring that other WTO states abide by the rules of the system. Acting on behalf of, and on the information provided by, EU businesses, the Commission screens and monitors other states' actions. The Commission keeps a database of every specific trade barrier and seeks their removal via the WTO system.

While the current WTO is flawed, the EU is keen that it be developed and improved to offer a fairer trading system for all participants. Thus, within the context of the current Doha Round, the EU is seeking further market opening, to aid the integration of developing states into the system and to ensure that all elements of society are aided by the process. In this way, the momentum behind internationalisation can be sustained.

THE CHALLENGE OF INTRA-INDUSTRY TRADE

The most notable feature of the EU's trade with other leading developed states is that it is largely intra-industry in nature. Intra-industry trade (IIT) is when a state (or region) imports and exports the same types of products. This type of trade runs counter to the conventional theories of trade which stress specialisation based on different factor endowments. IIT is derived from the existence of economies of scale that create the scope for a firm or a state to specialise in a narrow product line. Similarly, other states will focus on producing products that are similar but different. The result is that states seek to compete through product differentiation and consumers have the ability to access and purchase goods most akin to their requirements. These trends allow states and regions to become specialised within specific market segments with the result that it is possible that specific products grow increasingly complex in terms of breadth and depth. This added complexity in the development of markets leads to increased trade.

IIT is based around similarly endowed states and in 2004 represented around 60 per cent of global trade. There are three basic explanations for IIT: country specific (due to resources), industry specific (features of industry) and policy based (influenced by policy/institutional factors). In relation to country-specific factors, in large states with similar incomes, taste overlap and geographic proximity stimulates interaction and trade. This has links to the concept of psychic distance and explains why there is so much IIT within the EU. Industry-specific factors underpin IIT when one or more of the following are present: scope for product differentiation; scope for economies of scale; a trend towards monopolistically competitive conditions; scope for product market and/or technological differentiation; and when there is high involvement by MNCs. Policy-based drivers for IIT are based on lower barriers to market entry arising from reduced tariffs and non-tariff barriers and on a high degree of integration across the market involved.

Since the 1980s, the share of IIT as a percentage of total trade has been rising. Different types of trade are covered within the definition of IIT. These include:

- Horizontal trade in similar types of products (in similar class and product range): this involves a firm moving into niche segments by specialising in a particular type of products for a particular class of customers.
- Trade in vertically differentiated products distinguished by quality and price (such as importing high-quality textiles and exporting low-quality textiles): this may reflect different factor endowments, particularly skills or RTD capabilities.
- Vertical specialisation of production that results in trade of similar types of goods

at different stages of the product value chain: this can be driven by comparative advantage, for example, in unskilled labour.

Generally, IIT is stronger across manufacturing than across other broad product groupings and is especially marked for more sophisticated products such as chemicals, machinery, transport equipment and electronics (see Table 17.1). These sectors are more likely to benefit from economies of scale and are easier to differentiate to the final consumer. As a result, the potential for trade is easier in these cases, for as products get more complex, there is increased scope for differentiating products across states.

IIT trade is of particular importance for those European states where trade represents a high proportion of GDP such as Austria, Belgium and Ireland. Krugman (1995) argues that the emergence of states that rely upon such a high proportion of trade in GDP is a function of the possibility of an industries value chain to be sliced up across political borders. Furthermore, the new member states of the EU from Eastern Europe are demonstrating high and rising IIT. The Czech Republic underwent an 11 per cent increase in IIT between 1992 and 2000 and Hungary a 17 per cent increase over the same period: this has been driven by the high levels of FDI undertaken by MNCs in these states.

Intra-industry trade tends to be higher for the US (around 60 per cent) than it is for Japan (around 20 per cent). This is due to the idiosyncracies of Japan with regards to low cross-border trade (where trade is easier with adjacent states), a high population density and low natural resource endowment. Thus, Japanese trade flows are primarily inter-industry in nature.

Table 17.1 Manufacturing IIT in the EU-15 (%)

	1988–91	1992–95	1996–2000	Change
Germany	67.1	72.0	72.0	5
Portugal	52.4	56.3	61.3	8.9
France	75.9	77.6	77.5	1.6
Austria	71.8	74.3	74.2	2.4
UK	70.1	73.1	73.7	3.6
Belgium/Luxembourg	77.6	77.7	71.4	−6.2
Spain	68.2	72.1	71.4	3
Netherlands	69.2	70.4	68.9	−0.3
Sweden	64.2	64.6	64.7	3.1
Denmark	61.6	63.4	64.8	3.2
Italy	61.6	64.0	64.7	3.1
Ireland	58.6	57.2	54.6	−4.0
Finland	53.8	53.2	53.9	0.1
Greece	42.8	39.5	36.9	−5.9

Source: OECD 2002.

THE EU AND TRADE WITH THE TRIAD

As highlighted within Chapter 3, the EU is the single biggest trading entity within the global economy with a large proportion of its external trade and investment focused on the other triad regions – the US and Japan. Trade and investment relations between these states are not just significant in terms of inter-partner economics but important because harmony between these states is central to the effective functioning of the global trading system. In combination, these states shape the global trade and investment agenda. However, relations between these parties can often be fractious. This section will focus on the form and nature of the interaction between, first, the EU and Japan, and, second, the EU and the US.

The EU and Japan

Together, the EU and Japan comprise 40 per cent of global GDP while the latter accounts for 7.2 per cent of global trade. Over the past decade, trading relations between the EU and Japan have been cordial (especially compared to Europe's relations with the US) and, despite the ongoing economic stagnation within Japan, the EU's trade with Japan still represents a substantial proportion of its global trade. Japan is the EU's fifth largest trading partner behind the US, China, Switzerland and Russia. If Japanese production in China is included, Japan would represent the EU's second largest major trading partner. Despite this, between 2000 and 2004, trade between the EU and Japan declined 1.3 per cent, although it increased by 5.2 per cent between 2003 and 2004.

395

Japan's share of EU exports was 4.5 per cent and accounted for 11.1 per cent of the EU's agricultural exports, 4.3 per cent of its textiles exports, 20 per cent of chemicals and 17 per cent of transport materials. In addition, Japan represents 7.2 per cent of EU imports with the majority coming from the transport and machinery sectors. The EU is also important to Japan as its third largest importer and second largest exporter. The trend and pattern of EU–Japan merchandise trade is highlighted by Figure 17.1. This shows the EU's persistent and ongoing deficit in its merchandise trade with Japan. When services are included, the pattern is reversed with the EU running a trade surplus (see Figure 17.2).

Japan is an important investor in the EU. In 2003, 4.1 per cent of EU FDI inflows came from Japan. Indeed, by the end of 2003, Japanese investment represented over 5 per cent of the stock of FDI in Europe. In return, 0.6 per cent of outward EU FDI went to Japan which in total represented around 2 per cent of Japan's total stock of FDI. FDI in Japan is relatively low due to structural impediments. The pattern and trend of EU–Japan FDI stocks is reflected within Figure 17.3 which shows that the EU is a net recipient of Japanese FDI.

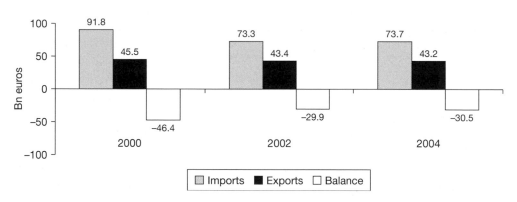

Figure 17.1 EU-25 merchandise trade with Japan

Source: Eurostat.

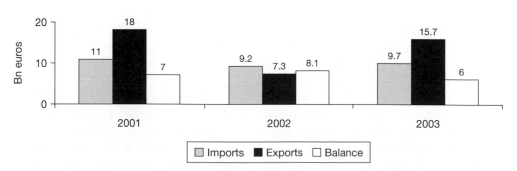

Figure 17.2 EU-15 trade in services with Japan

Source: Eurostat.

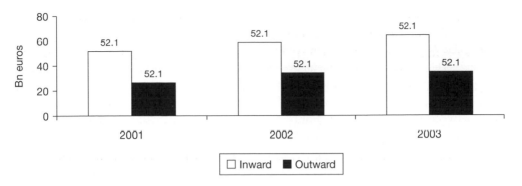

Figure 17.3 *EU-25 stock of FDI with Japan*
Source: Eurostat.

Traditionally, the trade relationship between the EU and Japan has been characterised by a strong trade surplus (especially in merchandise trade) in favour of Japan (see Figure 17.1). In more recent times, there has been a rebalancing, mainly due to the strong showing of EU service exports (see Figure 17.2). However, structural difficulties and a lack of a sustained programme of economic reform have made investment and trade with Japan comparatively difficult. Nevertheless, as Japan begins to look for a solution to its stagnation, it is beginning to accept the inevitability of economic reform and overseas competition. These changes have brought about a more cooperative relationship between the EU and Japan but the rate and pace of this change should not be overstated. These changes have been especially marked in FDI, although they have tended to be based on a small number of large-scale investments rather than on sustained interactions between these parties. Thus, the ability of EU firms to penetrate the Japanese market more fully has been limited, especially with regard to access by SMEs.

There are a number of informal means through which dialogue between these parties has been established. The EU–Japan summit in mid-2004 reaffirmed the importance of a strong strategic partnership, especially regarding the need to enhance trade and investment links. This is supported by the Regulatory Reform Dialogue which seeks to lower the number of regulatory barriers to trade and interaction between the partners. The result has been mutual participation in their respective reform efforts since 1995. Indeed, the EU has submitted an action plan to the Japanese to aid them in developing an environment that is more conducive to trade. Finally, efforts by EU exporters to sell to the Japanese market have been assisted by the Expom programme which offers concrete assistance to market entry in Japan. In other areas, there is a more cooperative atmosphere in both bilateral and multilateral fora. Within the framework of the WTO, the EU and Japan have worked together to develop common positions in areas where there is a common interest.

In terms of bilateralism, two major agreements have been signed. The first is the EU–Japan mutual recognition agreement which, from 2002, permits acceptance of conformity assessment conducted in either party in four product areas – telecommunications terminal equipment, electrical products,

397

good laboratory practice for chemical, and good manufacturing practices for pharmaceuticals. This is an important step in market opening. The second is an agreement for cooperation on anti-competitive agreements. However, despite the generally cordial relations between the EU and Japan, clear problems remain, not least of which are problems experienced by EU firms in gaining entry to the Japanese market place. Japan's trade balance remains positive which in no small part is due to these structural impediments.

The EU and North America

Trade with North America (the US, Mexico and Canada) represents 22.7 per cent of extra-EU trade. On its own, the US is the EU's major trading partner, accounting for 19.7 per cent of the EU's trade (while Canada accounts for 1.9 per cent and Mexico 1.1 per cent). As a result of this dominance, the following analysis focuses on the EU's trading relationship with the US which has, over time, been politically controversial and beset by trade disputes.

The EU's trade relations with the US are pivotal, not just for both partners but also arguably for the health of the global economy. Together, this bilateral relationship represents 37 per cent of global merchandise trade and 45 per cent of trade in services. The US and the EU are also the world's largest source and destination of FDI, accounting for 54 per cent and 67 per cent of inflows and outflows, respectively, in 2000. The US represents nearly 25 per cent of EU exports and just over 15 per cent of its imports. The US has a 32 per cent share of the EU's trade in services and the EU is a major recipient of US investment. In return, the EU is the US's biggest trading partner, representing over 20 per cent of total trade flows. Imports and exports are highest in machinery and transport equipment and represent a good example of intra-industry trade. Merchandise trade shows a small surplus for the EU (see Figure 17.4) while trade in services shows approximate equality with the EU registering a small surplus (see Figure 17.5) in later years.

Investment links between the US and the EU are even more substantial and each is

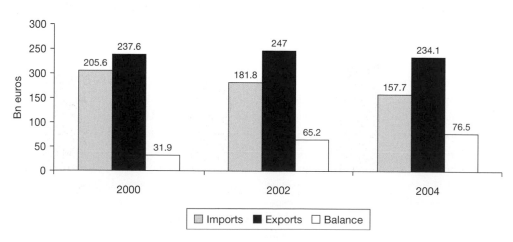

Figure 17.4 *EU-25 merchandise trade with the US*

Source: Eurostat.

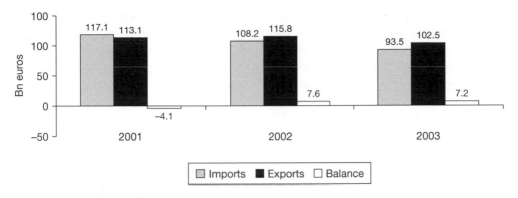

Figure 17.5 EU-15 trade in services with the US

Source: Eurostat.

the other's largest investment partner. The US represents 52 per cent of EU FDI while the reciprocal flows represent 61 per cent of inwards FDI. The EU's total investment in the US economy exceeds €1.4 trillion, accounting for 75 per cent of US FDI. Figure 17.6 indicates the flows of FDI between the US and the EU and reflects the fact that the former is becoming a net recipient of funds from the latter. The result is a high degree of interdependence between the two partners. The inter-relationship is pivotal for both parties, generating as many as 12 million jobs across the US and the EU with many of these jobs in high-wage, high-skilled, knowledge-intensive sectors. This mutual interest in the health of the global trading system has resulted in a number of actions at both bilateral and multilateral levels.

Bilateral action has centred on a 'New Transatlantic Agenda' (NTA), which set out the form of the relationship from the mid- to late 1990s and which is intended to reduce barriers to trade and investment through closer regulatory cooperation. The aim is to focus on areas where goodwill exists and where convergence of rules and standards is promoted, and to act as an early warning

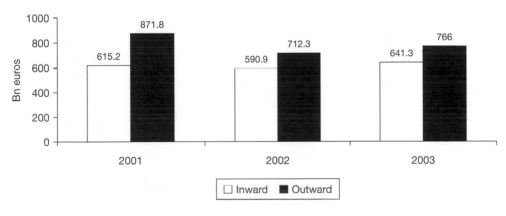

Figure 17.6 EU-25 FDI with US

Source: Eurostat.

mechanism for possible disputes. These processes were enhanced in 2004 as both parties looked to find an amicable solution to the trading problems between them. The NTA reflects the fact that trade is only a small part of the political and economic interaction between the states. Trade consists of less than 20 per cent of economic activity between these states: the rest is made up largely of FDI. The priorities for cooperation between the EU and US are:

- *regulatory cooperation*: with the aim of sharing experience across a number of areas;
- *the creation of an open aviation area*: the aim is to create a common regulatory framework between the EU and the US to replace existing bilateral deals (see Case Study 17.1);
- *competition policy*: (see Chapter 5) to create consistency between authorities and credible, predictable decisions;
- *government procurement*: to improve mutual market access;
- *intellectual property*: to promote innovation and counteract piracy;
- the reduction of business and legal costs;
- safer and securer borders;
- freer movement of travellers.

In terms of multilateral action, the EU and the US worked together to launch the Doha Round of trade talks and have agreed common positions in a number of areas. The shared objectives of the EU in terms of the multilateral trading system include: full implementation of WTO commitments; full opening of service markets; support for multilateral reform of agriculture; trade facilitation; and establishing common approaches in relevant multilateral fora on investment cooperation. The aim is to create regular dialogue between parties to ensure close cooperation on WTO issues.

Despite this mutual importance, the trade relationship between the EU and the US has often been fractious. In the early to mid-1980s, there was a sharp escalation in trade friction between the parties which was reflected in the rising level of disputes between them within GATT (General Agreement on Tariffs and Trade). This was driven by macro-economic difficulties in both the US and the EU, although the latter did not experience as sharp a rise in the trade deficit as the former. Disputes in this era centred on agriculture (90 per cent of the complaints by the US to GATT about the EU were concerned with this sector) and steel. The former has proved controversial due to the high subsidies given by the EU to its suppliers and their effect on third parties and their exports. In steel, disputes centred on dumping concerns that resulted from both structural and cyclical changes in the global economy.

In the 1990s (especially after 1995), there was a sharp increase in trade tension between the EU and the US. Indeed, the number of complaints filed at the WTO increased threefold between 1995 and 2001. Thus, while EU–US trade accounts for around 10 per cent of global trade over this period, it accounted for 20 per cent of complaints. While (as mentioned) agriculture remains a constant source of complaint by the US, the nature of the disputes has changed. Since 1995, the US has filed no action against the use of subsidies. This is the direct result of the Uruguay Round and improvement of the WTO subsidies code. However, any complaints against subsidies have been overshadowed by two major disputes:

- *Beef hormones*: this started in 1989 when the EU banned the use of growth hormones used to enhance growth in cattle and banned imports containing this

Case Study 17.1

EU AND US OPEN SKIES NEGOTIATIONS

The airline industry is a competitive anomaly. It is subject to explicit state subsidies and a number of international cartels. As a result, the market place for air travel has been char-acterised by a large number of unsustainable flag carriers sustaining their position in the international market place through competitive distortions. The source of these distortions is a network of bilateral agreements between governments. These control market entry and access and thereby control which airlines can fly where. In addition, many of these agree-ments cover frequency and the number of seats per flight and, in extreme cases, prices.

The current system of the control of aviation is based on the Chicago Conference of 1944 in which states established the legal and technical rules for international air transport post 1945 based upon the IATA (International Air Transport Agreement). Many states saw aviation as a matter of prestige and sovereignty with the result that a series of bilateral deals emerged between states that controlled traffic between them as well as rights of cabotage (which defined the rights of carriers to carry passengers from the destination to third states). Alongside this was a tariff setting agreement under the IATA which worked as a de facto cartel that controlled the price of tickets.

Overtime, progressive deregulation, the expansion of networks and the emergence of niche operators (especially in areas of low-fare, point-to-point networks) has made such cartels anachronistic. As Europe started to liberalise (see Chapter 10), the US began to develop a series of bilateral agreements with individual EU states (the first was in 1993 with the Netherlands), allowing the respective carriers access to each others' markets. These agreements tended to work more in favour of the US than the EU airlines. Under the bilat-eral deals, US airlines were allowed to fly from anywhere in the US to anywhere in the EU while the EU signatory could only fly from its home base. As a result, these agreements limited European integration due to the controls on the operations of EU airlines' transat-lantic operations. In addition, transatlantic mergers were not possible as foreign ownership of US carriers was limited to 24.9 per cent whereas the EU limits non-European ownership to 49 per cent. In addition, EU carriers were limited in their ability to deliver passengers in one US city and pick up passengers and deliver them to another US city.

On 1 October 2003, talks began between the EU and the US to replace the series of bilat-eral agreements between individual states and the US with a single agreement covering all EU members. The aim of this discussion was the liberalisation of transatlantic traffic. In 2002, the Commission won a court ruling that bilateral deals were unlawful as such a frame-work discriminated between signatories and non-signatories. Thus, the Council of Ministers gave the Commission the right to negotiate an EU-wide deal. The US aims to extend the existing 11 bilateral deals and extrapolate them into the rest of the EU via a single agree-ment. Europe wants a more ambitious agreement that removes remaining restrictions, including on ownership, and gives its operators open access to the high-value internal US market. The end point of such an agreement would be the creation of a single aviation area covering the EU and the US. In the immediate term, the US wants better access to key hubs.

Over the longer term, this could change the nature of the aviation market, moving it from a regulated market of protected national flag carriers to a true global business comprised of a series of mega-carriers.

The fact that many US and EU airlines are of questionable financial solvency should be a direct stimulant to the process. The emergence of low-cost operators has eaten away at profitable segments of these 'flag carriers'. Thus, in many ways, the move towards such a deal represents the last stages of a liberalisation process that has been under way for nearly a decade in Europe and over two decades in the US. Prior to the agreement, there had been limited attempts to promote consolidation between EU operators. These have often been curtailed by the rights enjoyed by flag carriers at their respective hubs as well as the rights enjoyed by operators elsewhere. Many states were keen to protect the preferential access rights given to their airlines at key national hub airports.

Clearly consolidation is linked intimately to the change in ownership rules. However, such rules can only be changed by the approval of the US Congress. In some parts of Congress, there is a reluctance (for both political and strategic reasons) to allow such a change if it means the loss of US airlines to overseas rivals. Congress appears to want to limit foreign involvement in US airlines to control, not ownership. Thus, they are prepared to accept a foreign chief executive and/or other top managers but are reluctant – within the current political climate – to cede any more control to overseas interests.

The tentative agreement, which was signed on 18 November 2005, allows every US and EU airline to fly between every city in the US and the EU. It allows US and EU airlines to determine the number of flights according to market demands and to enter freely into cooperative agreements with other airlines. The US eliminated the nationality clause which was in the bilateral deals and which meant that an EU airline's flights no longer have to begin or end in that airline's home state. The deal is currently subject to the approval of the EU-25 states but the European Council is concerned that the US's concessions on ownership restrictions are still too limited and is likely to defer approval of the deal until there is some shift in this policy.

Case questions

1 On what basis have states traditionally protected their airline industry?

2 Are such controls still justified?

3 What are the advantages and disadvantages of an Open Skies agreement between the EU and the US?

product. This was motivated by concerns over the health aspect of these hormones which had been linked to cancer. This led to the US filing a GATT lawsuit and, later, a WTO dispute settlement case in 1996 (as well as against other beef exporting nations). This resulted in retaliatory tariffs by the US of US$117 million per annum.

■ *Bananas*: in 1993 and in the wake of the SEM, the EU established an EU-wide system of quotas for bananas to replace the existing system of national quotas.

This was to favour African Caribbean Pacific (ACP) states at the expense of US and Latin American suppliers. The result was two lawsuits by the US (as well as other Latin American states) and, later, two WTO dispute settlement cases. The WTO found that the measure compromised the EU's WTO obligations and the US was authorised to impose retaliatory tariffs on EU imports to the value of US$191 million per annum.

These two cases are important as retaliation was authorised by the WTO. Furthermore, despite other states being involved, these disputes were largely seen as the US versus the EU. The cases are also important as they underline that if retaliation through compensation is going to work as an effective constraint on state action, the threat has to be credible and there has to be a capacity to retaliate. This is based on the size of the retaliator and the direct threat to the terms of trade of the offender.

Steel has maintained its controversial place in US–EU trade with the former filing a large number of complaints against producers from many states (including the EU). The outcome of these complaints was the imposition of anti-dumping and countervailing duties by the US upon a number of states' steel imports. The result was a flurry of complaints to GATT/WTO. These complaints by the EU about US behaviour continued into the new millennium. This problem was compounded by the Byrd Amendment in 2000 which gave the revenue raised by the extra duty to the affected firms. This gave the EU (as well as other states) an extra incentive to complain. This protection was enhanced even further with more safeguards by the US on special types of steel and the deliberate exclusion of its NAFTA (North American Free Trade Area) partners from such meas-

ures. Again, these further measures stimulated complaints by the affected parties and the WTO found such measures were inconsistent with the US's WTO commitments (under the subsidies code). The US response was to narrow the field of affected steels, with the result that the EU softened its stance. Despite this, the US continued to enhance the safeguard measures on imports, causing the EU finally to give up on the WTO structure and implement its own retaliatory measures independent of the formal framework. Thus, over nearly four decades the EU and the US have made little progress in settling trade disputes, especially in an area as controversial and politically salient as steel.

Over the past decade, two further EU–US disputes have unsettled trade relations between these parties:

- *Foreign sales corporations*: this is based on the tax treatment of Foreign States Corporation (FSC) which allowed under US tax emption for foreign sales income. The EU believes these are tantamount to trade/export subsidies. The WTO agreed. The US appealed the FSC states but replaced it with a new Extra territoriality Act which the EU also complained about. Again, the WTO agreed with the EU's objection. The US is struggling to offer support to business while maintaining its WTO commitments.
- *Genetically modified organisms (GMOs)*: since 1998 the EU has applied a moratorium on GMOs which has had the effect of reducing US exports to the EU of agricultural and food products. The US argues these rules are too ad hoc and there are no formal rules to assess these products. The EU disagreed.

The case of GMOs highlights how regulatory regionalism (Isaac and Kerr 2003) can lead to

Case Study 17.2

AIRCRAFT SUBSIDIES

Over the past decade, Airbus has overtaken Boeing as the world's leading civil aircraft maker (see Case Study 6.1, p. 129). However, the US claims that this market transformation has been aided by the level of financial support (in the form of launch aid) given to Airbus by European governments. The US argues that the use of up-front subsidies has given Airbus a risk-free source of capital, allowing it to undercut Boeing in the global market place for civil aircraft. In 1992, the US and the EU effectively agreed to turn a blind eye to subsidies through an agreement to set launch aid for Airbus at 33 per cent of the development costs of a new plane while indirect support for Boeing was to be limited to 4 per cent of its turnover. By 2002, the US argued that such launch support could no longer be justified when Airbus holds the majority of the market for civil aircraft. As a result, the US wanted the EU to end all future subsidies while allowing existing financial commitments to remain.

The US claims that Airbus has received at least US$15 billion in launch aid from the constituent governments. This took the form of loans that were offered at interest rates at below market levels. Furthermore, these loans were repayable on the basis of future aircraft sales. If a product should fail, the loan will not have to be repaid. As a result, Boeing claims that Airbus has avoided around US$35 billion of debt, although Airbus will have to continue paying royalties to governments long after the loan and interest on it have been repaid. The EU counter-claims that Boeing has received around US$23 billion in aid since 1992, largely through defence and space contracts. These defence contracts, the EU alleges, have not only been deliberately overpriced but Boeing was also given preferential access to government procurement sources. The EU also plans to challenge the tax reduction given to Boeing by Washington over the next 20 years to support the launch of new products – a gift of some US$2.3 billion. In addition, the EU claims that Boeing gets a subsidy from Japan as the Japanese government has offered subsidies to three domestic businesses supplying Boeing with core components for its products.

Initially, the US sought to solve this problem through bilateral negotiation but turned to the WTO (via its dispute settlement mechanism) when these efforts failed. Importantly the uncertainty generated by the dispute is likely to spread beyond these states as the construction of civil aircraft is complex as it is based on a network of partners and suppliers across multiple states and continents. Thus, there is the danger that the trade dispute could impact beyond these two companies to the host of suppliers that work for both airlines. For example, six US companies are working for the A380 Airbus programme while a similar number of European businesses are working for Boeing. However, the real danger is that the dispute escalates and results in extensive sanctions between these trade partners. This could add a substantial form of instability to the global economic system.

However, many argue that the timing of this trade dispute was political. The filing of the case with the WTO coincided with the US election campaign and with the need for the US president to be seen to be tough on trade disputes. The US is losing manufacturing jobs, a trend that the government wishes to reverse through tough action on 'unfair' trade practices.

In addition, Boeing has drawn on political support to pursue its case with vigour especially now since it is losing market share to its rival. The EU also suspects that the dispute has been driven by the erosion of Boeing's market share and the launch of the A380 to challenge Boeing's cash cow – the 747. However, the US's use of the WTO to resolve the dispute has confused many as any victory would only affect new subsidies. In addition, recourse to the WTO dispute settlement mechanism could result in protracted uncertainty for the aircraft sector as well as offering the potential to poison trade talks elsewhere. There are also uncertainties as to whether the WTO is the best mechanism for dealing with a dispute of this gravity.

In early 2005, the US and EU called a truce and agreed to seek a bilateral deal. However, by March, these talks had broken down as the EU demanded that the aforementioned Japanese support be included in the talks. Some suggested that these talks were a delaying tactic by Boeing to prevent the rash of new Airbus products and to allow it to catch up with its development of rival products. At the time of writing, the dispute looks as intractable as ever. While the launch of bilateral talks was a step forward, there has been a change in personnel within the respective trade delegations since this dispute was initiated. The result is that the cordial relations between the respective trade delegations have deteriorated, meaning that an absence of goodwill may limit the potential for a swift resolution of this issue.

Case questions

1 To what degree was the launch aid given to Airbus justified?

2 Do you agree with Boeing's claim that as market leader such support to Airbus is no longer warranted?

3 Is the WTO the right place to settle this dispute?

trade disputes: differences in the regulations on particular products can and do lead to trade barriers. These products are governed by the Risk Analysis Framework which was developed to deal with advanced technology products (based on there being a large information gap between producers and consumers). However, this is operationalised differently by both the US and the EU. In the US, science was placed at the forefront of considerations while the EU takes a more precautionary approach.

In the WTO between 1995 and 2004, the EU was the defendant against the US in three cases (GMO, beef and agricultural trade) and was the complainant in ten. While disputes between the two change their respective behaviour, there is also the unintended impact that the dispute can have on third parties via trade diversion. Despite the profile of these disputes, it is important to stress that they affect less than 2 per cent of total trade between the parties. In addition, both have agreed on the core compliance produces through the WTO, want to avoid a trade war and appreciate the need to agree for the good of the global trading system.

At the time of writing (spring 2006), there are still evident disparities between the EU and the US over trade in agriculture and aerospace (see Case Study 17.2). In terms of the former, despite attempts to find a common position, the EU still asserts that the US offers an implicit subsidy to its exporters as it has been buying surplus production and offering it as aid, which, in turn, distorts global prices. However, there are combined barriers to entry into the US by US producers in a number of areas such as beef and poultry exports. In addition, the US claimed that the extension of the EU to the east increased trade barriers in a number of key areas. These relate to import policies (in areas such as wine, pharmaceuticals etc.) standards, labelling and certification (beef, poultry etc.), government procurement, export subsidies, IPR as well as services and investment barriers.

CONCLUSION

The majority of the EU's trade relations are with other developed states and the majority of this trade is intra-industry in nature. The intra-industry nature of trade defines the core competitive threat to European business. As a consequence, trade with other developed states is often surrounded by controversy. Over the past decade, there have been a number of high-profile disputes between the EU and its major trading partners, most notably the US. However, instead of resorting to trade wars, these disputes have normally been settled within the multilateral framework of the WTO.

KEY POINTS

■ The focus of global trade and investment within the global economy is based around the 'triad' of Europe, North America and East Asia.

■ The EU's major trading partners are other developed states based within this triad.

■ Much of the trade between these states is of an intra-industry nature. As a result, the EU often competes in the same industry areas as other developed states.

■ The EU's trade policy towards these states is guided by the CCP which – within the context of the WTO framework – commits it to fair trade.

■ Over the last two decades numerous trade disputes have arisen, notably between the US and the EU. These disputes are important to the development of the global trading system.

ACTIVITIES

1 Choose a particular type of product and explore who are the major import and export markets for it.

2 Research an EU trading partner and explore the form and nature of trade and investment with that state.

3 As a group, discuss the case for and against the use of protectionism.

406

4   Divide into two groups and assess the case for and against the special protection given to agriculture and its justification.

QUESTIONS FOR DISCUSSION

1   How do you explain and account for the emergence of the 'triad'?

2   Compare and contrast inter- and intra-industry trade.

3   What is the difference between direct and indirect foreign investment?

4   Assess the claim that the EU is more sinner than sinned against in international trade.

5   How do you account for the fact that the EU's major exports are now services?

SUGGESTIONS FOR FURTHER READING

de Burca, G. and Scott, J. (eds) (2003) *The EU and the WTO: Legal and Constitutional Issues*, Oxford: Hart Publishing.

Dicken, P. (2003) *Global Shift: Reshaping the Global Economic Map in the 21st Century*, 4th edn, London: Sage.

Dillon, S. (2002) *International Trade and Economic Law and the EU*, Oxford: Hart Publishing

Fogarty, E. and Aggarwal, V. (eds) (2004) *EU Trade Strategies: Regionalism and Globalism*, Basingstoke: Palgrave Macmillan.

Greenaway, D. (1987) 'The New Theories of Intra-industry Trade', *Bulletin of Economic Research*, 39 (2), pp. 95–120.

Isaac, G. and Kerr, W. A. (2003) 'GMOs at the WTO: A Harvest of Trouble', *Journal of World Trade*, 37 (6), pp. 1083–95.

Krugman, P. (1995) 'Growing World Trade: Causes and Consequences', *Brookings Papers on Economic Activity* (1).

Meunier, S. (2005) *Trading Voices: The EU in International Commercial Negotiations*, Princeton, NJ: Princeton University Press.

Poon, J. P. II., Thompson, E. and Kelly, P. (2000) 'Myth of the Triad? Geography of Trade and Investment Blocs', *Transactions of the Institute of British Geographers*, 25(1), pp. 127–44.

Rugman, A. M. (2000) *The End of Globalization*, London and New York: Random House.

Petersmann, E. and Pollack, M. (eds) (2003) *Transatlantic Economic Disputes: The EU, the US and the WTO*, Oxford: Oxford University Press.

Van Bael, I. (ed.) (2004) *Anti-dumping and Other Trade Protection Laws of the EC*, The Hague: Kluwer Law International.

Chapter 18

Europe and emerging economies

Opportunity or threat?

No nation was ever ruined by trade.

Benjamin Franklin

This chapter will help you:

- understand the growing importance of the EU's relations with emerging economies;
- identify key differences in the EU's relations with the three largest emerging economies;
- understand the competitive challenges facing European business as a result of the rapid integration of China and India into the world economy;
- consider how European business can respond to these competitive challenges;
- identify opportunities for European business as a result of the rapid integration of China and India into the world economy.

The United States is Europe's biggest trading partner (see Chapter 17) and has been for some time. However, European policy makers and businesses are giving greater attention to what are commonly termed 'emerging' or 'transitional' economies. These are economies that are undergoing some form of fundamental change that is enabling them to engage more with the outside world in terms of trade and investment in particular. Examples of the type of change involved include a shift from a closed to a more open, liberal economy such as has happened in India or the transition from a state/command economy as in CEE (see Chapter 16), Russia and China. These economies are in the process of developing key market institutions and are engaged in ongoing economic reform. They also exhibit trade, investment and GDP growth rates way above the average of the developed world.

The impact of the bigger transition economies on the rest of the world in general, and on Europe in particular, is significant. From the perspective of European business, these emerging economies pose a twofold challenge. First, they intensify the degree of competition in both domestic and export markets, which results either in efforts to rise to these new competitive pressures or campaigns to impose protectionist barriers. Second, the opening of such potentially significant economies provides a range of trade and investment opportunities which gives European business an interest in improved access to these markets. For EU members and institutions, the challenge is to update and upgrade formal relations with emerging and transition economies to reflect the new reality, rather than the reality of two to three decades previously when these economies were not merely relatively isolated from the global economy but were, in some cases, ideologically opposed to Europe both politically and economically.

This chapter explores Europe's developing trade and investment relationship with the world's three largest emerging and transitional economies – China, Russia and India. It outlines the development of formal links between the EU and these countries: it is these formal links that shape the environment in which European business develops its strategies for engaging with the transition economies. In the process, the chapter discusses how the commercial relationship has developed, identifies areas where there are tensions or problems and puts forward examples of the response of business to these rapidly developing links.

CHINA

China began the long process of transforming itself from a command into a market economy in 1979 and the task of liberalisations and the development of market institutions continues to the present day. China rapidly began to reap the benefits of reform

and has grown at an annual average rate of over 9 per cent since 1980 (see Table 18.1) – a rate that is four to five times greater than that of the eurozone. China's growth has been strong in manufacturing, averaging nearly 12 per cent per annum during 1990–2003 (compared to 1.6 per cent in the eurozone over the same period). Growth in services output was particularly strong at 13.5 per cent per annum during the 1980s, the first decade of reform. Chinese services growth has been less rapid since 1990, but at 8.8 per cent per annum, it is still significantly above that in Europe.

Export growth has been an important aspect of Chinese development. According to World Bank figures, total Chinese exports grew at an annual rate of 13.9 per cent per annum during 1980–90 and at 14.1 per cent per annum between 1990 and 2003 in volume terms and at 12.9 per cent and 14.1 per cent in value terms for 1980–90 and 1990–2003 respectively. Between 1997 and 2004, China's share of world exports grew from 3.3 per cent to 6.5 per cent and its share of world imports from 2.5 per cent to 5.9 per cent – significant increases in a relatively short space of time.

Chinese exports to the EU have also grown rapidly and at a faster pace than EU exports to China (see Figure 18.1). Consequently, the EU–China trade balance is heavily in China's favour. Indeed, the EU's trade deficit with China is its biggest with any single trade partner – a factor that goes some way to explaining why calls for protection against Chinese exports to Europe have been particularly loud.

The composition of China's trade reveals that the stereotype of Chinese exports as primarily labour-intensive, low value-added goods is inaccurate. Table 18.2 shows that the value of Chinese exports with a high technology content far exceeds the value of

Table 18.1 Output growth in the big three emerging economies and in large European economies

	GDP (% growth p.a.)		Agriculture (% growth p.a.)		Manufacturing[b] (% growth p.a.)		Services (% growth p.a.)	
	1980–90	1990–2003	1980–90	1990–2003	1980–90	1990–2003	1980–90	1990–2003
China	10.3	9.6	5.9	3.5	10.8	11.7	13.5	8.8
India	5.7	5.9	3.1	2.7	7.4	6.5	6.9	7.9
Russia	–	−1.8	–	−1.7	–	−3.2	–	0.2
Eurozone[a]	2.4	2.0	1.1	1.1	–	1.6	2.9	2.4
Germany	2.3	1.5	1.6	1.5	–	0.1	3.0	2.5
France	2.4	1.9	1.3	1.3	1.3	2.6	3.0	2.2
UK	3.2	2.7	2.1	−0.2	3.1	1.1	3.1	3.4
Italy	2.5	1.6	−0.5	0.8	2.1	1.2	2.9	1.8
Spain	3.1	2.8	3.1	0.7	–	3.6	3.3	2.9
Poland	–	4.2	–	1.1	–	7.7	–	4.1

Notes:
a   Eurozone = the 12 original members of the eurozone.
b   The UK and Russian figures refer to industry not manufacturing.

Source: World Bank, *2005 World Development Indicators.*

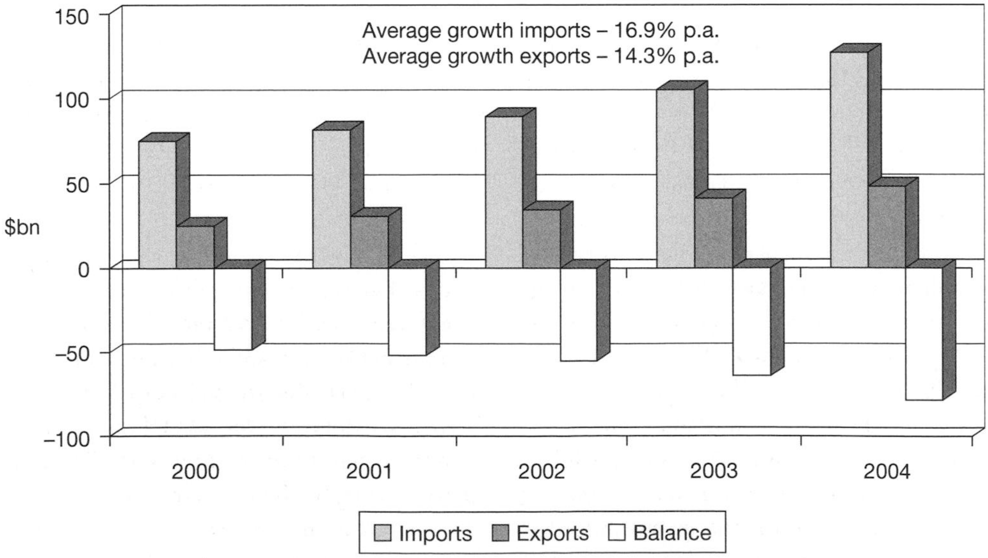

Figure 18.1 EU merchandise trade with China, 2000–04
Source: Eurostat.

Table 18.2 Value of total Chinese exports by major commodity (US$ billion)

	2004	2005	% change
Machinery and electronic products	323.4	426.7	32.0
High-technology products	165.5	218.2	31.8
Automatic data-processing equipment and components	59.9	76.3	27.4
Clothing	61.6	73.9	19.9
Yarn, fabric and products	33.5	41.1	22.9
Spare parts for automatic data-processing equipment	23.9	28.4	18.8
Wireless telephone	14.2	20.6	45.7
Footwear	15.2	19.1	25.3
TV, radio and telecommunications components	12.0	18.2	50.8
Integrated circuit and microelectronic components	11.0	14.4	30.9
Furniture and parts	10.2	13.5	32.8
Steel	8.3	13.1	56.9
Plastics products	9.2	11.3	22.9
TV sets	5.5	8.4	53.3
Travel goods and bags	6.2	7.3	17.2
Toys	4.4	6.6	49.2
Digital cameras	4.9	5.5	13.9

Source: Ministry of Commerce of the People's Republic of China, http://english.mofcom.gov.cn, accessed April 2006.

Chinese exports of textiles, clothing, footwear, toys, etc., notwithstanding the fact that the value of the latter exports runs into many billions of dollars. Although a substantial proportion of China's high-value exports is from affiliates or joint ventures of foreign multinationals, these figures suggest increasing competition across a whole range of sectors. Over time, a greater proportion of exports will come from Chinese firms that have benefited from technology transfer and have been able to build up their own brands. Lenovo, which in early 2005 bought IBM's personal computer business, is entering export markets in a big way and is merely one of the first of many Chinese companies that will develop an international outlook and increase the competitive threat to European business. In short, although trade disputes between the EU and China have tended to focus on labour-intensive sectors (such as textiles and clothing (see Case Study 18.2)), the protectionist clamour could spread beyond these sectors.

In 2004, the EU became China's single biggest trading partner. This trend continued into 2005 when the EU accounted for 15.3 per cent of China's trade compared to 14.9 per cent for the US and 13 per cent for Japan. However, the EU takes on a less prominent role in terms of inward FDI into China. During the first nine months of 2005, both in terms of numbers of projects and the value of contracts, the EU accounted for about 5 per cent of total inward FDI into China. Hong Kong, Taiwan, South Korea,

411

Case Study 18.1

EUROPEAN MULTINATIONALS IN CHINA

The imperative to establish a major presence in China is driving many of Europe's multi-nationals. This case study outlines the experience of just two of them – Philips from the Netherlands and Siemens from Germany – two of the world's biggest electronics and electrical companies.

The involvement of both companies in China goes back many years. In 1872, Siemens exported pointer telegraphs to China and in 1899 built China's first electric tram in Beijing. In the early twentieth century, Siemens built power plants, steelworks and China's first high-voltage line and by the 1930s, Siemens China Company was Siemens' largest company outside Europe. Philips' first involvement with China goes back to the 1920s when it dispatched medical equipment to China.

However, contemporary involvement with China for both companies can be traced back to 1985 and the early days of China's economic reforms. In 1985 Philips established its first Chinese joint venture. Since then, it has invested more than US$3.4 billion into 35 joint ventures and wholly owned subsidiaries and has established over 60 offices nationwide. In 2004, Philips employed about 20,000 workers in China and generated total sales of over €6 billion, two-thirds of which were exports. The company aims to double its revenues to €12 billion by 2007. In 1985, Siemens signed a Memorandum of Comprehensive Cooperation with China's machinery, electrical and electronics industries regarding technology and know-how transfer. Since then, Siemens has established over 45 operating companies and 51 regional offices in China with more in the pipeline. In fiscal year 2005, Siemens' China sales reached €3.2 billion (or 4.2 per cent of total sales and a 15 per cent increase on the previous year) and received new orders worth €4.1 billion. Siemens' workforce in China amounts to 36,000 or 9 per cent of its workforce.

All the main business units of both Philips and Siemens are active in China. In the case of Philips, this means semiconductors, consumer electronics, medical systems, lighting and domestic appliances and personal care products. Philips claims to be (or aims to become) a top three player in each market in which it is active in China. In 2004, it claimed to be number one in China's lighting market, third in medical systems and third in semiconductors. Siemens' main business segments are information and communications, automation and control, power, transportation, medical and lighting as well as household appliances. Given this profile, Siemens has been particularly active in major Chinese infrastructure projects and in industrial modernisation. Siemens, for example, supplied 15 machine transformers for the Three Gorges Dam Project on the Yangtze, the largest dam construction in the world and, in the summer of 2005, it received a €100 million order for a high-voltage, direct current power transmission line that will transport electricity from western China to eastern Guangdong Province by 2007.

As well as becoming a centre for production and supply and a key location in the global supply chains of both companies, China is also becoming a centre of R&D activity for them. China has been an important R&D base for Siemens in mobile communications since 1998 and, indeed, is Siemens' largest R&D location for communications outside Germany. In 2003, Siemens registered over 500 patent applications with the Chinese State Intellectual Property Office, making it one of the most prolific corporate patent applicants in China and testifying to its R&D commitment in China. Siemens plans to expand its communications research in China with a major emphasis on designing and developing products to meet the needs of the local market. Siemens is also active in research in its other business segments in China and has established cooperation with 16 of China's top universities to promote R&D, encourage knowledge sharing and to help develop scientific and technological talent.

Philips is not to be outdone in its R&D commitment in China. In 2004, it maintained 15 R&D centres in China employing almost 900 staff. These comprised two technology R&D centres to serve global as well as Chinese markets – Philips Corporate Research East Asia which investigates digital TV, optical storage and connectivity, and the Medical Development Centre. The remaining 13 centres have been established for product and process development for the Chinese and regional markets in lighting, semiconductors and engineering support in particular. An important development in the mid-2000s was the establishment of the Philips Shanghai Innovation campus which is intended to bring all the various research facilities scattered around Shanghai together both to encourage collaboration between them and to open Philips' facilities and technologies to partners. Philips remains committed to expanding its R&D capacity in China further.

After the uncoordinated moves into China during the late 1980s and the 1990s, Philips has entered a more mature phase of its China development and has begun to look at its interests in China in a more holistic way with a view to streamlining them to build deeper, broader and more integrated foundations for future growth. This more considered China strategy has a number of elements. Notably, the company is developing central services to support its various business operations and to boost efficiency. Under this 'One Philips' principle, the following common functions of its joint ventures are being brought together under a common and coordinated management structure:

- human resources and talent;
- government and public relations;
- streamlined brand management;
- information technology support;
- financial and accounting functions.

Harmonising the 'multi-China' strategy among the five product divisions present in China will enable them to share 'China expertise', avoid duplication and help reap synergies between various activities. The process is managed by a China Strategy Board on which the heads of its five business units sit together with the President of Philips China, the chief marketing and technology officers and a representative of the IPR division. The Board's remit is to formulate a strategy for Philips in China – a change from the previous practice when the company had only a global strategy and the role of the individual business units was to execute this strategy in China.

Case questions

1 What does the significant and growing presence in China of Philips and Siemens, two
   multinationals whose competitiveness depends on being world leaders in appropriate
   technology, tell us about the nature of the future competitive challenge facing Europe?

2 Identify the potential advantages and disadvantages of Philips' shift to a coordinated
   China strategy compared to its previous strategy of individual business units
   independently implementing Philips' global strategy in China.

3 What is the significance of the commitment of Philips and Siemens to R&D in China?

4 Choose another big European multinational and research its involvement in China.

Japan and the US all easily exceeded European investment in China during that period, as has been the case throughout the reform period. In short, despite the efforts of big European multinationals such as Philips and Siemens (see Case Study 18.1), European firms have generally been much slower to invest in than trade with China.

China's economic development and its increasing integration into the world economy have stimulated formal relations between the EU and China. Just as greater commercial transactions between the two place the formal aspects of the relationship in the spotlight, so a healthy official relationship helps shape the business environment and can facilitate or hinder business developments.

Formal diplomatic EU–China relations began in 1975, following the US's normalisation of its relationship with China. By 1978, the EU and China had signed a trade agreement that included the creation of an EU–China Joint Committee which provided a forum for debate about key commercial issues. In 1985, this process was taken a stage further with the signature of a Trade and Economic Cooperation Agreement. In the 1980s bilateral cooperation between the two

partners was extended into areas such as scientific cooperation, business management, training and rural development, and in 1988 the EU opened its delegation in Beijing. This greater closeness was temporarily halted in 1989 following the suppression and deaths of protestors in Beijing's Tiananmen Square and the subsequent freezing of EU–China relations, including the imposition of sanctions.

By 1992, relations had been normalised again with the exception of the arms embargo which remains in force. In 1995, the European Commission's first Strategy Paper on EU–China relations was adopted and in 1998, the first of the annual EU–China Summits was held. As part of the process of WTO accession, bilateral negotiations take place between the applicant and any existing WTO member that requests such talks. The EU–China bilateral pre-accession talks concluded in 2000 and eased access to the Chinese market for European producers in a number of ways (see Box 18.2). In 2003, China published its first policy paper on its links with the EU and in September 2005, the Eighth Annual EU–China Summit agreed to negotiate a new China-EU Framework Agreement 'to reflect the full breadth and depth of the strategic partnership between

MILESTONES IN EU–CHINA LINKS

BOX 18.1

1975   Formal diplomatic relations established between the EC and China

1978   EC–China sign Trade Agreement – includes the creation of an EC–China Joint Committee

1979   European Commission President Roy Jenkins visits China

1988   EU delegation opens in Beijing

1989   Events in Tiananmen Square lead to freezing of relations and the imposition of sanctions

1992   Relations normalised in most areas but arms embargo remains

1995   First European Commission Strategy paper on EU–Chinese relations

1998   First annual EU–China Summit

2000   EU–China conclude bilateral talks relating to China's WTO accession

2003   First Chinese policy paper on the EU

2003   EU adopts Commission paper *A Maturing Partnership – Shared Interests and Challenges in EU-China Relations*

2004   The EU becomes China's biggest trading partner and China, the EU's 2nd biggest

2005   Eighth EU–China Summit

China and the EU. This commitment promises to place the EU–China relationship on a more formal basis, possibly in the direction of the Partnership and Cooperation Agreement with Russia.

Given the inexorable intensification of the EU–China relationship, both on a business and an official basis, what do Europe and China want from each other? The EU's interest in China is largely economic, although its stance can be influenced by political interventions from the US (such as the continuation of the arms embargo). China's rapid economic development poses opportunities and challenges for European business. China has a large private sector, providing investment and partnership opportunities. The world's biggest steel and telecommunications markets are in China, again providing markets and investment opportunities. China has also become the world's largest

energy consumer behind the US and its energy demand growth is likely to continue given China's ongoing economic growth.

Corporate Europe needs the removal of barriers to trade and investment in China. Although European firms have not invested in China to the same extent as firms from Asia and the US, those European firms with a presence in China have shown a deep level of commitment to China, including significant investment in R&D (see Case Study 18.1), the business function that is frequently the last to transfer overseas. For China, such strategies assist the process of technology transfer and generally enhance its technological skills and capabilities. In relation to investing in and trading with China, European firms frequently allude to the need for further improvements in intellectual property protection in China – a need that is becoming increasingly important for Chinese

415

BOX 18.2

MAIN POINTS OF EU–CHINA AGREEMENT PRECEDING CHINA'S ACCESSION TO THE WTO IN 2001

Telecommunications

- Acceleration of timetable for opening mobile telephony market
- Opening up of leasing market
- Gradual easing of restrictions on foreign investment

Insurance

- Foreign brokers allowed to operate upon accession
- Seven new licences to European insurers
- Foreign participants in life insurance joint ventures to be allowed effective management control

State trade monopolies

- State monopoly of silk exports (China accounts for 70 per cent of world silk production) to be removed by 2005
- State monopoly on importing crude and refined oil and NPK fertiliser to be gradually opened to private traders

Tariffs

- Tariffs reduced on over 150 major European exports. Agreed levels about 8–10 per cent

Motor vehicles

- Greater flexibility for European car manufacturers in China to choose the type of vehicles they build
- End of joint venture restrictions on engine production

Distribution

- Joint venture restrictions on large department stores and on chain stores lifted

Agriculture

- Improved market access for EU products such as rape-seed oil, dairy products, pasta, wine and olives

Horizontal measures

- China to cease measures that distort trade, including local content requirements and industrial export subsidies
- More transparent procurement system

Other

- Improved market access in banking, legal services, accountancy, architecture, tourism, construction, dredging and market research firms themselves as they develop their own technological base. Standardisation is another area where collaboration can further the mutual interests of both sides. European firms complain of lack of clarity and conflicting information about Chinese standards. In many areas, China is developing new standards as it moves into new areas of production. Given the export orientation of much of Chinese industry, the adoption of international standards is helpful to both Chinese importers and exporters. In telecommunications, for example, European multinationals have been working closely with Chinese counterparts to develop the next generation of standards. It is in such ways, that commercial interaction between China and Europe will continue to flourish.

China's aspirations for its links with the EU are both political and economic. In the post-cold war era, China's preference is a multipolar world in which there are alternative spheres of influence to the US rather than a unipolar world in which the US is dominant. This vision is shared by several European countries. More developed and comprehensive relations between China and the EU help foster alternatives to the US. On an economic level, China wants access to European markets for traded goods and, increasingly, for investments in line with China's growing outward investment.

In October 2003, China published its first policy paper on the EU. Following a general preamble in which China asserts 'there is no fundamental conflict of interest between China and the EU' and that 'the common ground between China and the EU far outweighs their disagreements', the paper goes on to identify actions to strengthen relations in the three fields of politics, culture and economics. Politically, China wants to intensify and increase political contact at all levels with the EU. More specifically, China emphasises the 'one China' principle in relation to Taiwan, for which it wants the EU's support, and wants to 'promote the EU's understanding of Tibet'. Cultural objectives centre upon cooperation in science and technology, education and medical care and personnel and cultural exchanges.

In the economic sphere, China wants to increase cooperation with the EU in all areas. It is seeking fewer restrictions on high-technology exports and would like to see the reduction or even abolition of anti-dumping duties, an unlikely outcome given that anti-dumping duties are a legitimate trade instrument within the WTO and that their use appears to be currently popular within Europe (see Case Study 18.2). China is also prepared to seek compensation for any losses arising from EU enlargement, another objective that is unlikely to meet with EU agreement. However, some of China's economic objectives are being met more positively by the EU, including increased EU–China coordination in WTO negotiations (providing common ground can be found); a stronger dialogue on investment; and more EU assistance in areas such as the environment and human resource development. China is also seeking greater sectoral cooperation in financial services, agriculture, IT (China wants Europe to participate in the creation of the Information Society in China and to engage with the creation of Chinese IPR and technical standards), energy and transport, especially maritime and civil aviation.

In practice, in recent years the EU and China have started to engage in 'sectoral dialogues' in over 20 different areas involving officials (specialists from 19 different Directorate Generals of the European Commission are engaged in regular contact with their Chinese counterparts), politicians, business organisations and private companies.

417

Case Study 18.2

'BRA WARS' – ANATOMY OF A TRADE DISPUTE

On 1 January 2005, quotas on imports of textiles and clothing into European and North American markets were finally removed, giving WTO members unrestricted access to them. As part of the agreement concluding the Uruguay Round of multilateral trade talks in 1995, this act reflected the effective demise of the Multifibre Arrangement introduced in the 1970s to 'temporarily' shield the textile and clothing industries of the developed world from competition from developing countries.

As a result of this market opening, there was a surge in EU imports of textiles and clothing from China between January and June 2005, with some categories increasing by over 500 per cent. However, the value of Chinese textiles and clothing imports did not rise as quickly, implying a significant drop in the unit price of items. In the case of dresses, for example, the implied price fall was 62 per cent, undermining EU producers and other suppliers further.

As part of the agreement governing China's WTO accession, the EU had the right to impose temporary limits on Chinese textile imports to give European manufacturers time to adapt to their new trading environment. Accordingly in June 2005, the so-called 'Shanghai Agreement' was reached between the EU and China by which quotas were imposed on ten items of textiles and clothing (see Table 18.3) that had been particularly affected by the original lifting of quotas. The June 2005 quotas were to be increased on a yearly basis until the end of 2007 when they would be removed. As Table 18.3 demonstrates, the June 2005 quotas still represent a major increase on 2004 imports from China. The intention of the June 2005 agreement was to allow a reasonable growth in Chinese imports while providing European producers with space to prepare themselves for total liberalisation – despite the fact that it had been known for ten years that textiles and clothing quotas would be removed on 1 January 2005.

Table 18.3 Products and quotas included in the June 2005 Shanghai Agreement

	Quotas agreed in June 2005 as a percentage of 2004 imports
Cotton fabrics	188
T-shirts	247
Pullovers	251
Men's trousers	429
Blouses	269
Bed linen	177
Dresses	302
Bras	153
Table and kitchen linen	154
Flax or ramie yarn	167

Source: European Commission, DG Trade.

However, the June 2005 agreement soon ran into trouble because the quotas were rapidly breached by huge shipments of textiles and clothing items arranged before the regulation came into force. By the beginning of August, the quota limits on pullovers and men's trousers had already been reached and were quickly followed by the quotas on blouses, T-shirts, bras and flax yarns. Companies that had legitimately ordered goods in preparation for the autumn season found their goods stranded in warehouses and were unable to acquire import licences for them. An estimated 75–80 million Chinese textiles and clothing items were waiting to be let into the EU. At this point, retailers faced the prospect of empty shelves and rising prices in their shops if the goods were not released.

A deal was reached in early September whereby all the goods in European warehouses were allowed into the European market but half of them counted against the 2006 quota. Moreover, China agreed not to export any more pullovers, trousers or bras to Europe in 2005. The September Agreement begs a number of questions, not least whether, by 'borrowing' from the next year's quota, the problem has been put on hold rather than resolved.

The whole episode illustrates how trade disputes bring into conflict a range of different stakeholders. The original disagreement occurred because EU producers and member states (notably, France, Spain, Italy, Greece, Spain, Portugal and Lithuania) lobbied the European Commission to restrain Chinese textiles and clothing imports on the grounds that they were being driven out of business by cheap imports following the lifting of quotas in January 2005.

In practice, the initial surge in imports from China appeared to be at the expense of traditional EU suppliers, notably from Asia, Africa and other ACP states rather than of EU producers. Significant falls in textile and clothing exports to Europe by Pakistan, Indonesia, Thailand, South Korea, Philippines, Taiwan etc., ranging from 10 per cent in the case of Pakistan and 60 per cent for South Korea, were recorded. Moreover, textile exports from ACP countries fell by 20 per cent and Mauritius and Morocco saw a 20 and 11 per cent drop, respectively, in the value of their textile exports to Europe. Conversely, these traditional suppliers rather than EU producers were the main beneficiaries of the imposition of restrictions on Chinese textiles and clothing. Unable to source Chinese products because of the June restrictions, European retailers switched to other low-cost production from Turkey, Romania, Bangladesh, Sri Lanka, etc.

The European producers' case was opposed by European retailers and consumers' organisations. They were supported by several member states' governments, including Germany, Denmark, the Netherlands, Finland and Sweden who argued that protectionism does not work and damages the interests of consumers who merely end up paying more for goods. Given that about one-quarter of the world's clothing is currently produced by approximately 35,000 factories along the Yangtze and Pearl River Deltas, all the big fashion retailers, including retailers at the higher end of the market, were affected by the dispute. The lure of sourcing from China is not only driven by price but also by the ability of Chinese manufacturers to transform catwalk fashions into products for mass market retail outlets within three to four weeks, the most rapid turnaround in the sector, thereby posing even greater challenges to European producers and other traditional suppliers. The position of the retail sector was summed up by Stuart Rose, Chief Executive of Marks & Spencer, who said: 'People want cheap goods and Italy does not make them. Protectionism does not work.'

The September 2005 Agreement has, for the time being at least, taken the sting out of the issue of Europe's textile and clothing trade with China. However, further trade disputes are anticipated. At the time of writing, the EU is set to impose anti-dumping duties on footwear imports from China and Vietnam. Moreover, in March 2006, Italian and German furniture producers are preparing a complaint to the European Commission about alleged dumping of Chinese-made furniture in the European market. However, the trade challenge from China is increasingly going to come not only from labour-intensive, lower value-added products such as textiles, clothing and footwear but also from higher value-added products with a significant high technology content. Europe urgently needs to find a way to respond to this without resorting to protection.

Case questions

1   What does the textiles and clothing case tell us about the effectiveness of protection?

2   'The real answer [to increased Chinese imports] is to allow access to the EU for goods produced in China and for EU producers to adapt to the competitive challenge this presents' (Sir Digby Jones, Director General of the Confederation of British Industry).

- ■ Discuss the above statement in relation to the increasing trade challenge to Europe from China.
- ■ The above statement was made by the head of the main British employers' organisation. Does such a statement from someone in this position surprise you?

3   China finds itself as the subject of protectionist initiatives by its main trading partners. Imagine you are (a) involved in forming Chinese trade policy; (b) the head of a Chinese enterprise whose products are the subject of, or are threatened by, import restrictions in key markets such as the EU. What strategy would you adopt to minimise the impact of such actions?

Although not headline grabbing, these dialogues help remove potential obstacles to trade and investment, increase understanding and provide a detailed, technical basis for further development of the EU–China relationship. At the end of 2005, sectoral agreements and dialogues were in place in the following areas: science and technology, satellite navigation, customs cooperation, maritime transport, nuclear research, tourism, energy, environment, the Information Society, enterprise and industry policy, trade policy, employment and social policy, agriculture, textile trade, space science, macroeconomics, regional policy, civil aviation, transport in general, education and culture, competition policy, intellectual property and geographical designation and product safety and sanitary and phytosanitary regulations.

The competition dialogue provides a good example of how these dialogues can work in practice. China is continuing to develop its market economy institutions and, as part of this process, has drafted its own comprehensive competition laws. In May 2004, China and the EU agreed a permanent mechanism for consultation in the area of competition policy and there have been extensive contacts between both sides at official level. Consequently, it is unsurprising that China's draft competition laws have much in common with the European model. This apparent convergence of approach could prove invaluable when, as appears likely, international competition cases concerning cartels or mergers occur involving interests from both China and the EU.

Moreover, the Chinese market, given its size and uneven levels of development, is fragmented. In order to gain the maximum benefits from a large internal market, China wishes to end this fragmentation and facilitate free movement of goods, services and people and open up procurement. The EU can offer technical assistance and expertise in this area and, in the process, secure better access to Chinese markets for its own businesses.

RUSSIA

Russia's post-millennium growth rates, buoyed by high energy prices, have been impressive but, over a much longer period (see Table 18.1), the opposite has been the case. Indeed, the Russian economy contracted during the 1990s and the EBRD has estimated that Russia's real GDP in 2004 was still only 82 per cent of its 1989 levels. Moreover, unlike China where economic performance is becoming increasingly broadly based, Russia's economic fortunes remain overly dependent on one sector – energy. Indeed, Russia's oil revenues exceeded US$100 billion in 2005, over three times the level of 2001, and regularly account for over half of Russia's export revenues and more than 40 per cent of state budget revenues. The big jump in the value of Russia's exports to the EU between 1999 and 2000 demonstrates the impact of higher energy prices on this important bilateral relationship (see

Figure 18.2). Until 2000, EU–Russia trade was roughly in balance, with the EU showing only a small deficit. Since 2000, the EU's trade deficit with Russia has become more substantial. Without energy, Russia's remaining economic sectors would not be able to sustain the economy for any period. Nevertheless, despite the absence of a balanced economy and persistent question marks over the policy direction of the country, Russia remains a key partner for the EU, for both economic and political reasons.

For several years after the end of the cold war and the disintegration of the Soviet Union, it was difficult for the EU to develop a consistent policy towards Russia given the political and economic twists and turns that have made Russia's transition into a market economy much less straightforward than the USSR's former satellites in CEE. However, two factors make Russia an important partner for the EU – proximity and energy. As the EU has enlarged, its borders have moved further east and a much greater proportion of the EU's eastern border is with Russia than hitherto. The presence of such a potentially powerful economy as a direct neighbour makes the forging of good relations with Russia imperative.

In terms of their relative importance to each other, on the face of it, the EU is a much more important trading partner for Russia than Russia is for the EU. As Figure 18.3 shows, almost 60 per cent of Russia's exports are destined for the EU and half of Russia's imports originate from the EU. In short, the EU is Russia's main trading partner by an extremely large margin. On the other hand, Russia is the EU's fourth most important trading partner, accounting for only 6.3 per cent of the EU's trade. This imbalance in the relative importance of trade is a reflection of the EU's greater diversity and maturity of its market economy.

421

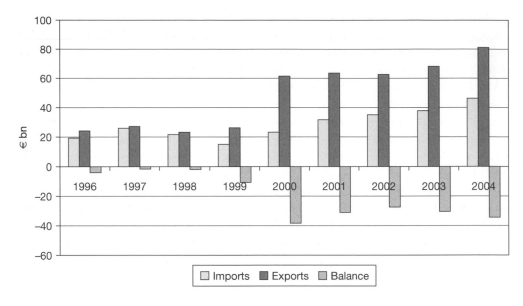

Figure 18.2 EU merchandise trade with Russia, 1996–2004

Source: Eurostat.

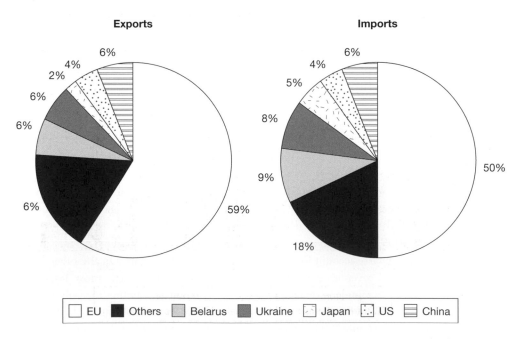

Figure 18.3 Russia's main trading partners, 2004

Source: Eurostat.

Russia's more modest share of EU trade does not, however, tell the full story of the importance of Russia as an economic and commercial partner to the EU. Figure 18.5 illustrates how the EU's imports from Russia are dominated by oil and gas. In 2004, for example, 85 per cent of the EU's imports were composed of energy. This is particularly important given the EU's growing dependency on imported energy (see Chapter 11). Europe's exports to Russia are much more diversified (see Figure 18.4).

As is the case with the EU's links with China, EU–Russia relations are affected not only by immediate economic imperatives. A broader political framework establishes the context for economic and business relations. After the break-up of the Soviet Union and the shattering of the long-held assumptions of the cold war era, the EU's initial concerns about Russia focused around traditional 'hard' security issues in general and individual issues such as the war in Chechnya. European states have dealt with these matters on a bilateral basis or through other institutions, such as NATO, the Organisation for Security and Cooperation in Europe (OSCE), the Barents Euro-Arctic Council and so on, and not through the EU. For most of its existence, the Soviet Union adopted a comprehensive approach to the West and did not differentiate between or deal with individual Western nations apart from the US. Therefore, Europe's relationship with the Soviet Union was largely determined by cold war rhetoric, with the tone set by the state of play between Washington and Moscow. Any diplomatic contacts between Western European countries and the Soviet Union were on a bilateral basis. As far as Moscow was concerned, the European Community's role was limited to trade policy.

As Russia's economic reform became more urgent, the economisation of Russia's external relations also grew more pressing. Russia was seeking to transform its economy into a market-led economy, and needed to reach out beyond its conventional trading

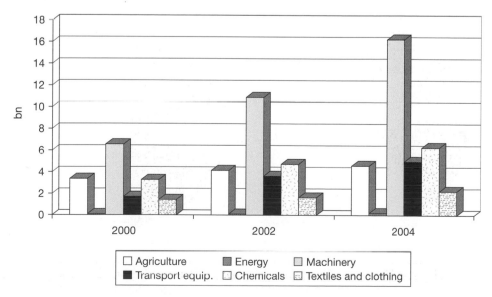

Figure 18.4 EU exports to Russia

Source: Eurostat.

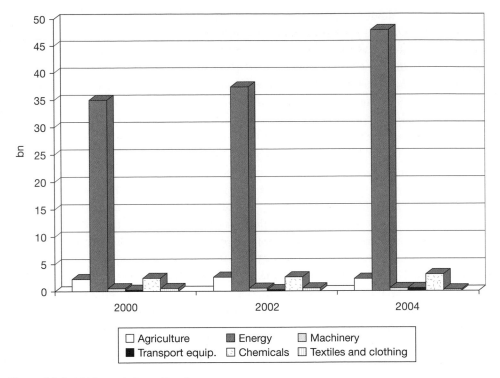

Figure 18.5 EU imports from Russia

Source: Eurostat.

partners, especially as the closed circle of Comecon links had collapsed. The 'economisation' of Russia's external relations, therefore, created room for the EU to step in as a partner of its Eastern neighbour.

The current formal legal basis of Russia's relationship with the EU is the PCA which came into effect in 1997. The PCA has a lifespan of ten years but its automatic extension beyond 2007 is anticipated. The PCA's objectives include:

1 the provision of 'an appropriate framework for the gradual integration between Russia and a wider area of cooperation in Europe';
2 the creation of 'the necessary conditions for the future establishment of a free trade area between the Community and Russia

covering substantially all trade in goods between them, as well as conditions for bringing about freedom of establishment of companies, of cross-border trade in services and of capital movements'.

Although the first objective is fairly general in that it does not define exactly what aspects of the EU–Russia relationship should be integrated or exactly how wide the area of cooperation should be, the second objective is more specific and, as a result, potentially more ambitious. Not only does it refer to the establishment of a free trade area, it also refers to free movement of capital and liberalisation of services trade.

More specifically, the PCA makes a commitment that both parties will extend Most Favoured Nation (MFN) treatment to the

BOX 18.3

MILESTONES IN EU–RUSSIA LINKS

1991   EU delegation established in Moscow
1997   Partnership and Cooperation Agreement (PCA) in force
1999   EU Strategy Paper on Russia
2000   Energy Dialogue launched
2001   High-level Group on Common European Economic Space (CEES) set up
2005   EU–Russia Summit adopts roadmap on CEES
2007   Automatic extension of PCA

other independently of WTO membership. It also makes provision for the principles of national treatment and freedom of transit, for freedom of establishment, with exceptions for various transport modes, and free movement of capital (with Russia still able to apply restrictions for outward direct investment by Russian residents). The most telling and ambitious provision for enhancing integration and interdependence between the two PCA signatories is Article 56 which states that:

> The Parties recognise that an important condition for strengthening the economic links between Russia and the Community is the approximation of legislation. Russia shall endeavour to ensure that its legislation will be gradually made compatible with that of the Community.

The list of laws at which this approximation would be aimed is extensive and envisages company law, banking law, company accounts and taxes, protection of workers at the workplace, financial services, rules on competition, public procurement, protection of health and life of humans, animals and plants, the environment, consumer protection, indirect taxation, customs law, technical rules and standards, nuclear laws and regulations, transport. The PCA also alludes to Russia's infrastructure problems, speaking about the 'modernisation of energy infrastructure including interconnection of gas supply and electricity networks', and the strengthening of the transport and telecommunications infrastructures.

The PCA also established the institutional arrangements that manage the EU–Russia relationship. These include two summits each year involving the heads of government of Russia, EU member states, the President of the European Commission, and the Secretary-General/High Representative for the CFSP; annual cooperation councils at a ministerial level and cooperation committees of senior officials that meet on an ad hoc basis. Nine sub-committees deal with technical level issues at a working level. A joint parliamentary committee provides a regular forum for members of the EP and the Duma to discuss current issues.

The PCA remains at the heart of the EU–Russia relationship but, in 1999, the European Council adopted a Common Strategy on Russia. The strategy sets out the EU's vision that 'a stable, democratic and prosperous Russia, firmly anchored in a united Europe free of new dividing lines is essential to lasting peace on the continent'. Achievement of this vision requires an 'open and pluralistic democracy in Russia, governed by the rule of law and underpinning a prosperous market economy'. Of particular potential interest to European business is the prospect of the integration of Russia into a 'common European economic and social space' (CEES).

In response to the EU's strategy, Russia published its own common strategy for dealing with the EU. The strategy is driven by two concepts: the establishment of a multipolar world, an aspiration shared by some EU members, and the promotion of economic security in Russia, a goal largely shared by the EU on the grounds that an economically secure Russia will enhance peace and stability on its borders and will also provide major commercial and economic opportunities for EU members and their businesses.

The Russian common strategy, although confirming the mutual economic and security benefits of close EU–Russia cooperation and the attraction of a strategic partnership with the EU, also exhibits some important differences. First, the Russian strategy locates its European strategy in a much broader context than its EU counterpart. In describing itself as 'a world power situated on two continents', and by reminding the EU of its role as a Euro-Asian state and of its status as the largest country in the Commonwealth of Independent States (CIS), Russia is signalling the importance of its broader international role, thereby making it more difficult for the EU to dictate the terms of the relationship to it.

Second, Russia's strategy contains a long list of how Russia can help the EU. The list includes additional EU growth and employment through enhanced trade and investment; the provision of long-term and stable energy supplies and raw materials; greater scientific cooperation and commercialisation

of Russian research in European markets; greater integration of key transport and energy infrastructures and information systems; collaboration in space research; strengthening of the international role of the euro through including it in Russia's foreign currency reserves; military and technical cooperation and joint initiatives to prevent local conflicts; and combating organised crime. The inclusion of such a long list reflects Russia's determination to be perceived as the EU's equal. In particular, when discussing the issue of harmonisation and approximation with EU legislation in key areas of cooperation, the Strategy emphasises 'the independence of the Russian legislation and legal system', the need to promote broader application of ISO (International Standardisation Organisation) standards and the mutual recognition of certificates. In other words, the EU cannot expect Russia to change everything to conform to EU practices.

Notwithstanding Russia's reservations, initial exploratory steps have been taken regarding the development of a CEES. The concept of the CEES is based on the neo-liberal economics that underpin the SEM and promises Russia access to a massive market, helping it to recover lost ground in CEE and explore new opportunities in Western Europe. Regulatory convergence will allow business to operate according to common rules in key sectors across an area of over 500 million consumers.

In May 2001, the EU–Russia Summit established a joint High Level Group (HLG) on the CEES chaired by then Commissioner Patten and Russian Deputy Prime Minister Khristenko. The HLG's mandate was to elaborate a concept for 'a closer economic relationship between Russia and the EU'. The HLG has agreed:

that the overall aim is to bring the EU and Russian economies – including the rules and regulations within which they operate – closer together . . . so as to form the basis for an EU–Russia medium/long term economic integration commensurate with the size and complementarity of the EU and Russian economies, as well as their geographical proximity and the overall EU–Russia strategic partnership.

In practical terms, the HLG has been looking for sectors where the trade interest of the EU and Russia is strong and where co-operation and regulatory approximation will boost trade and investment. They have come up with standards, technical regulations and conformity assessment, customs, financial services, accounting/auditing, transport, space launching services, public procurement, telecommunications, competition, industry and agriculture.

In May 2005, the EU–Russia Summit agreed a roadmap on the CEES and in December 2005, the EU and Russia agreed two permanent frameworks, within the context of the roadmap, to reduce the trade and investment barriers between them. These are:

1 *the regulatory dialogue*: to promote the harmonisation of technical standards on industrial products;
2 *the dialogue on industrial and enterprise policy*: to improve the administrative, regulatory and investment environment for companies operating in Russia.

Working groups will cover a number of industrial sectors, including telecommunications and information technologies, automobiles, textiles, chemicals and pharmaceuticals.

In short, the CEES appears to be shaping up to extend the SEM, if not in its entirety,

at least a significant part of it, to Russia. The problem with this approach is that it relies on harmonisation of regulations, and the adoption by Russia of much of the *acquis communautaire*. From the Russian point of view, this is unacceptable if Russia does not gain a say in designing those regulations. On the other hand, the EU rejects the idea that non-members participate in the EU's internal decision making or that the EU should move closer to Russian standards.

INDIA

India has long been overshadowed by China as an emerging economy but in the first years of the twenty-first century, India is increasingly recognised as an awakening sleeping giant as a result of growth rates consistently over 6 per cent for a number of years and the growth of skill-intensive, large-scale industries and services, particularly in telecommunications, services and outsourcing of back-office functions.

Although its formal trade links with India are less developed than those with China or Russia, greater focus on India by the EU and by European business can be expected in the future.

India's emergence into the international economic arena has been based on two decades of gradual but persistent economic reform. Prior to the early 1980s, the Indian economy was built on import substitution; extensive public involvement in key industries; controls over the private sector through investment licensing, import licensing, foreign exchange controls and credit and price controls; and extensive labour protection laws. From the early 1980s, reforms began to remove some of the controls on the domestic private sector. These reforms included import liberalisation, especially of intermediate and capital goods; export incentives; improved access to credit and foreign exchange; relaxation of industrial licensing requirements; and the removal of controls on some administered prices. Reforms continued in the 1990s and included the abolition of industrial licensing; a reduced number and scope of public sector monopolies; liberalisation of FDI; wide-ranging trade liberalisation, including the end of import licensing and the reduction of non-tariff barriers; financial services liberalisation and liberalisation of trade and investment in key service sectors such as telecommunications. Reform has, however, not yet been attempted in the labour market or agriculture.

In the mid-2000s, India is not so integrated with the world economy in terms of trade and investment as China but the above reforms should help bring about change. China's development has been based on industry whereas India's has been driven by services. China's reform has been more consistent and has involved heavy investment in physical infrastructure, an area in which India still encounters many problems. However, India is widely held to have a better institutional infrastructure and corporate governance than China, factors that are increasingly regarded as crucial in long-term development. In short, China is currently far ahead of India in its development but the expectation is that the combined impact of India's reforms, further reform in key areas and the momentum and interest created by the already successful areas of India's economy will accelerate India's development.

The EU is India's biggest trading partner, accounting for almost one-quarter of its imports and exports in 2004. The EU is also a major supplier of India's relatively small inflows of FDI (in 2004, for example, India's FDI inflows totalled only 10 per cent of China's FDI inflows of US$60 billion). India, however, accounts for less than 2 per cent of the EU's total trade and is the destination for only 0.3 per cent of the EU's FDI outflows. EU imports from India are concentrated in

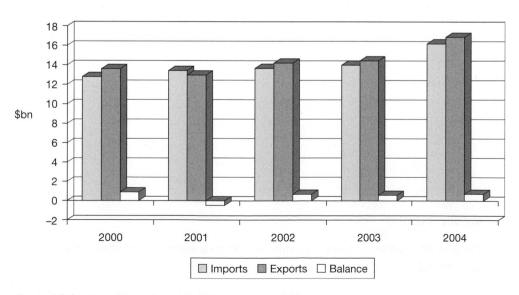

Figure 18.6 *EU merchandise trade with India, 2000–04*

Source: Eurostat.

BOX 18.4

POTENTIAL SECTORS OF INTEREST IN INDIA FOR EUROPEAN BUSINESS

Infrastructure

Infrastructure inadequacies have been identified as holding back India's overall develop-ment. The prospects for engineering and construction companies look promising. Opportunities for European involvement in alliances, joint ventures or as sole contractors could arise in the following infrastructure areas:

- *electricity*: major capacity expansions are anticipated and needed for many years;
- *oil and gas*: major investments in refining capacity, oil and gas pipelines and LNG capacity are anticipated;
- *ports/airports*: expansion of existing facilities and the construction of new airports (e.g. international airports at Hyderabad and Bangalore) are planned;
- *urban infrastructure*: serious investment in water supply, urban transportation and housing is planned;
- *roads*: investment of over US$55 billion is planned in the construction of new roads and the improvement of existing ones.

Information technology

One hundred per cent FDI is allowed in this sector which has grown at an average rate of nearly 30 per cent since 2000. Growth is expected to continue at high rates. India's IT strengths come from its position as an outsourcing hub, from low costs and from involve-ment in high-level research as a result of its pool of skilled personnel. India already exports a high value of IT and IT services but large scope to develop these activities further remains.

Pharmaceuticals

India is one of the world's most important manufacturing bases for generic drugs. Drugs can be manufactured in India at a fraction of the cost in the developed world and research capabilities in this sector are constantly being upgraded. Opportunities for European companies exist in clinical trials, research and manufacturing. Aventis from France and Novonordisk from Denmark have, for example, engaged in clinical trials in India.

Manufacturing

The gradual reduction in taxes and tariffs is increasing India's attractiveness as a manu-facturing hub.

BOX 18.5

MILESTONES IN EU–INDIA LINKS

1963   India establishes diplomatic relations with EEC

1973   Launch of EEC's GSP scheme – India is a beneficiary

1981   EEC–India 5-year Commercial and Economic Cooperation Agreement

1983   EC delegation established in India

1996   Commission Communication – *EU-India: Enhanced Partnership*

2000   First annual EU–India summit

2005   6th EU–India summit issues Joint Action Plan setting out steps needed to transform bilateral ties into strategic relationship

textiles and clothing, agricultural products and chemicals whereas EU exports to India are dominated by machinery and chemicals (see Figure 18.6). Unlike with China, however, the EU's trade with India is roughly in balance.

Simplification and liberalisation should yield more FDI in India but restrictions still remain in key sectors such as telecommunications, insurance and banking and the retail sector. European companies are represented in industrial machinery, electrical goods and electronics, chemicals, the automotive industry and infrastructure. Food processing and horticulture have also attracted a European interest. European companies have also invested in India's dynamic services sector, including IT, financial services and education.

In short, European–Indian commercial contacts, although growing, are underdeveloped given the size of the Indian market. The Indian government will unilaterally continue to play an important role in creating an appropriate business environment to encourage its indigenous entrepreneurs and to attract foreign investors. However, the development of EU–India links can also nurture and facilitate the development of European–Indian business ties.

India and the EC first established diplomatic links in 1963 and India was one of the first beneficiaries of the EU's Generalised System of Preferences (GSP) scheme introduced in 1971. During the 1970s and 1980s, the EC and India signed various Commercial and Economic Cooperation Agreements to facilitate their commercial relationship. For many years, the relationship continued at a relatively low-key level. In 1996, the European Commission adopted and the Council approved the communication *EU-India Enhanced Partnership* and, in 2000, the first annual EU–India summit was held. In 2002, the Commission brought forward its Country Strategy Paper to guide its India policy for the period 2002–06 and at the Sixth annual EU–India Summit in 2005, the EU and India issued a political declaration and a Joint Action Plan setting out the detailed steps needed to take the relationship further.

The Joint Action Plan deals with political and cultural issues but the main interest for business lies in the economic sphere. Many initiatives involve enhanced technical and expert cooperation in areas such as the environment, industrial policy, energy, transport, pharmaceuticals and biotechnology, science and technology, finance and monetary affairs, ICT, agriculture, customs, employment and social policy and business and development cooperation. The Joint Action Plan recognises the growth in trade and investment between Europe and India but acknowledges that 'they remain below potential'. Accordingly, the EU and India have agreed to set up an HLG to explore how they can deepen and extend their relationship in both trade and investment. The Action Plan raises the possibility of the nego-tiation of a wide-ranging trade and investment agreement.

Overall, the EU–India relationship is not as structured or as formalised as that of the EU and Russia. It has evolved in a relatively low-key, ad hoc manner. The Joint Action Plan is important because it brings the whole gamut of initiatives together and in the proposals for trade, at least, there is the possibility of major developments in the relationship.

KEY POINTS

■ China, Russia and India are all important emerging and transitional economies but they present different challenges to the EU.

■ The EU's commercial links with China are already developing quickly. This provides substantial opportunities for European business but also requires European business to meet the competitive challenge posed by China.

■ Russia's immediate importance to the EU comes from its status as an energy supplier but it is in the EU's longer term interest to have an economically prosperous and stable Russia on its borders.

■ India is seen by many as 'the new China'. India's growth and general performance is not yet at the level of China's but the potential is there and the intensity and extent of European–Indian commercial interaction is likely to increase in the coming years.

■ Russia and the EU have developed formal framework which helps shape the business environment between the two. Greater focus by the EU on formal relations with first China and then India is probable.

ACTIVITIES

1 Choose one of the sectors in Box 18.4 and research it further in relation to the opportunities open to European investors in India in your chosen sector. Which European companies are already involved in the sector and why have they chosen to operate in India?

2 Identify inward investment into Europe from either China, Russia or India. What trends are apparent (for example, investment growth, sectoral composition of investment etc.)? How do you explain such trends and what are the prospects for future investment?

3 Make a list of why European firms may wish to invest in Russia and a list of why they may be reluctant to do so.

4 Compare the relative attractiveness of the Chinese and Indian markets for European investors and exporters.

QUESTIONS FOR DISCUSSION

1 European business is coming under increasing competitive pressure as a result of the emergence of China and India on the world economic stage. Discuss ways in which European business can and should respond to this pressure.

2 Who loses and who gains in the case of a trade dispute (such as the 2005 Bra Wars between China and the EU)?

3 Assess the EU's policy approach to the three emerging economies discussed in this chapter. Discuss ways in which the EU can improve the environment in which European business conducts it trade and investment in these three countries.

4 Russia is the least economically successful of the three emerging economies discussed in this chapter but it is of crucial importance to the EU and to European business. To what extent and why does the EU need Russia and, similarly, to what extent and why does Russia need the EU?

5 Identify the main issues shaping the EU–China or EU–India relationship and assess the implications for business.

SUGGESTIONS FOR FURTHER READING

Amber, T. and Witzel, M. (2004) *Doing Business in China*, 2nd edn, London: Routledge.

Antonenko, O. and Pinnick, K. (eds) (2005) *Russia and the EU: Prospects for a New Relationship*, London: Routledge.

Arora, A. and Gambardella, A. (eds) (2005) *From Underdogs to Tigers: The Rise and Growth of the Software Industry in Brazil, China, India, Ireland and Israel*, Oxford: Oxford University Press.

Barysch, K. (2005) 'Embracing the Dragon: Can the EU and China be Friends', *CESifo Forum*, 6 (3), pp. 8–15.

Chee, H. with West, C. (2004) *Myths About Doing Business with China*, Basingstoke: Palgrave Macmillan.

Choi, C. (2005) 'The Chinese Market and European Countries: Pricing and Surviving the Local Competition', *European Business Review*, 17 (2), pp. 177–90.

European Bank for Reconstruction and Development (2005) *Transition Report 2005: Business in Transition*, London: EBRD.

European Commission (2003) 'A Maturing Partnership – Shared Interests and Challenges in EU-China Relations', COM (2003) 533.

Gamer, R. (ed.) *Understanding Contemporary China*, 2nd edn, Boulder, CO: Lynne Rienner Publishers.

Johnson, D. and Robinson, P. (2005) *Perspectives on EU-Russia Relations*, London: Routledge.

Meyer, K. (2004) 'Perspectives on Multinational Enterprises in Emerging Economies', *Journal of International Business Studies*, 35 (4), pp. 259–76.

Ministry of Foreign Affairs of the People's Republic of China (2003) *China's EU Policy Paper* (an English translation), http://www.fmprc.gov.cn/eng/, accessed 23/02/2006.

Ohmae, K. (1985) *Triad Power: The Coming Shape of Global Competition*, New York: Free Press.

Phansalkar, S. (2005) *Opportunities and Strategies for Indian Business: Preparing for a Global India*, New Delhi: Response Books.

Roubal, G., Wieweg, H. and Taube, M. (2005) 'The Chinese Challenge to the EU25', *CESifo Forum*, 6 (3), pp. 37–42.

Index

Page references in **bold** indicate tables and figures; page references in *italic* indicate case studies and boxes.

Communism: collapse 361; legacy of past in CEE
 359, 360, 363; Polish joke 359; threat of Soviet
 bloc during Cold War 30
Community Charter of the Fundamental Social
 Rights of Workers 296
companies *see* business enterprises; firms;
 multinational companies/enterprise
 (MNCs/MNEs)
competition: airlines' strategies to improve 225–6;
 challenge of emerging economies 409; and
 competitiveness 103, 137; effect of globalisation
 59; in EU industrial policy 137, 138, 143; EU
 measures affecting road haulage 219; extension
 beyond EU borders 137; impact of SMEs 146,
 154; and importance of efficient transport 212;
 investment responses of firms 55–6; and
 investment in telecommunications 197; and
 need for labour flexibility 30–8, 308; need to
 start at home 18; objectives of energy policy
 235, 236, 238, 239–49; problems for
 manufacturing in Italy 175; role of Lisbon
 Strategy 19; role of SEM 4, 84, 85
competition policy 55, 103, 136; core features
 105–7; criteria and agreements for CEE 364,
 365; EU–China mechanism for consultation
 420–1; EU policy instruments *106*; implications
 of EU enlargement 385; implications of SEM
 81, 86, 98; international aspects 113–21; need
 for coordination with consumer policy 344–5;
 new era of reform 107–9, 111; role of ECJ in
 issues of 51; themes for longer-term goals
 109–13, 137; theory and types 104–5
competitiveness 103, 128, 137; and business
 performance 15–18; challenges for CEE
 countries 363, 376; and challenges of EMU 172;
 comparison of world economies *64*; and
 consolidation of industry structure 76–7; energy
 policy *239*; and entrepreneurship 158; and
 environmental policy 312, 316, 317, 320, 325;
 hindrance of labour immobility 307; and
 industrial policy 124, 125–31, 132, 134, 135,
 137–8, 142–3; and information economy
 263–6, 270, 281; key importance of TENs 193;
 and need for flexible labour market 290, 308;
 new member states 183; perceived link with
 scale 153, 156; and performance of EU
 economy 63–4, 127; pressures of emerging
 economies 409; problem of 'Eurosclerosis' 34;
 problems for Italy 175, 176; and REACH
 proposal for chemical industry *315*; recent
 initiatives in competition policy 109–11; role of
 SEM policies 81, 85, 94, 98, 101; role of SMEs
 149; sectoral issues 138–42; states and firms
 14–15; and transport systems 211, 212

Completing the Internal Market (White Paper, 1985)
 34–5, 35, 85, *86*, 218, 240, 241
computers 265; *see also* e-commerce; Internet
Constitution *see* draft constitutional treaty
construction sector **9**, 148
consumer policy 338–9; emergence 341–3;
 emergence of EFSA 346–51; financial services
 354–5; Internet and consumer protection
 352–4; legislation 351–2; principles for
 consumer protection 343–5; role of consumers
 339–41, 343, 344
consumer rights 92, 93, 97, 339, 340–1, **340**, 341,
 344, 351, 354
consumers: benefits of competition policy 112;
 choice in sourcing energy supplies 242; global
 61; and GM foods *350*; importance for
 European integration 338–9, 339, 352; and
 price convergence 90; and problems with euro
 345–6; reaction to BSE crisis *348*; role in
 consumer policy process 339–41, 343, 344;
 SEM measures 91–2, 92, 93
Convention on the Future of Europe 41
cooperation: bilateral agreements 114–15;
 consumer protection 344; environmental issues
 329–30; EU agreements with CEE countries
 364; EU–China agreements 414; in EU
 competition policy 107, 113; EU–Japan trade
 relations 397–8; EU–Russia relations 424–5,
 426, 427; EU–US trade relations 399–400;
 procedure introduced by SEA 35
Copenhagen Council (1993) and criteria 364–5,
 365, 367, 385
Coreper (Committee of Permanent
 Representatives) 48
corporate culture: and energy liberalisation
 255
corporate governance 135, 344
corporate reform and restructuring 73–6, 79
corporate social responsibility (CSR) 209
corporations *see* multinational
 companies/enterprises (MNCs/MNEs)
Council for Mutual Economic Assistance (CMEA)
 361, 363, 364, 368, 370, *375*
Council of Ministers 46, 47–8, 322; changes in
 Amsterdam Treaty *40*, *302*; changes in TEU 37;
 and CTP 52, 215–16, 218; effect of right to
 veto policy 33; European Parliament's move
 towards parity with 50–1; and EU–US open
 skies negotiations *401*; and guidelines for TENs
 193; lack of support for opening up rail sector
 230; and WTO 392
Court of Auditors 45, *49*
Croatia 359, 387
cross-border strategies 54–5; TENs 195, 205

451